NONVERBAL COMMUNICATION

STUDIES AND APPLICATIONS

SIXTH EDITION

Nina-Jo Moore
APPALACHIAN STATE UNIVERSITY

Mark Hickson, III
UNIVERSITY OF ALABAMA, BIRMINGHAM

Don W. Stacks
UNIVERSITY OF MIAMI AT CORAL GABLES

NEW YORK   OXFORD
OXFORD UNIVERSITY PRESS

Oxford University Press is a department of the University of Oxford. It furthers the University's
objective of excellence in research, scholarship, and education by publishing worldwide.

Oxford   New York
Auckland   Cape Town   Dar es Salaam   Hong Kong   Karachi
Kuala Lumpur   Madrid   Melbourne   Mexico City   Nairobi
New Delhi   Shanghai   Taipei   Toronto

With offices in
Argentina   Austria   Brazil   Chile   Czech Republic   France   Greece
Guatemala   Hungary   Italy   Japan   Poland   Portugal   Singapore
South Korea   Switzerland   Thailand   Turkey   Ukraine   Vietnam

For titles covered by Section 112 of the US Higher Education
Opportunity Act, please visit www.oup.com/us/he for the
latest information about pricing and alternate formats.

Published in the United States of America by
Oxford University Press
198 Madison Avenue, New York, NY 10016
http://www.oup.com

Oxford is a registered trade mark of Oxford University Press.

Library of Congress Cataloging-in-Publication Data
Moore, Nina-Jo.
   Nonverbal communication: studies and applications / Nina-Jo Moore,
Appalachian State University; Mark Hickson, III, University of Alabama,
Birmingham; Don W. Stacks, University of Miami at Coral Gables.—Sixth edition.
      pages cm
   Includes bibliographical references and index.
   ISBN 978-0-19-999025-2
   1. Nonverbal communication. I. Hickson, Mark. II. Stacks, Don W. III. Title.
   P99.5.H53 2014
   302.2'22—dc23
                                                          2013009377

Printing number: 9 8 7 6 5 4 3 2 1

Printed in the United States of America
on acid-free paper

BRIEF CONTENTS

CONTENTS

PREFACE

The overall message of this textbook is that nonverbal communication is important in all settings. Since the majority of the messages we receive and send have a nonverbal communication component to them, we look at how even the most minute aspect of nonverbal behavior can influence a message.

Authors always make decisions about how they will write a textbook. Since this is a sixth edition, many decisions have been made over the years in the writing of this textbook. In order to have you, our readers, understand why we have done some of the things we have in this new edition, we offer you some explanations here.

New to the sixth edition:

1. More than 275 new sources, most published since the fifth edition was completed (2009).
2. New sources include studies from many disciplines, not just communication. This should make the textbook more functional for other disciplines as well as communication.
3. We continue to take a research-based approach to our material, but in this textbook we have moved our chapter on research methodology to an appendix. This was done to facilitate use by programs that do use a research-based approach when they teach the course as well as programs that do not take that approach. This was done in deference to critiques we have received on prior editions.
4. We continue to keep our historical grounding, because it is this material that lays the path for the contemporary studies. For that reason, you will see that we cite both historical and contemporary work.
5. We have added some material about computer mediated communication (CMC), because this one issue has greatly affected our communication practices over the last decade. Indeed, many people in today's society struggle with how to use CMC effectively and respectfully.
6. As more research and findings have become available about sex and gender differences, we have included more up-to-date and relevant studies in those areas.

7. We have added "Student Voices" to each chapter. These "voices" are from students who have applied what they have learned while studying Nonverbal Communication to "real-world" settings.

As you read this text, you may discover that you recognize much of what you read. If this perplexes you at first, you will soon discover that much of what we consider "nonverbal communication" is a norm of human communication and that its nonverbal form is more complex than the term denotes. Chapter 1 provides an understanding of the norms of nonverbal communication. Part I, "Studies and Subcodes," examines each subcode[1] in some depth. A subcode is a specific area or type of nonverbal communication. Earlier editions of this text relied heavily on referenced material, providing a history of the study of each of these areas. This edition focuses more on individual applications of the contemporary research findings. With this "application orientation," we ask you a number of experiential questions designed to have you apply these theories, to actually go out and either observe or experiment with the theories discussed. We include numerous "Observational Studies" in each chapter to give you a chance to apply what you are learning to a variety of contexts. From these experiences you can explore on your own how much you really know about nonverbal communication and apply that knowledge to specific situations you encounter.

Many textbooks end there; readers must take what they know and try to apply it to the world beyond the classroom and the textbooks. We, however, feel that there is enough information to move beyond that point, and so we offer Part II, "Applications." Inclusion of "Applications" continues a tradition of this text that goes back four editions and twenty-five years of trying to present nonverbal communication in a usable way. Part II is based on what you will have studied earlier, and it examines how each subcode operates, both alone and in conjunction with other subcodes. We look at this in several contexts, and we include "Observational Studies" here also.

Our original editions included a chapter at the start of the textbook (Chapter 2 in the last few editions) that looked at the research techniques necessary to delineate the norms and create the theories of nonverbal communication. This edition still includes that material, but we have moved that to an appendix. We did this because we know that some courses that use our text do not use a research-based approach and having that material at the start of the text causes some dis-fluency in the flow of the material. But we also know that many of our users do take the research approach to teaching nonverbal communication; indeed, we (your authors) take that approach, so we still wanted the material to be a part of this textbook. We have included the same educational approach in this appendix, and it is our hope that your professors will use the material so that you understand where all of the theories you will be studying this semester come from.

Some other nonverbal communication textbooks organize their materials in a visual order, starting with physical appearance and moving on to body movement and gestures, space, touch, voice, and environment. That is, the subcodes are ordered according to what you *see* first and recognize as nonverbal communication. We choose to order our materials to accord with what we believe many people *think* about first when they start to consider how nonverbal communication is used. Allow us to explain.

We look at the study of nonverbal communication more from what we consider a "sensory" perspective, meaning how nonverbal communication is processed through our five senses. We begin with the sense that many people feel is one of the senses that communicates the most to us, rather than *about* us: the sense of touch. Then we lead into the study of space (we define touch as the lack of any space between interacting communicators or "zero proxemics"). We move next to the sense of sight, meaning nonverbal issues that we process by seeing them. Here we also discuss humans' use of space, plus physical appearance, body movements, and the environment. From there we move to the sense of hearing, where we discuss how people use their voices to communicate. Next, we look at how the sense of smell communicates to us. Finally, we add a factor that we believe is also an important subcode of nonverbal communication—the use of time.

We use a process of allowing you to see how many research studies actually exist in the discipline of nonverbal communication. At the end of each chapter, we include a list of further references. In hopes that we pique your interest at least a little, we supply those resources so you can study the subject further. The appendix on research methods, although more elementary than any research methods course you might take, we include because we hope that some of the things you read about in this textbook might excite you and that you might try your hand at researching the subject further. Good research cannot be completed without a good review of literature, thus our reason for including as many references (both in-text and at the end of the chapters) as possible. You will see that much of the research is not as contemporary as we would hope for, although we did include the newest and most recent studies published. We do need to point out, however, that the historical research we do cite sets the base of knowledge from which we teach nonverbal communication. We believe that it will be our students of today who further the scholarship of this field tomorrow.

Key features of the sixth edition:

- The chapters continue to be written in a more conversational tone, as a discussion with the readers (written in first person more than any other "voice"). This was done consciously to try to engage the readers with what we are discussing.
- Each chapter includes up-to-date and historical references to studies done in each of the nonverbal subcodes.
- Each chapter includes Observational Studies—several per chapter—that allow for students to apply the knowledge ascertained by reading to various contexts and situations.
- Each chapter contains Student Voices, which exemplify the concepts being discussed as former students have recognized in their everyday lives.
- Each chapter ends with Questions for Thought in hopes of having professors use those for discussion, or that the readers themselves will read them and discuss them with each other.
- Each chapter includes a section of Additional References, which provides the students with more resources to study should they wish to look into any specific subcode in more depth. This section in each chapter is organized by subtopics that fit the discussions within the given chapter. Since some professors will take a research approach to teaching this course, these sources may prove to be invaluable.

- The textbook includes an Appendix that deals solely with research methods that might be used for teaching research approaches to studying nonverbal communication. Although not intended to be a course in research methods, this appendix will give enough of a background that students can understand how researchers have developed their theories on the use of nonverbal communication behaviors/skills.
- The textbook includes an updated Glossary of terminology used in the textbook and in the subdiscipline of nonverbal communication.

As you read through this textbook, it is our hope that your minds will be opened to new possibilities of what you might do with this knowledge. Regardless of what fields you hope to enter, you will work with other individuals; understanding some of the information we present here will be helpful in your professional lives. Those of you hoping to go into fields such as advertising or public relations will have more pragmatic uses for some of this material, such as how to design an advertisement to sell a specific product, or how to create an image for an organization based on the nonverbal message it needs to promote.

As authors, we invite you to question, experiment with the theories, argue with the findings of others, and become critical thinkers about this topic of human communication.

ACKNOWLEDGMENTS

The authors would like to thank the people who assisted in the review process and gave valuable input into the changes and editing of this edition: Edith E. LeFebvre (California State University–Sacramento), Julie Mayberry (North Carolina State University), Diana Karol-Nagy (University of Florida), Charles H. Tardy (University of Southern Mississippi), Jane B. Teel (Auburn University), Nancy Hoar (Western New England College), Carolyn M. Anderson (University of Akron), Ross Buck (University of Connecticut), Christopher Carey (Portland State University), Steven Duck (University of Iowa), Norah E. Dunbar (California State University, Long Beach), Kory Floyd (Arizona State University), Ken Frandsen (University of New Mexico), Alan J. Fridlund (University of California, Santa Barbara), Jerold Hale (University of Georgia), Marvin A. Hecht (Oracle Corporation), Bill Huddleston (University of North Alabama), Maureen Keeley (Texas State University, San Marcos), Paul Krivonos (California State University, Northridge), Jeff Lewis (Pitzer College), Karen Lovaas (Institute for Global Communications), Matt Martin (West Virginia University), Barbara Penington (University of Wisconsin, Whitewater), Shelby Taylor (California State University, Fullerton), Carol L. Thompson (University of Arkansas, Little Rock), William Todd-Mancillas (California State University, Chico), Merry Buchanan (University of Central Oklahoma), Gina Jensen (Webster University), Elizabeth Munz (SUNY at New Paltz), Judith Tenney (University of Maryland), Rosalind Kennerson-Baty (Baylor University), Richard West (University of Texas at San Antonio), and Jeffrey McQuillen (University of Texas at Pan American).

ANCILLARIES PROVIDED WITH THE SIXTH EDITION

- An Instructor's Manual which includes:
  - In-depth chapter outlines
  - Sample test questions
- PowerPoint lecture slides for use in teaching classes. The slides are editable, so the user can either use the notes provided or narrow them down and can change the pictures used.

NOTE

1. Some communication scholars use the term *channel* instead of *subcode;* the terms are virtually interchangeable. We mention this because if you choose to research nonverbal communication outside of this textbook, you will find *channel* used more commonly than *subcode.*

ABOUT THE AUTHORS

Nina-Jo Moore is Professor of Communication at Appalachian State University, and the former Associate Dean of the College of Fine and Applied Arts. She received her B.A. from the University of South Florida, her M.A. from the University of Georgia, and her Ph.D. from the University of Maryland. For many years she has taught nonverbal communication in addition to other interpersonal, organizational, intercultural, and public communication courses. She has published in the area of distance learning, mentoring, and rhetoric and public address. Active in professional organizations for 40 years, Dr. Moore has served as president of the Southern States Communication Association and the Carolinas Communication Association, in addition to many other leadership roles within these organizations as well as the National Communication Association. With a strong interest in intercultural communication, she spent a year abroad teaching in Warsaw, Poland, and leads summer-study abroad programs to Poland and the Czech Republic for Appalachian State University.

Mark Hickson III received his Ph.D. from Southern Illinois University. He is a professor in the Department of Communication Studies at the University of Alabama at Birmingham. Dr. Hickson has been published in the disciplines of psychology and sociology in addition to communication. He has taught in Bangkok, Thailand, as well as at five colleges in the United States. He has had more than 100 articles published in journals ranging from *Communication Monographs* to *Psychological Reports*. Dr. Hickson is currently undertaking research on the biological foundations of the communication process.

Don W. Stacks received his Ph.D. from the University of Florida in Communication Studies in 1978. He is Professor of Public Relations in the Department of Strategic Communications at the University of Miami. Dr. Stacks teaches a variety of courses but primarily research methods, public relations administration and management, publication writing and design, persuasion, communication theory, and mass communication in society. His current research interests include tourism and hospitality management, crisis management, public relations education, integrated communications, listening, and the neurological impact of communication. Professionally, Dr. Stacks is the author or co-author of eight books and more than 250 articles, chapters, and professional chapters. His latest book, *Primer of Public Relations Research*, and a second, *A Practitioner's Guide to Public Relations Research, Measurement, and Evaluation* with David Michaelson, have received critical acclaim. He also co-founded the *Journal of Applied Communication Research*. Dr. Stacks is married to the former Robin Hickson (sister of his primary co-author and co-founder of the *Journal of Applied Communication Research*). They have three children.

INTRODUCTION

We authors consider that "nonverbal communication" is a norm of human communication, and that the nonverbal form of communication is more complex than the term denotes. For that reason, we begin with a discussion of exactly what nonverbal communication is, how different communication scholars approach the subject, and the components of this area of our discipline. We next look at the subcodes that are considered a part of this field of study and how nonverbal communication functions. Chapter 1 discusses the relation between perception and nonverbal communication, which helps in understanding the factors that assist us in filtering the nonverbal messages we receive. In addition, we look at how we use nonverbal communication and how our brains process it. Finally, we look at other factors that affect how we use and interpret nonverbal messages, including age, cultural backgrounds, race, status differences, and sex and gender differences.

We believe that research is an important aspect of the study of nonverbal communication, so we briefly discuss the importance of basic research methods here. Later in the text, in Appendix A, we present a whole section approaching how to conduct nonverbal communication research. Earlier editions of this textbook included a chapter on this topic early in the book, but we have opted to rearrange our approach in this edition. Your professors may ask you to read Appendix A prior to starting your study of the nonverbal subcodes, or perhaps your professor will have you look at it at a point later in your semester. Regardless, we hope the material in Appendix A will be helpful for you to understand the "hows and whys" of nonverbal communication theories and perhaps become a nonverbal communication scholar yourself. After reading the introductory chapter, you may wish to study the appendix prior to reading the rest of the textbook if you wish to make better sense of the research you will be reading about throughout the rest of the book.

Before we begin our journey in Part 1, we need to accomplish the following:

- Agree on what nonverbal communication is.

You should be able to define nonverbal communication and know how verbal and nonverbal communication differ from each other with respect to several important dimensions.

- Understand the historical foundations of what we call nonverbal communication.

One fact that cannot be stressed enough is that nonverbal communication cannot operate within a vacuum. Nonverbal communication usually functions along with the verbal aspects of communication to "create a message."

- Explain how nonverbal communication clarifies what we communicate verbally.
- Acquire a basic understanding of the nonverbal subcodes that are studied in later chapters of this text.

The chapters you will be reading in this book are based on research conducted by social scientists who use various methods in conducting their studies.

This first section, then, provides the foundations for what we later examine in detail. We will attempt to identify several significant aspects of nonverbal communication for later study. As noted in the Preface, much of what we authors examine may seem rather obvious and may be something you already know. What might surprise you, however, are the deviations and the effects of violating expectations based on the nonverbal subcodes. You might also be surprised by how much you are continually being influenced—and are influencing others—by means of nonverbal communication. For those reasons, throughout this textbook we will look at how you use nonverbal communication to affect others, and also at how you are influenced by it.

CHAPTER 1

FOUNDATIONS OF NONVERBAL COMMUNICATION

KEY CONCEPTS

- Definitions, Processes, and Problems
- Approaches
- Verbal–Nonverbal Distinctions
- Nonverbal Functions
- Nonverbal Subcodes
- Communication Functions
- How the Brain Processes Communication
- Age, Culture, Race, and Status Differences
- Sex and Gender Differences

OBJECTIVES

By the end of this chapter you should be able to:

- Define nonverbal communication.
- Distinguish between various approaches that researchers take in studying nonverbal communication.
- Distinguish between verbal and nonverbal communication.
- Explain nonverbal communication filters, such as age, culture, race, status, sex, and gender differences.

For Francesco, a typical sophomore communication major at a university similar to yours, it is a typical Monday morning. The electric alarm clock makes its familiar blast of music at exactly 7:00 a.m. Francesco, in the middle of a snore, turns over to his other side. His roommate, Will, awakens slowly.

Quietly, Will steps across the bedroom floor to the shower. The familiar creeping sound awakens Francesco once again, and this time he gets out of bed. While Will is in the shower, Francesco goes to the dresser to select his socks and underwear. He can hardly distinguish the black socks from the blue but reasons that if he can't tell, no one else can tell either. Francesco slowly picks up the electric razor and begins to change his physical appearance.

Meanwhile, Will completes his shower and shampoo. He gets out of the shower and dries his hair, brushes his teeth, puts on deodorant, shaves, and splashes on a little cologne. He puts on his underwear and walks back into the bedroom.

Francesco takes over the bathroom to begin a similar process of getting ready while Will is choosing his wardrobe of the day. Will is particularly careful on this Monday, because he wants to impress Rachel, the woman who usually sits next to him in his 9:00 a.m. computer science class. In a matter of 45 minutes or so, the young men are on their way to the cafeteria for breakfast.

Immediately, the two can see that they will need to "reserve" a table. Their usual table has been taken, the one they really consider "their table," so they choose one nearby. Each places his book bag on a chair at this table, believing that leaving their possessions there reserves their places. That done, they get in the cafeteria line, each selecting his own breakfast.

M any of the actions performed by Will and Francesco seem typical. You may have noticed that much of their morning has been spent in **nonverbal interactions**, or behaving without words. You may think this behavior is typical of the beginning of the day but that it does not continue. The fact is, however, that we receive much of our emotional meanings through nonverbal subcodes. In addition, we spend a considerable amount of time in nonverbal communication. Historically, the most commonly cited statistics still stand today. Mehrabian (1968, 1981), observing how feeling is transmitted in messages, found that as much as 93 percent of emotional meaning is transmitted nonverbally. Mehrabian's research further indicates that in face-to-face interactions the total affective (or emotional) meaning may be sent as follows:

- 38 percent of the emotional meaning of the message is *vocal*
- 55 percent of the emotional meaning of the message is expressed via *facial expression*
- 7 percent of the emotional meaning of the message is expressed *verbally*

Most researchers looking at the impact of nonverbal communication believe that Mehrabian's 93 percent figure may be a little high, but at the same time these researchers do accept the relatively high impact of the "other-than-words" dimension, which this text calls *nonverbal communication*. In general, we authors accept Birdwhistell's (1970) and Philpott's (1983) approximations, which say that nonverbal communication accounts for 60 percent to 70 percent (or approximately two-thirds) of what we communicate to one another. It should be noted that this statistic has been widely accepted and reported by most contemporary nonverbal communication textbooks and scholarly articles.

If this information is accurate, you are probably asking yourself, "Why haven't we studied this important phenomenon before?" This question is an excellent one, especially because everyone studies *verbal* communication from infancy through college. Although we all have had many courses in learning verbal "language," most of us have never had a specific course in nonverbal communication. You probably know something about nonverbal communication, especially if you have taken other communication courses, but what you know about it is probably not systematic, organized, or based on the ability to critique research. This text is designed to give you systematic, organized information about nonverbal communication.

In our study of nonverbal communication, we will find that nonverbal communication tends to be more elusive, is more intangible, is more difficult to define, and is more "natural" than verbal communication, yet we do not think about it as much as we think about the more symbolic, verbal form of communication. As Ekman and Friesen (1968) noted more than 45 years ago:

> [Most people] do not know what they are doing with their bodies when they are talking, and no one tells them. People learn to disregard internal cues that are informative about their stream of body movements and facial expressions. Most interactive nonverbal behavior seems to be enacted with little conscious choice or registration; efforts to inhibit what is shown fail because the information about what is occurring is not customarily within awareness. (p. 181)

In summary, we are not always aware of the nonverbal communication of others, and we are sometimes unaware of our own nonverbal communication. This is not to say that *all* or even *most* of our nonverbal communication takes place unconsciously. Most of the time we simply act or react to an event, person, or object spontaneously; however, on occasion, the reaction may have been planned or rehearsed. Although we discuss this later in this chapter, we must realize that nonverbal communication is not totally symbolic. What we communicate nonverbally cannot, in most cases, symbolize something that is not present, but it may be the "trigger" that causes symbolic communication to occur. Verbal communication, as we will see, is more symbolic (although not totally) and more conscious in terms of its presentation. For example, Will might talk about Rachel, the woman he is interested in, by using a verbal description of what she looks like. That, in turn, triggers the other person's mind to create a nonverbal picture of the absent woman. Of course, when that person finally meets Rachel, the nonverbal picture will almost always change. The nature of nonverbal communication, then, is something we often take for granted.

BASIC DEFINITIONS

For you to understand nonverbal communication, we need first to define what we mean by the term *communication*. We believe that **communication** is an interactive process whereby people seek to induce some form of change in attitude, belief, or behavior. We also agree with J. K. Burgoon, Buller, and Woodall (1989, 1996), who suggest in their original edition of their nonverbal communication textbook, as well as later editions, that communication is a "dynamic and ongoing process whereby people create shared meaning through the sending and receiving of messages via commonly understood codes" (p. 12; see also J. K. Burgoon, Guerrero, & Floyd, 2010). We look at communication as the process of senders stimulating meaning in the minds of receivers and then having the receivers respond to the message they have received and interpreted (feedback). Although we believe that most communication is intentional, we also contend that intent is not absolutely necessary in order for communication to take place. The receiver of the message often perceives intent, even though the sender had no intention of sending the message received. In short, the sender of the message may not have meant what you thought he or she meant. When you are motivated to get your nonverbal message across to your receiver, you will be much more intentional with your nonverbal behaviors.

We also believe that *communication* is a reciprocal process, creating a *norm of reciprocity* (or a *dyadic effect*). This concept says that we should expect those with whom we communicate to respond in a manner similar to our original communication. For example, in nonverbal communication, if you use a positive nonverbal indicator (such as your tone of voice, your posture, or a smile), you should expect a similar positive response from the person with whom you are communicating. If you use negative nonverbal indicators, you should expect a negative response. This does not always happen, however, and those phenomena are discussed later in this textbook, when the *expectancy violations theory* is discussed.

What, then, is nonverbal communication? To begin this definition, we can say that the *nonverbal part of communication is that aspect of the communication process that deals with the transmission and reception of messages that are not a part of the natural **language** systems.* Whether they are spoken or written, words are considered part of verbal communication. Any aspect of communication that does not include words is considered part of the nonverbal code. This does not mean that you do not combine verbal and nonverbal codes to create a message; indeed, much of nonverbal communication occurs in conjunction with verbal communication. This textbook deals with those aspects of nonverbal communication that are perceived through the five most commonly known human senses: sight, touch, hearing, smell, and taste (Figure 1.1).

Nonverbal communication may come via the characteristics of the speaker (hairstyle, vocal characteristics, appearance, behavioral displays); it may come via the characteristics of the receiver (obvious boredom, dress, audible sighing); or it may rest in the features of the situation (cold room, institutional cream-colored walls, burned-out light bulbs). Nonverbal communication often occurs through the interaction of all three of these: **the speaker** (dress, voice, distance maintained), **the receiver** (posture, facial expression, distance maintained), and **the situation** as perceived by the sender and/or receiver (the context, the environment, the time of the interaction). For example, look at two of your classes, say, Biology and Psychology. Compare the differences between the two professors, your conduct in those two class settings, and the physical classroom settings. Can you see how differences between the nonverbal aspects of those two situations can result in very different communication in those settings? Surely you can, and that means you are well on your way to understanding some of the effects of nonverbal communication.

By now you should have a basic idea of what nonverbal communication is. It is something more than being merely "beyond words" or, as Sapir (1949) once suggested, "an elaborate code that is written nowhere, known to none, and understood by all" (p. 556). Nonverbal communication is complex because it creates communication by use of nonverbal behaviors, either by themselves or combined with words. It may be shared *between* people (interpersonally) or *within* a person's thoughts (intrapersonally). It may be intentional or unintentional. It may also be used without words, or it may take on meaning only when it is used in combination with words.

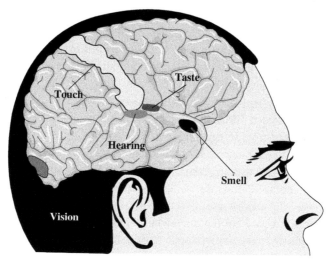

FIGURE 1.1   Sensory organs.

CONSIDERATIONS FOR DEFINITIONS

Before we clarify what we believe nonverbal communication to be, we must address some of the considerations just mentioned. In this subsection we examine behavior versus communication, intentionality, signs versus symbols, which leads us to understand how people process nonverbal communication.

BEHAVIOR VERSUS COMMUNICATION

First, we distinguish between nonverbal behavior and nonverbal communication. Some scholars do not make this distinction, but we believe that it is an important one for understanding the scope of nonverbal communication. The perception of cream-colored walls is part of nonverbal communication. The walls may be said to "communicate" only because living things—people—perceive and interpret them in certain ways and act accordingly. Only living things behave. In a given context, the size of a room may communicate; you probably feel quite awkward when you have a class of five students in a room designed to hold two hundred. At the same time as we say that inanimate objects *may* communicate, as just defined, human beings might behave without communicating. It is true to say that people cannot not behave; it happens as a natural process of being a living human being. We believe, however, that people who are behaving are not necessarily communicating. In our discussion, we use the word *communication* only when a receiver has *interpreted* a message as having some meaning. For communication to occur, a receiver must be present and must interpret (decode) the transmission of symbols (messages). Some theorists would not agree with this position, so we present it as a foundation for understanding our approach in this textbook. These messages may be either verbal or nonverbal; as long as a receiver has interpreted a message, whether it was sent intentionally or not, communication has taken place.

You can communicate nonverbally with yourself (*intrapersonally*), which is actually being your own sender and receiver, and in that case there may be a fine distinction between behavior and communication. As Dittman (1972) points out in an early study of nonverbal communication, a message may be controlled by the person and yet be below the level of consciousness (or subliminal) and not actually perceived. For example, suppose you are driving down the highway. You look around and see that there are no cars approaching. There are no other people around, so you pick your nose. Is this action nonverbal communication or nonverbal behavior? In this incident, it is nonverbal communication. Why? It is nonverbal communication because you yourself interpreted the behavior as a *message*. You checked around to see if anyone might see you do this action, knowing that it would not be considered socially acceptable; it would be against societal norms to be caught in the act of picking your nose, even if it was by someone you did not know. You were weighing the social consequences of the act; you were having social cognition. Social cognition also includes issues other than weighing consequences, such as decision making, the perceptions of others, and the attribution of characteristics to a specific nonverbal behavior. We focused on weighing consequences because it is one of the more obvious aspects of social cognition. If you had merely acted and not thought about the act, then that act would have been simply a nonverbal behavior.

BOX 1.1 OBSERVATIONAL STUDY

As you walk around campus, explore the various considerations discussed and decide if what you observe is nonverbal behavior or nonverbal communication. Perhaps look especially at people talking on their cellphones. What led you to decide whether the "acts" you observed were communication or behaviors? Are there some that are easier to determine than others? Why?

INTENTIONALITY

It is important to understand **intention** as it relates to nonverbal communication. In verbal communication, we often think about what we say, although some might argue with that position. In the nonverbal system, however, there is often unintentional transmission of messages. For example, if you have an itch, most often you will scratch it. In the event that you think about it and you deem it inappropriate to scratch that particular part of your body in front of other people, you may make the decision not to scratch that itch. If you do not think about it, you might just reflexively scratch whatever itches. In doing this, you create the difference between intentional behaviors and unintentional ones. The actual decision not to scratch makes the absence of scratching intentional intrapersonal communication. Scratching without thinking and sending a message to those who see you scratch that you are crass would be unintentional interpersonal communication.

A good example of this difference is the head scratch. Usually you scratch your head in a general context, and it means nothing. In the early 1980s, however, the Head and Shoulders shampoo advertisers created a new meaning for head scratching—dandruff and all the negative connotations, according to the commercial, of having a "flaky" scalp. In later years,

PHOTO 1.1   Is sleeping in class considered nonverbal behavior or nonverbal communication? What if your instructor saw you falling asleep and thought the lecture must be boring you? Did nonverbal communication occur?

NIX and RID advertisements for ridding hair of head lice and Scalpacin's contemporary advertisements for "Stress Itch" added to the social unacceptability of scratching your head in public. What had been a simple reaction (behavior) to a felt need may now be interpreted as an intentional (and negative) communication between you and receivers (those who actually see you scratch your head).

The *perception* of some form of intent is enough for an act to be considered communication. In the head-scratching example, communication did occur, although it may not have been the intended message that was transmitted. Nonverbal communication occurs when a message is decoded (or interpreted) as having some meaning, *regardless of the sender's intent*. Most *verbal* communication carries with it a greater amount of intent, but *nonverbal* communication tends to be more primitive and less controllable than its verbal counterpart.

Researchers believe that intention is necessary for communication to take place. This does not mean that you will not receive and interpret events that were not intended for you as communication; you will. You will also be sent messages that you do not interpret as messages; this is another intentionality issue in and of itself. Suffice it to say that effective communication is often dependent on the intentions of the sender.

Nonverbal communication is rarely as easily understood as verbal communication is. The problem is that whether or not the source intends the message (be it nonverbal or verbal) is secondary; as long as the receiver perceives intent, then communication has occurred. Often sources simply behave—they do not consciously think about the ramifications of a specific behavior—but others perceive that the source has done the behavior on purpose. It often gets confusing and, more often than not, leads to misunderstanding. *There are times, however, when neither the source nor the receiver perceives intent; in this case, the act falls under the category of behavior, not communication.*

BOX 1.2 OBSERVATIONAL STUDY

Go to class and look around at your surroundings and the people in your class. Write down five nonverbal behaviors you notice that you believe were intentional and five that you believe were unintentional. Try to decide what makes the difference.

SIGN VERSUS SYMBOL

Verbal and nonverbal communication guides or directs people through the use of signs and symbols. Verbal communication, because of its symbolic nature, includes a code (language) upon which we must agree if communication is to take place. We must create a socially shared system of agreement—a language in which words take on "meaning." If we are to be understood, then people must comprehend the symbols we use to communicate. The perceived intention of verbal communication creates a need to share with others what we mean when we use words. For example, look up the word "dog" in a dictionary. How many different meanings can be taken from the use of a simple three-letter word? Does meaning differ when "dog" is used as a noun as compared to a verb? Add connotations (or emotional meanings) to the definition of "dog," and you have a whole different issue to add to the topic of the meaning of verbal communication.

Nonverbal communication may be symbolic or nonsymbolic. One of the more difficult areas in discussing the distinction between verbal and nonverbal communication is the distinction between *signs* and *symbols*. In the verbal code we have a **symbol**; that is, the word takes the place of something else—the word represents an abstraction, such as *beauty*, *God*, *wealth*, or even *dog*. The symbolic nature of verbal communication is inherent in language; words are abstractions of actual things that may or may not be seen by the receiver. Most of us have heard the childhood phrase, "Sticks and stones may break my bones, but words can never hurt me." Most of us are also well aware that this phrase is wrong. If I call you a "rat," you know you are not really a rat. You may not even think of yourself as a "ratty" person. Yet you react to the word with emotional responses, such as hurt, anger, or indignation, or perhaps even laughter if I have said it, nonverbally, in a teasing tone of voice.

A **sign**, on the other hand, is a natural representation of an event or act. Fever is a sign of one's being ill. A cross on a building is a sign of a church or, if a person wears a cross we view it as a sign of someone who professes Christianity. The "$" sign is a sign of money and sometimes wealth, although that may indeed take on new meaning with the financial crisis of 2008, or the "fiscal cliff" of 2012. Much of what we call nonverbal communication falls under the rubric of a signal, though nonverbal communication is sometimes considered symbolic by receivers. People expressing emotions do so nonverbally. They may smile, cry, or frown; when they do, we label the nonverbal behaviors with a symbol—*happiness*, *sadness*, or *displeasure*. What we try to do in many cases is to infer meaning from a sign. With the verbal code, which must depend on socially shared meanings, the process of *inferring* meaning is not usually necessary. When we infer meanings without being sure of what was meant, we can damage communication. The crying, for example, may have been a sign of happiness, not sadness at all.

Although the verbal code is quite *explicit* about what it represents—meaning more precise or specific—nonverbal communication is more *implicit,* meaning more implied or understood. Mehrabian (1981) first distinguished between explicit and implicit communication by noting that "Verbal cues are definable by an explicit dictionary and by rules of syntax, but there are only vague and informal explanations of the significance of nonverbal behaviors" (p. 3). Nonverbal communication would be much easier to understand if we did have a dictionary and syntactical rules for nonverbal signals. We take Mehrabian's dichotomy of explicit and implicit communication one step further: We note that most nonverbal communication involves expectations on both the senders' and receivers' parts. These expectations become the *norm* in given situations or relationships, and they generate both appropriate and inappropriate behaviors. Distancing zones (or space usage), appropriate dress, hair length, speech rate, amount of touch, and other nonverbal elements differ by culture and subculture. They take on normative expectations that people can choose to either maintain or violate. Violations of norms, as discussed in later chapters, can yield both beneficial and hazardous results.

Let us look back to Will and Francesco. When they got up to prepare for classes, they began a series of behaviors that are the norm for many of us: They showered, they cleaned up, dressed, went to eat, reserved their places with their book bags, and generally behaved as *expected* of college students. Over a period of time such habits become so normal that they govern behavior and communication patterns. Would you have thought their behaviors were so normal if Will had worn a tuxedo to impress Rachel? Although verbal communication is symbolic and must be analyzed when it is used—we must *think* about what we are going to say, or at least wish we had said at times—the nonverbal code is less symbolic and is more normative in nature. We often do not think about what we do nonverbally, yet most of us could name what is acceptable and what is not acceptable in specific situations. Waving hello to one of your good friends with your "upraised middle finger" (the proverbial "flip off") may be perfectly fine, whereas doing the same to your professor, your boss, a judge in a courtroom, your clergy, or your parents would probably have some negative consequences. A rule of thumb by which you should begin your study of nonverbal communication is: *What is the norm in one context may not necessarily be so in all situations.* In other words, when you try to attribute meanings to anyone's nonverbal behaviors, be sure you know both the context and the person. Your unwritten rule should be: *Unless I know both the context and the individual(s), I run the risk of being incorrect in my perceptions.* The better you know the context and the individual, the more accurate your perceptions are likely to be.

Because we have expectations, we sometimes assume (often inappropriately) that nonverbal communication is less calculating and a more accurate reflection of our feelings than verbal communication. Exploring nonverbal communication in more detail reveals that the relationship really does not exist in the ways we might imagine. In the case of Will and Francesco, unless there is a particular reason for changing their thinking about their communication, they usually act and react in accordance with everyday normative expectations. These actions often mold their verbal communication as well.

At this point, we would define **nonverbal communication** by going back to our earlier definition of communication (p. 5): *A process of creating meaning in the minds of receivers, whether intentionally or unintentionally, by use of actions other than, or in combination with, words or language. Nonverbal communication includes norms and expectations, usually imposed by society, for the expression of experiences, feelings, and attitudes.* In other words, nonverbal communication occurs when some nonverbal subcode (e.g., appearance, touch, space, body movement) creates meaning for a receiver, which can happen on purpose or unintentionally.

Nonverbal communication, then, operates in much the same way as verbal communication. It provides us with a means to control our communication, although it takes place in a more subtle, spontaneous, and natural way. Aspects of nonverbal communication make it possible, however, for receivers to be mistaken in interpreting a message, especially if the receiver perceives that message as having been sent on purpose. A shrug meant to convey "I don't know" may be interpreted as "I don't care." Nonverbal messages, while containing at least as much information as verbal messages, may lose their specificity of content, for a number of reasons. A nonverbal message by itself may be ambiguous or unclear; in many instances, it needs the verbal message to complete the process of communication.

There seems to be agreement among scholars about what subcodes are included in nonverbal communication, but there are considerable differences of opinion about how to approach their study. Part II of this book looks at the different approaches that appear regularly in the study of nonverbal communication.

APPROACHES TO NONVERBAL COMMUNICATION

To *approach* means to get close to a subject—in this case, nonverbal communication. Our approach to nonverbal communication suggests several factors. First, it implies that we either include or exclude several elements in our study. Second, our approach "colors" how we see the event and may even determine whether we can see the event at all. Third, our approach involves some research methodology (a method of classifying what we are observing), a way of understanding what we see based on that classification, and finally a basis for predicting future behaviors. As you might guess, there are many approaches to the study of nonverbal communication; ours is simply one of them (see Figure 1.2).

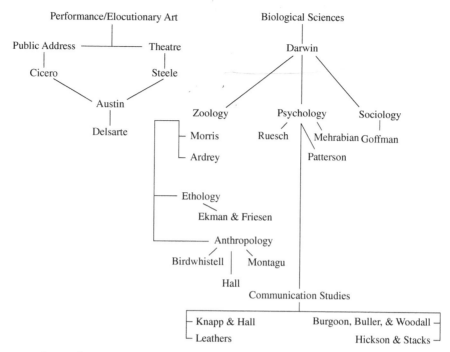

FIGURE 1.2 Approaches to nonverbal communication. *Source:* Adapted and extended from M. Hickson and D. W. Stacks, *NVC: Nonverbal Communication Studies Applications* (Dubuque, IA: Wm. C. Brown, 1985), p. 13.

An *approach* is often identified by one of three related, but different, factors. The first factor is one's theoretical point of view; the second is one's field of study or discipline; the third is one's methodology for undertaking research.

THEORETICAL APPROACHES

Many researchers think nonverbal communication is learned. People taking this perspective advocate the *nurture approach.* Traditionally, anthropologists and sociologists (such as Birdwhistell, E. T. Hall, Montagu, and Goffman) have used the nurture approach. We learn our nonverbal communication norms from sources that nurture our education. In opposition to this approach is the *nature approach,* developed by Darwin in *The Expression of the Emotions in Man and Animals* (1871/1998). Darwin assumed that nonverbal behavior is part of the genetic structure of human beings as well as of other animals. In other words, the nature approach claims that our nonverbal communication skills are part of our heredity, and that they are innate. A third approach, the *functional approach,* assumes nothing about genetics or learning behavior. It focuses instead on the types and functions of nonverbal communication. Psychologists and communication researchers (such as Mehrabian, J. K. Burgoon, Leathers, Knapp, J. A. Hall, E. T. Hall, Richmond and McCroskey, and Floyd, among others) have emphasized the functional approach. This approach looks more specifically at how we use nonverbal channels to accomplish the function of our communication encounters.

While these theoretical approaches reveal something about the nature of nonverbal communication, more can be learned by looking at the disciplines (or areas of study) of the researchers.

DISCIPLINARY APPROACHES

Perhaps the oldest discipline to consider the effects of nonverbal communication began in considering delivery in public speaking contexts. The early Greeks and Romans, and Cicero in particular, were the first to analyze delivery as one of the five important components of effective public speaking: invention, organization, memory, style, and *delivery*. Management of the voice and of gestures was a focus in the consideration of delivery (Corbett 1971). This focus on voice and gesture was known as the *elocutionary movement,* and it brought about an emphasis on the proper use of voice and gesture, which was prescriptive in nature. It provided specific vocal expressions and gestures based on how people should read or recite words. Steele (1779/1968) developed a musical staff analogy, in which he wrote "music" for speeches, poetry, and literature. Austin (1966) suggested a similar prescription for gestures. The prescriptive approach may be referred to as the "performance/elocutionary art" approach to nonverbal communication. Today, this approach is considered antiquated, and, with the exception of some broadcasting and theater programs, it is rarely taught. Today we look more at the substance of a public message when we teach Public Speaking than at its delivery. Because it was primarily a learned systematic approach to using specific nonverbal channels, it may be considered a *nurture view.*

Such a *nurture view* is held by many social scientists, who feel that the nonverbal code is similar to the verbal code and that all we need to do is to understand the structure of the nonverbal code. These scholars do *not* accept the notion that nonverbal communication is universal. Just as language differs, they argue, different cultures have different nonverbal coding systems. Nonverbal messages that are normal in the United States may very well have a completely different meaning in an Asian culture, and quite often may be considered socially unacceptable. There are some universal nonverbal codes, such as a smile, but for the most part we cannot be sure that all people we encounter will understand our nonverbal messages the same way.

Within the social and behavioral sciences we find many contemporary nonverbal communication researchers, although most of these researchers claim communication studies as their home discipline. Those closest to the *nature view* follow a biological science approach and are best represented by Desmond Morris (1977) and Robert Ardrey (1966). They are followed by ethnologists, who compare and contrast human behavior with that of other animals. Probably best known are Ekman and Friesen (1969), both having closely followed Darwin's beliefs. Psychologists often take different approaches from those of communication theorists. Some, like Mehrabian and Ruesch, take a *functional view;* others take a more psychological (or *nature)* view. Morris, for example, was a zoologist by profession, and he took the *nature view* in some instances. Some social anthropologists, such as Birdwhistell, take a linguistic (or language) view. We present these examples to show that there is no one correct way to study nonverbal communication.

METHODOLOGICAL APPROACHES

The methods used in the study of communication help us understand the many approaches to studying nonverbal communication. Typically, those who take a *nature view* observe the similarities in behaviors of humans and other animals. The establishment of territoriality is a good example of this approach; both human beings and animals establish their own territories. Those who take a *nurture view* observe over a period of time how nonverbal communication occurs in groups. For example, someone might videotape a group, and by viewing the tape again and again, the researcher may discover underlying systems of nonverbal communication (e.g., nodding, blinking, and winking). Functionalists focus on specific functions of nonverbal communication to determine how they work in specific contexts. For example, this approach may be used to study different greeting behaviors. More specific issues about methodologies are discussed in the appendix, where we discuss applying them to specific nonverbal subcodes.

This book, while reviewing the contributions of all approaches, uses a functional approach to nonverbal communication, combined with teaching you how to apply what you learn about those functions (what we referred to in the preface as an application orientation). This approach, we believe, will allow you to see how nonverbal communication functions in interactions with other individuals and will allow you to use the functional approach yourself. To develop such a view, we must first examine in more detail what constitutes nonverbal communication, its subcodes or channels, and its functions.

NONVERBAL FUNCTIONS AND SUBCODES

To this point, we have talked about what nonverbal communication is. We can look at many actions or expressions and call them "nonverbal communication." What we choose to study and how we group these subjects together reflect both our definition and our approach to the study of nonverbal communication. We believe it best to examine the subcodes, those different component parts of the overall nonverbal code, as dimensions of five areas: touch and space, physical appearance, gestures, vocalics, and covert body/temporal communication (or those nonverbal issues that are not seen or heard). We feel that these five areas, each with its own appropriate subareas, constitute nonverbal communication. After this examination, we look briefly at the traditionally held functions of human nonverbal communication.

TOUCH AND SPACE

We communicate within an environment or physical setting. Because of this, our examination begins with an analysis of how touch is used and how it is a component of using *zero space*. Zero space is when two people are touching and there is no space or distance between them. Next we analyze how people use their own personal space and then how the environment affects communication, helping to establish the context (or situation) of the communication. Later in the text, we examine the influences of the environments' physical dimensions (e.g., furniture, architecture), color and aesthetic appreciation, environmental size and shape, and temperature and humidity. Within environments, we structure the space around us in two ways: We establish territories, and we expect certain amounts of personal space to be available to us. Thus, the text looks at how we structure our territory and our personal space, what types of communication can be expected in each of these two, and what the norms are regarding both of these aspects of proxemic behavior, or the use of space. We examine the total lack (absence) or violation of space as well as touch behavior. The term is commonly referred to as haptics or "zero-proxemics." Finally, we examine the impact of violating the norms and expectations of someone with respect to both space usage and touch.

PHYSICAL APPEARANCE

We examine how our body affects communication. We look at body shape and size, body image, physical attractiveness, clothing, and accessories, including all types of objects we carry or use. We consider how the body is used as a communicative tool and how we perceive the bodies of others. Stereotypical judgments, relationships between body size and I.Q., salary discrepancies, and expectations are examined for their day-to-day impact. We also examine how accessories, such as jewelry, book bags, hats, etc., affect people's perceptions of others. Included in this analysis is the impact of advertising on our society's view of what is physically attractive. We also include how the birth and the prominence of social media affects issues in the study of nonverbal communication.

BODY MOVEMENTS AND GESTURES

Kinesics is the study of communication that is engendered by bodily behaviors that can be visually observed. These may be gross or exaggerated movements or minute, almost imperceptible movements. Kinesics is explored through Birdwhistell's "kinesic system," which looks structurally at the use of body movements. It is then explored through Ekman and Friesen's more "meaning-centered approach" to bodily movement. We examine the blending of kinesic behaviors to create different emotional messages. We also look at the relationship between eye behavior and communication, both between people and as an analysis of the brain's activity during communication.

VOCALICS

The fourth subcode examined is the unique contribution the voice makes to our "vocal expressiveness." We explore some of the stereotypes we have of others that are based on voice—masculinity, femininity, assuredness, and cooperativeness, to name but a few. We look at sound and its attributes—loudness, pitch, duration, articulation, and silence. We examine the "paravocal" aspects of voice qualities—what is a "good" or a "bad" voice, how it is used, and with what effect, characterizers, and qualifiers. Finally, we examine the effects of dialect, accent, rate, and nonfluencies, and we consider their correlation with such characteristics as body shape and appearance.

COVERT BODY/TEMPORAL COMMUNICATION

The final chapter in Part II examines phenomena we usually do not see: the impact of the olfactory system (scent and smell), as well as perceptual aspects of nonverbal communication, including possible detection of deception. We then examine the impact of time (chronemics) on our communication, looking at biofeedback rhythms and cultural expectations of how we use and perceive time.

NONVERBAL FUNCTIONS

As noted earlier, nonverbal communication does not operate in a vacuum. Nonverbal communication often performs one of several functions in relationship to verbal communication. These functions help us to understand and use communication more effectively. We have identified six functions for which nonverbal communication is used.

1. *Identification and self-presentation.* We use nonverbal devices to let others know who we are. Those who know us well can identify us by our voices on the telephone. Some people call and say, "Hey, it's me." When we know that voice well, we know who "me" is. We also present ourselves through physical appearance, by facial expression, by vocal tone, by postural stances or sitting, by our olfactory signature (how we smell), by our use or misuse of time, among many other factors. We can tell when other people are "dressed up," when they appear excited, and when they sound depressed.

2. *Control of the interaction.* We use the nonverbal channel to take the floor so that we can speak; we regulate many interactions by nonverbal channels. Instead of saying, "I have a question," we may raise our hand or show a look of puzzlement. In an interpersonal setting, we are likely to raise our index finger and lean forward to signal our desire to take the floor. We also let others know when it is their turn to speak by slowing down our rate of speaking and pausing, by leaning back, or by using silence, among other tactics. All these nonverbal devices, and others, regulate our interactions.

3. *Relationship of interactants.* We illustrate to others how well we know a person by how closely we stand or sit to him or her, whether we smile and wink at the person, whether we whisper to him or her. Holding hands illustrates a particular type of relationship. For two teenagers, it may mean, "We're together [for now]." For a father and son, it may mean that the father is taking care of the son. If the son tries to pull away, the hand holding may mean that the father is in charge. Employees may assume a stiffer posture in the presence of their bosses than with their coworkers. If you are "in charge," say, as a parent, you may fold your arms across your chest and tap your foot to show impatience with your child, yet you are not likely to use the same nonverbal behaviors with your boss because the relationship is different.

4. *Display of cognitive information.* We use nonverbal communication to send specific information to the receiver; consider the use of a hand to communicate. A display of fingers may mean, "Okay." Another display, a hand held up by a road worker, may mean, "Stop!" When you allow someone to pull into the line of traffic in front of you, the same hand signal may mean "Thanks!" Thumbs up may mean "Great!" Obscene signs may be delivered

in an angry way or a friendly way. Recall the earlier example where you might "flip off" a good friend just to say hello; not everyone you did that to would take it as a friendly gesture. A specific uniform may tell others, "I am a police officer." A stethoscope around one's neck illustrates that one is a health care worker.

5. *Display of affective (emotional) information.* We use nonverbal communication to let others know how we feel. Also, our innate knowledge of nonverbal communication allows us to interpret the emotions of others. When we first meet a person, we establish a "baseline" of his or her emotions. Does the person appear nervous, anxious, stressed? When we meet that person again, we use that first occurrence in evaluating how we think that person feels. The better we know someone, the more accurate we are with our suppositions.

6. *Display of deception.* We also use nonverbal communication to show others that we feel a certain emotion when we actually do not feel it. We try to detect deception in others through their nonverbal behaviors. We tend to think of excessive pauses and "ahs" as indicators that the other person is lying. As we discuss later, behaviors that we have long thought are cues to deception are not good indicators (Park, Levine, Harms, and Ferrara 2002).

These six nonverbal functions provide us with a basic set of tools for the examination of nonverbal communication. Other scholars may provide other functions, but we believe these six meet our criteria for teaching about nonverbal communication. Before we begin to examine these functions, we need to look at the general communication process. The following review will form a background for the examination of our functional approach to communication, which is based on what we believe to be the purposes of nonverbal interaction.

NONVERBAL COMMUNICATION AND PERCEPTION

Most researchers agree that the communication process begins with **perceptions**. Perceptions are derived from the way we look at things—through (1) sensation and (2) interpretation. A sensation takes place through one of the five senses: touch, or the tactile sense; sight, or the visual sense; sound, or the aural (hearing) sense; smell, or the olfactory sense; and taste, or the gustatory sense. After a stimulus has been sensed by one or more of our sensory organs, the brain interprets this stimulus and places it in our "memory bank of perceptions." Through this process of perceiving, the external world becomes a part of what we refer to as knowledge.

To look at how perception affects communication processes, let us analyze an example. Recall a class you have had where there were students who felt they always had to participate in class discussions by either asking questions or sharing their thoughts whenever the professor asked a general question of the class. You may have perceived these students to be *brown nosers and royal pains*, and because the professor always allowed these students to speak up, you may have believed that the professor was "falling for it." The professor, however, might have perceived these students to be people who were unsure of themselves and of their worth as students. The professor may have believed that those issues prompted these students to try to prove to themselves that they were smart enough to be there. The students, however, may have perceived themselves to be active participants in the class simply because they liked the subject matter and they wanted to "take in" as much of it as possible in the short time allotted to class meetings. The only way they knew how to accomplish that goal was to be active participants. Although the students' self-perception may have been correct, does that mean the professor's or your perceptions were incorrect?

Just contemplating that small communication example, you can see how much perception affects how we interpret messages. For that reason, we always suggest checking your perceptions with the communicator, not with other observers of the communication. When you wish to know the actual message a communicator means to send, you need to consult with the communicator to clarify the meaning of the message.

In nonverbal communication, knowledge is typically related to *how we intend to evaluate the message*. Nonverbal communication provides us with a *metamessage*—a message about the message. Nonverbal communication tells us, for example, whether people are being serious, joking, or sarcastic when they say, "I love you." Now take this same expression and repeat it in these manners: sincerely, sarcastically, and playfully. Can you tell the difference? This evaluation of the meaning is based on the vocal tone and facial expressions used when the message is sent.

BOX 1.5 OBSERVATIONAL STUDY

Find an opportunity to carry on a conversation with someone you are comfortable conversing with (e.g., roommate, best friend, boyfriend/girlfriend, parent, etc. . . .). Observe the nonverbal messages of this person, watching carefully for nonverbal cues. Then try experimenting with your own nonverbal messages; try sending one that is sincere, then one that is sarcastic or humorous. Take note of whether or not your conversational partner received the message you believe you sent. Take note of whether you think that person understood your message because of how well they know you and/or because of the context in which you were communicating.

There are a number of factors that **filter**, or influence, our perceptions or interpretations. These filters include the function or purpose of the communication, as already discussed, as well as process structure, age, culture and race, status, and sex and gender. These five perceptual filters, discussed in the following paragraphs, do influence how we perceive others' communications, and it is crucial to always keep them in mind when communicating with others.

PROCESS STRUCTURE

Process structure refers to how the brain processes incoming sensations. Some texts use the term *hemispheric differences* (more commonly known as left brain/right brain) to refer to processing differences; however, we prefer *hemispheric style*. The left hemisphere of the brain is responsible for most people's verbal communication. This side of the brain is specialized in an abstract, logical, and analytical way that is best used for the analysis of language.

The left is also known as the side of the brain that most often processes the cognitive information you receive. The right hemisphere (sometimes called the "minor" hemisphere) is specialized for the spatiotemporal, gestalt, emotive forms of communication for which nonverbal communication is best suited. The right is often called the side of the brain that processes more of the affective (or emotional) information as well as more of the creative information received (Prochnow et al. 2013; Alibeik, Angaji, Pouriamanesh, and Movallali 2011; Morimoto et al. 2008). For many years it was thought that one side of the brain dominated the other. More recently, we have begun to realize that each hemisphere's specialization includes a small share of the other hemisphere's specialty (Stacks and Andersen 1989). This means that some language will be processed in the right hemisphere, which may be done automatically or because it is tied to some emotions. The left hemisphere also processes some nonverbal communication.

It is essential to note that each hemisphere of the brain is specialized to analyze either verbal or nonverbal communication. To explain this difference, we look at a model suggesting that nonverbal communication is more spontaneous, whereas verbal communication is symbolic. According to Buck (1982, 1984), spontaneous communication is related to the right hemisphere, is an automatic reflexive response, and is nonpropositional (lacks logical analysis) in nature. Buck's dichotomy is presented in Table 1.1.

One final approach to hemispheric processing has been proposed by Stacks (1982). Stacks postulates that the two brain hemispheres differ only in terms of style; that is, each is best suited for either verbal or nonverbal communication. Stacks theorizes that each hemisphere contains the process necessary for language, but language processed in the right hemisphere is unconscious or repressed by the left hemisphere (which is the analytical, logical aspect of reality).

How each hemisphere of the brain operates also helps determine what type of material is being processed. Based on the work of Watzlawick, Beavin, and Jackson (1967), J. K. Burgoon and Saine (1978) concluded that verbal communication is more digital, much like a computer's

TABLE 1.1 SUMMARY OF THE CHARACTERISTICS OF SPONTANEOUS AND SYMBOLIC COMMUNICATION

Characteristics	Spontaneous Communication	Symbotic Communication
Basis of signal system	Biologically shared	Socially shared
Elements	Signs: Natural, externally visible aspects of referent	Symbols: Arbitrary relationships with referent
Intentionality	Spontaneous: Communicative behavior is an automatic or a reflex response	Voluntary: Sender intends to send a specific message
Content	Nonpropositional motivational/emotional states	Propositions; Expressions capable of logical analysis (test of truth or falsity)
Cerebral Processing	Related to right hemisphere	Related to left hemisphere

Source: R. Buck, "Spontaneous and Symbolic Nonverbal Behavior and The Ontogeny of Communication," in *Development of Nonverbal Behavior in Children*, ed. R. S. Feldman (New York: Springer-Verlag, 1982), p. 38. Reprinted with permission of Springer Science + Business Media.

information: It is highly arbitrary, discrete, and found in finite units. Nonverbal communication, however, is more continuous and natural. Burgoon and Saine label this kind of communication as **analogical**, which means that the code material is composed of continuous, infinite, and natural representations of what people observe. A metaphor for the analogical nature of nonverbal code material is the color spectrum. It consists of a finite number of colors, from white (a combination of all colors) to black (the absence of all colors), but our symbolic representations of the color spectrum are arbitrary and discrete (e.g., aquamarine, tangerine, lilac, navy blue). In the same way a gesture is continuous and infinite, analysis forces us to "create" a meaning for that gesture. That meaning will be arbitrary, and it may change by culture or subculture, from relationship to relationship, from situation to situation. Take, for example, the "okay" symbol—creating a circle with the thumb and forefinger and extending the other three fingers upward. In our culture it means "okay." In some other cultures the same symbol is an expression of what "flipping someone off" is in our culture. Those definitions are arbitrary and are based on the norms of the culture. Richmond and McCroskey (2000) take this processing of information in a similar direction, but the distinctions they note are a little different. Two distinctions they make, among others, are the **linguistic distinction** and the **continuity distinction**, showing processing distinctions similar to those of J. K. Burgoon and Saine (1978). The **linguistic distinction** is discussed as relying on language, whereas nonverbal communication does not rely on language. This does not deny, however, that verbal and nonverbal communication do work in conjunction with each other. The **continuity distinction** looks at verbal communication as discontinuous, meaning that a verbal interaction has a start and a finish. Nonverbal communication is continuous, meaning it is ongoing and does not need a verbal component to have meaning. Even the absence of nonverbal behaviors can send a message (e.g., the "silent treatment" when you are angry).

Finally, we must examine the structure of the two codes. As might be expected, nonverbal communication is much less structured than verbal communication. Many researchers believe that nonverbal communication has no particular set of rules, no grammar, and no syntax. Other nonverbal communication scholars would disagree with that statement, however, and say that we actually do create rules for what is nonverbally acceptable and what is not. The verbal code can be indicative of the past, present, and future, and it can also be expressed in a number of different languages. Nonverbal communication has no written set of rules (although some are probably understood), grammar, or syntax; it is bound to the present, and is its own natural language. For example, although speakers can talk about speeches they give or will give (about how good or bad they were or will be), they cannot do so nonverbally without first providing a context through verbalizing. Consider a smile. What does it reflect? Without some other information, say about the topic being discussed or the situation at hand, we have no idea. Although we may infer many things from that smile, a verbal message is needed to understand what the emotion is.

Nonverbal communication, because of its rather singular need to be in the present, tends to be highly *contextual*. Different situations or environments produce different nonverbal messages. Your nonverbal communication will likely be different at a funeral than it is at a party, although a funeral in New Orleans might be a different experience from what we normally think of as funereal. The way you act in class or while hanging out with a friend would probably not be proper in a job interview or at work. The context helps us to decide what norms and rules to follow.

AGE

As we discuss in later chapters, age is a primary factor in the communication process. For example, children stand closer to one another when they are younger. You will usually allow a 3-year-old to climb into your lap, but would you allow the person sitting next to you in this class to do the same? People who lose some of their hearing as they age will stand closer to people so they can hear, yet adults generally tend to stand farther away from people. These are norms for our society, and such standards will always be contextually based. Individuals whose sight has weakened may have difficulty observing the gestures and facial expressions of others and so may move closer to others. As people get older, they tend to put more distance between others and themselves. We often see children as "space invaders," and we may have a tendency to avoid getting anywhere near senior citizens, almost as if old age were contagious. We should also point out, however, that these are standards of our culture; other cultures that revere their aged members do not avoid coming in contact with the older generation. It is Knapp and Hall's (1992) belief that we are more likely to move closer to others of our own age group.

Age may also affect other aspects of nonverbal communication. Physical appearance is one area where age may play a role. Children of preschool age may not yet be aware of clothing trends and may, therefore, be less concerned with their physical appearance than when they grow into their school-age years. As people age into senior citizens, they may become less concerned with appearance again, perhaps becoming more concerned with the people they are than how they appear. It would be stereotypical to make any blanket statements about how age affects appearance, because each person will certainly make personal choices based on his or her preferences. Can you think of any senior citizens who are overly concerned with their physical appearance and attributes, including the trendy dress of the day? Conversely, can you think of any young children who are similarly concerned with the same issue? Your answer will likely be yes to both of those questions, just proving that you need to be careful about the nonverbal subcode of physical appearance when you analyze it using this perceptual filter of age.

CULTURE AND RACE

Nonverbal aspects of communication vary widely according to culture and race. In some cultures people stand very close to one another; in others, men kiss one another's beards; women do not shave their legs and underarms in some cultures; some cultures' pace of life is very different from ours in the United States. With the many cultural and racial differences, we may find that dress can be different, as can touch, space, scent, usage of time, gestures, and so forth. In addition, some theoretical differences will greatly affect nonverbal communication between people from different cultures.

We should take note of cultural variables that can influence nonverbal interactions. One specific variable that would influence nonverbal communication is whether a culture uses **high-context** or **low-context communication**. High-context communication, according to

Samovar, Porter, McDaniel, and Roy (2013), is seen where most of the information is either in the physical context or internalized in the coded, explicit, transmitted part of the message. What this means is that high-context communication is more indirect, ambiguous, and far more dependent on the nonverbal code. Low-context communication is seen when the mass of the information is vested in the explicit code. Low-context communication is more direct, precise, clear, and dependent on the verbal code for message transmission.

Another cultural variable that researchers should determine when studying nonverbal communication is whether a culture is **individualistic** or **collectivistic** in nature. Samovar et al. (2013) tell us that cultures that are more individualistic are ones where individuals' goals take precedence over the group's goals; they are more likely to promote self-realization, and they see each person as having a unique set of talents and potential. In individualistic cultures, according to Gudykunst (1998), people are expected to look after themselves and their immediate families only; the "I" identity takes precedence over the "we" identity. In collectivistic cultures, the group's goals take precedence over individuals' goals, which re-quires that individuals fit into their groups. Emphasis is placed on collectivity, harmony, and cooperation within the group. In collectivistic cultures "people belong to in-groups or collectivities which are supposed to look after them in exchange for loyalty" to the group (p. 47); the "we" identity is more important than the "I" identity. These two variables can significantly influence the importance of nonverbal communication. Using dress as an ex-ample, we can see that people from individualistic cultures may dress in unique styles. Someone from a collectivistic culture, wanting to fit in with the group, might dress like others in the same culture. In some cultures, collectivism is forced on the population, as in Communist China. The government, especially in some work settings, can prescribe dress, and many people in cultures like that of China dress in identical clothing styles and colors.

There are other cultural variables that are also important when studying nonverbal com-munication. **Power distance** is one variable that affects the use of nonverbal communication in situations involving interactions between people of different statuses. Some cultures' norms say that people who are more powerful should be in control, and their nonverbal communication behaviors will reflect this. This norm is called **high power distance**. The United States is deemed a culture that practices **low power distance**, which means that Americans believe people should be treated as equals, even if there are status differences between them (Samovar et al., 2013; Gudykunst, 1998). Most of us know some nonverbal behaviors that are expected of us when we are in a subordinate role, so it is easy to see how this variable could affect nonverbal communication norms and expectations. If you are a subordinate in a high power distance culture, you will assume postures that indicate less power, such as shrinkage of your body, whereas the boss might use an expansive posture. You might not initiate eye contact or touch if you are in a subordinate role in a high power distance culture; that privilege is reserved for the person in the higher status role.

Another cultural variable we would do well to understand is **high** and **low uncertainty avoidance**. Samovar et al. (2013) define this concept to be how comfortable we are with being uncertain about how communication progresses in our society, and in our case here we'll look at nonverbal communication. Cultures high in uncertainty avoidance have many unwritten rules about what is acceptable and what is not. For example, making direct eye contact in the culture of the United States is acceptable and even expected. Doing the same in the Japanese culture (a high uncertainty avoidance culture) is considered rude when there is a status differential; lower status individuals are considered rude and disrespectful for making direct eye contact with persons of higher status. Should you go to Japan to work when you graduate from college, these are "rules" you would do well to know.

The final cultural variable that would cause communicators to modify their nonverbal communication would be **masculinity** and **femininity**. In cultures that are considered more masculine, gender roles are clearly distinct. Men are supposed to be assertive, tough, and focused on material success, whereas women are supposed to be more modest, tender, and concerned with the quality of life. People in highly masculine cultures value things, power, and assertiveness; they emphasize differentiated sex roles, performance, ambition, and independence; they tend to have little contact with members of the opposite sex when growing up, and they tend to see same-sex relationships as more intimate than opposite-sex relationships (Gudykunst 1998). In cultures considered more feminine, gender roles overlap; both men and women are supposed to be modest, tender, and concerned with the quality of life. People in highly feminine cultures value quality of life and nurturance; they value fluid sex roles, service, and interdependence (Gudykunst 1998). The authors of this text believe that there is also a "middle of the road" position on this issue—that there are also **androgynous** cultures, which means that they reject the rigid sex roles often imposed by society (Wood 2012). A culture that is androgynous would have characteristics of both masculine and feminine cultures.

When deciding how to communicate with people who are culturally or racially different from us, we need to take many things into account. Culture and race are clearly important filters that help us understand nonverbal communication.

STATUS

How we interact nonverbally with superiors may differ entirely from how we interact with subordinates. In addition, our nonverbal communication sending and receiving processes vary depending upon whom we are interacting with. We may have relaxed kinesics while interacting with our peers, but when in the presence of our "boss" we become more formal. A superior may initiate touch with you by putting a hand on your shoulder after a successful project, for instance, but would you be likely to do the same if he or she had similar success?

In 1994, C. B. Johnson reported that there are reasons to believe that the purpose for which we use nonverbal communication depends on position of legitimate authority. That is, bosses tend to use nonverbal communication to manipulate and even control, while subordinates use it to comply and show deference (or respect) to a boss's authority. Later in this textbook, we discuss more ways status is communicated, and it will become even more obvious that status also serves as an important filter for understanding nonverbal communication.

GENDER

We, like many communication scholars, differentiate between *sex* and *gender*. We define sex as the biological determination of male and female. Gender we define as a psychological and sociological determination, and we consider it to be a continuum, with masculinity at one

PHOTO 1.2 Does your posturing differ when interacting with a professor or advisor than with your roommate?

end and femininity at the other. The midpoint of the continuum would be androgyny, which is having both masculine and feminine psychological traits. In 1977, Henley published *Body Politics: Power, Sex, and Nonverbal Communication.* In her book, Henley argues that males are the dominant and domineering sex and that males indicate their dominance through a number of channels, including nonverbal communication. Tannen (1990) and Wood (2012) wrote that males typically use the communication process as a method of *control,* which complemented Henley's analysis. At the same time, Tannen suggested that females generally use the communication process to *negotiate,* and Wood's research on "women's speech" confirms that finding. Over the last decade, many researchers have studied the differences between male and female communication, and the discipline of nonverbal communication is not a stranger to that research. This book looks at how gender affects the many subcodes that we use.

When looking at status differentials, we need to refer to Johnson's (1994) findings mentioned in the preceding section about status. These findings can be applied especially to work environments employing both males and females. As the make-up of the work force becomes more and more that of both sexes, in both superior and subordinate roles, the nonverbal communication will change. For now, however, the majority of research on gender issues in the workplace indicates that the "superior" nonverbal behaviors are those considered typically male (Wood 2012). In the course of covering the different subcodes in this text, we point out some of those specific findings.

There appear to be several positions regarding the relationships between power, gender, and nonverbal communication, and they should be considered as positioned along a continuum. We summarize these positions by saying that some scholars report no differences in how males and females use power, while others take the position that there are no similarities. Some of the positions point to differences but say those differences exist as a result of legitimate authority being exercised, not because of gender. Some say that males always dominate females and that nonverbal communication is just one such area. Others point to the idea that both men and women exhibit power, but it is not to be viewed as dominance. Power is certainly one area where we see differences between genders, if not in the manifestation of power, surely in the range of findings we discovered when surveying the literature on this theme. We look at this issue a number of times in our study of the subcodes of nonverbal communication, allowing you to draw your own conclusions.

Henley (1977) saw significant differences in nonverbal communication when a male boss dominated a female secretary by using nonverbal communication. A situation with a male boss and a female secretary was typical when Henley undertook her research in the early 1970s. Today, while such a relationship may still be somewhat typical, there are also others that are much different (e.g., a female boss with a female secretary, a male boss with a male secretary, and a female boss with a male secretary). Johnson (1994) attempted to determine gender-based differences in light of the legitimate authority of the individual. She found that, with the exceptions of smiling and laughing, one's position in authority was more important than gender. Even with smiling and laughing, the gender composition of the group being studied was more important than the sex and gender of the boss. Today Henley would probably find different results, the differences traceable solely to the changes prescribed by federal Affirmative Action and Equal Opportunity laws. What might have been acceptable in the workplace 20 years ago may not be acceptable today, and most of our society has been educated about this topic. Most people in positions of authority today are very careful about using any discriminatory nonverbal behaviors based on sex for fear of the consequences. We could hope that these changes came as a result of more nonverbal sensitivity, since that would indicate that more effective communication practices were being learned, but the reality is probably that these changes have come about as a result of subtle coercion by our society. Nevertheless, most would attest that the outcome is still positive.

To better understand some of the gender differences found in nonverbal communication, we briefly explore several factors that previous research has indicated as dominating and deferent (acquiescent, obedient, submissive) behaviors. Using the control of interaction function, we might see that there are several ways to dominate a conversation. It may be done by talking too much, interrupting, changing the topic, and by the use of silence. Each of these methods has been viewed as a dominating mechanism.

AMOUNT OF TALK

James and Drakich (1993) and Wood (1998), among others, have reported that men talk more than women in mixed-sex interactions. Tannen (1990), however, suggests that in public situations, males ask more questions, ask longer questions, and typically ask the first question; Wood's (2012) research confirms those findings. Tannen suggests further that males talk more in public and females more in private situations, referring to male talk as "report talk" and female talk as "rapport talk."

INTERRUPTIONS

There are three types of interruptions: positive, negative, and neutral. Positive interruptions include those where a question is asked for clarification purposes (communication function). Neutral interruptions include those that are "asides" (e.g., "Please pass the butter.") Negative interruptions are often referred to as **overlaps**, although some overlaps are not considered to be negative. Overlapping, by definition, means that you overlap someone's speech with your own; it is sometimes seen as a sign that you are interested and that you are following the conversation. Let's consider what we know thus far about the amount of talk and regulation of conversation between males and females, and then consider how interruptions are a part of the process of communication. We know that men talk more than women in public situations, asking the first questions, asking more questions, and asking longer questions (which are often preceded with a statement or statements; Tannen 1990). With that in mind, let us assess how interruptions add to this:

1. Men interrupt more often (A. T. Beck 1988; Bohn and Stutman 1983; Esposito 1979; J. A. Hall 1984; C. West and Zimmerman 1983).
2. Interruption is often seen as dominance (Youngquist 2009; Samar and Alibakhshi 2009; L. P. Stewart, Stewart, Friedley, and Cooper 1990; Tannen 1983, 1990).
3. Interruption has also been seen as a signal of interest as opposed to dominance (C. West and Zimmerman 1983).
4. Women will interrupt more with questions, men with statements (LaFrance and Carmen 1980; Wood 2012).
5. Interruptions and overlaps are different, according to some theorists (Bennett 1981).
6. Overlaps are not gender related (Zimmerman and West 1975).
7. Seventy-five percent of the time, overlaps are cooperative (Tannen 1990).
8. Sometimes overlaps are simply conversational "duets" (Falk 1980).
9. Men use interruptions more to control conversation; women use interruptions more to indicate interest and to respond (L. P. Stewart et al. 1990; Wood 2012).
10. Men more often consider interruptions as normal and good-natured, at least within masculine environments, so it carries over into all environments (Wood 1998, 2012).

If you are thinking that some of these points contradict each other, you are correct. The body of research on the topic of interruptions has never been clearly conclusive about which gender uses more of them and how they are used. Perhaps further research into this nonverbal and verbal field will be more forthcoming with its results, but for now, suffice it to say that interruptions do occur and are used by both sexes. We look at these more closely when we discuss the vocal subcode in Chapter 10.

SILENCE

If silence means the lack of interruption, it is interesting that some researchers have found that males use silence as a method to dominate. Silence has long been considered a vocalic subcode factor that communicates much information. Sattel (1983) has noted that silence can be used as an instrument of power. While Tannen (1990) has indicated that some males use silence as a "taciturnity of spirit" (meaning being subdued or reserved), there appears to be no research to support males using silence as a manipulative tool.

Power is not the only issue in the use of silence. Richmond and McCroskey (2000) point out that people use silence to communicate many things. We may use silence to establish interpersonal distance, to put our thoughts together, to show respect for another person, or to modify others' behaviors. Most research in the area of gender differences, however, has not determined that either sex uses silence for one of those functions more than the other sex.

DEFERENCE

At the other end of the regulation-of-interaction spectrum is the concept of deference, meaning that we can expect subordinates to defer to their superiors in terms of conversations and other communication interactions. One of the most significant means of deferring is through nonverbal gesturing. When the boss is "lecturing," a subordinate may be compelled to nod his or her head in agreement. Goffman (1976) discussed deferential behavior at length in his studies of advertising. Goffman found that marketing and advertising specialists had taken advantage of the common stereotypes of gender differences. Goffman found six general types of *gender-isms* in advertisements: (1) males were larger than women in relative size; (2) women were portrayed as outlining and touching objects more often than men (the feminine touch); (3) males were portrayed as having the more executive, superior, or active role (function ranking); (4) the family was often used, but whereas sons were shown as inferior to fathers, mother–daughter combinations generally displayed more equality; (5) females were found to physically lower themselves to males (ritual of subordination); and (6) women were found to be depicted as withdrawn psychologically from the social situation at large, not oriented to it, and dependent on the goodwill of others. We might think that these findings have changed in recent years. Although there have been some changes, the majority of advertisements still send the same message (Wood 2012). When we view an advertisement that shows something out of the "ordinary," in relation to gender roles, it stands out. The Coca-Cola advertisement where the women working in an office building ogle the attractive construction worker outside or the man who bakes biscuits for his football-watching buddies (which is the exact opposite of that which we usually think of as "the norm") would be some examples. Another might be some of the advertisements where a man is discussing bathroom-cleaning products.

The mass media apparently reflect the gender roles of our society and also contribute to them. D. Archer, Kimes, and Barrios (1976) noted some factors similar to Goffman's findings. Studying photographs in newspapers and magazines, they observed that more of the bodies of females were shown, whereas pictures of males contained mostly faces. Still other researchers look at election campaigns where there are female and male candidates. Media will often pay attention to what the female candidate is wearing, but the male candidate does not receive the same scrutiny (Wood 2012). Think of the 2008 primary and how often the media pointed to the clothes Hillary Clinton was wearing at different events, or when she was in a bar and drank a shot of whiskey as if it was something women do not do. Was the same done to Barack Obama? Consider, also, the attention Sarah Palin received about how much money she spent on clothing for the 2008 presidential campaign. Did John McCain receive the same scrutiny? The 2012 primary season was spared that treatment, but that was based solely on the fact that there were no female candidates. Such differences make it clear why, in almost any social situation, we have a certain set of expectations about how our own sex and gender should communicate.

BOX 1.6   OBSERVATIONAL STUDY

Choose to watch a half-hour television program that is on a commercial television station. Observe the advertisements that accompany the program. How many were there? How many used stereotyped gender roles for both men and women? How many did not? What nonverbal messages did these ads send about the roles of men and women in our society today? Were the depictions of both sexes accurate? Why or why not?

An overview of gender differences research reveals that males and females differ in terms of facial expressions (women reveal more emotions); posture and bearing (women are more relaxed and sit differently; men expand more, women use shrinkage behaviors); eye contact (women employ more); gesturing (men use more and are more expansive in their use of gestures; women use more in approval-seeking situations); clothing, grooming, and physical appearance (women put more importance on their appearances, and society places more importance on their appearance); use of space (women are approached much more closely); and touch (men often interpret women's touch as sexual, more so than women do men's touch; women are touched more in same-sex interactions than men are). In terms of vocalics, there are gender differences in sound development (female children start speaking earlier, mothers vocalize more to female children); physiology (males have larger larynxes and longer and thicker vocal cords; more males have speech defects); and pronunciation (more females speak standard American dialect, more males, nonstandard, blue-collar English); pitch (lower pitch for males); volume (males generally speak more loudly); and vocal typecasting (males have more problems verbalizing emotions).

Identifying an individual's sex can often be determined solely on the basis of the voice. Although there are gender differences in how messages are transmitted, there are also gender-related differences in perceptions of others' nonverbal communication. Vocally, women are generally perceived in terms of sociability, and men are perceived in terms of physical and emotional power. Vocal quality cues are used more in judging women than in judging men. As a general conclusion, we can also state that *women are more accurate in their interpretation of nonverbal cues and are more responsive to nonverbal cues than are men.*

Additional research has examined how males and females perceive each other. L. Powell, Hill, and Hickson (1980) had students view a videotaped speech given by a speaker of the same sex and one of the opposite sex. Participants evaluated speakers for attitudinal similarity, credibility, and interpersonal attraction. The only differences between males and females were found for females who viewed a female speaker, and then only on the assessment of the female speaker's *social attraction.*

It is our position that understanding differences in power and gender is important to effective communication, especially when dominance in an interaction is considered. Just as with all nonverbal communication, it would be impossible to generalize about entire populations just because some findings indicate that certain behaviors are used by the majority of one group. Such a generalization would be stereotyping at its worst, and it would not allow for the individuality of human beings. Such general differences, however, can be important and helpful in learning to communicate effectively with others.

THE IMPORTANCE OF RESEARCH

We believe it is important for you to acquire a basic understanding of how nonverbal communication has been researched and studied, and how theories have been derived through research processes. First, all research is only as good as the methods used by researchers to answer the questions they set out to answer and the hypotheses being tested. Learning about how research is conducted helps you to better understand the strengths and weaknesses of the research reported. Second, you may wish to repeat some of the research procedures or test some of the researchers' assertions and hypotheses that we report in this text. An understanding of research methodology will, at least informally, help you find the answers to your questions. For that reason, we suggest that at this time you look at the appendix for what is a brief review of what researchers of nonverbal communication have gone through to derive at the theories you will study in this textbook. We hope that this lends credibility to what you will study for the semester in this course.

SUMMARY

Introductory information on this significant topic of nonverbal communication is crucial to your understanding the rest of what we discuss in this textbook. Nonverbal communication is important; it accounts for 60 percent to 93 percent of the communication we have with others in face-to-face interaction, depending on which theorist one cites. Several theoretical and methodological lines of thought developed for the study of nonverbal communication have been presented here, in the hope of making the concept of nonverbal communication clearer for you. Realize, too, that although nonverbal communication and verbal communication differ in many ways, the two systems function together. After reading this introduction, you should be able to distinguish between nonverbal communication and nonverbal behavior. It is our hope that you are now able to identify and define nonverbal communication in terms of four basic dimensions: overt (kinesic and vocalic) communication, spatial use (proxemics, haptics/tactics), physical appearance, and body/temporal communication (covert, olfactory, chronemic). In addition, environmental factors become an important part of our study of nonverbal communication.

It is important to understand that we both receive and send the nonverbal code to others through a number of filters. Our filters assist us in interpreting the various stimuli that we sense. These filters include the purpose of the interaction (according to each of the interactants), the sex or gender of the interactants, the brain processing of the nonverbal code, and the age, culture, race, and status of the interactants. As you go through the chapters of this book, you should remember that these filters help determine what you gain from a nonverbal encounter. To understand the studies we cite in Part II, we review in the appendix how nonverbal communication research is conducted. Enjoy the adventure you embark upon here!

QUESTIONS FOR THOUGHT

1. What is nonverbal communication? Nonverbal behavior?
2. How much difference is there in the ways males and females use nonverbal communication?
3. How do the two code systems (verbal and nonverbal codes) work to create "communication"?
4. In your mind, how do the five purposes of nonverbal communication relate to the total communication process?
5. Given what you have learned in this chapter, how effective are you as a nonverbal communicator? Why?
6. What do you think is the role of media in setting the nonverbal roles for individuals? Are the roles they create realistic for you and people in your age group? What about for young children? Senior citizens? Middle-aged adults?

FURTHER REFERENCES

Nonverbal Behaviors Versus Nonverbal Messages

Infante, D., Rancer, A. S., and Womack, D. F. (2003). *Building communication theory* (4th ed.). Prospect Heights, IL: Waveland.

Theoretical Approaches

Ekman, P. (1965). Communication through nonverbal behavior: A source of information about an interpersonal relationship. In S. S. Tompkins and C. E. Izard (Eds.), *Affect, cognition, and personality* (pp. 390–442). New York: Springer.

Infante, D., Rancer, A. S., and Womack, D. F. (2003). *Building communication theory* (4th ed.). Prospect Heights, IL: Waveland.

Process Structure

Andersen, P. A., Garrison, J. D., and Andersen, J. F. (1979). Implications of a neurological approach for the study of nonverbal communication. *Human Communication Research, 16*, 74–89.

Birdwhistell, R. L. (1967). Some body motion elements accompanying spoken American English. In L. Thayer (Ed.), *Communication: Concepts and perspectives* (pp. 53–76). Washington, DC: Spartan.

Birdwhistell, R. L. (1974). The language of the body: The natural environment of words. In A. Silverstein (Ed.), *Human communication: Theoretical explorations* (pp. 203–220). New York: John Wiley & Sons.

Birdwhistell, R L. (1983). Masculinity and femininity as display. In A. M. Katz and V. T. Katz (Eds.), *Foundations of nonverbal communication: Readings, exercises, and commentary* (pp. 81–86). Carbondale, IL: Southern Illinois University Press.

Bodary, D. L., and Miller, L. D. (2000). Neurobiological substrates of communicator style. *Communication Education, 49*, 82–89.

Bowers, D., Bauer, R. M., and Heilman, K. M. (1993). The nonverbal affect lexicon: Theoretical perspectives from neuropsychological studies of affects perception. *Neuropsychology, 7*, 433–444.

Hall, E. T. (1959). *The silent language.* Garden City, NJ: Doubleday.

Hall, E. T. (1972). Proxemics: The study of man's spatial relations. In L. A. Samovar and R. E. Porter (Eds.), *Intercultural communication: A reader* (pp. 205–220). Belmont, CA: Wadsworth.

Hall, E. T. (1976). *Beyond culture.* Garden City, NY: Anchor.

Stacks, D. W. (1982, May). *Hemispheric and evolutionary use: A re-examination of verbal and nonverbal communication and the brain.* Paper presented at the meeting of the Eastern Communication Association, Hartford, CT.

Stacks, D. W., and Andersen, P. A. (1989). The modular mind: Implications for interpersonal communication. *Southern Communication Journal, 54,* 273–293.

Stacks, D. W., and Sellers, D. E. (1989). Understanding intrapersonal communication: Neurological processing implications. In C. Roberts and K. Watson (Eds.), *Intrapersonal communication processes: Original essays* (pp. 243–267). Auburn, AL: Spectra Publishers.

Gender Issues

Cline, R. J. (1986). The effects of biological sex and psychological gender on reported and behavioral intimacy and control of self-disclosure. *Communication Quarterly, 34,* 41–54.

Cline, R. J., and Musolf, K. E. (1985). Disclosure of social exchange: Anticipated length of relationships, sex roles, and disclosure intimacy. *Western Journal of Speech Communication, 49,* 43–56.

Eakins, B. W., and Eakins, R. G. (1978). *Sex differences in human communication.* Boston: Houghton Mifflin.

Farris, C., Treat, T. A., Viken, R. J., and McFall, R. M. (2008). Perceptual mechanisms that characterize gender differences in decoding women's sexual intent. *Psychological Science, 19,* 348–354.

Hall, J. A. (1984). *Nonverbal sex differences: Communication accuracy and expressive style.* Baltimore, MD: Johns Hopkins University Press.

Hewig, J., Trippe, R. H., Hecht, H., Straube, T., and Miltner, W. H. R. (2008). Gender differences for specific body regions when looking at men and women. *Journal of Nonverbal Behavior, 32,* 67–78.

Jones, S. E., and Yarbrough, A. E. (1985). A naturalistic study of the meanings of touch. *Communication Monographs, 52,* 19–56.

Kramer, C. (1978). Women's and men's ratings of their own and ideal speech. *Communication Quarterly, 26,* 2–11.

LaFrance, M., and Mayo, C. (1979). A review of nonverbal behaviors of women and men. *Western Journal of Speech Communication, 43,* 96–107.

Menz, F., and Al-Roubaie, A. (2008). Interruptions, status and gender in medical interviews: The harder you brake, the longer it takes. *Discourse & Society, 19,* 645–666.

Reeder, H. M. (1996). A critical look at gender difference in communication research. *Communication Studies, 47,* 318–331.

Rosenthal, R., Hall, J. A., Di Matteo, M. R., Rogers, P. L., and Archer, D. (1979). *Sensitivity to nonverbal communication: The PONS test.* Baltimore: Johns Hopkins University Press.

Thorne, B., and Henley, N. (Eds.). (1975). *Language and sex: Differences and dominance.* Rowley, MA: Newbury House.

Von Neuforn, D. S. (2007). Gender gap in the perception of communication in virtual learning environments [Electronic version]. *Interactive Learning Environments, 15,* 209–215.

Wood, J. T. (2012). *Gendered lives: Communication, gender and culture* (10th ed.). Belmont, CA: Wadsworth/Thompson Learning, Inc.

PART

1

STUDIES AND SUBCODES

With a basic understanding of what constitutes the nonverbal code, we can now examine in more detail the nonverbal subcodes. Chapter 2 begins with what we consider the most appropriate issue: the use of touch (also known as zero space/proxemics or **haptics**). In addition to the sensory approach we have chosen to follow, as discussed in the Preface, we establish this starting point for the nonverbal subcodes because we believe that we always communicate in some medium or environment, and that environment is the basis for our definition of territory or personal spacing zone (also known as **proxemics**). We separate the proxemic issues into personal space in Chapter 3 and territoriality in Chapter 4. Sometimes, however, people within an environment misread the cues we establish to convey what we expect of them in terms of communication. Sometimes such a misreading leads to a person touching us against our will. Your knowing what the **normative expectations** are for touch and for space usage will provide you with the initial information you need to study nonverbal communication.

Physical appearance is covered in Chapters 5 and 6. It should not surprise you that the way we perceive another person is greatly influenced by that person's physical appearance. Since physical appearance is so important, we attempt to change such characteristics as our body images, attractiveness, and body types by using clothing, accessories, and body adaptors. What the physical appearance subcode conveys to us is a major determinant of whether or not we want to communicate with someone. Communication with an attractive person is also influenced by the environment and the distance we maintain (if we think someone is attractive, we may try to get closer and may even invade his or her territory and personal space).

In Chapters 7 and 8, we examine what many people would consider the most important nonverbal subcode, **kinesics**, or body language. This subcode has been popularized and is considered by many to be typical of nonverbal communication. When you tell people you are taking a course in nonverbal communication, how many say to you, "Oh, that's body language, isn't it?" The kinesic subcode deals with such subjects as the communication of emotion, both in terms of what that emotion is and how intensely it is held, and with communication through gesture, including face and eye behaviors as well. Beyond that, however, the kinesic subcode can give evidence of status, attitudinal character, warmth, and quasi-courtship behaviors (flirtation). In many instances the gestural/kinesic subcode provides us with the information we need to better understand what others "mean" in their communication.

Chapter 9 examines the vocal aspects of nonverbal communication (**vocalics** or **paralanguage**), a second feature of the body's communication. Most of us have probably heard, "It's not what you say but how you say it that matters." Depending on *how* we say things, the meaning of what we say may be altered. Such communication outcomes are based on stereotypical judgments we make regarding such variables as pitch, breathiness, raspiness of the voice, and so forth. Many times we use our voices to contradict, such as sarcastically telling someone how *much* we admire his or her hairdo. The verbal communication may indicate one thing while the vocal communication may be entirely different. This chapter explores the effects of such vocal segregates as dialect, accent, and rate of speech. The vocal subcode, then, serves to stereotype or identify people, and it enables them to alter the impact of their verbal messages.

Finally, in Chapter 10 we examine some of the less obvious, yet nevertheless important, aspects of nonverbal communication. For example, the use of time (**chronemics**) and smell (**olfaction**) in everyday communication are discussed. Consideration is also given to less understood and less acceptable aspects of nonverbal communication, such as perceptual and biofeedback systems. This examination looks at internal states and their possible impact on our communication.

Once you have completed this section, you will have the information necessary to begin to understand how nonverbal communication operates. As noted in Chapter 1, however, nonverbal communication does not operate in a vacuum but is considered to be multichannel/multimessage oriented. Nonverbal communication always depends upon the context in which it is studied and upon the norms prevailing in that context. By this we mean that the artificial division of nonverbal communication into subcodes, as we have done, makes the study of this complex subject seem simpler than it really is. Knowing where and how the various subcodes function, however, enables us to make predictions as to what the effects of each subcode are in a given context. For that reason, we continue to include "Observational Studies" to keep you, the reader, active in looking at how these subcodes influence a variety of communication contexts in which you find yourself. Always remember that the better you know the people involved and the context, the more accurate you will be when "reading" others' nonverbal communication.

CHAPTER 2

HAPTICS (TOUCH)

KEY CONCEPTS

- Zero-Proxemics
- Touch
- Tactile Development
- Comparative Studies
- Human Studies
- Functions of Touch
- Influencing Factors
- Substitutions for Touch
- Frequency of Touch
- Touch Violations
- Functional Approach to Touch

OBJECTIVES

By the end of this chapter you should be able to:

- Define haptics.
- Explain the importance of touch in normal social development.
- Discuss how and why people touch where they do and with what frequency.
- Explain the different types of touch and the functions that touching others has in human communication.
- Discuss the factors that influence touch and touching behavior.
- Explain the effects of violating haptic expectations.
- Discuss how people substitute other behaviors for their haptic needs. *Haptics (tactics) touch & tactile behavior*

The study of touch and touching is most commonly known as **haptics**, although some research calls it **tactics** (in reference to tactile behaviors). Most of us can define touch quite easily; it occurs when some portion of someone else's body comes into direct contact with our own. Some touch we find acceptable, and some touch we deem unacceptable.

We can also refer to touching as "zero-proxemics" (recall that proxemics is the study of the use of space), meaning there is no space between persons. Early in the study of nonverbal communication, a substantial number of research studies were conducted on the issue of touch. Unfortunately, fewer and fewer research studies have been conducted over the years. For that reason, there are only a few contemporary studies to direct you toward as you study this important topic. Many of the more recent nonverbal studies are more contextually based (such as looking at workplace communication, at social gatherings, etc.). The earlier studies isolated and focused on specific subcodes (such as touch and space) and studied the subcodes more as individual variables than many of today's studies do. The impact of the early studies, however, is not lessened by this problem; the research from the earlier years is sound, and the findings still are applicable today. Contextual variables may have changed over the years, but touch behaviors still exist much as they did in the early studies. This should have you thinking about conducting some of your own research studies (as we discuss in the Appendix). Let us begin by telling you what we do know about touch and how it communicates.

Weitz (1974) says, "the logical end of proxemics [study of space] is touching. Once two people touch they have eliminated the space between them, and this act usually signifies that a special type of relationship exists between them" (p. 203). We begin with touch because, as Montagu (1971) points out, it is the mother of all senses. It may be the most important nonverbal communication subcode in terms of social and personal development. It certainly is the subcode we react most strongly to when it is violated.

Adler and Towne (1975) pointed to the importance of touch when they noted:

> Besides being the earliest means we have of making contact with others, touching is essential to our healthy development. During the nineteenth and early twentieth centuries a large percentage of children born every year died from a disease called *marasmus,* which translated from the Greek means "wasting away." In some orphanages the mortality rate was nearly one hundred percent, but even children from the most "progressive" homes, hospitals, and other institutions died regularly from the ailment. They hadn't been touched enough, and as a result they died. (pp. 225–226)

Contemporary research has shown that Adler and Towne's dramatic statement has validity, and their more recent editions of their interpersonal communication textbook (Adler and Proctor 2010) continues to espouse the same position. Anthropologists have noted that something as natural as breastfeeding versus non-breastfeeding often has severe consequences for children. Montagu (1971) found that non-breastfed children had four times the respiratory infections, twenty times more diarrhea, eight times as much eczema, as well as more hay fever, asthma, and other diseases than did breastfed children. Recent studies have also returned to this topic. Breastfeeding has been at the forefront of the public agenda as recently as of this writing; stories about its effect on child development were the topic of television news, newspapers, news magazines, as well as family-oriented magazines. After a careful search, however, there does not seem to be any definitive scientific research that says breastfeeding is an *absolute* necessity for the development of a healthy and happy child, nor do any studies show that it was touch that caused the positive results in the studies. It may have been the babies' consumption of breast milk instead of formula, or the touch they received, or, more than likely, a combination of both (Daniels and Adair 2005). We mention this because further research is essential to take any definite position such as *every child should be breastfed*. It is always important to point out possible shortcomings of research studies, so further research can be conducted to obtain more valid and reliable results (see the Appendix pp. 420–421 about reporting shortcomings of research studies).

Being deprived of touch has also been associated with learning problems involving speech, with symbolic recognition difficulty, and with lack of trust and confidence (Bowlby 1961; Despert 1941). These studies have shown a correlation between a lack of touch and these negative outcomes. Hollender (1961, 1970) described female psychiatric patients who resorted to "sexual enticement" because of the need to be held. Henley (1977) concluded that ". . .despite extremes of touch-avoidance, it is probably true that people fervently wish, even need, to be touched, and satisfy this desire in whatever way they can" (p. x). This "wish to be held" has also been associated with depression, especially in females (Sanfilipo and Stein 1985). Punyanunt-Carter and Wrench (2009) added to the base of knowledge when they reported that touch deprivation was related to, among other things, a person's self-esteem and depression. Clearly, touch can have both positive and negative effects on human beings.

Before fully examining tactile communication among humans, we briefly review several historical classic studies carried out on other animals. Specifically, we consider how touch deprivation affects their growth and development.

ANIMAL STUDIES

There are similarities between studies of lower animals and human studies regarding healthy development. In a classic study on the impact of touch, H. F. Harlow and Zimmerman (1958) studied the physical contact between a monkey mother and her infant. In natural settings, infant monkeys spend much time clinging to their mothers. Harlow raised baby monkeys in the laboratory; the babies clung to cloth pads researchers had placed in their cages. When the researchers attempted to replace the pads, the infant monkeys engaged in "violent temper tantrums." Harlow then built a terry cloth "surrogate" mother with a light bulb behind her to radiate "body" heat and a second surrogate mother made of wire mesh. In half the cases the wire mother provided milk and the terry cloth mother did not; in the other half, the situations were reversed. Figure 2.1 demonstrates how the infants spent their time. In general, it was found that the infants spent time with the cloth mother for tactile "affection," as opposed to the wire mother even when "she" provided food.

Touch is an important factor in the communication of lower animals. In newts, sex recognition and courtship involve tactile signals as well as other aspects, such as visual and chemical signals. For example, Thorpe (1972) reported that among certain parasitic water mites, sexual recognition can only be made through tactile communication. These and other examples of lower animals' use of touch appear regularly in the touch research (Leathers 1997; Montagu 1986). As Leathers (1997) reported, "Touching is a requirement for the healthy development of animals" (p. 113).

Aside from its sexual and courtship aspects, touch plays an important role in animal development. Two significant activities that adult animals, especially the female in most

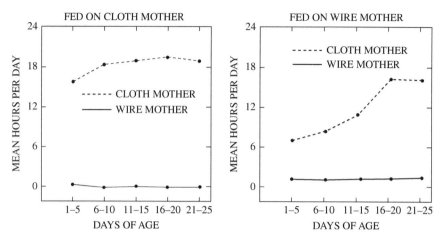

FIGURE 2.1 Comparison of time spent on surrogate mothers. *Source:* H. H. Harlow and R. R. Zimmerman, "The Development of Affectional Responses in Infant Monkeys," *Proceedings of the American Philosophical Society* 102 (1958), 501–509.

species, engage in at birth are *gentling* and *licking* behaviors. Hammett, in 1921, found that stroking or touching newborn rats, gentling them, yielded a gentler and less frightened rat than those not gentled. According to Malandro, Barker, and Barker (1989), licking behaviors in animals immediately after birth serve to stimulate certain bodily functions, such as excretion. Although this line of thought has not been extended to humans, the "maternal bonding" between a human mother and her infant and its effects are still rather controversial, as are such actions as warm water immersion immediately after birth. Some hospitals now include a period during which a newborn is slowly acclimated to the normal temperature of the room, rather than simply placing the infant on an unheated bed (along the lines of Harlow's findings), which more simulates a mother's touch in a sterile environment. Touch is clearly an important component in the life of animals, including human beings.

TACTILE DEVELOPMENT AND HUMANS

The early portion of human life is extremely dependent upon touch. Touch's effect on development and well-being has been known for quite a while. In an early study of tactile communication in American children, Clay (1966) found that children 14 months to 2 years old received more touching than infants younger than 14 months. Of course, immobile infants must wait for someone to come and touch them while toddlers can approach others to receive touch. He also found that female children received more tactile affection than baby boys. It has been known for some time that, of the available forms of communication, touching is the first form developed in infant children. The child's first orientation toward the world is discovered through tactile communication (Frank 1957). Babies explore their own bodies and their environment through touch. As children grow older, they become more dependent on symbolic communication, including verbal communication and other forms of nonverbal communication. Infants are given a feeling of vibration, touch, and rhythm even before they are born. As Desmond Morris (1971) notes, ". . . before birth the baby is undoubtedly capable of hearing (and feeling) the steady thump of the maternal heartbeat, seventy-two times every minute. It will become imprinted as the major sound-signal of life in the womb" (p. 14). He postulates that the heartbeat rhythm is so important that the ideal rocking speed for a cradle is 60 to 70 beats per minute. Touching, according to Morris (1971), continues to be a significant aspect of communication throughout life. "If the baby's message was 'hold me tight,' and the child's message was 'put me down,' that of the adolescent is 'leave me alone'" (p. 31). Then, with the young lovers, the cycle moves back to the baby's "hold me tight." Clearly, the touching needs of human beings evolve and revolve throughout their lives.

According to classic research, your development as a "healthy" individual seems related to the amount of touch you received as an infant. If we examine Harlow's findings and suppose that they can be transferred to human beings, then we can conjecture that the amount of touch a child receives in infancy may affect later development. This may or may not be true, which makes it an open area for research, but most people do believe that touch is a crucial element in the raising of a child. F. N. Willis and Hoffman (1975) found that as a child moves through life, from infancy on, the amount of touch declines. This finding has been reported in many nonverbal communication textbooks and articles throughout the last three-plus decades. J. K. Burgoon and Saine (1978) conjecture that touch needs that are met in infancy result in four major values: biological, communicative, psychological, and social. The importance of biological value is found both in Harlow's studies and in modern delivery-room techniques and refers to the vulnerability of an infant and its need for protection. The communicative value comes from behavior much like that of Harlow's monkeys: When the mother feeds, assures, and cuddles the infant, she touches her or him. At the earliest stage of life, the only communication between the infant and an adult is either touch or crying. You may observe that the quickest way to quiet a crying baby is to touch it (the same may be true for adults). Psychologically, the infant, through self-exploration, begins the process of achieving self-identity, environmental identity, security, and well-being. Finally, the social value of touch can be found, just as in the Harlow studies, in research that indicates what lack of touch may result in. These findings include marasmus, from the Montagu study, and also increased speech and learning difficulties in later life. Prescott (1975) conducted studies on cross-cultural pleasure and how touch was important to the cross-cultural context. Prescott's findings support the relationship between violence and pleasure, with pleasure being positively associated with touch. Such findings as reported here support the notion that the more touch you received as an infant during development, the better adjusted you should be as a child, an adolescent, and an adult.

TYPES AND FUNCTIONS OF TOUCH

Just as research indicates that we experience different frequencies of touch, we also experience different types or kinds of touch. Two studies, in particular, point out the differences we perceive in types of touch. In 1975, Argyle reported that 16 types of touch occur commonly in Western culture (see Figure 2.2). He argued that the various touches communicate attitudes, regulate the interaction, or fall into a "meaningless" category.

At about the same time, Heslin (1974) argued that we could classify touching behavior into five categories based on the nature of the interpersonal relationship between toucher and touchee. Most nonverbal communication theorists use these same categories today to classify types of touching, including us. Think about these categories in terms of a continuum. At one end of the continuum there is very little interpersonal relationship, and at the other end is a very intimate relationship. At one end, we have the *Functional/Professional* level; this level includes such actions as touch from a nurse, a doctor, a hairstylist, or even a cashier who places change in your hand. This is touch that is both functional (it is doing something for you) and professional (it is impersonal). Moving toward an interpersonal level, we have *Social/Polite* touches, which in the culture of the United States are represented by handshakes and other socially prescribed touching behaviors. In other cultures, *Social/Polite* touches may include a perfunctory kiss on the cheek or a hug. Heslin theorizes that such touch acts to neutralize status differences between people. The next category is called *Friendship/ Warmth*, a type of touch that is most difficult to interpret because it is easily mistaken for love or sexual attraction, especially in the issues of gender differences in communication. Further, it is often carried out when the toucher is alone with the other person. This type of touch can take the form of touching in a more personal way, such as putting a hand on someone's forearm in a friendly way, hugging a close friend, or putting your arm around someone's shoulders. The last two categories are *Love/Intimacy* and *Sexual Arousal*. *Love/Intimacy*

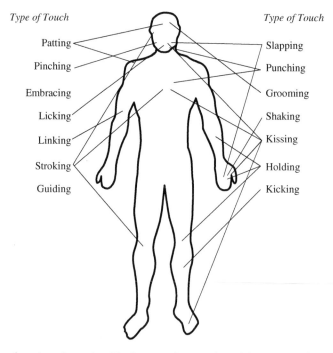

FIGURE 2.2 Type of touch and associated body areas. *Source:* Adapted from M. Argyle, *Bodily Communication* (New York: International Universities Press, 1975).

PHOTO 2.1 In which of Heslin's categories would you classify these two people?

represents touches indicative of intimacy and requires appropriate interpersonal contexts. It can be seen in many ways, depending on the relationship between the interactants. An example might be a longer caressing touch, holding someone's hand, or a touch on someone's face or hair. *Sexual Arousal* touch, the opposite end of the continuum from functional/professional touch, is probably the most idiosyncratic and variant type of touch and is obviously the most intimate. It probably does not need specific examples for you to understand its nature. It should be pointed out, however, that these last two areas of touch are where males and females differ in their interpretations of what is being communicated. These issues are discussed later in more detail.

Heslin (1974) argues that as you move from the Functional/Professional level of touch to other levels, you increase the individuality of the relationship and "humanize" the other person. He says that the strongest appreciation of others is shown at the middle level of touch categories, Friendship/Warmth touch. Along this same line, research indicates that touch added positively to the "foot-in-the-door" technique often used by salespeople. Goldman, Kiyohara, and Pfanners (1985) demonstrated this by having a confederate touch participants while asking for directions in one instance and in recruiting volunteers for a telephone survey in another. Siminoff, Traino, and Gordon (2011) found similar results when requesting that individuals become tissue donors. In all instances, the confederates achieved greater compliance from the participants when they touched than when there was an absence of touch. Those of you going into professions where sales or recruitment will be important to you (whether it be of products or of your ideas) should begin to take note of these findings. Touch does influence many outcomes of interpersonal encounters.

FACTORS INFLUENCING TOUCH

The works of Wood (2012) and others discussed in Chapter 1 indicate that your gender and relationship to others affect the amount of touch you both give and expect to receive. In addition to gender and relationship, other variables that affect the amount of touch and your reaction to it include the extent to which you like the other person, the extent to which the other person likes you, the type of touch itself, your culture, and the attractiveness of the other person. Various theorists have attempted to show how important these factors are in communication encounters.

IMMEDIACY

Both Anastasi (1958) and Mehrabian (1971a, 1971b, 1981) concluded in separate studies that the tendency to have tactile contact with others is consistent with the idea that touching is one way to communicate liking. Closely related to Mehrabian's (1981) concept of liking is his concept of *immediacy,* where "people are drawn toward persons and things they like, evaluate highly, and prefer; and they avoid or move away from things they dislike, evaluate negatively, or do not prefer" (p. 1). This immediacy principle and its relationship to touch are consistent with the available literature on interpersonal attraction; that is, we tend to touch people we like and avoid those we dislike (see also Thomas-Maddox 2003). The concept of immediacy has been likened to "approachability" by many theorists, and it is an extremely important idea to consider when looking at what factors of nonverbal communication make us more immediate or less immediate.

Richmond, Gorham, and McCroskey (1987) found that the principle of immediacy and touch is especially important in classroom teaching. They found that factors such as vocal expressiveness, smiling in class, and having a relaxed body position had a "high positive association" with pupils liking the teacher. However, *touch was found to have a relatively low effect* in comparison with other immediacy variables, meaning that touch does not seem to be very important in the classroom for a teacher to be perceived as immediate. This lack of importance may be a function of the perceived "correctiveness" of touching behavior in the classroom, which can be defined in two ways. First, touch coming from a teacher is often perceived as serving a corrective function. Take, for example, the child who is disruptive or misbehaving in the classroom. Often the teacher will put a hand on the child's shoulder to calm that student down. Second, in today's society it has unfortunately become taboo for teachers to touch children, especially children of the opposite sex; therefore, students do not receive much touch in the classroom setting, despite the fact that most research says it is important (see also Kerssen-Griep and Witt 2012; Finn and Schrodt 2012; and Trad et al. 2012) . These two issues alone should make it obvious that touching in the classroom would have far less of an impact on a teacher's perceived immediacy than the other factors mentioned previously.

The concept of immediacy, defined as the appearance of being approachable, has been further examined. C. E. Thomas, Richmond, and McCroskey (1994) suggest that immediacy has been associated with "responsiveness" to students in the classroom. The question they addressed was whether immediacy is something beyond being physically close. In this light, they associated "assertiveness" with such nonverbal behaviors as direct eye contact, direct body position, moving physically closer, raising one's voice, and so forth. In short, their "assertiveness" may be considered "dynamism." The question is, then, can a teacher be just as immediate using a "masculine," assertive approach as using a "responsive," feminine approach, where the responsive approach is defined as helpful, sympathetic, compassionate,

PHOTO 2.2 Touching can communicate immediacy when used between friends.

sincere, and friendly? Their results indicate that immediacy can be effective using either approach. Richmond and Gorham (1998) found similar results and have published a prescriptive approach to accomplishing immediacy in the classroom, including the use of touch. Teven and Gorham (1998) also found that touching was a part of perceived nonverbal immediacy in their study of how college students perceive the immediacy of their professors. Teven and Gorham did find, however, that touch was not a significant factor in determining whether a teacher is immediate or not. There are many more significant nonverbal issues relating to immediacy, and we discuss these in the course of this textbook. It may be that students seek out teachers whose teaching approach is consistent with that teacher's personality. *It may also be that students seek out teachers who use other nonverbal cues that act as surrogates for touching behavior,* which is not approved in the classroom beyond the elementary level. If students cannot receive positive reinforcement in the form of touch, they look for it in positive personalities of their teachers; verbal "stroking," therefore, replaces physical touch.

Another study has found that immediate messages are perceived as more pleasant than non-immediate messages (Manusov 1991). Recall that immediacy has been defined as the appearance of being approachable, likeable, and open. Manusov described immediate messages as smiling, forward leans, head nods, and open body position. Non-immediate behaviors included lack of eye contact, backward leans, closed arms, unpleasant facial expressions, and unpleasant vocal tones. Again, touching was not found to be an important variable in her study. Nevertheless, an effective, immediate teacher seems to take one of two stances: (1) a dominant, organized, dynamic, definite approach or (2) an open, flexible, sensitive approach. Both of these approaches may substitute for touch where touch is not possible in today's classroom, since both approaches show liking and caring for the students. (If we have sparked your interest in touch behaviors and how they communicate, perhaps you might like to conduct some of your own research about touch.) Other studies in the field can tell you something about the use of touch and immediacy, and reading those studies would be a place to begin.

AREA OF BODY TOUCH

Nguyen and associates (M. L. Nguyen, Heslin, and T. Nguyen 1974, 1975, 1976) examined the meaning of various types of touch as they are applied to different parts of the body. Their research participants were opposite-sex, unmarried friends. The researchers were concerned with four types of touch: the pat, squeeze, brush, and stroke. Examining how the different types of touch were related to 11 areas of the body (top of the head, face, shoulders and top of back, chest, arms, stomach, genital area, thigh, buttocks, legs, and hands), they found that touch is generally considered a positive phenomenon. Strokes usually communicate warmth and sexual desire, pats communicate friendship and playfulness, whereas brushes and squeezes are ambiguous.

Responses of males and females were also found to differ, according to Nguyen et al. Females discriminated among their body parts more than males. The touching of breasts, for example, was not seen as friendly or playful. Females perceived the squeezing of hands as loving and friendly. Males were less concerned with specific body parts; males felt that almost any meaning could be derived from touching almost any area of the body. Touching of the thighs and buttocks tended to be better suited to communicate playfulness, while the genital area was reserved for sexual desire. Males were more concerned about the type of touch than the area of the body touched. Both sexes agreed about which kinds of touching indicated sexual desire. However, males related sexual desire to pleasantness and love, while females considered sexual desire the opposite of playfulness, friendliness, pleasantness, and love. Wood (2012) discusses this in her coverage of how males and females interpret touch differently.

While thinking about these findings, you should remember that touching in intimate relationships is much different than in friend or acquaintance relationships. In friendship or acquaintance situations, we are likely to be accepting of touch on the forearms and hands, shoulders, and in some cases the upper back and the knee area. In intimate relationships, we are likely to allow (and sometimes even expect) touching in other areas in addition to the aforementioned ones, such as the head, face, and hair area, the small of the back, on the thigh, as well as other, more sexually related areas. Think about the person who sits next to you in this class. Would you appreciate it if she or he touched you in an area that you deem intimate? Or what if your professor came up and began to run his or her hands through your hair? We have specific norms for touch behavior, and we do not easily accept violations of these norms.

COMFORT TOUCH

Looking at another context, Stolte and Friedman (1980) examined the type of touch expectant mothers received and their perceptions about that touch during labor. What they found further supports the notion of immediacy and suggests a relationship with anxiety. Their participants were full-term pregnancy patients who were interviewed as soon after childbirth as possible. Each was asked 10 questions concerning how she felt about touch and her perceptions of touch during the labor period. In general, touch was thought to be positive during labor. Women ages 20 to 34 viewed touch more positively, however, than 14- to 19-year-old women. Whites perceived touch more positively than nonwhites; single or divorced women perceived touch more negatively than married or separated women. The most frequently touched area during positive experience was the hand; the most negative touch was reported to be the physician's touch in the abdomen or pelvic area. Those reported as providing the most positive touch were husbands and family members, followed by the nursing staff. Hence, both physical and attitudinal immediacy, along with perceived professionalism, contributed to the pregnant women's perceptions of touch behavior. Family members, health-care professionals, and friends could probably help provide an easier labor for an expectant mother if they were aware of these findings.

Touch is also seen as "comforting behavior." A study by Dolin and Booth-Butterfield (1993) asked students how they might comfort others by means of nonverbal behaviors. Not surprisingly, they found that haptics (hugs, pats, and increased miscellaneous touch) comprised three of the top six responses. In order of ranking, the students listed hugs, proxemics, facial expression, attentiveness, increased miscellaneous touch, pats, eye contact, crying, emotional distancing, instrumental activity, gesturing, and vocalics. Further, they found that males and females differed in how they would use the haptic communication; males reported that they would use more pats than females, and females reported greater use of miscellaneous touch and hugs. Interestingly, the comforting strategies reported as ranking highest are also the most immediate. Most recent research into comfort touch is published in medical fields (Aucoin and Lane 2004). It is clear that doctors and nurses today also see the importance of what is known as "healing touch"; from autism to HIV to cancer treatment to treatment of elderly patients, medical professionals turn to the use of touch to comfort patients (see Stepanikova, Zhang, Wieland, Eleazer, and Stewart 2012; Kozlowska and Doboszynska 2012; Gleeson and Higgins 2009).

STUDENT VOICES

Zachary: The other day I was walking through campus and sat down to just rest for a few minutes until my next class. I saw a girl who was very upset from an unknown cause. I sat and watched as a guy walked up to her and kneeled down to talk to her about what she was upset about. He proceeded to put his arm around the girl in order to issue her some comfort since she was upset. This type of touch was used just to issue the girl some comfort. It was an appropriate touch for the situation and after doing so and talking to the girl for a few minutes, she didn't seem as upset as she was before. As he walked off, she told him thank you for taking time out of his day to comfort her while she was upset and they both went on their way. I guess this info we are learning is starting to make sense.

SAME-SEX TOUCH

F. N. Willis and Rawdon (1994) found some cultural effects when they studied participants' attitudes toward same-sex touch across four cultures. They found that, in order, the most positive feelings were from American, Spanish, Chilean, and Malaysian students. J. K. Burgoon, Walther, and Baesler (1992) reported that feelings toward touch are also related to the interpersonal attractiveness of the toucher. In their study, they used a confederate in the same conditions, except that in half the cases the confederate was perceived as high "valence" (attractive, high status, expert) and in the other half as low valence (unattractive, low status, inexpert). Participants were more surprised by touches from the high-valence confederate. In all instances, touching was viewed as positive when the confederate and participant were doing a problem-solving task together. Researchers have come up with other findings concerning same-sex touch behaviors. Derlega, Lewis, Harrison, Winstead, and Costanza (1989) found that men fear same-sex touches more than women do. Most commonly, this difference was because men were more homophobic than women. J. K. Burgoon and Walther (1990) and Major (1981) reported that men will avoid affectionate touch to avoid the appearance of being feminine. You must keep in mind that these studies are commonly conducted from the heterosexists' viewpoint and that homosexuals will not necessarily interpret same-sex touching the same way as heterosexuals do. Knöfler and Imhof (2007) discovered in their study of homosexual nonverbal communication that the only real area where homosexual and heterosexual dyads differed in the area of touch was in the area of self-touch. Homosexual dyads, both males and females, were found to touch their own faces and other body parts significantly more frequently than heterosexual dyads. This topic alone, the use of the subcode of touch and homosexuals, is one area of study that deserves more attention. Morman and Floyd (1999) also found that when fathers and sons expressed affection, including touch, the amount was dependent on how nonverbally affectionate the son was, not the father. Suffice it to say, same-sex touching has long been an issue of discussion in the study of zero-proxemics, and it is likely to be a topic for a long time to come.

Thus, recent research indicates that the amount of touch and your reaction to touch are related to your feelings toward the other person, the type of touch, the context of that touch, and the attractiveness of the other person. As has been mentioned, attitudes toward touch are also related to your gender and the gender of the toucher, your cultural identity, as well as your relationship with the other person(s) involved in the touching.

GENDER ISSUES

Three other studies looked at gender as a factor in touch attitudes. Struckman-Johnson and Johnson (1993) tested whether females had a more negative view of opposite-sex touch than did males. They found that females *anticipated* more negative feelings about opposite-sex touch than males; this was true whether the type of touch anticipated was gentle or forceful. Females had similar anticipatory feelings about same-sex touch. Males, however, had strong negative attitudes about same-sex touch, whether gentle or forceful. Both males and females considered same-sex touch negative, with related feelings of violation and harm. A contrary finding is reported by Sanfilipo (1993), who found that females reported the "wish to be held" more often, with corresponding positive feelings about touch from males. Gender touch study results further found that males scored higher on homophobia and that they touched the same sex less often than females (Roese and Olson 1992). Further, homophobia and lack of same-sex touch were highly correlated for both males and females, although it appears that females are much more accepting of same-sex touch than males are (Dolinski 2010). Think about your own heterosexual male and female friends for a minute. Which of them would be more accepting of being touched by someone of the same sex? How would they respond if touched by someone of the same sex? What about your homosexual friends? Being careful not to stereotype, would same-sex touch be more acceptable than opposite-sex touch for your homosexual friends?

Other findings about gender differences show that women and men perceive touch differently (Guéguen 2010). Many nonverbal communication theorists report that females are more likely to discriminate about where their bodies are touched, and males are more discriminating about the type of touch they receive (pats, caresses, rubbing). Deaux (1976) and Leathers (1997) found that women are more likely to initiate hugs and touches to express affiliation (support, affection, and comfort), and that men are more likely to use touch to assert control or power (direct others, interrupt, express sexual interest). Buss (2001) also reported that men are more likely to overinfer women's sexual desire for them when women are simply touching casually. These differences can generate many misunderstandings. Indeed, some researchers have found that these touch differences between genders may be the root of many sexual harassment cases (J. K. Burgoon, Buller, and Woodall 1989). The results of these studies could have been very different had they been conducted in another culture. For example, the male and female touch norms in countries of Arabic origin are considerably different from those in the United States. Suffice it to say that when persons of one sex have different touch norms from the persons they touch, there are bound to be misunderstandings, regardless of whether the two are of the same or of opposite sexes. It is no mystery, then, that we have a hard time communicating across genders when it comes to the issue of touch.

Research has also explored touch and the relationship of the interactants. Salt (1991), for instance, found a negative relationship between a son's age and the amount of touch the son received. Both fathers and sons were accepting of the fathers' touch during pre-adolescence. Both fathers and sons stated that touch was important in their relationship, but sons were less accepting of touch. F. N. Willis and Briggs (1992) found that males were more likely to initiate touch during courtship and females were more likely to initiate touch after marriage. Morman and Floyd (1999) and Guerrero and Andersen (1994) offer similar findings: that the upbringing of a male child is affected by his father's use (or nonuse) of affection. Some male children are brought up in families with higher touch norms, meaning they were touched more (including by their fathers), so their adult norms will be different from that of males who were brought up with a lower level of touch.

We can conclude, then, that factors influencing touch include the type of touch, degree of liking or disliking in a relationship, and the situation at hand. Additionally, Maines (1977) found that touch is associated with the degree of perceived similarity between interactants. That is, people prefer to be touched by others of the same race and sex. Other scholars contradict this finding, particularly regarding sex. S. E. Jones (1986), for example, contends that females initiate touch (touches meant to control behavior) more often than males and females initiate control touches over males more often than males initiate control touch over women. Jones' findings are inconsistent with Henley's (1977) findings reported earlier. It may well be that women do initiate control touches over males, but, as indicated by Maines, males may not like it. Another interesting finding was that Hertenstein and Keltner (2011) found that male children were more likely to communicate anger through the use of touch than their female counterparts. Storrs and Kleinke (1990) found, for instance, that in interview situations the status or sex of the interviewer who touched them did not influence females. Males, however, were less favorable toward equal-status and female interviewers who touched them. Another issue to consider is that women usually will wait until the male initiates touch for the first time. Once that barrier is broken, women usually touch more than men. This often occurs because women have been socialized not to be the "initiator" in male/female situations, lest they be seen as "fast" or "loose." Touch norms seem to be changing from the "Victorian morals" that your parents most likely learned from their parents, but there are still some residual societal norms that parents continue to pass on in order to try to teach their children what they believe is right and wrong. Other research reports that females touch more often among elderly nursing-home patients (Rinck, Willis, and Dean 1980). This study shows that the older generation in nursing homes does seem to have different touch norms than people of college age, or even younger people.

The concept of whether we do or do not like to be touched is a significant one. As has been pointed out, there are many variables that affect perceptions of touch, of which age, race, and religion—as well as same-sex versus opposite-sex interactions—seem to be important. We seem not to mind touch in most *professional* situations, for example, a handshake from coworkers, a doctor's touch, or a cashier returning our change to us. In addition, we seem to like touch if that touch is consistent with the relationship and message(s) of the moment. At other times, however, we feel that we have been violated by someone's touch. Many of us do not like being touched by people we do not know, or do not know well, and by people we think are unattractive or whom we do not like. One other violation is when we are touched in what we evaluate as a more intimate zone than we deem the relationship warrants. For example, women often mention men (with whom they are not intimate) putting their hand in the small of their backs as one of the most disconcerting touch violations that men make. Men, on the other hand, often do not realize that it is a violation because it is one of the types of touches men have been taught is polite to do when a man is walking through a doorway with a woman. Women see this as a more "intimate touch zone," perhaps because they are taught to protect what is "below the belt," and they wonder why a man with whom they are not intimate is touching them in an area reserved for intimacy. Since the small of the back is close to the buttocks, women often see this as heading toward a violation of casual touch norms. The most serious of touch violations, of course, is in the form of assault and battery, but we also dislike being touched unexpectedly and when message and touch do not match.

Aylor and Dainton (2001) found that negative communication, including touch, can occur in situations of jealousy between men and women. Interestingly, women were shown to use more violent communication than men did in situations of jealousy, including "violence toward objects." Although the researchers did not mention actual hitting as a form of violent communication, the results still should be considered here, since violence is often demonstrated through the use of touch. Aylor and Dainton caution their readers that their findings are inconclusive and that the study needs to be replicated to determine how reliable their findings were. If we have piqued your interest in conducting research, this could be a study you might want to replicate.

BOX 2.2 OBSERVATIONAL STUDY

Consider the use of touch of your closest same-sex friend and your closest opposite-sex friend. What are the touch norms of each? Do their touch norms seem to confirm the norms for males and females in our society? (Remember that their sexual preference may affect their answers here.) Do their touch norms seem out of the ordinary? Does either of them ever violate your touch norms? If so, how do you communicate to them that they have done so?

FREQUENCY OF CONTACT

A significant aspect of touch is how often people touch each other. As noted in Chapter 1, there are a number of filters that influence how we use nonverbal communication, with culture being a major filter in human use of touch. Jourard (1966, 1968), for instance, counted the frequency of body contact between couples in various cafes in different cities and countries. He found differences among cultures, exemplified by the following number of body contacts per hour:

San Juan, Puerto Rico: 180
Paris, France: 110
Gainesville, Florida: 2
London, England: 0

Realize that these are generalized results, and that the different communities within countries often vary significantly. You can still conjecture from these statistics, however, that the United States is a lower touch culture, although not as low as England. Jourard was also interested in which parts of the body were touched the most often. For this reason, he asked students to complete a questionnaire that listed 24 body parts and provide information about who is touched according to sex and relationship in the United States. Some 45 years later, Jourard's studies, as well as other nonverbal theorists', are still cited by us as the premier studies on cultural touch differences. Other variables related to touch include status, positive attitude toward the other, immediacy, and the perceived meaning of the touch. These are variables that also might have piqued your research interests in this area, or perhaps you might like to apply the theories we have already discussed to these variables.

In another study, L. T. Huang, Phares, and Hollender (1976) examined the influence of cultural attitudes on the wish to be held. They examined the touch preferences of five groups of women living in Malaysia. Their participants consisted of the following groups: Chinese-educated Chinese, English-educated Chinese, Malay-educated Malay, English-educated Malay, and English-educated Indians. They found that Chinese-educated Chinese had the lowest body contact and most often regarded the wish to be held as "something to be kept secret." Interestingly, this group preferred being held to talking while angry. English-educated Chinese were the least likely to regard being held as something secretive and were least likely to prefer holding to talking. The other nationalities and educational backgrounds followed the Chinese-educated in this order: English-educated Indians, English-educated Malay, and Malay-educated Malay. Thus, we find strong touch preference differences even *within* a specific culture. Research continues in Chinese cultures with the works of Yang (2007, 2011), who describes different uses of nonverbal communication, especially touches, in the Mandarin culture of China.

In yet other studies, Remland, Jones, and Brinkman (1991, 1995) found that southern Europeans engage in more touch than northern Europeans. Their studies observed nearly 1,000 couples at train stations in 15 different countries. They found that the highest incidence of touching occurred, in descending order, in Greece, Spain, Italy, and Hungary. D. E. Williams and Hughes (2005) confirmed those findings of the presence of more touch in settings such as restaurants and bars, especially in Italy. The lowest touch-oriented culture, in ascending order, was found in the Netherlands, Austria, England, Belgium, and Germany. It should be noted at this point, however, that many of these differences could be dependent on other factors, such as gender, context, personality, and the relationship. Remland (2000) reports that many studies that try to determine cultural differences "fail to find them or find only limited evidence for them" (p. 161). It is very hard to generalize about cultural differences, except to say that some do exist and that some cultures seem to touch more than others. You would do well to determine what the differences are if you travel to a culture unlike your own—assuming, of course, that you wish to be the best communicator you can be.

BOX 2.3   OBSERVATIONAL STUDY

What is the impact of touch on children in your cultural or subcultural region? Observe how adults and children touch each other and the impact of that touch. Can you draw any conclusions based on your findings that are related to: (1) culture, (2) the sex of the adult toucher, (3) the sex of the child touched, or (4) the age of the child touched?

VIOLATIONS OF HAPTIC EXPECTATIONS

Little is known of what happens when we violate touch expectations. Much of what we do know suggests that three variables are important in evaluating the touch we receive from one another: the **location** of the touch, its **duration**, and its **intensity**. For instance, if we specify the location as the facial cheek, the duration as long, and the intensity as soft, we are defining a positive touch; the relationship between the toucher and touchee, then, is intimate. On the other hand, if the location is the same, but the duration is extremely short and the intensity hard, we ascribe a negative meaning, especially if the relationship is a superior toucher and a subordinate touchee. When we examine the impact of touching behavior, we should keep in mind location, duration, and intensity, as well as the nature of the relationship.

What does the research indicate? Despite how much people use touch communication, not much research on violations of touch norms has been conducted. What we do know, however, seems to indicate that accidental touch, or touching another person "accidentally," leads to more positive evaluations of the toucher. Accidental touch can occur when one person either squeezes another person's hand too strongly during a handshake or is too "feminine" (a "wet fish" handshake), resulting in impressions that may not have been intended. The "American handshake," for example, is supposedly one that is firm but not too firm, and usually consists of two and one-half shakes. A whole new area for studying the handshake is now being discovered in the concept of "digital handshakes" (Ballenson and Yee 2007; and Bartz 2011) or handshakes that are simulated over computer-mediated communication. Other norms include contextual ones. For example, you are more likely to touch as the persuader than as the persuadee; when you are giving advice rather than receiving it; or when giving orders rather than receiving them. You are more likely to be touched when getting "worry" or "concern" messages. You are more likely to touch or be touched when you are involved in deep conversations, in social settings, and when signaling excitement and enthusiasm. Think of yourself in each of these settings. Do those norms seem to be true for you?

Researchers have attempted to study the impact of touch on both attitude and credibility. In a study conducted by J. D. Fisher, Rytting, and Heslin (1976), librarians provided "incidental" touch to randomly selected students checking out books. The researchers found that the librarians were evaluated more positively after incidental touch than after no touch. Another study (Stacks et al. 1980) had male and female confederates "interview" students in randomly selected areas of a college campus, each interview beginning with one of three types of handshakes: (1) a "normal" handshake (see previous comments), (2) a "hard" handshake (practiced by the confederates until the excessive pressure was applied equally by both male and female confederates), and (3) a "soft" handshake (only the thumb, index, and middle finger touched the participants). The researchers sought to discover whether the interviewees' perceptions of the interviewers' credibility was affected by the type of handshake. Findings indicated no differences for male interviewers across the three handshakes, although the mean responses were best for the normal handshake, followed by the hard and soft handshakes. For females, however, the hard handshake produced significantly higher perceptions of credibility. In a search for newer, more recent studies on this subject, however, no newer studies were found. Perhaps this is an area in which you might like to conduct your own research studies?

BOX 2.4 OBSERVATIONAL STUDY

Observe a one-hour television program. Note all touch used by the program's actors/participants. Do they confirm the norms of touch as discussed thus far in this chapter?

What violations of touch norms do you note? What messages do you think are being sent by the actors/participants? Does touch seem to matter to the message of the show?

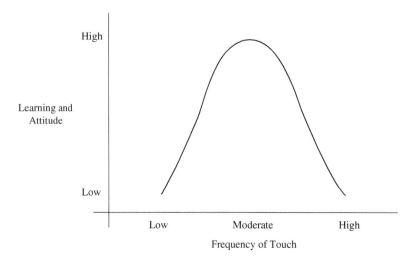

FIGURE 2.3 Frequency of touch and outcome.

Pressner (1978) undertook one study that merits discussion. She was interested in the effect of touch both on attitude toward clinical sessions in speech pathology and on learning. Her study was simple. She had clinicians use normal touch (operationalized from observations of the number of touches clinicians used on a number of patients) at one of the three levels of touch: low, moderate, or high. Touch was defined as contact (usually manual) with the patient during the clinical session in random form: 0 to 6 touches per session was low, 7 to 16 touches was moderate, and 17 to 25 touches per session was high. Her general findings were that touching in moderation seemed to produce the best results, although the number of patients studied may have been too small to detect any real differences. Figure 2.3 indicates the predicted relationships among touch, attitude, and learning. Low amounts of touch are expected; moderate amounts may indicate interest and an interpersonal awareness of the patient and may be seen as immediacy behavior; a high amount of touch offers too much "reward," and the frequency becomes expected rather than rewarding.

STUDENT VOICES

Chris: Oh my do I have an example of disliking touch! My friend set me up on a blind date and within 30 minutes of being on the date, the guy was rubbing my leg and back. He was playing with my hair and was far too "touchy-feely."

Trying to be polite, I said nothing but tried to make it known by my body language that I was not enjoying it. At the close of the date he walked me to my door and asked if we might go on a second date. I declined respectfully and explained to him that he came on a little too strongly.

SUBSTITUTES FOR "REAL TOUCH"

As we grow up, various senses achieve a different sequence of precedence, from most to least important. As children, our senses tend to follow the sequence (1) touch, (2) vision, and

(3) hearing. As adults, and with the learning of language, the precedence changes to (1) vision, (2) hearing, and (3) touch. How many times as children did your parents tell you, "Look but don't touch"? This warning is based on the fact that parents recognize that a child's first instinct is to touch things, especially when the child wants to look at that thing. Thus, as adults, we Americans tend to become "touch-starved."

Because we become starved for touch, we tend to buy "touch-for hire" (Morris 1976). Morris has stated that we hire "licensed touchers," such as hairstylists and masseuses, to take care of our need for bodily contact in a socially acceptable way. Other substitutes are used, such as petting a dog or cat, sucking a thumb, or smoking a cigarette. This lack of intimacy that we Americans ordinarily experience, and its substitutes, Morris (1971) calls a major social disease; we need touch as adults, just as we did as infants, but the need is satisfied in unusual and unnatural ways. Researchers have also noted that when we receive these more intimate types of touches, we communicate on a more intimate level than with a regular acquaintance. Hairstylists report of hearing "more intimate" stories from their customers than many other service professions. One of your authors of this text conjectures that this greater intimacy is a result of the touch the customers are receiving; the head and hair area is usually reserved for touching by people with whom we are more intimate, people with whom we open up more. A massage situation might create the same response as a result of the type of touch received and the areas of the body touched.

It appears that adults want to touch and be touched, yet there are social norms in American society that pressure us to avoid touching. Perhaps one reason for such a norm is that few people work with their hands, the lack of touch creating a population much more touch avoidant than some other cultures. Most college students, if asked, say they are in college to avoid getting their hands "dirty." As noted in Figure 2.4, there may be a

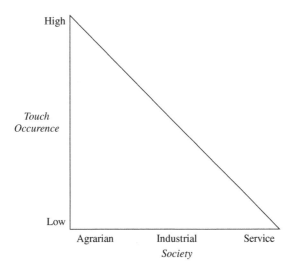

FIGURE 2.4 Relationship between touch and type of society.

relationship between the type of society (agrarian to service-oriented) and the amount of touch expected. Societies in which people work with their hands seem to find touch natural. Societies that have progressed beyond this point, as America has, find touch less attractive.

It is interesting to note that Clynes (1988) found that people could transmit emotions to others who speak a different language through touch and gesture. Investigating this notion in the laboratory, however, Trussoni, O'Malley, and Barton (1988) failed to find similar findings, perhaps because touch behaviors are idiosyncratic and are not as predictable as we social scientists would like to believe they are.

FUNCTIONAL APPROACH TO TOUCH

In Chapter 1 we presented a number of functions for nonverbal communication. In examining touch we find that—in regard to the functions of **identification** and **self-presentation**— some people are more "touchy-feely" than others. Such behavior might be considered a trait of a particular individual, although, as we have seen, factors such as gender, culture, and age can affect the person's traits. Such people typically stand closer to others, have greater eye contact with others, and so forth. Regarding regulation of interaction, we have found that when two people are near one another, reaching out and touching another's forearm or holding another by the upper arm may be used as a method of interruption rather than using vocalics to "request a turn." This behavior has been found particularly in Brazil. The simple act of a female touching a male may also regulate interaction.

From the available research, it appears that touching is used to illustrate the **relationship of the interactants**. As discussed earlier, several studies have found that males initiate touch more often during the early stages of a relationship, while females take on the initiator role more often in later stages. **Display of instructional information** can be made using touch, especially when parents gently slap the hand of youngsters to prevent them from touching an object or from taking a particular action. The **display of liking** (affection) is illustrated by the work of Mehrabian (1971a, 1971b), as well as recent research by Booth-Butterfield and Booth-Butterfield (1994). They found that we are more likely to touch others, as well as to accept touch from others, whom we like. The research on immediacy, however, especially in the teacher-student context, reveals less information about touch, perhaps because touch in the school setting has become taboo in today's society. Finally, how can touch be used to *deceive*? Such actions as shaking the hands of a person you dislike, or even greeting that person with a hug, illustrate that deception is sometimes used in the haptic subcode.

BOX 2.5   OBSERVATIONAL STUDY

Observe a half-hour television show and consider the advertisements. What functions of touch are used within the ad? What messages are sent about the product by those uses of touch? Are all the portrayed touches what we would consider typical or customary in the United States? If not, what reaction do you have to those touches?

SUMMARY

Touch is a prominent aspect of our development and occurs as a major form of communication. Although cultures differ in their expectations of what amount, type, and location of touch is appropriate, the need for touch is always there. Touch is essential in our development as humans; it is needed in the development of intimate relations. Touch, although so urgently required, is also approached with puritanical avoidance, especially in North American culture. Learning about how touch operates and its significance should make you a better communicator.

QUESTIONS FOR THOUGHT

1. Why do Americans approach touch as we do in our culture?
2. How correct is Morris when he asserts that Americans turn to "licensed touchers" to fulfill their needs for touch? Can you provide some examples of such people in your life? Such people in the lives of your friends?
3. Why do males and females differ in their approaches to and perceptions of touch? Are these differences genetic or social?
4. If you were to carry out your own research project on touch avoidance, how would you go about doing so? What would be your independent and dependent variables? How would you operationalize touch?
5. Of all the research presented in this chapter, what findings surprised you the most? Why?

FURTHER REFERENCES

Birth and Touch Studies

Lamb, M. E. (1982a). Paternal influences on early socio-emotional development. *Journal of Child Psychology*, 23, 185–190.

Lamb, M. E. (1982b). The bonding phenomenon: Misinterpretations and their implications. *Journal of Pediatrics*, 101, 555–557.

Lamb, M. E. (1982c). Early contact and maternal-infant bonding: One decade later. *Pediatrics*, 70, 763–768.

Moszkowski, R. J., Stack, D. M., and Chiarella, S. S. (2009). Infant touch with gaze and affective behaviors during mother-infant still-face interactions. *Infant Behavior & Development*, 32, 392–403.

Touch Effects in Childhood

Bowlby, J. (1961). *Maternal care and mental health.* Geneva: World Health Organization.

Despert, J. L. (1941). Emotional aspects of speech and language development. *International Journal of Psychiatry and Neurology*, 105, 193–222.

Rogels, P. L. J., Roelen, E., and VanMeel, J. M. (1990). The function of self-touchings, posture shifts, and motor discharges in children from 3 to 6 years of age. *Perceptual and Motor Skills*, 70, 1169–1178.

Touch Functions

Erceau, D., and Gueguen, N. (2007). Tactile contact and the evaluation of the toucher. *Journal of Social Psychology*, 147, 441–444.

Farris, C., Treat, T. A., Viken, R. J., and McFall, R. M. (2008). Perceptual mechanisms that characterize gender differences in decoding women's sexual intent. *Psychological Science*, 19, 348–354.

Patterson, M. L., Powell, J. L., and Lenihan, M. G. (1986). Touch, compliance and interpersonal effect. *Journal of Nonverbal Behavior*, 10, 41–50.

Sauter, D. (2010). More than happy: The need for disentangling positive emotions. *Current Directions in Psychological Science*, 19, 36–40.

Thayer, S. (1988). Touch encounters. *Psychology Today*, 22, 31–36.

Thompson, E. H., and Hampton, J. A. (2011). The effect of relationship status on communicating emotions through touch. *Cognition & Emotion*, 25, 295–306.

Factors Influencing Touch

A. Gender

Jones, S. E., and Yarbrough, A. E. (1985). A naturalistic study of the meanings of touch. *Communication Monographs*, 52, 19–56.

Jourard, S. M. (1966). An exploratory study of body-accessibility. *British Journal of Social and Clinical Psychology*, 5, 221–231.

Rosenfeld, L. B., Kartus, S., and Ray, C. (1976). Body accessibility revisited. *Journal of Communication*, 26, 27–30.

B. Immediacy

Berscheid, E., and Walster, E. H. (1969). *Interpersonal attraction*. Reading, MA: Addison-Wesley.

Chory, R. M., and McCroskey, J. C. (1999). The relationship between teacher management communication style and affective learning. *Communication Quarterly*, 47, 1–11.

Folwell, A. L. (2000). A comparison of professors' and students' perceptions of nonverbal immediacy behaviors. *Journal of the Northwest Communication Association*, 29, 41–58.

Frymier, A. B. (1993). The impact of teacher immediacy on students' motivation: Is it the same for all students? *Communication Quarterly*, 41, 454–464.

Gendrin, D. M., and Rucker, M. L. (2007). Student motive for communicating and instructor immediacy: A matched-race institutional comparison. *Atlantic Journal of Communication*, 15, 41–60.

Huston, T. L. (Ed.). (1974). *Foundations of interpersonal attraction*. New York: Academic Press.

Myers, S. A., Mottet, T. P., and Martin, M. M. (2000). The relationship between student communication motives and perceived instructor communicator style. *Communication Research Reports*, 17, 161–170.

Plax, T. G., Kearney, P., McCroskey, J. C, and Richmond, V. P. (1986). Power in the classroom VI: Verbal control strategies, nonverbal immediacy, and affective learning. *Communication Education*, 35, 43–55.

Same-Sex Touch

Floyd, K., and Mormarn, M. T. (2000). Reacting to the verbal expression of affection in same-sex interaction. *Southern Communication Journal*, 65, 287–299.

Knofler, T., and Imhof, M. (2007). Does sexual orientation have an impact on nonverbal behavior in interpersonal communication? *Journal of Nonverbal Behavior*, 31, 189–204.

Morman, M. T., and Floyd, K. (1999). Affectionate communication between fathers and young adult sons: Individual and relational-level correlates. *Communication Studies*, 50, 294–309.

Gender

Andersen, J. F., Andersen, P. A., and Lustig, M. W. (1987). Opposite-sex touch avoidance: A national replication and extension. *Journal of Nonverbal Behavior*, 11, 89–109.

Andersen, P. A. (1999). *Nonverbal communication: Forms and functions.* Mountain View, CA: Mayfield Publishing Company.

Andersen, P. A., and Leibowitz, K. (1978). The development and nature of the construct touch avoidance. *Environmental Psychology and Nonverbal Behavior*, 3, 89–106.

Andersen, P. A., and Sull, K. K. (1985). Out of touch, out of reach: Tactile predispositions as predictors of interpersonal distance. *Western Journal of Speech Communication*, 49, 57–72.

Farris, C., Treat, T. A., Viken, R. J., and McFall, R. M. (2008). Perceptual mechanisms that characterize gender differences in decoding women's sexual intent. *Psychological Science*, 19, 348–354.

Guerrero, L. K., and Andersen, P. A. (1991). Nonverbal involvement across interactions with same-sex friends, opposite-sex friends, and romantic partners: Consistency or change? *Journal of Social and Personal Relationships*, 8, 147–165.

Hall, J. A. (1984). *Nonverbal sex differences: Communication accuracy and expressive style.* Baltimore: Johns Hopkins University Press.

Hall, J. A. (1996). Touch, status, and gender at professional meetings. *Journal of Nonverbal Behavior*, 20, 23–44.

Hall, J. A., and Veccia, E. M. (1990). More "touching" observations: New insights on men, women, and interpersonal touch. *Journal of Personality and Social Psychology*, 59, 1155–1162.

Jones, S. E., and Brown, B. C. (1996). Touch attitudes and touch behaviors: Recollections of early childhood touch and social self-confidence. *Communication Monographs*, 52, 19–56.

Martin, M. M., and Anderson, C. M. (1993). Psychological and biological differences in touch avoidance. *Communication Research Reports*, 10, 141–147.

Roese, N. J., and Olson, J. M. (1992). Same-sex touching behavior: The moderating role of homophobic attitudes. *Journal of Nonverbal Behavior*, 16, 249–260.

Cultural Differences

Dolinski, D. (2010). Touch, compliance, and homophobia. *Journal of Nonverbal Behavior*, 34, 179–182.

McDaniel, E., and Andersen, P. A. (1998). International patterns of interpersonal tactile communication: A field study. *Journal of Nonverbal Behavior*, 22, 59–75.

Ping, Y. (2011). Nonverbal aspects of turn taking in Mandarin Chinese interaction. *Chinese Language & Discourse*, 2, 99–130.

Schmidt-Fajlik, R. (2007). Introducing nonverbal communication to Japanese university students: Determining content. *Journal of Intercultural Communication*, 15, 2.

Wang, D., and Li, H. (2007). Nonverbal language in cross-cultural communication. *US-China Foreign Language*, 5, 66–70.

Touch Substitutions

Andersen, P. A., and Sull, K. K. (1985). Out of touch, out of reach: Tactile predispositions as predictors of interpersonal distance. *Western Journal of Speech Communication*, 49, 57–72.

Pisano, M., Wall, S. M., and Foster, A. (1986). Perceptions of nonreciprocal touch in romantic relationships. *Journal of Nonverbal Behavior*, 10, 29–40.

CHAPTER 3

PROXEMICS (PERSONAL SPACE)

- Proxemics
- Personal Space
- Classification Schemes
- Definitions and Need
- Factors Influencing Distancing Expectations
- Violations of Personal Space
- Other Violations

OBJECTIVES

By the end of the chapter you should be able to:

- Define proxemics.
- Demonstrate how different classification schemes operate.
- Discuss the various factors that influence distancing expectations.
- Explain how personal spacing violations operate.
- Discuss Goffman's notion of "modalities of the self." *zero - proxemics/proxemics*

Chapter 2 discussed touch as a basic nonverbal element that is part of proxemics, which is also referred to as zero-proxemics. Certainly, most of us consider touch a significant factor in terms of our space; therefore, we touch and are touched by relatively few people. As this chapter moves from touch to a discussion of personal space, we consider the nonverbal communication aspects of that space, which we carry around with us like an invisible bubble. This bubble, or "zone," has received considerable attention and has been found to differ in terms of the amount of space we expect and give as a function of several things.

"zone" (or bubble) = personal space we give & expect

PROXEMICS

E. T. Hall (1966) defined proxemics as "the interrelated observations and theories of man's use of space as a specialized elaboration of culture" (p. 1). Hall's definition remains the definitive one today, despite the passage of more than 45 years. One can hardly dismiss the importance of all types of space. Land values are going up every year (even when the economic situation was bleak from 2008 to the time of this writing, land value was still high), funeral plots are becoming more expensive, traffic congestion characterizes urban areas during morning and evening drive times, and people are queuing up everywhere to see the latest hit movie, rock group, or selected politician (see B. Schwartz 1975), to name just a few issues. Space is important to all of us, and, in Western culture, there are many laws about space. Individuals have different concepts of space, as do different cultures, racial groups, sexes, and ages. The situation, or context, also greatly affects our usage of space. Proxemics is best defined, however, in terms of the two major subareas that constitute how we use the space around us: personal space and territory. In this chapter we turn first to the study of personal space; in Chapter 4 we look at territory and the general environment.

PERSONAL SPACE

Edney (1976) has classified the use of space into three basic categories: (1) individual, (2) small group and interpersonal relations, and (3) communities. Much of the research in this area has been strongly influenced by anthropologist Edward T. Hall, who first noted the communicative potential of personal spacing as it affects interactions between individuals.

CLASSIFICATION SCHEMES

Hall (1968) classified space in the United States according to the distance between two individuals in the process of communication, and these classifications are still used today by most nonverbal communication theorists. The closest distance is referred to as **intimate** space. This distance is measured from zero-proxemics (touching) to 18 inches in the United States. It is space that is reserved for people with whom we are very close, our significant others, sometimes family members (depending on our family's use of touch), and very close friends. **Personal** space ranges from 18 inches to about 4 feet. Generally, we allow our friends and people whom we like into this range. Social space ranges from 4 to 10 feet and is also sometimes called the "business" zone. It is reserved for our business associates and people with whom we feel little or no interpersonal relationship. Finally, **public** space ranges from 10 feet to about 25 feet. Within each distance "zone," we have units, or **proxemes**. These units are generally classified as "inner" or "outer" zones. The inner proxeme of the personal zone, for instance, might run from 18 to 25 inches; the outer proxeme for that same zone might run from 32 to 48 inches. The proxemes allow us to establish subranges within each distancing zone. Despite the more than 45 years that have elapsed since this original research was done, Hall's space zones are the most commonly used measurements for how scholars classify personal space zones. Hall's guidelines for personal space zones are closely adhered to in communication textbooks across our discipline. From nonverbal to interpersonal to small group texts, these space usage zones appear over and over again.

Take a look around you as you read this (or, if you are alone, notice the next time you are in a room with someone else). How close is the nearest person? Which zone would that be? What is the relationship between you and that person? Then, think of your classroom setting for this class. How closely placed are the students? Does this spacing bother you? Usually the closest person in a classroom setting will be in your intimate zone. How far away is the professor? Does this distancing seem correct? You can see that these "zones" are affected by many variables, and these are looked at more closely in Chapter 4.

Personal spacing is based on the intimacy of the topic of conversation; as it becomes more intimate, we reduce the space between us. Also, other people viewing you and another person conversing at an intimate distance will conclude that the conversation is an intimate one. If we see someone sitting close to someone else—say, within the range of 0 to 18 inches—we often perceive a degree of intimacy between the interactants. We may believe they are "significant others," especially as we observe their use of space and touch functions, or we may think they are very close friends. How many times have you perceived there was "something romantic going on" between two of your friends long before they ever "went public" with their relationship? At the other end of the continuum, how many times have you perceived there was an argument going on between a couple on the basis of their use of space? Everyone makes judgments about relationships based on the interactants' use of space.

Hall also associates a number of factors with the various distances we adopt in daily interaction. There are numerous features other than intimacy that contribute to our perception of personal space. Hall includes *postural-sex identifiers*. Sex refers to the biological sex (male/female) of the two people involved in the interaction; postural refers to whether the interactants are prone, seated, or standing. Men and women will assume different postures and establish different distances depending on the person with whom they are interacting and the gender and status of that person (among other variables, such as the topic being discussed or how public or private the setting is). Postures are discussed in more detail in Chapter 7, where we discuss kinesics.

A second factor that is associated with distance is the *sociofugal–sociopetal axis.* As indicated in Figure 3.1, this factor refers to the "angle formed by the axis of the interactants' shoulders."

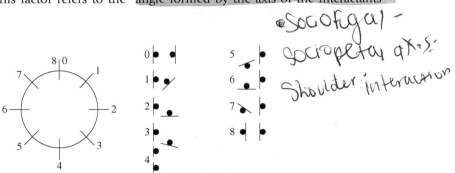

FIGURE 3.1 Sociofugal–Sociopetal axes. *Source:* E. T. Hall, "A System for the Notation of Proxemic Behavior," *American Anthropologist,* 65 (5), 1963. Reproduced by permission of the American Anthropological Association.

At level 0, the interactants are face-to-face (maximum sociopetality); at level 8, they are back-to-back (maximum sociofugality). Although not as practical as the postural-sex identifiers, it is a fascinating aspect of the history of the study of proxemics.

— Amount of *touch,* ranging from none to mutual caressing (on a six-point scale), is the third factor. *Kinesthetic* features (parts of the bodies touching) is the fourth factor. The *visual code* (amount and kind of visual interaction, or what can be seen) is based on areas of the eye, specifically of the retina. The *thermal code* includes the amount of heat detected by the people in the interaction, as given off by the body. Have you noticed how you do not appreciate the body heat of someone sitting too close to you when the weather is hot, but when the weather is cold, the proximity of others is something you want? The *olfactory code* identifies the detection of body odor and breath. And, finally, *voice-loudness* refers to the volume of the oral aspect of verbal language. All these factors are related to the distances people adopt, and they help explain why we have certain distancing preferences or norms with different people at different times. Consider the distance you kept from someone who had a bad body odor or someone you could not hear very well. Think of the last time you got closer to someone when it was cold in order to absorb some body heat. These would all be factors of proxemics.

The interaction of these factors and the intimacy of topic allows us to examine why people adopt spatial distances. As distance increases or decreases, however, other nonverbal codes come more or less into play. The interaction of Hall's factors results in an *equilibrium* among the nonverbal behaviors (Argyle and Dean 1965). There are a number of other factors that influence distancing: age, sex, culture, race, task, degree of relationship, personality, and environmental structure help determine what distances we adopt with others.

STUDENT VOICES

Tom: The other day I was out to dinner with my roommates, and I happened to notice my "crush" across the restaurant with another man. I kept thinking, "But her communication to me has always been such a come-on to me." How could I have misread her so much? She was sitting close to the guy, what I learned in my nonverbal class was "intimate space." I was so disappointed. Then, on her way out, she saw me and stopped by and introduced her younger brother to me. I must admit, I stereotyped what I saw and should have thought that there might be some other explanation before I jumped to conclusions.

DEFINITIONS AND NEED

Before we begin to examine the other factors that influence distancing, we need to establish which distancing zones really concern us here. The emphasis of much of the rest of this section is on the personal spacing zone. Although we also consider the intimate and the social, much of our interpersonal communication is found in the personal spacing zone.

DEFINITIONS

Personal space is referred to either as an "invisible, flexible bubble that surrounds us" (Dosey and Meisels 1969) or as a "body buffer zone" (Horowitz, Duff, and Stratton 1964).

PHOTO 3.1 Think about a time when someone violated your personal space. What nonverbal behaviors did you use to adapt to the situation?

Our personal space expands or contracts depending on other variables, such as the situation, gender, personality, and the relationship of the interactants. Personal space seems to be attributable to the need to protect our body territories. In that regard, personal space is a "body buffer zone," a zone of space—unmarked, unlike territories—that serves to protect us from the intrusion of others. Personal space is also flexible; it surrounds the individual but is usually larger in the rear, with less distance needed in the front and to each side, although even that will vary (especially with heterosexual dyads). Hayduk (1978) adds that horizontal and vertical factors (such as how close the ceiling is, or how close the walls are) influence personal space. What we have, then, is a sphere of space that surrounds us totally, from the floor to the ceiling, from front to back, and from side to side.

[handwritten margin note: horizontal is vertical factors]

NEED FOR SPACE

Just as we need territory, we need personal space. **Body buffer zone** implies a definite psychological need. Other researchers have found, through the use of electrocardiogram, electroencephalogram, galvanic skin response, and other physiological indicators and from actual physical response, that people react to personal space physiologically (Argyle and Dean 1965) as well as psychologically (see Albert and Dabbs 1970). Indicators of strong psychological and physiological needs are found in reactions to other people as compared to relations with inanimate objects, in verbal and nonverbal reports of anxiety, and in the placement of figures based on expected distances in given scenarios (Hickson and Stacks 1991).

Perhaps one of the best indicators of the need for personal space is the research first reported by Felipe and Sommer (1966) and later replicated by Krail and Leventhal (1976), Ahmed (1979), and Agnosto, Paone, and Ipock (2007). This research examined the impact of violating another person's space in a library. Felipe and Sommer first studied the expectations of females studying at a table alone. In this research a male confederate sat in one of several different seats at the same table as the studying female. When the confederate sat close to the female subject, a series of behaviors occurred: The student would almost always (1) engage in eye contact with the confederate and give "dirty looks"; (2) build barriers (establish markers on the desk with such items as books, purses, paper, pencils); (3) exhibit body shifts (moving the body around, as if uncomfortable); (4) use the body as a barrier by turning away from the confederate; (5) use subvocal expressions or mutter; (6) engage in decreased eye contact (eye contact would go to the material in front of her); (7) assume a nonperson orientation (react as if the confederate were an extension of the chair or another object); (8) exhibit anxiety movements, such as drumming of fingers, variant eye contact, and so forth; and (9) finally, leave the table (give up her space and established territory) within 10 to 30 minutes. Clearly, these were strong reactions arising from the student's feeling of having her personal space invaded.

Krail and Leventhal (1976) and Ahmed (1979) each replicated this study but added several variations. First, they had males and females invade the territories of students of both sexes who were studying alone in the library. Second, they introduced a verbal claim to the space. They found that the same reactional behaviors occurred but were much faster when the confederate was of the *same* sex. They also reported that females gave up their space more readily than did males when verbally challenged. (The researchers suggested that females are taught socially to share more than are males, who are taught to defend things that they possess.) In another context, during their menstrual periods, females distance themselves farther from males but not from other females (O'Neil, Schultz, and Christensen 1987). In any case, these studies (as well as many others) indicate a strong need for space, with both psychological and physiological reactions when someone "violates" a spatial expectation or norm. Perhaps this is an area where you might like to conduct studies on your own?

BOX 3.1   OBSERVATIONAL STUDY

How do people demonstrate their need for body space? According to a theory proposed by Argyle and Dean (1965), as we change one nonverbal behavior, we compensate for that change by changing other nonverbal behaviors. Thus, as we move closer to or farther from someone, we may also change our body lean, eye contact, our level of touching, vocal loudness, and so forth. Try a simple test of this theory with your friends. As you carry on a conversation with a friend, change the distance you adopt and observe changes in, first, your friend's nonverbal behaviors (including trying to maintain the distance you originally established), and then observe how you were compensating for changes in distances.

FACTORS INFLUENCING DISTANCING EXPECTATIONS

Many factors influence people's expectations about how much space to maintain between themselves and others. The general factors include the interactants' demographics (such as age, sex, culture, race, and personality). In addition, the structure of the environment appears to make a difference.

AGE DIFFERENCES

In general, as the age of a person increases, so does the expected distancing; however, this holds true only where there is a discrepancy in the ages of the interactants. With same-age people, distancing expectations are closer than with those who are older or younger. Several studies lend support for this generalization. Tennis and Dabbs (1975), for instance, found that older subjects (among students enrolled in the first, fifth, ninth, and twelfth grades and college sophomores) preferred greater interpersonal distances than younger subjects. They also found that corners were a preferred place to carry on conversations only among first graders. Aiello and Aiello (1974) reported that students from ages 6 to 16 maintained greater interaction distances as age increased, but this distancing trend leveled off at about the seventh grade, and distances did not increase significantly after that grade level.

When you think back to your junior high or middle school years, you probably can recall beginning to really worry about people invading your space. You probably established new personal space zones about that time of life, and it is likely they have not changed much in the years that have passed since then. In yet another study, researchers found that invasion of personal space in the refreshment line of a drive-in theater was influenced by the age of the invader (Dean, LaRocco, and Willis 1976). With a 5-year-old invader, adults were facilitative; with 8-year-olds there was no particular response; with 10-year-olds the adults displayed avoidance and excess motor activity (i.e., fidgeting and other negative behaviors). Apply this to yourself for a minute by picturing this scenario in your mind. You probably would not be upset if a small child, 3 to 6 years old, came up and invaded your space by climbing into your lap. Would you react the same way if the person sitting next to you in this class did the same?

A number of studies have found that up to about age 7, sex is not an important factor in distancing norms. After that age, closer distances, at least for heterosexuals, are found for

PHOTO 3.2 Does technology sometimes affect how much space you maintain between someone else or where you position yourself?

female–female and male–female interactions, and farther distances are found with male–male interactions. Recall that researchers (Derlega, Lewis, Harrison, Winstead, and Costanza 1989) found that aversion to male–male touch was a result of heterosexual men being more homophobic than heterosexual women. Logic would have you apply the same reaction to the space usage reported here. Floyd (2000b) also found similar results when testing whether college-age students who observed romantic or affectionate posturing (including both close proximity and touching) perceived male–male affection more positively than female–female affection or vice versa. The students responded more negatively to the male–male affection they observed than to female–female affection.

S. E. Jones and Aiello (1973) found that black and white elementary school children adopt different distancing norms. First-grade blacks adopted less personal space than whites, but by third grade the difference between the races began to diminish and began to finally reverse by the fifth grade. In the 35 years since that study, changes in the racial culture of the United States have taken place, and these findings may no longer hold true. One author of this text always discusses the racial differences in proxemics when discussing this topic in class. Almost without fail, the female African Americans point out that they find Caucasian women move closer to their Caucasian women friends than they do to their African-American women friends. This leads the discussion to Jones and Aiello's study, where they also reported sex differences in distancing norms.

SEX DIFFERENCES

As noted, distancing preferences for either males or females are influenced by age. However, there are some generalizations that can be made based solely on the sex of the individual. Tennis and Dabbs (1975) found that males usually prefer greater distances when interacting with one another than females require with each other (pp. 386–387). As early as 1966, F. N. Willis reported that speakers usually stood closer to women than to men. Rosegrant and McCroskey (1975) found that in an interview situation, male–male dyads established greater distances than any combination containing at least one female. Not all research has confirmed these findings; Pedersen and Heaston (1972) and J. D. Fisher and Byrne (1975) have reported contradictory findings. It would seem from most studies that females prefer less distance when interacting than do males. It would be a mistake to make this a blanket generalization, however. Some scholars of nonverbal communication believe that females really would like more space when interacting but that they are less likely to be accorded that space. Because people in the United States tend to believe this generalization about females, they are more likely to move closer to females than to males.

Several studies indicate that males tend to approach females more closely than females approach males, but this may be affected by the angle of the approach. Pedersen and Heaston (1972) reported that females allowed others to approach closer to their sides than to their front; males allowed others to approach closer to their front than to their sides; males were allowed to approach both males and females more closely off-center to the left than were females, although no difference was found for approaching off-center to the right. Hendricks and Bootzin (1976) noted that males reported significantly more discomfort in approaching a female confederate than did females. Tipton, Bailey, and Obenchain (1975) found that traditional females maintain greater distances from males than do feminists but do not differ in their approach distances with other females, although there have been other studies that have found these results reversed (Wood 2012). Perhaps these changes in attitudes and norms can be accounted for by the more than 25 years between the studies; much has changed in our society in that span of time.

Banziger and Simmons (1984) reported that the level of attractiveness of the confederate seems to affect interpersonal distance. In a simple but effective research design, they measured street-crossing times and reported the emotions of male and female street crossers who were approached—intruded upon—by either an attractive or an unattractive female. Another female confederate then approached the participants *after* they had crossed the street and asked what two emotions they felt in response to the intruder. Positive emotions were more prevalent when the intruder was attractive, and negative emotions were more prevalent when the intruder was unattractive. The researchers theorized that spatial invasion increases arousal, but whether the arousal is positive or negative depends upon the attractiveness of the invader. J. K. Burgoon (1978, 1983, 1991) and her associates in many other studies defined attraction in several ways and also tested this finding. In short, it appears that the more attractive a *space invader* is, the more we are willing to accept his or her violation of our proxemic norms.

Males and females will approach another person differently depending on whether or not the approached person is looking at them. Males will move closer to "non-lookers"; for females, moving closer will depend on the gender of the other person. Females move closer to male "non-lookers" and closer to female "lookers" (J. D. Fisher and Bryne 1975; J. Hughes and Goldman 1978). As you can see, males and females respond differently to other people moving into their personal space zones. Responses often depend on the sex of the persons approaching them as well as other nonverbal indicators, such as eye contact.

Perhaps one of the most important studies of nonverbal communication to introduce here is J. K. Burgoon's (1978) development of the *expectancy violation model.* She believes that we will react to another's invasion of our space, especially if it is unexpected. Once our spatial expectations are violated, our attention is aroused and we will pay attention to whether that person can offer rewards or positive reinforcement. If the invader has a high level of positive reward value (such as status, appearance, or even material goods), Burgoon conjectures that we will be more likely to have a positive response to the violator and are more likely to reciprocate the positive invasion. The opposite is likely to occur if the person has a low reward value. As you can well imagine, this model is greatly affected by sex differences. We discuss this model in more detail later in this chapter.

Generally, sex differences play a major role in determining distancing norms. Males tend to expect and receive more space when interacting with other males, especially when the interaction is between heterosexual men. The attractiveness of the invader does influence how much arousal a person whose space is invaded experiences; this arousal can be either positive or negative. Males tend to approach females more closely than females approach males, and, although it is not possible to explain exactly why, approaches seem to differ by angle or side of approach. Clearly, sex differences do affect our responses to invasion.

BOX 3.2 OBSERVATIONAL STUDY

Observe your closest male friend and your closest female friend over the next week. Since you likely know their space norms, violate those norms and take note of their reactions. Behave as you normally do with the exception of violating the space norms of your relationship with

those persons. Or choose someone whom you do not know well (such as a classmate) and violate what you have learned is a sex-based space usage norm. Did you notice any sex-based differences like those reported by researchers? If so, what were the sex-based norms? If not, why do you think there were none?

CLOSER
former vs latter

CULTURAL DIFFERENCES

The main thrust of cultural research by anthropologists maintains that two types of cultures exist, either "contact" or "noncontact"; the former maintain closer distances than the latter (E. T. Hall 1959). Whether these differences really exist has been questioned. Several researchers have maintained that this distinction is not viable and may be a feature of faulty analysis. Others have found that significant differences do exist between contact and non-contact cultures (Shuter 1976, 1977). Cultures differ in their expectations of what distances *should* be maintained when people interact. The differences, however, may be more country specific than culture specific. E. T. Hall and Hall (1976) have suggested that Americans generally do not like interacting with people who get too close and breathe on them. Americans often go to great lengths to avoid spatial violations. As an extension of this notion, Hall states that some cultures have no words for "trespassing."

An examination of different cultures offers doubt that all countries in a given culture operate on the same distancing norms. L. C. Baxter (1970), for example, noted that Mexican Americans maintained closer personal spacing than did European Americans, who in turn maintained closer personal spacing than did African Americans in a natural setting. Machado-Casas (2012) discovered that often Latinos will employ a "chameleon effect" (changing how they act or react when faced with a communication difference from their own cultures), especially in situations where there is a status differential. Lorenz (1976) examined the cultural norms of three nationalities and found that the placement of figurines in relation to each other was largely contingent upon culture: South Americans had the largest personal spacing and Iraqis the smallest, with Russians being intermediate.

Roger and Schalekamp (1976) investigated the body zones, or personal space bubbles, of South-African black prisoners and found that South-African blacks have larger body zones than American black prisoners. They attributed the difference in terms of contact versus noncontact cultures, with the American culture being more prone to contact than the South-African culture. The differences between the two cultures were also viewed as possibly the result of cultural anomie (personal unrest, alienation), because South-African blacks at that time represented the opposite status of whites and rejected values forced upon them by the minority white population. An alternative explanation is that the blacks may form a distinctly noncontact *subcultural* group and, as a result, may maintain greater personal space norms (Engelbretsen and Fullmer 1970). Although not mainstream culture, these findings still tell us some things about cultural differences in the use of space. Scholars can learn much from the study of a broad spectrum of examples when it comes to studying the use of any nonverbal subcode, and this information should make it clear to you how important it is to pay attention to context.

Shuter (1976) noted that differences occur in personal spacing within a large culture. From observations made in Costa Rica, Colombia, and Panama (all presumably contact cultures), he found that Costa Ricans interacted closest and Panamanians at the greatest distance; Colombians maintained an intermediate distance. He also investigated the interaction patterns in Germany, Italy, and the United States (Shuter 1977). In this study, he observed dyads of males and females and found no significant differences between cultures with respect to male–female, male–male, or female–female dyads, although Germans interacted least directly in both-sex pairs. In terms of male–female dyads, Italians interacted at a more direct angle than did Americans; however, American female dyads communicated at a more direct angle. More recent studies confirm these findings (e.g., D. E. Williams and Hughes 2005).

In an observational study of seating patterns on park benches in three different cultures, A. Mazur (1977) found no difference between the distances adopted by strangers. His results, however, may have been an artifact of measurement owing to differing bench lengths in different cultures. In several other studies, methodological problems also have contributed to such findings. For instance, Forston and Larson (1968) found no significant differences in interpersonal distancing between contact and noncontact cultures. However, the study participants were noncontact people who had been living in the United States for a period of time prior to the study and who had probably assimilated into the norms of its culture.

It appears that cultural and subcultural differences do exist in spacing expectations. The fact that they do not necessarily create a dichotomy as large as "contact" or "noncontact" should not surprise us. We may have a stereotypical view of appropriate interpersonal distancing, but, as Shuter found, that stereotype may or may not be accurate, depending on what nationality or subculture we are studying.

It is best, then, not to generalize about people's use of space on the basis of their cultural identity but rather to know how an individual responds to different space zones. One author of this text has spent a great deal of time in Eastern Europe over the last 15 years, in countries that were once behind the Iron Curtain. In public spaces in Poland, for example, people will invade your personal space continually, which makes most Americans very uncomfortable. In interpersonal settings, however, most Polish people have the same space distancing as Americans (Hall's space zones, mentioned earlier). It is alright to make or almost make body contact on public transport or to push into someone while you are "queuing up" to purchase something (such as in a grocery store, a clothing store, train ticket windows, even the post office), but when conversing with someone who is not a close friend, Hall's "personal zone" is what is expected. Many Polish people say that this is a "leftover" from when they were Communist-ruled; they needed to line up to get any "goods" they wanted. If they were able to push their way to the front of the line, their chances of getting the desired product were greatly enhanced. Others say that this has long been an action those cultures have practiced. To generalize about all Polish people on the basis of their use of space in the public setting would be incorrect and could lead to a breakdown in interpersonal communication. It would be just as wrong to generalize about any culture on the basis of only a few studies or known examples about them.

RACIAL DIFFERENCES

No clear-cut generalizations can be made regarding racial differences and personal spacing expectations. Part of this problem of determining racial differences emerges out of our discussions of cultural, sexual, and age factors, but in most cases the results of research are mixed. In one study, for instance, L. C. Baxter (1970) found that in the United States about one-third of the explanation for distancing expectations could be attributed to race. Other researchers have found that the distance between interactants was greater for African Americans than for Caucasians, although a number of factors (age, sex, culture) may also enter into the interpretation. With college-age students, however, Bauer (1973) found that blacks stood closer to one another than whites did. This was basically the same finding reported by Rosegrant and McCroskey (1975), except that the sex of the individual also affected the interaction distances. Rosegrant and McCroskey found that in an interview situation, "Female-black interviewers established closer interpersonal distance to all interviewees than did any other sex–race interviewee combination" (p. 408). Based on this, J. K. Burgoon, Stacks, and Woodall (1977) suggested that same-race interactions would result in closer interpersonal distances than opposite-race interactions, but they failed to support such a hypothesis. Thus, at this time no clear-cut conclusions can be made about race and personal space. You need to discover a person's individual space preferences by interacting with them, regardless of race. Only then can positive interpersonal interactions occur.

BOX 3.3 OBSERVATIONAL STUDY

Watch a half-hour television show where the actors/participants are from different racial or cultural backgrounds than yours (e.g., *The Hughleys, Boy Meets World, Moesha, Parkers, The Office, Ugly Betty, Baldwin Hills,* etc.), and study their use of personal space. Are there stereotypical space usage issues utilized by the actors? Are there any atypical ones you notice? What messages about those races or cultures did you receive?

STATUS, PERSONALITY, AND LIKING

Several factors that influence our distancing expectations are brought to the interaction with us—an individual's status or personality or the degree of liking one holds toward the other. In general, people of higher status expect and receive more interpersonal distance than those of lower status (Lott and Sommer 1967). Dabbs and Stokes (1975) had a female confederate stand next to a wide sidewalk. The confederate was first dressed as a high-status person (business suit, heels) and later dressed as a low-status person (blue jeans). People tended to walk more closely to her when she was dressed as the low-status confederate than when she dressed as the high-status one. Think of your own use of space in situations where there is a status differential, for example, with a boss or professor. Then think of yourself with your peers or friends. To whom do you get the closest? Chances are that you will get closer to your peers and friends than to your professor or boss. Mehrabian (1981) found that it is more likely that you will have your space invaded by your bosses or professors than that you will invade their personal space. Think about your own situations; are you more likely to encroach upon the space of your boss, professors, and other persons in charge, or are they more likely to invade your proxemic territory? Chances are good that your answer will mirror these research findings.

~~Personality~~ differences also function to create different personal spacing expectations. Although there is a rather large body of research in this area, the variables that affect the process of establishing spacing expectations are still not completely identified. What we know, however, seems to indicate that introverts and extroverts differ in their spatial use, with extroverts using less space. Anxious and neurotic individuals tend to prefer more space but perceive less space to exist between them and others than do less anxious and neurotic individuals (Malandro, Barker, and Barker 1989). Aberrant or deviant personalities also affect the distancing patterns between people (Fast 1970). Violent people need more space than do nonviolent people. Schizophrenics use and expect others to use space differently than non-schizophrenics (Lambrey et al. 2011). S. Park et al. (2009) found that schizophrenics even used increased personal space in virtual social environments. Finally, emotionally disturbed people use space differently than do non-emotionally disturbed people. If the emotional disorder is one that is manifested in violent behaviors, greater spatial preference is observed by those disturbed people (Roger and Schalekamp 1976). Clearly, many issues determine how individuals use proxemics, and we have barely scratched the surface with what we have mentioned here.

Finally, the degree of liking in the interaction helps determine personal spacing expectations. Liking, however, can be viewed as more than simple "liking" and is related to such things as physical attraction, degree of acquaintance, and approval. In general, we approach others we see as being physically attractive more closely than we approach those we perceive as less attractive; when we wish to demonstrate liking, we also establish closer physical distances (Norum, Gergen, Peele, and van Ryneveld 1977). Moreover, people tend to establish closer distances from someone they are acquainted with than from someone who may be a stranger (D. J. A. Edwards 1972). Think about yourself at a social gathering, such as a party or some other type of group gathering. To whom do you move closer? People you perceive as more attractive? Your friends? How close do you stand to people you find unattractive, or do you not even approach them? How close do you get to your friends as opposed to someone to whom you have just been introduced? The answers to these questions will probably give you a better idea of how these theories apply to your own life.

An area that has received less attention is the finding that people maintain greater distances from others who have stigmas. Goffman (1963) noted that one who has a stigma is one "possessing an attribute that makes him different from others in the category of persons available for him to be, and of a less desirable kind—in the extreme, a person who is quite thoroughly bad, or dangerous, or weak" (p. 184). Stigmas may be of two basic types: physical or social. *Physical stigmas* include being in a wheelchair, being blind, being an amputee, having a scarred face, and so forth. One group of researchers, for example, found that pedestrians allowed a legally blind person with a white cane 33.8 inches of personal space as opposed to 5.6 inches when there was no cane (Conigliaro, Cullerton, Flynn, and Rueder 1989). *Social stigmas* include reputations such as being an ex-convict or having a social disease (one that cannot be seen—an STD, for instance). In general, we maintain more space between ourselves and those with stigmas. Examples of combined physical and social stigmas would be someone who is obese or someone with HIV. Owen (2012) found that people often keep their distance from overweight individuals, adding to the stigma (see also Merrill and Grassley 2008). These findings indicate that stigmas may result in an unwillingness to move closer to individuals with any such stigmas.

The last time you saw someone with a stigma, how did you respond? Did you give them a "wide berth," thinking they probably wanted it or needed it? As you can imagine, persons with a stigma receive this distant spatial treatment continually, yet their human needs are likely similar to those of all other human beings. If you have never paid attention to this phenomenon, position yourself somewhere where you can observe it, say, in front of a hospital or clinic entrance and see what you discover. If you were to do this in the town square of Morristown, New Jersey, where the Seeing Eye, Inc. foundation and training facility is located, it would not take you long to see the "wide berth" accorded to this sightless population. Attending a Special Olympics gathering, you would also see some of the same sorts of behaviors. This distancing became such an issue for Special Olympics that they established volunteer "huggers" for the athletes when they finish an event in an effort to send the message of "job well done" and to communicate that people are not averse to approaching another human being who happens to have what society considers a human deficiency.

BOX 3.4 OBSERVATIONAL STUDY

Take a magazine that is targeted toward your sex and look at the advertisements with more than one person in the ad. What use of personal space do you notice? What does the use of space by the advertiser tell you about the relationships between the individuals in the ad? What does the use of space by the advertiser tell you about the personalities of the individuals in the ad? What does the use of space tell you about the product/concept the advertiser is trying to sell? Is it effective or not?

ENVIRONMENTAL STRUCTURING

The way an environment is structured obviously has an impact on personal spacing. In fact, personal space research often seems to be mislabeled, especially when the subject is seating preferences and furniture arrangement. However, if we think of such arrangements as way of expressing ourselves by means of the distances we either choose or are made to choose, then we can begin to better understand how personal spacing expectations and norms are structured.

In a classroom setting, Heston and Garner (1972) found that distances between students fell within Hall's intimate zone, with seating preference for a U-shaped arrangement. This

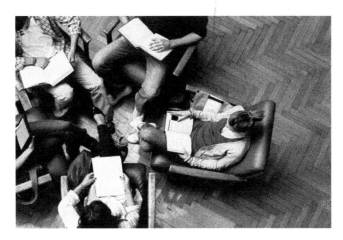

PHOTO 3.3   How does the way that people structure their environment impact their personal spacing?

arrangement seems to direct attention away from immediate neighbors and may explain the closeness of the preferred distance. Hirst and Cooper (2008) discovered that students do respond and react to the ways teachers spatially set up their classrooms. Think again about the classroom where you take this course. How close is your neighbor? As suggested earlier, is he or she in your intimate zone? If so, what is your level of intimacy with your neighbor? Chances are that most of you in this close zone are only acquaintances. Research in task- and social-oriented interactions indicates that the purpose of the interaction along with the environmental constraints may dictate distance between interactants and seating arrange- *Seating arrangement* ments. Several studies report that the kind of interaction (i.e., casual or conversational, cooperative, competitive, or co-active) produces different preferences for seating arrangements that reflect different distances between individuals. Corner or adjacent seating preferences are found normally in cooperative task situations. Opposite seating arrangements are usually found in competitive situations, where a greater distance keeps other people from surveying one's progress.

For co-acting people (for example, people completing a jigsaw puzzle together), a greater distance is preferred (G.T. Lang, Calhoun, and Selby 1977). Cook (1970) notes that in bars, where the conversation is intimate or social, seating preference is for the side-by-side or adjacent cross-corner arrangement. When the purpose of dining is added, the preference is for larger distances and an opposite-seating arrangement. In dining situations, participants tend to divide the table (in their imaginations) into half for each. Indeed, most people think it strange when intimate couples sit next to their significant others in a "booth" setting in a restaurant, although the closer distancing would definitely indicate the intimacy between the two. Riess and Rosenfeld (1980) found that when specific impressions were desired in a group interaction around a table, the position taken helped to indicate that impression. They had people choose one of several seats around a table to convey the impression of (1) leadership and dominance, (2) nonparticipation, (3) attraction, and (4) dislike. To show leadership, 80 percent of the people in the study took one of the two end chairs. To show nonparticipation, 64 percent chose one of the corner seats, farthest from the head. To present themselves as attracted to other group members, they chose chairs in the middle. To show themselves as disliked (cold, unfriendly), they chose the farthest seating possible. Other researchers on group processes report similar findings. Leadership comes from the ends of the table, where there are fewer chairs on one side of the table and usually one chair at the end of the table; leadership also comes from the side of the table with fewer chairs. One reason for these findings is that those physical positions control eye contact, and so people who are in the leadership roles (or the more powerful positions) will choose those seats (Jackson and Engstrom 2004).

In other situations, such as being outdoors, the type of environment may affect personal spacing expectations and norms. Edney and Jordan-Edney (1974) found that the size of groups and the place they are meeting may be significant factors in determining personal spacing. They observed spacing on a large, open beach. Their concern was how naturally occurring groups divided their territory and the use of space within the territory. They found that (1) group territories did not necessarily grow with group size; instead, individuals decreased their personal space; and (2) females claimed less territory than males.

The use of territory and personal space communicates many things. Territory is more fixed or marked than the more flexible personal space zone around us. The concepts are related, however, because personal space is an outgrowth of our need for some form of protection from others (we protect our bodies by erecting a psychological barrier, a physical one, or both). Many factors influence the amount of space around us, including the type of territory we are in. The best conclusion is that we form expectations based on norms associated with such characteristics as sex, race, culture, personality, status, location, and so forth. Like the environment, space helps communicate perceptions of relationships and indicates how we perceive others.

BOX 3.5   OBSERVATIONAL STUDY

How do factors such as age, race, culture, and environment influence the distancing norms we adopt? Several researchers have used dolls to test "distance placement" between interactants. In a test to see how valid such studies are, take several dolls and dress them according to different cultural standards. Ask friends to place these dolls in standing positions where they would be if they were engaged in a normal conversation. Measure the distances between the dolls in various dress and see what differences are obtained. If you can, do the same for age differences, sex differences, and environmental manipulations.

VIOLATIONS OF PERSONAL SPACE

In general, we perceive a violation of expectations as either positive or negative, depending on several factors. In this section of the chapter, we examine in some detail the dimension of space and how people react when we violate others' expectations based on personal space.

Research indicates that people, as well as other animals, have concepts of territory and personal space. Within cultures and subcultures, there is recognition of this "right to space." As in other societies, residents of the United States have proxemic norms (Leathers and Eaves

2008; Leathers 1997). Most of the research on proxemic norms has consisted of field experiments in which a confederate violates the space of subjects. Probably the most familiar of these studies includes the Felipe and Sommer (1966) investigations of library invasion noted earlier and similar investigations.

When someone violates our territory, we humans tend to react with defensive devices. Again, the research of Felipe and Sommer (1966) is concerned with such invasion; however, if that territory is either the person's home or body, then reactions become more violent. In most states the act of "defending" home or body is defined in such a way as to make homicide "legal" ("self-defense"). For the most part, however, research has focused on less intensely held territories and has found that we engage in the following behaviors when our territory is invaded: (1) We avoid conversation (we do *not* challenge unless challenged, and even then it will depend upon the sexual configuration of the interaction); (2) we avoid eye contact (in cases where a stranger sits down at a restaurant table with us, after the initial glare, we look almost exclusively at our plate); (3) we place objects between ourselves and the other person; and (4) we focus our attention, body orientation, and eye contact elsewhere.

Not all spatial violations are territorial. Just as unnerving are personal spacing violations. Because we have no real markers around us, we form an expectation of appropriate distancing and then expect that this distance will be maintained. It is precisely this type of thinking that led Burgoon and her associates (J. K. Burgoon 1978, 1991; J. K. Burgoon and Hale 1988) to propose the theory of personal space expectations and their violations, known as the *expectancy violations* theory, discussed earlier. This theory postulates that we can predict the outcome of a spatial violation on the basis of three factors: (1) the "reward" power of the violator (what aspects he or she brings to the interaction: attraction, power, and/or status, for instance); (2) the direction of the violation (closer or farther than expected); and (3) the degree of the deviation (how much closer or farther). Let us look at the theory in a little more detail now.

This theory contends that violators who are able to reward others will produce better outcomes than will nonrewarding violators (see Figure 3.2). The outcomes, however, also depend on the amount of deviation and direction. If the violator deviates too closely, meaning the violation is noticeable, the impact of reward is not strong enough to reduce the tension, uneasiness, anxiety, and pressure associated with extremely close distances. If the violator is rewarding and deviates in moderation, then generally positive outcomes are observed. If the violator is nonrewarding, however, any deviation from the expected norm produces lower, even disastrous, outcomes. Partial support for this theory has been demonstrated for such outcomes as perceived attraction, credibility, and persuasiveness. This simply means that in positive reward situations, positive violators will be perceived as more attractive, credible, and persuasive; in negative reward situations, the violators will be seen as less attractive, credible, and/or persuasive. This may be a simple theory, but the consequences are far more complex than many people are willing to acknowledge, especially in the business world.

Such research results point to strategies that seem worth examining in more detail. For instance, suppose you know that others perceive you as being rewarding. This spatial

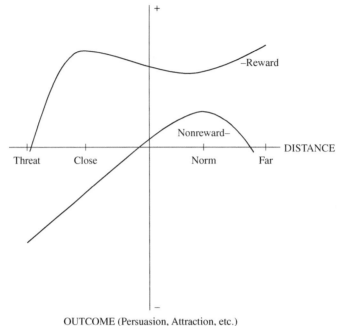

FIGURE 3.2 Predicted outcomes for violating or maintaining a spatial expectation.

theory implies that you will be perceived as more credible, attractive, and more persuasive if you deviate in moderation from the expected distance. On the other hand, if you know that you are "nonrewarding," then you should maintain whatever distance is "agreed" upon. Research has indicated that these findings can be used in both two-person (dyadic) and small-group contexts. However, before depending on your self-perception to determine how rewarding you are, realize that we are often much more severe in our self-evaluations than are others in evaluating us (especially physically). We discuss this again in Chapter 5; be sure your self-evaluation is accurate by checking it out with a person you love and respect.

Research has also indicated that attractiveness of the person is a factor in spatial violations in many contexts, including gender, status, culture, background, and communication apprehension. Gender and status, however, have relatively limited effects on spatial expectations and violations. Attractive females are expected to be relaxed or erect in their use of space, but not tense. Regarding cultural differences, for example, spatial invasions among Turks are much less than have been reported in the research literature (Arik 2012; Ozdemir 2008). Finally, some researchers report that communication-apprehensive people are aroused when closely violated. Other researchers have disputed that such persons have defensive reactions to spatial violations. Simply put, these scholars found that apprehensive people who are violated may feel defensive when their space is violated, but they do not necessarily react in a defensive manner.

OTHER VIOLATIONS

Goffman (1971) identified numerous types of violations of the territories of the self. His first violation is spatial invasion: the infringement of actual body space. Second is using the body, including the hands, to inappropriately touch the skin or clothing of another. Third, he discusses the visual violation. This is the glance, the penetration of the eyes; staring is an example. The wink, however, can be considered as a visual approach to decreasing personal space. No matter how close or how far apart two interactants are, a wink tends to bring them closer in a psychological sense—if they perceive the other person positively, of course. The wink, then, is an element in *proxemic* relationships (Argyle and Cook 1976), and it is discussed in more detail in Chapter 8, where we discuss eye behaviors.

Goffman has also indicated that there are violations of acoustic space. Perhaps an example will help make this phenomenon clear. Suppose that you go to a restaurant to have lunch with a business associate. In addition to having lunch, it is your intention to discuss business. You sit down, order from the menu, and begin your business talk. After about five minutes, music starts blaring throughout the restaurant. Certainly, you would feel that other people have infringed upon your acoustic space. A similar phenomenon is found in the volume of some people's automobile radios, especially the "booming basses" of some cars driving down the street. Has someone ever disturbed you with his or her noise level? If you have ever lived in a dormitory setting, or in an apartment with walls that do not block out all sounds from your neighbors, you may also experience acoustic violation of your space when they "crank up" their stereo or have a party while you are trying to study for a big test or sleep. Many college students mention acoustic violation as a huge issue when they are trying to study for tests or write papers.

Kendrick and MacFarlane (1986) found that horn honking, as an acoustic spatial violation, was related to environmental temperature. Their study was conducted in Phoenix, Arizona, on 15 consecutive Saturdays between April and August. They found that at temperatures over 100 degrees Fahrenheit, 34 percent of the people observed honked their horns when a red light turned green. When the temperature was 90 degrees or less, there was no honking. Additionally, they observed that young males accompanied by other young males usually did the honking. Several of the honkers integrated their horn honking with verbal and nonverbal signals of hostility. This form of acoustic violation can be very frustrating, so much that large cities (such as New York City, Los Angeles, Chicago, etc.) in recent years have tried to curb its use by making honking of car horns, especially by taxis, a violation of traffic laws.

A final category of violations, according to Goffman (1971), is related to body excreta. Goffman identifies four types of bodily excreta as personal violations. First, there are those that can be transmitted by direct touch: "spittle, snot, perspiration, food particles, blood, semen, vomit, urine, and fecal matter" (p. 47). Second, there are various odors, including bad breath, body odor, and flatus. Third is body heat transmitted in a number of places mentioned by Goffman. The final element Goffman discusses—plate leavings on the table—either food left on the plate or that has fallen off the plate onto the table. He mentions another interesting phenomenon to consider, and that is that knives perform an interesting function in this regard: if a child bites into a cake, it can easily be detected, whereas if he/she slices off another slice, it cannot. If we find a bite mark of someone's mouth on the cake, we consider that a violation, but we would not likely be offended if the piece has been sliced off (if we even noticed). How many times have you been violated by what Goffman called someone else's body excreta—perhaps someone sneezed on you? Perhaps someone spoke to you in class prior to having brushed his or her teeth? Interestingly, we rarely speak up when someone performs such violations, perhaps because the culture has made it taboo to broach these subjects with other individuals (unless we are *very* close, and even then, it may not be easy to discuss). Many, if not most, of these body excreta violations are based more on societal norms than on logical reasoning, like many other proxemic expectations. Goffman provides us, then, with some of the norms that may affect our reputation with others and therefore our ability to communicate effectively.

Some of you may be asking, "How can I tell if I have violated someone's space norms?" One suggestion is to be especially perceptive and to watch how people react when you approach them. There may be an almost imperceptible movement backwards of the whole body or just the neck or head. Another tell-tale sign is that when you come too close, persons who feel you are encroaching on their space will often look down or away from you, and they are slow to return eye contact with you (if at all). When you see these types of reactions, you have definitely invaded someone's space in some way and need to respond accordingly by bathing, brushing your teeth, being quieter, allowing them more space, or so forth. When you become more perceptive in settings such as this, you will become a better communicator.

STUDENT VOICES

James: On our campus buses, when it gets really crowded and people have to stand in the aisle, I always see the people who are sitting down, lean over as far as they can away from the people standing. To the people who are sitting down, the person who is standing, has their bottom half at eye level, so they try and get as far away from them as they can. It also makes the persons sitting on the inside more uncomfortable, because now their space is violated as well. It's an ongoing issue and happens all the time on the buses with people standing and sitting. It does give me a good laugh, though, to see some of the facial expressions the people sitting down make.

FUNCTIONS OF PERSONAL SPACE

We provide information about **self-presentation** and **identification** by how close or far we stand in relation to others. From this chapter, we know that older children tend to stand farther away from each other than younger children. We know that males of all ages tend to desire more space than females. Males especially desire significantly more space when interacting with other males. Many heterosexual males may associate close proximity among males with homosexuality and tend to avoid close proximity. Heterosexual females appear to be less homophobic and less concerned about space. Recall the earlier discussion about gender research saying that many women desire more space but in this society are not often accorded it. Because of this, women do not react as negatively or as forcefully as men when someone violates their space norms. Conversation is rarely *regulated* by spacing; however, we can demonstrate a desire to end a communication by starting to back up or by simply walking away. Spacing also indicates the *relationship of interactants*. When we are physically closer to one another, we are more likely to have a personal or intimate conversation. There is little opportunity to *display instructional information* through the use of space. In addition, the *display of affective information* is influenced only in minor ways by the use of space. When we like a person, we usually stand or sit closer to him or her than to persons we do not like. Finally, the *topic of conversation* affects distancing norms. For example, when you expect the topic to be positive for both you and others, you are likely to stand or sit closer to the others.

SUMMARY

When looking at proxemics, or the science of how we use space, keep in mind that generalizations about whole classes of people can be dangerous. When we say that "all" (or even "most" or "many") men, women, Latinos, African Americans, senior citizens, or blind people use space in a certain way and act on that information, we are setting ourselves up for possible communication breakdowns. As with all nonverbal subcodes, the better you know someone, the more accurate your predictions about how he or she uses space will be, thereby improving communication.

The thrust of this chapter is on space immediately beyond touch, or zero-proxemics, and how we use it to communicate. We looked at how we establish and preserve a certain amount of space around us—a body bubble or spatial zone—that serves to protect us against others. That same space, however, also establishes the norms we expect to observe when interacting with close friends, acquaintances, and strangers. Violating that spatial expectation often has extreme consequences. Finally, we looked at a different kind of spatial violation, one based on Goffman's (1971) "territories of the self." The next chapter takes a look at space as we expand our "zones" or "bubbles" to create territories found in different environments.

QUESTIONS FOR THOUGHT

1. How do people demonstrate their need for space when interacting? When not interacting?
2. In how many ways can you differentiate personal spacing expectations and norms at your college or university?
3. Based on your observations, how do your friends establish personal spacing expectations? What criteria, if any, do they use in establishing personal space?
4. What impact does violating personal spacing expectations have? How do you think space could be manipulated to affect perceptions of credibility, attraction, or persuasion?
5. Just how does Goffman's notion of "territories of the self" fit with the discussion of personal space and personal spacing expectations and violations?
6. Identify the last time your space norms were violated. What are some possible reasons this was a violation for you? What space norms did the violator breach?

FURTHER REFERENCES

Need for Space

Burgoon, J. K. (1978). Further explication and an initial test of the theory of violations of personal space expectations. *Human Communication Research*, 4, 129–142.

Doering, N., and Poeschl, S. (2007, May). *Nonverbal cues in mobile phone text messages: The effects of chronemics and proxemics*. Paper presented at the meeting of the International Communication Association, San Francisco, CA.

Fong, L. (2007). Playing keepaway. *Psychology Today*, 40, 15.

Hickson, M. L., and Stacks, D. W. (1991). *Nonverbal communication: Studies and applications* (3rd ed.). Dubuque, IA: Brown and Benchmark.

Spence, P., Westerman, D., Skalski, P., Seeger, M., Ulmer, R., Venette, S., and Sellnow, T. (2005). Proxemic effects on information seeking after the September 11 attacks. *Communication Research Reports*, 22, 39–46.

Stacks, D. W., and Burgoon, J. K. (1979, April). *The persuasive effects of violating spatial distance expectations in small groups*. Paper presented at the annual meeting of the Southern Speech Communication Association, Biloxi, MS.

Factors Influencing Distance Expectations

Age

Lerner, R. M. (1973). The development of personal space schemata toward body build. *Journal of Psychology*, 84, 229–235.

Lomranz, J., Shapira, A., Choresa, N, and Gilat, Y. (1975). Children's personal space as a function of age and sex. *Developmental Psychology*, 11, 541–545.

Pedersen, D. M. (1973). Developmental trends in personal space. *Journal of Psychology*, 83, 3–9.

Sex Differences

Burgoon, J. K., and Aho, L. (1982). Three field experiments on the effects of violations of conversational distance. *Communication Monographs*, 49, 70–88.

Burgoon, J. K., and Jones, S. B. (1976). Toward a theory of personal space expectations and their violations. *Human Communication Research*, 2, 131–146.

Burgoon, J. K., and Walther, J. B. (1990). Nonverbal expectancies and the evaluative consequences of violations. *Human Communication Research*, 17, 232–265.

Hall, J. A. (1984). *Nonverbal sex differences: Communication accuracy and expressive style*. Baltimore: Johns Hopkins University Press.

Hayduk, L. A. (1983). Personal space: Where we stand now. *Psychological Bulletin*, 94, 293–335.

Madden, S. J. (1999). Proxemics and gender: Where's the spatial gap? *North Dakota Journal of Speech & Theatre*, 12, 41–46.

Pedersen, D. M. (1973). Developmental trends in personal space. *Journal of Psychology*, 83, 3–9.

Piercy, M. (1973). *Small changes*. New York: Doubleday.

Slavutzkaya, A. Gerasimenko, N., and Mikhailova, E. (2012). Recognition of spatially transformed objects in men and women: Analysis of behavior and evoked potentials. *Human Physiology*, 38, 238–248.

Stacks, D. W., and Burgoon, J. K. (1979). *The effects of violating spatial distance expectations in small groups*. Paper presented at the meeting of the Southern Speech Communication Association, Biloxi, MS.

Tannen, D. (1990). *You just don't understand: Women and men in conversation.* New York: William Morrow and Company.

Thomas, D. R. (1976). Interaction distances in same-sex and mixed-sex groups. *Perceptual and Motor Skills,* 36, 15–18.

Cultural Differences

Aliakbari, M., Faraji, E., and Pourshakibaee, P. (2011). Investigation of the proxemic behavior of Iranian professors and university students: Effects of gender and status. *Journal of Pragmatics,* 43, 1392–1402.

Antonijevic, S. (2008). From text to gesture: A microethnographic analysis of nonverbal communication in the second life virtual environment. *Information, Communication & Society,* 11, 221–238.

Arik, E. (2012). Space, time, and iconicity in Turkish sign language (TID). *TRAMES: A Journal of the Humanities & Social Sciences,* 16, 345–358.

Dolphin, C. Z. (1988). Beyond Hall: Variables in the use of personal space in intercultural transactions. *Howard Journal of Communications,* 1, 23–38.

Ellis, R. (2009). Understanding interpersonal relationships in the Chinese context. *Journal of Intercultural Communication,* 20, 3.

Ozdemir, A. (2008). Shopping malls: Measuring interpersonal distance under changing conditions and across cultures. *Field Methods,* 20, 226–248.

Roger, D. B., and Schalekamp, E. E. (1976). Body-buffer zone and violence: A cross-cultural study. *Journal of Social Psychology,* 98, 153–158.

Semnani-Azad, Z., and Adair, W. L. (2011). The display of "dominant" nonverbal cues in negotiation: The role of culture and Gender. *International Negotiation,* 16, 451–479.

Subramani, R. (2010). Insight through body language and non-verbal communication references in Tirukkural. *Language in India,* 10, 261–271.

Williams, D. E., and Hughes, P. C. (2005). Nonverbal communication in Italy: An analysis of interpersonal touch, body position, eye contact, and seating behaviors. *North Dakota Journal of Speech & Theatre,* 18, 17–24.

Yun, Y., Xiaoyi, H., and Jie, Z. (2007). A research on sexual difference in the resident space. *Canadian Social Science,* 3, 92–100.

Racial Differences

Bass, J. K., and Lambert, S. F. (2004). Urban adolescents' perceptions of their neighborhoods: An examination of spatial dependence. *Journal of Community Psychology,* 32, 277–293.

Jones, S. E., and Aiello, J. R. (1972). *The acquisition of proxemic norms of behavior: A study of the lower-class black and middle-class white children at three grade levels.* Unpublished paper.

Jones, S. E., and Aiello, J. R. (1973). Proxemic behavior of black and white first-, third-, and fifth-grade children. *Journal of Personality and Social Psychology,* 25, 21–27.

Status/Liking/Personality

Allgeir, A. R., and Byrne, D. (1973). Attraction toward the opposite sex as a determinant of physical proximity. *Journal of Social Psychology,* 90, 213–219.

Barrios, B. A., Corbitt, L. C., Estes, J. P., and Topping, J. S. (1976). Effect of a social stigma on interpersonal distance. *Psychological Record,* 26, 343–348.

Fisher, R. (1967). Social schema of normal and disturbed children. *Journal of Educational Psychology,* 58, 58–92.

Floyd, K. (2000a). Attributions for nonverbal expressions of liking and disliking: The extended self-serving bias. *Western Journal of Communication*, 64, 385–404.

Hildreth, A. M., Derogatis, L. R., and McClusker, K. (1971). Body buffer zone and violence: A reassessment and confirmation. *American Journal of Psychology*, 127, 77–81.

Horowitz, M. J., Duff, D. F., and Stratton, L. O. (1964). Body buffer zones. *Archives of General Psychiatry*, 11, 651–656.

Leipold, W. (1963). *Psychological distance in dyadic interviews.* Unpublished dissertation, University of North Dakota.

Little, K. B. (1965). Personal space. *Journal of Experimental Social Psychology*, 1, 237–247.

Mallenby, T. W. (1974). Personal space—Direct measurement techniques with hard of hearing students. *Environment and Behavior*, 6, 117–121.

Mehrabian, A. (1968). Relationship of attitude to seated posture, orientation, and distance. *Journal of Personality and Social Psychology*, 10, 26–30.

Mehrabian, A., and Williams, M. (1969). Nonverbal concomitants of perceived and intended persuasiveness. *Journal of Personality and Social Psychology*, 13, 87–58.

Nechamkin, Y., Salganik, I., Modai, I., and Ponizovsky, A. M. (2003). Interpersonal distance in schizophrenic patients: Relationship to negative syndrome. *International Journal of Social Psychiatry*, 49, 165–173.

Novelli, D., Drury, J., and Reicher, S. (2010). Come together: Two studies concerning the impact of group relations on "personal space." *British Journal of Social Psychology*, 49, 223–236.

Patterson, M. L., and Holmes, D. S. (1966). Social interaction correlates of the MPI Extroversion–Introversion Scale. *American Psychologist*, 21, 724–745.

Reiman, T. (2008). First impressions really matter. *Communication World*, 25, 28–31.

Russo, N. (1967). Connotation of seating arrangements. *Cornell Journal of Social Relations*, 2, 37–44.

Slavutzkaya, A, Gerasimenko, N., and Mikhailova, E. (2012). Recognition of spatially transformed objects in men and women: Analysis of behavior and evoked potentials. *Human Physiology*, 38, 238–248.

Tucker, I. (2010). Mental health service user territories: Enacting "safe spaces" in the community. *An Interdisciplinary Journal for the Study of Health, Illness, and Medicine*, 14, 434–448.

Williams, J. L. (1963). *Personal space and its relation to extroversion–introversion.* Unpublished master's thesis, University of Alberta.

Worthington, M. E. (1974). Personal space as a function of the stigma effect. *Environment and Behavior*, 6, 289–294.

Environmental Structuring

Gardin, H., Kaplan, K. J., Firestone, J., and Cowen, G. A. (1973). Proxemic effects of cooperation, attitude, and approach-avoidance in a prisoner's dilemma game. *Journal of Personality and Social Psychology*, 27, 13–18.

Gillath, O., McCall, C., Shaver, P. R., and Blascovich, J. (2008). What can virtual reality teach us about prosocial tendencies in real and virtual environments? *Media Psychology*, 11, 259–282.

Hare, A. P., and Bales, R. F. (1963). Seating position and small group interaction. *Sociometry*, 26, 480–486.

Hearn, G. (1957). Leadership and the spatial factor in small groups. *Journal of Abnormal and Social Psychology*, 54, 269–272.

Howells, L. T., and Becker, S. W. (1962). Seating arrangement and leadership emergence. *Journal of Abnormal and Social Psychology*, 64, 148–150.

Kendon, A. (1976). Some functions of gaze direction in social interaction. *Acta Psychologica, 26,* 22–63.

Mehrabian, A., and Diamond, S. (1971). Effects of furniture arrangement, props, and personality on interaction. *Journal of Personality and Social Psychology, 20,* 18–30.

Norum, G. A., Russo, N. J., and Sommer, R. (1967). Seating patterns and group task. *Psychology in the Schools, 4,* 240.

Russo, N. (1967). Connotation of seating arrangements. *Cornell Journal of Social Relations, 2,* 37–44.

Stodtbeck, F. L., and Hook, L. H. (1961). The social dimensions of a twelve man jury table. *Sociometry, 24,* 397–415.

Violations of Personal Space

Buller, D. B. (1988). Communication apprehension and reaction to proxemic violations. *Journal of Nonverbal Behavior, 11,* 13–25.

Burgoon, J. K. (1978). Further explication and an initial test of the theory of violations of personal space expectations. *Human Communication Research, 4,* 129–142.

Burgoon, J. K. (1982). Privacy and communication. In M. Burgoon (Ed.), *Communication yearbook 6* (pp. 206–249). Beverly Hills, CA: Sage.

Burgoon, J. K., and Aho, L. (1982). Three field experiments on the effects of violations of conversational distance. *Communication Monographs, 49,* 70–88.

Burgoon, J. K., and Jones, S. B. (1976). Toward a theory of personal space expectations and their violations. *Human Communication Research, 2,* 131–146.

Burgoon, J. K., Buller, D. B., and Woodall, G. W. (1996). *Nonverbal communication: The unspoken dialogue.* New York: McGraw-Hill.

Burgoon, J. K., Stacks, D. W., and Burch, S. A. (1982). The role of interpersonal rewards and violations of distancing expectations in achieving influence. *Communication, 11,* 114–128.

Burgoon, J. K., Stacks, D. W., and Woodall, W. G. (1977, December). *Personal space expectations and reward as predictors of recall, credibility, and attraction.* Paper presented at the meeting of the Speech Communication Association, Washington, DC.

Burgoon, J. K., Stacks, D. W., and Woodall, W. G. (1979). Personal space expectations and reward as predictors of recall, credibility, and attraction. *Western Journal of Communication, 43,* 153–167.

Burgoon, J. K., and Walther, J. B. (1990). Nonverbal expectancies and the evaluative consequences of violations. *Human Communication Research, 17,* 232–265.

LePoire, B. A. (1991). Orientation and defensive reactions as alternatives to arousal in theories of nonverbal reactions to changes in immediacy. *Southern Communication Journal, 56,* 183–145.

Novelli, D., Drury, J., and Reicher, S. (2010). Come together: Two studies concerning the impact of group relations on "personal space." *British Journal of Social Psychology, 49,* 223–236.

Rustemili, A. (1988). The effects of personal space invasion on impressions and decisions. *Journal of Psychology, 122,* 113–118.

Other Violations

Jason, L. A., and Jung, R. (1984). Stimulus control techniques to handicapped-designated parking spaces. *Environment and Behavior, 16,* 675–686.

Kleck, R., Buck, P. L., Goller, R. S., London, J. R., Pfieffer, J. R., and Vukcevic, D. P. (1968). Effect of stigmatization conditions on the use of personal space. *Psychological Reports, 23,* 111–118.

Milgram, S., Liberty, H. J., Toledo, R., and Wackenhut, J. (1986). Response to intrusion into waiting lines. *Journal of Personality and Social Psychology, 61,* 683–689.

CHAPTER 4

PROXEMICS (TERRITORY AND ENVIRONMENT)

KEY CONCEPTS

- Territory
- Territoriality
- Territorial Types
- Correlates of Territory
- Animal
- Human
- Territorial Claims
- Purposes
- Functions
- Environment
- Environmental Structure
- Environmental Perceptions
- Categories
- Uses
- Structuring
- Functions

OBJECTIVES

By the end of the chapter you should be able to:

- Define and distinguish between territory and environment.
- Discuss different types of territory as defined by researchers.
- Compare and contrast human and animal studies relating to territory.
- Explain environmental categories and how they influence communication.
- Explain how and why humans mark out and use territory.
- Discuss how humans structure their environment for specific purposes.

When two or more human beings occupy the same environment, they usually establish social norms in terms of what objects within that environment belong to whom. Many fathers have their own chairs in the living room. Most of us have a designated space at the dinner table at home. Have you ever tried to sit in your "father's seat"? What was the reaction? Even some pets have their own space. Animals in their natural habitats also define territory relative to one another. Wolves, chimpanzees, bees, birds, dogs, cats, and squirrels have established means for marking their areas. **Territoriality** is the concept that an animal, which includes human beings, "lays claim to an area and defends it against members of its own species" (Hall 1966, 7). Territoriality, especially in the case of animals, assures the propagation of the species by regulating density.

TERRITORY

Historically, Lyman and Scott (1967) identified four types of human territories on the basis of their accessibility, and these are still widely accepted as the types of human territory more than 45 years hence. The first is **public territory**, where individuals freely enter. Public territory is subject to temporary ownership, although people are likely to protect its accessibility strongly. Government buildings, schools, hospitals, and commercial enterprises generally allow individuals such access. You should note, however, that the notion of "public" is legislated. The school you attend, the class you sit in, is designated "public" in many states but in reality is restricted to those who have a *legitimate use for that space* (try to sit in on a class without permission and observe the reactions as you violate the "public" space). Consider, also, going to a dance club/bar that is open to the public and claiming a table as yours. You then go out to dance, and return to find some other people sitting in "your" seats. How strongly do you react? If you have placed something to mark the space as your own, your reaction will be much stronger than if you did not mark it. However, if it really is space open to the public you are less likely to react as strongly as you might have had it been space that legitimately belonged to you.

The second type of territory is **interactional**, which is a mobile area where individuals congregate informally, the boundaries of which are likely to move. In terms of access, interactional territory is more restricted; generally, someone exercises control. Examples of such territories are a movie theater, a restaurant, and your classroom. Interactional territory, however, is also viewed as a more mobile or indefinite territory, such as the space you have as you walk on a sidewalk, or a small group's claim to a territory at a party. Note that the boundaries here are not explicit and that other people may invade or "defile" that territory by walking through it. Consider for a moment walking to classes. How often have you seen people congregated for a discussion in the middle of a walkway, hallway, or stairwell? Do you allow them to claim that interactional territory by going around them? Or do you push through them? There is also the issue of claiming interactional territory when people actually block passage. How do you react then? Interestingly, the "blockers" of passage rarely see it as their duty to excuse themselves when they block passageways, yet most of us will excuse ourselves when we must pass through the interactants' space.

The third type of territory is **home territory**. In the home, we find free interactions by individuals who claim the territory; however, others may not have free access. In most places in the United States, homes are locked when the occupants are away; they are also locked at night. In most states, trespassing laws provide us legal recourse should others intrude upon our home territory. In some states you can legally defend your home territory with the use of deadly force *if the intruder is breaking into the home.* We even construct fences to keep others out of our yards. The concept of home territory, then, includes legal, physical, and social barriers. Outsiders usually do not enter our homes or use areas or objects within the home without the express permission of someone who lives there. One of the major problems for people who live with others occurs when a roommate invites someone the other roommates do not like into the home. In this case, the roommates' perception is that the home has been "defiled." Home territory goes beyond these concepts, however, and includes the concept of "feeling at home" in a territory. For example, ~~Comfort~~ is there a favorite restaurant or bar where you and your friends congregate often and "feel at home"? Or have you ever had friends in whose house you felt just as much "at home" as in your own? These would also be examples of home territory. Students who live in apartments and dormitories often mention how some of their fellow students who live in the same building "make themselves at home" in their apartments/rooms. This encroachment can be a source of frustration if the encroachers do not take into account that the space really does not belong to them but is someone else's home territory. Sinha and Mukherjee (1996) found similar results; people living in dormitory settings do not like their territory encroached upon, and the more roommates per living space (e.g., dorm room or apartment), the less tolerant the students were. How many times have you felt encroached upon in your living space? ~~Body territory~~

The last spatial area is **body territory**, the space immediately surrounding us. Body territory is usually marked by the skin or by the clothing with which we cover our bodies. Body territory can be seen as an imaginary area or radius around our bodies, an area that may be small for some people and larger for others. When one enters another person's body territory, there is a spatial violation. Because Americans do not like our body territory violated, we tend to have larger body areas surrounding us than do people in some other cultures. This represents personal spacing expectations. Chapter 4 was about personal proxemics, which could also be called the study of body territory.

BOX 4.1 OBSERVATIONAL STUDY

Before your class meets next time, gather a few members of the class and go out into the hallway and begin an interaction. Be sure to block passage of other individuals who need to get by to get to their classes (or leave their classes). Take note of how many individuals excuse themselves to get by and how many do not. How many send you a message that your blocking of the hall is inconsiderate? How many go to great lengths to go around your group rather than have to pass through it?

ANIMAL CORRELATES OF TERRITORIALITY

Territory is important for all animals; two sets of other animal species studies lend support for its importance. Although we authors hesitate to compare other species' behavior to our own, there are some remarkable parallels between behavior in humans and that in some other animals.

CALHOUN'S STUDIES OF RATS

Calhoun (1950, 1962) observed the conditions of overpopulation of Norway rats. He observed three generations of rats over a period of 28 months. The rat population, in a quarter-acre pen, stabilized at 150. The rats "organized" themselves into 12 or 13 colonies of about 12 rats each and were allowed to live as normally as possible in a carefully controlled experimental setting. Human intervention was minimal, except that the pens were constructed to preclude other animals from entering. In other words, the rats were provided with plenty of food and water but had no predators or enemies.

During the experiment, the rats developed an area in which gross distortions of behavior occurred, which Calhoun has referred to as a "behavioral sink." In the sink, these "deviant" behaviors were observed disrupting normal nest building, courting behaviors, reproduction, and social organization. The development of the sink was strongly related to the density of the rat population within the territory. As density increased, as Figure 4.1 indicates, behavior began to deviate from accepted norms until it reached the lowest common denominator: the sink. As territorial density decreased, behavior became more "normative," that is, what appeared to be normal for the rats.

Most of the deviant behavior involved social actions. Female rats normally undertake most of the nest building. In the normal area, the rats had no problems; however, females in the sink were unable to complete the nest building. Several types of distorted behavior occurred with male rats in the sink. They mounted other males, young females, or unreceptive females. Others retreated from sexual intercourse entirely.

Litters became mixed; some of the young were stepped on by other rats and hyperactive males devoured some. Extensive fights between males marked the sink behavior. Only

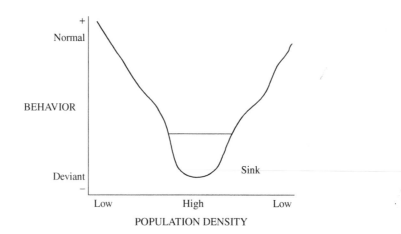

FIGURE 4.1 Relationships between behavior and population density.

one-fourth of 558 young rats survived to be weaned. Miscarriages increased, and various sexual disorders were found. There were also cases of unprovoked tail biting.

It is important to note that there was enough food to support all the rats, but there was not enough space or privacy. Parks and Bruce (1961), for example, indicated that the presence of a second male rat could block pregnancy, meaning the other male's presence kept the rats from copulating, or that he would not allow the other male near the female. Thus, at least in the case of Calhoun's Norway rats, the lack of territory caused social deviation and physiological problems. Whether this outcome can be compared to human nature is a topic for later discussion.

SIKA DEER STUDY

A second study on the effects of lack of animal territory concerns deer found on James Island in the 1950s (Christian 1963; Christian and Davis 1964; Christian, Flyger, and Davis 1961a, 1961b). James Island is about one mile off the Maryland coast in Chesapeake Bay. The size of the uninhabited island is 280 acres (about half a square mile). In 1916, four or five Sika deer were placed on the island. By 1955, the population had grown to between 280 and 300; support for such a population was no problem, given the adequate supply of food and water. About this time, however, a die-off occurred. J. J. Christian, a biologist, shot several deer for histological studies prior to the die-off. During the first three months of 1958, 161 carcasses were recovered, and the population had stabilized at around 80 deer.

Histological studies of the carcasses indicated that the deer had not died of starvation. Christian and his associates found, instead, that the deer had enlarged adrenal glands, and they attributed the enlargement to a high level of stress. They concluded that the lack of relief from confinement caused stress, which accounted for the increased size of the adrenal gland; the adrenal gland, in turn, increased the supply of adrenaline to the deer, resulting in death. Thus, Christian's studies support the idea that for the Sika deer the lack of space produced stress that resulted in death.

[handwritten marginal note: Density & crowded]

The major issues of the Sika deer study are density and crowding, which we discuss in more detail later in this chapter. We define density, as most nonverbal communication theorists do, to be the number of living beings present in a given area. Crowding is an issue of perception; it occurs when living beings perceive restrictions on their ability to move freely in a given area because of the presence of too many other beings to feel comfortable in that environment. In the Sika study, the deer had ample resources to survive, yet the increase in population per square foot, Christian conjectured, caused a response from crowding. The outcome was a negative physical response—in this case, death. We return to this topic of density and crowding later, when we discuss how humans respond to those factors.

It should be noted that even today, researchers in many fields—social sciences, psychology, communication—still look at animals' use of territory to draw conclusions about how humans use their territories. Schonfield, Taylor, Boutin, Humphries, and Andrew (2012) conducted a study on how red squirrels defend their territories, and they discovered things similar to Calhoun's rats and Silka's deer. These researchers found that the squirrels were more likely to use "highly conspicuous territorial vocalizations" (p. 372), defined as "rattles," to establish their own territories, and also to alert the other squirrels that interlopers were nearby. And although their relating these findings to human territoriality is vague, at best, the idea of the study being published in a scholarly journal about behaviors of animals and humans makes clear the intent that we are able to do some comparisons between animals' and human beings' use of territory.

BOX 4.2 OBSERVATIONAL STUDY

How similar are animal studies to human studies? Test this for yourself by observing your friends' behaviors (or even your own) at a packed athletic event or concert. How do they "react" to the lack of territory? Can you find results similar to those with the rats, deer (but not quite as severe), and squirrels in dormitories around midterm and final times?

HUMAN CORRELATES OF TERRITORIALITY

Although we tell you about these studies so you can see any similarities between animals and humans, it is essential to note that the conclusions of animal studies cannot be directly transferred to human beings. Humans in crowded nonlaboratory situations adapt by moving to other areas, but there are some situations in which departure is not possible. In this sub-section, we examine numerous research projects demonstrating that humans can suffer from a lack of territory similar to the reactions of lower species of animals.

PRISON STUDIES

Research on humans has been conducted in situations similar to that which Calhoun created for the rats: the penal institution. McCain, Cox, and Paulus (1976), for instance, observed crowding in prison environments. They observed inmates at a prison and in a county jail to determine whether crowding/stress produced increases in illness complaints. Prior to visiting the prisoners, the researchers obtained detailed housing and medical histories of the preceding six-month period. Most of the illness complaints in their medical histories involved back pain, nausea, rash, sinus, constipation, chest pain, and asthma. In general, they found more illness complaints from inmates living in dormitory housing than from those living in single or two-person prison cells. They concluded that the higher social density factor (total number of people in the unit) rather than the spatial factor (amount of space per person) accounted for the stress. In a similar study, D'Atri (1975) found that both systolic and diastolic blood pressure readings, as well as pulse rates, were higher for prisoners living in dormitories than for those in one- or two-person cells.

Bonta (1986) has severely criticized prison-crowding studies, arguing that little effort was made to show the overall relationship between population density and other factors in the prison environment. He suggests that a prisoner's age and length of exposure to the prison environment might be important variables to consider when interpreting territoriality in such environments. Other variables that Bonta suggests might affect territoriality findings include noise level, temperature, inmate turnover, and difficulty of surveillance. Franklin, Franklin, and

Pratt (2006) also conjectured that there is not definitive results-oriented research that shows prison crowding is responsible for inmate misconduct. In short, to conclude that only crowding affects the health, both physical and mental, of prisoners would probably be unsound reasoning, although social density certainly plays a role in the health and well-being of prisoners.

COCOONING BEHAVIORS

A series of studies was conducted in the late 1960s and early 1970s to gauge human reaction to territory size. Research by Altman (1973, 1975) as well as others vividly demonstrates the problems associated with confinement to a particular territory for a long period of time. Such confinement effects might be equated with the behavior found in nuclear submarines on patrol for long periods of time or during long periods of confinement in bomb shelters. Altman's research indicated that when two people were confined to a small room for periods of 10 to 21 days (thus becoming "home" territories), a strict division of territory quickly occurred, and in many cases the individuals were unable to complete the confinement. Those who did, however, withdrew into their "own areas" after working hours. This behavior, **cocooning** or withdrawing into oneself, is known as a "territorial behavior." We find cocooning today in individuals' private studies, workshops, and other spaces that other people without "ownership" are not allowed to enter freely.

Such cocooning is common, even without confinement. Do you ever need to just get away from roommates or other pressures and find yourself "cocooning" in your own room (or your side of the room) for a period of time? Some contemporary writers (such as John Gray in his *Men Are from Mars, Women Are from Venus*, 1992) include this topic in discussions of male/ female communication differences. For example, Gray explains the concept of cocooning as retreating to one's cave and has pointed out that men are more likely to do this. Wood (2012) mentions that her students initially disagreed with the conclusion that men are more likely to cocoon. The students pointed out that their mothers also had their own spaces. When asked to describe the space their mothers had, the majority of the students identified the kitchen, a sewing room, or other spaces where things are done for other people, not just for themselves. Other academic research, which we find to be more credible than the popular findings of Gray, has also shown that men are more likely to "cocoon" (Wood 2012). Simply put, men seem to have the need to cocoon more than women. Regardless of gender, most people occasionally need time away from others, and cocooning is a natural way to do this.

TERRITORIAL CLAIMS

According to Goffman (1971), human beings make several types of territorial claims. In each case there is individual variation, cultural variation, sexual and ethnic variation, and variation by age. Finally, there is variation according to situation. Goffman notes, "to stand or sit next to a stranger when the setting is all but empty is more of an intrusion than the same act would be when the place is packed and all can see that only this niche remains" (p. 31). Hickson and Self (2003) tell us that the concept of territoriality is universal; it will vary according to the same things Goffman notes, but everyone will have some form of territorial claim. You can observe this if you are the only person in a movie theater or large lecture room. A second person enters and sits right in front of you, although there are hundreds of remaining seats. This occurrence is probably upsetting, and you may even become defensive. On the other hand, if the only remaining seat in the room was directly in front of you, you probably would not have a second thought about the newcomer's sitting there. Have you ever observed in a movie theater how some people will come in, choose a seat, and then try to expand that space by placing items in chairs next to or in front of them? Sometimes they will even put their feet up on the backs of the chairs in front of them to try to keep people from sitting in those chairs. In both of these situations (movie or lecture hall), the situation changes with each new arrival and departure. Another example familiar to all of us is the elevator. Each time another person enters or leaves, the entire spatial configuration in the elevator changes. What is happening is that the occupants are "re-dividing" the territory in the elevator each time. Thus, with three occupants, each has one-third. When one leaves, the two that remain each have half, and they are likely to reposition themselves to show those halves.

BOX 4.3   OBSERVATIONAL STUDY

Find a place where there are not many people within that territory (e.g., the library, a bus, a fast-food restaurant, a movie theater). Take a seat as close as possible to a person you do not know, or do not know well. How did the person seem to react? Did he or she move quickly? Did he or she give you dirty looks? Did he or she sigh audibly? If so, why do you believe he or she did so? If not, why not? If you feel comfortable explaining to that person what you are doing, see if you can get him or her to tell you how he or she felt when you moved in closer than what is normal (when there is other space available to you).

TERRITORIES OF THE SELF

Goffman (1971) also discussed eight **territories of the self**. The first is **personal space**, which is essentially the same as Lyman and Scott's (1967) concept of body territory. The extent to which someone violates this territory is dependent upon how large this personal space is from the perspective of the individual. Some individuals do not mind being touched by others, and some people do not like others within, say, 18 inches of them. Be sure to use the tip given in the preceding chapter to watch for an almost imperceptible pulling or leaning away as evidence that you have entered someone's body territory. If this happens, adjust your use of space accordingly.

The second type of territory is the **stall**. This is a well-bounded space, usually for use by one person at a time. The restroom stall, a single bed, a beach towel space, a telephone booth, and a parking space are examples. The desk you use at work or to study also qualifies as a stall; usually, only one person at a time works in this space.

The third type of territory discussed by Goffman is **use space**. Such areas are claimed by individuals within your line of vision, or areas that may be outside strict boundary lines but are instrumental in performing a function. For example, areas around a tennis court, space around a golfer swinging a club, space between you and a magazine rack, and the space between you and a television set are all prime examples of use space. We will avoid this space if we know it is being used for some purpose. If we do discover that we have violated it, we will usually excuse ourselves.

Goffman's fourth category is more a temporal rather than a spatial dimension; it is called the **turn**. "Ladies first" and "children first" are basic examples, although our society has created more complex versions. Turn taking requires not only an ordering rule but a claiming mechanism as well (p. 35). Thus, we must queue up or we must hold a ticket number to assure ourselves of space at a certain time. This, by the way, is more of an American phenomenon than a universal one; indeed, many foreigners say, "Americans will line up for anything." While traveling abroad in Poland with American university students, one of the authors of this text had to explain numerous times to the students traveling with her that they would need to vigorously defend their places in lines (at food counters, ticket counters, or loading trains and buses). If they did not, someone would be likely to try to push in front of them, a tactic all of the American students had been taught was poor manners. Indeed, the professor's aggressiveness in some of these situations was seen by the students as abnormal, as well as rude according to American norms, and the students looked embarrassed when the professor defended their places in line. Taking turns may be normal for our culture, yet it does not seem to be commonplace in some foreign countries. Good students of cultural communication differences would do well to know this fact about other cultures to which they might travel; such knowledge could lessen the possibility of conflict.

The **sheath** is the fifth type of territory. This territory includes the skin that covers the body and the clothing that covers the skin. The sixth classification is **possession territory**. This territory refers to objects we view as our own, our "personal effects." Jackets, hats, gloves, umbrellas, and cigarette packs are examples. Interestingly, Belk (1988) found that the most important possessions relative to a sense of self-identity were body parts, followed by objects, collections, memories, and finally, people and pets. Richmond and McCroskey (2000 reported that the more personal a possession (object) is, the more other people see it as an extension of the actual person, and the less likely they are to invade it. Your jacket or purse is less likely to be invaded than your newspaper or soda can.

The final two types of territories deal with self and others. The seventh area is called the **information preserve**. It includes territories that contain facts about the self that we wish to control. Our thoughts, diaries, letters, pockets, e-mail accounts, computer files, and personal desks are examples. Some preserves appear with sexual maturity because they are associated with puberty. Females begin to control access to their purses, and males begin controlling access to their billfolds.

The final area is the **conversation preserve**, which involves those who summon us into an office or area to talk as well as those times when we can be called on or are required to talk (Goffman 1971, 29–41). This type of territory may be associated with the person's status, power, or credibility. We have norms that we think should apply in these conversation preserves, such as topics discussed. Who wants to go to a fine dining restaurant and listen to the people at the next table discuss their intimacies in great detail, or argue? How many of us believe that if we are to be reprimanded by a boss or professor, it should be done in a private setting, not in front of our co-workers or fellow students? A newer phenomenon in this area is the use of the cellphone and how using it in public places encroaches on others' space. More so, though, would be the issue of the "conversation preserve," meaning who really wants to listen to other people's phone conversations, especially if they are personal in substance? Yet, how many times have you either been subjected to that violation or subjected others to that encroachment?

TERRITORIAL DEFENSE: MARKERS, OFFENSIVE DISPLAYS, AND TENURE

To maintain a claim of these various territories, we need a visible sign of ownership. Goffman (1971) calls these signs **markers**. There are three basic methods of identifying areas or possessions as our own, and all are closely related to the "possession territory" just discussed. The most typical is probably the *central marker*. This is a sign used to indicate a claim radiating from the center. Thus, a drink left on a bar means to others that we shall be returning to that seat to maintain ownership. Leaving a theater program in a seat is another example. If you leave your sunglasses and suntan lotion on a space at the beach, you have left a central marker. The second category of markers is the *boundary marker*. Instead of radiating from a center, they establish boundary lines. For example, bars are often used on checkout counters in supermarkets to identify which groceries "belong" to whom. There are lines between seats or numbers identifying the seats on benches in a football stadium; fences are used between yards to indicate boundaries. Finally, the third category is the *earmarker*. This sign indicates a trademark, initials, or a name to signify ownership: a label. Name plates on doors and desks (even inside automobiles), personalized license plates, and monograms on dress shirts are examples of earmarkers. Animals are branded or tagged with "earmarkers" as well. As Ardrey (1966) notes, "A territory is an area of space, whether of water or earth or air, that an animal or group of animals defends as exclusive preserve" (p. 3). An invasion of territory comes when someone violates the boundary of a territory. Childress (2004) discovered that teenagers are especially likely to claim their territory by marking it, yet they are most likely to have their territorial markers ignored or removed by adults. Childress does believe that this may come because teenagers try to claim spaces that the adults in their lives (parents) do not recognize as the teens' legitimate territories.

Sommer (1969) adds offensive displays and tenure to the ways we maintain our body territories. **Offensive displays** can be accomplished by the posture you assume, the stance you take, or gestures you use. If you are talking with someone you do not care for (perhaps the person has a tendency to invade your space every time he or she talks with you), you may put a foot out in front of you and perhaps cross your arms. Perhaps you put the foot out in front of you, and then you proceed to back away, step-by-step. That would be an offensive display. All of us know some gestures that would keep people away from us, such as shaking a fist at someone, "wagging" an index finger, and even the often-used middle finger raised at others when you wish them to stay away (or go away).

Tenure is another way to maintain your territory. If someone perceives that you have a "claim" on a certain space and that you have had that space for some time, the person is not as likely to invade "your space." Take, for example, your classroom. Most of you probably return to the same seat every class period, regardless of whether there is assigned seating or not. Your fellow classmates begin to associate you with that seat, and they do not take it. Even if it is empty when they arrive, they think, "That is Rod's seat," and move on to the one they have claimed for themselves. This classroom situation is referred to as **secondary space**, meaning space that you deem important but could "live without." Costa (2012) discovered similar results in a study conducted in Italy, so it is important to note that this really is more of a universal phenomenon than first thought in studies conducted in the United States. Such tenure happens not only in classrooms but in restaurants, on park benches, in bars, and so forth (see also Mortensen 2009). In Boone, North Carolina, there was a homeless man who claimed a bench on the main street just about every day. Local people and most students knew this and accorded him tenure, and when the man appeared they gave up the bench to him. Visitors (and there are many in this resort area) were often surprised because this man would ask them to move when he arrived at that bench. When you get comfortable in what you consider to be your own space, you try to protect and defend that space.

BOX 4.4 OBSERVATIONAL STUDY

Choose a public setting on your campus, such as a cafeteria, a coffee house, a pub, or the Student Union, and experiment over a few visits. Choose busy times. One time, "mark" a space with a school newspaper and see if that space is taken. The next time, "mark" that space with your book bag and/or other personal items. See if that space is taken. What is the difference? Do you do the same thing when you see a "marked space"?

PURPOSES OF TERRITORY

We have looked at why territory is important in a general sense, but we should briefly discuss the purposes of territoriality among animals. Rosenfeld and Civikly (1976) suggest that territory is significant in that it does the following:

1. Defines an area for gathering food.
2. Ensures an adequate food supply.
3. Provides an area for mating and caring for the young. Most animals tend to mate only with others within their areas.
4. Provides an escape from enemies.
5. Provides an advantage in fighting enemies.
6. Helps in the regulation of population density.
7. Helps regulate the spread of disease. (p. 148)

In *Human Territoriality,* Edney (1974) reached several conclusions regarding how human beings purposively use territory. First, our use of space is variable; we use space differently at different times. Second, the association between territory and aggression is not clear-cut; we do not always increase aggression as density increases. We name territory and defend that territory if it takes on certain psychological identities. *Motherland, fatherland,* and *country* are three terms that we defend. Consider how defensive Americans became about our *homeland* after September 11, 2001. Indeed, we Americans even coined a new national term: *Homeland Security.* Third, territory aids in providing food, shelter, recreation, and so on. Fourth, we maintain several territories. Often we have territories at work, at home, and at play that differ. In some cases the three territories just mentioned may be the same; only the name changes (e.g., an office at home). We "time-share" temporary territory and invade others' territory. (The notion of "time-share" has received attention in resort communities where you "buy" a week or two at a resort and others buy the remainder of the year. You actually "own" a week or two with all the associated privileges, but you do not own the property.) Finally, Edney notes that we are the only animals that, in most cases, "visit" without antagonism.

Territory is important to people based on a number of dimensions. For example, the amount and location of territory one has may be an indication of that person's status or power. Like other animals, humans attempt to maintain more territory than is actually needed for them to survive; this is referred to as "super territory" (Zahavi and Zahavi 1997, 29). Territory is important to animals and humans alike to show intimacy, to demonstrate power, or to illustrate ownership.

BOX 4.5   OBSERVATIONAL STUDY

Survey your different territories, from your room to your apartment to your seat in class. What about that specific space makes it your territory rather than someone else's? How can people tell it is your territory? What are some differences between your separate territories?

CROWDING AND PERCEPTION OF TERRITORY

Before reading about the Sika deer study earlier in this chapter, had you ever considered what the difference is between *crowding* and *density*? Recall that *crowding* has been defined as an issue of perception; when you perceive that there are restrictions on your use of space due to the presence of too many other people (or objects), then you feel crowded. Further, *density* has been defined as the number of people present in a given area. J. L. Freedman (1971) believed that crowding received unwarranted negative publicity through some of the studies carried out on animals. Freedman attempted to answer two questions: (1) What effect does density have on performance of simple and complex tasks? (2) What role do temporal factors play? (p. 61). To answer these questions, subjects were placed in small, crowded rooms and large, less crowded rooms, with one to four persons in each room. Their behaviors were judged for a period of four hours; in some cases, participants returned the next day for an additional four hours. The room sizes ranged from 35 to 180 square feet. In the high-density rooms (for example, four people in 35 square feet) each person had a chair. There was enough room for the people to be able to sit without touching, but there was no additional space. A less dense room allowed for as much as 15 to 20 square feet per person.

Freedman found no significant differences in the ability to perform tasks as related to population density. He did find, however, that density influenced certain types of interpersonal behavior. Among high school students, boys competed more than girls when in a

PHOTO 4.1   People expect and accept crowding as a norm in certain situations.

crowded room or a room with high density. With other age groups, similar results were reported. In general, females liked the smaller room better, and males disliked the more limited territory. Freedman concluded that it is not the population density but the number of individuals with whom one must interact that produces the feeling of being crowded and thus substantially changes human behavior. Similarly, O'Brien (1990) found that people preferred increased density in mission task situations that called for it. Therefore, in most situations, both the finite space (in O'Brien's study, a submarine) and the nature of the task may cause people to accept undue density and thus crowding. Which situation do you work or learn best in? If you ask neighbors, their perception might well be the opposite of yours. Do you learn as well in your classes where every desk is taken? Or do you function better in a classroom where there are some empty spaces between students?

Several researchers have postulated that crowding is related to more factors than the number of people present in the territory. Willems and Campbell (1976) note that many variables lead to perceptions of crowding. They infer that the interactive effect of such factors as number of people, spatial density, social density (perceived amount of space per person), environmental constraints, and physical variables (objects, placement of objects) affects perceptions of crowding. Even in the case of urban crowding, perception plays a part. Bagley (1989), for example, found that murder rates in Bombay and New York City increased with population growth; however, Bombay's murder rate increased "only moderately" while New York City's increased "dramatically," despite Bombay being far more densely populated than New York City.

Perception of the environment or type of territory also seems to play a role in perceiving crowding. Fried and DeFazio (1974), for instance, found that people expect smaller territories in public buses (where you cannot claim or own a territory unless you are physically present) than in an automobile (which is viewed by most as a form of home territory). In general, the research on crowding is mixed, and the results may be dependent on how the individual researcher defined crowding. Take note of your own perceptions of crowding and those of people with whom you are close. It may make a difference in effectively communicating with those persons, or it may give you explanations about why you and they respond in different ways to different settings.

Richmond and McCroskey (2000) report that there are three factors in the perception of crowding: **surveillance, behavioral constraint**, and **stimuli overload**. Surveillance occurs when you perceive that you are being watched or observed by strangers, which can cause a crowded feeling and "dis-ease." Behavioral constraint occurs when your freedom of movement is reduced. For example, have you ever been on a crowded bus and were not able to "spread out" as you prefer to do? Stimuli overload occurs when there are just too many things (such as noises, sights, sounds, people talking) going on and you feel bombarded by their presence, creating unease in that setting.

STUDENT VOICES

Samantha: Space can be breached with the simplest of ease. I was working on a project with a classmate at the library when I found out that he did not know how to respect other people's space. We were working on the same computer, which put us in close proximity of each other to begin with, but the fact that he was constantly touching my things and me and was leaning on me was in no way okay with me. I made my excuses, then left to work at home, where my things were not touched by someone else, nor was I!

Crowding, or a perception of crowding, influences family relations and human sexual behavior. Booth and Edwards (1976), for instance, found that the concept of "love" in the family was unaffected by crowded conditions but that crowding influenced the extent to which parents played with their children. Although neighborhood congestion does not affect sibling quarrels, mothers in crowded households reported more sibling quarrels than those in uncrowded households. These researchers undertook a second study to investigate the effects of crowding on sexual behavior (Edwards and Booth 1977). Four types of crowding were considered in the study: objective (real) household congestion, subjective (perceived) household congestion, objective neighborhood congestion, and subjective neighborhood congestion. These researchers were concerned with how crowding related to marital relations, extramarital involvement, homosexuality, and incestuous relations. They interviewed people in all four types of crowding conditions to determine the effect of privacy on relations, the frequency of intercourse, and the extent to which intercourse was withheld.

Edwards and Booth found that lack of privacy has an influence on marital intercourse, but it is the influence of perceived crowding, not the actual density, that has the effect. Only under stressful conditions was the frequency of intercourse affected by crowding. However, men and women reported greater sexual involvement *outside of marriage* when they were living in crowded conditions. With the interaction of stress and crowded conditions, more extramarital relations tended to occur. Finally, there was no significant relationship between crowding and homosexuality or incest.

Although all these studies on crowding and density are significant, we should remember several facts. First, humans are not rats or deer. The differences between animal and human studies suggest that we can adapt to stressful conditions, whereas lower animals may not be able to. Second, laboratory studies cannot be undertaken on human beings for extended periods of time as they can with animals. Third, as the research indicates, variables other than the simple size of the territory affect how we behave and communicate. Territory, like the environment, affects our communication; as with the environment, we are not always aware of how territory operates or that it is operating. Finally, in today's society, the prevalence of being connected practically 100 percent of the time, whether it be through the internet, social media, smart phones, etc., or in person, can create that same perception of being crowded. We should not conclude, however, that crowding causes extramarital affairs, nor should we blame that behavior on crowding, but crowding does seem to be at least one factor that exists when surveying people who have participated in extramarital relationships. Knowing what types of territory we are in (e.g., Lyman and Scott's 1967) and our claims to territory (e.g., Goffman's 1971) should help us better understand our communication and the communication of others, at least within those territories.

TERRITORIAL DEFENSE

Perhaps you are wondering what makes you defend your space more intensely at some times, while at other times you do not seem to care if it has been invaded. Knapp and Hall (1992) report seven issues that can affect how, as well as whether, you respond to territorial invasion:

1. Who was the person that violated the territory, and what is his or her relationship to you?
2. Why did that person violate your territory?
3. What type of territory was it?
4. How did he or she actually violate your territory?
5. How long did he or she remain in your territory?
6. Do you expect that person to violate your territory in the future?
7. Exactly where did the violation occur? (p. 151)

Put yourself in scenarios with different people (either actual people or types of people) answering these questions. How would you react? How strongly would you defend your territory if your boss were the intruder? Your boyfriend? A classmate whom you were not fond of? What if it was "your" seat in the classroom? Your bed? Your section of the refrigerator in your apartment? The variables could be listed ad infinitum; suffice it to say that you will defend your territory in different ways depending on at least these seven general factors, plus other ones that are important to you personally.

BOX 4.6 OBSERVATIONAL STUDY

Choose a few territories that you know "belong" to someone else (e.g., your father's chair in the den, a fellow classmate's seat, a table in your school's dining room where a specific group always sits), and "invade" those spaces. Watch for reactions from those people and make note of them. Did your family members or close friends react more defensively than people you didn't know? Did groups of people react more defensively than a single person did?

ENVIRONMENT

Look around you. What you see right now is your immediate environment. Until now it has been subconsciously influencing your behavior; we're about to make that conscious influence. Most environments were designed for some reason; they serve to tell you how you should communicate and behave. If you stop and consider it, the environment has quite an impact on you. All interactions between people take place in some environment—an area you attempt to structure, in which you attempt to create a mood or a response. When you are studying, your environmental preferences are different than when you are looking for a good time. You may expect a quiet, relaxing environment for study; you expect a little more noise, sensory input, and tension when having a good time. Thus, you structure your environments for your preferences, and in turn, others structure environments according to what they consider appropriate for some expected outcome. There are many ways to structure your environments. For example, in the last two decades, the United States has seen an escalation of the use *of feng shui* (an Asian approach to arranging environments for "positive" energy within them) to develop environments, especially in homes. Regardless of how they are structured, most environments have some form of organization to their configurations, and how they are organized creates perceptions of them for people who enter those environments.

Knapp (1978) has concluded that the environment is perceived in six ways. His system examines the environment in terms of formality, warmth, privacy, familiarity, constraint, and distance. Think of them as continua: What we look for in any environment are the degrees each "framework" possesses. At opposite ends you would, for example, have formality and informality, warmth and cold, private and nonprivate, familiar and unfamiliar, constrained and not constrained, and close and far. An office should be formal, somewhat cool (in terms of temperature), private (if meant for one person), familiar (we all know how to behave in familiar surroundings), and fairly easy to leave (yet not "too easy" to leave), and it should put us in a power position by distancing us from others. This may sound strange, but look at the environment you are in right now and see how it operates in terms of formality (informal to formal), warmth (comfortable to uncomfortable), privacy (private to open to others), familiarity (known area to unknown), constraint (temporal/changing to permanent), and distance (how far away others are). Now, take another environment and do the same. If the two environments have been designed for the same purpose, they should have similar "ratings." If not, they will differ along one or more of Knapp's "frameworks," and you will find you communicate differently in each. How you communicate in a courtroom will be completely different from how you communicate in your favorite hangout with your friends.

A second way of examining the environment is offered by J. K. Burgoon and Saine (1978). They postulate that each environment is differentiated by nine dimensions: size or volume of space, arrangement of objects within the environment, materials used in the environment, amount of linear perspective, lighting and shading, color, temperature, noise, and sensory stimulation. Knapp's frameworks and Burgoon and Saine's dimensions are structured to produce an aesthetic feeling. By taking the nine dimensions, we create the frameworks identified by a combination of the two (see Figure 4.2).

ENVIRONMENTAL ANALYSIS

I. Perceptual Features

	1	2	3	4	5	6	7	

Informal ___:___:___:___:___:___:___ Formal (FORMALITY)
Uncomfortable ___:___:___:___:___:___:___ Comfortable (WARMTH)
Open ___:___:___:___:___:___:___ Private (PRIVACY)
Unusual ___:___:___:___:___:___:___ Usual (FAMILIARITY)
Temporary ___:___:___:___:___:___:___ Permanent (CONSTRAINT)
Others Close ___:___:___:___:___:___:___ Others Far (DISTANCE)

II. Environmental Features

Low ___:___:___:___:___:___:___ High (VOLUME OF SPACE)
Low ___:___:___:___:___:___:___ High (ARRANGEMENT/OBJECTS)
Low ___:___:___:___:___:___:___ High (MATERIALS)
Low ___:___:___:___:___:___:___ High (LIGHTING/SHADING)
Low ___:___:___:___:___:___:___ High (LINEARITY)
Low ___:___:___:___:___:___:___ High (COLOR)
Low ___:___:___:___:___:___:___ High (TEMPERATURE)
Low ___:___:___:___:___:___:___ High (NOISE)
Low ___:___:___:___:___:___:___ High SENSORY STIMULATION)

III. Environmental Patterns

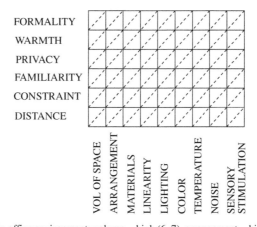

Example: Formality, as in office environment: volume = high (6–7), arrangement = high (6–7),
materials = high (5–7), linearity = moderate (4–5), color = moderate (4–5),
temperature = moderate (4–5), noise = low (1–2), sensory stimulation =
moderate (4–5), would be an example of a middle/lower high-level manager's office.

FIGURE 4.2 Environmental analysis.

These frameworks and dimensions occur in several ways. E. T. Hall (1972) suggests that the environment can be divided into three basic categories: dynamic, semifixed, and fixed-feature. **Dynamic** is the type of space that is involved with people communicating; it changes as the people change. The hallways between classes, as discussed in the previous chapter, are an example of dynamic space. **Semifixed** features are those that enable people "to increase or decrease (their) interaction(s) with others, and to control the general character of (their) transactions, to some degree" (p. 210). People do this primarily by arranging furniture and other objects in the environment. Consider for a moment how your living room or den is arranged. Do the chairs face each other for easy conversation? Do they face the television? What do these arrangements communicate about that environment? A **fixed-feature** environment includes two phases: "internal, culturally specific configuration, and external environmental arrangements such as architecture and space layout" (p. 210). Consider the classroom building where you take this class. What does its architecture and layout communicate? Look at the local courthouse, church, synagogue, mosque, or other place of worship. What about your favorite hangout with your friends? Despite the 40-plus years that have passed since this original research, these dimensions still exist today. They may vary due to our use of more electronic devices, but all-in-all they remain the same.

Depending upon the desired outcome, how we structure our environment includes all three of Hall's categories. For instance, suppose you wanted to design a room just for one purpose. How would this best be accomplished? First, ask yourself how you would like the person who enters it to respond to Knapp's (1978) six frameworks: Is the environment to be formal/informal, warm/uncomfortable, and so forth? Then take J. K. Burgoon and Saine's (1978) nine dimensions (e.g., size, arrangement of objects) and create that feeling.

Several of these dimensions/frameworks influence how we are expected to communicate in a particular environment. These include room color and aesthetic appreciation, room size and shape, temperature and humidity, and environmental structuring. As we examine each in greater detail, you should begin to understand how people use the environment to manipulate others or to create a first impression.

BOX 4.7 OBSERVATIONAL STUDY

Conduct an environmental analysis of your own room (either at home or school). First, employ Knapp's (1978) system alone. Then employ Burgoon and Saine's (1978) system alone. Third, approach it from E. T. Hall's (1972) category system. What similarities do you find? What differences? Finally, see if you can combine and compare all three systems and interpret what you observed as a whole picture.

ROOM COLOR AND AESTHETIC APPRECIATION

Room color and the degree of attractiveness associated with a room are important environmental considerations. Maslow and Mintz (1956) examined the impact on human behavior of three rooms, each differing in degree of "beauty." The three rooms were engineered to be "beautiful" (with carpeting, drapes, and so forth), "average" (a professor's office), and "ugly" (giving the impression of a janitor's storeroom). People were then placed in one of the three rooms and asked to rate their negative perceptions of a print photograph of faces. The photographs were rated as more attractive in the "beautiful" room. Both the experimenters and the subjects reported more fatigue and a greater need to escape while in the "ugly" room. Would "beauty" be the same in today's society? Would the outcomes be the same?

PHOTO 4.2 (A) AND (B) Most environments are designed with purpose, indicating how you should communicate and behave. How might your nonverbal communication and behavior differ between these two environments?

Kitchens, Herron, Behnke, and Beatty (1977) studied the interpersonal attraction of a confederate in a "live" situation. To determine the influence of the aesthetics of the room upon ratings of interpersonal attraction, Kitchens and colleagues asked people to rate a *live* communicator rather than photographic negatives. The "unattractive" room had walls of dull green, light bulbs were unshaded, and the furniture was splattered with paint. A green couch with a broken leg and torn seat cushions was placed in the room. The "attractive" room was freshly painted and had been decorated by a professional interior designer. A regular classroom was used as a control to measure the impact of each room. The results of this study supported the conclusions of Maslow and Mintz (1956), that the environmental aesthetics of a room influence both our behavior and our communication.

What is aesthetically pleasing to one may not be to another. Hence, we structure our environments partially to please ourselves and partially to please others. This difference may come from our geographic residence, personality, status, and so forth. Would you, for example, eat a meal in an environment that was formal, uncomfortable, nonprivate, somewhat familiar, nonconstraining, and cramped, allowing only a short distance (say 6 to 12 inches) between people? If you have ever eaten at a fast-food restaurant, you already have. Most fast-food restaurants appear rather large, with seats arranged to maximize the number of people who can be seated at once; they also tend to use the hardest material possible to sit on. These features of the environment, when combined with a linear perspective—bright to harsh lighting, cooler than needed temperature, high noise level, and maximized sensory stimulation—all have one purpose: to serve as many people as quickly as possible. To sit and have a "chat" is simply not the purpose of this type of environment. The proprietors want you to enter, buy your food, and consume it as quickly as possible, and move on so they can serve the next person. Eaves and Leathers (1991) found just this in an examination of 10 fast-food restaurants. They found that not only were there behavioral differences in involvement and discomfort but that those differences were dependent on the specific fast-food chain they observed—McDonald's or Burger King. Try it yourself. Go to a fast-food restaurant and sit with a friend for at least a half-hour *without* getting up; it's difficult. Note also how involved customers are in their conversations with each other, and note how long they remain in that environment.

A second factor involved in aesthetic appreciation is room color. As noted in the research of Maslow and Mintz (1956) and of Kitchens et al. (1977), *room color* may play a determining part in how we perceive an environment. Wexner (1954), for instance, found that certain colors were associated with certain moods. Thus, red was considered exciting and stimulating, blue was identified as secure-comfortable or as tender-soothing, and yellow was described as cheerful-jovial-youthful. J. K. Burgoon and Saine (1978) have identified various mood and symbolic meanings that we associate with different colors. If you are in a classroom, you might note that none of the colors are "exciting" or "stimulating." Instead, the colors you see are pastels, shades meant to subdue rather than excite the student. The halls, however, are usually more colorful and contrasting; consequently, there is more talk and behavior than in the classroom (where you are expected to sit and "soak it in").

ROOM SIZE AND SHAPE

A second feature of the environment is the size and shape of the room where interaction takes place. Sommer (1969) studied the effects of size and shape of classrooms on behavior. He observed that various types of classrooms (seminar rooms, laboratories, windowless rooms, and rooms with an entire wall of windows) produce various reactions. Sommer found that both students and professors disliked windowless rooms and laboratories. He noted that in seminar rooms, fewer people participated, but they participated for longer periods of time than in other settings. In seminar rooms, most of the participation came from those seated directly across from the instructor. In straight-row-seating classrooms, more participation came from students within range of eye contact with the instructor. Sommer found that participation decreased as class size was increased; in addition, most of the participation came from those seated near the front or directly in front of the instructor. Look at your class's environment for an example. Who participates the most? Where do they sit? Do you think this style of participation is a matter of seating, personality, or both? (Perhaps they chose their seating because of their personalities, or perhaps those seats were the only ones available to them when they entered the classroom.)

Other researchers have examined the impact of whether a room can be altered and the resultant effects on communication. High and Sundstrom (1977), using dormitory students, found that people who could not alter their environments (beds, desks, and other major features were fixed) had fewer friends visit and did not stay in those environments as long as those who could change their environments. Generally, High and Sundstrom found that the center of social life revolved around the more changeable room. Imagine living in a room over which you have little control; many of us could not live in such a room.

Room shape does not appear to have a major influence on us; however, nonverbal communication is culture-bound. We Americans are used to an environment where our rooms are mostly linear; that is, we tend to prefer our environments to be square or rectangular. Living in a 12-foot by 24-foot block building would not bother most of us; however, people from cultures in which the rooms are circular—or the corners are rounded (as in some Spanish-style housing)—would find such a linear perspective odd. Generally, Americans perceive the size of a room as more important than its shape. We notice other shapes of rooms as being different and perhaps may even label them as interesting, but they rarely affect our perception of communication within that environment. Other cultures may have different views.

TEMPERATURE AND HUMIDITY

A third feature of the environment is the perceived temperature and humidity—"perceived" because several factors can change how hot or cold we think a room is. For instance, the colors red and white produce different perceptions of temperature (Griffit 1970). White rooms are almost always perceived as cooler (as much as five degrees cooler than red rooms). What effects do temperature and humidity have on people? How many violent acts can you think of that occurred in November, December, January, or February? Now, compare your analysis with that of the summer months. It should not be surprising that riots in the 1960s came during the hottest summer months on record. Indeed, many people believe that the heat of summer flared tempers more than would have occurred in the winter months.

What is known about temperature and humidity makes good sense. For example, Griffit (1970) found that as temperature and humidity increased, impressions of others' interpersonal attractiveness *decreased*. Another researcher noted that the outdoor temperature is more suitable for mental vigor if it ranges in the 50s or 60s rather than in the 70s. McClelland (1961) found that achievement motivation was higher when the mean annual temperature was between 40 and 60 degrees Fahrenheit. We must temper these findings, however, by noting that they were conducted in external environments cooler than some parts of the country. Anyone who has survived a Southern summer knows that 80 degrees can feel as cool as 50 degrees would to a Northerner, considering the higher heat and humidity of the South. A parallel might be that anyone who has survived a New England winter knows that a 40-degree day in the middle of winter feels as balmy as a 75-degree day elsewhere. Rosenfeld and Civikly (1976) concluded in a study of indoor environments that 64 to 68 degrees Fahrenheit might be the most ideal temperature for an indoor environment. How much do you enjoy being inside when you are either so cold you must "bundle up" or so hot that it makes you tired or irritable?

Knapp (1980) summarized much of the research that had been done on temperature and environments. Knapp found that monotonous weather is likely to affect your moods. You usually do your best work in late winter, early spring, and fall. When the sky is blue for prolonged periods of time, you will be less productive, and an ideal temperature should average about 64 degrees Fahrenheit (p. 58).

ENVIRONMENTAL STRUCTURING

Structuring refers to how the environment and the objects within it are arranged and for what effect. People generally structure an environment purposefully, with an idea about its effect. The environment may serve as a **metamessage**, which is a message suggesting how to behave or communicate. The absence of an ashtray should tell a smoker not to smoke. The position of a chair should indicate how the conversation will go, how formal it may be, or the status differences between people. Why, for example, is the pharmacist usually at a higher level than you are? We probably have as much research in this area as in any area of the environment, and it all deals with either self-presentation or manipulation.

Consider, for example, an office arrangement; if the desk is in the center of the room and faces the door, some type of power signal is being transmitted. Korda (1975) and Cooper (1979) discuss how to structure your environment to increase your perceived power and status. Both stress the need to understand how the environment is structured. In general, the more permanent the environment, the more "plush" and spacious it is, the more powerful the occupant. Within the office there are emblems of power: diplomas, pictures, plants (the larger the plant, the more power is suggested), size of desk, comfort of chairs, paneled rather than painted walls, access to windows, and so forth. Visit the office of a professor that you feel comfortable talking with; how has he or she arranged it? Then do the same with a professor with whom you are less comfortable. Can you find any differences? Do their office arrangements affect the types of communication that take place within the offices?

The structure of the environment also tells visitors how they are supposed to act. Anyone who has ever walked into a "bachelor's pad," or tried to put one together, knows that the subdued lighting, the shape of the couch, the texture of material, the carpeting, and mood music are all tips as to what behavior is expected. Other environments are structured: a dentist's office, a professor's office, a church (especially one with great spaciousness that makes you feel insignificant), and a bar. Each is structured to induce you to feel and act in a predetermined manner. The fast-food restaurant is another example of environmental structuring. In addition, note the differences between the flooring in a Wal-Mart or K-Mart and the flooring in a high-quality clothing store.

Have you examined other environments for their impact? Freeman, Roach, and Gladney (1980) examined the environmental structuring in a supermarket. They found that the most expensive items were placed at eye level. The attraction value of vegetables was important; notice that they are usually shining green, yellow, red, and so forth because they have been watered several times. Indeed, many stores now run sprinkler systems over their fresh vegetables to keep them looking moist and fresh. One supermarket in Mobile, Alabama, found that by randomly placing Coca-Cola in the line of vision throughout the store, it sold more of the soda. Many stores place "sale" items in the front so that you see them as you enter. Have you ever noticed that their price is the same as, if not higher than, those items on the shelves? It is no accident that supermarkets try to lead you to pass by the bakery as soon as possible (some stores even give cookie "credit" cards to children in order to attract them). In clothing stores, the most expensive items are often placed at the front of the store, and you must pass them to get to the "bargains," which are usually crowded together on racks in the back.

All these are examples of how people are manipulated by the environment. Other features that could be mentioned include music in the store or room (with faster music getting you in and out faster, slower music inviting you to spend more time), lighting, and temperature. Although physicians' offices are often cold for health reasons, the cold also distracts the patients from the amount of time they have been waiting. The critical intent, however, is that we communicate in and through our environments. Environments form the first line of communication, indicating how we should act and how we should view the inhabitants of the environment. More recent research is looking more at how environments need to be arranged for better access by senior citizens and especially health-challenged seniors (Vergados 2010). Furthermore, studies are being done in how mentally challenged and mentally ill patients come to depend on certain aspects of a territory to better function in health care situations (Tucker 2010). Suffice it to say that we have many uses for the studies of environments that are done and looking at how environmental structuring affects communication.

BOX 4.8 OBSERVATIONAL STUDY

Take a print magazine and look at no less than 10 advertisements that include the surrounding environment in the pictures found in the ads. Look first at what you see in the environmental structuring the advertisers use.

What messages do these ads send about the products? About the people in the ads using the products? What would you have done differently with the environment if you had designed the ads?

ARCHITECTURE

A final area to consider when thinking about how the environment can communicate is the area of architecture, meaning how people build our buildings, how we landscape, the actual rooms, and other structural aspects of an environment. If someone were to ask you what your ideal house would be, what would you describe? Would you have a large house? Would there be a fireplace? Swimming pool? Would it be more than one story high? And if it were, what would your staircase look like? Would you have a large deck or a porch? What color would the house be?

It is probably not news to you that how people structure their physical environments communicates something about them, whether it is an individual or a company, a restaurant or a store, a movie theater or a bar. Studies have also reported that architecture within environments is designed to express how people are feeling and also to send a message (K. D. Fisher 2009). Consider the buildings on your campus. What do they communicate about your school? Are they old? Are they made to appear older than they are? This choice of a bygone architectural style often occurs on college campuses that try to send the message of a long tradition of fine education. Consider the formal restaurant that you frequent the most (not fast-food); what does its architecture communicate about the atmosphere of the restaurant? Compare it with a fast-food restaurant. What are some of the communicative differences between the two?

In one of the best-known historical studies about work environments, Bruneau (1973) studied the design of office spaces in educational organizations, looking at how office designs affected the communication of both the people who "owned" the office space and those who

PHOTO 4.3 With the largest manmade waterfalls in North America cascading into reflecting pools set within the footprints of the original Twin Towers, architects designed the National September 11 Memorial to convey a spirit of hope and renewal.

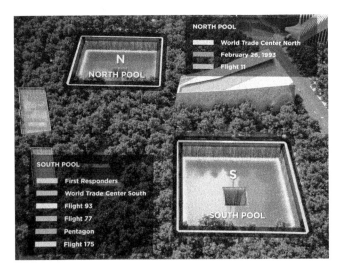

PHOTO 4.4 Not only does the sound of water drown out the noises of the city, creating an environment suited for reflection; the arrangement of the victims' names, in what designers call "meaningful adjacencies," adds to the feeling of intimacy and contemplation.

visited it. He noted that as the status of the "owner" increased, one would have to pass through more space to get to see that person. Students' behavior was also much more controlled while in the environment of a high-status person. Other findings about architecture are that the larger the office space someone has and the closer his or her office is to the boss, the more status and power he or she is perceived to have.

Architecture tells us much about what takes place in the building, about the people who work there, about aesthetics, as well as many other things. You would do well to think about this topic when you think about how your environments communicate to others.

STUDENT VOICES

Ryan: I am at the point where I am starting to think of what I would like in a house—what it will look like, what it will say about me, etc. . . . I think I will want a two story house, with large bay windows in the front, a huge yard for the many children I plan to have to play in, a pool and a Jacuzzi tub, and a fireplace in the living room as well as the master bedroom. That will be the epitome of romance for me. Now, I guess I'll have to try and find a career that will afford me that opulence; right now it's looking like a one-bedroom apartment. . . .

BOX 4.9 OBSERVATIONAL STUDY

With some of your friends, sit and brainstorm about your ideal home. How much do you and your friends agree on? How much do you disagree? Try to discover why these friends think the way they do, and why they prefer certain things when designing a house.

FUNCTIONS OF TERRITORY AND THE ENVIRONMENT

Territory is demonstrated through spatial factors. For example, those of higher status tend to take up more space. Their *self-presentation and identification* illustrate their status, often through large offices and barriers (such as desks) between the higher-status person and the visitor. Because of the larger distance, higher-status persons present a *regulation* mechanism in that most of the time you will assume that you have less time to make your case. Though you may easily enter an office assistant's territory—even touch the desk—when you get to the boss' office, you typically "wait" at the door to be invited into the room. Research in interviewing techniques suggests that when told to proceed to the interviewer's office, you should knock before entering even if the door is open, which clearly communicates the status and power of the interviewer (C. J. Stewart and Cash 2003). The *relationship of interactants* is illustrated by how you feel about violating the territorial expectations of others. For example, many workers feel they can grab, throw, and peruse items on a secretary's desk, presuming they are of higher status and, in a sense, "own" whatever is on that desk. If you have ever talked with (or been) a clerical worker, you know that this behavior communicates to the secretary that the person feels superior to the secretary and that the secretary is not worthy of the same respect that other employees enjoy. (A tip to remember is that in any place of business, the administrative assistants are the ones to "make friends" with, as they are usually the gatekeepers to many things you will either need or want. Begin interacting with them by communicating their worth nonverbally.)

Through the environment, you can *display instructional information* by how clean or messy your office and desk appear. We usually presume that a person's organizational skills, or lack thereof, are reflected by what we see in his or her office. Also, if your office provides a chair next to the person behind the desk, it indicates a more responsive individual and perhaps a less assertive one. Of course, these items can be *deceptive,* characterizing your space in a way that is different from your personality. It is best not to assume what a person's personality is on the basis of these factors. As always, get to know the individual before passing judgments.

SUMMARY

As you have read, the environment can be a major nonverbal communicator, yet how many of us have never considered this as an aspect of communication prior to studying it here? Although not a forgotten topic, it is not what we usually think of when we hear the words "nonverbal communication." We would do well to pay attention to environmental factors as part of our nonverbal communication "package."

This chapter has examined the study of space and how we use it to communicate. We looked at the environment and how, through its structuring and manipulation, we communicate to others information about ourselves, about how we expect others to act, and about how we should act. The environment, we noted, is the first line of communication, and its manipulation can alter other aspects of our communication. Territory consists of spaces or areas that are marked, have boundaries, and suggest ways to act and communicate. The territory we occupy—like the personal space we expect and maintain (see Chapter 4)—is influenced by a number of factors, each operating in conjunction with the others to produce expectations of appropriate behavior and communication.

QUESTIONS FOR THOUGHT

1. What is the relationship between lower animals' and humans' use of territory and environment?
2. How does territoriality function to affect human communication?
3. Contrast territoriality with Goffman's "territories of the self" in terms of both theoretical understanding of territory and territoriality and practical implications.
4. How do humans structure their environment as both messages and metamessages?
5. What factors exert the strongest influence on our perceptions of a communication environment? Which would you manipulate to create an "atmosphere of communication"?

FURTHER REFERENCES

Types of Territory

Hickson, M. L., III, and Self, W. (2003). Biological foundations of territoriality: Nonverbal communication, language, and the law. *Journal of Intercultural Communication Research, 32*, 265–283.

Knowles, E. S. (1972). Boundaries around social space: Dyadic responses to an invasion. *Environment and Behavior, 4*, 437–445.

Sobel, R. S., and Liffith, N. (1974). Determinants of nonstationary personal space invasion. *Journal of Social Psychology, 97*, 39–45.

Human Correlates of Territory

Altman, I. (1973). An ecological approach to the functioning of social groups. In J. G. Rasmussen (Ed.), *Individual and group behavior in isolation and confinement* (pp. 241–269). Chicago: Aldine Press.

Altman, I. (1975). *The environment and social behavior: Privacy, personal space, territoriality, and crowding.* Monterey, CA: Brooks/Cole.

Altman, I., and Haythorn, W. W. (1967). The ecology of isolated groups. *Behavioral Science, 12*, 169–182.

Altman, I., Nelson, R. A., and Lett, E. E. (1972). The ecology of home environments. *Man-Made Systems*, 2, 189–191.

Altman, I., Taylor, D. A., and Wheeler, L. (1971). Ecological aspects of group behavior in isolation. *Journal of Applied Social Psychology*, 1, 76–100.

Fong, L. (2007). Playing keepaway. *Psychology Today*, 40, 15.

Frieze, H., and Ramsey, S. J. (1976). Nonverbal maintenance of traditional sex roles. *Journal of Social Issues*, 32, 133–141.

Novelli, D., Drury, J., and Reicher, S. (2010). Come together: Two studies concerning the impact of group relations on "personal space." *British Journal of Social Psychology*, 49, 223–236.

Crowding and Density

Sinha, S. P., and Mukherjee, N. (1996). The effect of perceived cooperation on personal space requirements. *Journal of Social Psychology*, 136, 655–657.

Wenz, F. V. (1984). Household crowding, loneliness, and suicide ideation. *Psychology: A Quarterly Journal of Human Behavior*, 21, 25–28.

Room Color and Aesthetic Appreciation

Hirst, E., and Cooper, M. (2008). Keeping them in line: Choreographing classroom spaces. *Teachers & Teaching*, 14, 431–445.

Leathers, D. G. (1997). *Nonverbal communication systems: Principles and applications* (3rd ed.). Boston: Allyn and Bacon.

Luscher, M. (1971). *The Luscher Color Test* (I. A. Scott, Ed. and Trans.). New York: Pocket Books.

Mintz, N. L. (1956). Effects of esthetic surrounds: II. Prolonged and repeated experience in a "beautiful" and "ugly" room. *Journal of Psychology*, 41, 459–466.

Murray, D. C., and Deabler, H. L. (1957). Colors and mood-tones. *Journal of Applied Psychology*, 41, 279–283.

Room Size and Shape

Adams, R. S., and Biddle, B. (1970). *Realities of teaching: Explorations with video tape*. New York: Holt, Rinehart, &Winston.

Becher, D., Sommer, R., Bee, J., and Osley, B. (1973). College classroom ecology. *Sociometry*, 36, 514–525.

Bodin-Danielsson, C., and Bodin, L. (2008). Office type in relation to mental health, well-being, and job satisfaction among employees. *Environment & Behavior*, 40, 636–668.

CHAPTER 5

PHYSICAL APPEARANCE: IMPRESSIONS OF THE BODY

KEY CONCEPTS

- Physical Appearance
- Physical Attractiveness
- Impact on Social Interaction
- Impact on Sex Appeal
- The Body
- Body Shape and Size
- Body Image
- Stigma

OBJECTIVES

By the end of the chapter you should be able to:

- Explain the significance of physical appearance in today's society.
- Explain how one's physical appearance influences social interaction.
- Discuss the concept of "sex appeal" and its relationship to attraction and physical appearance.
- Differentiate between body types.
- Explain how one's weight and height influence one's own and others' perceptions of personality.
- Discuss the impact of body image on daily interaction and the things people do to alter those images and their effects on both themselves and others.
- Explain the concept of stigma as it relates to physical appearance.

Physical appearance is often the first nonverbal factor we notice in meeting people. In fact, when we see an individual we have met before, our immediate reaction often is "I don't remember the name, but I remember the face." Physical appearance refers to more than just facial features, of course; it includes such dimensions as body shape, body image, physical

facial features   body image
body shape

physical appearance dimensions

attractiveness, clothing, cosmetics, hair, and accessories. We cannot help but form impressions based on these dimensions of physical appearance.

How important is physical appearance? According to some researchers, physical attractiveness may be the major reason two people communicate (C. R. Berger and Calabrese 1975). When people must communicate with strangers, most prefer to talk with ones they find attractive. In general, we have a tendency to gravitate toward individuals we perceive as attractive and away from those we find unattractive. In sum, we tend to categorize people at one end of an attractiveness continuum or the other; either they are attractive or they are not, although most of us probably lie somewhere between these extremes.

Why is physical attraction important? Many people would like to say that *inner beauty* is more significant than physical attraction in judging another's worth. It would be nice to think that that is true, but, unfortunately, what goes on in American society does not confirm that position. Study after study has shown the reality of how important physical attractiveness is. Numerous research papers have shown that beauty is a commodity. People who are perceived to be more attractive are better liked, are able to obtain better jobs, have more social power, have higher self-esteem, have enhanced financial values, receive higher grades, engage in classroom interactions with teachers more frequently, are more often communicated with, are perceived to be more persuasive, are less likely to be convicted in courts of law, are more talented, are more successful, and so on. The body of research on this topic spans a number of decades. A. J. Huang (2001), in a discussion of the link between beauty and plastic surgery, tells us that "the American public is arguably just as concerned about physical attractiveness" as it was in 1907, when doctors began to surgically improve the appearance of individuals (p. 2158). Everywhere you look today, you still see the same message being sent—physical attractiveness is crucial in our society. From the media to scholarly research to your interactions with others, you are continually being sent this message.

Langlois and Roggman (1990) and Langlois, Ritter, Roggman, and Vaughn (1991) add to the concept of how important physical appearance is in our society. In their definitive research on the importance of attractive faces, they found some interesting results. They discovered that infants between the ages of 2 months and 8 months can discriminate between women's faces that have been rated by young adults as being attractive or unattractive and that infants pay more attention to the attractive faces. These researchers replicated their experiments a number of times, which is important to good research (as is discussed in the Appendix, p. 416), and the results were similar each time. Langlois and colleagues suggest from these findings that a universal standard of attractiveness may exist in our society. A few researchers disagree with that notion, though, and believe there to be no universality of attractiveness, especially across age brackets (Zebrowitz and Rhodes 2004). You have probably discussed this subject with some of your peers and have found that there are some similarities in what each of you finds attractive. Perhaps you have found the opposite of each other.

2–8 month infants can identify attractiveness

In researching, evaluating, and studying physical appearance, we are reminded of the numerous clichés that seem trite but are nevertheless meaningful: "Beauty is in the eye of the beholder," "Blondes have more fun," "Clothes make the man," "Beauty is only skin deep," and "Black is beautiful." Some of these sayings confirm the position that physical attractiveness is an individual perceptual phenomenon and that individuals have different standards for beauty. Others send the message of a universal standard of beauty. Which of those is true? Probably both, since most of us will have our own preferences for beauty, yet we would agree with some universal standards of beauty, such as a nice smile (including teeth), pretty eyes, clean and well-kept hair, and so on.

Beautification is a continuing project. Much money is spent every year by individuals simply to alter their physical appearance. Why? As students of nonverbal communication, we believe that people are concerned about their physical appearance because they wish to communicate a "better" message about themselves. In the United States, we seem to have bought into the concept of the *beauty myth*—that beauty is of utmost importance to survival in our society. Walk through any department store—from the toniest to the discounters— and see just how much of what they sell centers on trying to make ourselves more attractive. How we look, how we are shaped, and what we wear tell as much about us as anything else, and yet it is told without our uttering a word.

Physical appearance operates in several ways. Of primary concern to most of us is the *visible* aspect of our physical appearance: how we look naturally, including our body shape, height, weight, hair, teeth, complexion, and other natural endowments; and how we look in different types, styles, and colors of clothing. The importance of such perceptions is discussed in this chapter when we consider such things as body shape, body image, clothing, and other accessories. First, let us discuss the importance of physical attractiveness.

[handwritten margin note: Visible aspect - naturally, without altering features]

BOX 5.1 OBSERVATIONAL STUDY

For the next 24 hours keep track of how many things you do to enhance your physical attractiveness. Then, choose another day on which you know you are going to try to impress someone (e.g., an interviewer, a boss, someone

you think is "hot" or "fine"), and keep track of how many things you do on that day to enhance your physical attractiveness. What, if any, are the differences between the two days? Does this seem to be the norm? Did the enhancement of your physical appearance serve its purpose?

PHYSICAL ATTRACTIVENESS

Defining physical attractiveness in terms of absolutes is impossible. The old cliché "Beauty is in the eye of the beholder" seems to apply to some degree. Although there are no absolutes in defining physical attractiveness, there is a high level of agreement as to what constitutes physical attractiveness. When asked to rate photographs of African American women taken from *Ebony* and *Sepia* magazines by a researcher (J. G. Martin 1964), 50 black American males and 50 white American males reached a high degree of consensus on which women were most and least attractive. Although not specified, since a 1964 study would not have likely asked the participants their sexual preference, it is assumed that these were heterosexual men. A similar study conducted in Great Britain questioned more than 4,000 subjects who varied in age, sex, occupation, and place of residence (Illife 1960). Again, a high level of agreement was found as to which female faces were "pretty."

In both studies, however, it should be noted that what constitutes beauty for these men was culture-related. In the case of black beauty, a separate Nigerian sample chose different women as being most attractive; those with predominately Negroid features were preferred to those with Caucasoid features (J. G. Martin 1964). Also, specific ideals of attractive women or men undoubtedly vary over time. Women considered attractive by old-world painters (Rubens, in particular) would no longer be considered beautiful; instead, most would currently be classified as overweight! Additionally, we need to take into consideration location. Hensley (1981), for example, found that well-dressed females received more money (for a telephone call) in airports, whereas poorly dressed confederates received more money at bus stations.

It is important to remember that attractiveness is a perceived factor, meaning someone must perceive it in someone else; it actually does not exist on its own. When discussing what is considered attractive, you must always remember that what you perceive as physically attractive may not be so for your best friend. How many times have you looked at a couple and asked yourself, "What does he or she find attractive about that person? I find that person to be most unattractive." You may find blondes with blue eyes more attractive than redheads with green eyes. Someone else may find the opposite to be true. You may find the standards of what you judge to be attractive to be based on people of your same sex, race, or socioeconomic background. Or you may set those standards by looking at people of the opposite sex, another race, or any cultural difference. Attractiveness is perceived, and therefore the old adage "Beauty is in the eye of the beholder" takes on new meaning as we begin to study physical attractiveness. Recall that we have said there may be some universal agreement about certain physical attractiveness factors and about what is attractive and unattractive. As we look at this aspect of nonverbal communication, we will try to point out the factors that comprise these standards.

Physical attractiveness has a major impact on how other people perceive us as similar to themselves, a concept known as **homophily**. Because physical attractiveness affects evaluations of our credibility, sociability, ability to work with others, and so forth, it merits considerable study.

Let's consider two studies that explored the "use of physical attractiveness by females as a manipulative device to obtain higher grades from college professors" (J. E. Singer 1964; J. E. Singer and Lamb 1966). Singer found a high positive correlation between firstborn, attractive females and grade point average. He also determined that firstborn, attractive females engaged in more "exhibiting" behavior, such as sitting at the front of the classroom, talking to the professor after class, and making appointments to see professors in their offices. These may or may not be tied only to attractiveness, but since Singer and Lamb's studies were mostly on the effect of attractiveness on various factors, it appears that attractiveness is at least an important variable here, even if it is not the only one at work in these settings.

Singer and Lamb wanted to determine whether the better grades of these attractive females were a result of intentional manipulation or were due to luck. Consequently, Singer conducted a survey in which females were asked to estimate their own body measurements and ideal measurements. A "manipulative intent" hypothesis was confirmed. Findings indicated that (1) firstborn females more accurately estimated their own body measurements, (2) firstborns were more accurate in estimating the ideal female measurements, and (3) firstborns were more likely to distort their own measurements in the direction of the estimated ideal measurements than were later-born females (Singer and Lamb, 1966). It may be that later-born females have had more realistic ideals about female measurements because they

first born perceptions of body shapes

have the opportunity to see their older sisters' bodies not camouflaged by clothing. The first-born, however, must compare herself with idealized attraction standards. Again, attractiveness may not be the only variable influencing the outcomes of this study, but it is a recognizable one; thus, we point it out here. The Singer studies have yet to be replicated using male subjects, but the findings would surely be interesting should they be conducted again with a male population. Pompper, Soto, and Piel (2007) have studied the appearance of males in magazines and discovered that there is the *ideal man projected*, although men are more *ideal men projected* ambivalent about that image than women are. In addition, times have changed since 1966 in regards to publicly judging women and men based on their physical attributes. Finally, E. Mazur and Richards (2011) discovered that "emerging adults" (college-age folks like you) and adolescents looking to establish online relationships do look for different aspects of homophily when they are deciding whether or not to establish online relationships. The outcome of replicating these studies would surely show some changes.

Other studies have shown that in the educational setting, teachers interact less with unattractive students and respond to comments from more attractive students more readily (Leathers 1997). It has also been found that students do the same; they are less likely to interact with less attractive students. Misbehavior in a classroom is even perceived differently by teachers. Unattractive children are likely to be judged as having chronic behavior problems, whereas the more attractive children are believed to have only a temporary behavioral problem.

is about familiarity culture

PHOTO 5.1 In 2013, Gwyneth Paltrow was named *People's* Most Beautiful Woman in the World despite *Star Magazine* putting her at the top of their list of *The Most Hated Celebrities*, calling her phony, condescending, and pretentious. Is it possible to be considered physically attractive at the same time as having other unattractive qualities? Have your ever changed your opinion about someone's physical appearance the more you communicated with each other?

Mills and Aronson (1965) conducted a study in which a woman delivered the same speech to two audiences. For one audience, the woman dressed attractively (properly applied makeup, neat and well-fitting dress); for the other audience, she dressed unattractively (no makeup, loose-fitting clothing, messy hair, oily complexion). Mills and Aronson showed that men were more persuaded by the attractive female than the (same) unattractive female.

One group of researchers found that women do not put as much emphasis on physical attractiveness when looking at other people as men do (Graziano, Jensen-Campbell, Shebilske, and Lundgren 1993). They found that women tend to look more for ambition and social status than for mere physical appearance. Another researcher (Feingold 1992) found that there are stereotypes whereby physically attractive people are perceived as more dominant, sociable, socially acute, and mentally healthy, when not all are. Some scholars believe that the stereotypes can actually come to reflect reality, because attractive people are treated as if they have those qualities and therefore become that type of personality. Another study found that assessments of physical attractiveness are made very quickly (Locher, Unger, Sociedade, and Wahl 1993). Locher and associates showed black-and-white slides of the face and shoulders of college students (who were less than 30 years old) to other college students, who were asked to rate the target slides for physical attractiveness, suitability for a job for which the person was supposedly applying, and expectation of cooperation on the job. The researchers not only found that the participants could make such judgments quickly and with only the information contained in the slides, but that both males' and females' judgments were consistent with the researchers' opinions of physical attractiveness. But lest you think all studies find that, some researchers find that many people are discriminating between social attractiveness and physical attractiveness. Chambers and Sparks (2009) discovered that individuals with better personalities were rated as more physically attractive, and also that they were remembered better. This should get us thinking that it is not always physical attractiveness that is the most important characteristic of other human beings.

BOX 5.2   OBSERVATIONAL STUDY

Choose three of your friends or close acquaintances of both sexes and ask them what they find to be physically attractive characteristics of the opposite sex and of the same sex. Take notes and compare the lists. Are heterosexual women better able to give characteristics for the same sex than are heterosexual men? Why do you think this is true? Do homosexual men and women give beauty standards for people of the same sex or of the opposite sex? Why do you think that happens? Are there any universal physical characteristics that most of these people found to be things they find physically attractive?

SOCIAL INTERACTION

Other research indicates that attractiveness has a significant influence on perceptions of social interaction. Widgery and Webster (1969) concluded that physically attractive people, regardless of sex, were rated higher on the character dimension of credibility than were unattractive persons. In a related study, Eiland and Richardson (1976) found that differences in credibility and interpersonal attraction ratings of individuals are, in large part, determined by race, age, and sex. Physical attractiveness does increase how likable one is perceived to be; however, it does not inherently increase one's status. They also found that lonely men were perceived as less attractive than men who were not lonely. However, women were perceived no differently in physical attractiveness, whether they were lonely or not. People who provide more spontaneous, uncensored nonverbal information appear more extroverted, and they were also viewed as more physically attractive. Kang and Hamilton (2003) found that even in advertising, the use of more attractive—in particular, sexually attractive—models results in more positive attitudes toward the advertisement as well as the product. Be it credibility, likability, or loneliness factors, perhaps you can see yourself or your friends in one of these contexts that we report here.

Ries, Nezlek, and Wheeler (1980) were interested in the impact physical attractiveness had on social interaction in general. They concentrated on the everyday activities of people of varying degrees of attractiveness. Rather than undertaking the usual experimental study of highly attractive versus unattractive people, they had college students keep a journal of their daily activities and related the journal entries to the students' physical attractiveness, which was rated independently. Their results indicated five conclusions. First, physical attractiveness is strongly related to the quantity of social interaction for males, but not so for females. For heterosexual males, the interactions were rated more positively if the other person was female; if the other person was male, the interaction was rated more negatively. Second, for both sexes (and in particular for cross-sex interactions) satisfaction increased over time when the others were physically attractive. Third, females rated as moderately attractive seemed to enjoy socialization more than others. Fourth, males who were rated as physically attractive reported more mutually initiated interactions with the opposite sex than self- or other-initiated interactions. Finally, attractive males spent more of their time conversing and less in activity, and attractive females spent less time in task interactions and more time on dates or at parties. Have you noticed any of these findings in your own life? Or in the life of friends you find attractive?

More recent studies have identified that social interaction is still greatly affected by perceived physical attractiveness. As mentioned already, Chambers and Sparks (2009) found that attractiveness was important, but they also found that positive social attributes are important to finding someone physically attractive. With the prevalence of the use of social media in today's society, we would be remiss not to mention that even on social media sites (i.e., Facebook. LinkedIn, etc.), physical attraction plays an important role in social interactions, and especially in establishing relationships. Wang, Moon, Kwon, Evans, and Stefanone (2010) found that people who use social media to build (or perhaps to even create) friendships actually used the photos posted on Facebook to determine if the person was attractive enough to "make friends" with them. This, of course, leads to another area of research on how people use deceptive photos on social media websites (Toma and Hancock, 2010; Ramirez and Wang, 2008).

In classroom interaction, researchers have found that teachers associated personality characteristics with their judgments of their students' attractiveness. Turning the tables, Romano and Bordieri (1989) examined students' perceptions of the physical attractiveness of college professors. The attractive professors were seen as better teachers, as more likely to provide assistance, as less likely to be blamed for a student's failing a course, and as more likely to be recommended to other students. Female professors were rated higher than their male peers. Obviously, *physical attractiveness influences our perceptions of social interaction and how we structure that interaction* (Kenealy, Frude, and Shaw 1988). How do you rate your professors, and can you see any of these same types of responses when you look at how you react to them? As R. Wilson (2010) points out, even the well-known *RateMyProfessors.com* allows for the attractiveness factor by allowing you to rate your professors with a chili pepper if you think they are "hot."

In a study seeking to determine the relationship between attractiveness and liking, K. K. Dion and Berscheid (1972) studied nursery school children. They asked the children to name the classmates they liked best. The youngsters not only preferred the more attractive children but also perceived the unattractive children as mean and aggressive. The relationship of attractiveness to other traits also has been explored. One study found significant differences in subjects' perceptions of physically attractive and unattractive individuals on 15 of 17 personality dimensions (Bar-Tal and Saxe 1976). People who were rated low in attractiveness were perceived as having negative and undesirable traits, whereas attractive individuals were judged significantly more positively with respect to these traits.

We often say that it is shallow to evaluate people based on how physically attractive they are, yet the results of past studies and studies conducted today show that we do make judgments about people based on their attractiveness to us. Several researchers have studied the effects of attractiveness and intelligence. Clifford and Walster (1973), for example, asked fifth-grade teachers to evaluate a hypothetical student's academic record. The record included a photo of either an attractive or an unattractive student, but the record was the same for both students. They found that the teachers perceived the attractive children as being more intelligent, as being more likely to attain advanced education, and as having parents who were more likely to be concerned with academic achievement. Marwit (1982) also noted that physical attractiveness affected teachers' perceptions of transgressions made by students. He examined whether a student's physical attractiveness had any effect on teachers' ratings of transgressions and found that physically unattractive students were rated more severely than physically attractive students. Additionally, he found the effect to be more pronounced for black than for white students. These findings, however, are not without their inconsistencies. Felson (1981), in an examination of the role of physical attractiveness and deviance, found that physical attractiveness was not related to grades given to students for conduct, sociometric ratings of aggression by classmates, and student reports of teacher disciplinary actions. Even with this finding, it appears that physically attractive people receive less harsh treatment, are more persuasive, and are perceived to be more intelligent. Thinking back to your elementary school years through your high school years and even now in college, can you recall any situations where you believe this to be true?

Apparently, physical attractiveness not only affects people's perceptions of future success but can also have a profound impact on immediate achievement. May (1980) conducted a study involving attractive and unattractive waitresses. His results indicated that attractive waitresses received higher tips than did their unattractive counterparts. The effect of physical attractiveness has also had a demonstrated effect on perceptions of journalists as to whether an individual was likable. Infante, Rancer, Pierce, and Osborne (1980) had students read articles associated with either an attractive female's picture or an unattractive female's picture. Results indicated that they felt that the attractive writer would more likely succeed as a writer than would the unattractive writer and that the attractive writer's academic achievement was higher. Finally, they found the attractive writer was perceived as having a better chance of obtaining a job with a major magazine.

As introduced earlier in the book, a relationship has been established between proxemics and physical attractiveness. Dabbs and Stokes (1975), for example, found that pedestrians walked closer to unattractive females than to attractive females, perhaps finding them less intimidating. As reported earlier, J. K. Burgoon's (1983) expectancy violation theory, as it applies to spatial norms, is heavily dependent upon the reward "valence," or value of the initiator of a deviation from an expected distancing norm. Interestingly, however, J. K. Burgoon, Stacks, and Burch (1982) observed that high reward could have a "boomerang" effect. For a southern U.S. sample, they found that enhanced physical attraction was viewed as less persuasive than "normal" physical attraction. Stacks (1983b) later hypothesized and supported this relationship in a field study. He had each of two students dress either attractively or unattractively and go out and ask students to sign a petition, after providing a number of arguments in favor of the petition. Preliminary tests indicated that the two female confederates were perceived as being significantly more ttractive when in the "physically attractive" condition than in the normal condition. However, attitude change was greater with the normal attraction condition than with the physically attractive condition.

Clearly, physical attractiveness is an important asset. In receiving money for tips and telephone calls, attractive females were more successful. In other persuasive attempts, physically attractive persuaders were more successful and were rated higher on credibility scales. Academic achievement, too, appears to be higher among attractive people from elementary school through college. A study of playgroup caregivers, however, found that attractive children 12 to 30 months old were not more likable or easier to deal with (Fogot 1991). The more attractive youngsters did not get along better with their peers. Thus, physical attractiveness has its merits and disadvantages, and sometimes it makes little or no difference in interpersonal relations.

In one study, researchers found that slides of attractive models (male and female) were more effective in persuasion attempts than were slides of "average-looking" models (Debevac, Madden, and Kernan 1986). When Heilman and Stopeck (1985) investigated attractiveness as a factor in evaluating an employee, they found that attractiveness was only beneficial to those whose job was *clerical*. In fact, they found that attractiveness was detrimental to favorable evaluations for female managerial employees. More attractive female managers were perceived to be less able to control the environments for which they were responsible. These findings do seem to resonate with cross-cultural research. Tsai, Huang, and Yu (2012) found that attractiveness was important for potential employees in Taiwan who were to work in high customer-contact jobs; however, they did find it not to be an important factor in those who were to work in lower customer-contact positions.

PHOTO 5.2 Research shows attractiveness in males and females to be an important asset, especially in persuasion, as evidenced in the film *Crazy, Stupid, Love.*

The attractiveness of a victim can be an influential variable in moot court decisions. Kerr, Raymond, MacCoun, and Rathborn (1985) found that a defendant was more often found guilty when the victim was unattractive and had a disfigurement unrelated to crime than under any other combination of these two variables, such as unattractive without disfigurement, attractive with crime-related disfigurement, or attractive without disfigurement. They contend that their findings are consistent with a "just world" hypothesis: Faith in the world subsides if a careful, innocent victim is harmed. Consequently, jurors put down attractive victims to resolve injustices they perceive to have occurred. On the other hand, Austad, Bugglin, Burns, Farina, and Fisher (1985) found that attractive institutionalized psychiatric patients (male and female) were better able to adapt to discharge and successful recovery in their communities than those who were unattractive. Innala and Ernulf (1994) presented photographs of attractive men and women depicting homosexuals and heterosexuals to participants who were judged not to be homophobic. The female participants rated the men more physically attractive when they were told the men were gay. The women were rated more physically attractive when the participants were told they were heterosexual. The researchers contend that the study illustrates the "gay-pretty-boy stereotype" (which might well be argued).

It appears that attractiveness is becoming a more universal concept. Even though all the participants in Cunningham's (1986) study were white males, they assigned similar attractiveness attributes to photographs of white, Asian, and black female confederates. The participants preferred large eyes, small noses and chins, and wide cheekbones. Although these results may reflect attitudes of the participants in the study, it would have to be replicated with Asian and black participants before any real sense of universality about attractiveness could be inferred (Keating 1985).

Just what does the "typical" attractive person look like? *Time* magazine put on its cover what it considered to be the "average" female in terms of the various racial and ethnic characteristics. That female has what *Time* magazine polls reported as the best characteristics of many racial and ethnic features. Interestingly, while we are able to make "good" guesses at what is attractive for females, we do not make similar decisions about males.

Attractiveness, then, has an impact on communication. What exactly constitutes attractiveness, however, is another question. For many, the concept has been associated with sexual attraction. Sexual attraction, however, is associated with many variables other than physical attractiveness. We need to always keep in mind the perceptual nature of attractiveness, and to recall that the findings are very much tied to the individuals judging physical attractiveness. Obviously, accuracy in judgments of sociability, intelligence, credibility, and effectiveness as an employee is likely to be low until we get to know the actual individual. The old adage "Don't judge a book by its cover" may be what we should espouse, but chances are likely that the "cover" will still be judged.

BOX 5.3   OBSERVATIONAL STUDY

How important is physical attractiveness to social interaction? Ask some of both your male and female friends to describe the physical attraction of someone whom they find attractive enough to approach to begin a conversation with that person. What similarities and dissimilarities did they report? How do these descriptions fit with the research presented in this chapter? Try doing the same exercise again, but this time ask your friends to describe someone of the same sex whom they find attractive enough to approach for a conversation. What is the outcome in this situation?

SEX APPEAL

Just as there are no absolutes in defining physical attractiveness, there are no absolutes in identifying sex appeal. Sex appeal is a result of an individual's experiences, attitudes, and preferences. Judgment of others' sex appeal is affected by such factors as (1) whether the person is known or is a stranger, (2) whether the perceived chances of "success" in a sexual encounter are high or low, and (3) early love experiences (Knapp 1978).

In a 1978 survey, Eakins and Eakins asked heterosexual respondents what they noticed first about the opposite sex. Results indicated that females noticed overall physique first. A close second was grooming and neatness of appearance, followed by eyes. Males noticed breasts first, followed by a general body shape and eyes.

In advertising, Kang and Hamilton (2003) "found that sexiness of clothing, amount of sexual imagery, body language, wording, and amount of nudity" (p. 6) determined how sexy people were considered to be. Since much of the nonverbal research of the day has mass media as its focus of analysis, advertising is one place we turn to determine what we believe is sexy. Davies, Zhu, and Brantley (2007) found that we develop our own view of how sexy we believe we are from contact with others as well as media, but that media has a strong influence on whether or not we view ourselves as sexy.

Heterosexual women report being more interested in men with small buttocks and men who are slim and tall. "The favorite male physique had thin legs, a medium-thin waist, and a medium-wide chest" (G. Wilson and Nias 1976, 98). This description closely parallels the finding that heterosexual females preferred a thin male (Guy, Rankin, and Norvell 1980). Many wonder today, at a time when body building and being in shape has become more important, if this is still true. Heterosexual college women find a *buff* physique, meaning muscular with little to no fat, sexy. Think about what you prefer, since so much time has passed since these studies were done. If you are a heterosexual woman, what physical characteristics do you prefer in men? If you are a man, ask your heterosexual female friends what their preferences are. Do your findings bear out this research? Then consider beyond the research presented. If you are a homosexual woman, your preferences in determining attractiveness in men may be similar or different, since your standards may not be based on romantic interests. Compare your preferences with those of your heterosexual female friends; see if there are any similarities. You might be surprised at the outcome.

One way to determine what a heterosexual man finds appealing in a woman is to study various beauty contest winners. Another method is to determine each man's personality from standard personality tests. The characteristics desired by heterosexual men are correlated with their personalities (G. Wilson and Nias 1976). "Men who like large-breasted women were . . . active in sports and dated frequently. The men who opted for small breasts drank little, held fundamentalist religious beliefs, were submissive, and mildly depressed. The results suggested that large women attract men with a strong need for achievement who drink a lot, while petite women are pursued by persevering introverts" (p. 98). Of course, generalizing about heterosexual men's personalities by their choices in women would surely have its shortcomings, at least as far as accuracy is concerned. Again, if you are a heterosexual man, what do you prefer? If you are female, ask your heterosexual male friends what their preferences are. Do your findings bear out this research? If you are a homosexual man, what are your standards of attractiveness for women? Are they different from those of your heterosexual male friends, since your standards are not based on sexual interests?

Sex appeal is directly related to dating and marriage. Attractive college women tend to date more frequently, to have more male friends, to fall in love more often, and to have more sexual experiences than women of medium attractiveness. Walster, Aronson, Abrahams, and Rohmann (1966) conducted a study relating attractiveness and dating behavior. They considered many variables (height, race, self-esteem, academic rank, religious preferences, etc.), but physical attractiveness was by far the most important determinant of how much a date was liked by the partner and whether there would be subsequent dates. They further concluded that physical attractiveness is just as important of an asset for a man as for a woman. In the 1990s, when individual dating at the college level became almost obsolete and "group dating" was more the norm, there would undoubtedly be a few changes in these findings. Chances are good, however, that even groups that go out together for social interaction are based on attraction levels, including physical attractiveness.

A number of studies have supported a *similarity hypothesis*. That is, we tend to like those who do not distort our own view of ourselves (self-image) or who do not depreciate our own *(handwritten margin notes at top: "Similarity hypothesis" "we don't like those who don't match" "(depreciate) our level of attraction")*

level of attractiveness. Bailey and Schreiber (1981), for instance, found that college-age people like and desire to date partners who support or enhance their own self-view of physical attractiveness. They also found that heterosexual college students liked the opposite-sex person who matched their own level of physical attractiveness. Stretch and Figby (1980) found that people like physically attractive people better than unattractive ones and that males were more concerned with physical attractiveness than were females. Both of these studies were concerned with more immediate aspects of physical attractiveness, meaning how one sees attractiveness in the "here and now," not on a long-term basis. In addition, one study in the homosexual community discovered that this similarity hypothesis (homophily) was especially important for gay men when trying to determine suitability for relationships (Abel and Kruger 2011), although not as important for lesbian couples.

On a more long-term basis, two studies have established that physical attractiveness is also correlated with marital adjustment and success. J. L. Peterson and Miller (1980) studied middle-aged heterosexual couples and found that couples could be matched for physical attractiveness. Further, they found that attractiveness correlated with marriage adjustment; however, the correlation was stronger for husbands than for wives, meaning husbands mentioned it as a factor more often than wives did. R. M. Jones and Adams (1982) found that males perceived attractiveness as being more strongly associated with success for females than for males. They also found that for men and women, high self-assessed physical attractiveness was associated with the perceived importance of attractiveness to marriage selection and success for both sexes. Since we know that attractiveness is perceived, all of these studies need to be treated as relative and tied to the personal perceptions of the men and women who participated in them.

Finally, Tanke (1982) examined the heterosexual male stereotype for female physical attractiveness. She asked 204 male undergraduates to give their impressions of females of varying physical attractiveness. The result of her analyses was a four-dimensional model of attractiveness. Of the four factors she found, however, only "sexual/social excitement" was associated with physical attractiveness.

(handwritten margin notes: "sexual/social excitement" and "larger pupil size")

From these studies, it is fairly obvious that many factors influence sex appeal. Finkelstein and Walker (1976) conducted a study in which they concluded that larger pupil size of the eyes was perceived as more attractive than smaller pupil size. We must be careful, however, when examining pupil dilation research. Pupil dilation is regulated by the automatic nervous system, and we have very little control over it. Anything that we perceive as interesting will cause pupil dilation; this would include drawing an inside straight in poker, seeing someone we view as attractive, or seeing a piece of steak if we are hungry (Metalis and Hess 1982). The fact that we view dilated pupils as a sign of attractiveness goes back to the Middle Ages, when women used the drug belladonna to enlarge their pupils. Advertisers seem to take advantage of this attractiveness factor also. By "touching up" the size of the pupil in photographs of female models' eyes, they can create two "different" moods. The one with pupils dilated will probably be seen as more attractive and could sell emotional or nonlogical materials, whereas the constricted pupils would be more businesslike (A. S. King 1973). This topic is also taken up in Chapter 9, where other issues of eye behaviors are discussed.

PHOTO 5.3 (A), (B) AND (C) Johnny Depp, Brad Pitt, and George Clooney hold the record for being named *People* magazine's sexiest man alive. What factors do you think determined these men as having sex appeal? What makes someone sexy to you?

Other studies about physical attractiveness show many things. Kleinke and Staneski (1980) found that females with medium bust sizes were rated significantly higher in liking and personal attraction. Seiter and Dunn (2000) found that attractive females are more likely to be sexually harassed than unattractive ones. They also found that unattractive women are less likely to be believed when they report incidents of sexual harassment than attractive women are. Finally, Feiman and Gill (1978) showed that white males indicated a preference for lighter female skin coloration, whereas white females preferred darker skin coloration in men. Black and white North American males preferred lighter-colored black females over darker-colored black females (J. G. Martin 1964). With more education about skin health (e.g., the sun's role in skin cancer) and diversity issues, some of these findings have changed somewhat, although they probably have not changed exponentially (K. Thomas et al., 2011). For example, Sengupta (2000) more recently found that, at least for models in advertisements, race and the degree of darkness in the model's skin did not make a significant difference in evaluations of attractiveness for either black or white men. This may be different in face-to-face interactions, but the models used in ads still give a good picture of how men respond to differences in skin color, one that would be a change from the studies of the 1960s and 1970s. Today, with the election and re-election of an attractive, biracial U.S. president, with a lighter skin coloration, married to an attractive darker-skinned black woman, we will surely see some studies that change the view of what is attractive and sexy in other races. With the influx of the Latino population over the last 10 years, we no doubt will see some research about issues of coloration in that race, as well.

Whether one is sexually appealing or physically attractive, then, is dependent on a number of factors, probably the foremost being personal preferences of the individual making that judgment. One area where there is a paucity of research is in what homosexual men and women use for standards of attractiveness and whether or not those are correlated to what heterosexual men and women find attractive in potential romantic partners. We find research on issues such as use of touch and space, but there is a lack of research on physical attractiveness issues for the homosexual population. In the next sections, we focus on attractiveness factors as they relate to the body itself: body shape, body weight, and height. In addition, we discuss the importance of how people feel about their own bodies as well as their assessment of others' bodies.

STUDENT VOICES

Denna: Now on the topic of sex appeal, you might think it is listed on the job application and is a requirement to maintain employment. The combination of charm, self-confidence, personal style, intelligence, and the ability to mesmerize others sexually was summed up in one of my fellow employees, Katie. At 5'11" and hair that shampoo advertisers would pay some serious green for and legs that were digitally designed by a computer program, she is undoubtedly irresistible to the men around her. Her size and stature and electric green eyes are no match for the men that are eager to get an opportunity to get close to her. It is quite comical and embarrassing to witness as they stumbled over one another in an attempt to get her to notice them. She handles the situation with grace and charm and with an occasional smirk to her fellow cohorts.

BOX 5.4 OBSERVATIONAL STUDY

Choose a contemporary magazine for your gender (e.g., *Cosmopolitan, Men's Health, Vogue, Sports Illustrated, Elle, Maxim,* or whatever catches your attention that seems to be gender-based) and look at its advertisements.

What do the ads featuring sex appeal look like? What products are they selling? What messages do these ads send by their focus? Which products do you think would make you sexier?

THE BODY

We human beings notice the bodies of others. Males notice females, females notice males, and we observe the bodies of members of the same sex. Bodies are to be looked at. After all, body type is a prominent natural feature. Unlike a person's hair, face, eyes, or legs, the overall body shape can be observed and judged from a distance. It is vitally important in the formation of impressions. We must ask whether the stereotypes concerning body shape are true. Is the heavier person a jolly person? Is the well-built person a more adventurous person? Is the thinner person more nervous?

BODY SHAPE

Bodies can be classified according to their degree of muscularity, height, and weight. The three main body types are the endomorph, the mesomorph, and the ectomorph (Cortes and Gatti 1965). Although some feel that this research is dated, there still seems to be at least some degree of information we can glean from these body shapes and sizes, if for no other reason than to establish a starting point for how our body images effect our communication. Diagrams of the three body types and brief descriptions of each are listed in Figure 5.1.

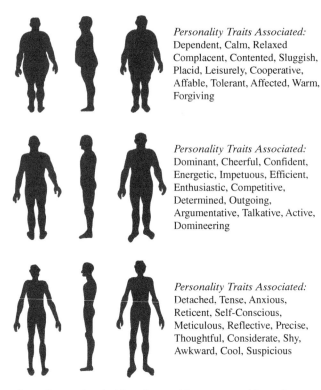

Personality Traits Associated:
Dependent, Calm, Relaxed
Complacent, Contented, Sluggish,
Placid, Leisurely, Cooperative,
Affable, Tolerant, Affected, Warm,
Forgiving

Personality Traits Associated:
Dominant, Cheerful, Confident,
Energetic, Impetuous, Efficient,
Enthusiastic, Competitive,
Determined, Outgoing,
Argumentative, Talkative, Active,
Domineering

Personality Traits Associated:
Detached, Tense, Anxious,
Reticent, Self-Conscious,
Meticulous, Reflective, Precise,
Thoughtful, Considerate, Shy,
Awkward, Cool, Suspicious

FIGURE 5.1 Personality traits associated with endomorphic, mesomorphic, and ectomorphic body types.

The **endomorphic** type is considered to be soft, plump, short, and round. The **mesomorphic** type is properly proportioned and athletic, trim, muscular, and average in height.

The **ectomorphic** individual has the tall, thin, frail body type. Because people can control their body weight and physical fitness, it is a popular assumption that body type is a message about individuals' personalities and interests.

Each body type encourages stereotyping by people in interpersonal situations. The endomorph is rated fatter, older, shorter, more old-fashioned, lazier, physically weaker, less good-looking, more good-natured, more agreeable, more dependent on others, and more trusting of others. The ectomorph is rated thinner, younger, more ambitious, taller, more suspicious of others, more tense and nervous, less masculine, more stubborn, more pessimistic, and quieter. The mesomorph is rated stronger, more masculine, better-looking, more adventurous, younger, taller, more mature, and more self-reliant (Lamb, Jackson, Cassiday, and Priest 1993). Some would argue that whether these stereotypes are true probably depends more on personalities than on body shape and size. It will take you, as critical thinkers, to discover your own answers to those arguments. Although we may examine the processes of stereotyping on the basis of possessing one of three body types, in reality we all have a little of each. In extreme cases there may be medical or psychological reasons for the body type—glandular problems, hypertension, or *anorexia nervosa* may have caused the particular body type. In many instances, however, we possess a combination of body types.

We can "measure" perceptions of our own body type (Millar and Millar 1976; J. K. Burgoon and Saine 1978, 76–77; Knapp 1978, 162–165). Sheldon proposes that we use a 1-to-7 scale for each of the three body types. At the low end (1 or 2), you possess none or very few of the characteristics defining that body type. At the high end (6 or 7), you possess many of those characteristics. For instance, a mesomorph would be rated something like this: endomorphism—2, ectomorphism—2, mesomorphism—6 or 7 (depending upon whether the individual is tall or compact). For long-distance runners, the ratings might go endo—1, ecto—6, meso—4. For an NFL lineman: endo—6, ecto—2, meso—5 or 6. Note that the endomorphic and ectomorphic traits tend to be bipolar.

STUDENT VOICES

Linda: One night around a fire pit, which is the central hub for a club we go to, a man fitting the endomorphic body description came and plopped down on the couch right next to me and began to share his life story. He struggled to light a cigarette [with one hand], trying to balance his beer in the other, and began to share the unfortunate circumstances he was handed throughout his 33 years of life. His body was frail and weathered, and at first I was hesitant to engage in any kind of conversation, immediately sensing he might be a little drunk. I personally enjoy meeting and conversing with new people from all walks of life; however, he was hindering and delaying my attention to the other scenarios taking place all around me. I listened to stories of how he was jilted and out of work for many years now. He was apparently intelligent and quite funny, and his conversation reeled me in for a short while. I finally had to excuse myself as my friends began to show up and I quickly wished him well. I had to get back to my comfort zone. To me, he fit the description of an endomorph; he was calm, relaxed, affable, and warm.

All the foregoing examples have dealt with men. How do women fit? The answer is, not very well. Most females would prefer a mesomorphic/ectomorphic body. This was brought out convincingly in the 1976 Olympics when a commentator asked the American female swimmers whether they would like to be more like the East Germans (who looked more masculine than some males, extremely mesomorphic); their almost unanimous response was "No!" They would rather look like a female. That would seem to hold true for today's society as well, although our female Olympic athletes do appear more mesomorphic and muscular, and thus more masculine, than they did more than 30 years ago.

In today's society, the media play an important role in how we perceive our bodies. White, Brown, and Ginsburg (1999) found some interesting facts when they surveyed prime-time television and afternoon soap operas. It is probably no surprise to you, but they found that women on television are "slimmer and more likely to wear revealing clothing than men" (p. 391) and that extremely thin and extremely heavy men and women are "less likely to wear revealing clothing or appear in romantic situations" (p. 391). White et al. were not alone in their findings; other researchers have discovered similar findings, namely that the media does influence how we think our bodies should look (Slevec and Tiggemann 2011; Bissell and Hays 2010). Luther (2009) found that this also occurs cross-culturally, in particular with Japanese teenagers. Does this carry over into actual society? Look around your classrooms and see if you can see the same. The researchers concluded, "[T]here is a lack of diversity in body types for women on television and an ideal is perpetuated. This ideal is more

TABLE 5.1   BODY TYPE AND GENDER BY REAL LIFE AND TV SAMPLE

Gender/Body Types	Real-Life Sample	Television Sample
Female Ectomorph	5.8%	7.7%
Female Ecto-mesomorph	25.5%	64.8%
Female Mesomorph	15.0%	14.8%
Female Meso-endomorph	28.3%	7.1%
Female Endomorph	25.0%	5.7%
Male Ectomorph	9.6%	4.9%
Male Ecto-mesomorph	10.6%	24.3%
Male Mesomorph	17.0%	37.9%
Male Meso-endomorph	47.9%	25.4%
Male Endomorph	14.9%	7.5%

Source: Adapted from White, S. E., Brown, N. J., & Ginsburg, S. L. (1999), Diversity of body types in network television programming: A content analysis. *Communication Research Reports*, 16(4), 390.

likely to be seen as attractive because of romantic interest and involvement and also because their bodies are more likely to be on display in tight clothing" (White et al., p. 391). If we survey our own society, outside the realm of the media, we would be likely to find the same results.

White et al. (1999) also found that television body types are significantly different from those of people in "real life." Table 5.1 shows you their findings: television body types are significantly thinner than real-life body types. Moriarty and Harrison (2008) found that television viewing of "ideal bodies" significantly predicted eating disorders for adolescent girls, but not for adolescent boys. If the media helps socialize us, it is easy to see the effect these body images can have on society. Issues such as eating disorders are one topic that deserves attention and further research in this area of study.

Finally, two studies indicate that perception of body type may correlate both positively and negatively. First, Lester (1981) found a positive correlation between suicide rate and endomorphism in 10 industrialized nations (as endomorphy increased, so did suicide); however, this held true only for males. A second study (Guy et al. 1980) found that meso-morphs were more often perceived as masculine. Interestingly, of the female perceivers, 56 percent found the ectomorph to be feminine, while only 25 percent found the meso-morph to be masculine. It would be interesting to see study results now, after the past few decades of almost all female supermodels or stars being ectomorphic and male ones being mesomorphic and buff.

WEIGHT AND ATTITUDE

Endomorphs and ectomorphs elicit negative reactions and teasing, whereas mesomorphs receive more positive reinforcement and are seen as more attractive. Along with the negative reactions that underweight or overweight children receive about their bodies, they also learn what behaviors are expected of them. Overweight children are supposed to be fragile and awkward. However, *Family Weekly* reported that extremely overweight children rated eight to ten points higher on IQ tests than did thin children.

In a study of prejudices toward weight conducted by Karris (1977), six male college students were divided into two groups. One male was obese; all the others were normal. Both groups visited 11 apartments available for rent. Five of the 11 landlords would not rent to the group including the obese male; three increased the rent; and two said the apartment had already been rented to someone else. Crandall (1991) found that overweight students received less financial support from parents than did other students. He indicated that this conclusion holds regardless of income, race, family size, or number of children attending college. Crandall concluded that this problem is attributable to stereotyping by parents, which generates what he calls an "anti-fat attitude." One might wonder if this statistic is not tied to the idea that endomorphs are often considered to be lazy and therefore are less likely to be successful in college. In a second study, Crandall (1995) found that the anti-fat attitude was similar to racism and suggested three commonalties between racism and "fatism." First, there is a similarity of values and beliefs and a rejection of those stereotyped. Second, he found an antipathy toward the rejected group. Third, he found a lack of self-interest among overweight participants. In other words, obese people were also prejudiced against other obese people. Have you ever experienced the phenomenon where you hear an overweight person disparage other overweight persons on the basis of their weight? Although Crandall felt that fatism was similar to racism, he found that the negativity was even greater in fatism.

In our society today, it does seem that fatism is more acceptable than any other "ism." Media fuels this by the models it presents as having an acceptable appearance for the public. Take, for example, how the media responded in 2013 to Princess Kate still having a "baby bump" when she and Prince William presented their newborn to the public on the steps of the hospital. How ridiculous was that to make those comments when she had given birth less than twenty-four hours earlier? This is an important aspect of nonverbal communication that we need to give attention to, lest we cause further stigmatization for overweight individuals.

In a sense, obese people are among the few against whom it remains socially acceptable to hold prejudices. Women feel weight is more important than do men; in addition, they also have more knowledge about obesity than do men (Harris, Waschull, and Walters 1990). Grugg, Sellers, and Waligroski (1993) found that among females depression was significantly correlated with rated body size. Self-esteem was related to perceived attractiveness. Baldaro et al. (2003) found that children who were suffering from obesity were less able to determine nonverbal emotions, and they also discovered that the mothers of these children were less able to decode the emotions of others. Even in health care situations, overweight patients report feeling less satisfied because of the responses they felt they received from health care providers (Merrill and Grassley, 2008). Clearly, obesity, which is so prevalent in our society today, does effect nonverbal communication.

College students' radical changes in eating habits often result in the opposite problem from being overweight, such as *anorexia nervosa* or *bulimia*. As a result, a number of studies have been conducted on eating attitudes and behavior. Brenner and Cunningham (1992), for instance, found that women displayed significantly more eating-disordered behavior than men. A. J. Hill, Oliver, and Rogers (1992), studying children and adolescents in Great Britain, found that dieting among females was related more to their perceived shape than to their actual body weight. They also found that children adopted their culture's perceptions of attractiveness by age 7. Interestingly enough, researchers have found similar effects about the ability to read nonverbal emotions that Baldaro et al. (2003) found with obese individuals. Zucker et al. (2013) discovered that individuals suffering from anorexia nervosa are less able to determine emotional nonverbal messages, and especially the emotions of sadness and anger.

One more recent area of research in the topic of body size is an area known as *fat talk*, meaning individuals who are likely to talk about their sizes and about dieting. Gapinski, Brownell, and LaFrance (2003) discovered that women who talked about being fat were more likely to self-objectify, which was then associated with more negative self-feelings as well as other negative outcomes (e.g., lower self-efficacy, lower intrinsic motivation, and diminished cognitive functioning). Craig, Martz, and Bazzini (2007) found that college-age females were likely to engage in fat talk when they were interacting with their peers as a form of impression management. Martz, Petroff, Curtin, and Bazzini (2009) found that women were more likely to engage in fat talk than men. This is not only a phenomenon in the United States, as Payne, Martz, Tompkins, Petroff, and Farrow (2011) found when they surveyed men and women in England and then made comparisons with the findings of the United States. In both countries, women are more likely to engage in fat talk than men. Finally, it needs to be noted that using *fat talk* is rarely a good thing for the health and well-being of the individuals using it. Arroyo and Harwood (2012) discovered that there are usually negative effects whenever individuals use *fat talk*. Since women are more likely to use it, think about the ramifications for women in our society. Think about your friends; who is more likely to engage in talk about their concerns of being overweight, your male friends or your female friends?

In an interesting study about how much we eat, Guarino, Fridrich, and Sitton (1994) measured subjects' conformity behavior while selecting food at a cafeteria. The situation was manipulated in terms of whether to have dessert. Women conformed to a confederate's behavior more than men did; women showed an even stronger tendency to conform to a same-gender confederate. In other words, if a female confederate is in line in front of another female, and the confederate selects a dessert, it is likely that the second female will also select a dessert.

C. D. Thomas (1991) studied the relationship of weight history (stable versus unstable) to body image and weight concerns of women. All of Thomas' participants were of average body weight at the time of the study. Thomas found that size and shape concerns were generally no different with a stable or unstable weight history; however, women with stable histories were more preoccupied with the size and shape of specific body parts. Neither group, however, was more likely to have been on diets or gained weight or lost weight within the past six months. H. J. Williams, Wagner, and Calam (1992) studied the eating attitudes of women who had encountered unwanted sexual experiences. They concluded that women who had had such experiences either overeat or undereat to ward off future unwanted advances. Brownwell (1991) and Gettleman and Thompson (1993) found similar results, and if we ask ourselves if we have found this to be true, either about ourselves or our friends, we would likely see some truth behind their findings.

Singh's (1993) studies focusing on waist-to-hip ratio (WHR) have added a whole new dimension to nonverbal communication research dealing with physical attractiveness. Singh's research has consistently shown that men find women with a lower WHR (a narrow waist and fuller hips) to be more attractive than those with a higher WHR (fuller waist and fuller hips). Singh also feels that this preference may not be a by-product of media messages about what women should look like but may be more of an innate issue. According to Singh, a low to moderate WHR would signal a healthier candidate to bear offspring, and so men may unconsciously choose this body shape and size. Psychologists have continued this line of study and have found similar results (Parsons, Manor, and Power, 2008). Also, some researchers are now studying if larger people, meaning those with a larger WHR, suffer from more stress when they reach middle age (Lasikiewicz, Hendrickx, Talbot, and Dye 2013). Lasikiewicz et al. discovered that people with higher WHR were subject to more stress, poorer memory function, and an overall decrease in cognitive functioning. As you can imagine, this adds even more to the debate we have discussed earlier about the nature-versus-nurture discussion in the nonverbal communication literature. It does not appear that this debate will be solved any time in the near future.

HEIGHT AND PERSONALITY

Although weight is a factor influencing how others perceive us, height is also a determinant. We look at people's heights to determine extroversion, attractiveness, self-esteem, status, and power, among other qualities. In a study by Elman (1977), college students were asked to assign trait ratings for a male college student on the basis of information in an application he purportedly filled out. When the form indicated that the applicant was tall, he was rated as more extroverted and attractive than when it was indicated that he was shorter.

Lechelt (1975) explored the possibility of a correlation of physical height and personal esteem within occupations such as accounting, clergy, clerk, and so forth. The results showed that males and females tended to rate the physical height of members of occupational groups similarly. Males' ratings of physical height and personal esteem were also highly positively correlated, meaning males who were tall rated their self-esteem as higher. Since we often think of tall males as being the norm, this should come as no surprise. Conversely, shorter men, since they do not meet the "norm," can suffer from low self-esteem, often known as the *Little Man Syndrome* or a *Napoleonic Complex* (Napoleon was a French emperor whose small stature, it is said, gave him the psychological need to conquer the world). You may have met some men labeled as such who always seem to be trying to prove themselves in one way or another. (Most men of shorter stature do not appreciate the reference to this phenomenon.)

There is a relationship between height and power, as Henley (1977) showed in her study of nursing students. The students were asked to estimate heights of known faculty and student members in their classes. The heights of staff members were overestimated, whereas the heights of students were underestimated. Similarly, when other undergraduates were asked to estimate the height of a man introduced to them as any one of five academic ranks, the estimated height increased as the ascribed status increased. The conclusion was that people infer that persons of higher status are taller than they actually are. The *New York Times* reported in 2008, that since 1900 the shorter of the presidential candidates had been elected seven times. The election of 2004, when George W. Bush defeated John Kerry, was the most recent case of the shorter person being elected, , since John Kerry is 6?4?. The election of 2008, however, returned us to the so-called norm, as Barack Obama is 6?1? and John McCain is 5?9?. Once again, for now an eighth time since 1900, in the election of Barack Obama in 2012, Obama was the shorter of the two candidates at 6? 1? and Mitt Romney is 6? 2? (Stulp, Buunk, Verhulst, and Pollet 2012). A survey at the University of Pittsburgh showed that shorter men are discriminated against with respect to job opportunities and salaries (Knapp 1978). In American society, at least in the past, there seems to have been a preference for the taller man.

Biernat (1993) studied kindergarten, third-grade, seventh-grade, tenth-grade, and college students. The students were asked to choose the taller of a series of male-female photographed pairs, which had been matched for height. At the end of the questionnaire, the participants answered questions concerning their beliefs about gender differences in height. They judged adult males as taller than adult females, but seventh-graders judged their seventh-grade peer females as taller than the males. The study supported the original hypothesis: that men are generally taller than women. Egolf and Corder (1991) found a similar result. They found that managers were perceived to be taller than non-managers; however, males were perceived as taller than females, regardless of job status. This stereotype seems to be normal for most people, regardless of how many shorter men or taller women they encounter.

BOX 5.5 OBSERVATIONAL STUDY

Watch your favorite television show. Take note of all the main characters and the lesser characters of the show, noting especially their body shapes and sizes, their weights, and their heights. Note personality traits tied to those characters. Do they seem to confirm the research findings reported here? If yes, how? If not, how do they differ?

BODY IMAGE

about how people perceive themselves

In day-to-day interactions, we do not typically describe ourselves as endomorphic, mesomorphic, or ectomorphic, or as any combination of the three. Rather, people tend to perceive their bodies in positive and negative terms, and they form attitudes toward their bodies that range from satisfied to dissatisfied. This is their *body image*. Body image is a concept that deals with the body as a "psychological experience" (S. Fisher and Cleveland 1968). Quite simply, it is how a person views his or her body, including his or her attitudes and feelings. Body image helps to explain personality characteristics of those who are physically handicapped. For example, after the loss of an arm, a person may become "motivated toward high achievement or develops negative feelings toward himself" (p. xi). A person's body image is both affected by and helps to influence others' perceptions of the personality, attractiveness, sexual activity, and other features of that individual.

PHOTO 5.4 In sharp contrast to the advertising industry standard that regularly alters models digitally to achieve unattainable perfection, Dove received worldwide attention for developing campaigns to combat negative body image.

NEGATIVE BODY IMAGE

The concept of body image developed from research in neurology. In their book, *Body Image and Personality*, S. Fisher and Cleveland (1968) described some fascinating distortions of the body. They reported instances in which a patient thought "his paralyzed leg belonged to the man in the next bed," felt that the left side of his body was "lined with iron making it too heavy to move," and believed his head to be "filled with bricks." They reported that some patients thought their left arms (which were paralyzed) were "strange, ugly, disfigured, artificial, enlarged, shapeless, thickened, shortened, or snake-like." One patient even believed that the left side of his trunk and limbs had been replaced with a board (pp. 3–8). Note that the negative body images became more object oriented, almost as if the patients were saying, "It's not a part of me; it's something added, like a hook." This psychological transformation was no doubt done to protect their self-image and esteem; if it were an object and not a part of them, then it did not have to be perceived as a positive or negative appearance factor.

Research in this area points out that people with negative body images have what Malandro, Barker, and Barker (1989) referred to as *body distortion* and they report reasons we are likely to understand for distorting their body images. The reason these theorists use the term "distortion" is simple. When persons have a negative body self-image, they are likely to have problems developing an accurate visualization of their appearance and, in particular, visualizing their physical features. Women are more likely to distort their body images (McCauley, Mintz, and Glenn 1988), which seems plausible since our culture places greater importance on women being physically attractive.

Regardless of these findings about negative body images, we need always to keep in mind that attractiveness is a perceived characteristic. We point this out numerous times because in our society it is easy to forget that point. When making self-evaluations, we apply the perceptions of what we think is attractive. Self-evaluations of attractiveness are simply a product of our own tastes and preferences, not any indisputable universal standard. Many people believe that we judge ourselves more harshly than others do, which leads us to an even more negative body image. This negative body image may be one of the main reasons for such issues as an increase in eating disorders, especially in women (Grugg et al. 1993). This type of harsh self-judgment is not likely to change much in the near future, especially since Americans continue to become more conscious of health and physical fitness. In addition, media's attention to this matter can also skew a person's self-judgment. Krcmar, Giles, and Helme (2008) discovered that exposure to the mediated images of fashion and fitness magazines had a negative effect on college-age women's image esteem. Many researchers today look at the effect of these mediated images (see also Silverstone 1990).

"NORMAL" BODY IMAGE

Not all the studies on body image have been as extreme as those cited. In 1973, Berscheid, Walster, and Bohrnstedt conducted a study on body image. Using a questionnaire, they surveyed approximately 62,000 readers of *Psychology Today* magazine to determine the relationship between body image and (1) attitudes, (2) self-esteem, and (3) experiences with the opposite sex.

Berscheid and her colleagues used 25 body parts to measure "satisfaction" with the body. Attitudes of overall body appearance and facial appearance were measured, as well as attitudes on hair, eyes, mouth, voice, complexion, extremities, torso, sex organs, height, and weight. Results indicated that only 7 percent of the females and 4 percent of the males responding to the questionnaire felt "extremely dissatisfied" with their body appearance. Twenty-three percent of the females and 15 percent of the males reported "slight dissatisfaction," whereas 45 percent of the females and 55 percent of the males were "extremely satisfied" with their body appearance. *The results indicated that fewer females than males were satisfied with their body appearance.* Women also felt that "physical attractiveness" was more important for social interaction than did males—32 percent and 24 percent, respectively. Results might be different if this same study were conducted in today's society, but chances are the results would be similar. Some 35 years later, Krcmar et al.'s (2008) study is a good example about how media affects this phenomenon. There would almost undoubtedly be a decrease in satisfaction due to the standards of acceptable appearance that exist today.

Considering the extent to which the American society emphasizes the importance of looking young and acting young, it could be assumed that older respondents would be more dissatisfied with their bodies than younger respondents. The results of the study by Berscheid and colleagues indicated that, in general, there were no significant satisfaction differences among respondents of varying ages, except that as males aged they became more satisfied with their body images, whereas females became less satisfied. These results have not changed in the forty years that has passed since that study was conducted (Balcetis, Cole, Chelberg, and Alicke 2013; Ashikali and Dittmar 2012).

In the facial area, the most dissatisfaction for both sexes was with the teeth, followed by complexion and hair. The most frequently indicated area of dissatisfaction for both males and females was in the torso area. Males were more dissatisfied with the size of the abdomen e <u>men,</u> abdomen

o <u>females</u>, hips

(47 percent) and buttocks (26 percent); females were most dissatisfied with the size of hips (71 percent), abdomen (69 percent), and buttocks (60 percent) (Berscheid et al. 1973).

Because of the emphasis placed on sex in our culture, it would be logical to assume that both sexes would be concerned with the size or appearance of their sex organs. According to the Berscheid et al. (1973) results, however, only one in four women reported some dissatisfaction with breasts. Of that quarter, only 9 percent were very dissatisfied. In addition, 15 percent of the males reported being worried about penis size, and 6 percent of those were very dissatisfied. An exception among male respondents was homosexuals. Male homosexuals reported a greater concern with size of their sex organs than did heterosexual males. No such distinction was found between female homosexuals and heterosexuals.

We would be remiss if we did not mention that the respondents in the Berscheid et al. (1973) study were self-selected. Had the survey been designed for a more random sampling, results could be relied upon for more accuracy. Still, these findings do give us some idea of how a specific population (those who read *Psychology Today*) views its body image, and allow us to compare their opinions to how we feel about these same physical characteristics of our own.

Studies by Berscheid 3 Klenke & Staluski!

In another study concerning attractiveness of body parts—this one in a more controlled setting—Lerner and Brackney (1976) asked males and females to judge the attractiveness of their own body parts. Their findings showed that men gave their highest mean scores to eyes, teeth, general appearance, and face. The lowest scores among males were for ankles and hair. Females gave their highest scores for eyes, general appearance, and teeth, whereas their lowest scores were for hair color, ankles, and height. It was further determined that females consistently rated their body parts higher than males, demonstrating a higher overall satisfaction with body parts. This finding seems to contradict, to some extent, the conclusions of Berscheid et al., perhaps because of the method of determining the sample population for study.

A study by Kleinke and Staneski (1980) related female bust size and first impressions. Males and females rated color photographs of females exhibiting small, medium, or large bust sizes. Major findings were that females with large bust sizes were consistently evaluated as being relatively unintelligent, incompetent, immoral, and immodest. Such findings are interesting in light of the fact that everyone knows intellectually that breast size has nothing to do with intelligence, competence, morality, or modesty, but people nevertheless attach personal judgments such as these to other's appearance. It also opens up some questions about the issue of breast augmentation. We wonder, if those who seek this procedure knew that this was the evaluation they would receive, would they still decide to have the operation? Surely, many would, especially if being sexually attractive is the person's main goal, but there might be others who would think twice about it.

satisfaction or dissatisfaction norms

The major emphasis in these studies of body image indicates that there is something we can use as a norm to judge satisfaction or dissatisfaction with our bodies. Several studies have found that body image perceptions may be affected by other factors. Lucker, Beane, and Helmreich (1981), for instance, note that sexiness, femininity, masculinity, and liking all have a strong correlation with physical attractiveness, especially for females. These factors are all closely related to body image. Higdon (1982), examining paranoid schizophrenic, non-paranoid schizophrenic, and nonschizophrenic females found that "in females, the paranoid phenomena may result from some factor such as a feeling of deficiency" (p. 399) in female attractiveness. Markham-Shaw and Edwards (1997) found that "university students stereotypically associate the adjective 'attractive' with women and 'independent' with men" (p. 60). Clearly, gender is one of those areas that affects perception of attractiveness.

BOX 5.6 OBSERVATIONAL STUDY

Open the same magazine you used in Observational Study 5.4, but this time consider body image. How many products advertised in the magazine are to enhance a person's body image? How many articles in that same magazine are concerned with improving your body image?

FURTHER ISSUES OF BODY IMAGE

Although the size of sex organs may not be extremely important to body image, body image is important to sexual behavior. Berscheid and associates (1973) report that positive body image results in (1) more sexual partners, (2) more sexual activity, and (3) greater enjoyment in sexual relationships. Negative body image results in difficulty relating to the opposite sex. According to Berscheid and associates, bachelors have more complaints about their body appearance than do married males. Apparently, unmarried males are more concerned with sexual performance; the lower their body image score, the more they feel that some body feature made them poor sexual partners and the more dissatisfied they were about penis size and shape. No such "satisfaction" distinction was found among married and unmarried females. It was further determined from the study that satisfaction with body appearance among males and females increased slightly for those reporting having had sexual relationships with 10 or more partners. Pujols, Meston, and Seal (2010) found that body image was an important aspect of women feeling sexually attractive and that this self-image was related to sexual functioning and sexual satisfaction. Whether the feeling of satisfaction came from the feeling of success in attracting others to be sexual partners or from personal body image is another question that should probably be answered in future studies.

Cash, Winstead, and Janda (1986) replicated Berscheid and associates' study in 1985–1986. They found that women were still less satisfied with their bodies' overall appearance than were men. Their findings supported the idea that women are more critical of their bodies than men are. The 1985 respondents were more dissatisfied with their bodies than the 1972 respondents, which, as mentioned earlier, may come from the change in society's emphasis (through advertisements, entertainment, media, and so forth) on a more ectomorphic female and a more mesomorphic male (White et al. 1999). In a related study, Cash, Noles, and Winstead (1985) found that individuals with a poor body image reported greater depression than individuals with moderate or high levels of body image. They also found that others do not perceive depressed people as less attractive than nondepressed people. They did find, however, that depressed people distorted their body images in a negative direction, whereas nondepressed people distorted their body images in a positive direction. Additional studies by Prabu, Liu, and Cortese (2003) support the contention that women overestimate their body weight and that women believe men have a greater desire for thin women than they actually do. Prabu et al. (2003) found that women who observed "plus-sized" models rated their body shapes to be slightly heavier. Cash and Green (1986) found that overweight participants did not differ significantly from others in estimating their own body size. Underweight subjects, however, significantly *overestimated* their own body size. The latter finding is consistent with research conducted by J. K. Thompson (1986), in which he found that 95 percent of women overestimate their body size. Cheeks, waist, thighs, and hips were most often found overestimated.

As reported earlier, the body image problem is especially important to those with eating disorders such as anorexia nervosa and bulimia. Not eating is just one way some people attempt to change the body to meet with the body image. This has become such an issue in the last two decades, especially for young adult females, that people have begun to criticize advertisers, movie producers, and so forth, for the public image created for the "ideal" woman. Goodman (2005) discovered that media pressure, along with peers' dieting talk and behaviors, had the greatest influence on individuals' awareness and understanding of what is thin, as well as about social comparison of the self to others, which then influenced individuals' dissatisfaction with their own bodies, often leading to eating disorders. In a recent study, Miller-Day and Marks (2006) discovered that parental communication that encourages the child to conform to parental directives, and in particular communication between the father and his children (both sons and daughters), may increase the child's likelihood of developing eating disorders. Arnold and Doran (2007) also studied parental effects on children, but their study looked at how mothers who had suffered from eating disorders themselves affected their children's eating behaviors. Moriarty and Harrison (2008) also looked at the effect television exposure has on eating habits of children. They discovered that television exposure was important to look at when trying to discover why both black and white preadolescent girls were more predisposed to eating disorders than preadolescent boys. Clearly, the area of eating disorders has received a great deal of attention in the last decade and will no doubt continue to be researched. Perhaps this is an area that interests you to conduct some research on your own.

[handwritten margin note: Eating disorders]

While most research has found that women are more dissatisfied with weight than men, C. Davis and Cowles (1991) found that men were equally dissatisfied with their weight. While women wanted to lose weight, men were equally divided between those who wanted to lose and those who wanted to gain weight. Age was not a significant factor. In terms of physical attractiveness, sexiness, body image, and body shape, we should not leave this area of research without reporting some other interesting studies. Age and physical attractiveness are areas that, if we have inspired you in any way to do research studies in nonverbal communication, are wide open for investigation. You might conduct studies into what has created these body images for both men and women. This would help add to the body of knowledge on this important topic.

We cannot move on from the topic of body image and human beings without considering how humor is used in the area of body image and physical appearance. Futch and Edwards (1999) asked 202 college students to assess scenarios where a response could be made with either humor or defensiveness. As Futch and Edwards discovered, appearance and weight are sensitive issues for women; although both men and women can find humor in some "comments made about their hair and eating a lot" (p. 94), men and women found those types of comments to be "more humorous than comments concerning their clothing"

(p. 94). Egan, Harcourt, and Rumsey (2011) also found that one of the most common coping techniques is to use humor when it comes to body image. One interesting gender difference, which may surprise some of you, is that "women responded more humorously than men to messages regarding physical and mental errors" (Futch and Edwards, 1999, 93). Suffice it to say that you should be aware of issues that some people do not find funny when you are making attempts at humor based on people's physical appearance. Consider what you personally appreciate when people tease you about your physical appearance. Ask yourself, "Would I find this to be humorous if someone said it to me?" and then act accordingly.

Cann (1991) studied the circumstances of individuals in a work situation and observed three things. First, those who had high social and professional competence received higher ratings of attractiveness. Second, competent individuals were rated as being taller. And, finally, socially competent females were rated as both being taller and thinner. In essence, this study supports the view that if you are competent, then you will be perceived as more attractive. In another study, Brownlow (1992) tested the persuasiveness of people based on whether they were "baby-faced" or "mature-faced." She found that baby-faced persuaders were more effective when trustworthiness was in question, but mature-faced persuaders were more effective when expertise was in question. All of this says that you need to know and understand the values of your expertise and your perceived physical attractiveness to be more effective communicators.

EFFECTS OF PLASTIC SURGERY

People who are dissatisfied with their appearance have the option to change it through plastic surgery, of which there are two basic kinds: (1) cosmetic or aesthetic surgery, which refers to improvements of the artistic and natural beauty of the face or body, such as face lifts, breast augmentation, liposuction, and now Botox injections; and (2) reconstructive surgery, which refers to repair of congenital or acquired defects such as cleft palates or scars (Dicker and Syracuse 1976).

PHOTO 5.5 The staggering increase in men obtaining cosmetic procedures seems to contradict the assumption that women are far more concerned about their appearance than are men. Explain this discrepancy.

People who are dissatisfied with their appearance and consult plastic surgeons have been remarkably consistent in their agreement as to what constitutes beauty (Wein 2002). Many such dissatisfied people may seek advice from several surgeons and attempt drastic changes to "improve" their appearance (Mirivel 2008). Sometimes these individuals have low self-esteem, grandiose ambitions too difficult to achieve, and vagueness concerning exactly what it is they are hoping to achieve. Frequently, plastic surgeons refer those patients to psychiatrists. By the beginning of the 21st century, it was clear that not all patients who seek cosmetic surgery need psychological treatment. Sarwer, Pertschuk, Wadden, and Whitaker (1998b) report that among those seeking plastic surgery, it is likely that there are as many people one would refer to as "mainstream Americans" as there are people with psychological problems. These days, plastic surgery has become more commonplace; it is seen as just another means of improving physical appearance (Jordan, 2004). The Sarwer et al. study does present questions for further study, and those are the questions that we look at here, as they apply to physical appearance and its relation to communication.

The motivation of the average patient seeking plastic surgery may arise from either internal or external pressures (Edgerton and Knorr 1971). External pressures include (1) a need to please others, (2) paranoid ideation (belief that he/she would please others), and (3) personal or social ambitions that seem obstructed because of personal appearance. The patient who is motivated primarily by *external pressures* might well be disappointed after surgery because the real cause of the patient's problem often is not a defect in personal appearance but is a much deeper-rooted psychological issue. The patient who is motivated by *internal pressures* is more likely to feel satisfied with the subsequent change in appearance. The most common inner motivations are depression and a sense of inadequacy. As a general rule, Erickson and Billick (2012) found that patients who were trying to align their physical appearance with their personal body image were most satisfied with the outcome.

Leathers (1976) inferred that plastic surgery results in changes in communication behavior. He reported a series of discussions and interviews with plastic surgeons, which reveal such changes in terms of self-image, body image, and communicative behavior. The following excerpt reflects the drastic changes that may occur after plastic surgery:

> Typically the change in communicative behavior after plastic surgery seems to manifest itself in a drastic reduction in inhibitions and in an openness, candor, and trusting type of behavior which is the ideal sought by so many authorities in interpersonal communication. For example, before plastic surgery some women with small breasts (those who later resort to plastic surgery) seem to "have a behavioral disorder . . . they will never dress or undress in front of women . . . [and] are very bashful in front of men. After surgery for breast augmentation, however, a stunning change in behavior takes place." (Leathers 1976, 107)

The same may be true of less dramatic changes such as having teeth capped, using "elevators" in shoes, simply changing hair color, or getting Botox® or Restylane® treatments to reduce facial lines or liposuction to decrease body fat. When these changes are made, modification of body parts leads to a new "personality"—or at least individuals begin to act the way they think that improved type of person would act. For instance, the Leathers study went on to say that the women with the breast augmentation surgery "undress at the drop of a hat in front of everybody" (p. 107). Although that surely is overgeneralized or exaggerated, it does seem plausible that they might well be less conscious of their "shortcomings" when they perceive that they no longer have what they perceived as a deficiency in the size of their breasts. It appears that in the early part of the new century the most requested and performed *aesthetic surgery* (what plastic surgeons have named cosmetic surgery) was liposuction. Matarasso and Hutchinson (2001) reported that the increase in the number of people requesting and obtaining liposuction had increased in staggering numbers in the preceding decade. The number of people obtaining liposuction had increased 27 percent since 1997. Between 1992 and 1998, the increase for women was 270 percent; for men it had increased 300 percent (Matarasso and Hutchinson 2001). The "Botox Party" scene was the next phenomenon that added a whole new dimension to the acceptability of plastic surgery. In April of 2002, The Food and Drug Administration (FDA) approved Botox® for use in some cosmetic surgery situations, most commonly for injections into the wrinkles on people's faces and hands, wrinkles due to natural aging or sun damage (C. Lewis 2002). At the start of the availability of Botox®, and because it was so readily available and easy to give and receive treatments, people were even holding "plastic surgery events," which include seminars, evening socials, and other gatherings, where doctors came and performed the Botox injections in the privacy of people's homes, or even held such gatherings in their offices. C. Lewis reported that one plastic surgeon even hosted "Botox Happy Hours" in his medical office (C. Lewis 2002). The concept of a gathering for this procedure allowed for groups of patients to attend and the procedure was made more affordable for each of them. *CBS* (2013) reported that today the most commonly requested plastic surgery is for breast augmentation; liposuction has slipped to fourth place, and Botox was nowhere in the rankings.

In recent years, more and more attention has been paid to the media's effect on the use of cosmetic enhancements. Nabi (2009) believed that an increase in reality television programs that highlighted "makeovers" (e.g., *What Not to Wear* and *Extreme Weight Loss*) created a situation of the public having unrealistic expectations of plastic surgery (see also Tait 2007). Conners (2007) believed that the public should be concerned about the ethics of such programs as they focus more on the positive outcomes than on the risks of surgery of any type. She felt that the programs focused more on the satisfaction the patient would attain after the surgery than perhaps other issues that need to be paid attention to. Conversely, Cho (2007) reported that the news media paid more attention to the safety and health hazards when covering news stories concerning plastic surgery. One can believe, however, that the stories about the positive aspects of cosmetic surgery receive more attention than those stories that deal with the risks and safety hazards.

The overall conclusions concerning the motivations for plastic surgery are that a change in physical appearance alters the very foundation of personality function: the physical or body image. Plastic surgery results in a change in the reflexive image, the self-image, and in the communication behavior of the patient (Castle, Honigman, and Phillips 2002). Plastic surgery is one of the means of voluntarily making changes in one's physical appearance that also tends to affect one's body image. Some physical (and social) disabilities are more difficult to overcome. We often refer to these as stigmas.

BOX 5.7 OBSERVATIONAL STUDY

How does the stigma of being physically unattractive operate in society? Find a friend whom you believe is physically attractive, and ask him or her to serve as a "confederate" in a study for you. Ask him or her to do whatever he or she usually does to enhance physical appearance and attractiveness. Then, stand somewhere public and have your friend ask people, "Can you tell me the time?" Afterwards, ask your "confederate" to discuss how he or

she felt when engaged in conversation with the people he or she engaged. Discuss what you and the person think might have happened had he or she been stigmatized as being physically unattractive. If possible, talk your "confederate" into doing the other side of this—do whatever it takes to make himself or herself physically unattractive and try the experiment again—in the same public space. Then discuss any differences in treatment either you or the confederate perceive.

STIGMAS

The concept of stigma was introduced in Chapter 4. As stated earlier, one "possessing an attribute that makes him different from others in the category of persons available for him to be, and of a less desirable kind—in the extreme, a person who is quite thoroughly bad, or dangerous, or weak" is one who possesses a stigma (Goffman 1963, p. 184). People who exhibit stigmas include psychiatric patients, ex-convicts, divorced women, obese individuals, prostitutes, wheelchair victims, AIDS victims, and blind people, to name just a few.

Stigmatization can have dramatic negative effects on an individual, especially if the stigma is physically evident. It may interfere with the stigmatized person's attempts to achieve steady and essential interpersonal relationships with others. The stigma may be a source of embarrassment for the individual and may encourage the person to avoid interactions that might reveal the stigma. A second effect of stigmatization is that the individual may develop a sense of guilt regarding the affliction. Guilt may arise particularly if the source of the stigma is believed to be within the control of the individual. If a stigma lasts for a long time, the individual is usually forced to alter his or her self-concept.

The central problem for the stigmatized person is how to attain "acceptance" from others. One method of seeking acceptance is to associate with "sympathetic others." These "others" are individuals who either share the stigma or accept it. A second method of coping involves the use of *disidentifiers*, methods of de-emphasizing one's handicap. Another technique for gaining acceptance from others is "passing." The individual who attempts to pass tries to pretend that he or she is not stigmatized. If the stigma is not severe, the individual may be able to pass as one who is not afflicted by a stigma and therefore, may be perceived as "normal" (Goffman 1963).

Nonstigmatized individuals are cautious when interacting with those perceived as having stigmas. Worthington's (1974) study, which was mentioned briefly in Chapter 3, is an example of this phenomenon. Worthington found that individuals had a willingness to help stigmatized persons, but they did not wish to "catch" whatever the stigmatized experimenter had.

In a related study, Barrios, Corbitt, Estes, and Topping (1976) found that individuals preferred to maintain an increased distance between themselves and a person with what they perceived to be a social stigma (in this case, bisexuality). This perceived stigma, therefore, had a dramatic effect on the proxemic behavior of individuals as well as the stigmatized individual's overall acceptance by others. Young, Henderson, and Marx (1990) found that nursing students had more negative attitudes toward homosexual AIDS patients than toward heterosexual AIDS patients. Rintamaki, Scott, Kosenko and Jensen (2007) found that people really do treat HIV/AIDS-infected persons in a nonverbally disdainful way, including subtle cues (avoiding eye contact, for example) to actual physical abuse. Merrill and Grassley (2008) reported that obese patients struggle to maintain their health care relationships, since many health care providers discriminate against them based on their obesity. Regardless of what the perceived stigmas were, in these studies people maintained their proxemic distances from the persons with the perceived stigmas.

We expand in this section upon Goffman's notion of stigma by noting that people in American culture who are not physically attractive are generally stigmatized. Although this area has been only tangentially researched in terms of attractiveness, there is a body of research suggesting that stigmas associated with lack of physical attractiveness may go much further than we think. Many of us can remember the buxom female who developed before others in high school or even in junior high. She was stigmatized for bust size in a rather negative way. Many of us can also recall the way a boy in high school was stigmatized for being too short. Stigmatization can be looked at in other instances. Adamczyk (2010) discovered that people often consider themselves to be physically ugly, and that people are treated accordingly due to that stigma of being considered less attractive than others. To look at a different type of physical stigma, in Wisconsin in 1977, the electorate recalled a judge because he noted that a female who had been raped was "looking for it" by the way she dressed (Woliver 1990). Obviously, the judge labeled the victim with a stigma, in this instance that of what he considered a prostitute or a "loose woman." Hopefully in today's society this would not happen, but it is historically where our country stood on the issues at one point in time. Interestingly, today the American culture is one of the few that legally recognizes this appearance factor as not being a stigma. For example, recently a group from an American university studying in Germany for the summer encountered this problem. The police refused to listen to a young woman's complaint of a "near sexual assault" because she was dressed provocatively and had been drinking. They likened these two factors to her "asking for it," and they would not take a report of any crime. As you know, in the United States sexual assault would be charged, regardless of how the woman was dressed or how much she'd had to drink.

A second area of stigmatization is described in research that examines compliance with a request. Much like Worthington's (1974) earlier research, these studies indicated that people are more likely to help or comply with the request of an attractive person (Kanekar, Mayundar, and Kolsawalla 1981). Other studies have examined the attribution process in courtroom trial situations. In almost every case, physical attraction was found to correlate with outcome. In a study presenting a hypothetical rape case in which the defendant was either physically attractive or unattractive, Dietz and Byrnes (1981) found a direct relationship between the amount of attractiveness and the defendant's ability to "manipulate" the jury. As attractiveness increased, so too did the defendant's influence. Lawyers, of course, coach their clients to appear attractive during a trial just for this reason, dressing up for the court session, cutting hair, shaving or trimming beards, and so forth. Finally, Hocking, Walker, and Fink (1982) reported that attractive females were perceived by a jury to be less

Stigmas as attractiveness

moral than unattractive females under the same immoral conditions. As with Stacks' (1983b) earlier findings, physical attractiveness does have its drawbacks, and these drawbacks can cause major communication problems.

In general, the relationship between physical attractiveness and a variety of outcomes resembles an inverted U. As physical attractiveness increases, outcomes are generally more positive; however, at some point the person becomes "too attractive" and is no longer provided the same positive rewards. This person, then, may be stigmatized by being too beautiful. Perhaps moderation is best, with just a little enhancement of one's physical attributes and endowments. After considering the ads in magazines for Observational Studies 5.4 and 5.6, however, you can probably see that the media in the United States (or at least the advertising portion of them) do not want to settle for "just a little enhancement."

Stigmas are often difficult to overcome through physical change. Most people with stigmas compensate through their interactions with others. Nevertheless, almost everyone wishes to make some changes in physical appearance from time to time. These changes are typically less drastic than undergoing plastic surgery but more involved than a change of clothing. Such changes can be made through **body alterations and coverings**, which are discussed in Chapter 6: hairstyle, skin changes, and additions.

FUNCTIONS

Physical appearance is one of the most significant aspects of nonverbal communication when it comes to *identification* and *self-presentation*. A person's appearance is often seen as a key to interaction, with many people interpreting how we look as keys to our personalities. Research has demonstrated that the way you present yourself physically—your body image in particular—significantly influences others' desires to interact with you; therefore, the way you look in general serves to *control the interaction* a great deal, especially in initial interactions among strangers. *Cognitive or instructional information* is also provided by our bodies—our shape, height, and weight—regarding personality cues and perceptions of sexuality. *Affective information*, or information about how we feel, is clearly indicated by how we "keep" our bodies and is found in the stigmas attached to negative body characteristics. Finally, we *deceive* others through our physical appearance, often using socially acceptable stereotypes dealing with expected behaviors based on our body type and shape. We look at how body alterations and coverings affect these functions in Chapter 7.

SUMMARY

This area of nonverbal communication is one most of us feel uncomfortable discussing as a part of our communication, probably because we have been taught all our lives that to "judge a book by its cover" is neither accurate nor productive. We do, unfortunately, make judgments of others based on their appearance, whether it is done consciously or subconsciously. If we know some of the factors discussed here and in the next chapter, perhaps these issues will have fewer negative effects on our communication with others.

This chapter has focused on the impact of the body as part of the physical attraction or appearance subcode. While previous chapters have examined the impact of environmental aspects of nonverbal communication (environment, space, territory, touch), physical appearance deals with a social dimension—something that we, as communicators, manipulate with certain gains in mind. Because physical appearance is the first nonverbal cue to be noticed, it will have a profound impact on your relationships with others. Physical appearance communicates "meaning," and many stereotypes are based on our first impressions of others' body shape and body image. The fact that our physical appearance is a major development in our self-image underscores its importance in healthy personal development. Chapter 7 explores an additional dimension of physical appearance—how we alter our body through clothing, cosmetics, artifacts, and additions.

QUESTIONS FOR THOUGHT

1. Just how important are body shape, weight, and height in your daily interactions? Why?
2. Are the stereotypes based on body type really true today? Do people you know change after they have gained or lost weight? After they have worked out at the gym?
3. Body image can have significant impact on how we interact with others. Where have you observed this, and what impact has it had? Focus in particular on how body image affects first impressions and initial contacts with strangers.
4. The plastic surgery industry is one of the fastest growing industries in the world. Given the aging of our society, what societal impacts can you envision coming from plastic surgery? Are they "good," "bad," or "indifferent" in regards to communication norms and expectations?
5. Is there a true stereotype for "beauty"? If so, is it pan-cultural, or do our stereotypes for beauty change by culture?

FURTHER REFERENCES

Importance of Physical Appearance

Adams, G. R., and Crossman, S. M. (1978). *Physical attractiveness: A cultural imperative*. Roselyn Heights, NY: Libra.

Bloch, P. H., and Richins, M. L. (1993). Attractiveness, adornments, and exchange. *Psychology and Marketing*, 6, 467–470.

Dion, E., Berschied, E., and Walster, E. (1972). What is beautiful is good. *Journal of Personality and Social Psychology*, 24 (2), 285–290.

Hu, F., and Wang, M. (2009, November). *Beauty and fashion magazines and college-age women's appearance-related concerns*. Paper presented at the National Communication Association, Chicago, IL.

Kang, Y., and Hamilton, M. (2003, May). *The effect of sex appeal on believability, attitude toward the advertisement and brand, and purchase intention*. Paper presented at the meeting of the International Communication Association, San Diego, CA.

Malandro, L. A., Barker, L. L., and Barker, D. (1989). *Nonverbal communication* (2nd ed.). Reading, MA: Addison-Wesley.

Molloy, J. T. (1975). *Dress for success*. New York: Warner.

Molloy, J. T. (1978). *The woman's dress for success book*. New York: Warner Books.

Molloy, J. T. (1988). *The new dress for success book*. New York: Warner Books.

Molloy, J. T. (1996). *New women's dress for success book.* New York: Warner Books.

Nitz, M., Reichert, T., Aune, A. S. and Velde, A. V. (2007). All the news that's fit to see? The sexualization of television news journalists as a promotional strategy. *Journal of Promotion Management*, 13, 13–33.

Patzer, G. L. (1985). *The physical attractiveness phenomena.* New York: Plenum.

Ye, Y., and Zhou, S. (2006, June). *Is it the content or the person? Examining sexual content in promotional announcements and sexual self schema.* Paper presented at the meeting of the International Communication Association, Dresden, Germany.

Social Interaction

Back, M. D., Schmukle, S. C., and Egloff, B. (2010). Why are narcissists so charming at first sight? Decoding the narcissism-popularity link at zero acquaintance. *Journal of Personality & Social Psychology*, 98, 132–145.

Burgoon, J. K., and Jones, S. B. (1976). Toward a theory of personal space expectations and their violations. *Human, Communication Research*, 2, 131–146.

DeBono, K. G., and Harnish, R. J. (1988). Source expertise, source attractiveness, and the processing of persuasive information: A functional approach. *Journal of Personality and Social Psychology*, 55, 541–550.

Friedman, H. S., Riggio, R. E., and Casella, D. F. (1988). Nonverbal skill, personal charisma, and initial attraction. *Personality and Social Psychology Bulletin*, 14, 203–211.

Kalick, S. M. (1988). Physical attractiveness as a status cue. *Journal of Experimental Social Psychology*, 24, 469–489.

O'Grady, K. E. (1989). Physical attractiveness, need for approval, social self-esteem, and maladjustment. *Journal of Social and Clinical Psychology*, 8, 62–69.

Rubin, M., and Sabatelli, R. (1986). Nonverbal expressiveness and physical attractiveness as mediators of interpersonal perceptions. *Journal of Nonverbal Behavior*, 10, 120–133.

Zakahi, W. R., and Duran, R. L. (1988). Physical attractiveness as a contributing factor to loneliness: An exploratory study. *Psychology Reports*, 63, 747–751.

Sex Appeal

Beatty, J. (1977). Activation and attention in the human brain. In M. C. Wittrock (Ed.), *The human brain* (pp. 63–85). Englewood Cliffs, NJ: Prentice-Hall.

Hess, E. H. (1975). The role of pupil size in communication. *Scientific American*, 222, 110–119.

Hess, E. H., and Polt, J. M. (1960). Pupil size as related to interest value of visual stimuli. *Science*, 132, 349–350.

Janisse, M. P., and Peavler, W. S. (1974). Pupillary research today: Emotion in the eye. *Psychology Today*, 7, 60–73.

Kang, Y., and Hamilton, M. (2003, May). *The effect of sex appeal on believability, attitude toward the advertisement and brand, and purchase intention.* Paper presented at the meeting of the International Communication Association, San Diego, CA.

Nitz, M., Reichert, T., Aune, A. S. and Velde, A. V. (2007). All the news that's fit to see? The sexualization of television news journalists as a promotional strategy. *Journal of Promotion Management*, 13, 13–33.

Taylor, L. D. (2008). Cads, dads, and magazines: Women's sexual preferences and articles about sex and relationships. *Communication Monographs*, 75, 270–289.

Wrench, J. S., and Knapp, J. L. (2008). The effects of body image perceptions and sociocommunicative orientations on self-esteem, depression, and identification and involvement in the gay community. *Journal of Homosexuality*, 55, 471–503.

Ye, Y., and Zhou, S. (2006, June). *Is it the content or the person? Examining sexual content in promotional announcements and sexual self schema.* Paper presented at the meeting of the International Communication Association convention, Dresden, Germany.

Body Shape

Fay, M., and Price, C. (1994). Female body-shape in print advertisements and the increase in anorexia nervosa. *European Journal of Marketing*, 28, 5–18.

Millar, D. P., and Millar, F. E. (1976). *Messages and myths*. New York: Alfred Publishing.

Sheldon, W. H. (1942a). *The varieties of human physique*. New York: Harper and Row.

Sheldon, W. H. (1942b). *The varieties of temperament*. New York: Harper and Row.

Sheldon, W. H. (1954). *Atlas of man: A guide for somatyping the adult male at all ages*. New York: Harper and Row.

Weight and Attitude

Brown, I., and Thompson, J. (2007). Primary care nurses' attitudes, beliefs, and own body size in relation to obesity management. *Journal of Advanced Nursing*, 60, 535–543.

Furnham, A., and Dias, M. (1998). The role of body weight, waist-to-hip ratio, and breast size in judgments of female attractiveness. *Sex Roles*, 39, 311–327.

Ogden, J., and Clementi, C. (2010). The experience of being obese and the many consequences of stigma. *Journal of Obesity*, 2010, 1–9.

Pliner, P., and Chaiken, S. (1990). Eating, social motives, and self-presentation in women and men. *Journal of Experimental Social Psychology*, 26, 240–254.

Portnoy, E. J. (1993). The impact of body type on perceptions of attractiveness by older individuals. *Communication Reports*, 6, 101–108.

Tassinary, L. G., and Hansen, K. A. (1998). A critical test of the waist-to-hip-ratio hypothesis of female physical attractiveness. *Psychological Science*, 9, 150–156.

Body Image

Avery, A. Pallister, C., Allan, J., Stubbs, J., and Lavin, J. (2012). An initial evaluation of a family-based approach to weight management in adolescents attending a community weight management group. *Journal of Human Nutrition and Dietetics*, 25, 469–476.

Brenner, J. B., and Cunningham, J. G. (1992). Gender differences in eating attitudes, body concept, and self-esteem among models. *Sex Roles*, 27, 413.

Elliott, R., and Elliott, C. (2005). Idealized image of the male body in advertising: A reader-response exploration. *Journal of Marketing Communications*, 11, 3–19.

Harrison, K., Taylor, L. D., and Marske, A. L. (2006). Women's and men's eating behavior following exposure to ideal-body images and text. *Communication Research*, 33, 507–529.

Jerslev, A. (2006). The mediated body. *NORDICOM Review*, 2, 133–151.

Lu, L., Kao, S., Chang, T., and Lee, Y. (2009). Individual differences in coping with criticism of one's physical appearance among Taiwanese students. *International Journal of Psychology*, 44, 274–281.

Rasnake, L. K., Laube, E., Lewis, M., and Linscheid, T. R. (2005). Children's nutritional judgments: Relation to eating attitudes and body image. *Health Communication*, 18, 275–289.

Rozin, P., and Fallon, A. (1988). Body image, attitudes toward weight and misperceptions of figure preferences of the opposite sex: A comparison of men and women in two generations. *Journal of Abnormal Psychology, 97,* 342–345.

Willis, J. (1994). *Beautiful again: Restoring your image and enhancing body changes.* Santa Fe, NM: Health Press.

Eating Disorders

Bissell, K. L., and Zhou, P. (2004). Must see TV or ESPN: Entertainment and sports media exposure and body-image distortion in college women. *Journal of Communication, 54,* 5–21.

Harrison, K., Taylor, L. D., and Marske, A. L. (2006). Women's and men's eating behavior following exposure to ideal-body images and text. *Communication Research, 33,* 507–529.

Heilburn, A. B., and Witt, N. (1990). Distorted body image as a risk factor in anorexia nervosa: Replication and clarification. *Psychology Reports, 66,* 407–416.

Hoek, J., and Gendall, P. (2006). Advertising and obesity: A behavioral perspective. *Journal of Health Communication, 11,* 409–423.

Houston, G. S. (2006). Ally McBeal as allegory: Setting the eating-disordered subject in opposition to feminism. *Communication and Critical/Cultural Studies, 3,* 288–306.

Lapinski, M. K. (2006). Starvingforperfect.com: A theoretically based content analysis of pro-eating disorder web sites. *Health Communication, 20,* 243–253.

Park, S. Y. (2005). The influence of presumed media influence on women's desire to be thin. *Communication Research, 32,* 594–614.

Zucker, N., Moskovich, A., Bulik, C. M., Merwin, R., Gaddis, K., Losh, M., Piven, J., Wagner, H. R., and Labar, K. S. (2013). Perception of affect in biological motion cues in anorexia nervosa [Electronic version]. *International Journal of Eating Disorders, 46,* 12–22.

Fat Talk

Engelin-Maddox, R., Salk, R. H., and Miller, S. A. (2012). Assessing women's negative commentary on their own bodies: A psychometric investigation of the negative body talk scale. *Psychology of Women Quarterly, 36,* 162–178.

Salk, R. H., and Engelin-Maddox, R. (2012). Fat talk among college women is both contagious and harmful. *Sex Roles, 66,* 636–645.

Salk, R. H., and Engelin-Maddox, R. (2011). "If you're fat, then I'm humongous!": Frequency, content and impact of fat talk among college women. *Psychology of Women Quarterly, 35,* 18–28.

Taniguchi, E., and Lee, H. E. (2012). Cross-cultural differences between Japanese and American female college students in the effects of witnessing fat talk on facebook. *Journal of Intercultural Communication Research, 41,* 260–278.

Tucker, K. L., Martz, D. M., Curtin, L. A., and Bazzini, D. G. (2007). Examining "fat talk" experimentally in a female dyad: How are women influenced by another woman's body presentation style? *Body Image: An International Journal of Research, 4,* 157–164.

Plastic Surgery

Chock, T. (2007, November). *Is it all in the looks? Approval of cosmetic surgery, gender role stereotypes, and the effects of graphic surgical depictions.* Paper presented at the National Communication Association convention, Chicago, IL.

Davis, K. (1995). *Reshaping the female body: The dilemma of cosmetic surgery*. New York: Routledge Press.

Doniger, W. (2000). The mythology of the face-lift. *Social Research*, 67, 99–125.

Edgerton, M. T., Jacobson, W. E., and Meyer, E. (1960). Surgical-psychiatric study of transsexual patients seeking plastic (cosmetic) surgery: Ninety-eight consecutive patients with minimal deformity. *British Journal of Plastic Surgery*, 13, 144.

Ericksen, S. J. (2012). To cut or not to cut: Cosmetic surgery usage and women's age-related experiences. *International Journal of Aging & Human Development*, 74, 1–24.

Gilman, S. L. (1998). *Creating beauty to cure the soul: Race and psychology in the shaping of aesthetic surgery*. Durham, NC: Duke University Press.

Gilman, S. L. (1999). *Making the body beautiful: A cultural history of aesthetic surgery*. Princeton, NJ: Princeton University Press.

Hamburger, A. C. (1988). Beauty quest. *Psychology Today*, 22, 29–32.

Knorr, N. J., Edgerton, M. T., and Hooper, J. E. (1967). The "insatiable" cosmetic surgery patient. *Plastic and Reconstructive Surgery*, 40, 285–289.

Markley-Rountree, M., and Davis, L. (2011). A dimensional qualitative research approach to understanding medically unnecessary aesthetic surgery. *Psychology & Marketing*, 28, 1027–1043.

Sarwer, D. B., Bartlett, S. P., Bucky, L. P., La Rossa, D., Low, D. W., Pertschuk, M. J., Wadden, T. A., and Whitaker, L. A. (1998). Bigger is not always better: Body image dissatisfaction in breast reduction and breast augmentation patients. *Plastic & Reconstructive Surgery*, 101 (7), 1956–1961.

Sarwer, D. B., Pertschuk, M. J. Wadden, T. A., and Whitaker L. A. (1998a). Body image and body dysmorphic disorder in 100 cosmetic surgery patients. *Plastic & Reconstructive Surgery*, 101 (4), 1644–1649.

Sarwer, D. B., Pertschuk, M. J., Wadden, T. A., and Whitaker L. A. (1998b). The psychology of cosmetic surgery: A review and reconceptualization. *Clinical Psychology Review*, 1, 1–22.

Sullivan, D. A. (2001). *Cosmetic surgery: The cutting edge of commercial medicine in America*. New Brunswick, NJ: Rutgers University Press.

Tait, S. (2007). Television and the domestication of cosmetic surgery. *Feminist Media Studies*, 7, 119–135.

Wein, B. (2002). The changing face of cosmetic surgery. *Biography*, 6 (7), 62–66.

Stigma

Brown, I., and Thompson, J. (2007). Primary care nurses' attitudes, beliefs and own body size in relation to obesity management. *Journal of Advanced Nursing*, 60, 535–543.

Kanekar, S., and Kisawalla, M. B. (1980). Responsibility of a rape victim in relation to her respectability, attractiveness, and provocativeness. *Journal of Social Psychology*, 112, 153–154.

Tompkins, C. J., and Perkinson, M. A. (2006). Are we really teaching our students an aging perspective when we use the term intergenerational? Are we encouraging the stigmas associated with aging if we use a "backdoor approach" in recruiting students to become interested in working with older adults? *Journal of Intergenerational Relationships*, 4, 109–112.

Wispe, L., and Kiecolt, J. (1980). Victim attractiveness and nonhelping. *Journal of Social Psychology*, 112, 67–74.

CHAPTER 6

BODY ALTERATIONS AND COVERINGS

KEY CONCEPTS

- Body Alterations
- Hair
- Hairstyles
- Skin Cosmetics
- Skin Colorings
- Tattoos and Body Piercing
- Clothing
- Purposes
- Functions
- Clothing and Success
- Accessories

OBJECTIVES

By the end of the chapter you should be able to:

- Explain the importance of body alterations to human communication.
- Discuss how hair (head/cranial, facial, body) influences communication.
- Discuss how clothing influences communication.
- Explain the various interpretations people make about you based on your dress.
- Discuss how cosmetics are used as a part of the physical appearance subcode.
- Explain how tattooing is used to embellish the body or establish a bond with others.
- Discuss the long-term effect that clothing has had on our perceptions of the successful businessperson.

Chapter 5 examined how the body establishes a social basis for communication. We now examine the altering of our bodies through a variety of means and the image others may have of our bodies. This area of study is restricted to American culture. A more in-depth coverage of how other cultures alter their bodies would no doubt reveal different means of body alterations and coverings, but space and time in a semester-long course do not permit those inclusions. Some of the alterations we discuss are simple, quick, and easily removed or changed to create a different impression. Some, however, are more permanent and, when removed, often leave scars and telltale indications of their previous existence. In this chapter, we also look at a phenomenon created in the late 1970s that took the business world by storm and is still a lingering but potent force in society: "dressing for success."

BODY ALTERATIONS

Body alterations affect others' perceptions about us as individuals, and there are numerous types and varieties of these alterations. Through our decisions about personal body altera- tions, we convey messages and offer hints and clues to our personalities. As with other fac- tors affecting our appearance, it is risky for a person to make use of body alterations without first understanding their implications. In a positive sense, body alterations can be indicators that a person's beauty is more than just skin deep. We often wish to change the way we look by dressing a certain way, manipulating the hair on our head (cranial hair), adding facial hair, altering our skin tone (tan or pale makeup), modifying the size of our body parts, gaining/losing weight, or wearing high-heeled shoes. All of these things are used to modify how we look to others to increase credibility, liking, and/or homophily (similarity of appearance); to enhance popularity; and to increase attractiveness. Few of us are attracted to people who do not properly alter their appearance and instead fit the "plain Jane" or the "scum bum" mold.

Some religious groups, such as the Pentecostal Holiness denomination, oppose the use of such alterations, especially among its female members. For example, female members of the Pentecostal Holiness sect historically have not been allowed to cut their hair or use lipstick, makeup, or other types of cosmetic treatments. Other extremes in the use and nonuse of makeup may be found among rock-and-roll performers. Over the years, a number of groups have taken on a particular "look" to popularize themselves or to create a unique identity. Consider the rock group KISS; their appearance over the last 40 years has altered, but it has always been a bit out of the ordinary and has been created almost entirely by makeup and clothing.

Changes made by an individual that affect his or her facial appearance seem of vital importance. If clothes can be used to highlight the body, body alterations are often used to emphasize the face.

HAIR AND HAIRSTYLES

Changes involving cranial, facial, and body hair received the most attention among researchers over the early years of nonverbal communication study. In 1976, K. Peterson and Curran found that short-haired men were rated as more intelligent, moral, masculine, mature, wise, and attractive than long-haired men. Beards appear to produce better effects than the clean- shaven look. Some studies have shown that college students attribute higher power and status to males who wear beards; however, this may not hold true in business.

Historically, Americans seem to go through cycles in preference of men's hair. About a hundred years ago, men had longer hair, beards, mustaches, and sideburns. In the 1920s there was a preference for a clean-shaven look and short hair. In the 1940s and 1950s, the "butch" and "flattop" haircuts became popular, and facial hair was almost nonexistent. About this time, the "Bohemian" look began to invade the American culture; hair became shaggier, and goatees sprouted, especially with the start of the "Beatnik" culture. In the mid-1960s, the Beatles, or "moppet," look became popular. During the unrest of the late 1960s and early 1970s, male hair became longer, and beards again flourished. The 1980s saw the return of flattops and crew cuts. The 1990s saw a conglomeration of styles, a sort of "anything goes" approach—short, long, dyed blue or bright pink, spiky, or flat. It is a little too early to say whether this cycle will repeat itself; however, some styles of hair might suggest that shorter hair is once again the "norm." In the first 12 years of the 21st century, though, we seem to still have a mixture of what hairstyles are considered normal.

In 1976, the University of Florida *Placement Manual* reported the results of a survey among 114 college recruiting officers and managers, determining which male hairstyles and beard styles had the most positive effect on hiring decisions. The short-haired, clean-shaven male received the most favorable ratings. Thus, it seems reasonable to conclude that hair and beard styles also influence the attribution of occupational status to the wearers. These styles survived over the previous 35 years; employers today seem to prefer the same styles (Richmond, McCroskey, and Hickson 2011).

According to Molloy (1978), hairstyles for the businesswoman of that era could be shoulder length but no longer. The hair could be wavy but not curly, and it could be short but not masculine. He suggested that a businesswoman's hair must lie neatly in place without constant attention. Notice how little has changed in the 30 years since Molloy published his findings. We still find materials that tell women to tie their hair back if it is longer than shoulder length (J. K. Burgoon, Buller, and Woodall 1996), and women do this, regardless of the fact that these directions seem to be outdated, as well as sexist.

In 1969, D. G. Freedman studied beardedness and offered some interesting insights into the issue, although the research should not be considered conclusive. It should also be noted that the studies were conducted in the late 1960s, a time when long hair and beards were seen as signs of rebellion. Today, a similar look may appear to be "blue collar" and politically conservative. Freedman asked a group of undergraduate students how they felt about facial hair. None of the males wore a beard. The majority of both men and women, 56 percent, used adjectives of youthfulness to describe the beardless male. Of the men, 22 percent described the personalities of the bearded men as independent, and 20 percent described them as extroverted. Women who were envisioning an idealized husband in describing bearded men chose the adjectives *masculine, sophisticated,* and *mature* 55 percent of the time. Freedman adds that people will stand closer to beardless men, and even bearded men report they are less tense with beardless male strangers than with other bearded men. Howard, identified by Freedman as a graduate student at the University of Chicago, investigated women's thoughts on describing a man with a beard and concluded that a beard heightens sexual magnetism. Perhaps if this study were done again today, the findings would be different. However, that is the nature of all studies done about hair, they can become outdated almost as soon as they

PHOTO 6.1   People's hair and the way it's styled affect others' perceptions of them, thereby communicating demographic and personality characteristics nonverbally, such as their socioeconomic status, their occupation, or how friendly or outgoing they might be.

are completed. Addison (1989) conducted a study at Eastern Illinois University. His 114 participants (55 men, 59 women) rated bearded men higher on masculinity, aggressiveness, dominance, and strength.

The subject of facial hair appears to be such a changing factor that in the updating of this 6th edition, very few new studies on hair (facial or cranial) could be found—at least in the communication discipline. One study found was a study of beardedness in advertising conducted by Guido, Peluso, and Moffa (2011). These researchers found that bearded endorsers of products being advertised were deemed to be more credible and to have a positive influence on people's intention to buy products. A study such as this, however, probably does not have much applicability for you deciding to grow facial hair or not. Another study found that men with facial hair were judged by women to be less trustworthy and less task attractive (defined as being the "degree to which we perceive another person as someone with whom we would like to work," Richmond & McCroskey, 1995, 17) than clean-shaven men, although they did have a degree of being judged more socially and physically attractive (Ebesu-Hubbard et al. 2009).

One interesting phenomenon that had its birth in 2003 is an initiative called *Movember*. This is a month-long "growing campaign," where men grow mustaches and beards for the full month of November. It had its inception as a campaign to raise awareness of prostate cancer and depression in men, but has expanded to include testicular cancer and other physical maladies of men (S. Wright 2012). It was started as a fundraising event, but has extended to become the impetus for men to discuss more openly the aspects of men's health that are often publically ignored. Although begun in Australia, it has spread to all parts of the world, including the United States. How many of you or your friends have participated in this? The authors of this textbook have noticed an increased number of their male students participating in this over the last few years.

In a 1973 study concerning facial hair, Pelligrini found a consistent pattern of description. The more hair on the face, the higher the ratings given to models on masculinity, maturity, self-confidence, dominance, courage, liberality, nonconformity, industriousness, and good looks.

Thourlby (1980) says beards, except for those belonging to persons in the areas of art, music, and education, are not recommended. Mustaches are not highly recommended but, when worn, should be kept trimmed and clean and should not curve around the mouth or come below the upper lip (Thourlby 1980). These standards may undoubtedly be relaxed somewhat, but they still are "safety catches" for men deciding on what they should do about facial hair. These findings are telling: People do respond to men with facial hair. All of these findings might be different today, but there undoubtedly would be responses of some type to bearded men.

Rich and Cash (1993) analyzed magazines to determine hair color of cover models in *Ladies Home Journal* and *Vogue* and centerfolds in *Playboy.* As they suspected, the proportion of blondes was much higher than all other hair colors shown and increased over a 40-year period. Another study (Forrester, Crumbley, Powell, Hill, and Hickson 1981), however, found that among college students there were no differences in perceived similarity, credibility, or attractiveness among blondes, redheads, or brunettes. Although the media still paints attractiveness in the form of "blondeness," in studies of actual human subjects in actual settings, there seems to be little consistency in how people are judged by their hair color.

In summarizing the subject of cranial and facial hair, it appears that the length of a man's hair is a significant characteristic and a personal statement on how he views himself. To most people, long hair connotes an artistic, aesthetic, romantic, and casual mode of life. Discipline, seriousness, and business ethics are not suggested by long hair. Very short hair usually

PHOTO 6.2 Facial hair on men sends messages of masculinity.

represents the energetic, precise, athletic, and youthful type, whereas moderate length suggests pragmatic, executive, businesslike, serious, and decisive qualities of an individual. Perhaps when you wonder why people give you directions about how your hair should be when you start employment interviewing, these findings can give you some answers. True, some of them are now outdated, but this body of research is where these suggestions originated. Perhaps some of you who have become interested in doing research studies in nonverbal communication can come up with more contemporary suggestions in this always-changing area of personal appearance. Since there is such a paucity of research done in this important area, you would surely be adding to the base of knowledge in nonverbal communication.

For facial and cranial hair, the amount, texture, length, style, and color can be varied to produce messages. Among females it has been noted by fashion experts and cosmetologists that the brunette is more of an authority figure, whereas the blonde is considered more of a popular figure. The "blondes have more fun" message in advertising, movies, and television shows still seems to be prevalent in today's society.

Another feature to consider is body hair. In this case, amount and location are the principal considerations. Some reports say that females prefer hairy-chested men to bare-chested ones. However, the fact that body hair in and of itself elicits feelings of either appreciation or repugnance is the critical point.

Morris (1977) has indicated that hairstyles vary considerably from culture to culture. Wigs, for example, have been with us for over 5,000 years. The ancient Egyptians shaved their heads completely and wore elaborate wigs. The early politicians in the United States during the late eighteenth century often wore wigs for formal occasions, and wigs still exist in the British courts of law. Film stars and others have used the wig as a substitute for their "real" hair over the past 40 years (Morris 1977, 222). Today, we find many people who wear wigs when they have suffered hair loss from natural or extreme causes, such as chemotherapy. Vingerhoets and Breed (2009) studied this phenomenon and discovered that most cancer patients find the loss of hair to be a burden, so they seek many different ways to try to avoid that loss; the most recent way has been to use "scalp cooling." Scalp cooling is a process whereby the scalp is cooled during the administration of chemotherapy. When the hair follicles are cooled, less of the chemotherapy drugs flow through them, which is thought to lessen hair loss. Vingerhoets and Breed report that when patients who attempt to use the scalp cooling system lose their hair anyway, they see the hair loss as even more burdensome than those who do not use the scalp cooling system. Clearly, the issue of hair loss is an important one, regardless of who is affected by it.

One issue that always seems to be mentioned when discussing hair in our nonverbal communication classes is that of cleanliness. Almost without fail, students who are asked to identify the most unattractive factor about hair answer, "poor hygiene." In order for us to consider hair attractive, regardless of length, color, or location, the majority of us believe it needs to smell and be clean. Many hair care products are advertised with scent as the main attraction for buying them.

A brief mention might be made of eyebrows as a part of facial hair. According to fashion trend magazines and other articles, eyebrows are best when little, if any, attention is called to them; heavy, thick eyebrows tend to overshadow the rest of the face. They may be distracting.

On the other hand, pale eyebrows tend to give an individual, especially a woman, a washed-out, weak look. Some women shave their eyebrows completely and use eyebrow pencils to draw their own eyebrows; others pluck what they consider to be the excess hairs. Some women even have permanent eyebrows tattooed on their foreheads; as you can imagine, this is not a "natural look." In the 1980s, when actress Brooke Shields was popular, thicker eyebrows became more acceptable. Eyebrows are especially noticeable when they do not "match" the color of cranial hair. We will return to the subject of eyebrows in Chapter 7, because they are clearly an important part of facial communication.

As you can see, hair, regardless of its length, color, or location, is important in our reactions to personal appearance. Attractiveness is often determined by hair, but realize how much of this attractiveness is perceptual. What you find attractive about someone else's hair may not be attractive to your peers.

BOX 6.1 OBSERVATIONAL STUDY

Take a magazine and look at the advertisements in it (use a different one than the one you used for Chapter 6). How many different hair colors are represented in the magazine? Lengths? Styles? How prevalent is facial hair on men? Does what you find reflect the norms for your culture today? Do the choices for these advertisements fit the theme of the magazine? The product being sold?

THE SKIN: COSMETICS AND COLORINGS

Another type of body alteration is the use of cosmetics. Makeup and other facial colorings, such as lipstick, cause people to form differing perceptions of others' personalities. Unfortunately, research on this area of body alterations is limited. In researching this new edition of the textbook, studies on makeup were virtually nonexistent. Fabricant and Gould (1993) found that people use makeup to give color to the human face, and Cash (1987) believed that women (who obviously use more cosmetics than men do) find makeup to be important to their psychological well-being. The applications of makeup, lipstick, and other skin colorings seem to be an extremely trendy issue, and the research on the effects of makeup and other colorings has yet to catch up with changes in cultural norms. One exception to that statement, however, was a study done by C. Harrison (2008) that looked at advertising for mascara for men. She reported that advertisers of this product are trying to create a message that men can use a traditionally feminine product such as mascara and still maintain their masculine identities.

Interested in the effects of lipstick, McKeachie (1952) had six male students interview six female students (three who wore lipstick and three who did not) and rate them according to personality perceptions. Women who wore lipstick were perceived as more frivolous and more overtly interested in males. This study, however, would seem to possess little validity today. First, wearing lipstick is more generally accepted now than it was in the early 1950s, and second, there are more colors and shades of lipstick on the market today. In addition, fashion trends show that the use of lipstick is widespread, unlike in the 1960s and 1970s, when the *au naturale* appearance (the use of little or no makeup) was more popular.

The effects of lipstick and other artifacts interact with those of clothing and facial, verbal, and bodily features, but under some yet unspecified conditions, makeup may be the primary source of information communicated about a particular person. How many times has someone's use of cosmetics stood out to you? Was it too much? Too little? What was your perception of that person based on the use of cosmetics?

In another study, P. N. Hamid (1972) focused on the interaction between makeup cues and the presence or absence of glasses. Females wearing makeup were rated as wearing shorter skirts than those without makeup; the same held true for those without glasses as opposed to those with them. Women wearing both glasses and makeup were perceived by males as artistic, intelligent, self-confident, and sophisticated but low in shyness, seriousness, and sentimentality. Females also saw such a person as intelligent but conceited and cold. A woman with glasses and no makeup (or neither) was generally perceived as conservative and low in individuality. A woman with makeup and without glasses was rated favorably on outward appearance but unfavorably on personal traits.

Fabricant and Gould (1993), in a more recent study, believed that a woman's choices to use specific makeup colors, how much makeup to use, and what kinds to use are really dependent on the role she is assuming at a given point in time. When she is "the boss," her choices are likely to be different than when she goes out after work with a man she is trying to attract.

BOX 6.2 OBSERVATIONAL STUDY

Do hairstyles and accessories really influence interpersonal impressions? Take advertisements out of several magazines that feature both male and female models and ask your friends to choose which models they would rather interact with on a serious discussion, or even take out on a date. Ask them why they think the way they do. Is there agreement between your friends on what is a favorable or good appearance?

One cosmetic change that may yield subtle results is eye color. In a study undertaken by Hickson, Powell, and Sandoz (1987), eye color was found to be a significant factor in determining physical appearance. They had participants view slides of a confederate. Half the participants viewed the confederate with brown eyes. The other half viewed the same confederate with blue eyes. In terms of physical attractiveness, participants preferred the blue-eyed confederate for social interaction but they preferred the brown-eyed confederate for working with on tasks. Eye color change today is relatively easy using tinted contact lenses or novelty lenses.

Molloy (1978) observed women ages 18 to 40 wearing a minimum of makeup that they had applied and then again wearing heavy makeup that had been applied by professionals. The results showed that out of a hundred men under age twenty-five, 92 percent picked the minimum makeup picture as the more appealing. Sixty-seven percent of the men aged 25 to 35 and 62 percent of the men from ages 35 to 45 also preferred the women in less makeup.

One author of this text asks her nonverbal communication classes to determine attractiveness and unattractiveness factors by observing people. Without fail, most men list "too much makeup" as a major "turn off" when it comes to attractiveness of women. This fact is interesting in light of how advertising tries to sell products; "more, not less" seems to be the norm in advertisements. If attractiveness is the aim of the product, and it appears that "less is better" when it comes to judgments of attractiveness, why do advertisers use the opposite?

Molloy, in 1978, suggested that women under 35 should wear lipstick and not much other makeup, but even the lipstick should not be overly obvious. Also, he said, eye shadow and eyeliner are out. Long fingernails and false eyelashes are for actresses, not for the professional businesswoman. Colorless nail polish should be the only kind used. Molloy also stated that mascara should be used with great discretion. As for skin coloring as a result of suntans, Molloy stated that the sun can do three things: increase your sex appeal, increase your authority, and increase your chances of getting skin cancer.

How valid are Molloy's findings today? Although many appear to be common sense, more recent research than Molloy's has validated some of those findings. Broadstock (1992), for instance, found that a suntan is an important feature for adolescents, who perceive a tan to be an indicator of health and attractiveness. The darker the tan, the healthier and more attractive the individual is perceived to be. These findings remain the same, according to Chung, Gordon, Veledar, and Chen (2010). Yung et al. discovered by having participants of their study rate pictures of both tanned and untanned individuals according to physical attractiveness. Yung, et al. discovered that females, especially, rate individuals who have a suntan as more physically attractive. Some say a tan in winter sends the message of affluence; if you can afford to vacation where you can get a tan in the winter, you must be wealthy. Another study (Keith and Herring 1991) performed in an African American community found that those with lighter skin were perceived as more educated. The participants felt that skin tone not only affected perceptions of education but also of personal income, occupation, and family income. Mucherah and Frazier (2013) found similar results when they looked at several issues of how women in the African American community perceived themselves as either attractive or unattractive. Banton (2012) discovered that African American men also prefer lighter skiined women for their romantic interests. Interculturally, we find this in many cultures. Parameswaran (2009) and Parameswaran and Cardoza (2007) discovered that in India the same phenomenon exists: people prefer light-skinned females when measuring beauty. In addition, they discovered that advertisers in India use lighter-skinned females in their advertisements for beauty products.

cultures
&
skin
color

The research suggests that cosmetic use and perceptions of the people who use them have remained fairly stable over the years. The popularity of some films and television programs, have made suntans more attractive among the young. The actors on *Baywatch*, a 1990's popular show that takes place on a California beach,did not tan in the sun or in artificial light; instead, they used a lotion that changes the color of their skin (*Orlando Sentinel*, 1997). Those who understand the impact of the sun realize that, besides skin cancer, the sun's effects including early wrinkles, a weathered look, and so forth—that is, damage to the skin. Who has not seen an older "sun god/goddess," especially from sunny climes such as Florida, Arizona, or California, and made comments about how *gross* their skin is? "Lizard skin" and "leathery" are just two descriptors used to show what people think of that kind of appearance. Dermatologists will be quick to tell you that the "suntanned look" is not healthy.

tanning

K. Thomas et al. (2011) found that part of the reason we are more careful with the sun is because the messages we receive in today's society about abusing our skin are effective. Perhaps the reason Botox became popular so quickly after the Food and Drug Administration approved it for cosmetic use has more to do with the issue of sun damage to skin than any other part of the aging process. Advertisers, however, have not yet embraced that message for their models. Not all messages of having a tan are positive.

ADDITIONS

Although little research is available on them, other body alterations include additions—padded bras, false breasts, false buttocks, pantyhose, shoe "lifters," and artificial tanning creams or lotions. In 1976, Mathes and Kempher found that the number of different sex partners for a female corresponded highly with the frequency with which she went braless. Today, few women go braless because health reports point to muscular damage leading to future negative appearance issues. Most women do not relish the thought of having "sagging breasts" later in life. Because of that, many bra manufacturers have designed bras that give a woman support but are designed to give a natural appearance.

The other items mentioned in this section seem less important in altering an individual's personal appearance. First, they are worn beneath the clothing, and second, if the clothing projects the correct impression of the individual, then these other items, or the features they either accentuate or hide, will be less prominent and noticed.

Body alterations (not of the surgical type) are relatively inexpensive compared to other factors that influence the overall body appearance. If used effectively, they can project a chosen personality type. If used haphazardly, they can cause an individual to pay a high price in lost appeal. We would do well to think about these effects before we make changes.

TATTOOS, BODY PIERCING, AND BRANDING

The 1990s brought an increased use of tattoos on virtually every part of the body, and that continues today. Tattoos, previously considered a "biker" or "blue collar" phenomenon, are today worn by both sexes and by virtually every socioeconomic class. In surveying college nonverbal communication classes, one author of this text often finds that more women in the class have tattoos than men. Horne, Knox, Zusman, and Zusman (2007) and Schulz, Karshin, and Woodiel (2006) discovered the same statistic, and reported that women sought tattoos for different reasons than men do. The business world has not yet accepted tattoos, as they are seen as a symbol of a rebellious spirit, which is not something businesses usually appreciate in their young employees.

Since tattooing as a body alteration has been occurring over the last decade, there has been considerable research done on this phenomenon and what tattoos can communicate about those who sport them. Resenhoeft, Villa, and Wiseman (2008) discovered that tattoos are likely to create perceptions of college students who have them, and that the actual depiction is likely to affect that perception as well. For example, they discovered that a dragon tattoo on a woman had a more negative perceptual effect on a woman than a dolphin did. Wohlrab, Stahl, Rammsayer, and Kappeler (2007) did not find relevant differences between individuals who had tattoos and body piercings as far as demographics go, but they did find significant differences in personality traits between those who choose to modify their bodies with tattoos and piercings and those who do not. Wohlrab et al. discovered that those who do choose to modify their bodies in these ways seem to be sensation seekers and that they follow a mating strategy that is less restricted than their counterparts who do not modify their bodies in these ways. This is one study, and you would do well not to stereotype people with tattoos, and women in particular, as easy prey when seeking a mate. In a more recent study, Wohlrab, Fink, Kappeler, and Brewer (2009) found that males who were tattooed were perceived to be more dominant, whereas females who were tattooed were believed to be less healthy.

Other tattoo studies report that people who do have tattoos are evaluated more negatively than those who do not have tattoos. Tate and Shelton (2008) found that tattooed individuals were evaluated more negatively on agreeableness and conscientiousness, but they were rated more highly on the need to be unique. Tate and Shelton warn, however, that it is best not to assume that someone will be evaluated negatively based solely on the fact that they have tattoos.

Various other findings have been discovered in the last few years since we published the 5th edition of this textbook. For example, Rivardo and Keelan (2010) discovered that college students with tattoos and piercings were more likely to be sexually active. Doss and Ebesu-Hubbard (2009) found that people are more likely to have visible tattoos when they wanted the message of the tattoos communicated, and more private tattoo messages were found on tattoos that are hidden by clothing. Bauman (2008) found that people with tattoos that are seen publically violate the norms of self-disclosure, meaning others find out intimate information about the person early on in a relationship as opposed to moving naturally toward deeper self-disclosure as you get to know someone. In the midst of many studies, researchers have discovered many things, and we suggest that if you are interested you read the research listed in the "Additional Resources" section of this chapter.

As far as reasons for tattooing themselves go, they are varied and there is little agreement about what causes people to tattoo their bodies. For example, Otte (2007) reported that in a post-Katrina study, many of those who experienced the devastating New Orleans hurricane of 2005 tattooed themselves with the fleur-de-lis symbol and other symbols indicative of what they had gone through. The reasons for those tattoos are probably fairly clear, whereas a pirate or dragon tattoo may need more explanation by the person who has chosen it. Further research will no doubt continue in this area of tattooing, if for no other reason than the prevalence of the practice in Western society.

STUDENT VOICES

Jerry: There is a gentleman that goes to the local coffee shop frequently. He has tattoos everywhere, including his face, neck, and hands. I personally think that this is a stupid decision, but on top of that he wears a visor hat upside down and backwards. . . . This gives me the non-verbal impression that he has had a rough life, and never cares to pursue a career in sales or any other customer-focused industry. I have tattoos, but mine are all easily covered. I purposely did this so that I would not give the nonverbal message from my tattoos of being a bum with a tat.

Body piercing

In addition to tattooing, body piercing has increased. Long prevalent in other cultures, Morris (1977) told us that nose, ear, eyebrow, and nipple piercing had become more common in American society in the 10 years preceding his publication. Now, in the 21st century, we find that the trend has continued. While ear piercing has been common among women in America for a long time, the piercing of noses, eyebrows, tongues, nipples, belly buttons, and genitals has become more popular. Prominent men such as Harrison Ford (the actor) and the late Ed Bradley (the news commentator on *60 Minutes*) wear and wore earrings on a regular basis. You may notice that even when playing serious parts, Ford wears an ear pin. Martino (2008) found that women with piercings in their eyebrows, ears, lips, and noses were judged to be more creative, artistic, and mysterious, but also less religious. Langman (2008) reported that individuals use the vehicle of body adornment, including piercings and tattoos, to show a form of resistance to what is going on in society. In a controversial study, J. R. Koch, Roberts, Armstrong, and Owen (2007) found that college women with body piercings (other than earlobes) reported greater frequency of sexual activity than college students without body piercings. Seiter and Sandry (2003) found that potential job candidates' hirability ratings decreased when a nose ring was present, although other jewelry did not affect that measure. Popularity, nevertheless, does not mean acceptance within the business community, although it is more acceptable today. Most materials on interviewing, however, still strongly suggest that men remove earrings for the interview process, indicating that the business community is still not accepting these practices in men. Time will likely change that when people of college age today become the CEOs of tomorrow, but for now it is best to think conservatively in this area of body adornment.

hiring decreases
— popularity increases

Some African American fraternities have required branding as part of the initiation process. The brand is most often on the upper left arm and shows the Greek letters of the fraternity. Many people view this form of body modification to be extreme and even refer to it as mutilation and as an aberration (Schramme, 2008). Again, although this practice is not well accepted in the business world, the issue may be moot since the upper arm is rarely seen in

PHOTO 6.3   Tattoos have become more acceptable for men and women of all socioeconomic classes in today's society.

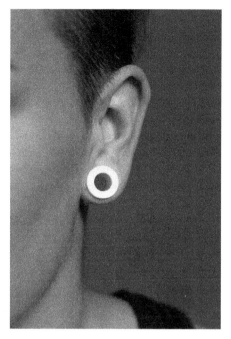

PHOTO 6.4 The trend of body piercing continues into the 21st century.

the business setting. On college campuses, more and more athletes (both male and female) are also acquiring tattoos, just as we see on professional athletes. It would not be surprising to see these trends changing or even disappearing in the next decade, only to change and reappear a decade later.

BOX 6.3 OBSERVATIONAL STUDY

Survey your nonverbal class by looking around the room. How many piercings do you see? Tattoos? Out-of-the-ordinary hairstyles? Ask your professor to poll the class for issues you cannot see (such as tattoos and piercings beneath people's clothing). What trends do you see? Are there gender-based differences? Any surprises?

CLOTHING

Clothing is a phenomenon of the human species. Although other species use various appendages (feathers, fins, antennae, crests, bands, and the like) for ornamentation, only human beings go to the trouble of garbing themselves in textiles.

— protection & modesty

PURPOSES OF CLOTHING

It is generally accepted that people wear clothes for protection and modesty; however, in his book *The Psychology of Clothes,* Flugel (1950) provided evidence to contradict these assumptions. Charles Darwin observed that the natives of Tierra del Fuego did not wear clothes despite the severe weather conditions, thereby dispelling the first theory for at least this group of people. The theory that people wear clothing for modesty's sake may be true for more complex societies, but it does not hold true for all cultures. As a matter of fact, Americans distinguish between being naked and being nude (Freed 1973). To be naked is to be deprived of clothes, which causes embarrassment. To be nude is to be confident about the body in an aesthetic sense.

If humans do not wear clothing for protection or modesty, which is an arguable position, then what is the purpose of clothing? As noted earlier, Birdwhistell suggests that only a third of human communication is accomplished through words; nonverbal communication accounts for the rest. Because what you wear is nonverbal communication, clothing is a means of communicating. You are constantly sending and receiving messages from other people based on dress alone, and we learn this early on in life. Boden (2006) asserts that we learn to build our social identities, including what clothing we should wear, as children. In her study, she determined that children especially are influenced by societal phenomena, and that sports and pop music have the greatest influence on children's clothing choices. Boden also believes that children are "educated" about the concept of fashion mostly through the media, in particular television and print media (such as magazine advertisements). In today's society, people are paying more attention to the environment, and that would include the types of clothing we choose to wear. Winge (2008) has found that people, and celebrities in particular, are becoming more eco-conscious and wearing more "ecofashions" than has ever occurred in the past.

FUNCTIONS OF CLOTHING

Although one purpose of clothing appears to be communication, the functions are varied. Clothing serves as a means of protection, sexual attraction, self-assertion, self-denial, concealment, group identification, and status and role indicator (Aiken 1963). Morris (1985) says that we dress the way we do for comfort and protection, concealment, and cultural display. Clothes can communicate many personal attributes, including such characteristics as sex, age, nationality, relation to opposite sex, socioeconomic status, group and occupational identification, mood, personality, attitudes, interests, and values (J. Kelly 1969). The attributes communicated by clothing have not changed over the years since Kelly reported this information.

Thourlby (1980) said there are 10 conclusions people make about each other based on clothing alone:

1. Economic background
2. Economic level
3. Educational background
4. Educational level
5. Level of sophistication
6. Level of success
7. Moral character
8. Social background

9. Social position

10. Trustworthiness

This list does not seem to have changed over the last 30-plus years.

If you read through the list just after you chose what you want to wear for the day (or for a party, an interview, and so forth), you will undoubtedly see how much those "conclusion makers" are a part of your choices.

At least one home economist has attempted to prove that the contents of a woman's wardrobe can indicate everything from her level of intelligence to her degree of sophistication (Gittelson 1975). Results of this less-than-scientific study showed that the "high-fashion woman" considered herself religious, considered herself well-to-do, disagreed less with her parents, and spent more money on clothes. The "low-fashion female" perceived herself to be the all-American girl, possessing natural good looks which she considered more important than money, clothes, or status. The "nonfashion female" thought of herself as conservative and usually came from a low socioeconomic background. The "counterfashion woman" viewed herself as more liberal, individualistic, and conscientious but less status-minded and the least sophisticated. Results also indicate that the high-fashion woman had the lowest grade point average, whereas the nonfashion woman had the highest. It would be interesting to conduct this study again, perhaps using a more scientific model, to see if the results would be the same. As always, we need to be careful about overgeneralizing.

(handwritten margin note: high fashion women)

CLOTHING AND STATUS

Fortenberry, Maclean, Morris, and O'Connell (1978) sought to determine which mode of dress best served as a perceptual cue for status. They placed one male and one female confederate in a hallway at conversational distance, similar to the directions in Observational Study 5.1. Anyone wishing to go by had to avoid them or pass between them. In one condition, the conversationalists wore "formal daytime dress." In the second condition, they wore

(handwritten margin note: "formal daytime dress." "casual attire")

PHOTO 6.5 Fashion designer Miuccia Prada said, "What you wear is how you present yourself to the world, especially today, when human contacts are so quick. Fashion is instant language." What do you think your clothing communicates about you?

"casual attire." There was a significant difference between the behaviors toward the conversationalists when they were formally dressed as opposed to when they were casually dressed. Positive behaviors were observed toward the perceived high-status couple, whereas negative behaviors were exhibited toward the perceived low-status couple. Hensley (1981) reported similar results in terms of requesting assistance from someone, and M. Walker, Harriman, and Costello (1980) found that people are more likely to comply with a request from a well-dressed person.

Finally, your authors know of academic department chairpersons who have been known to suggest that graduate teaching assistants dress more formally, wearing shirts and ties (if male) and dresses, skirts or slacks, and blouses (if female) to create a "teacher-status" effect and to appear older. Paralleling this, many male professors forgo the coat and tie and females the dresses and skirts or slacks and blouses to reduce the status difference in the classroom, although most wear more formal clothing the first few weeks of class to establish a status differential between the students and themselves. Many feel that they can relax their clothing styles once their position has been established. Regardless, even today, clothing choices are important to the message you send about your status.

BOX 6.4 OBSERVATIONAL STUDY

Consider the courses in which you are enrolled right now. What physical aspects of your professors promote learning for you? Which ones detract from your learning? Discuss your answers with a few of your classmates. Are your findings similar? If so, what reasons do you think there are for the similarities? If not, what reasons do you think there are for the differences?

CLOTHING AND WEARER CHARACTERISTICS

The history of the study of clothing shows a strong relationship between clothing worn and characteristics attributed to individuals. In 1963, Aiken tested 160 women to determine wearer characteristics. Decoration in dress (a more elaborate, eye-catching style) correlated with conformity, sociability, and non-intellectualism; comfort in dress (a more casual, loose-fitting style) correlated with self-control and extroversion; interest in dress correlated with social conformity, restraint, and submissiveness; and economy in dress (a more conservative style) correlated with responsibility, alertness, efficiency, and precision. Another study on wearer characteristics was made by Rosencrantz (1962), who found that working women with high clothing awareness were from the upper social class, belonged to many social and community organizations, had higher levels of education and verbal intelligence, had higher incomes, and were usually married to white-collar workers. In the 50-plus years since this research was done, nonverbal communication theorists still report similar findings about the ways women dress in the business world (Molloy 1995). Issues surrounding the use of clothing deserve continual study, since clothing norms change consistently. Perhaps, if you have become interested in researching areas of nonverbal communication, these topics might interest you. Interestingly enough, though, in researching the updating of this edition, there were not many new studies done on clothing effects.

Hoult (1954) undertook a study to determine how males were informally rated when raters gave no attention to attire. The males were then divided into three groups and judged again; this time special attention was directed to clothing. Results showed that clothing changes made no significant difference between the two ratings when the participants knew the men. These findings would undoubtedly remain the same if this study were replicated today; if we know the persons, we are less likely to judge them on their clothing.

In a second historical experiment, Hoult (1954) had photographs of the heads of 10 college-age men ranked according to attractiveness. He also had 10 photographs of outfits ranked according to their "appropriateness for college students." The photographs of the heads were then negatively correlated with the photographs of the outfits. When the heads were later viewed with the negatively correlated outfits, there was a marked difference in the attractiveness ratings from the first set of rankings. The attractiveness for heads initially rated low was improved when they were matched up with outfits originally rated high, and vice versa. These findings of 59 years ago would no doubt still be the same today.

Clearly, clothing is one of the major factors influencing how we judge others. We need to remember, however, the tips about accuracy and judging others (relative to nonverbal factors): The better you know the person, the more accurate your clothing-based perceptions will be.

CLOTHING AND ITS EFFECTS ON BEHAVIOR

What are the effects of clothes on interpersonal behavior? A series of classic studies suggests that clothing does, indeed, make a difference. Bickman (1974b), for instance, undertook two field experiments in which he observed the effects of clothes on behavior. In the first experiment, he wanted to test a person's "clothes-categorizing system" in regard to honesty. He enlisted three male and three female confederates, who dressed in either high-status or low-status clothing. One of the confederates would put a dime on the shelf of a public phone booth and leave. When a caller entered, the confederate watched to see whether the person took the dime. The confederate would then approach the booth and explain that he/she may have left a dime in the booth. Confederates in high-status clothing had 77 percent of the callers return the coin, whereas only 38 percent returned the dime to the low-status person. — *honesty — authority*

An interesting question to ask here would be about credibility. Did the person who found the dime more readily believe the confederate dressed in high-status attire? Think about yourself in this setting; would you have given the dime more readily to the person with a high-status appearance? The low-status one? Neither?

In a similar study, Bickman (1974a) wanted to find out whether uniformed individuals, acting outside their traditional roles, would still have greater authority than persons not in uniform. His confederates varied in dress and level of authority. The lowest authority figure was dressed as a civilian, the average authority figure was dressed as a milkman, an early to mid-1900's phenomenon of a person who delivered milk to your door, and a guard represented the highest level of authority. Bickman then set up three situations. In the first situation, the confederate stopped the participant and asked him or her to pick up a piece of litter. In the second situation, the confederate stopped the participant and asked him or her to put

PHOTO 6.6 Despite the power and influence of clothing, particularly in the work environment, clothing people choose says a great deal more than they are aware of.

a coin in a nearby expired parking meter. In the last situation, the confederate approached the participant and asked him or her to stand on the other side of a "No Standing" sign (which meant no parking in a bus stop zone).

Regardless of age or sex, participants were definitely more compliant with the requests made by the guard. As a matter of fact, 83 percent of the pedestrians obeyed the high-authority figure, while only 46 percent obeyed the low-authority figure. There were no significant differences in the compliance shown toward the civilian and the milkman (Hewitt and German 1987). These results probably are not surprising to you, because this seems to be normal in our society. We are a low power-distance culture, which means we believe that people in our society are relatively equal in perceived power (Samovar, Porter, McDaniel, and Roy 2013; Gudykunst 1998). Unless a person is in a definite hierarchical position above us, meaning one established by legitimate means (such as police, bosses, professors), we assume others are equal in status to us and we are less likely to defer to someone we think is *an equal*.

Lefkowitz, Blake, and Mouton (1955) were interested in people's conformity to violation. The chance of conformity happening seemed to increase if the original violator was perceived as someone of authority. The study took place at a traffic light where a male confederate, wearing high-status or low-status clothing, violated the "Do Not Walk" signal. Significantly more pedestrians followed the confederate when he was perceived to be a figure of authority. More pedestrians, however, violated the traffic signal when the confederate, regardless of perceived status, initiated the violation than when the confederate obeyed the law or was absent.

STUDENT VOICES

Sandy: The choice of clothing that I saw some of the women chose to wear out in public was a little unsettling. I watched as the men, and some women, sat down to watch a show at a club. It was like watching an X rated show, waiting for the moment they would bend over revealing intimate body parts. It is actually quite sad to watch because you see how others make assumptions and judgments about their character. Unfortunately in our society, we are judged and categorized based on our outward appearance. Those who are physically attractive based on body shape, height, weight, hair, teeth, complexion and clothing are treated and revered as more intelligent, powerful, and worthy of the good things in life.

BOX 6.5   OBSERVATIONAL STUDY

The uniform or dress studies clearly suggest that we are influenced by what other people wear. Replicate one of the studies reported in this section and see if clothing effects are as strong as they were 30 to 50 years ago. How did people respond to the uniformed confederate? The non-uniformed one?

Most of us wear uniforms of some type. Some are not as obvious as others; however, some of these uniforms may be more important than we think. They may be blue jeans and a t-shirt, your Greek letters, or your ROTC uniform. Regardless, they are a uniform of sorts. Huddleston and Huddleston (1986) studied the legitimacy and competency attributed to male and female judges based on whether they wore robes in making their judicial decisions. Although male judges were consistently rated higher than females, the males and females who wore robes were rated as being more competent than robeless judges. The highest ratings were given to male judges who wore robes. This may have altered somewhat over the last 20 years or so, with the influx of more female judges, but perceptual evaluations of people's status are likely to be slower to change than the actual change in rank.

CLOTHING AND SUCCESS

Molloy (1975, 1995) has extensively researched "wardrobe engineering." He has shown that what a person wears can determine ultimate success or failure in the business environment. His *Dress for Success* books describe the proper attire for the successful businessman. Suits represent authority, credibility, and likableness. Darker colors transmit more authority. Although darker colors are preferred, black should be avoided as it is too powerful for most men and has funereal undertones. Dark blue and dark gray suits build credibility. Molloy recommends solid colors, but pinstripes and chalk pinstripes are acceptable. Meehan (1999) has indicated that the fabric of clothing may be as important as color, and he shows a preference for wool suits.

Solid white shirts received better responses in terms of taste, class, credibility, and effectiveness. Pastel shades and simple, closely striped shirts are also acceptable. Molloy recommends that the shirt be lighter than the suit and that the tie be darker than the shirt. Solid ties have the best effect, but diagonal stripes are acceptable.

Molloy also wrote *The Woman's Dress for Success Book* (1978) and *New Women's Dress for Success Book* (1996). His research showed that the best outfit for a woman is a skirted suit and blouse. A medium gray or medium blue suit with a white blouse expresses the most authority. Navy blue, charcoal gray, and beige are acceptable for suit colors, and white on white, gray, and pink are acceptable colors for blouses. The "imitation man" look diminishes a woman's authority and should therefore be avoided entirely. These factors have changed somewhat over the past 30 years, but one thing remains the same: In order for a woman to be perceived as having more power, she must dress more formally and not casually. What we wear may say much more than we might realize. The more you understand about this component of non-verbal communication, the more effectively you will be able to communicate.

Interestingly, what Molloy described as "correct" was caught up by the business world. Consider, for example, what the average male bank executive still wears: blue or gray pin-stripes, white or off-white shirt, or pastel blue or brown, and a conservative tie (usually tied in a "false" Windsor knot). We encounter people who are carbon copies of each other. Significantly, those who were in charge seemed to set the "norm," even when no written dress code existed. This still seems to hold true today, although styles of formal clothing have changed. Go into any business and observe what dress codes you find. Most will be obvious, regardless of changes in what is acceptable workplace dress and what is not suitable. You, too, could use this power; conduct the research and write your own findings into a prescriptive approach to how people should dress. Molloy's most recent work was over 17 years ago for men and over 16 years ago for women; it's time for those of you who are excited about this research to write a new *Dress for Success* book for your generation.

Finally, as K. W. Watson and Smeltzer (1982) found, in interview situations the dress "code" has become an expectation rather than a hit-or-miss procedure. They noted that top Fortune 500 interviewers listed clothing high on their list of something to look for and that because of this and Molloy's influence, the actual impressions that were once made no longer prevail everywhere, that is, provided you do not violate the clothing "game." Further, they reported that interviewers tend to hire in their own image. To succeed in an interview, dress much like the interviewer, or some say dress "one step up" from the "normal" dress for that workplace. How would you know what the normal dress code is? Research the company, a tip all materials about interviewing tell you to do anyway.

Despite the work of Molloy and others, M. R. Solomon (1986) argued that we know little about appropriate dress in varying contexts. He suggested, however, that (1) there is a connection between those who think they are actors on life's stage and their dress habits; (2) some therapists suggest buying new clothes as therapy for some of their depressed clients; (3) those who are "dressed up" in interview situations think more highly of themselves in the interview; (4) people are more concerned about dress when they move into a new situation; and (5) according to business executives who interview women for managerial positions, "feminine grooming and dress" does not work. These findings confirm the fact that clothing does have a communicative impact, regardless of the situation.

People who travel abroad for business also need to pay attention to what clothing sends messages of power and success in other cultures. They should also learn what is acceptable and unacceptable dress in those cultures to which they will travel, especially if they hope to be successful in their business objectives. Stoykov (2007) tells his readers that there are many variables to which a person should pay attention. For example, Stoykov reports that businessmen always wear a shirt and tie and women dress conservatively. In Brazil, if you wear a three-piece suit you are sending the message that you are an executive, whereas the two-piece suit indicates that you are an office employee. It is fascinating to find these things out, but more importantly, it is crucial to your success in the business world. As Stoykov says, ". . . the lack of knowledge of its [corporate dress's] main codes, depending on the respective race, religion, ethnos, traditions and habits, can cause frustration, misunderstanding and even failure in communication between managers from different geographic spaces" (p. 1).

Richmond and McCroskey (2000) point out six important generalizations about judgments that are based on how people dress:

1. The accuracy of our judgments about others based on dress varies as a function of what type of judgment we make. Demographics are judged more accurately than personality, moods, values, and attitudes.
2. The dress of others influences our perceptions of them but is affected by whether they are strangers or acquaintances.
3. The perceptions we have of others are initially influenced by their dress.
4. If someone dresses similarly to us, then we are more likely to approach him or her to initiate an interaction.
5. If people want to be recognized as a part of a group they should wear clothing that imitates that group.
6. Clothing can denote our credibility. (p. 47)

If we accept these generalizations, then we must pay attention to both how we dress ourselves and how we make judgments of others.

BOX 6.6 OBSERVATIONAL STUDY

Watch television for a half hour, or at least view the advertising during a show. How are the models dressed for the ads? What does that tell you about the product? What message is the advertiser trying to get across to you about the product? Does it work?

ACCESSORIES

Like clothes, accessories can communicate many messages to an observer. Accessories can cast an individual into a specific role or group. Group identifiers include items such as wedding bands, fraternity/sorority pins, hearing aids, canes, crutches, walkers, and jewelry that reveal religious preference (Knapp 1978).

One type of group identifier is the occupational identifier, which is those accessories that signify a particular role or position. Police officers wear their uniforms, guns, badges, hats, and handcuffs. Laboratory coats and stethoscopes distinguish doctors. Some ministers wear collars and carry Bibles or prayer books; a rabbi might wear a yarmulke. Athletes suit up in gear designed for their specific sports. Those in the military are recognized not only by uniforms but also by colorful ribbons, stripes, insignia, and medals that distinguish the various branches of service as well as rank. Construction workers may use hardhats, gloves, and goggles as identifiers. College students may dress in the "college garb" of their era. At the writing of this edition, for example, Abercrombie and Fitch, American Eagle, Hollister, 7 For All Mankind, and Rock & Republic seem to be popular designers for many in the college-age group, although these choices have probably changed even before we went to print (since styles change so quickly in our society). In researching this edition, we discovered that young businesswomen (ones who have recently graduated from college) tend to like Ann Taylor, Anne Klein, and The Loft for their professional clothes. We also discovered that it is alright to purchase your clothes at the discount retailer Target, but not at Wal-Mart or K-Mart. The list of identifiers is endless, but regardless of what goes on the list, messages are communicated.

Jewelry alone can tell much about an individual. Besides classifying you as belonging to a certain group or occupation, jewelry can reveal your social status, economic background, self-image, religion, education, and availability for a relationship. According to Molloy (1995, 1996), businessmen should limit jewelry to a wedding ring and a thin, plain gold watch; businesswomen might consider wearing a wedding ring even if they are not married because the presence of a band projects an "all business" image. Many gender researchers today would argue strongly against Molloy's tip, partly because of the sexist nature of such a tip, and partly because of the ethics of such a decision. A thin watch and gold post earrings were the only other pieces of jewelry a successful businesswoman should wear, at least according to Molloy. Has this changed today? Research has discovered, for example, that wearing a watch is passé these days, that most of you use your cellphones for your "time-pieces" (Bilton 2011). It would be prudent for you to discover the answers to questions about what artifacts communicate the most about your professionalism before you begin your job search.

Eyeglasses play a large role in one's appearance. P. N. Hamid (1968, 1972), for instance, found that people who wear glasses were perceived as religious, conventional, and unimaginative. In an earlier study, he used waitresses wearing makeup and/or glasses as subjects and found that if they wore glasses and makeup, they received the most favorable ratings concerning the aforementioned qualities. When the waitresses wore neither makeup nor glasses, they received the poorest ratings. Beattie (1975) undertook another study, at Mississippi State University, and found no significant rating differences between students who wore glasses and those who did not. Today, however, we are seeing more and more designer eyeglasses which communicate more about your style of dress than your intelligence.

An optician by the name of Poll concluded that the way in which people handle their frames can make a statement about the wearer's mood and even the image he or she is trying to project (Levy and Poll 1976). The person who compulsively folds and unfolds his spectacles, for instance, may be indicating boredom; the one who bends his temple bar may be revealing inner agitation. Someone who touches both temple tips together may be expressing intense concentration. Chewing on the temple tip is common among people who are tense, nervous, or under great stress. Poll goes on to say that the way you position your glasses on your nose is also significant. For example, if you prop your glasses on your brow to look at a visitor with the naked eye, you may be demonstrating honesty and openness. By contrast, sliding your glasses to the tip of your nose and peering over the frame may be a nonverbal gesture for "You're putting me on."

Molloy (1995) recommended that a businessman should select heavy plastic or horn rims, which will make him look traditional, authoritative, and older. His glasses should enhance or offset the facial features so that the upper and lower face become a "compatible unit." Again, these issues seem to be "trend bound." The tiny sizes of lenses in the late 1990s and into the 2000s would need to be considered. In the case of the businesswoman, glasses will also make her appear more authoritative but less appealing; therefore, Molloy suggested that contact lenses be worn for social affairs. Chances are good, however, that studies conducted today would not give these same suggestions since they seem to indicate that women with glasses are less attractive in social settings, especially to men. This seems to tell women that they should manipulate their appearance to suit the desires of what men dictate as an attractive or businesslike appearance. This type of suggestion, at least formally, is less likely to occur today. First, the unlawfulness of such a statement would thwart someone saying such a thing. Second, just an awareness of human nature and of the underlying message should prevent someone from suggesting this.

glasses

Smoking artifacts may also be considered accessories. One study (Hickson, Powell, Hill, Holt, and Flick 1970), comparing pipe smokers, cigar smokers, cigarette smokers, and nonsmokers, found that the pipe smoker was perceived as high in credibility, high in similarity to peers, and high in attractiveness. Cigarette and cigar smokers were perceived as low in credibility, low in similarity, and low in attractiveness. The nonsmoker tended to fall between the pipe smoker and the other two groups regarding most factors; however, there were no significant differences among pipe smokers and nonsmokers. One shortcoming of this study was that subjects were not asked whether they smoked and, if so, what they smoked. When the study was replicated by Amsbary, Vogel, Hickson, Wittig, and Oakes (1994), all smokers were found to be less credible than a nonsmoker, as the popularity of smoking itself had decreased. In this case, the participants were asked whether they smoked. Even smokers rated other smokers less credible than a nonsmoker, and this trend seems to continue in the first decade of the 21st century. The recent popularity of cigar smoking has not increased the credibility of the smoker, according to any scientific research.

smoking artifacts

In addition, two physicians at the Bowman Gray School of Medicine in Winston-Salem, North Carolina conducted a study to have participants estimate the age of people in photographs. These doctors (Sherertz and Hess 1993) found that smokers were rated as 5 years older than their actual age, whereas the same was not true of nonsmokers. Whether they were judged older because their skin looks older, a known biological byproduct of smoking, or because of their smoking in the photographs per se would be an interesting facet to add to these findings. One interesting cultural difference about smoking would be a great area for future study. In most countries outside of the United States, a much higher percentage of the population smokes and finds smoking acceptable, although in 2012 that is starting to change in many foreign countries. If the taboos about smoking do not exist, what might the perception of smokers be? Would it be less negative? Would smokers still appear older?

Although they may be considered unimportant by themselves, accessories are vital to the overall communicative effect. They are used as a means of identification, as an indication of status, and as a medium for nonverbal communication. The cliché "It's the little things that count" is particularly relevant where accessories are concerned. Think of your book bag, your favorite t-shirt's motto/insignia, your hat, your jewelry, your style of glasses—what do they say about you? Does a t-shirt with your university's logo send a different message than a "Big Johnson" t-shirt? Is carrying an L. L. Bean book bag less prestigious or more prestigious than a Jansport or a leather bookbag? One of your authors had a college student in 2012 who carried a Spiderman book bag, which seemed a little odd; however, other students thought this was just fine and not odd in any way.

Although many of these studies on accessories generally have been carried out under scientific conditions, the studies on dress are more questionable. Much more scientific and controlled research needs to be undertaken on dress and the effects of dress, and it needs to be done periodically. For example, if studied today, would there be variations in the perceptions of dress among institutions and businesses such as banks, engineering firms, insurance companies, and book publishers? Is it possible that dress becomes more important in situations where the individual is coming up for promotion? When one gets a divorce? After one has been promoted to the top level? Most of the questions about "dressing for success" remain empirically unanswered and are open to new research studies. Styles change so often that we need to conduct studies in the area of artifacts more often if we are going to keep up to date. Unfortunately, the research that was done in the 1970s and 1980s seems to be the most recent available.

BOX 6.7 OBSERVATIONAL STUDY

For one day, take note of any artifacts you notice as you go through the day, either on humans you come in contact with or in advertisements. When you write one down, write the message it sends to you. What are the differences relative to gender? People with higher or lower status? People from different cultures? Your peers?

FUNCTIONS

The most important functions of physical appearance change are **identification** and **self-presentation**. These are the primary reasons for modifying one's appearance. On talk-show television, "makeovers" are a typical topic. The changes are usually cosmetics, hair color, hairstyle, clothing, and often weight issues. Sometimes the individual wants the change for himself or herself. In other cases, such as a parent dressing in younger, trendier fashions, the child wants the parent to appear "less provocative" or "more mature." Obviously, the **control of interaction** is influenced by one's physical appearance. An attractive person can initiate an interaction more easily, can maintain the floor longer, can take control of the floor more easily, and can prevent others from gaining the floor. How many times have you approached an unattractive person to begin an interaction? We do not ordinarily approach people we find unattractive. The **relationship of interactants** is certainly affected when one finds that a son or daughter wants to assure his or her friends that the person "with me" is my mother, not another friend. **Displays of affective information**, or what our emotional states are, are indicated by how we look. **Taking control** of one's appearance is indicative of someone certain about who she or he is. Finally, there is obviously **deception** involved in the modification process. One may wish to appear taller, or more sophisticated, or less sophisticated, or more casual, or older, or younger than one actually is.

SUMMARY

As you can imagine, this chapter has barely scratched the surface of how much is communicated by body alterations and coverings. We need always to recall the perceptual aspects of physical appearance issues—both the accuracy issue and what is communicated to specific people. The accuracy of our perceptions will be dependent on how well we know the persons and the context.

This chapter has been concerned with a second area of the social dimension of physical appearance—including body alterations, clothing, cosmetics, and artifacts—as it applies in American culture. A more in-depth coverage would include looking at other cultures' use of body art, alterations, and artifacts, but space limits our ability to go into great detail on those issues here. Changes in physical appearance, either intentional or unintentional, alter an individual's perceptions and the perceptions others have of him or her. Clearly, the addition of clothing and accessories to the body changes perceptions. As Molloy has pointed out, and others have demonstrated, clothing and accessories play a major role in "making" us the people we are. Combined with body shape and image (Chapter 6), these "body accessories" have incredibly strong influences over the perceptions we have not only of others but also of ourselves.

QUESTIONS FOR THOUGHT

1. What makes a person spend more time than usual in preparing/changing his or her physical appearance after waking in the morning?
2. What are the advantages and disadvantages of breast implants?
3. Do clothes "make the person"? Why or why not?
4. When would one want to "dress down"?
5. What effect does a "good" tan have on others' perceptions of a person? On self-perceptions? Why?
6. What suggestions would you give to someone about to make a first impression in such contexts as the job interview? A first date? A courtroom appearance? A sales call?
7. What body alterations do you find attract you to someone else? Which ones deter you from approaching other persons?

FURTHER REFERENCES

Hair and Hairstyles

Dixson, B. J., and Vasey, P. L. (2012). Beards augment perceptions of men's age, social status, and aggressiveness, but not attractiveness. *Behavioral Ecology*, 23, 481–490.

Hilton, S., Hunt, K., Emslie, C., Salinas, M., and Ziebland, S. (2008). Have men been overlooked? A comparison of young men and women's experiences of chemotherapy-induced alopecia. *Psycho-Oncology*, 17, 577–583.

Kolber, R. H., and Albanese, P. J. (1996). Man to man: A content analysis of sole-male images in male-audience magazines. *Journal of Advertising, 4,*1–20.

Neff, J. (2004). Marketers betting on big-hair bounce. *Advertising Age, 75,* 3–53.

Patton, T. O. (2006). Hey girl, am I more than my hair? African American women and their struggles with beauty, body image, and hair. *NWSA Journal, 18,* 24–51.

Peixoto, L. M. (2002). The Brazilian wax: New hairlessness norm for women? *Journal of Communication Inquiry, 26,* 113–133.

The Skin: Cosmetics and Colorings

Bagdasarov, Z., Banerjee, S., Greene, K., and Campo, M. (2007, May). *Indoor tanning and problem behavior theory: Systems of influence.* Paper presented at the meeting of the International Communication Association, San Francisco, CA.

Dixon, H. G., Hill, D. J., Karoly, D. J., Jolley,D. J., and Aden, S. M. (2007). Solar UV forecasts: A randomized trial assessing their impact on adults' sun-protection behavior. *Health Education & Behavior, 34,* 486–502.

Frith, K., Shaw, P., and Cheng, H. (2005). The construction of beauty: A cross-cultural analysis of women's magazine advertising. *Journal of Communication, 55,* 56–70.

Mak, A. K. Y. (2007). Advertising whiteness: An assessment of skin color preferences among urban Chinese. *Visual Communication Quarterly, 14,* 144–157.

Reynolds, K. D., Buller, D. B., Yaroch, A. L., Maloy, J., Geno, C. R., and Cutter, G. R. (2008). Effects of program exposure and engagement with tailored prevention communication on sun protection by young adolescents. *Journal of Health Communication, 13,* 619–636.

Walkosz, W., Buller, D., Andersen, P., Scott, M., Dignan, M., Cutter, G., and Maloy, J. (2007, May). *Increasing sun protection in outdoor recreation: A theory-based health communication program.* Paper presented at the meeting of the International Communication Association, San Francisco, CA.

Tattoos, Body Piercing, and Branding

Aguilar, A. (2007, November). *Tattoos as worldviews: A journey into tattoo communications using standpoint theory.* Paper presented at the National Communication Association, Chicago, IL.

Atkinson, M. (2004). Tattooing and civilizing processes: Body modification as self-control. *Canadian Review of Sociology & Anthropology, 41,* 125–146.

Bernstein, E. (2007). Laser tattoo removal. *Seminars in Plastic Surgery, 21,* 175–192.

Carmen, R. A., Guitar, A. E., and Dillon, H. M. (2012). Ultimate answers to proximate questions: The evolutionary motivations behind tattoos and body piercings in popular culture. *Review of General Psychology, 16,* 134–143.

Cheng, S. C. (2003, May). *My body is the book: An ethnographic study of the tattooing practice among U.S. youth.* Paper presented at the meeting of the International Communication Association, San Diego, CA.

Eason, K. A., and Hodges, N. (2011). Reading contemporary female body modification as a site of Cixous' L'ectriture Feminine. *The Journal of Dress, Body & Culture, 15,* 323–343.

Fenske, M. (2007). Movement and resistance: (Tattooed) bodies and performance. *Communication & Critical/Cultural Studies, 4,* 51–73.

Firmin, M. W., Tse, L. M., Foster, J., and Angelini, T. (2008). Christian student perceptions of body tattoos: A qualitative analysis. *Journal of Psychology & Christianity, 27,* 195–204.

Gueguen, N. (2012). Tattoos, piercings, and sexual activity.*Social Behavior & Personality, 40,* 1543–1547.

Harlow, M. (2008, November). *UnConventional beauty: Bodies that speak*. Paper presented at the National Communication Association, San Diego, CA.

Koljonen, V., and Kluger, N. (2012). Specifically requesting surgical tattoo removal: Are deep personal motivations involved? *Journal of the European Academy of Dermatology & Venereology*, 26, 685–689.

Martino, S. (2008). Perceptions of a photograph of a woman with visible piercings. *Psychological Reports*, 103, 134–138.

McNaughton, M. J. (2007). Hard cases: Prison tattooing as visual argument. *Argumentation & Advocacy*, 43, 133–143.

Modesti, S. (2008). Home sweet home: Tattoo parlors as postmodern spaces of agency. *Western Journal of Communication*, 72, 197–212.

Porter, H. H. (2012). Tattoos v. tattoo: Separating the service from the constitutionally protected message. *Brigham Young University Law Review*, 2012, 1071–1107.

Schiller, D. (2008). China in the United States. *Communication & Critical/Cultural Studies*, 5, 411–415.

Sims, C. (2008, November). *Living (body) art: Framing the art and losing the body*. Paper presented at the National Communication Association, San Diego, CA.

Skegg, K., Nada-Raja, S. Paul, C., and Skegg, D. (2007). Body piercing, personality, and sexual behavior. *Archives of Sexual Behavior*, 36, 47–54.

Stirn, A., and Hinz, A. (2008). Tattoos, body piercings, and self-injury: Is there a connection? Investigations on a core group of participants practicing body modification. *Psychotherapy Research*, 18, 326–333.

Van der Meer, G. T., Schultz, W., and Nijman, J. M. (2008). Intimate body piercings in women. *Journal of Psychosomatic Obstetrics & Gynaecology*, 29, 235–239.

Vevea, N. (2008, November). *Body art: Performing identity through tattoos and piercing*. Paper presented at the National Communication Association, San Diego, CA.

Woodstock, L. (2008, May). *Tattoo therapy: Gender and healing on reality TV*. Paper presented at the meeting of the International Communication Association, Montreal, Canada.

Clothing

Adamo, G. E. (2011). Nigerian dress as a symbolic language. *Semiotica*,184, 1–9.

Fowles, J. (1974). Why we wear clothes. *ETC: A Review of General Semantics*, 21, 343.

Harvey, J. (2007). Showing and hiding: Equivocation in the relations of body and dress. *The Journal of Dress, Body & Culture*, 11, 65–94.

Kaiser, S. (1990). *The social psychology of clothing: Symbolic appearances in context* (2nd ed.). New York: Macmillan.

Nathan, J. (1986). *Uniforms and nonuniforms: Communication through clothing*. New York: Greenwood Press.

Raiscott, J. (1986). *Silent sales*. Minneapolis, MN: AB Publications.

Reynolds, K. D., Buller, D. B., Yaroch, A. L., Maloy, J., Geno, C. R., and Cutter, G. R. (2008). Effects of program exposure and engagement with tailored prevention communication on sun protection by young adolescents. *Journal of Health Communication*, 13, 619–636.

Rosenfeld, L. B., and Plax, T. G. (1977). Clothing as communication. *Journal of Communication*, 27, 24–31.

CHAPTER 7

KINESICS: THE STUDY OF HUMAN BODY MOVEMENTS

KEY CONCEPTS

- Birdwhistell's Six General Principles
- Approaches to Kinesic Study
- Linguistic Analogy
- Derivation System
- Functional
- Cumulative Structure
- Meaning-Centered Approach
- Functions

OBJECTIVES

By the end of the chapter you should be able to:

- Explain Birdwhistell's six general principles of kinesics.
- Demonstrate the differences between the various approaches to the study of kinesics.
- Explain how kinesics approximates language and define its parts.
- Explain what is meant by a "meaning-centered" approach to kinesics and define the five key kinesic functions developed by Ekman and Friesen.
- Discuss how emotions are communicated through kinesic displays.

Kinesics may be defined as the study of human body movements, including such phenomena as gestures, posture, facial expression, eye behavior, and rate of walk. Some popular writers have used the term "body language" to refer to what is scientifically known as kinesics. Kinesics has been a significant part of nonverbal communication for thousands of years, but scientific interest was rekindled by the works of Raymond Birdwhistell (1960, 1967, 1970, 1974) and has continued until the present time. Birdwhistell outlined six general principles of kinesics based on a scientific approach to the study of bodily movement that still can be applied. We look in some detail at Birdwhistell's contributions to the study of kinesics, but we also examine a second, more subjective, method called the functional approach to kinesics. Each approach produces different interpretations based on how the researcher using it sees the study of kinesics. Many consider Birdwhistell to be the "Father of Kinesics," so we begin with his work, including his six general principles.

PRINCIPLES

In one of his more important publications, *Kinesics and Context,* Birdwhistell (1970) outlined six general principles of kinesics. Each principle deals with (1) how we study body movement and (2) how such a study leads to understanding communication.

1. *There is a high degree of interdependence among the five body senses (visual, aural, gustatory, olfactory, and tactile) that, together with the verbal, form the intracommunicational system.* Each of the five senses is important in the determination of nonverbal meaning in face-to-face interactions. At various times each of the senses may dominate an interaction. For example, when a person you have known to be "cold" hugs you in greeting, the tactile sense (or touch) may become most obvious to you. In many instances, however, the senses *interact,* each of them adding a little to the perception of meaning in the interaction—thus the interdependence. What if that hug was given with a stiff body posture, around the shoulder area, with an extreme forward lean? Would that communicate the same message as what you think of as a "warm" hug? The kinesic variables (posture, lean, and gesture expressed by where the person puts his or her arm) offset what your sense of touch is telling you. The same is true when someone says they like you but does not look you in the eye; the verbal and nonverbal messages contradict each other.

2. *Kinesic communication varies according to culture and even among microcultures (or subcultures).* Individual differences persist in kinesic messages as a result of cultural differences. K. R. Johnson (1972), for example, described two ways in which black Americans' kinesic behavior differs from that of their white counterparts. Johnson attributes much of the difference to the African heritage of black Americans. One of the differences is that blacks have been found to be more reluctant to look another person directly in the eye. The other is that blacks walk differently than whites. Johnson writes, "Observing young black males walking down ghetto streets, one can't help noticing that they are, indeed, in Thoreau's words, 'marching to the tune of a different drummer.' The 'different drummer' is a different culture; the non-verbal [*sic*] message of their walk is similar to the non-verbal [*sic*] message of young white males, but not quite the same" (p. 185). To stereotype all black Americans as walking this way, however, would be wrong. In the 30 years since this research was reported, more people have come to realize that to stereotype an individual on the basis of cultural differences can (and often does) spell disaster for effective communication interactions. K. R. Johnson reported in a more recent study (2004) that an African American who finds himself or herself in a subordinate role is likely to show disdain by rolling the eyes. Studies such as these just go to prove that you need to be observant of the people you are communicating with and gear your communication accordingly.

In addition to these cultural variations, there are differences in kinesic behavior between subcultures. Morris, Collett, Marsh, and O'Shaughnessy (1979) have discussed some of the differences in Western Europe, although they are too numerous to list here. Differences exist, too, even between microcultures, such as families. Some families, often those of higher socioeconomic classes, tend to be more "formal" in their kinesic behavior, while other families are more "huggy-kissy," or dramatic or animated. Although these are just a few examples, suffice it to say that cultural backgrounds do affect how people communicate through their use of kinesics. We suggest a course in intercultural communication not only to understand these differences but to become better communicators when you encounter those differences.

3. *There is no universal body language symbol.* The nature/nurture controversy (referring to whether kinesics are innate or learned) persists. Birdwhistell's view is that nurture (learning) is the sole responsible factor. Darwin, with his nature view (innate), and some contemporary researchers, who are discussed later in this chapter, have disputed this view.

Birdwhistell (1970) claims, "We have been searching for fifteen years and have found no gesture or body motion which has the same meaning in all societies" (p. 81). To exemplify this, an Arab may stroke his beard to convey the message, "There goes a pretty girl." A southern Italian, however, pulls his right ear lobe with his right hand to mean the same thing. To convey the same message, an American male may form the shape of a pretty woman by moving his hands in the air (Birdwhistell 1970). "As far as we know," said Birdwhistell, "there is no body motion or gesture that can be regarded as a universal symbol. That is, we have been unable to discover any single facial expression, stance, or body position which conveys an identical meaning in all societies" (p. 32).

4. *The principle of redundancy, as stated in information theory, is not applicable to kinesic behavior.* According to information theory, some gestures may be reinforcing (and therefore redundant or repetitious) for verbal communication. An example would be when one says, "A box is about 24 inches long," while simultaneously holding one's hands to indicate the 24 inches. Birdwhistell claims that kinesic behavior is *complementary to* (meaning "adds to") rather than *redundant with* (or repeating of) the verbal behavior; however, not all scholars accept his notion of this complementary function. A prime example is the smile. We are not always complementing or reinforcing when we smile; indeed, we may even be masking a contradictory or negative message.

PHOTO 7.1 Some gestures do not need words to be understood, although meanings can vary from country to country.

5. *Kinesic behavior is more primitive and less controllable than verbal communication.* Although both kinesic behavior and verbal communication are learned, it seems that we pay less attention to what our nonverbal communication is "saying." There are numerous reasons for this, but one account is perhaps the most common. It says that we learn the use of verbal communication very early as a conscious process; however, we are not aware of our learning to "speak" nonverbally. Parents get very excited about their child's first words, but do they get as excited about a child's first gesture? Although we pay attention to the kinesic behavior of others, we may not monitor our own nonverbal communication. This lack of self-monitoring is probably most evident when a person takes a public speaking class. Although we "speak with our hands" naturally, when we get up in front of an audience those gestures seem to disappear. Students must be "re-taught" to use gestures in such situations. In many instances, a speaker who is anxious about the speaking experience grabs the lectern and "hangs on for dear life." Also, many beginning public speakers have been literally taught (often by their parents) that they should *not talk* with their hands; such teaching is a major disservice, since the use of hand gestures sends a message of dynamism. There is an optimum level of gesturing, however, and when you go beyond this optimum level, you move to a point of distraction, not dynamism.

6. *We must compare and contrast nonverbal codes time and time again in context before we can make accurate interpretations.* When we meet strangers, we tend to evaluate them. These evaluations are often based largely on nonverbal behavior. We often agree with each other as to what stereotypes we see on the basis of kinesic behavior alone. Barker (1942) found, for example, that people can make similar (but not always accurate) judgments about others, based on just visual and proxemic information. In principle number 6, Birdwhistell (1974) warned that we should attempt to evaluate kinesic behavior only after having significant information about the person behaving. Even then, we should consider the social context, or situation, when making an interpretation. This means that we should have some baseline behavior as a norm *before* making a judgment. What we authors have found, based on comments made by our students, is that other people will assume that because you are taking a course in nonverbal communication, you can "read body language." Although you may be tempted to show off, you should remember that what you interpret from the other's gestures is only as valid as what you know about the person and the context or situation. If you don't know the person at all, it may be, at best, an educated guess at this point in your studies. Would you like others evaluating you on the same basis?

PUTTING PRINCIPLES TO WORK

Birdwhistell's six underlying kinesics principles provide a basis for studying body movement, even some 50-plus years later. In this chapter, we review the principles of the science, together with the different ways in which men and women send and receive messages, and how these messages can be interpreted in and out of context. Body movement varies with language and culture. Aspects of status, facial expression, and eye behavior should be considered. Pupil size, conscious and unconscious facial expressions, and even our place in the chain of command help to convey nonverbal messages. It should be noted before we begin this study of kinesics that human dominance in nature (over other animals) has come about as a result of the ability to communicate thoughts and to control oneself, the environment, and other people through communication. As we become better able to understand the complex communication processes observed in others, we can better understand those processes in ourselves.

CATEGORIES IN KINESICS

Kinesics is a nonverbal area that is approached in a number of ways. Knowing these approaches and understanding how each differs in the interpretation of behavior makes possible better and more refined explanations of communication. This knowledge also enables us to understand better how others may interpret communicative behavior.

BIRDWHISTELL'S LINGUISTIC ANALOGY

Birdwhistell (1974) claimed that there is an analogy between kinesics and linguistics. He says that **parakinesic phenomena** (meaning everything involved in the actual overall use of kinesics, including minute movements we may never notice) are similar to factors that influence our verbal expression. He has further theorized that three factors are included in all parakinesic phenomena: (1) the degree of muscular tension (intensity); (2) the length of time involved in the movement (duration); and (3) the extent of the movement (range). These three phenomena yield a system of kinesic study that examines the *structure of the movement* and, based upon that structure, creates a "meaningful" statement, much like the building of a sentence from its parts.

For purposes of analysis, Birdwhistell defined what he referred to as an **allokine**, the smallest unit of kinesic behavior, generally too small to be meaningful. Birdwhistell noted that allokines are rarely perceptible to the human eye, and there are 20,000 allokines in the facial area alone. When observing people, we must use **kines**, which are combinations of allokines. This level of analysis, however, is still beneath the meaningful (it also is too small for analysis) and must be combined with other kines to allow substantial analysis. The next largest unit (the combination of kines) is the **kineme** (a group of kines) but may be used interchangeably without affecting the social meaning. General American movement contains about 50 or 60 kinemes; most of these are in the head and face area. Kinemes combine to form **kinemorphemes**, which are sequential movements. These categories may be considered analogous to categories in language from allophones to sentences.

Some social scientists say that the comparison of kinesics to the linguistic system is simple; others would disagree. Allokines and kines are equivalent to the allophone and phone. Kinemes are equivalent to the morpheme; morphemes combine to form words, and kinemes combine to form kinemorphic classes. Birdwhistell postulated that these can be analyzed by means of a coding system. Critics of Birdwhistell's system say that it is not easy to determine each part of the process. They further say that if an allokine cannot be perceived as sending a message, then why try to determine what an allokine is? Critics also point out that what Birdwhistell developed to simplify the understanding of kinesics really did nothing more than complicate the science. The major criticism is found in the position that it simply is not possible to treat physical movements in the same way one treats verbal language (see Dittman 1971).

BOX 7.1 OBSERVATIONAL STUDY

Observe a simple interaction and write down whatever communication you saw (it may be best to video a few minutes of interaction—since most smartphones today have that capability, this should be easy to do). First, simply describe what you saw in terms of specific body-part behaviors. Second, attempt to devise symbols that describe the kinesic behaviors you observed. Do the same for the verbal portion of the interaction. What do you discover about this phenomenon? Are the symbols and the verbal portion (language) connected? If so, how? Do they contradict each other? If so, which messages are more believable, the verbal or the nonverbal? Why do you think this contradiction happens?

MORRIS' DERIVATION SYSTEM

Morris (1977) suggests that there are five categories of *actions*. These categories are inborn, discovered, absorbed, trained, and mixed. Morris states, "Human behavior is not free-flowing; it is divided into a long series of separate events. Each event, such as eating a meal, visiting a theatre, taking a bath, or making love, has its own special rules and rhythms" (p. 11). One category of actions is *inborn* actions; these actions are innate and exist at birth. One example is a newborn baby's "reacting immediately to its mother's nipple by sucking" (p. 13). A second category is *discovered* actions, actions that we discover (such as folding one's arms) but that are limited because of the genetic structure of our bodies (in this case, our arms; p. 17). Absorbed actions are those that "we acquire unknowingly from our companions" (p. 18). Many of these actions are acquired in an unconscious attempt to synchronize our actions when we are with others; in short, we have a tendency to use the same behaviors that our companions use (also called the reciprocal or dyadic effect). Scheflen (1964) actually recognized this idea before Morris labeled it as *absorbed action*; he called it *postural echo* and *postural congruence.* Scheflen believed that when two people shared the same figurative position (i.e., ideological beliefs), they would also share the same literal postural position, in essence *echoing* the other person's posture. E. T. Hall (1976) suggests that *absorbed* actions occur at an early age. (Examples are the synchronized behavior of elementary school students on a playground, such as skipping, dancing, and jumping.) In a study trying to see if participants would "match" the confederates' nonverbal immediacy, S. M. Jones and Wirtz (2007) found that the condition did not matter (either high, low, or moderate immediacy displayed). They found that the participants would try to mirror the confederates' nonverbal behaviors regardless of the condition. In addition, Jones and Wirtz discovered that females are much more likely to try to "match" the confederates' nonverbal messages than men are. Similarly, Kimbara (2008) found that people are likely to try to match their gestures when describing something when they can see the other person to whom they are speaking. She placed pairs of speakers together and asked them to describe cartoons together to a video camera. When they were placed with a partner whom they could see, their gestures were similar. N. Hall, Millings, and Boucas (2012) found similar results when they looked at people who are "attachment oriented"—meaning they feel the need to be attached to certain individuals in their lives. N. Hall et al. discovered that people who were high in attachment orientation were more likely to imitate (or "mimic") the behaviors of those with whom we are communicating. Holler and Wilkin (2011) also discovered the same sort of thing when considering whether people would mimic speechmaking gestures when they engaged in face-to-face conversations. Clearly, we do have a tendency to synchronize nonverbal behaviors in many situations, just as we discussed in Chapter 1—the idea of the *norm of reciprocity* or the *dyadic effect.*

Trained actions are those that people have to learn from others; walking on one's hands is an example. Finally, *mixed* actions are those we *acquire* in a number of ways from a mixture of sources. Infantile crying, for example, is changed as we become adults in an attempt to "cover up" such behavior. Thus, Morris' categories are based upon how we acquire a particular nonverbal behavior. Even though it has been a long time since these studies were conducted and the categories were established, the categories still are used in today's studies of nonverbal communication. Can you think of any of your own kinesic behaviors and determine into which category they fall? Since much kinesic behavior is not done consciously, this task may be hard to accomplish.

MEHRABIAN'S FUNCTIONAL APPROACH

Other nonverbal communication theorists were researching kinesics in the earlier years of formalized study of the discipline; and although they took a different approach, their work is equally important to the study of kinesics. Mehrabian (1972, 1981) categorized kinesic behavior into functional groups. These categories include: (1) a pleasure–displeasure dimension (liking–disliking), (2) a dominance–submissiveness dimension (high status–low status), and (3) an arousal–nonarousal dimension (intense–relaxed). In his research on body orientation, Mehrabian found differences between people who liked one another and those who did not. *Body orientation,* for instance, may be defined as "the degree to which a communicator's shoulders and legs are turned in the direction of, rather than away from, the addressee" (Knapp 1978, 221). Mehrabian found that a male interacting with another male has less direct body orientation with a well-liked person. Female communicators used a very indirect orientation with intensely disliked persons, relatively direct with persons they liked, and the most direct with neutrally liked persons. There was no difference in the openness of arms and legs, whether the two communicators liked each other or not. Mehrabian's general conclusion on his **pleasure–displeasure** *(liking)* dimension is that relaxation is extremely low when one is talking to a disliked person; relaxation is moderate when one is talking with a friend. Naturally, the context—in addition to how well one knows the person—affects the accuracy of one's interpretation of someone's posture. Do not just assume that because others take a certain posture they are sending a specific message.

Mehrabian's second dimension is **dominance–submissiveness**, or what we might refer to as *status* or *power difference.* Mehrabian found that people stand with a more direct body orientation when talking to a higher-status person. People in inferior roles often lower their heads. Individuals' legs and hands are more relaxed when they are of higher status talking with a lower-status person. A higher-status person uses a sideways leaning posture more often when talking to a subordinate. All are indicative of a relationship between the two interactants of differing status.

Mehrabian's research on status has induced others to view status as directly related to the sex of the individual. Henley (1977), for example, hypothesized that females nonverbally communicate from a lower-status position, whereas males gain and maintain their higher status through the use of nonverbal symbols. Goffman (1976) found some support for Henley's hypothesis in his research on advertisements. Finally, Argyle and Williams (1976) suggested that one reason for sex differences in status may be derived from the perception of where the nonverbal behaviors are *attributed*. They believe that females generally attribute nonverbal actions as feedback from themselves. That is, they take on a perceivee role; they take the responsibility for their nonverbal actions. Males tend to attribute nonverbal actions to others or to the environment. That is, they take on a perceiver role; they think their nonverbal actions are caused by outside sources. This line of reasoning could be further extended to infer that any minority (implying here that females may perceive themselves as a "minority" in terms of status, equated with, for example, Blacks, Hispanics, or others) might classify the nonverbal actions as feedback from themselves, or as feedback from powerless, low-status people.

Over the years, research has often shown that male nonverbal behaviors are more dominant than that of females, especially in bigendered situations. Research shows that men will expand their posture to take up more space, especially in sitting and standing; women have been found to use shrinkage behaviors, taking up less space (L. V. Harper and Sanders 1975; Wood 2012). Take a look around your classroom and look at the posturing exhibited by both the males and females. Do you notice the differences? A favorite example to discuss in nonverbal communication classes is an airplane situation. Ask women how they feel about being placed in airplane seats next to men who expand their posture into the women's seats. You might be surprised at how women respond to this invasion of space, and how often men are oblivious to the encroachment since they are just using their normal posture in this setting. The female author of your text has always wanted to say, "I paid for this seat, you paid for that seat; you stay in your seat, and I'll stay in mine." The findings about expansive male posture seem to occur over and over again in each subsequent study conducted over the years.

Mehrabian's third category is the **arousal–nonarousal** dimension, or *responsiveness*. High levels of arousal are shown both internally and externally. When we are interested in something or someone, we have higher blood pressure, higher pulse rates, and increased muscle tension; we respond to the stimulus through an aroused feeling. When aroused, our pupils enlarge (dilate), and we engage in more bodily movement. Recently, researchers have referred to *immediacy*, a factor that is both an arousal and a liking function. Immediacy, as you will recall, is the concept of appearing more open, likable, and approachable, in this case by your use of kinesics. Immediacy involves not only kinesic cues but, as Mehrabian has suggested, spatial cues, verbal cues, touching, loudness of voice, and the like. For immediacy,

Physical Violence/Verbal Hostility/Neutrality/Immediacy/Intimacy

FIGURE 7.1 The place of avoidance-oriented to approach-oriented behaviors.

these verbal and nonverbal cues must work together. Richmond, McCroskey, and Hickson (2011) argue that immediacy can be found on a continuum, with physical violence at one end and intimacy at the other (see Figure 7.1).

Obviously, when two people engage in a fistfight, they are close in space and they are "touching" one another, but they are not immediate. R. G. Powell and Harville (1990), for example, saw immediacy as behaviors reducing physical and psychological distance between people. They studied differences in what constitutes immediacy across ethnic groups, as it relates to teacher clarity (how a teacher's clearness is perceived by students).

Interestingly, the health care environment has not received a lot of research attention when it comes to the study of kinesics. Blanch-Hartigan (2011) found that there was a way to measure how well health care providers were able to recognize emotional messages of kinesic behavior, and that health care industries would do well to pay attention to teaching these skills when they are lacking. One study by Gorawara-Bhat, Cook, and Sachs (2007) found some interesting outcomes of how the health care providers positioned themselves as well as their kinesic behaviors when working with elderly patients. Gorawara-Bhat et al. determined kinesic behaviors in the health care setting to be: stance, eye contact, facial expressions, gestures, and touch. They found that patients responded better to environments where the doctors used some of the positive kinesic attributes, and they believe that doctors would do well to structure their examination rooms to facilitate such kinesic behaviors.

If we look at immediacy as a form of nonverbal responsiveness, there are many findings that support its use or nonuse (see G. B. Ray and Floyd, 2006). As we begin this discussion, since there is no *one* standardized method of measuring learning, realize that findings are mixed about whether or not the actual differences in learning are attributable to immediacy and teaching styles. Because of this, it makes it a bit more difficult to compare results from different studies, but we point out some salient issues here so that you can think about what some researchers have found on this important topic of nonverbal immediacy. Sanders and Wiseman (1990) found that teacher immediacy enhanced students' cognitive, affective, and behavioral learning. Their study's participants were white, Asian, Hispanic, and black. The relationship of immediacy to affective learning (or the emotional responsiveness aspect of learning) was more common in the Hispanic students. Other researchers (Kearney, Plax, Smith, and Sorensen 1988), looking at immediacy in the learning context, found that students reported a greater likelihood of resistance to teachers if the teacher's techniques were *unexpected*. According to perceived immediacy, the teachers appeared less immediate and, therefore, the students were less responsive. Kerssen-Griep and Witt (2012) discovered that the immediacy of teachers affects the students' perception of teacher fairness with his or her students. J. K. Burgoon and Newton (1991), in a study on relational messages, found that *high involvement* and the specific nonverbal cues associated with it conveyed greater intimacy.

including immediacy and affection, than did low-involvement nonverbal cues (see also L. Powell, Hamilton, Hickson, and Stuckey 2001).

Mehrabian presented three dimensions of nonverbal behavior: (1) liking, (2) power and status, and (3) responsiveness. Each of the three may function alone or may interact with another to communicate messages to another person. Regardless, all of these dimensions are important in communication.

BOX 7.2 OBSERVATIONAL STUDY

Choose a place where you can sit and observe people for 10 to 15 minutes (or more). Note the bodily movements of the people you observe. Do they seem to be using movements on purpose? How many of the movements appear nonpurposive (or not intended to send a message)?

What messages do you see sent about the people you observe? If they are animated, do you think they are extroverted? Does your interpretation of those behaviors change if you take Morris's kinesic perspective? Mehrabian's perspective? Why?

EKMAN AND FRIESEN'S CUMULATIVE STRUCTURE

Ekman and Friesen (1969) have taken a more precise approach to kinesic behavior, and although their initial study was conducted more than 40 years ago, it is still considered the definitive research of this topic. Most contemporary nonverbal textbooks still cite Ekman and Friesen's study when they define kinesics, as do contemporary studies published in professional journals. This approach is sometimes called the *meaning-centered* approach to the study of kinesics because Ekman and Friesen were most interested in the meanings associated with bodily movement. They state that body movement can be analyzed in terms of five functions or categories of behaviors: (1) emblems, (2) illustrators, (3) regulators, (4) adaptors, and (5) affect displays. Because the approach is less "structure" oriented, it is easier to comprehend, but because of that same quality it is more difficult to determine what specific behavior might be equated with what meaning. (There are also some competing theories to Ekman and Friesen's, most recognizably Russell's [1994] theories, which are discussed in detail in Chapter 8.)

EMBLEMS

Ekman (1976) writes that emblems have direct translations into verbal communication (usually a word or two or a phrase). Most people in the culture are familiar with the word or phrase and with the emblem; emblems, then, are sent with conscious intent. The receiver knows that he or she is the recipient of the message, and the sender usually takes responsibility for the message. Some examples are the American emblem for "OK"; pointing one's finger like a pistol to indicate suicide; and rubbing one's index fingers from back to the tip, one on top of the other, to mean "shame on you." One of the most common messages in the United States is the emblem of "the finger." Its meaning is generally interpreted as "screw you," but the negative intent usually associated with it may be dampened when accompanied by a smile and transmitted by a friend. We do, however, find this emblem used considerably

PHOTO 7.2 What type of gesturing appears to be taking place here?

in situations of anger and rage. Cayanus, Martin, and Weber (2005) conducted a research study on college-age drivers, their levels of anger while driving, and their aggression traits. Cayanus et al. discovered that many things are likely to cause a high level of anger with college-age drivers (construction, slow drivers, police presence, discourteous driving), and that when the level of anger increases, assertive negative gestures—such as the middle finger—are more likely to be displayed. Again, contexts and relationships will greatly affect the meanings of emblems.

In their European studies of gestures, Morris and others did not find "the finger" to be a dominant gesture. They found a number of substitutes, however, including the forearm jerk, the vertical horn-sign (index and pinky fingers up while the thumb holds down the middle and ring fingers), the fig (the thumb between the index and middle fingers), the peace or victory sign with the back of your hand facing the receiver, and what we Americans know as the "OK sign" (thumb and forefinger placed in a circle with the other three fingers extended in the air). There are many ways to offend people of other cultures when using emblems we find common in our culture, so be sure you know the unacceptable ones in cultures you plan to travel to (see Morris et al. 1979).

ILLUSTRATORS

Ekman and Friesen's second category is **illustrators**. These gestures are used to support what is being said verbally, usually serving the *complementary* or redundant function discussed earlier. They are used particularly when giving directions. Cohen (1977) investigated the use of illustrators and found that (1) they were used more often in face-to-face interaction, and (2) they were used regardless of how familiar the communicator was with the directions. In general, there are several classes of illustrators:

- Those that emphasize words or sentences (such as shaking your fist while telling another person *how* mad you are).

- Those that represent the thought processes (such as rolling the hand over as if trying to get a thought out or snapping a finger to create the impression of knowledge suddenly retrieved at a point in time). These gestures are sometimes called *ideographs*, to indicate your attempt to get the idea out.
- Those that "draw" the shape of objects in space (such as drawing a circle with your fingers or calling someone a "square" while outlining one in the air) and represent some form of bodily action, sometimes called *pictographs*.

In addition, other researchers have found that the use of gestures helps the listeners (or decoders) to retain the message over time (Church, Garber, and Rogalski, 2007). Lozano and Tversky (2006) discovered that the use of gestures not only assisted in retention but also in the actual process of problem solving. Gregersen, Olivares-Cuhat, and Storm (2009) indicated in their results of an experimental study of college-age Spanish-class students that people do use illustrators (as well as other gestures related to the verbal message being sent) to enhance the meaning of their messages.

REGULATORS

The third category developed by Ekman and Friesen is **regulators**. These gestures allow us to regulate when to talk and when to allow others to talk.

Regulation refers to a person's desire to enter, exit, or maintain the floor in an interaction. Kendon and Ferber (1973) provide six stages of general interaction that serve to regulate or use the regulation function:

1. *Sighting, orientation, and initiation of the approach.*
2. *The distant salutation.* This is the "official ratification" (1) that a greeting sequence has been initiated and (2) of who the participants are. A wave, smile, or call may be used for recognition. Two types of head movements were noted at this point. One, the head toss, is a fairly rapid back and forward tilting movement. Some people, however, tend to lower the head, hold it for a short while, then slowly raise it. Some scholars report that this movement occurs only in American culture; the head-toss back is more likely to be done by African Americans, and head lowering, by Caucasians.
3. *The head dip.* This movement has been noted by researchers in other contexts as a marker for transitions between activities or shifts in psychological orientation. Kendon and Ferber did not observe this movement if the greeter did not continue to approach his or her partner.
4. *Approach.* As the greeting parties continued to move toward each other, several behaviors were observed. Gazing behavior probably helped signal that the participants were cleared for talking. An aversion of this gaze was seen just prior to the close salutation stage, however. Also observed at this point were grooming behavior and the moving of one or both arms to the front of the body.
5. *Final approach.* Now the participants are less than 10 feet apart. Mutual gazing, smiling, and positioning of the head not seen in the sequence thus far can now be seen. The palms of the hands may also be turned toward the other person (see also Palanica and Itier 2012).

6. *Close salutation.* As the participants negotiate a standing position, we hear the more stereotyped, ritualistic verbalizations so characteristic of the greeting ceremony, for example, "Hi, Steve! How ya doin'?" and so on. If the situation calls for body contact or ritualized gesture (handshakes, embraces, a kiss, and the like), it will occur at this time.

Once the two parties have entered into conversation, decisions must be made about who talks when *(turn-taking)*. Although a large portion of turn-taking behavior is vocalic, there are certain kinesic behaviors that control the flow of communication, and these differ from culture to culture. In an interesting study in Sweden, Brumark (2010) found that in family dinner table talk, little children need more direct regulators used with them, such as direct questions, but that older children (as well as adults) understand and react to nonverbal regulators. For the North American culture, as Duncan (1972, 1975, 1983) points out, the turn-taking sequence is typically me-you-me-you-me-you. Within the interaction, we typically find such kinesic behaviors as gaze direction, head nods, forward leans, gesturing, and facing behavior (facing the other person, or turning away) used to control the flow of communication (Wiemann and Knapp 1975). These kinesic behaviors have several functions: They may indicate a desire to continue with the conversation if you are speaking; they may signal a desire to turn the conversation over to you if you are listening; or you may use them to keep the other person talking. You may also signal a desire to take over the conversation (or a desire to enter). An interesting example of how this is often done in interpersonal interactions is by the raising of the index finger. Some scholars conjecture that we do this because we are conditioned to "raise our hands" to gain the floor in the classroom setting, so we raise a part of our hand in interpersonal settings. Take note of how often you use this regulatory body movement over the next few days; it is usually surprising to most people that they do use this gesture.

STUDENT VOICES

Chihiro: As an exchange student from Japan, I have had to learn a lot about the greeting behaviors used in the U.S.A. I learned at home to greet people with a bow, but when I do that here in the U.S.A., my fellow students laugh at me. I wish they could see that this is how I have been raised—it is a part of my culture—and I will be expected to do this when I return home. I wouldn't laugh at those who laugh at me when they try to greet my fellow Japanese friends with a handshake.

Keeping the other person talking is usually the regulatory function of **backchanneling** behaviors, behaviors engaged in (1) to make the speaker feel he or she is being listened to and (2) to confirm interest in the speaker (Duncan 1972). Li (2006) added to that list a third function: recall of what is being discussed. With backchanneling cues you can set the pace at which the speaker speaks with your head nods and smiles. More succinctly, when you backchannel, you respond to the speaker in some way. Head nods (usually accompanied by "um-hmms") often accomplish those three functions. These backchanneling cues are not unique to the culture of the United States. Li (2006) discovered that in a cross-cultural study between Canadian doctors and patients and Chinese doctors and patients, backchanneling cues improved recall of what was discussed when Canadian doctors communicated with

Back Channeling

Gender
Di Alvereal

Canadian patients, and when Chinese doctors communicated with Chinese patients. The same results did not occur when the groups were mixed—when Chinese doctors communicated with Canadian patients and Canadian doctors communicated with Chinese patients. J. A. Dixon and Foster (1998) found that there are gender differences in backchanneling, and that females use more backchanneling behaviors than males do. Often backchanneling is done subconsciously, but if we know that there is the possibility of these positive functions occurring, we would do well to manipulate these behaviors.

BOX 7.3 OBSERVATIONAL STUDY

Explore the backchannel in class or in the hallways. As a speaker talks to you, slowly begin to backchannel with head nods; slowly increase the frequency of the head nod and note what the speaker's pace is. Does she or he stop and turn the "floor" over to you? Slow down the backchannel; what is the speaker's frequency of speech now?

Several studies demonstrate the impact of other influences on turn-taking. Since turn-taking is a part of the regulatory function and usually includes body movements and eye behaviors, as well as vocalics and proxemics, we look at it here. Iizuka (1993), for example, divided Japanese participants into dyads composed of either one man and one woman or two women and had them watch a movie and review it. Iizuka found that the participants used vocal inflection shifts, no eye contact during the pause, and repetition of words to indicate that they wanted the speaker to continue his or her turn. While some turn-taking cues were similar to those used by Americans speaking English, some were different. Iizuka points out that there are cultural and linguistic differences in turn-taking cues. In a study with American participants, Ayres, Hopf, Brown, and Suek (1993) found that the level of communication apprehension also affected turn-taking cues; however, the differences were related more to turn-requesting than turn-yielding behaviors. Females also employed different cues than did males; females not apprehensive about speaking used considerably different cues than very apprehensive males. This apprehension variable tends to place less value on gender than perhaps Henley (1977) and others indicate. Such an analysis might appear to indicate that females were seeking the floor for what Tannen (1990) refers to as "positive interruptions." Such an interaction might appear as:

PERSON 1: "I was on Oak Street trying—"
PERSON 2: "Aren't the cherry blossoms beautiful there?"

J. K. Burgoon, Buller, and Woodall (1996) report a study in which the regulation of conversation took on a synchronous form. People are synchronous in their behavior and communication when the "flow" of their actions takes on a continuous flow: The conversation flows back and forth in a rhythm (the you-me-you-me format mentioned earlier). Although this research did not deal specifically with kinesics, the form of synchrony observed brought the interactants into a face-to-face, reciprocal gaze during the synchronous part of the conversation, which included smiling. The lack of synchrony was indicative of tension in the interaction; the interactants were uncomfortable for one reason or another.

ADAPTORS

Ekman and Friesen's fourth category is **adaptors**, gestures that are learned in childhood; some research calls them "nervous habits." Picking one's nose, scratching the body, or playing with hair or an earlobe are adaptors; they serve to satisfy a bodily function. When attention is focused on such behavior, we sometimes turn to objects instead. Hence, the fondling of rosary beads, the thumbing of a stone, playing with one's jewelry or clothing, rubbing one's forehead, or nail biting all function to reduce some felt stress or need. People who quit smoking turn to other object adaptors such as pens, pencils, their fingers, or candy. Wolfe (2005) discovered that a student technical writing group used adaptors, in particular pen fidgeting, not only as nervous movements, but also as a form of regulator. It seemed to Wolfe that the students used these adaptive behaviors to control conversational space and to call attention to themselves as writers.

Adaptors, then, are used to adjust the body, to satisfy some bodily need, or, at times, to satisfy some emotional need. These are also often caused by nervousness, negative arousal, or boredom. Look around your classroom and see how many people are using some form of an adaptor, such as tapping their pens, playing with their clothing, or covering their mouth with their hands. These are common behaviors and can be seen in many different settings.

BOX 7.4   OBSERVATIONAL STUDY

In your next class, observe your fellow classmates for their use of adaptors. How many do you notice? How many are self-focused? How many are object-focused? Speculate on what sort of emotion has caused these adaptors (Nervousness? Boredom?). (Recall that making judgments without knowing the person or the context will affect your accuracy.)

AFFECT DISPLAYS

The final category is that of affect displays, or emotional displays. Ekman and Friesen (1975) undertook a number of research studies in this area (see Hickson and Stacks 1991 for a review of those studies). Using participants from a number of cultures, Ekman and Friesen found seven emotions that are universally expressed in facial expression: (1) fear; (2) anger; (3) surprise; (4) disgust; (5) contempt; (6) sadness, and (7) happiness.

Usually when we look at affect displays, we associate the specific emotion with the face and with the degree to which that emotion exists in the body. The body, by its tenseness, is indicative of what degree of emotion is being exhibited. As the body tenses, the emotion is usually greater. The body, then, tells us much about a person's emotional state, but we usually combine it with facial expressions. When identifying the specific emotion, however, we still rely on the face. According to Ekman and Friesen (1975), we can examine the face for emotion by the area or region of the face from which the cue originates. This technique is called the *Facial Affect Scoring Technique,* or *FAST.* A second technique is the *Facial Meaning Sensitivity Test,* or FMST, developed by Leathers and Emigh (1980). Although both tests are

Universal facial expression.

According to a 1960's study by psychologist Paul Ekman, all cultures associate these seven facial expressions with the same seven emotions.

Disgust.
R. Clenched nostrils.
S. Pursed lips.

Happy.
T. Primarily, a smile.

Contempt.
U. Primarily, tight lips, raised slightly on one side.

Rest.

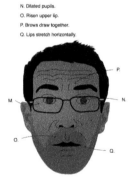

Sad.
L. Primarily, a frown (or a furrowed brow).

Anger.
A. Flushed face.
B. An inward and downward brow movement.
C. A hard stare.
D. Flared nostrils.
E. Clenched jaw.

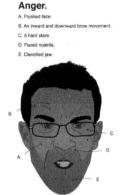

Fear.
M. Widening eyes.
N. Dilated pupils.
O. Risen upper lip.
P. Brows draw together.
Q. Lips stretch horizontally.

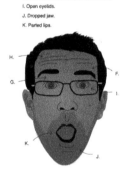

Surprise.
F. Raised and curved eyebrows.
G. Stretched skin below the eyebrows.
H. Horizontal wrinkles across the forehead.
I. Open eyelids.
J. Dropped jaw.
K. Parted lips.

PHOTO 7.3

concerned with affect displays, FAST looks mainly for a categorization of the specific emotion, whereas EMST looks for the meaning within such a categorization found in FAST. Both are useful.

Within the FAST are three areas or regions. Region I contains the eyebrows and forehead; Region II is the area from the eyelids on down to the bridge of the nose; Region III comprises the nose, cheeks, mouth, and jaw. Morris (1985) refers to these as blends, blending areas of the face together to create an emotional message; this phenomenon is discussed in more

PHOTO 7.4   People's posture, combined with facial expressions, convey many things.

detail later. Within these regions, we can identify the seven emotional facial expressions
Ekman and Friesen found. The best area in which to identify *fear* is from the eyes and eyelids,
the upper eyelid usually being raised and the lower eyelid tensed and drawn up. Fear may
occur simultaneously with other emotions such as sadness, anger, or disgust. Varying from
something minor to something life-endangering, the causes of fear can be physical, psychological, or both. The psychological object of fear may be the loss of friendship, attacks on
one's worth, or damage to one's self-esteem and sense of security.

Anger is usually expressed through the cheeks, mouth, brows, and forehead. Unless anger
is registered in all three facial areas, there is ambiguity. Anger is usually aroused by frustration, physical threat, psychological hurt, or violation of moral values. Some of the usual
signs of anger are an increase in blood pressure, a change in one's breathing, and a rising
tension in the person's body (Boucher and Ekman 1975). Some researchers believe that men
show more negative emotions than women do, and that women are often the recipients of
negative affect displays. Many have gone about trying to show this to be true. S. C. Koch
(2005) is one such scholar, and she discovered that in small group task contexts, women
group leaders did receive more negative affect, even when both the males and females were
evaluated to have equivalent group facilitation skills. LoBue and Larson (2010) found some
interesting results when they tried to discover if adults or children read an angry emotional
expression on someone's face as more threatening than other facial expressions. Their results
showed that both adults and children read angry faces as threatening.

Two other studies found that the anger emotion is also displayed in other ways. Deffenbacher, Oetting, and Lynch (1994) found that people displayed facial expressions of anger
when driving an automobile. They constructed a "driving scale" composed of six subscales:
hostile gestures, illegal driving, police presence, slow driving, discourtesy, and traffic obstructions. Men were angrier when there was a police presence and when others were driving
slowly. Women were angered by illegal behavior on the part of other drivers and traffic
obstructions. Overall, however, the male and female anger scores were similar. It would be
interesting to have someone replicate this study to see the results today, since "road rage" has

[handwritten margin notes: "Area for fear" and "Anger region"]

become such a prevalent issue in our society. The Cayanus et al. (2005) study found similar results about what causes road rage, although they were looking more specifically at the use of emblematic gestures as affect displays.

Surprise is the briefest of the seven emotions that Ekman and Friesen consider to be universal. Surprise is triggered by the unexpected and by what might be called the "misexpected" event. An unexpected surprise is an unusual event that is unanticipated, occurring when the surprised person is not expecting anything in particular to happen. In a mis-expected surprise, the event need not be unusual to be surprising; it is the contrast with what is expected at the moment that is surprising. Surprise is not limited to the physical; it can also be in reaction to ideas, concepts, or words. When it is not experienced as isolated emotion, surprise is usually followed by another emotion. It is the subsequent emotion that gives a positive or negative tone to the experience, fear being the most common sequel. It is most often shown in the eye region, including eyebrows, and the mouth area. Surprise may be used to mask or cover other emotions when you want to conceal how you are truly reacting or feeling.

The emotion of *disgust* often blends with surprise. Disgust is a feeling of repulsion, as a reaction to something or someone, and it usually involves getting-rid-of and getting-away-from responses. The intensity of disgust may vary and can be closely related to *contempt*, a sentiment that is experienced only in relation to people or the actions of people. Disgust can appear in reaction to other people, ideas, actions, situations, or oneself, or in reaction to the sight, taste, smell, or touch of something. Contempt is an indicator of "I'm not going to do what you ask me to do" or "What you are saying is ridiculous." The most common of the gestures indicating the latter issue, for example, is rolling the eyes up. Recall the earlier reference to the rolling of the eyes in the African-American culture that K. R. Johnson (2004) reported.

The *disgust* emotion is somewhat more complex than some of the other emotions. Rozin, Lowery, and Ebert (1994) found that when they had college students match disgust faces with verbal situations that described possible disgust emotions, several different behaviors were exhibited. The nose wrinkle was associated with bad smells (and to some extent, bad taste). Our favorite bad smell is liver, but it probably depends on your own taste. Eye gape and tongue extrusion were associated with food offense and oral irritation. General disgust irritants (especially those reminding us of our animal origins), aversive interpersonal contacts, and moral offenses were associated with a raised upper lip. Sometimes a crinkling of the nose combined with the raised upper lip also indicates disgust.

Sadness is expressed when the "inner corners of the eyebrows are drawn up. The skin below the eyebrow is triangulated, with the inner corner up. The upper eyelid inner corner is raised. The corner of the lips are down or the lip is trembling" (Ekman and Friesen 1975, 126). *Happiness* is shown when the "[c]orners of the lips are drawn back and up. The mouth may or may not be parted, with the teeth exposed or not. A wrinkle (the naso-labial fold) runs down from the nose to the outer edge beyond the lip corners. The cheeks are raised. The lower eyelid shows wrinkles below it, and may be raised but not tense. Crow's-feet wrinkles go outward from the outer corners of the eyes" (p. 112). One of the most prominent aspects of the emotion of happiness is the smile. Women, for example, use smiling to appease others but also to try to be responsive to others, which women do more readily than men in most situations (Wood 2007).

It appears that women smile more often than do men. Studies show that men are less likely than women to show teeth when they smile. Actually, males and females use smiling differently. In telling the truth or lying, males smiled more in telling lies than in telling the truth, but females' facial expressions of smiling do not vary much in either case. Forgas and East (2008) found that a person's mood can effect whether or not they believed the smiles being observed were genuine. In a study, they found that a more positive affect (or mood) increased the belief that the smiles the participants observed were genuine; conversely, when the affect was more negative, the belief that the smiles being observed were genuine decreased. Many people believe they are skilled at detecting lying, but most are actually not very good at detecting deception. Many theorists believe that this is true because most people look only to the face and eyes to detect deception. They would be much better at discerning lying if they looked at changes in body movement from the person's norm, not just at face and eye behaviors.

A "contagion hypothesis" was tested concerning the smile. Hinsz and Tomhave (1991) were interested in determining whether the folk adage "Smile and the world smiles with you; frown and you frown alone" is actually true. They found it is true; people returned smiles as greetings, acknowledgments, and as a reciprocal response. They did not return frowns the same way. Bailey and Henry (2009) discovered that even the older generation mimics angry and happy facial expressions. Other researchers (Schneider and Josephs 1991) found that preschool children smiled after achievement situations regardless of whether they failed or succeeded. In taking photographs, participants smile more often when they are asked to do so; it makes no difference what the gender of the photographer is or how much one ordinarily smiles while taking a photograph (Brennan-Parks, Goddard, Wilson, and Kinnear 1991). These findings add more to the *norm of reciprocity* concept; we are likely to mirror the emotions we observe in face-to-face settings.

Ekman and Friesen conducted a great deal of research in an attempt to discover whether there are other facial expressions of emotion that are pancultural (exist across cultures). One phenomenon observed was the expression of *contempt* and the startle reaction. Regarding contempt, the researchers found that, contrary to prediction, a contempt expression exists in Estonia, Germany, Greece, Hong Kong, Italy, Japan, Scotland, Turkey, the United States, and Sumatra (Ekman and Friesen 1986). Previously, Ekman and Friesen had thought that the emotion was simply a variation of disgust.

Unlike the other six emotional expressions, contempt has not been found among other primates, and two of four such expressions of contempt involve unilateral facial actions, meaning it is shown as one emotion across the entire face. The other six involve bilateral facial actions, meaning they are shown in at least two *separate* areas of the face. In their study of the startle, Ekman and Friesen (1985) studied whether people reacted to the firing of a blank pistol. In addition, they forewarned their subjects and asked them to suppress their startle reaction. They found the startle to be a *reflex, not an emotion.* To this point, then, Ekman and Friesen have found *seven facial expressions of emotion:* happiness, sadness, disgust, anger, fear, surprise, *and* contempt.

Other nonverbal communication theorists have referred to the primary emotions by the acronym of SADFISH, standing for sadness, anger, disgust, fear, interest, surprise, and happiness, making these emotions easier to recall (Leathers 1997; Richmond and McCroskey 2000; Richmond, McCroskey, and Hickson, 2011). You will note that they include interest and not contempt. Some researchers originally listed these as universal emotions, or ones that can be recognized universally, but that issue is addressed in Chapter 8.

One area that has become one of major interest in the field of communication is how emotions can be communicated through computer-mediated communication. Walther, Loh, and Granka (2005) found that there was a dearth of information on how affective messages are communicated in online communication. Antonijevic (2008) found that computer users who are aware of the nonverbal cues they are using—or attempting to use—in computer-mediated communication are usually more successful in conveying the emotional meanings of their online messages. Parkinson (2008) found that in a more computer-oriented communication culture we must pay attention to the different styles of communication we use to send emotional messages. Today, with so many using "in time" video capabilities of such programs as *Skype* and *FaceTime*, the sending of emotional messages via computer-mediated vehicles has become easier. The question that comes to mind here, of course, is how many people actually think about the nonverbal message that is likely to be conveyed by an online message that you send via video-assisted communication media? More and more educational institutions are attempting to teach students about this facet of computer-mediated communication by offering classes in what is usually called "Internet Communication."

BOX 7.5   OBSERVATIONAL STUDY

Observe a television show or a movie of your choosing and take note of the emotions the actors are portraying. What emotions are they attempting to communicate?

How effective are they at doing this? What type of things do the actors do to send that message (face and eye, body posture/movement)?

STUDENT VOICES

Charlotte: I have a friend that is really good with covering her anger with smiles. People can never tell when she is going through hard time because she knows how to hide all of her negative emotional reactions. I do not think this is a bad thing; in fact, I think it is good because people can never know what is going on—all they can do is assume.

I also have a friend that when she is sad, it is very hard for her for her to hide it because it shows all over her face. Her eyes get really puffy, her face is red, and even if she smiles she appears fake. Another example I observed is another one of my friend's facial expression when she is in fear or scared; her cheeks turn red and her eyes get watery when upset.

AFFECT BLENDS

Ekman and Friesen (1975) also argue that an expression often shows two emotions at the same time; they label these affect blends (see also J. K. Burgoon, Buller, and Woodall 1989; Ekman, Friesen, and Tomkins 1971). Ross, Reddy, Nair, Mikawa, and Prodan (2007) say that blended emotions on faces come from looking at different sections of the face to read emotions. In their study they looked at the upper and lower face compared to the right- and left-hand sides of the face, and found that emotions are more accurately portrayed on the upper and lower portions of the face. They also contend that there is a *neutral* expression. Predicated upon these various categories of nonverbal communication, we can apply some of the principles suggested by Birdwhistell, and others' interpretations or reinterpretations of them, to the variables involved. (For instance, Ekman and Friesen's notion of universality of emotions runs counter to Birdwhistell's principle of no universally held gesture.)

In opposition to Birdwhistell, Ekman (1982) contends that Darwin's theory of universality of some emotions (and their innateness) is valid. He argues that there is evidence of universal facial expressions for such emotions as happiness, anger, disgust, sadness or distress, fear, surprise, and other sentiments. Ekman infers that cultures create "display rules," or norms, for where and when it is appropriate to reveal a facial expression of an emotion. Who has not been told by a parent (or a significant other), "Don't look at me that way," and perhaps even been punished for the look on their face? Such facial expressions, however, have been measured on the basis of *surface appearances.* Ekman and Friesen (1982) have also developed a second facial expression measurement system based on *muscle movement:* the Facial Action Coding System (FACS). The FACS was developed to allow researchers to classify units of facial expressions that can be distinguished anatomically and that are distinguishable by visually observing them. The FACS distinguishes expressions on the basis of (1) muscle appearance change, (2) muscle capability for independent action, and (3) feedback circuits that allow us to be aware of our own facial movement. Other tests developed by Ekman and Friesen include the Requested Facial Action Test (REFACT), which requires people to imitate facial expressions they have viewed on videotapes. The importance of such tests as the Facial Affect Scoring Technique (FAST), Facial Meaning Sensitivity Test (FMST), FACS, and REFACT depends on how well emotional expression is recognized and encoded and, just as useful, on the way conversational signals that emphasize such elements as linguistic comma, question, or exclamation point are employed. The facial expression is also used to signal agreement/disagreement or understanding/lack of understanding.

Ekman's research, especially regarding affect blends, was one of the most heuristic areas (meaning an aid to learning, discovery, or problem-solving) of study in nonverbal communication in the 1980s and 1990s. There is a controversy, however, over whether only seven basic or primary emotions are expressed in the facial area. The controversy has brought about the following questions. How well can people encode and decode facial messages? How do cultural differences relate to the concept of universal expression of emotions? Does Ekman uncover other emotions that should be added to the seven?

Skill in encoding and decoding nonverbal communication certainly affects the results of studies on facial expression. Coding abilities have been tested in regard to sex differences and personality. One researcher found that males and females were equally capable of decoding anger (Biaggio 1989). Others found females generally more accurate in encoding emotions of all types (Akert and Panter 1988; Tucker and Riggio 1988). Extroverts were more accurate in decoding facial expressions of emotion and were more confident in their assessments;

PHOTO 7.5   Studies show that women tend to smile more readily than men.

however, others might argue with those findings. Generally, *females are considered better encoders and decoders of emotion through facial expression* (a study that showed women to be superior encoders and decoders has been reported by Rotter and Rotter 1988).

Other researchers (T. Hill, Lewicki, Czyzewska, and Schuller 1990) found that knowledge of another's personality creates a bias in the decoding of that person's nonverbal messages. When you know a person, the accuracy of your decoding of his or her nonverbal message will be more accurate. In addition, children appear to learn to encode and decode more accurately as they get older.

There appears to be a cultural bias in some of the research in this area of decoding emotional expression. Cultural bias can occur in research findings when researchers from one culture study people from their own culture and then try to generalize their findings to people of other cultures. Makaremi (1990) found that Iranian students used crying as an angry reaction against their parents, peers, and teachers. These Iranian adolescents used verbal aggression more often with their peers. However, the overall aggressive behavior of Iranian adolescents was less than might have been anticipated by Western researchers. Matsumoto (1991) has expressed a more general concern with such cultural problems indicating that more research needs to be undertaken on the role of culture in formulating display rules. Sogon and Masutani (1989) observed some emotions as decoded by Americans and Japanese. They used as the seven emotions: joy, surprise, fear, sadness, disgust, anger, and contempt. If one considers joy as similar to happiness, these categories are similar to Ekman's, although they delete interest and separate disgust and contempt. They also added what they called three "affective-cognitive structures": affection, anticipation, and acceptance. Sogon and Masutani found that Japanese and Americans expressed anger, fear, and sadness in similar ways. This shouldn't be surprising, since these are considered universal emotions, or emotions that are usually recognized in most, if not all, cultures. Joy and surprise, however, were more culture-bound. Japanese subjects could not recognize disgust or contempt. (As has already been mentioned, Ekman also had some difficulty in separating these two.) Affection, anticipation, and acceptance were culture-bound and less likely to be universally recognized. Keep in mind one important point about the use of these emotional expressions; each culture will have its own *display rules.* Display rules tell us when it is appropriate or inappropriate to display certain emotions. For example, we usually find it appropriate to show happiness and joy when we are at festive social gatherings, but the same expressions might be inappropriate in a courtroom or when you are being disciplined by your employer.

Some scholars believe there are additional emotions, which are sometimes referred to as *blended emotions* or *conglomerates* since they blend two or more of the primary emotions to create one general emotion. Examples would include love, hate, depression, and stress, among others. One general type of these blended emotions that has received a great deal of attention is shame/embarrassment/guilt. Margalit (1977) found that there are cultural differences and even subcultural differences in the display of shame by mothers of severely handicapped children in Israel. Sharkey and Stafford (1990) found that display of embarrassment was situational and that, in large measure, such displays are related to the responses of the others who are present. Thus, the notion that embarrassment is a universal expression of emotion has been found not to be the case. From a more specific physiological perspective, Shields, Mallory, and Simon (1990) have investigated blushing. Blushing is more of an involuntary expression than some of the emotions discussed here. P. J. Lang, Bradley, and Cuthbert (1990) refer to affect blends as responses, but they claim there are also *reflexes.* Their specific example is the *startle reflex,* which occurs, for example, when one hears a gunshot. Pictures or memory images that are elicited when the sound is heard rather than overt, external stimuli, such as the gunshot, prompt the startle reflex at the time of the reflex.

BOX 7.6 OBSERVATIONAL STUDY

Take a magazine and look at at least 10 different faces in advertisements, or on models posed for a story's title page. What emotions do you recognize? How many are primary emotions? How many are blended emotions? If the pictures are from an ad, what messages do the facial expressions send you about the products? If the pictures are from a story, what messages do the facial expressions send about the story to follow?

FUNCTIONS

We withhold our discussion of kinesic functions until the next chapter. At this time it is sufficient to say that there are a number of ways we can approach kinesics, each providing information regarding the functions laid out in Chapter 1. It is clear that **identification** and **self-presentation** can be communicated through kinesics. How identification and self-presentation are interpreted, however, depends greatly on the kinesic approach taken. **Control of the interaction** is clearly found in the turn-taking, turn-yielding, and turn-requesting cues we employ when interacting with others. **Display of cognitive and affective**

information is found in all kinesic approaches, with emblems being the primary tool for illustrating cognitive information. **Deception** is found in some approaches, primarily in Ekman and Friesen's meaning-centered approach, but in today's society we find many studies being done trying to codify deception detection techniques. Chapter 8 presents a much more detailed functional analysis of the kinesic subcode.

SUMMARY

The kinesic subcode examines the impact of gestures on human communication. Gestures can be defined as any bodily movement, including highly visible motions and more subtle ones, such as facial expressions. When we look at how people communicate by use of their kinesics, we discover many things about them, from their personalities to their emotional states of mind. Pay special attention to facial communication, since when we communicate with others, we generally look at their faces.

In this chapter we examined several perspectives relative to the study of nonverbal communication, with major emphasis on Birdwhistell's and Ekman and Friesen's approaches (the most prolific and renowned researchers in this subject area). In so doing we have set the groundwork for Chapter 8, which presents a more interactive interpretation of kinesics, one that first examines the variables that influence kinesic communication. We then present a functional analysis of kinesic communication.

QUESTIONS FOR THOUGHT

1. Some would argue that kinesics, or body language, is the form of nonverbal communication that is most important. Do you agree? Why or why not?
2. Birdwhistell's six principles of kinesics provide a background for the study of all kinesic communication and perhaps even most of nonverbal communication in general. How influential was Birdwhistell's contribution to the study of nonverbal communication?
3. Thinking back over the various approaches to kinesics offered in this chapter, which approach makes the most sense to you? Why?
4. Ekman and Friesen's meaning-centered approach to communication has generated a lot of research and supplemental theory. On a scale of 0 to 10, with 10 being the most important, where would you put it? Where would you put the other approaches?
5. Emblems have garnered a lot of attention in modern society. What emblems do you know of that are universal for American culture? How do you think they developed and became universal?
6. What emblems do you use that are known to only a *select few* of your friends? How did you develop them? Have you ever used them to communicate covertly with those select few in the presence of others who did not know the meanings? What sort of message does that send to the *non-select few?*
7. Adaptors are an important part of kinesic communication. Some adaptors are received by others positively, while others are not. Why is this the case? Does culture or subculture have anything to do with how adaptors are perceived and interpreted?
8. Considering the communication functions of kinesics, and looking at someone you know, which functions have you noticed before? Why do you believe that you noticed these functions? Was it the movement, the individual, or both? Why do you believe these functions were noticeable to you? Given this same person, would other people notice the same things? Why or why not?

FURTHER REFERENCES

Principles of Kinesics

Castelli, L., Carraro, L., Pavan, G., Murelli, E., and Carraro, A. (2012). The power of the unsaid: The influence of nonverbal cues on implicit attitudes. *Journal of Applied Social Psychology, 42*, 1376–1393.

Henley, N. M. (1977). *Body politics: Power, sex, and nonverbal communication.* Englewood Cliffs, NJ: Prentice-Hall.

LaFrance, M., and Mayo, C. (1979). A review of nonverbal behaviors of women and men. *Western Journal of Speech Communication, 43*, 96–107.

Mehrabian, A. (1972). *Nonverbal communication.* Chicago: Aldine-Atherton.

Shuter, R. (1977). A field study of nonverbal communication in German, Italy, and the United States. *Communication Monographs, 44*, 298–305.

Tannen, D. (1990). *You just don't understand: Women and men in conversation.* New York: William Morrow and Company.

Wood, J. T. (2007). *Gendered lives: Communication, gender and culture.* Belmont, CA: Wadsworth/Thompson Learning, Inc.

Functional Approach

Casasanto, D., and Jasmin, K. (2010). Good and bad in the hands of politicians: Spontaneous gestures during positive and negative speech. *PLoS ONE, 5*, 1–5.

Dunbar, N. E., and Burgoon, J. K. (2005). Perceptions of power and interactional dominance in interpersonal relationships. *Journal of Social and Personal Relationships, 22*, 207–233.

Goldin-Meadow, S. (2005). The two faces of gesture: Language and thought. *Gesture, 5*, 241–257.

Kana, R. K., and Travers, B. G. (2012). Neural substrates of interpreting actions and emotions from body postures. *Social Cognitive and Affective Neuroscience, 7*, 446–456.

LePoire, B. A. (1991). Orientation and defensive reactions as alternatives to arousal in theories of nonverbal reactions to changes in immediacy. *Southern Communication Journal, 56*, 183–145.

Melinger, A., and Levelt, W. J. (2004). Gesture and the communicative intention of the speaker. *Gesture, 4*, 119–141.

Mottet, T. P., and Beebe, S. A. (2002). Relationships between teacher nonverbal immediacy, student emotional response, and perceived student learning. *Communication Research Reports, 19*, 77–88.

Myers, S. A., Monet, T. P., and Martin, M. M. (2000). The relationship between student communication motives and perceived instructor communicator style. *Communication Research Reports, 17*, 161–170.

Othony, A., and Turner, T. J. (1990). What's basic about basic emotions? *Psychological Review, 97*, 315–331.

Sime, D. (2006). What do learners make of teachers' gestures in the language classroom? *International Review of Applied Linguistics in Language Teaching, 44*, 211–230.

Singer, M., Radinsky, J., and Goldman, S. R. (2008). The role of gesture in meaning construction. *Discourse Processes, 45*, 365–386.

Streeck, J. (2008). Depicting by gesture. *Gesture, 8*, 285–301.

Cumulative Structure

Arendsen, J. (2008). Garrick Mallery (1891): Greeting by gesture. *Gesture, 8*, 386–390.

Aviezer, H., Trope, Y., and Todorov, A. (2012). Body cues, not facial expressions, discriminate between intense positive and negative emotions. *Science, 338*, 1225–1229.

Beek, Y., and Dubas, J. (2008b). Decoding basic and non-basic facial expressions and depressive symptoms in late childhood and adolescence [Electronic version]. *Journal of Nonverbal Behavior*, 32, 53–64.

Brennan-Parks, K., Goddard, M., Wilson, A. E., and Kinnear, L. (1991). Sex differences in smiling as measured in a picture taking task. *Sex Roles*, 24, 375–382.

Buck, R., Miller, R. E., and Caul, W. F. (1974). Sex, personality and psychological variables in the communication of affect via facial expression. *Journal of Personality and Social Psychology*, 30, 587–596.

Elfenbein, H. A., and Eisenkraft, N. (2010). The relationship between displaying and perceiving nonverbal cues of affect: A meta-analysis to solve and old mystery. *Journal of Personality and Social Psychology*, 98, 301–318.

Gueguen, N. (2012). Gait and menstrual cycle: Ovulating women use sexier gaits and walk slowly ahead of men. *Gait & Posture*, 35, 621–624.

Halberstadt, A. G., Hayes, C. W., and Pike, K. M. (1988). Gender and gender role differences in smiling and commitment consistency. *Sex Roles*, 19, 589–604.

Hawhee, D. (2006). Language as sensuous action: Sir Richard Paget, Kenneth Burke, and gesture-speech theory. *Quarterly Journal of Speech*, 92, 331–354.

Koppensteiner, M., and Grammer, K. (2011). Body movements of male and female speakers and their influence on perceptions of personality. *Personality and Individual Differences*, 51, 743–747.

Matsumoto, D. (1980). Face, culture and judgments of anger and fear: Do the eyes have it? *Journal of Nonverbal Behavior*, 13, 171–188.

Motley, M. T. (1993). Facial affect and verbal context in conversation. *Human Communication Research*, 20, 3–40.

Pell, M. (2005). Prosody-face interactions in emotional processing as revealed by the facial affect decision task. *Journal of Nonverbal Behavior*, 29, 193–215.

Saarni, C. (1988). Children's understanding of the interpersonal consequences of dissemblance of nonverbal emotional-expressive behavior. *Journal of Nonverbal Behavior*, 12, 275–293.

Sharifabad, M. R., and Vali, S. (2011). A comparative study of native and non-native body language: The case of Americans' kinesics vs. Persian English speakers. *Journal of Intercultural Communication*, 26, 6.

Tronick, E. Z. (1989). Emotions and emotional communication in infants. *American Psychologist*, 44, 112–119.

CHAPTER 8

A PRACTICAL FUNCTIONAL APPROACH TO KINESICS

KEY CONCEPTS

- Influencing Variables
- Culture
- Sex
- Handedness
- Language
- Decoding
- Eye Behavior
- Functions

OBJECTIVES

By the end of the chapter you should be able to:

- Explain how kinesics is influenced by variables brought to an interaction.
- Explain how individuals influence kinesic communication.
- Explain the impact of kinesic decoding differences on communication.
- Describe how the eye influences our communication with others.
- Demonstrate how kinesic communication functions in daily interaction.
- Explain the process of *quasi-courtship behavior* as it relates to healthy communication.
- Describe how people deceive others through their kinesic communication.

The previous chapter discussed kinesic researchers who developed systems for understanding human nonverbal behavior. Many of these researchers took a functional approach, as we did earlier in the book. In this chapter, we describe how other research falls into the functional categories previously discussed through the kinesic subcode. Again, the nature-versus-nurture debate arises, as it applies to how you acquire/learn your kinesic behaviors. Also, no universal position yet exists as to which approach is more "acceptable." This debate will no doubt be with us for as long as nonverbal theorists research this discipline.

VARIABLES THAT INFLUENCE KINESICS

Kinesics, like personal space, is influenced by a number of variables, including culture, sex/gender, left- and right-handedness, language behavior, and the ability to decode or interpret, especially for decoding eye behavior. The following paragraphs illustrate how some of these variables might be important for studying the role of gestures in communication.

CULTURE

Perhaps one of the most influential variables in kinesic communication is culture; culture includes the various subcultures found within our larger cultures. Subcultural differences may be manifested in how we stand or walk, the gestures we choose to employ, and the emotions we display or hide.

K. R. Johnson (1972) integrated kinesic investigations with a detailed analysis of black nonverbal communication patterns. Johnson's hypothesis was that African American/Caucasian American kinesic differences resulted from different cultural backgrounds, the African Americans' patterns having some distant relation to African body movement. Johnson's research dealt mostly with walking behavior. According to him, young African Americans, particularly males, show defiance of authority by adopting a limp stance, which develops gradually during a conflict encounter: the head is lowered, the body extremely relaxed and motionless. In contrast, young Caucasian American males assume the opposite stance in such a situation: body rigid, legs spread, arms still at their sides, and the hands forming fists. The young African American's limp stance communicates that the authority is talking to thin air and might as well give up because the message is not being received. As mentioned in the previous chapter, K. R Johnson followed up with a study (2004) about how young blacks use their eye behaviors when confronted by a person in an authority position. African American young people are more likely to roll their eyes to show disdain for that authority, similar to the "limp stance" just mentioned. Recently, however, society has seen changes in how some Caucasian American males respond, with young Caucasian Americans adopting the "hip hop" dress in an attempt to imitate gestural patterns of young African Americans. In a more recent study, Tuminello and Davidson (2011) discovered that African American children were equally proficient in recognizing facial emotions when looking at both Caucasian American ("European American") photos and African American photos, whereas Caucasian American children were not as proficient when trying to read the emotions in photos of African American facial expressions. Consequently, the researchers believe that African American children are better decoders of emotional facial messages, which is helpful when communicating with others.

At this point, we should mention a few issues about research conducted regarding African American culture. Orbe (1995) criticized the research of the communication discipline for the limitations of research done about this ethnic subculture. Orbe said most of the existing research is highly Eurocentric, or done by Caucasians of European descent, so the perspective is limited. In addition, he said, most studies have been conducted at colleges and organizations where African Americans are in the minority, which further distorts the findings. Orbe asserted that the studies create a polarization of African American communication and Euro-American (Caucasian) communication, creating a comparison approach as opposed to searching for similarities between the subcultures. Orbe believes that all these shortcomings are troublesome since they create or perpetuate stereotypes of African Americans. We mention this point because some of the findings we report (such as the ones in the preceding paragraph) may have some of those shortcomings; we wish always to keep you from assuming stereotypical nonverbal characteristics of others. Orbe has continued his theoretical approach to research on African Americans in our society, following up his original study with many more. We also remind you that the accuracy of your judgments will always be based on how well you know the other person(s) and how well you understand the context.

In a more historical study, Michael and Willis (1968) examined cultural differences between socioeconomic classes and sexes in the United States with respect to the development of nonverbal interpretation and transmission skills in young children. A dozen gestures were chosen for which there was an agreement as to meaning, and these were presented to some children with no schooling and to some with one year of schooling. The interviewer made a gesture and asked the child, "What does this mean?" Low and middle socioeconomic groups were compared; all groups were racially mixed. Results indicated that middle-class children were "superior" to lower class ones in both transmission and interpretation; boys were found to be superior to girls in interpreting gestures. Michael and Willis found that for the interpretation of gestures, the first year of school is more important for lower-class children than for middle-class children, most likely because of the socialization process that occurs when children begin the schooling process.

Other researchers have observed a number of differences in how various cultures use gestures and what those gestures mean. Bosmajian (1971), for example, has identified 13 verbal expressions that have different nonverbal gestures in different cultures. Other research indicates that the simple greeting can have many different gestures assigned to it. In French Canada, for instance, typical "American" greetings are found: handshaking for males, embracing for females if they are close friends (Culturegram 1981d). In Puerto Rico, women often greet by grasping the other's shoulders and kissing the cheek (Culturegram 1981c). In Italy, persons of the same sex can walk arm-in-arm, and women often greet each other by kissing both cheeks (Culturegram 1981b). In Saudi Arabia, the most common greeting is a handshake with the right hand. Males will frequently follow up the handshake by extending the *left* hand to the other's right shoulder and kissing the right and left cheeks (Culturegram 1982). In China, where people usually do not like to be touched, a nod or slight bow usually serves as a greeting, but the handshake is also acceptable (Culturegram 1981a).

Those of you who have traveled to places outside your own culture can probably give many other examples. In Poland, for example, the common greeting between friends is a "kiss on the cheeks" (alternating sides), or a handshake with nonfriends. Interestingly enough, though, it is a three-time kiss, not what we find in other countries when there will be a two-time kiss—one on each cheek. Plus, it is still quite common when a woman is introduced to a man, especially a man 60 or older, for the man to take the woman's hand and kiss the back of it in the old chivalrous style. This is something that would likely raise the ire of feminists in our culture. Indeed, the younger generation of women in Poland even finds it outdated and scoffs at it.

In terms of gestures used in other cultures, there are a number of differences. In Canada, most gestures are similar to those of the United States, with the exception of western Canada, where the smile seems more important, and touching of the other person as a gesture is more allowable. In Puerto Rico and Korea, fingers waved downward generally mean "come here," but in the United States that same gesture means "goodbye." A question about what is happening is sometimes associated with the wiggling of the nose in some cultures, and in other cultures people often point with the lips puckered rather than pointing with the finger. In Italian culture, gestures with two hands are not appropriate, and one should use only one hand for emphasis. In Saudi Arabia it is impolite and offensive to point or to signal Saudis with your hand. Left-handed people must be careful not to eat, gesture, or send gifts or items with the left hand in Saudi Arabia, as the left hand is considered dirty and is to be used only for bodily functions. Pointing the soles of your shoes (such as the American way of putting the feet on the desk) at a Saudi or crossing your legs is considered a sign of disrespect. Surely you will recall when the journalist in Iraq threw his shoes at President George W. Bush in late 2008; that was a high insult from that culture, but for those of us who don't see that as an issue, we probably didn't realize how much of an insult it was. In most Eastern European countries, it is considered rude and disrespectful to carry on a conversation with your hands in your pockets. Finally, in China, a smile is the gesture preferred over a pat on the back or handshake. Hand holding with the same sex is common, and the Chinese use their open hands rather than a finger to point. They beckon others with their palms down, similar to those gestures in Puerto Rico and Korea. Orton (2006) found that the differences between Chinese nationals and Westerners could cause some problems in the area of kinesics. She found that what the Chinese find as appropriate for their culture is not necessarily acceptable for Western culture; thus the Chinese run the risk of being evaluated negatively due to their more reserved kinesic behaviors. Semnani-Azad and Adair (2011) discovered that Canadian negotiators used far more relaxed kinesics than Chinese negotiators. Wing (2010) also discovered that monolingual American English speakers are much more likely to use gestures when speaking than monolingual Chinese, and that bilingual Chinese were more likely to use more gestures.

Russell (1994) critiqued the work of Ekman (1993) by arguing that there is no universality of emotions. Ekman (1994), of course, disagreed with Russell's comments. Izard (1994) also challenged Russell, supporting Darwin's (1871/1998) work on the universality of emotions. Ekman (1994) suggested nine factors that must go into the study of emotion in the facial area:

1. We must study emotion.
2. We must consider both the nature and nurture approaches.
3. We must search for emotion-specific physiology.
4. We must specify which events precede the emotions.
5. We must examine ontogeny [the development of an individual organism].
6. We must study the use of face and voice among infants before verbal communication is available.

7. We must consider that emotions are families of emotions.
8. We must consider that emotions are discrete entities.
9. We must consider expression in determining how many emotions there are.

Tracy and Robins (2008) set out to discover if the emotion of pride could be recognized across cultures, in particular between a pre-literate tribe in Burkina Fast, West Africa, and American Caucasians. They found that pride does generalize across cultural lines of both male and female individuals of African, Asian, and Caucasian descent. Mesquita and Frijda (1992) have suggested that the differences in cultures are a result of when and where certain emotions are used.

Montepare and Zebrowitz (1993) suggest that different cultures perceive walking gaits differently. They observed differences in Korean and American views on walking gait. A slower and older gait was perceived as low dominance by Americans but as high dominance by Koreans. This difference could be explained by the fact that the Korean culture (as well as other Far Eastern cultures) places a higher value on its senior population. There are still serious questions about kinesics as related to culture. It is quite possible that some, but definitely not all, gestures are universal.

In the Appendix, we discuss some "pop" books published by people who have not conducted scientific research. Most college professors look at such books suspiciously since the conclusions are usually not verifiable and therefore are not as reliable as a study conducted under controlled situations. Roger E. Axtell (1991), however, has put together an interesting guide to kinesics for travelers entitled *Gestures: The Do's and Taboos of Body Language around the World*. He describes acceptable and unacceptable gestures and body movements used in other cultures. In the years since that publication, Axtell has written several other books of a similar nature—how to communicate nonverbally in foreign cultures—and those would be good sources as well. If you are going to travel somewhere, or wish to know about how cultures outside the United States communicate through kinesics, we suggest taking a look at these resources. We authors are not alone in suggesting this; other contemporary nonverbal communication textbooks also cite Axtell's work when they discuss intercultural communication.

Lest we think that all cultures communicate differently, we should be sure to look at a study by Sharifabad and Vali (2011). These researchers found that there is no significant difference between Persian-speaking (from Iran) students' kinesics tied to language use than U.S. native speakers of English. We mention this to point out that if you plan to communicate within a foreign culture, or with people from a culture other than your own, you need to research that culture to find out what differences, if any, may exist in their communication styles.

Finally, one can examine work environments as cultures or subcultures of their own. According to Reinhold (1999), emotional expression on the job is both good and bad. Reinhold's advice regarding emotional displays, such as crying, is that while it may provide an emotional release, it should be done discreetly. Tarrant (1999) goes one step further. According to him, "if anything, things [workplace expectations] have become worse. Any type of emotional display—joy, sorrow, laughing—is frowned upon. People are expected to be even-keeled" (p. 1F). What is an emotionally appropriate display may depend on the culture the organization has created (Hickson, Stacks, and Padgett-Greely 1998; Morgan 1997).

BOX 8.1   OBSERVATIONAL STUDY

What do you think of people who display emotions in the "workplace"? How are emotional displays interpreted at your school? Are people "allowed" to demonstrate

emotion? If so, under what circumstances and when? Does the culture or subculture have anything to do with emotional displays and reactions to them?

 SEX/GENDER

Just as culture produces differences in kinesic behavior, the sex of the person also affects how he or she acts and reacts. Recall the difference between *sex* and *gender*. Sex refers to the biological determination of an individual; gender refers to the psychological and sociological determination (Wood 2012). Males and females are the only sexual classification; with gender, we change the classification to masculine and feminine and add androgyny, which is seen when individuals have sociological and psychological characteristics of the opposite sex as well as their own sex. In short, androgynous persons exhibit both stereotypically male and female characteristics regardless of what their biological determination is. Many people believe that sex is *assigned* by genetics, and gender is *assumed* through the nurturing (or learning) process. Also, sex is an "either-or" concept, and gender is more of a continuum (with masculine and feminine at opposite ends of it and androgyny in the middle). In most cases, you can only be male or female, but your gender might fall anywhere along that continuum. You should keep in mind that much of the "sex-based" research is more about gender differences than it is about sex differences, yet the bulk of the research in communication labels it as "sex." And much of the research labels it as "gender" when they are really talking about sex.

Facial expression is a result of training from childhood and is also a type of sex stereotyping. Boys watch adults and decide they cannot cry because it is not tough and manly, or because adults tell them that. What boy has not been told that it is *sissy* to cry? Girls are taught that frowning makes them less pretty. Both sexes learn that when they pout, get mad, cry, or seem sad, they do not look attractive. This lesson is reinforced more for girls, and as a result Richardson (1981) found that most girls smiled or maintained a bland, expressionless face in an attempt to look pretty. In a more recent study, Woodzicka (2008) found that women were more likely to use false smiles to hide their negative emotions and to appear more enthusiastic in a mock job interview setting than men were. In addition, she found that women were evaluated more harshly when they did use the false smile than men were. In addition, Hugenberg and Sczesny (2006) found that smiling women are more easily categorized as being happy than men are. Further studies are warranted after more than 30 years of the *gender revolution*. Plant, Kling, and Smith (2004) were able to find, in two separate studies, that evaluators of facial expressions often, and more consistently, leaned toward stereotypical judgments of women's emotional facial expressions.

In essence, children of both sexes are encouraged not to show *negative* emotions, and women are taught this to a greater extent than men. Richardson (1981) reported that men communicate authority, activity, and independence, but women communicate submissiveness, passivity, and dependence through their kinesic behavior, although these behaviors may also be changing. Research of male and female postures has shown that American women give off gender signals by bringing their legs together, keeping their upper arms close to their trunks, carrying their pelvises rolled forward, and presenting their entire bodies as moving wholes. American men, however, tend to keep their legs apart, move their arms away from their bodies, carry their pelvises rolled slightly back, and present their trunks as moving independently from the arms and hips. These postures were discussed earlier in terms of shrinkage and expansive behaviors. In general, men tend to assume open, relaxed postures and expand into available space, while women tend to assume tense, deferent postures, taking up little space (Birdwhistell 1970). We would be remiss, however, not to point out that androgynous individuals would have a tendency to use both stereotypically male and female kinesic behaviors, expanding in some contexts and shrinking in others.

It is generally thought that women have more body sway while walking than men do. Studies by Birdwhistell (1967), however, indicate that the opposite is true. The male may subtly wag his hips in a light right-and-left presentation with a movement that produces a twist at the base of the thoracic cage and at the ankles. The female may present the length of the entire body as a moving whole; the male does not, but moves his arms independently of his trunk. Henley (1977) found in her study that "When around men, many women cross and uncross their legs incessantly, modify their voices, open their eyes dramatically, signifying animated interest in the male, and may also play with their hair" (p. 138). Hence, some stereotypic kinesic behavior may hold true for one sex and not for the other, but remember the dangers of stereotyping, this time based on the sex/gender of an individual.

PHOTO 8.1(A) AND (B) According to Birdwhistell (1970), men tend to expand their postures and women tend to shrink theirs.

During a conversation women watch and look while listening to their partners (Neijer 1991). This may be the primary reason why women have been reported to be more sensitive to kinesic messages and to respond to them more readily. Women may be taught what to look for; the female is better able to send kinesic messages also. Women, more than men, tend to smile, nod their heads, and produce a generally higher level of gestural activity. For example, when seeking approval, women tend to nod and smile, both of these being positive yet submissive signs. Consequently, women send more backchanneling cues, more commonly thought of as direct feedback during a conversation (J. A. Dixon and Foster 1998).

BOX 8.2   OBSERVATIONAL STUDY

Choose your closest friend of the same sex and your closest friend of the opposite sex. Note the nonverbal kinesic behaviors they use and indicate if they use more masculine or more feminine behaviors. Discuss your findings with them and try to discover where they developed these behaviors. If they use many of the opposite sex's stereotypical behaviors, try and find out if they consider themselves to be androgynous.

STUDENT VOICES

Dan: My sister has an ever-occurring roll of her eyes if something doesn't go her way. She always rolls her eyes if she is told no, or told something she doesn't want to hear. My brother and I are so used to it now, we communicate to each other exactly when it will happen. It went from being an aggravating eye behavior to one that was pretty funny, depending on the situation. She is a very prissy individual when she doesn't get what she wants, and her facial expressions and eye behaviors communicate this to everyone. I'd hate to say it was because she is female, but my brother and I have not adopted this behavior, and we grew up in the same household.

LEFT- AND RIGHT-HANDEDNESS

The bulk of research on brain hemisphere dominance has been conducted using only right-handed participants. There has been much concern recently about left-handers. Cornell and McManus (1992), for instance, reviewed the research on handedness and surveyed both left- and right-handers. Left-handers responded to the survey more quickly than right-handers. They also found that more women than anticipated counted themselves among the lefties. Left-handers were most enthusiastic about answering questions about handedness. These authors postulated that left-handedness may be genetic. Casasanto (2011) reported that changing people's use of their right and left hands causes them to think in a different manner. In another study, Pool (1991) found that among baseball players, lefties' life spans were an average of 8 years shorter than that of right-handers; in the general population the average difference was 9 years. Pool also found that lefties tend to have more accidents and are more prone to autoimmune diseases and are more often born prematurely. Pool compared being left-handed to smoking two packs of cigarettes a day. In a fascinating study comparing human infants and baboons, Meunier, Vauclair, and Fagard (2012) discovered that the majority of both human infants and adult baboons were likely to use their right hands, utilizing their left-hemisphere for processing, showing one more relationship between animal studies and human studies. If you are wondering why we include these findings here, we believe handedness is important for nonverbal behavior because so little research has been undertaken on those who predominantly use their left hands. In researching this new edition of this textbook, no new studies concerning the communication aspects of human left-handedness were discovered, just the one study mentioned previously. Perhaps it is time that more theorists look into the communicative impact of this interesting human phenomenon.

RELATIONSHIP WITH LANGUAGE

Blake and Dolgoy (1993) studied the development of gestures in infants. Their subjects were Parisian-French infants, all firstborns, who were filmed in natural settings with their parents and caregivers. The children were given picture books in which they could point to objects, as well as a wind-up toy. Blake and Dolgoy found that both informative and request functions of nonverbal communication became more sophisticated with the development of language. Matsumoto and Assar (1992) studied participants who spoke English and Hindi. The researchers concluded that those who spoke Hindi detected anger and fear more easily, and those speaking English more easily detected sadness. Both men and women were more accurate in English than in Hindi; however, this was true *only* when a confederate was Caucasian. Anger was rated more intensely in Hindi; sadness was rated more intensely in English. In another study looking at Japanese speakers and native English-speaking adults, S. D. Kelly and Lee (2012) found that sometimes using gestures is not to the advantage of the speaker, that sometimes the use of gestures can skew the meaning when trying to learn and use complicated language.

[handwritten margin note: Detecting emotions based on language]

Knuf (1992) found that the relationship between language and nonverbal communication has its bases far back in history. Knuf studied the ritual of spitting. He discussed an 1892 article that listed five different applications of saliva. First, spitting was used to ward off bad luck. Second, it was used to ward off the "Evil Eye." Third, spitting was used to ward off infection. Fourth, it was used to cure diseases or to transfer an infection to others. Finally, spitting was used to seal a bargain. As discussed later in the book, kissing has also been used to seal a bargain. Clearly, spitting has several messages, which have changed in the last hundred or so years; a person seeing someone spit must stop to decode which message is being sent. In the United States, most women think spitting is crude, and men think it is just a natural action, which also is cause for miscommunication. In other cultures it is as commonplace as breathing the air. As an example, recall the 2008 Olympics in Beijing when the Chinese government had to issue directives and orders for their Chinese nationals to refrain from spitting publicly. It is important to remember, however, that nonverbal gestures are closely related to rituals and to the language of the sender and the receiver, and that many things can affect interpretation.

DECODING

Our discussion of kinesic behavior has thus far focused on the encoding—or sending—of nonverbal messages. We now turn briefly to what we know about the decoding of nonverbal messages, especially in terms of facial expression and eye behavior. The primary conclusion we draw is that decoding ability is related mainly to the sex of the decoder. Generally speaking, *women have been found to be more accurate than men in decoding honest nonverbal communication.* This conclusion is supported in almost all research associated with decoding differences (see Begley 1997; McClure 2000; Schmid, Schmid-Mast, Bombari, and Mast 2011; Wood 2012). However, one study found that men could better decode anger, while women could better decode sadness. Additionally, depressed patients of both sexes have been found to be less accurate in nonverbal decoding, except for the emotion of sadness (Bhattacharya and Mandal 1985).

Accuracy in kinesic decoding is related to Ekman and Friesen's emotions (Weisel 1985). Happiness is the most accurately decoded emotion, followed by surprise, disgust, anger, sadness, and fear. Research has also found that vocal cues that might accompany emotion do not appear to enter into kinesic decoding. Deaf individuals and hearing individuals are no different when it comes to kinesic decoding, although it appears that the pleasantness of the emotion being displayed does make a difference in the accuracy (the deaf are more accurate in unpleasant affective decoding, whereas hearing people are more accurate in pleasant affective decoding). Additionally, people from low-expressive families have been found to be more accurate decoders than those from more expressive families (see Bull and Connelly 1985; Halberstadt 1986).

One other issue that we believe bears mentioning here is what Ekman and Friesen (1975) referred to as *micro-expressions* (or micro-kinesics). These are defined as expressions that occur much more rapidly than the normal 1- to 4-second duration that most expressions last; they occur in a fraction of a second. Regardless, they do *leak out*, and when they do they provide the person who "catches them" with a reliable source of information. We senders of the messages often think we have not disclosed our true feelings, usually because we have been taught to "lie" with our faces, but in reality the split-second expression can tell a great deal about a person's internal emotional states.

A body of research is beginning to develop in the area of patient–patient and patient–doctor relationships. Blanch-Hartigan (2011), as mentioned in Chapter 7, has recommended that health care workers use the Patient Emotion Cue Test (PECT) to be more efficient in decoding facial expressions of patients, and therefore serve their patients better. In addition, researchers have studied the greeting behavior of Swedish psychotherapists at their first-time meeting with a new patient (Astrom, Thorell, and D'Elia 1992). Patients used facial communication significantly less with male psychotherapists than with female psychotherapists. However, psychotherapists with at least 13 years of experience appeared to be shown no gender differences. Using psychiatric patients as decoders, Archer, Hay, and Young (1992) found that schizophrenic and depressed patients had a significantly lower ability to decode facial expressions than did a nonpatient control group. In a facial recognition test, other researchers have found several factors that affect facial identification: depth of processing, target distinctiveness, exposure time, and retention interval (Dinardo and Rainey 1991). They found that illumination of the room was a significant factor in such recognition also.

Using "facial mimicry" (i.e., where a patient attempts to imitate the facial expression of another), Berenbaum and Rotter (1992) found that females were better at decoding negative clips from two films *(Raiders of the Lost Arc* and *Alien)*. Females scored higher on mimicry in general; males scored higher on facial intensity response, or how strongly the emotion is exhibited. Mufson and Nowicki (1991) found that females were better at decoding facial affect (i.e., emotions), especially displays of fear and disgust. Miura (1991) found that participants with an active imagination scored higher on Archer's decoding test, a test designed to interpret facial expressions. Manusov (1992) observed participants' responses to the concept of attribution of motive (i.e., what did the participant believe was the intent of the other?). She found that, when participants were allowed to make their own attributions about facial expressions, they found their partners' behaviors as somewhat intentional. They also felt that the others were more competent and interpersonally attractive than when the researcher led them to believe that the partners acted deliberately. In other words, we tend to like those whom we feel are not trying to manipulate us, especially with their use of facial expressions.

All this research shows that women are better at some decoding than men, and men are better at other decoding. Recall that, for everyone, accuracy is going to be affected by how well one knows the person being observed and the situation.

DECODING EYE BEHAVIOR

Decoding is especially important in the area of eye behaviors. Studies on the decoding of eye behavior have yielded results in three general areas of investigation: eye contact/gaze, pupil size, and eye direction.

EYE CONTACT/GAZE

Studies indicate that women engage in more eye contact than do men. In 1963, Exline conducted an experiment with groups of three women and groups of three men; these groups were asked to carry on discussions focusing on solving a problem. Group members were asked to find a name for a newly developed soap product. Each individual had privately selected a name prior to the group discussion. Visual interaction among group members was then observed through a one-way mirror as members tried to complete their task. Observers who were experienced in scoring visual behavior determined from this study that women engaged more in both mutual and nonmutual gaze and held the mutual gaze longer than did men. In later studies, using male and female partners instead of partners of the same sex, it was revealed that women did more looking than men. "Female subjects looked more than males while speaking, while silent, during the interviewers' speaking, and in informal discussions following the interview" (Exline 1963, 80).

In relationships in daily life, eye contact can send important nonverbal information to others. "We look to the eyes for meaning, and find them so significant that our popular culture would have us believe that masking the eyes alone, while leaving all other personal characteristics—face, hair, clothing, body size, shape and gait—observable is enough to cloud the identity" (Henley 1977, 151). Eye contact has its positive and negative aspects. Experiments have shown that when people viewed videotapes of "engaged" couples, the couples that looked at one another the most received the highest positive ratings. Other studies conclude that more eye gaze make you more attractive as a communicator

(Ewing, Rhodes, and Pellicano 2010). On the negative side, our parents teach us that it is impolite to stare at others. "We don't like to be stared at, and believe it's impolite for us to stare at others" (Henley 1977, 152). Research shows that people dislike being stared at when the other person cannot be seen. An example of this is the resentment sometimes felt toward people with sunglasses, and more recently, toward people who have the bill of a baseball cap shielding their eyes. We need to be able to see the other person's eyes in order to receive the important visual information relayed through them, and it is often frustrating when we cannot see a person's eyes. The stereotype of "law enforcement" or "hell's angel" associated with chromed sunglasses prompted Stacks and Stacks (1982) to suggest that Auxiliary Coast Guard members remove their chromed sunglasses prior to conducting courtesy boat inspections. In short, if we cannot see people's eyes when we are interacting with them, communication is strained at best. In many cases, communication is ineffective because the person feels "cheated" out of direct contact with the other interactant.

The authors of this textbook, who are also professors, find the lack of eye contact to be frustrating in a classroom setting. If eye contact cannot be made with the students, the professor has no clue as to what is being understood and processed and what isn't. For that reason, some college professors have established classroom standards where sunglasses and ball-caps are taboo. In public speaking classes, or classes where public presentations are a part of the course requirements, this is an important thing to remember: Eye contact with your audience is important and sends the message that you care about them and that you are a credible source. The bill of a baseball cap hides your eyes from an audience, from a teacher, and from anyone who is not standing in close enough proximity to see under the brim.

Eye contact is also useful in the regulation of interaction, most notably as a turn-taking signal for speech. Eyeball watchers have established that a speaker, when nearing the end of an utterance, looks away from the other briefly, then, on ending, returns the gaze to the other, in effect conceding the floor (Duncan 1972). This turn-taking signal is used by whites only. Conversations between black and interracial conversations use other nonverbal cues; in fact, the cues are almost the opposite. "A naturalistic observation of 63 black and 63 white dyads (same-sex and mixed-sex) corroborated the finding that black listeners gaze less at the speaker than do white listeners" (Henley 1977, 159). This finding seems to have remained constant over the years, although there do not seem to be any updated studies available to attest to this at this writing.

Additionally, Beebe (1974) found that an increase in the amount of eye contact generated by a speaker in a live public speaking situation often enhances listeners' perception of the speaker's credibility. Somewhat ironically, in one-on-one situations, Ellsworth and Carlsmith (1968) found that eye contact simply *emphasizes* the content of the message. With positive verbal content, frequent eye contact produced positive evaluations of the message, but with negative content, eye contact produced negative evaluations. Similarly, Greene and Frandsen (1979) found that a person's self-esteem is related to the amount of eye contact he or she maintains with others relative to the favorability of the message he or she is receiving; for people with high self-esteem, increased eye contact was found in the presence of a positive message, whereas decreased eye contact was found in the presence of a negative message; for people with moderate self-esteem, eye contact was found to be decreased for both types of messages; and people with low self-esteem used more eye contact when receiving negative messages than when receiving positive ones. That is, eye contact becomes a gatekeeping mechanism whereby certain types of information yield more eye contact and others yield less. Abele (1986) found that gaze decreased as the other person's behavior became more *predictable;* in other words, averted eye contact by the listener might mean he or she is bored. Kleinke (1986) reports that with high gaze of prolonged eye contact, a person is evaluated as attentive, competent, and dominant; high gaze is also associated with perceptions of the person having good social skills, being mentally healthy, and having intense feelings. The opposite, low gaze, would be evaluated on opposite ends of the continuum from the positive evaluations.

BOX 8.3   OBSERVATIONAL STUDY

For 10–15 minutes, place yourself in a spot where people will need to pass by you (e.g., lobby of a classroom building, the student union, the library). Make direct eye contact with as many people as you can, whether you know them or not. See how many acknowledge you in some way—by a "Hello," a head nod, a small wave, a dirty look. What causes this to occur?

J. K. Burgoon, Manusov, Mineo, and Hale (1985) found that there are at least two types of deviation from the expected conversational pattern in interview situations: (1) gaze aversion and (2) constant gaze. Gaze aversion by an interviewee reduces the likelihood of the interviewee being hired. Interviewees exhibiting an aversive pattern were seen as incompetent, uncomposed, unsociable, and passive. With constant gaze the interviewee earned more favorable endorsements. The constant-gaze interviewee was described in terms opposite to those used in describing interviewees with averted gaze patterns. J. K. Burgoon, Coker, and Coker (1986) further supported the aversion-gaze effect in another study, although constant gaze was *not* perceived as yielding significantly favorable results. Along this line of research, Mulac, Studley, Wiemann, and Bradac (1987) investigated male and female gaze in same-sex and opposite-sex dyads. They found no significant differences in gaze

PHOTO 8.2   Where people direct their gaze communicates something about what they are thinking.

behavior of male–male and male–female dyads. They found, however, that female–female dyads exhibited more mutual gaze/mutual talk, more mutual gaze/mutual silence, and less individual gaze/small talk than other dyad combinations (see also Iizuka 1994).

BOX 8.4 OBSERVATIONAL STUDY

Go to a place where you normally socialize with other people (your dorm, apartment, local hangout, club meeting, or the like). Act as you normally do, but avoid eye contact with the people you normally make eye contact with. How hard do you find that to be? Why do you think this happens? How do the people with whom you are communicating react? Why do you think they react that way?

PUPIL SIZE

It has been said that nonverbal communication accounts for more than three-fourths of all human communication. This includes paralanguage (the use of the vocalics), gestures, eye contact, use of space, and various other behavioral patterns. Even features as seemingly insignificant as the pupils of the eyes have a bearing on what a person communicates. Studies have shown that people who possess larger pupils are perceived as more attractive than those with smaller ones. Albert King (1973), a researcher who studied pupil size and physical attraction, took identical photographs of a woman and enlarged the pupils in one photo. He then showed the two photos to a large sample of people and asked them which picture they preferred. In almost every instance, those tested chose the photo with the larger pupils. When asked *why* they had selected one photo over the other, they could not give a reason. Interestingly enough, in the researching of this new edition, no new studies in the discipline of communication could be found, the most recent having been done in the 1980s. Perhaps this is something you might like to try your hand at studying.

Photographers today are preoccupied with the phenomenon of pupil size. Many fashion photographers for women's magazines attempt to enlarge the pupils in their photos, especially for headshots in makeup and perfume advertisements. The photographer completely darkens the studio so the model's pupils dilate, then uses a sudden bright flash (as the photo is taken) before they can constrict. The larger pupils tend to radiate warmth and can, in fact, be persuasive. "The fashion photographer makes his pictures more explicitly sexy because the climate of today's world is sexually liberated" (Korn 1971, 130).

Many other factors cause pupil dilation. The drug belladonna, derived from a poisonous Eurasian plant, also enlarges the pupils. The powder or tincture derived from the leaves and roots of this plant is also used to treat asthma, colic, and hyperacidity, as well as being used for various cosmetic purposes. Use of this drug enlarges the pupils and creates a more physically attractive person. On the other hand, people perceive those with small pupils to be untrustworthy, deceptive, and rather cold.

One researcher has shown how the size of pupils can affect perception of another's emotional state (E. H. Hess 1985). E. H. Hess hypothesized that pupil size does not become a relevant variable in a person's perception until puberty. Because girls reach puberty before boys, more girls than boys of the same age should react to pupil size. In an experiment,

121 students aged 11 to 16 years judged which of two pictures of a teacher's face expressed a greater degree of positive attention and esteem toward students. The two pictures were identical except for pupil size. All age groups rated the pictures with larger pupils more positively. Sex differences occurred in the ratings made by 11- to 12-year-olds, with females rating the photographs with larger pupils more positively.

E. H. Hess (1975) found that the size of a person's pupils indicates the level of interest; the more interest there is, the more the pupils dilate. Metalis and Hess (1982) found that when people experience extreme interest in something, from food to other people, their pupils dilate. One interesting thing to note is that although pupils dilate for these aforementioned reasons, you must be careful. Of course, pupils also dilate for physiological reasons, such as darkness, drugs, and alcohol. Spying a "hottie" at a dark bar and believing she or he is interested in you because of dilated pupils would not be an "educated guess" for you.

Ambler (1977) notes that in 1964 a researcher experimented with four graduate and eight undergraduate students. Stimuli in the form of a series of two-digit numbers were presented to the subjects through headphones. The subjects were asked to listen and repeat the numbers in order. It was noted that subjects' pupils constricted during the period between listening to the numbers and repeating them. When repeating the stimuli, the subjects' pupils were dilated as if to "let out" the information. The error rate and pupil *dilation* increased as knowledge of *information* decreased; therefore, it can be inferred that pupil dilation corresponds positively with the number of internal transformations to be made (i.e., an internal psychological response to whatever stimuli might cause the response).

Another interesting aspect of eye behavior is the correlation between lying and pupil size. Many researchers have identified pupil dilation as a byproduct of lying and deception (O'Hair, Cody, Wang, and Chao 1990; Zuckerman, DePaulo, and Rosenthal 1981). Though watching someone's eyes to tell whether the person is lying may seem like an old wives' tale, this concept has been supported by a number of researchers in the field of nonverbal behavior. Lying definitely requires some internal transformation, and is accompanied by smaller pupil diameters while the lie is being conjured up. Larger pupils were evident while the lie was being told. Heilville (1976) observed that people's eyes are more dilated during deceptive answers than they are during truthful ones. This and other evidence implies that the dilation of the pupils reflects the amount of mental effort required to perform a task.

However, we do not ordinarily train ourselves to observe pupil dilation; we rely instead on the frequency of gaze when looking for deception.

BOX 8.5 OBSERVATIONAL STUDY

Take a fashion magazine for either sex and look carefully at the eyes of models. Remember, photographing models is usually done with bright lighting, which causes pupils to constrict. How many models appear to have dilated eyes?

What sorts of products are being sold with ads where pupils appear dilated? Are the products relying on sex appeal? Or does the pupil dilation show up with any type of product?

EYE DIRECTION

We already know that the brain is divided into two hemispheres, left and right, and that each hemisphere controls the opposite side of the body. The amount of information one can derive from this is remarkable. As a general review, the right side, or hemisphere, of the brain controls the emotional and subjective actions; the left side controls the objective and rational functions (Stacks, Hill, and Hickson 1991). The logical person uses his or her brain's left side most, whereas the emotional person tends to use the right side. This usage preference may be called *dominance* or *preferred style,* as noted earlier. The engineer who calculates all day is probably left-hemisphere dominant, using the left hemisphere more often than the right. The artist who paints or sculpts all day is usually thought to be right-hemisphere dominant.

The question arises as to how one may determine which is the dominant hemisphere. One of the ways is eye direction. Everyone uses what are known as lateral shifts of their eyes, known as Conjugate Lateral Eye Movements (or CLEMs), to either the right or left (Richmond and McCroskey 2000). A person will look in one direction relatively consistently when asked a numerical question. This indicates which side of the brain is dominant for that function. If a person looks to the left, the right hemisphere may be more dominant, and if to the right, the left hemisphere may be more dominant. There is also a tendency for a person to look in different directions for different types of questions. In a study by Weiten and Etaugh (1974), four categories of questions were asked: verbal, numerical, spatial, and musical. The numerical and musical questions were the most obvious. The subjects most often looked right to answer numerical questions (they were consulting their left hemisphere) and left to answer the musical questions (consulting their right hemisphere). Some researchers report that 75 percent of individuals' CLEMs are in one direction (Richmond and McCroskey 2000). This predominant direction would tell you something about which side of your brain predominates in your thought processing. Still other researchers found that people's CLEMs will differ with the actual sitting position they are in when conversing with someone (Baker and Ledner 2004).

At least one stereotype can be related to these concepts. The origin of the idea that males are more adept at engineering and that females are more adept at liberal arts is possibly illustrated in a study that found that, no matter what the question was, the males tended to look to the right. This indicates that they were consulting with the left, or numerical-objective, side of the brain. Females, on the other hand, seemed to be using the other, more abstract hemisphere. How much of this left brain/right brain activity comes from *nature* or *nurture,* of course, would deserve some attention in future studies. Since there is a clear paucity of research studies produced on this topic, this is also a possible research area for you to pursue.

As for the psychological aspects of eye movement, the right hemisphere has been associated with nonverbal and passive behavior. It follows, then, that the left hemisphere is more verbal and active. Gur and Gur (1975) conducted a study to determine whether eye movement would indicate which defensive mechanisms one would be most likely to use. They tested for five defense mechanisms: (1) turning against others; (2) projection;

(3) principalization; (4) turning against the self; and (5) reversal, repression, and denial. Those with left dominance (those who looked right) tended to project and to turn against others as a defense mechanism. Those who looked left (or right dominance) used reversal or repressed things and denied them. Principalization and turning against the self had no relation to eye movement.

Eye behavior is a real and visible aspect of kinesic communication; indeed, we can learn much about people just by watching their eyes. As you notice other factors of nonverbal communication, see if you don't realize how salient (or prominent) people's eye behaviors are to you.

BOX 8.6 OBSERVATIONAL STUDY

Test the eye direction hypothesis yourself. Take a number of advertisements from the print media that include male and female models. Check to see (1) what is being sold— does the product have emotional overtones or not—and (2) the eye direction of the models. What, if anything, does this communicate to you?

FUNCTIONS

So far, we have presented a number of related kinesic studies that point toward systems of understanding human nonverbal behavior and ultimately communication. Many of the researchers cited have taken what we labeled in Chapter 1 as a functional approach. This section describes how other research falls into the functional categories we introduced in Chapter 1 and have discussed in other chapters.

IDENTIFICATION AND SELF-PRESENTATION

We usually can accurately detect some characteristics of a person by his or her physical appearance; however, we can also determine who a person is by how he or she walks, the expansiveness of his or her gestures, and the like. Much of self-presentation and identification is related to the status of the person. Researchers have found that many of the kinesic cues of a higher-status person differ from those of a lower-status person. Most of us have roles where we are the higher-status person as well as roles where we are the lower-status person. If you want to look at some examples of status clues, look at your professors. Most times, their postures are ones where they stand over you, because you are sitting in a class. They also may use a more expansive torso position, such as their hands on their hips with their elbows away from the body. Do you, when you are in the role of the student, assume the same posture with your professors? Consider similar examples with your bosses, your parents, and your siblings.

Ridgeway, Berger, and Smith (1985) investigated the effects of power in accordance with expectations of status difference. Eye gaze was used as the power indicator. As hypothesized, male participants could perform tasks more easily when the confederate/observer who maintained eye contact was a female than when the confederate was a male. In both instances (male and female participants), participants performed better at a specific task when they were under the impression that the confederate was a superior. Research has long determined that people will perform differently when being observed, especially if they are being observed by someone they believe has more skill than they do at the observed activity. Although the researchers "linked" the condition of being male with the perception of the role of being superior, this should not necessarily be a condition for undertaking such a study. In fact, as a replication and extension of their findings, an interesting study might be to "link" higher status with the female confederate. Carre, McCormick, and Mondloch (2009) did find, however, that men are more likely to show aggressive and power-laden facial expressions than women are.

STUDENT VOICES

Deb: As part of an interviewing class this semester, I have learned that you may be a great interviewee, but if your posture is unprofessional, your credibility will deteriorate. Posture helps to present someone as marketable, responsible, and professional. Someone with bad posture in an interview displays himself or herself as lazy, unwilling, and unprofessional. As part of my interviewing class, we had to interview different people that we found to be interesting. I interviewed a student who has Tourette's. During the interview her posture stayed attentive which ensured me she was willing to continue with the interview.

Power in intimate relationships is sometimes harder to determine. Most of us know someone whose partner in their intimate relationship tries to show nonverbally any type of power they believe they have. Sometimes it is done by posturing, sometimes by interrupting, sometimes by lack of eye contact. Bodie and Villaume (2008) discovered that even the posture couples use when holding hands can send the message of who believes they have the most power in the relationship. Bodie and Villaume found that the participants in their study believed that the person who places his or her hand in the dominant position sends the message of being the person with more power in that relationship.

Status is not equal to power, but it is often difficult to differentiate between them. Related to power, status refers to a person's social position and judgments made of the person by his or her social group (Henley 1977). A person's attitudes about characteristics such as physical attractiveness, age, and sex reflect the power of that person's status. Mehrabian (1972) discovered, for instance, that posture is more tense (or erect) in higher-status people, and the inferior status person tends to lower his or her head. The arms and legs of a higher-status person are more relaxed when talking to a lower-status person. Some believe that this is not necessarily true, that a reasonably relaxed posture assumed by a lower-status individual sends a message that the person is confident and of higher status.

An individual's place in the chain of command may affect nonverbal communication. A study in Japan by M. H. Bond and Shiraishi (1974) applied kinesic behavior measurements developed in the United States to interactions among the Japanese. They were interested in how the variables of posture, status, and the participant's sex would affect nonverbal behavior. In certain situations it was the status variable that most affected responses. For the male and female participants combined, higher-status interviewers elicited shorter pauses, more eye contact, more hand and head gestures, and greater total speech. Females were more responsive to the status manipulation than were males. The researchers interpreted these results as being generally consistent with the American findings, except that greater tension was not seen in persons interacting with high-status interviewers. Head and hand gestures are indicative of relaxation, but they increased when interacting with high-status persons, apparently caused by nervousness. The higher-status figure initiates the distance or closeness of the relationship. This person also directs looks of greater duration toward those of lower status, and the lower-status person breaks eye contact first. The manner in which a person is addressed depends upon the degree of familiarity or the equality of the acquaintance.

Closely related to status is dominance and persuasiveness. Kinesic variables influence perceptions of both. When seeking to persuade, we use more eye contact (especially if the person to be persuaded is a female), more head nods, more gesturing (especially if the person persuading is a female), more facial expression and activity, moderate relaxation (but if the person to be persuaded is a female, slightly more tense posture), smaller reclining angles, and differences in body orientation (male persuaders use indirect orientation; female persuaders use direct orientation, but if the person to be persuaded is a male, more indirect orientation). Finally, persuaders try to use some "open" gestures—gestures that are outward rather than inward (see Breed and Porter 1972; H. S. Friedman and Riggio 1981).

Dominance, as expressed by kinesic cues, takes on several aspects. First is eye contact or gaze (Ho and Mitchell 1982). Dominant people are those who can establish eye contact. However, whether an interaction is to be warm or cold will depend upon the eye contact, warm being more eye contact, smiles, and head nods, versus head shakes, which are considered cold (Ho and Mitchell 1982). Dunbar and Burgoon (2005) found that when individuals in intimate relationships perceived power differentials with their conversational partners, they would try to display more dominance nonverbally. In another study, B. Schwartz, Tesser, and Powell (1982) found that elevation—being physically above others in an interaction—increased power and perceived dominance. They had subjects look at pictures of people sitting or standing, and also sitting or standing but elevated. They found that elevated people were regarded as more powerful, regardless of whether the lower figure was standing or sitting. When both people in the illustration were sitting, the one elevated was perceived as more powerful. This would seem to confirm Ken Cooper's (1979) more anecdotal advice that to be perceived as powerful in a business setting, you should arrive late and sit on something that will elevate you above the rest of the interactants. This elevation tip does not always hold true, however. One of your authors can describe an interview situation where the interviewee was asked to sit on a barstool-type chair, which elevated the interviewee above a group of eight interviewers. The interviewee reported being the most uncomfortable she had ever been in an interview situation, and because she teaches interviewing techniques, this seemed strange to her. The only variable to which she could narrow the source of intimidation was the elevated position above the interviewers.

In two separate experiments, the effects of facial feedback on impression formation were tested. Ohira and Kurona (1993) found that participants were rated more negatively when they exaggerated their negative facial expressions. The impressions are more favorable when positive emotions are displayed; however, when emotions were concealed, the impression was more favorable than all the other groups. DePaulo (1992), conducting similar research, found that adults regulate their nonverbal behavior for self-presentation and that this self-presentation is learned behavior. Burton and Bruce (1992) found that most of us remember people's faces but not their names. However, they found that we usually remember some other pieces of information, such as occupations, associated places, or hobbies.

BOX 8.7 OBSERVATIONAL STUDY

Watch a television show where you know there are some status differences between the characters (e.g., *Parks and Recreation*, *Law and Order: Special Victims Unit*, *NCIS*, *The Simpsons*, *Survivor*, *American Idol*, *Bones*). Note how the directors have the actors show the status differentials. How were the actors placed in the territories? What kinesics did you notice of the high- and low-status characters? Touch? Use of personal space? Appearance? Do these seem to confirm what you have read thus far? (You could do the same in a "real-life" setting, but be aware that publicly scrutinizing a person of higher status can have some uncomfortable consequences.)

CONTROL OF THE INTERACTION

The control of conversation is similar to Ekman and Friesen's notion of *regulators* discussed in the previous chapter. These are nonverbal attempts to enter, exit, or maintain the floor in a verbal or nonverbal conversation. Greetings and farewells fall into this category (see Hadar, Steiner, and Rose 1985). One of the authors of this textbook found an interesting concept while visiting Rio de Janeiro. People there often grab one another just above the elbow to get a chance to speak rather than interrupting verbally, while in the United States much of the control is determined through vocal cues, such as a "stutter start" ("uh-uh-uh"), an audible intake of breath, or a clearing of the throat.

Students raise their hands to get a chance to speak when they are in a large class. In smaller classes, students may simply speak out or try to gain the teacher's attention through eye contact or by leaning in toward the teacher. If you wish to begin a conversation with someone at a social gathering, you make eye contact with that person first. Also, we have already mentioned the lifting of your index finger as another signal of a desire to enter conversations. Thus, we see that culture and context affect how we try to control an interaction.

RELATIONSHIP OF INTERACTANTS

The relationship of interactants will affect whether parties are trying to avoid one another, show others that they are with one another, or some behavior between those. One of the most positive affinity-seeking behaviors (showing liking) is what Albert Scheflen (1965) has referred to as **quasi-courtship behavior.**

Scheflen (1965) has provided a process model of what he refers to as quasi-courtship behavior, wherein both sexes note a sexual interest in one another. The model consists of four general steps or stages: (1) courtship readiness; (2) preening behavior; (3) postural cues; and (4) appeals to invitation. Each of these steps involves specific types of behavior. For example, courtship readiness is expressed by increased muscle tone, reduced eye bagginess, less slouch, and decreasing belly sag (note that some of these cues are functions of the autonomic nervous system and others of the central nervous system). **Preening** behavior may be stroking the hair, rubbing the chin/beard area, rearranging makeup, glancing in a mirror, stretching one's clothes, leaving buttons unbuttoned (especially at the chest), adjusting suit coats, tugging at one's socks, and readjusting knots in ties. **Positional cues**, or postural cues, are using the shoulders and legs to "position others out" of the invitation. Here you turn your body toward the object of your interest, closing others out of your interaction. **Appeals to invitation** include flirtatious glances, gaze holding, rolling of the pelvis, crossing legs to expose the thigh, exhibiting the wrist or palm, and protruding one's breasts. Both sexes, then, use nonverbal cues in an attempt to attract another of the opposite sex. Moore (1985, 1995) developed a list of other behaviors that women practice in quasi-courtship interactions. Moore said that women use these behaviors to express their interest in a possible mate, what we would probably call *flirting* behaviors. A partial list of these behaviors includes room-encompassing glances, prolonged eye contact, hair flips, head tilts, head tosses, smiles, animated gestures, body leans, provocative walks, suggestive touches, and so on—she lists a total of 52 behaviors (see also Yeomans 2009; Moore and Butler 1989). Regardless of how long the list is, the conclusion is the same: People do use behaviors of this type to interact with others, and often with members of the opposite sex if you are heterosexual, and with the same sex if you are homosexual.

Quasi-courting occurs in nearly all situations when the participants know one another and are engaged in the common objective of courtship (or attraction). It can also be observed in situations when there is confusion over gender, that is, when we behave in a way that is inappropriate to our gender. Moreover, quasi-courtship behavior is still present when we have been excluded or have withdrawn from the interaction.

Quasi-courtship behavior has a definite purpose in our interactions with others. It helps to provide a positive attitude and increased attentiveness or readiness to relate to the group or other person. It can make the participants feel more at ease with others. Scheflen (1965) writes that the result of quasi-courting is that "a group can become animated and cohesive enough to work together to complete a dull or tedious task" (p. 255). The task may be to simply keep a conversation going, but quasi-courting helps bring forth activity and, therefore, new ideas. Quasi-courting also has an interpersonal dimension; by engaging in quasi-courtship behaviors, we make others feel attractive and needed and make ourselves feel needed. Attraction is certainly a primary element in quasi-courtship behavior.

Other relationships, beyond courting ones, have also received attention in nonverbal communication research. Guéguen (2008) discovered, in a simple study in a bar, that women who smile more are much more likely to be approached by men. Berry and McArthur (1986) found that adult facial structure that resembles that of a child carries particular characteristics. People with this facial structure are perceived as possessing qualities such as warmth, submission, less strength, more naïveté, less threat, and more honesty, which increases the likelihood of establishing a relationship with those people. Additionally, heightened eyebrows, dilated pupils, and wide smiles were perceived as attractive to females. The female face was generally perceived to be indicative of submission, warmth, naïveté, and weakness, also increasing the likelihood of establishing relationships.

Looking at other types of relationships, other researchers hypothesized that people who provided more spontaneous, uncensored nonverbal communication, what we would call extroverted behavior, were perceived to be more attractive than others (Sabatilli and Rubin 1986). A positive correlation was found between physical attractiveness and nonverbal *encoding;* however, a negative correlation was found between physical attractiveness and non-verbal *decoding.* What this means is that people who were able to put together these more extroverted messages were perceived as more attractive than those who did not, thus making those who send extroverted messages more likely to establish relationships with others.

BOX 8.8   OBSERVATIONAL STUDY

Attend a social event where you know people will be so-cializing and perhaps hoping to meet someone they think is "fine." Observe for quasi-courtship behaviors. How many do you notice? If any of your friends use these

behaviors, check with them later to see if they realized they were using them. If it is you, see if you are aware of it when doing it; see if you are able to recall doing any of these behaviors at a later time (when you sit down to analyze the outing).

DISPLAY OF COGNITIVE INFORMATION

When we discuss displays of cognitive information here, we refer to the presentation of in-formation through Ekman and Friesen's *illustrators* and *emblems.* In the first case, illustrators are gestures used *to support* or complement verbal information. We use these to illustrate what we are discussing, so the interactants have a clearer idea of what we are saying. In es-sence, we try to make others *see* what we are saying. In the case of emblems, gestures are used to *substitute* nonverbal information for verbal information. The decoders of the emblems do not need the words to interpret the message (we discussed these earlier, with examples such as the "OK" sign or "the finger").

DISPLAY OF AFFECTIVE INFORMATION

Display of affective information is seen in Ekman and Friesen's *affect display.* It is used to show others what one feels at a particular time: happiness, sadness, surprise, fear, anger, disgust, or contempt. We see these displays especially in posture, facial expressions, and even in gestures (as well as other nonverbal subcodes). We discussed this in more detail in Chapter 7.

DECEPTION AND LEAKAGE

There are a number of reasons why we may wish to know whether others are telling the truth or lying. Lying, to some extent, is related to acting. The difference, of course, is that in acting the audience *expects* the actors to be deceptive. The actors are not, in fact, the people they *represent.* In fact, a "good" actor is one who always *appears* to be the person he or she represents. In everyday life, however, deception is a totally different situation. Most impor-tantly, if we are trying to decode another's nonverbal communication, deception totally destroys the intended meaning. For example, when it is time to leave for school, a child

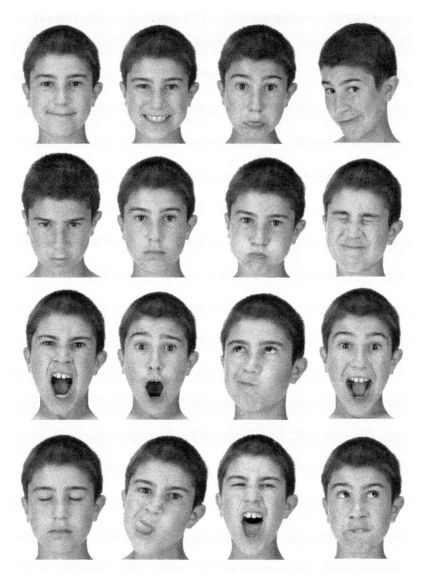

PHOTO 8.3 The face is our primary means of expressing emotion, which we often rely on when decoding how others are feeling. How successful are you with knowing how others feel based on their facial expressions? How can you tell the difference between someone communicating a true emotion and a falsified one?

might say, "I don't feel good." Of course, the parents try to determine the truth of the statement by asking questions, but the parents also look for nonverbal behavior consistent with hurt or pain.

As an example of this, consider a study by Poole and Craig (1992). They studied genuine, suppressed, and faked expressions of pain by asking participants to view videotapes they had prepared of people in pain or faking and asking them to judge the amount of pain. The participants were also given verbal information. They found that participants could distinguish genuine pain from the other forms. However, they attributed more pain to fakers than to those who suppressed their pain. Facial expression was also given more credence than the verbal information provided with the videotapes. The problem, then, would be a case where a child is in pain but indicates that he or she is not in pain.

Other cases where deception might be looked at could be where a police officer tries to determine whether a person is guilty of a crime; when a spouse is trying to determine if the other is having an extramarital affair; or simply whether a person is offering a true emotion or a falsified one. In this section we discuss both self-deception and the deception of others. Self-deception is similar to Ekman and Friesen's *adaptors,* or those movements we think of as "nervous habits" (e.g., playing with objects, our own bodies, shaking our limbs). Such behavior is often a message to oneself that an error has been made or that one is tense in the situation. Although the intention is that these messages be limited to the transmitter, the receiver often detects and interprets them. Stromwall and Willen (2011) conducted a study with criminals and discovered that criminals are often adept at using many kinesic strategies when trying to be deceptive. Those who work in law enforcement should be aware of the many different ways to detect deception, not just the stereotypical face and eye behaviors.

S. Goldberg and Rosenthal (1986) for example, investigated self-touching behavior (a form of adaptor) in the job interview. They used four males and females to serve as interviewers in a variety of situations and found that during a formal interview, self-touching seemed to be suppressed. Male interviewers tended to rate applicants higher when they showed a high rate of self-touching than did female interviewers. Foot touching by the male interviewees (where a man crosses his legs ankle-to-knee and places his hand on his foot) was a significant factor of favorable hiring.

S. Friedman and Mehrabian (1986) studied fidgeting behaviors, another form of adaptor. Fidgeting was positively and significantly correlated with the tendency to engage in a variety of extraneous activities; fidgeting was also associated with unpleasant and arousable temperament. Other extraneous activities associated with fidgeting include binge eating, daydreaming, physical activities, consuming alcoholic beverages, and cigarette smoking.

The deception of others has received much attention of late. Deception here is defined as an attempt on the part of a sender to cover up true information or the affect that he or she feels at that moment. Ekman (1989) notes that children begin to lie at around age 4, usually to avoid punishment. As they get older, their views about lying change. They do not necessarily lie more, but they do improve at it. He suggests that adults should examine the sound of the voice, the look on the face, and consistency between the movement of the hands and the words being said to discern deception.

Because deception is probably the most complex of all kinesic factors to determine, and because of the importance of searching for consistencies, we discuss both kinesic and vocal factors involved in deception here (see D. D. Winter, Widell, Truitt, and George-Falvy 1989). When we discuss vocalics in the next chapter, we ask you to refer back to this chapter's material when thinking about deception. Although it may seem strange to organize the material this way, it has been found that the best places to detect deception are in the kinesic and vocalic subcodes. Since so many of us have learned to deceive others by using our faces, we wish to tie the other kinesic areas and vocal behaviors together so that you have a larger picture of deception as it relates to nonverbal behaviors.

Greene, O'Hair, Cody, and Yen (1985) found that an important variable regarding truth-telling and lying was the *type of lie*. There are *prepared lies* and *spontaneous lies* (see also Stromwall and Willen 2011). Prepared lies are those in which a liar knows that he or she is going to be asked something. The spontaneous lie is one in which a surprise question is asked. The purpose of Greene et al.'s study was to determine deception by the latency (length of time it takes to respond) and duration of response, eye contact, and body movement with immediate spontaneous lies and delayed spontaneous lies. Greene et al. asked that participants respond to specific questions either truthfully or deceitfully to a confederate. Their responses were surreptitiously videotaped for later analysis. The results indicated that liars exhibited shorter response latencies, less leg/foot movement, less hand movement, fewer illustrators, less affirmative head nodding, and less eye contact than truth tellers. Immediate spontaneous liars were similar to nonliars in response latency but exhibited significantly more head nodding, laughing, and smiling. It appears, then, that liars who were prepared to do so were better able to overcome the stereotypical nonverbal indicators of deception.

Other researchers (Zuckerman, Driver, and Guadango 1985) found that, even without audio cues, subjects could distinguish deceptive messages from honest ones. Levine, Asada, and Park (2006) reported that people who were telling known lies engaged in less direct eye contact. O'Hair, Cody, and Behnke (1985) studied deception as related to *communication apprehension* (unwillingness to communicate). Highly apprehensive deceivers had higher levels of vocal stress when telling a lie than when telling the truth. Those with low apprehension did not seem to be affected in telling lies versus telling the truth. DeTurck and Miller (1985) found a number of differences between liars and people who were simply tense. They found that liars spent more time adapting and gesturing with their hands, exhibited longer pauses and response latencies, and spent less time answering questions. Liars *increased* rates of gestures and response latencies; aroused truth tellers *decreased* behavioral rates for the same cues. Table 8.1 displays the results of these studies, which were similar to those of Ekman (1985).

There are discrepancies among the studies as to how we can detect deception. Generally, we can conclude that facial expressions are not always valid clues to deception; that there is less eye contact and more averted gaze in deceivers; that messages (particularly answers to questions) are shorter; that adaptors increase; and that there is more time between a question and a response in deception. In addition to these kinesic cues, deception also varies from culture to culture. Deception is better detected when probing questions are asked (the questions shift a prepared liar to a spontaneous liar); when the liar is a friend or intimate rather than a stranger; when the decoder (receiver) is a male; and when there is more than one interview (see, for example, Bond, Omar, Mahmoud, and Bonser 1990). Finally, deception is also detected through vocal cues working with kinesic cues and verbal content.

In general, most research suggests that we should look at such vocalic cues as speech rate, speech errors, pitch variation, response latencies, and pauses as major predictors of deception (Mehrabian 1971a). Tone of voice has also been associated with deception, as DePaulo, Zuckerman, and Rosenthal (1980) and Streeter, Krauss, Geller, Olsen, and Apple (1977) found.

TABLE 8.1 A COMPARISON OF PREPARED LIARS' AND SPONTANEOUS LIARS' NONVERBAL COMMUNICATION VERSUS THE TRUTH-TELLER, USING TRUTH-TELLING AS THE NORM

Variable	Prepared Liars	Spontaneous Liars
Time to answer	Shorter	No difference
Leg/foot movement	Less	More
Hand movement	Less	More
Illustrators	Fewer	
Adaptors	30% more	300% more
Head nods	Fewer	More
Laughing/smiling		More
Facial expressions		Not a reliable cue
Pauses		Longer/more
Speech errors		More

Researchers have explored the deception function in more detail. These studies indicate that the process of deception is a complex one influenced by several factors. Vocal cues, however, still seem to be relied on heavily by people attempting to detect deception. In a study examining the impact of deception in face-to-face interaction, Stiff and Miller (1986) asked people to judge whether another undergraduate they interviewed was lying or telling the truth. The researchers created the deception conditions by having confederates involved in the study ask someone to cheat on a test. In the truthful conditions, where students knew it wasn't a true request, no cheating was observed. Those making the judgments were then interviewed about the "strategies" the dyad had used to do so well on their task. Findings indicated that the observers relied on several vocal cues. Specifically, the researchers found that observers associated longer pauses and short responses with deceptive communication.

DeTurck and Miller (1985) found that several nonverbal cues were associated with deception in both aroused (an environmental noise was added to the interaction) and non-aroused (no noise) conditions. Specifically, they found that deceivers encoded more speech errors and pauses, and engaged in increased response latencies and shorter messages; non-deceivers decreased rates on each cue and engaged in longer messages. (The noise in the environment did not seem to influence these two groups separately.) This finding is similar to that of Greene et al. (1985), who found that liars used significantly shorter response times when delivering a planned lie.

What impact does deceptive communication have on the encoder? O'Hair et al. (1985) examined the vocal stress associated with deception in interview settings via a physiological measure of voice stress. They also examined whether a person's apprehension about an upcoming communication interaction differed from that of a nonapprehensive person's communication. As part of the study, researchers told participants that they could earn $25 either by lying about their most recent employer (deceptive condition) or by telling the truth (honest condition). Questions asked by the interviewer (a confederate) were also manipulated so that deceivers would encode a prepared lie ("What was your most recent employment?"), a spontaneous lie ("What were your duties in this position?"), and a delayed deception asked later in the interview ("By the way, what was a typical day like at your most recent job?"). Their results indicated that only the highly apprehensive deceiver produced significantly greater vocal stress in the deception, and only in the prepared lie condition. Spontaneous and delayed deceptions failed to yield any differences in vocal stress. The vocal stress of people with low apprehension did not differ across the three conditions.

Females and males decode deception differently. Powers (1993), for instance, found that females rate deceivers lower on sociability than do males (with same-sex encoders). Levine, McCornack, and Avery (1992) also found that deception was more unacceptable to females, in terms of both friendships and romantic relationships. Swann, Stein-Seroussi, and McNulty (1992) found that people with negative self-concepts were rarely given negative verbal information about themselves, but others "leak" to them negative information through nonverbal channels. Those with negative self-concepts, however, are often unable to perceive the negative nonverbal feedback from others. C. F. Bond et al. (1992) found that, both in the United States and in India, decoders read "weird nonverbal behaviors" (arm raising, head tilting, and staring) as deceptive. The researchers raise the point that this may be where we get the concept, "fishy-looking." In addition, there has been some disagreement about the effects of training on improving the ability to detect deception. Ekman, O'Sullivan, Friesen, and Scherer (1991) declared that "gifted observers" could do a better job at detecting deception; short-term training alone would make no difference in deception detection. Studying and training police officers, Vrig (1994) found that having a baseline for deception (similar to a lie detector) helps in detecting deception. He also found that deception training was more useful for detecting spontaneous lies. DeTurck, Bodhorn, and Texter (1990), however, indicate that training does improve detection.

These studies demonstrate that deceptive communicators provide vocal cues that may give away a deceptive performance; however, the studies also indicate that many other factors are present in the deceptive performance. It is also apparent that being able to see the verbal portion of the message presented is still more effective in detecting deception than the vocal approach. In daily interactions, one still may examine vocal cues (speech rate, speech errors, and tone of voice) as indicators of *possible* deception. If one finds a possible deception occurring, then one can study other kinesic and verbal cues to determine whether one is being deceived.

We would be remiss in not pointing out that deception is difficult to discern and that there are no universal cues to detecting deception, a conclusion most nonverbal theorists espouse (see Feeley and Young 1998). One of your textbook authors disliked the television program *Lie to Me* because it sent the message that people can determine deception easily, in one or two short interviews. Indeed, Paul Ekman (whom we have cited numerous times throughout this textbook) indicates that it is important to know the context and the individual prior to determining if the person is lying or not. We point out again the importance of context and of how well you know the possible liar when employing any equation of deception detection. We should remember that when we try to codify any form of interpersonal communication, there are no "cut-and-dried" rules and regulations; human nature does not allow us that capability. We refer you also to the many studies in the "Further References" section of this chapter should we have caught your attention.

SUMMARY

When you think about why you are studying nonverbal communication, we hope you have some concerns about how you might use some of the findings we report to you. We hope the practicality of understanding how kinesics are used in communication interactions will be important to your becoming better encoders and decoders and thus better communicators. A focus on a practical functional approach to the study of kinesics becomes important to this understanding.

Kinesic variables such as culture and sex, which affect how we might interact with others, are important to understanding this subcode's influence on communication. In a desire to help you understand, we have looked at the decoding of kinesic behaviors, with major emphasis on eye behaviors, the eight functions associated with kinesics, as well as the research substantiating these functions and their impact on human communication. The kinesic subcode helps us all better understand our communication with others.

QUESTIONS FOR THOUGHT

1. Other than the variables discussed in this chapter, what things influence how people perceive kinesic communication?
2. As noted in the chapter, culture is a major determiner of kinesic communication. However, very little research has been undertaken as to how culture influences detection deception. Why?
3. What makes a good liar? What makes a good detector of deception?
4. Quasi-courtship behaviors are considered both natural and good. Can you think of any situations where this may not be the case? Why?
5. How do eye direction and pupil dilation operate in the advertising industry today? Do you think that manipulation of the eyes can really work in both print and nonprint media? Why or why not?
6. Where can you personally use the information you discovered here? Family? Friends? Work? How would you use it in those (and other) contexts?

FURTHER REFERENCES

Culture

Axtell, R. E. and Fornwald, M. (1997). *Gestures: The do's and taboos of body language around the world.* New York: John Wiley & Sons, Inc.

Bockler, A., Knoblich, G., and Sebanz, N. (2011). Observing shared attention modulates gaze following. *Cognition*, 120, 292–298.

Elfenbein, H. A. (2006). Learning in emotion judgments: Training and the cross-cultural understanding of facial expressions. *Journal of Nonverbal Behavior*, 30, 21–36.

Hopson, M. C., and Orbe, M. P. (2007). Playing the game: Recalling dialectical tensions for black men in oppressive organizational structures. *Howard Journal of Communications*, 18, 69–86.

Orbe, M. P. (1996). Laying the foundation for co-cultural communication theory: An inductive approach to studying non-dominant communication strategies and the factors that influence them. *Communication Studies*, 47, 157–177.

Orbe, M. P. (1998). An outsider within perspective to organizational communication: Explicating the communicative practices of co-cultural group members. *Management Communication Quarterly*, 12, 230–280.

Orbe, M. P. (2008). Representations of race in reality TV: Watch and discuss. *Critical Studies in Media Communication*, 25, 345–352.

Orbe, M. P., and Warren, K. T. (2000). Different standpoints, different realities: Race, gender, and perceptions of intercultural conflict. *Qualitative Research Reports in Communication*, 1, 51–57.

Patterson, M., Iizuka, Y., Tubbs, M., Ansel, J., Tsutsumi, M., and Anson, J. (2007). Passing encounters east and west: Comparing Japanese and American pedestrian interactions. *Journal of Nonverbal Behavior*, 31, 155–166.

Watts, E. K, and Orbe, M. P. (2002). The spectacular consumption of "true" African American culture: "Whassup" with the Budweiser guys? *Critical Studies in Media Communication*, 19, 1–20.

Sex and Gender

Beek, Y., and Dubas, J. (2008a). Age and gender differences in decoding basic and non-basic facial expressions in late childhood and early adolescence. *Journal of Nonverbal Behavior*, 32, 37–52.

Callen, V., and Gallios, C. (1986). Decoding emotional messages: Influences of ethnicity, sex, message type, and channel. *Journal of Personality and Social Psychology*, 51, 755–762.

DuBrin, A. J. (1991). Sex and gender differences in tactics of influence. *Psychological Reports*, 68, 635–645.

Ellsworth, P. C., and Ludwig, L. M. (1972). Visual behavior in social interaction. *Journal of Communication*, 22, 375–403.

Fernandez-Dols, J., Wallbott, H., and Sanchez, F. (1991). Emotion category accessibility and the decoding of emotion from facial expression and context. *Journal of Nonverbal Behavior*, 15, 107–123.

Graham, G. H., Unruh, J., and Jennings, P. (1991). The impact of nonverbal communication in organizations: A survey of perceptions. *Journal of Business Communication*, 28, 45–62.

Gullberg, M., and Kita, S. (2009). Attention to speech-accompanying gestures: Eye movements and information uptake. *Journal of Nonverbal Behavior*, 33, 251–277.

Hall, J. A. (1984). *Nonverbal sex differences: Communication accuracy and expressive style.* Baltimore: Johns Hopkins University Press.

Hewig, J., Trippe, R., Hecht, H., Straube, T., and Miltner, W. (2008). Gender differences for specific body regions when looking at men and women. *Journal of Nonverbal Behavior*, 32, 67–78.

Kirouac, G., and Dore, F. Y. (1985). Accuracy of the judgment of facial expression of emotions as a function of sex and level of education. *Journal of Nonverbal Behavior*, 9, 3–7.

Palchoudhury, S., and Mandal, M. K. (1985). Perceptual skills in decoding facial affect. *Perceptual and Motor Skills*, 60, 96–98.

Patterson, M. L., Iizuka, Y., Tubbs, M. E., Ansel, J., Tsutsumi, M., and Anson, J. (2007). Passing encounters East and West: Comparing Japanese and American pedestrian interactions. *Journal of Nonverbal Behavior*, 31, 155–166.

Patterson, M. L., and Tubbs, M. E. (2005). Through a glass darkly: Effects of smiling and visibility on recognition and avoidance in passing encounters. *Western Journal of Communication*, 69, 219–231.

Schmidt, K., Ambadar, Z., Cohn, J., and Reed, L. (2006). Movement differences between deliberate and spontaneous facial expressions: Zygomaticus major action in smiling. *Journal of Nonverbal Behavior*, 30, 37–52.

Stanners, R. F., Byrd, D. M., and Gabriel, R. (1985). The time it takes to identify facial expressions: Effects of age, gender of subject, sex of sender, and type of expression. *Journal of Nonverbal Behavior*, 9, 201–211.

Pupil Size

Hess, E. H. (1965). Attitude and pupil size. *Scientific American*, 212, 46–54.

Hess, E. H., and Polt, J. M. (1960). Pupil size as related to interest value of visual stimuli. *Science*, 132, 349–350.

Hess, E. H., Seltzer, A. L., and Schlien, J. M. (1965). Pupil responses of hetero- and homosexual males to pictures of men and women: A pilot study. *Journal of Abnormal Psychology*, 70, 165–168.

Wilbur, M. P., and Roberts-Wilbur, J. (1985). Lateral eye-movement responses to visual stimuli. *Perceptual and Motor Skills*, 61, 167–177.

Functions of Kinesics

Gregory, S. W., Jr., and Webster, S. (1996). Communication accommodation and social status perceptions. *Journal of Personality & Social Psychology*, 70, 1231–1240.

Guéguen, N., and Jacob, C. (2002). Direct look versus evasive glance and compliance with a request. *Journal of Social Psychology*, 142, 393–396.

Heisel, M. J., and Mongrain, M. (2004). Facial expressions and ambivalence: Looking for conflict in all the right faces. *Journal of Nonverbal Behavior*, 28, 35–52.

Kleinke, C. (1980). Interaction between gaze and legitimacy of request on compliance in a field setting. *Journal of Nonverbal Behavior*, 5, 3–12.

LaCrosse, M. B. (1975). Nonverbal behavior and perceived counselor attractiveness and persuasiveness. *Journal of Counseling Psychology*, 22, 563–566.

McClave, E., Kim, H., Tamer, R., and Mileff, M. (2007). Head movements in the context of speech in Arabic, Bulgarian, Korean, and African-American vernacular English. *Gesture*, 7, 343–390.

McGinley, R., LeFevre, R., and McGinley, P. (1975). The influence of a communicator's body position on opinion change in others. *Journal of Personality and Social Psychology*, 31, 686–690.

Mehrabian, A., and Williams, M. (1969). Nonverbal concomitants of perceived and intended persuasiveness. *Journal of Personality and Social Psychology*, 13, 37–58.

Patterson, M. L., and Tubbs, M. E. (2005). Through a glass darkly: Effects of smiling and visibility on recognition and avoidance in passing encounters. *Western Journal of Communication*, 69, 219–231.

Pell, M. D. (2005). Nonverbal emotion priming: Evidence from the "Facial Affect Decision Task." *Journal of Nonverbal Behavior*, 29, 45–73.

Riby, D. M., Doherty-Sneddon, G., and Whittle, L. (2012). Face-to-face interference in typical and atypical development. *Developmental Science*, 15, 281–291.

Ruys, K. I., and Stapel, D. A. (2008). Emotion elicitor or emotion messenger? Subliminal priming reveals two faces of facial expressions. *Psychological Science*, 19, 593–600.

Shariff, A. F., and Tracy, J. L. (2009). Knowing who's boss: Implicit perceptions of status from the nonverbal expression of pride. *Emotion*, 9, 631–639.

Deception

Bauchner, J. E., Kaplan, E. A., and Miller, G. R. (1980). Detecting deception: The relationship of available information to judgmental accuracy in initial encounters. *Human Communication Research*, 6, 253–264.

Buller, D. B., and Aune, R. K. (1987). Nonverbal cues to deception among intimates, friends, and strangers. *Journal of Nonverbal Behavior*, 11, 269–289.

Buller, D. B., Comstock, J., Aune, R. K., and Strzyzewski, K. D. (1989). The effect of probing on deceivers and truthtellers. *Journal of Nonverbal Behavior*, 13, 155–170.

Burgoon, J. K., and Buller, D. B. (1994). Interpersonal deception III: Effects of deceit on perceived communication and nonverbal behavior dynamics. *Journal of Nonverbal Behavior*, 18, 155–184.

Caso, L., Maricchiolo, F., Bonaiuto, M., Vrij, A., and Mann, S. (2006). The impact of deception and suspicion on different hand movements. *Journal of Nonverbal Behavior*, 30, 1–19.

Harrison, A. A., Hwalek, M., Raney, D. F., and Fritz, J. G. (1978). Cues to deception in the interview situation. *Social Psychology*, 41, 156–161.

Hillman, J., Vrij, A., and Mann, S. (2012). Um . . . they were wearing. . . . The effect of deception on specific hand gestures. *Legal & Criminological Psychology*, 17, 336–345.

Hocking, J. E. (1976). *Detecting deceptive communication from verbal, visual, and paralinguistic cues: An exploratory experiment.* Unpublished doctoral dissertation, Michigan State University.

Hocking, J. E., Bauchner, J. E., Miller, G. R., and Kaminski, E. P. (1979). Detecting deceptive communication from verbal, visual, and paralinguistic cues. *Human Communication Research*, 6, 33–46.

Hurd, K., and Noller, P. (1988). Decoding deception: A look at the process. *Journal of Nonverbal Behavior*, 12, 217–232.

Hurley, C. M., and Frank, M. G. (2011). Executing facial control during deception situations. *Journal of Nonverbal Behavior*, 35, 119–131.

Knapp, M. L., and Comandena, M. E. (1979). Telling it like it isn't: A review of theory and research on deceptive communications. *Human Communication Research*, 5, 270–285.

Knapp, M. L., Hart, R., and Dennis, H. (1974). An exploration of deception as a communication construct. *Human Communication Research*, 1, 15–29.

Leal, S., and Vrij, A. (2010). The occurrence of eye blinks during a guilty knowledge test. *Psychology, Crime & Law*, 16, 349–357.

Leathers, D. G., and Hocking, J. E. (1982, November). *An examination of police interviewers' beliefs about the utility and nature of nonverbal indicators of deception.* Paper presented at the meeting of the Speech Communication Association, Louisville, KY.

O'Sullivan, M., Ekman, P., and Friesen, W. V. (1988). The effect of comparisons on detecting deception. *Journal of Nonverbal Behavior*, 12, 203–213.

Porter, S., ten Brinke, L., and Wallace, B. (2012). Secrets and lies: Involuntary leakage in deceptive facial expressions as a function of emotional intensity. *Journal of Nonverbal Behavior*, 36, 23–37.

Stiff, J. B., and Miller, G. R. (1986). "Come to think of it . . .": Interrogative probes, deceptive communication and deception detection. *Human Communication Research*, 12, 339–357.

Stiff, J. B., Hale, J. L., Garlick, R., and Rogan, R. G. (1990). Effect of cue congruence and social normative influences on individual judgments of honesty and deceit. *Southern Communication Journal*, 55, 206–229.

Stiff, J. B., Miller, G. R., Sleight, C., Mongeau, P., Garlick, R., and Rogan, R. (1989). Explanations for visual cue primacy in judgments of honesty. *Journal of Personality and Social Psychology*, 56, 555–564.

Vrij, A. Mann, S., Leal, S., and Fisher R. (2010). "Look into my eyes": Can an instruction to maintain eye contact facilitate lie detection? *Psychology, Crime & Law*, 16, 327–348.

CHAPTER 9

VOCALICS (PARALANGUAGE)

KEY CONCEPTS

- Definitions
- Sound
- Paravocal Communication
- "Normal" Conversations
- Voice Types
- Vocal Recognition
- Disturbances
- Sequencing

OBJECTIVES

By the end of the chapter you should be able to:

- Distinguish between vocal and verbal aspects of communication.
- Discuss the voice set and vocal qualities people use in daily interaction.
- Explain how the voice operates in a "normal" conversation.
- Discuss the six vocalic functions as they relate to daily communication.

Closely related to the study of bodily gestures (kinesics) is the study of the vocal "gestures," or sounds that are not language. Over the years, the term paralanguage has been used to mean oral and vocal expression or as a synonym for vocalics. Some researchers have labeled the study of the voice, and its impact on communication, vocalics, noting that paralanguage is sometimes confused with other kinesic (facial) expressions. We use the two terms synonymously. It is important to realize that although we treat vocalics as a separate nonverbal subcode, many researchers do not.

DEFINITIONS

Vocal refers to how we say words and includes accent, emphasis, vocal quality, pitch, rate, pause (including silence, a form of vocalic behavior), or anything that adds to the meaning of verbal communication. In addition, sounds such as grunts, screams, laughs, gasps, sighs, and even silence fall under the purview of vocalics. In short, vocalics refers to the nonverbal messages of the voice that add to the meaning of verbal communication, or that can stand alone as a meaning-making entity. The voice itself has major communicative value, and we are interested in this nonlinguistic aspect of communication. Perhaps you think it strange to find a chapter on voice in a nonverbal communication textbook. Vocalics are often what give verbal messages their full meaning, but vocalics are not the words. Thus, paralanguage is considered a nonverbal communication issue.

SOUND AND ITS ATTRIBUTES

The main topic here is the *sound produced* during speech or conversation. There are eight attributes, or areas, of sound that contribute to the vocalic meaning associated with the speech produced. These are loudness, pitch, duration, quality, regularity, articulation, pronunciation, and silence as functions of the vocal cues people use. **Loudness** deals with the intensity of the voice; here loudness is more than simply volume. You can be loud without raising your voice. In many cases, lowering the voice produces the desired result. **Pitch** is the range your voice uses during conversation and is associated with the frequency of a sound. Most of us have certain *pitch ranges* (extreme high pitch to extreme low pitch) in our voices. We do not think of pitch much, unless there is a "break" in the smoothness of transition from one pitch level to another (often found in teenage boys) or a different pitch is used for some effect (as when we are excited).

Duration relates to how long the sound is made. It may also be considered as a *juncture,* or dividing point, between speech clauses (R. G. Harper, Wiens, and Matarazzo 1978). Voice **quality** is judged by the speaker's timbre, tonality, and production of airflow through the glottis (opening in the throat where the sound is made). **Regularity** (sometimes called tempo) is the rate at which we speak and may include stress within the speech (increase or decrease of loudness within a speech clause). **Articulation** concerns the clearness and control of the sounds being produced. **Pronunciation**, closely related to articulation, deals with the clearness and control of the sound, the rhythm, and the rate of speech. Finally, **silence** refers to the absence of sound.

What our voices are, how they are interpreted, and how we use them for effect are related to these eight sound attributes. These properties can make the way we talk and the words we use convey different meanings.

PARAVOCAL COMMUNICATION

One school of the study of vocalics refers to it as "content-free speech." The concept of vocalics as content-free speech would seemingly produce an area that does not lend itself to study. After all, if the area is content-free, what can we examine? This problem still perplexes some researchers; however, Trager (1958) proposed a way to examine this content-free area and to bring the voice back into relationship with language:

When language is used it takes place in the setting of an act of *speech*. Speech ("talking") results from activities that create a background *voice set*. This background involves the idiosyncratic, including the specific physiology of the speakers and the total physical setting; it is in the area of prelinguistics. . . . Against this background there take place three kinds of events employing the vocal apparatus: language; variegated other noises, not having the structure of language—*vocalizations*; and modifications of all the language and other noises. These modifications are the *voice qualities*. The vocalizations and the voice qualities together are being called paralanguage. (pp. 1–12)

In essence, then, speech is not truly without content, but the study of the use of voice often separates the voice from the content aspect. Just as Trager proposed more than 55 years ago, there are many ways to investigate this topic in the field of nonverbal communication.

The **voice set**, or prelinguistic area of vocalics, establishes a context from which the voice is to be evaluated. The voice set provides the background against which we hear the voice. Just as you talk about different personal-spacing zones creating different levels of intimacy, your voice also differs in various contexts. Evaluating a voice without considering the context in which it is used results in faulty interpretation and often miscommunication. Your voice is different in a quiet, indoor area than it is on a busy street or in a nightclub with loud music. You use a different voice during a football game than during a speech. The context itself may create a different voice; your pitch levels may change after yelling and screaming at a game; you sound different in one situation than you do in another. One last issue of voice set is the identification aspect; people whom you know well will recognize you by your voice set, and vice versa. Think about when you receive a phone call from your mother. Does she need to say, "This is your mother"? You just recognize some people by their voices. These are all issues of voice set, and your own voice set often identifies you.

Voice qualities are modifications of the voice. These modifications are specific features of the voice itself and tend to be associated with particular people. Trager (1958) identified eight vocal qualities that accompany speech:

1. *Pitch range:* the range in terms of frequency of pitch (highness or lowness) of the voice.
2. *Vocal/lip control:* degree of raspiness or hoarseness of the voice.
3. *Glottis control:* the amount of air passing through the throat; ranges from breathy (too much air) to thin/tense (not enough air).
4. *Pitch control:* degree to which the frequency of pitch is controlled during transitions ("broken" voice is the image conjured up when one thinks of someone with poor pitch control).
5. *Articulation control:* degree to which the speaker is precise and clear in forming the sounds; yields an impression by pronunciation.
6. *Tempo control:* rate of the voice (normal speaking rate is approximately 125 words per minute for the total American culture. Southerners may speak slightly slower than this; Midwesterners or Northeasterners, slightly faster).
7. *Resonance:* amount of reverberation in the head cavity, which helps to determine the timbre (i.e., quality, tone) of the voice.
8. *Rhythm control:* the phraseology of the voice in degrees of smoothness; most of us have a particular rhythm to our speech, ranging from a jerky presentation to an almost sing-song phraseology (some stutterers can reduce their stuttering by adopting a sing-song phraseology when feeling a stutter coming on).

PHOTO 9.1   Good speaking voices are important in many professions, like politics, broadcasting, and the law.

Contemporary nonverbal theorists list the same or similar voice qualities in their coverage of vocalics. Each one of these voice qualities tends to identify a particular speaker, and, as we shall see, may induce stereotypical judgments based on vocal qualities.

Vocalizations are specific features of the voice that characterize a specific voice at specific points in time. Trager (1958) stated that there are three categories of vocalizations. (1) **Vocal characterizers** are nonlanguage sounds that can be placed on a continuum (usually from positive to negative). Vocal characterizers include laughing, crying, whimpering, yelling, sneezing, moaning, groaning, belching, and voice breaking. We often recognize different people by their characterizers. Have you ever heard a laugh and even though you could not see that person, you knew exactly who it was? That laugh is part of that person's characterization. (2) **Voice qualifiers** are similar to the vocal qualities already discussed but fall into three categories: *intensity* (loudness), *pitch height*, and *duration* (extent of held sound). These qualifiers can depend on the situation, so we must take into consideration the contextual features of the sound's production, such as echo, size of room, indoors or outdoors, temperature—all factors that affect sound production. (3) **Vocal segregates** are nonwords used to fill pauses, sometimes called *fillers*. Formerly, speech teachers taught public speaking students never to fill a pause; in real life, we use many vocal segregates, often to let the other person know that we are still speaking. Vocal segregates include such nonsense words as *uh-huh, um, ah, like, you know* (when used to fill a pause), *whatever,* and so forth. Some more recent words used as vocal segregates are *actual* or *actually* and *really*, which have meaningless places in the sense of communication; often they are redundant. A television weatherperson might say, "It's *actually* going to rain tomorrow." The sentence would make as much sense without the segregate "actually."

Trager's system allows us to understand how vocalics contribute to meaning. Consider the voice qualities, for example. By manipulating these qualities, we can negate or change the meaning associated with a verbal statement. The following three phrases are indicative of how we use the voice to emphasize, de-emphasize, or change the meaning of the verbal statement:

1. Love you.
2. Hate you.
3. Gee, you're nice.

Try saying each of these: (1) sincerely, or as the absolute truth; (2) sarcastically; (3) humorously; and (4) with sadness. How you vocally say each will change the semantic meaning associated with it.

BOX 9.1 OBSERVATIONAL STUDY

For the next day, with your roommates and close friends, keep track of paravocal communication issues just discussed that you hear them use. What messages did you get from their use of these? Were you able to tell someone's emotional state because of their use of their voice set? Did any vocal segregates distract you from the meaning?

Other ways of studying how vocalics contribute to communication have been proposed. These include the temporal (timing) characteristics of the vocalization—duration, interruption, reaction time latency (response time)—and such aspects as silences, pauses, hesitations, disturbances and disfluencies, and other ways that we can examine the voice over units of time (R. G. Harper et al. 1978).

VOCALIC FUNCTIONS

Much like the study of kinesics, vocalics can be examined for how it functions with the verbal message. These functions, however, are much less refined than those identified with kinesics. Krueger (1986) suggests that vocalics exists as a small "window of presence," without a past or a future. This window is limited further by having to rely totally on auditory cues. These cues allow for no "second look" at the communication, as is possible when studying things that can be seen (i.e., kinesics, space, touch, eye, and so forth). Also, because the focus of study is on the voice, which is an aural (or hearing) dimension of communication, judgments of meaning will necessarily be less refined than with other nonverbal subcodes.

How do vocalics function with the verbal message? The first function concerns **identification** and **self-presentation** of the speaker. This function deals specifically with the type of voice we use in the particular situation and with our perception of the effect of the voice. When we answer a telephone call, how do we "know" who it is? How do we "know" how that person feels? If we know the person, we can usually tell by voice set and by vocal characterizers. The second function is **controlling the interaction**; for those involved in the interaction, it focuses on such vocal cues as hesitations, pauses, and interruptions. The third function concerns our **relationships with the other interactants**, which often affects the voice we choose to use. The fourth and fifth functions deal with **displaying cognitive and affective information**. The sixth function concerns **deception**.

Before turning to the first function, we need to examine briefly what the "normal voice" in "normal conversation" is like. Here, we look at the temporal dimensions of the voice and at how it is used in normal conversation over a period of time.

THE "NORMAL" CONVERSATION

Krueger (1986) examined normal vocalic communication *patterns* over time and with a variety of different people. His research was unique in that it used a measuring instrument that was attached to the participant and that recorded data at preset intervals over a selected period of time. His instrument, LOGOPORT, measured three vocalic parameters: duration of talk, pause between talks, and speech rate per talk (percentage of time a person speaks within a given talk). The LOGOPORT, then, measured nonlanguage variables associated with day-to-day interaction. In essence, it allowed the researchers to examine what "normal talk" might be like from a vocalic point of view.

Krueger's data describe the talk patterns of 66 people (male and female students between 20 and 30 years of age) talking over a period of one day. He reported that people, at least in the mid-1980s, had between three and five talks per day. Since people are using more electronic forms of communication these days, that number has probably decreased. Krueger also reported that talks have a typical form: a slow beginning period, an intensive speaking period, and a period he describes as "fading out." He notes that this form was not deviated from in any of the interactions analyzed, which suggests "a highly ritualized interaction behavior" (p. 8). In further analysis, Krueger concluded that the talk patterns were of a particular form and also that, within talks, people exhibited highly stable speech behavior, regardless of the context in which the talk was conducted. Krueger referred to these patterns and stable behaviors as *normal talk*. Think about your last face-to-face conversation; did it follow this pattern?

Let's turn to an examination of the six vocalic functions identified thus far, to better understand what is *normal* in communication interactions, in terms of vocalics.

STUDENT VOICES

Katie: I guess I never really thought about the idea of voice set. My dad once called the house and when I answered, he thought I was my mother because he mistook my voice for my mom's. We sound very much alike. His voice set changed when he realized that he was talking to me. He went from what sounded like being all "lovey dovey" to being like he was my father, not my husband. Since we have talked about this subject in class, I reminded him of this, and we have all had a good laugh about it.

IDENTIFICATION AND SELF-PRESENTATION

An important function of vocalics is to help identify others and to aid in interpreting their self-presentations through the type of voice chosen for effect, or the voice type selected for a specific purpose. In general, voice types are usually used for some sort of effect, often to approach an "idealized" voice pattern. A second aspect deals more with a socialization process than with the self-presentation effect. These are specialized vocal segregates that are associated with dialect and accent.

VOICE TYPES

People often use their voices for effect. *Most* of us possess certain voice qualities that tend to stereotype us one way or another. The fact that we sometimes use such stereotypes to characterize others or to play roles indicates that the voice type is ingrained in this culture. How many of the following stereotypes have you heard? Males with a breathy voice are effeminate, whereas females with a breathy voice type are sexy; people who speak fast are brighter than those who speak slowly; people who have no rhythm in their voices (i.e., whose voices are flat) are boring; people with high-pitched voices are weak, nervous, and argumentative; people with low-pitched voices are athletic or stoic. These voice types and the stereotypes are typical in this culture. Several researchers have examined the relationship between voice type and perceived personality; their results, however, have not always been consistent, supporting the contention that most of these personality perceptions come from stereotypes, not from fact.

In 1964, Heinberg theorized 11 voice types based on the degree of pleasantness or unpleasantness associated with the voice. Of the 11 voice types and their stereotypes, only one is perceived as "good." The other 10 are perceived as "bad" or "unpleasant." The good voice type is associated with proper breathing, articulation, tongue position, control of pitch and resonance, and so forth. This is the voice we may ascribe to a professional announcer.

Unpleasant voice types are generated from one's own specific vocal qualities. In most cases, these fall into one or more of the voice types. As you read the following, note which are recognizable:

1. *Breathy:* females perceived as sexy and spacey; males as younger, artistic, and effeminate.
2. *Tense:* older, anxious, nervous, uncooperative, less intelligent, and high-strung.
3. *Breathy-tense:* four types, all of which are perceived as weak and nervous: husky, harsh, hard, and strident.
4. *Nasal:* whiny, argumentative, lazy.
5. *Denasal:* stuffy, as if the speaker had a cold.
6. *Orotund:* energetic, pompous, authoritative, proud, humorless.
7. *Flat:* bored, sluggish, withdrawn.
8. *Thin:* immature, emotional, sensitive (mainly for females).
9. *Throaty:* sophisticated, less intelligent, careless, older.
10. *Fronted:* artificial, aloof.

Malandro, Barker, and Barker (1989) suggest that both males and females hold voice types and stereotypes. They infer that five major vocal areas influence stereotypes: nasality, screeching (shrillness of the voice), softness, monotone voice, and speed (rate). These areas do contribute to stereotypical judgments, but such judgments are made on additional vocal features also, which are discussed later in the chapter.

IDEAL SPEECH

Kramer (1977, 1978) and Giles, Scholes, and Young (1983) reported that vocal traits may yield an *idealized* voice. Kramer's research used a questionnaire consisting of 51 language traits (both verbal and vocal) based on actual content derived from high school and college students. In one study, Kramer (1977) asked 466 students from two high schools and a university to rate each of these speech traits as they compared to male and female use; hence she tapped the stereotypical "language" used. Table 9.1 presents the 51 traits found. Note that the overwhelming majority are vocal in nature (marked with an asterisk), although Kramer's main focus was on the verbal issues tied to those traits. The nonverbal aspects of these seemingly verbal traits lie in how we perceive the underlying message, or the *unspoken* message of these words. Kramer also found that males and females differed on many characteristics (see Table 9.2), with males differed on 16 traits, females on 20 traits. Hence, stereotypical vocalic (and language) traits we can associate with each sex exist. Much like the voice types discussed earlier, however, these traits are probably most identified with strangers, because the better we know someone, the better we judge the messages of that person's vocalics.

TABLE 9.1 SPEECH CHARACTERISTICS IDENTIFIED BY KRAMER

*Demanding voice	*Militant speech
*Enunciate clearly	Use slang
*Deep voice	*Emotional speech
Boastful speech	*Authoritarian speech
*High pitch	Use many details
Use swear words	*Serious speech
Use hands and face to express ideas	*Forceful speech
*Dominating speech	Lounge, lean back while talking
Gossip	*Smooth speech
*Loud speech	Open, self-revealing speech
*Relaxed speech	*Enthusiastic speech
Concern for listener	Explain things thoroughly
Interesting speech	Smile a lot when talking
*Gentle speech	*Stutter
*Fast speech	*Patient speech
*Persuasive manner while speaking	Good grammar
*Show anger rather than concealing it	*Logical speech
Talk about trivial topics	*Polite speech
*Wide range in rate and pitch	*Nervous speech
Look at listener directly when talking	Opinionated speech
Straight to the point	*Casual speech
*Friendly speech	*Aggressive speech
*Talk a lot	Gibberish
Large vocabulary	*Confident speech
Assume listener knows what speaker is talking about	Blunt speech
*Vocal characteristic	Sense of humor in speech

Source: Cheris Kramer, "Perceptions of Male and Female Speech," *Language and Speech*, 20 (1977), 156–157. Reprinted with permission.

In a second study, Kramer (1978) sought to extend this finding to discuss what idealized speech was. Here she was interested in two things: (1) whether her subjects agreed on what an ideal speech type would be and (2) where males and females differed in their stereotypical perceptions. She found that males and females did not differ about ideal speech types on 50 of the 51 characteristics identified. The only difference between male and female perceptions of the idealized voice was that males thought it should be a *deep voice*, whereas females did not. This finding strongly suggests that Kramer's high school and college students perceived the *same* characteristics in their idealized voices. A second concern of her research was to see what males and females identified to be the ideal voice. She found that males were less likely to identify the idealized voice characteristics when looking at 41 traits, whereas females were less likely to identify idealized voice characteristics on only 34 of the characteristics. What this means, at least according to Kramer, is that women seem to be a little more adept at coming to an agreement over what was an idealized voice characteristic than men were. Hinkle (2001) found that vocal variety, pronunciation, speech rate, and volume were important to creating nonverbal immediacy. Think about your friends, both male and female; would they be considered as having an ideal voice?

The vocalic characteristics that did not differ between males and females included a wide range in pitch and rate, authoritarian speech, serious speech, and casual speech. Further, males' perceptions of ideal voices did not differ from what was considered the ideal in high pitch, talking a lot, and emotional speech. Females' perceptions did not differ from what was considered the ideal characteristics in dominating speech, loud speech, gentle speech, show anger, militant speech, forceful speech, and aggressive speech. Finally, Kramer found that males and females differed on 7 of the 51 characteristics, with females differing significantly from the ideal on the ideal characteristics (females were different from their ideal, whereas males were not different from their ideal). Females saw themselves as significantly less deep voiced, lower in terms of a sense of humor, higher on gossip, higher on trivial-topics conversation, and higher on talk a lot. Males differed from the ideal on two of the characteristics that the females did not: males saw themselves as stuttering more and as being more boastful than the ideal speaker.

These findings show that (1) stereotypical (idealized) voice characteristics exist, and that (2) males and females perceive themselves fairly stereotypically. How valid are these results? In other words, would the presence of an actual *voice* have changed the results? Attempting to answer this question in part, Giles et al. (1983) replicated Kramer's studies with a British sample of 80 undergraduates. Their results were similar to Kramer's findings: 39 differences between ideal male and female characteristics, with an overlap of 32 characteristics; males and females rated themselves as significantly different from the opposite sex on 46 and 34 characteristics, respectively. Again, actual voices were not used; the method employed measured reaction to characteristics rather than to actual voices. However, both sets of research do indicate that fairly strong vocalic stereotypes exist—and they exist across cultures. Those vocalic stereotypes are why we include this information here. Even when there is an absence of voice sound, we are likely to stereotype the type of voice we expect when we think of those characteristics.

Other researchers have looked at the concept of the ideal voice and have found that vocal attractiveness is just as influential as physical attractiveness in daily interaction. In 1993,

TABLE 9.2   SPEECH CHARACTERISTICS DIFFERENTIATING MALE AND FEMALE SPEAKERS
FOR BOTH MALES AND FEMALES

Traits Characteristic of Male Speakers	Traits Characteristic of Female Speakers
*Demanding voice	*Enunciate clearly
*Deep voice	*High pitch
Boastful speech	Use hands and face to express ideas
Use swear words	Gossip
*Dominating speech	Concern for listener
*Loud speech	*Gentle speech
*Show anger rather than concealing it	*Fast speech
Straight to the point	Talk about trivial topics
*Militant speech	*Wide range in rate and pitch
Use slang	*Friendly speech
*Authoritarian speech	*Talk a lot
*Forceful speech	Use many details
Lounge, lean back while talking	*Emotional speech
*Aggressive speech	*Open, self-revealing speech
Blunt speech	*Enthusiastic speech
Sense of humour in speech	Smile a lot when talking
*Vocal Characteristic	Good grammar
	*Polite speech
	Gibberish

Source: Cheris Kramer, "Perceptions of Male and Female Speech," *Language and* Speech, 20 (1977), 157. Reprinted with permission.

Zuckerman and Miyake examined the ideal voice and concluded that eight subjective measures were the best indicators of the ideal voice for attractiveness: pitch, pitch range, shrillness, loudness, loudness range, monotonousness, resonance, and deepness. They reported that these eight factors accounted for almost three-fourths of the voice's attractiveness. They have indicated that voice attractiveness does not have the impact that physical attraction does because the voice is assessed for factors other than attractiveness, whereas the face primarily demonstrates attractiveness (Zuckerman, Hodgins, and Miyake 1990). Regardless, voice is an aspect of overall nonverbal attractiveness.

It appears, however, that a "bad voice" can be a relationship *disqualifier* in a fashion similar to bad physical appearance. Berry (1990, 1992) found that vocal attractiveness increased strength, assertiveness, invulnerability, and dominance in the male voice, while female attractive voices were rated as warm, honest, and kind. She also found that, in general, people with attractive voices are considered more competent, warm, and honest than people with unattractive voices. People with babyish voices were rated less competent and

PHOTO 9.2   A positive tone of voice and a good sense of humor help to create good conversations.

less powerful, but more honest and warm, than those with mature voices. In another study, Berry and colleagues found that young children with babyish voices were again rated honest and warm, but low on competence, leadership, and dominance (Berry, Hansen, Landry-Pester, and Meier 1994). Nasal voices are also considered to be "bad voices." Consider the reactions Fran Drescher, formerly of the TV series *The Nanny*, gets when she speaks. When surveying nonverbal communication classes about which public figure has the most annoying, unpleasant voice, almost unanimously Drescher is elected. In 2013, in the popular online media of the day, this still seems to be the top annoying voice of our time (Weiss 2013).

BOX 9.2   OBSERVATIONAL STUDY

Advertisers have focused on finding attractive actors with ideal voices. Can you name some? Listen to some television ads and some radio ads. What is it about those voices that makes them "ideal" for broadcasting or for advertising products? Are there some ads where you think the advertisers made a poor decision? Why?

In terms of speech rate and volume, several studies have demonstrated vocalic influences on individuals' perceptions of the speakers. Kimble and Seidel (1991), for instance, found that individuals who were confident about what they were saying talked louder and faster than those who demonstrated less confidence. S. M. Smith and Shaffer (1991) also found that people who talked quickly were perceived as more credible than those who talked at a normal rate. Such rates tended to suppress interruptions either of a counter or an agreeable nature. Buller and Aune (1992), however, found that moderate speech rates were preferred by most people and that people tend to prefer speech rates similar to their own. Other researchers have found that medium and high rates of pitch variation increase a person's perceived dynamism and that a person's credibility can be hurt by nonfluencies. Specifically, Engstrom (1994) found that vocalized pauses (e.g., "The Senate . . . uh . . . budget"), repetitions ("is is now"), and tongue-slip corrections ("Forty-foot seal-sailboat") lowered ratings of competence; dynamism, however, was not affected by these, nor was information recall.

In terms of the ideal speaker, there are differences between what males and females perceive to be idealized speech. The ideal speaker, however, appears to be a moderately loud, fast talker, a mature-sounding speaker, a speaker without nonfluencies, a speaker who does not stutter and who speaks at a moderate to fast rate, and a speaker who has a wide pitch range (G. B. Ray, Ray, and Zahn 1991). Think about the people of whom you think highly, then consider their vocal qualities. Do they have some of these ideal characteristics of voice? Do you have ideal vocal characteristics? Some research studies have shown that if we were able to observe our own vocalic behaviors, we would be able to identify our paralanguage weaknesses. Zick, Granieri, and Makoul (2007), in a study where first-year medical students were asked to evaluate videos of their health care interviews with patients, were able to identify their vocalic weaknesses: particularly they found that tone, rate, volume, and disfluencies such as "uh," "um" affected the health care interview situation.

BOX 9.3 OBSERVATIONAL STUDY

What characterizes your speech? Ask several friends to rate your speech on Kramer's (1977, 1978) speech characteristics and then compare them to what she reported for your gender. Record a short segment as you read from some book and then play it back to 10 friends. Give them a sheet of paper with Kramer's speech characteristics, and ask them to check those that fit you. What did you find? How much agreement did your raters have?

VOCAL RECOGNITION AND VOICEPRINTS

Based on the discussion thus far, it should be apparent that we can use our voices for a number of purposes. One purpose of the voice that has received some attention is the voiceprint. The idea behind the **voiceprint** is that an individual's voice is unique, much like a fingerprint, and that it is possible to identify people on the basis of certain vocal qualities. Although we can identify some people by their voices, as we mentioned earlier, the relative accuracy with which we do so is questionable. With technological advances of the last decade, voiceprints are becoming more and more reliable, and will continue to do so in this 21st century. In the course of a week of programming, between the educational television stations, such as The Learning Channel, Discovery, Arts and Entertainment, Investigative Discovery, and TRU-TV, there will always be at least one program that centers on finding criminals by using this technology. Voiceprinting, along with DNA analyses, created a new wave of forensic science, which is not likely to disappear soon.

When a voiceprint is taken, the voice is analyzed with a spectrometer, which displays a graph of the spoken language. What you actually obtain is a series of waves, some "thicker" than others, and blank spaces. This, then, becomes your identification. As you may surmise, however, the print is only as good as the voice that created it, and one must assume that it is as "true" as the person who created it; in other words, if we disguise our voices, the print will be distorted.

> . . . [I]t often happens [mistaking someone's voice for another] when I call my typist, Barbara Gombach, that I mistake the voice of another woman in her office for hers. Their actual voices are more distinctive than their telephone voices, however, probably because the telephone filters out many important voice characteristics and only carries sound in a narrow frequency range. (Weitz 1979, 227)

Weitz notes that the voiceprint has been used in some criminal investigations (notably recorded telephone conversations). Although some people claim that under proper conditions, "better than ninety-nine percent accuracy can be expected in matching voice samples," the methods used have been severely criticized (Weitz 1979, 227). Typically, past studies reported that accuracy ran only a little better than 50 percent (Reich, Moll, and Curtis 1976). More recent research reports that this technique is being refined and used more often in courtrooms than when Weitz originally researched the topic (Read and Craik 1995). Although people may claim to be able to identify voices, McGehee (1937) reported that accuracy drops off rather rapidly. After about 5 months passing since the last hearing of the voice, the accuracy of individuals identifying people by their voices is only about 13 percent.

The recent technological advances in this area have increased the accuracy, at least in the use of mechanical or computerized voice printing. This improvement can even be seen in new technology that uses voiceprints (as well as handprints) to allow individuals entry into "gated" areas. The individual says his or her name over an intercom and is allowed entry by comparison with a voiceprint. After the terrorist events of September 11, 2001, and the establishment of the concept of *Homeland Security*, this will probably be a type of technology all of us will have contact with in our futures. In addition, many banks are experimenting with voiceprinting for automated telephone banking. The most recent studies that have been done in the area of voiceprinting all seem to be in the area of financial institutions using the technology as a way to avoid fraudulent practices in banking (see Gunson, Marshall, McInnes, and Jack 2011; Gold 2010).

Voiceprint technology, like other technologies, can be the victim of scams. Some companies have been selling pencils as "lie detectors." Actually, these pencils are miniaturized stress evaluators. They supposedly pick up the stress in a voice, which they claim indicates lying. Can you imagine being told to report to your boss for no apparent reason, being informed that some money was missing, and then being asked whether you took it? Your voice might indicate some stress, which would be picked up by the detector, but this stress would be natural. Instead of recording the natural stress, the pencil detector would indicate lying (a little light would go off, indicating the lie/stress). Obviously, there can be misuses of any new technology, and this is something about which you should become aware.

In view of what we know about the voice and our ability to "mask," or to use the voice for effect, the voiceprint should be approached with caution. As the techniques for identifying those features that make our voices "unique" have improved, the voiceprint is becoming more of an everyday tool than it once was, although it has not yet become so common as to find it everywhere. Until this science is perfected, however, we should remember that a person can alter the voice enough to confuse others. Often a simple thing such as a cold will create enough difference in the voice to deceive others.

How good are we at voice recognition without the help of mechanical aids? Some research indicates that we are not very good at recognizing voices, and that the blind are not any better than the sighted, which would seem to debunk the idea that with blindness we become better at vocal cues. Winograd, Kerr, and Spence (1984) had students listen to 20 masculine and feminine voices saying both the same message and a different message. In one part of their experiment, they found no differences in ability to recognize the various voices. In a second part of the study, they added a new message along with the old message; findings here indicated that participants tended to recognize the old voice with the old message rather than the new message. Participants reported that the old messages sounded more familiar when speakers of the same sex said them. The third part of the study examined sighted versus blind subjects' ability to recognize voices, but the researchers found no differences.

It appears that we are fairly poor recognizers of voices. It also appears, however, that as we become familiar with the voices and messages we hear, some increase in accuracy is obtained. Some say that accuracy increases with the depth of the relationship; the better we know the persons, the more likely we will be able to accurately identify them by their voices. In some cases, especially in brain-damaged individuals, voice recognition has been studied carefully to see if there is any correlation between the impaired brain function and ability to recognize voices. Studies to date have not found such a correlation. Garrido et al. (2009) report a study they conducted with a 60-year-old female patient who had extreme difficulty with voice recognition. She had no medical signs of brain damage; she just was virtually unable to recognize voices. So, if you are one of those people who has trouble with voice recognition, realize that there are some people who do not have this ability.

BOX 9.4 OBSERVATIONAL STUDY

Make five phone calls to people you know well—family, close friends, roommates, your significant other—and do not identify yourself. Also, try not to identify yourself by the topic you choose to discuss, at least for the first minute of the conversation. See how long it takes before they recognize it is you, or ask who you are. What does this tell you about your voice? About others' abilities to recognize voice set?

ACCENTS AND DIALECTS

Trager (1958) defined a group of vocal characterizers as "non-words." These vocal segregates can have a dramatic impact on the evaluation of another person's speech. We will take Trager's definition and expand it to include several other nonword classes: dialect, accent, nonfluency, speech rate, response latency, duration of utterance, and interaction rate. Each of these non-word classes, in its own way, influences the positive or negative quality of the vocal message.

All of us speak with a special dialect or accent. We distinguish the two terms, as others have done: *Accent* is how the words sound as they are pronounced by individuals; *dialect* is the use of unique words or phrases common to a specific group (e.g., "soda," "pop," and "coke" all refer to "soft drinks," but their use varies depending on which area of the United States you come from). You need to realize that some researchers use the two terms synonymously, even though a good deal of research exists to show that they are two separate but interconnected concepts. We include both concepts here because they are interrelated. These identifiers tend to stereotype us according to some grouping. In the United States, for instance, there are three general *dialects:* Southern, Eastern, and general American. Of the three, the general American is by far the most dominant. There have been at least 10 major regional dialect areas identified: Eastern New England, New York City, Middle Atlantic, Southern, Western Pennsylvania, Southern Mountain, Central Midland, Northwest, Southwest, and North Central (C. K. Thomas 1958).

People from dialectical regions other than our own are often perceived to be different. A number of studies show that people react to others' dialects and/or accents on the basis of expectations. That is, we expect someone to possess a certain accent or dialect, and if that accent or dialect is present, we evaluate it positively (Knapp 1978). Drawing on a number of research studies, J. K. Burgoon and Saine (1978, 182–183) presented seven findings based on the credibility of a given speaker's dialect:

1. People don't have a preference for their own regional dialect; they don't consistently rate it highest.
2. General American speech (what Midwesterners speak) is generally viewed as more credible than Southern or New England speech.
3. The speech of native-born speakers is rated as more dynamic, more aesthetically pleasing, and reflective of higher sociointellectual status than that of speakers with foreign accents.
4. Both African Americans and Caucasian Americans rate speakers of Standard English higher than speakers using a nonstandard dialect (including African American dialect). African American speakers who use Standard English are assumed to be Caucasian Americans.
5. People speaking with a New York accent are rated more dynamic but less sociable than those with a Southern drawl.
6. People speaking with a New York accent or Central United States pattern (which is equivalent to General American speech) are rated as more competent than speakers with a New England or Southern accent (where competency is also a part of credibility ratings).
7. Finally, the effects of dialect on a receiver's judgment are short-term.

Mulac (1976) indicates that we evaluate others' dialects along three primary dimensions. His research examined a number of dialects, both foreign and regional, and found that people evaluated others' dialects on the basis of (1) sociointellectual status (status, occupation, income, literacy), (2) aesthetic quality (how pleasing or displeasing the accent or dialect is), and (3) dynamism (how aggressive, strong, loud, or active the voice is).

PHOTO 9.3 Do you think that Arnold Schwarzenegger's accent affects people's perceptions of his credibility as an actor? How about as Governor of California? Do you think his voice is immediately recognizable?

Some researchers believe that accent or dialect has an impact on how people are perceived. Jensen and Rosenfeld (1974) reported that teachers rate children whose accents are different from the subcultural norm as culturally disadvantaged. Other research indicates that dialect and accent may have subtle influences; Giles (1970), for instance, tested whether standard speech (that which is normal for the given area) would lead to higher perceptions of credibility and expertise for speakers attempting to influence others. He found that although the standard speech was more influential, it was influential only over the less prestigious accents and dialects found in the region. This finding may suggest that we identify with and prefer a normative accent much like that discussed earlier. It may be that certain accents—relative to our own subcultural accent—are more or less acceptable. Accents closer to our own will be perceived as more rewarding (more credible, sociable, influential) than those more noticeable because of their differences.

We have mostly been pointing out findings about accent; let us consider dialect separately here for a short time (recall that many scholars use the two terms interchangeably). Many issues of dialect are grammatical issues and therefore serve as another point of evaluation. One dialectical issue that appears to be changing in *all* regions of the United States was originally thought of as a *Southernism*. That dialectical expression is seen when someone refers to himself/herself and another person, saying "Me and _____." (Fill in your choice: him, her, my friend, and so on). Most people have been taught that this is grammatically incorrect, and it clearly is incorrect; yet it seems to be used consistently by educated individuals, as well as those who are not. There was a time when, if you used this expression, you were perceived to be "backwoods" or "uneducated." Today its use is widespread—used even by news broadcasters, talk show hosts, best-selling authors, and so forth. One of your textbook authors teaches about this issue when discussing vocalics, and many students are incredulous that this is grammatically incorrect, and appalled that someone might perceive them to be "less than intelligent" because they use it. Many take great offense when it is written on their speech or mock interview critique sheets to avoid the use of this dialect (as well as other examples, such as "he/she don't," "it don't," wrong forms of irregular verbs such as "went" and "gone," and so forth) because of being perceived as unintelligent because these are grammatically incorrect. Using this verbal example may have you asking, "How is that nonverbal communication?" It is clearly both verbal and nonverbal communication. The nonverbal aspect comes in the overall perception of the use of the terms, coupled with the accent issues, which creates a nonverbal perception.

The impact of accent and dialect, then, can have an effect on our perceptions of others. Although these perceptions may be short-term, they influence our initial interactions—even create an impression that may be totally wrong—resulting in not communicating with the other person. Initial impressions are very difficult to change, which is why first impressions you knowingly make are very important. How specific the accent and dialect are and how good you are at identifying it depends upon how perceptive you are. It is not uncommon for people who deal with others from all over the United States to be able to place someone within 10 to 50 miles of where he or she grew up. One of your authors, while serving in the Army, met someone who could place individuals within a 50-mile radius of their homes, not an uncommon phenomenon for people who study accent and dialect and understand it.

Other dialectical issues we point to are word choices, such as we mentioned in the "soda" example. These dialectical differences can cause confusion for communicators who are not familiar with the word choices being used by the speaker. For example, in the rural South, "old timers" will call a grocery bag a "poke" (some of you may call it a "sack"—making our point for us). Can you imagine waiting on a customer in a store where you work and having your customer ask you for a "poke"? In Maine, the word "wicked" is used as a highly positive term, such as "That was wicked good!" Can you imagine your new-found friend coming up to you and telling you that you are "wicked" and feeling complimented by that label? In the Northeast, some people refer to galoshes or rain boots as "rubbers." All of these are issues of dialect; can you think of more?

We would be remiss if we did not point out that in the updating of this textbook (in 2013), no new research on accents and dialects could be found. It seems that it has become either passé or impolitic to discuss such differences. Perhaps this is because when we do, we seem to be trying to decide which race or class of people have more standard dialects and accents, which leads to subtle racism or regionalism. Southerners, for example, do not care a whole lot for people who say they are stupid because of their accents and rate of speech, or even because some of their "dialecticalisms" are grammatically incorrect. The same is true for African Americans, Latinos, and other minority groups.

BOX 9.5   OBSERVATIONAL STUDY

For the next 24 hours take note of all the different accents you hear, either in your interactions (with friends, in classes, at work, etc.) or in the media (television and radio). How many different accents do your recognize? Also, listen for the dialectical differences—either in language structure or in word choices—and take note of those. What were some of the ones that stood out to you more than others?

VOCAL EXPRESSIVENESS AND BODY SHAPE

Typically, we expect that certain body shapes (somatotypes) produce certain vocal qualities. We expect the large male to sound like a large male; if he does not, we label him. Mike Tyson, for example, former world heavyweight boxing champion, has a voice quite incongruent with his size (and profession). Indeed, Tyson has become the brunt of many jokes because of his vocal characteristics. Many people say he fights and behaves crudely and aggressively in public to compensate for his effeminate voice.

Research indicates that judgments relating to body shape and voice should be accepted with caution. Lass and Harvey (1976), for instance, found some relation between voice and body shape, but not as great as might be expected. N. P. Solomon, Helou, Dietrich-Burns, and Stojadinovic (2011) discovered that obese persons did not have many differences in their voices, in particular the strain, pitch, and loudness of the voice, when losing weight and decreasing body mass index (BMI), even though many people thought there would be significant differences. Most of the time, our expectations are based on physical rather than physiological factors. The large person may have a higher-pitched voice than the smaller individual. We expect the opposite, however, and attach stigmas to those who do not meet our expectations. This attitude seems to be developing in regard to female athletes; we seem to expect them to sound more like athletes, with deeper voices and more guttural vocal expressions.

CONTROLLING INTERACTION

A second vocal function concerns the flow and control of a conversation. This section explores the regulating and controlling function: first, through the impact of disturbances within the flow of communication and, second, through the impact of interruption, speech rate, and talk duration.

DISTURBANCES

Two areas of vocalics that have received some attention are speech disturbances and temporal aspects of speech—that is, nonfluencies, speech rate, latency of response, duration of utterance, and interaction rate.

In the area of speech disturbance, Mahl (1956) concluded that speech disturbances could be classified into eight categories (see Table 9.3). His categories suggest that anxiety can be measured by a *speech disturbance ratio*, which is determined by the number of speech disturbances divided by the total number of words spoken. As noted in Table 9.3, speech disturbances range from the use of the *ah* and *non-ah* (incoherent) sounds to the correction of sentences as an interruption. A review of the research using Mahl's ratio indicates that the *ah* and *non-ah* speech ratio most frequently define speech disturbances associated with anxiety. Interestingly, a study found that males engage in more speech disruptions of the *ah* or *non-ah* variety than do females (Beckman 1975). It was speculated that society's role for the male of assertion and dominance may be stressful and produce more speech disturbances.

Other research gives us a better idea of the vocal disturbance phenomenon. In a developmental study, Dauterive and Ragsdale (1986) found that both children and adults used hesitations such as *ahs* and unfilled pauses to cover hesitations in thought. They also found that the *ah* phenomenon increased with age, especially among females. Among the children studied, females decreased unfilled pauses, and males increased pauses as age increased, indicating a smoother emergent speech pattern for females. Dauterive and Ragsdale also reported that stuttering showed increased peaks at ages 3, 7, and 8. The implication here, when combined with earlier research, is that females' speech patterns smooth out as they get older, whereas males' patterns tend to become more disruptive. Earlier research assumed that as males began to fulfill societal roles of assertion and dominance, they would indicate such change through their speech patterns. This study clearly supports such a view. Realize, however, that as females continue to assume societal roles of assertion and dominance, their speech patterns should similarly change.

TABLE 9.3 SPEECH DISTURBANCE CATEGORIES

Category	Definition
Sentence correction	Correction in form or content perceived by listener as interruption of word sequences
Sentence incompletion	Interrupted expression with communication continuing without correction
Stutter	Stutter
Intruding incoherent sound	Unrecognizable sound that does not alter the form of expression
Tongue slip	Neologisms, transposition of words from correct sequences, substitution of unintended for intended word
Omission	Words or parts of words omitted; generally terminal syllables of words
Filled pauses; repetition	Unnecessary serial repetition of one or more words
Ah	Definite occurrence of the "ah" sound

Source: R. G. Harper, A. N. Wiens, and J. D. Matarazzo, *Nonverbal Communication: The State of the Art* (New York: John Wiley, Interscience, 1978), 41. Reprinted with permission.

Verbal fluency has also been examined from both encoding and decoding perspectives. From an encoding approach, research indicates that speech patterns with the encoding of a message are less fluent (contain more pauses, filled pauses, hesitations) when psychological involvement in the conversation is low and when the communication topic is novel or is presented by people who are not trained in how to prepare a message, especially a public one (Coker and Burgoon 1987). From a decoding perspective, more fluent verbal presentations have been identified with source authoritativeness, attractiveness, and professionalism. Verbal fluency, however, also has a down side. Hosman and Wright (1987) found, for instance, that whereas perceptions of witnesses' authoritativeness and attractiveness increased with fewer hesitations, guiltiness attributions *increased*, presumably because the witness was perceived as a *smooth talker*.

BOX 9.6 OBSERVATIONAL STUDY

Attend two public speeches of some type (either a formal one, or a class where the teacher is lecturing, or even speeches being made in one of your classes). Keep track of the "speech disturbances" in the persons' speaking—

nonfluencies, awkward pauses, correcting speech, etc. Then, compare the two speakers. Which one was better? Did she or he have fewer speech disturbances? What messages did the speech disturbances send you?

TEMPORAL DIMENSIONS

The temporal (or time-related) aspects of vocalics were studied in some detail by Harper et al. (1978) and their colleagues. This body of research concentrated on the impact of the duration of utterance, the reaction-time latency (amount of time between two speech units), and the number of interruptions in conversation. These studies used interviews, with the interviewer manipulating the frequency of these three variables. The researchers found that by manipulating the duration of utterance, one person can influence how long another's utterance will be; the frequency of interruption by an interviewer produced a similar interruption frequency by the interviewee. Gregory and Webster (1996), in a different experimental setting using interviews, discovered a similar outcome; the lower status person was more likely to accommodate to the higher status person's vocalic behaviors. We can expect, then, as we make our utterances longer or shorter, that we unconsciously influence others along a similar line. In terms of interruption behavior, the more or less we interrupt, the more or less will others. This would seem to confirm the idea of the dyadic effect (or the norm of reciprocity), which says *how I communicate with you, I should expect to receive in return*. We have discussed this concept in the other nonverbal subcodes we have covered thus far, so it should be no surprise that it occurs with vocalic issues as well. In a fascinating study, M. L. Ray and Webb (1966) found that the frequency of President John F. Kennedy's response rate to a reporter's questions correlated highly with the length of questions posed. Other research indicates that interruptive behavior is associated with less empathic listening behavior and lower interpersonal orientations toward another (Street and Murphy 1987). As these theorists discovered, the temporal issues can have an effect on how the interaction progresses.

Finally, there may be racial and gender differences in temporal speech. Booth-Butterfield and Jordan (1989) observed vocalic behavior among African American and Caucasian American females in same-race and mixed-race groups. They found that African American females in all-African American groups were more nonverbally expressive than their Caucasian American counterparts in all-Caucasian American groups and that the African American females interrupted other African American females more than Caucasian American females interrupted each other. When the interaction was mixed, however, the African American participants' level of interruption changed more than did the level of the Caucasian participants; the interruption level decreased from the African American same-race group more so than occurred in the Caucasian American same-race group.

Gender differences in temporal behavior are less than conclusive. Although it has been reported that males have longer talk periods than do females (Beckman 1975) and interrupt more than do females (Mulac, Wiemann, Widenmann, and Gibson 1988), such findings have been questioned (Dindia 1987). In a study that reexamined these findings, Dindia (1987) had 30 male and 30 female undergraduates engage in unstructured conversations (they were not told what to talk about) in same- or opposite-sex dyads. Unlike earlier research, she found that (1) men did not interrupt more than women and that women did not get interrupted any more than did men; (2) interruptions were asymmetrically distributed in both same- and opposite-sex dyads, but it was not the male who interrupted more in opposite-sex dyads; and (3) women's less assertive behaviors were not interrupted—nor were their interruptions less assertive—and women's responses to interruptions were as assertive as males'. Like the research reported by Kennedy and Camden in 1983, Dindia found more interruptions occurring in opposite-sex dyads than in same-sex dyads, but both males and females were more likely to interrupt and be interrupted by an opposite-sex partner than by a same-sex partner. And, unlike earlier findings, interruption was not a function of sex (C. West 1979; Zimmerman and West 1975). Whether a person interrupts seems to be linked more to his or her personality than to sex or gender.

Dindia (1987) also found that male and female interruption behavior differed according to the type of conversation being carried out. In supportive conversations (where one partner seeks or gives agreement, acceptance, or approval), females were less likely to interrupt, but they were more likely than males to interrupt when the conversation was informational in nature (where one partner gives or seeks information, suggestion, or opinion), regardless of the sex of the person they were interrupting. Males in opposite-sex dyads were more likely than females to use disconfirming interruptions, and they were more likely to use disagreeing interruptions when interrupting another male than when interrupting a female (and were more likely to use disagreeing interruptions than if it were a female interrupting a male or female). Finally, Dindia found that males and females were *equally* likely to reinterrupt when interrupted; hence, interruption begets interruption, again confirming the dyadic effect, regardless of the sexual composition of the interaction.

One final gender interruption issue is the issue of why either males or females interrupt. L. P. Stewart, Stewart, Friedley, and Cooper (1990) found that men use interruption more to control conversation; women use it more to show support, encourage the other person to talk, or to acknowledge the other person. Stewart and colleagues were not alone in that finding; other scholars noted the same effect. Wood (1998) gave a different explanation when she asserted that men generally interrupt more. She believes that interruptions are seen as a norm and as pleasant conversational style within masculine speech communities.

One final area in gender issues, that of interaction rate (or how much each sex communicates), implies that the stereotypical expectation that females interact more and talk longer than males do is not true. *A significant body of research now indicates that men not only speak longer, use more words in the total interaction, and participate more in group discussions, but they also talk more than do females in public situations* (see Aries 1987; Wood 2007). These findings may be interpreted as stemming from a culture in which males have been expected to be more domineering and assertive than females (Courtwright, Millar, and Rogers-Millar 1979). It is interesting to note that women are stereotyped as being more talkative, but studies have shown over and over again that men are more likely to speak up in public situations than women are.

Street, Brady, and Lee (1984) provided further support for the rate of speech effects. Their research seems to show that perceptions of male and female sources' rate of speech are influenced by the context of the communication. They found that males were rated as significantly more competent and socially attractive when the rate of speech was fast to moderate. For females, however, only perceptions of competence increased with faster rate. Moreover, the speakers were perceived as more competent on the basis of rates of speech when they were engaged in normal conversation than when they were in an interview setting (see also Bradley 1980). In continuing this line of research, Street (1984) reported that speech rate contributed to evaluations of interviewer competence and social attractiveness. His findings also indicated that male interviewer/male interviewee dyads converged on their vocal cues (meaning they responded in similar ways—their vocal cues began to mirror each other—the dyadic effect again), whereas male interviewer/female interviewee dyads diverged on their vocal cues. Vocalics has become so important in law enforcement interview settings that the Federal Bureau of Investigation has even published information giving instructions to agents on how to establish better rapport with crime witnesses through their use of vocalics (Sandoval and Adams, 2001).

Speech rate has also been correlated with personality. G. Ray (1986) tested how the voice related to personality types and perceptions of competence and benevolence (i.e., kindness, compassion, goodwill). He found that rates of speech were related to judgments of competence, with rapid rates associated with more competence. The model competent speaker also exhibits a higher pitch range and is louder. The model benevolent speaker exhibits a low rate and a high-pitched speech.

What is your most preferred rate when listening to others? Is it situational? Chances are that it is dependent on context as well as your preferences. We usually prefer faster rates when we must listen to someone who has the potential to lose our attention (e.g., your professors), but probably a slower rate when we are hanging out with our friends, shooting pool (or the breeze), and drinking a beverage. Rate of speaking is an interesting phenomenon because people's personal preferences are so varied. Given the very small amount of current research on this topic, this might be one you would like to pursue if you are looking for topics in nonverbal communication to study.

REGULATING THE CONVERSATION

Perhaps the major function of vocalics is the regulation of a conversation. These turn-taking cues—cues indicating that we want to maintain a synchronous (back and forth) interaction pattern, that we want to maintain our turn, that we want to get rid of our turn, or want someone else's turn—are examined in terms of Starkey Duncan's (1972, 1975) cultural turn-taking signals and through work on terminating interaction.

According to Duncan, we structure our interactions according to a cultural rule that goes something like this: I have a turn, you have a turn, I have a turn, and you have a turn. This structuring of interaction is called **sequencing**. As long as the sequencing is synchronous, as long as the change from my turn to your turn is smooth, the structure of the interaction follows the cultural norm. There are times, however, when that sequencing breaks down; although a number of things can disrupt the sequencing, usually one of two major reasons can be found. First, one of the participants does not want to take his or her turn in the conversation, thus yielding a long "switch pause." Second, one of the participants interrupts, or crosses over into the other's turn. We examine instances of the first type.

Table 9.4 presents a graphic representation and a verbal sequencing of proper and improper turn-taking. Note that each turn represents the total speaking time each person has in the interaction (defined here as a simple interaction of four utterances). The spaces between the turns are pauses.

As long as the sequencing is moving synchronously, there are no problems; however, as the sequencing becomes more ragged or unsynchronized, problems may arise between interactants.

The impact of sequencing can be observed in the conversations of people who are of varying degrees of acquaintance. Saine (1976) maintains that the proper sequencing of an interaction may be in part a function of the similarity or level of agreement in the interaction. This he calls synchronous behavior. Obviously, in times of stress or in interactions between strangers (where similarity is low), synchrony may be low. The degree of synchrony in a relationship may be indicative of the relationship level of the *interactants.*

TABLE 9.4 STRUCTURING THE INTERACTION

A. Proper sequencing:

$Turn_{1.1}$ $Turn_{2.1}$ $Turn_{1.2}$ . . . $Turn_{2.2}$ $Turn_{1.n}$ $Turn_{2.n}$

B. Improper sequencing

$Turn_{1.1}$ $Turn_{2.1}$ $Turn_{1.2}$

C. Example of proper sequencing:

Jerry:	Hi, how ya' doing?
Bill:	Fine, how's Nan and the kids?
Jerry:	Doing good. And Ashley?
Bill:	Great. Hope to see you again soon.

D. Example of improper sequencing:

Jerry:	Hi, how ya' doing?
Bill:	Fine, how [INTERRUPTION]
Jerry:	How's Ashley?

TURN CUES

Within a conversation you usually play one of two roles. You are either the speaker or the listener (sometimes called *auditor*). When you have your turn, there are certain cues you use to maintain that turn or to signal the listener that you are ready to let that person talk. The other person may accept (and he or she becomes the speaker), or that person may indicate that you are to keep the "floor." Within each of these roles, certain cues may be used to signal a desire to keep, to give up, or to refuse the turn. These cues fall into the categories of turn-maintaining cues, turn-yielding cues, turn-suppressing (or denying) cues, and turn-taking (or requesting) cues (Jaffe and Feldstein 1970; Wiemann and Knapp 1975). We now look at each of these regulating functions separately.

TURN-MAINTAINING CUES

When you are speaking and the listener seems to be signaling an attempt to take your turn (interrupting or engaging in turn-taking behavior), you can suppress the other person by engaging in several paralinguistic cues. Taking an audible breath, using a sustained intonation pattern (falling or rising intonation patterns, such as at the end of sentences or questions, signal a willingness to stop talking), speeding up your rate, and using vocalized or filled pauses should inhibit the other's attempt (Duncan 1972). Duncan suggests that the use of only a single turn-suppression cue will usually stop interruptions by the listener.

TURN-YIELDING CUES

When you want to stop speaking, there are several vocal cues available. First, create a rising intonation pattern, one that suggests a question has been asked. Second, use a falling intonation pattern or draw out the final syllable of the clause at the end of your statement. Third, stop speaking; in the Western culture, silence usually induces the other to take the "floor."

TURN-SUPPRESSING CUES

Suppose that you do not have anything to add to the conversation or that you are afraid to speak, so you wish to deny your turn. What cues can you use? When Ekman and Friesen's (1975) approach to kinesics was discussed, you may recall, head nods and smiles were called *backchanneling* cues. You can do the same with vocalic cues; the cues you use in this case to indicate agreement with the speaker would fall in the vocal segregate class. In this manner you would use such nonwords as *uh-huh*, *yep*, or *ahhh*, each confirming the speaker and indicating, "all right, agree, keep on talking." In an effort to deny your turn, you would backchannel at a slower rate, a rate that would keep the speaker talking.

TURN-TAKING CUES

Perhaps you want to say something, but the other person will not let you speak. Most of the turn-taking (requesting) cues seem to be kinesic in nature—eye contact, facing behavior, leaning, raised hand or finger, straightening of the back, and so forth (Wiemann and Knapp 1975)—but there are at least three vocalic cues available. One is called a stutter-start;

you try to break in with a "b, b, b, but" or similar cue. The second is the *interruption*, in which you cross over into the speaker's turn and continue speaking. Remember, however, that interruptions seem to foster interruptions. A third would be to *increase the rate of the vocal segregates* you are using for backchanneling purposes. Just as slowing down the rate of them denies (or suppresses) your turn, speeding them up indicates a desire to say something, to take your turn.

One other technique you might use to request your turn is what Mortenson (2009) calls *vocal markers*. These can be heard when you take an audible intake of breath, signifying that you would like to be the next speaker. Keisanen and Rauniomaa (2012) discovered that people are likely to use this vocal signal to request their turn when making a request, and that they will also orient their bodies toward the other person when they use this vocal marker.

One other vocal turn-taking cue is socially unacceptable, and that is using a loud "Ahem," similar to a clearing of your throat. This one is sometimes used by someone trying to get control of the conversation, say, to conduct a meeting or a class. This type of turn-taking cue is more of a control-taking cue than simply requesting a turn.

PAUSES

One of the ways we can examine the structure of an interaction is by the use of pauses. Pauses allow the speaker to maintain turns, or they allow the listener a chance to gain a turn. In general, a **pause** is a silence in the turn or between turns. If it is within the turn it may be a *hesitation*, which is either filled or unfilled. A second type of pause is the *switch pause*, the silence found between turns, switching from one person to another. The third type of pause is that imposed by others, *imposed pauses;* pauses of this nature are usually governed by some norm or rule. Bruneau (1973) states that such imposed pauses are either a function of the environment (hospital zone, funeral, classrooms during tests) or in response to some role expectation. In other words, we pause because we think we are supposed to; the context dictates that we should pause at that point in time.

Sometimes the type of pause yields the turn ending. The switch pause usually signals a synchronous exchange of turns. This type of pause results in closed turn endings; these turn endings are very short. Two other forms of endings are the *interruption*, which is an overlap of one turn over the other, and the *open turn*. Open turns are overlong spaces between turns; usually they seem awkward, and are indicative of nonsynchronous sequencing. These open turns are usually found when relationships are just beginning or when stress is placed on one or more of the people interacting. They also can happen in situations where there are status differentials between the interactants.

IMPACT OF TURNS

A number of researchers have examined how turns operate in day-to-day interaction. As discussed earlier, turns are related to the synchrony of conversation between people. This synchrony is apparently learned early in life, even before formal education is begun (see P. A. Andersen, Andersen, and Mayton 1985). Such a finding should not be surprising since conversational *coherence* is something that we pick up early in life. What child has not been told at a very early age, "Don't interrupt," "Wait your turn," and "You can talk as soon as I'm finished"? Indeed, children who don't conform to these rules are deemed ill-behaved and mannerless. We also find parents who do not teach their children this synchrony as a norm to be less than effective in teaching their children widely accepted manners. The impact of appropriate turn-taking and turn-yielding, however, was associated with such personality-related variables as interpersonal orienting, self-monitoring, and self-disclosing. Street and Murphy (1987) reported that people who are low in interpersonal orientation, especially males, are less vocally active and engage in less consistent communication (as measured by turn duration and backchannel responses). Their speech fails to converge with the other persons' speech. The implications of this study are twofold. First, a person's interpersonal orientation is expressed through paralanguage cues, which are directly related to the structure of the interaction. Second, highly interpersonally oriented people "may be able to perform some behaviors, such as vocal and certain nonverbal behaviors, more consistently and to modify others' behaviors, such as self-disclosures, to a greater extent than individuals less concerned with self-presentations [low interpersonally oriented people or low self-monitors]" (p. 58).

The implications of such a finding have been demonstrated in a study by Coker and Burgoon (1987). They were interested in finding what nonverbal cues were present when conversations become more involving. They hypothesized that increased involvement in a conversation would produce increased nonverbal cues on several dimensions, including vocalic. They asked students to engage in dyadic (two-person) conversations. After a few minutes, the dyads were separated, and one of the students was asked to act as a confederate in the next stage with the same partner by either increasing or decreasing conversational involvement. The researchers found not only that increased involvement yielded more vocal expressiveness and relaxed laughter, but that the interaction was better managed. Specifically, they found fewer silences and response latencies between turns and, in general, more coordinated speech. This finding is similar to Street's (1984) finding, mentioned earlier, of male–male convergence on turn duration and male–female divergence in an interview setting. Street's results may be due to perceptions of similarity and involvement on the part of male–male dyads.

Finally, there has been some research suggesting that turns taken around some types of silence (meaning the turns that follow some type of silence) follow a particular backchanneling pattern. In 1982, McLaughlin and Cody found that conversations in which an "awkward silence" occurred as a result of a "minimal response" were repaired by a question/answer response. This finding suggested that participants engaged in backchanneling behaviors (question/answer sequences) to repair the damage done to the conversation's coherence (see also McLaughlin 1984). Dindia (1986) attempted to replicate these findings (in light of methodological and statistical advances unavailable to McLaughlin and Cody in 1982), but she failed to replicate the repair sequence. Although she found that minimal responses did predict silence in an interaction, it did not predict much of the reason for that silence, nor was she able to find McLaughlin and Cody's question/answer repair sequence. It would appear that synchronous turn-taking behaviors are a function of many nonverbal behaviors.

Research on vocalic cues and personality variables associated with turn-taking indicates that although the voice is important in conversations, there are a multitude of other variables of equal or more importance.

BOX 9.7 OBSERVATIONAL STUDY

Choose a half-hour television show, preferably a "sitcom," since most sitcoms contain back-and-forth type conversations. Watch it and take note of the conversational turn-taking that takes place. Do the actors use any of the turn cues discussed here? Do they violate any conversational rules? Do they use any of the stereotypes that may not be accurate (such as men interrupting more)? Do you notice any other issues, such as temporal dimensions, voice set, or vocal characterizers?

PHYSIOLOGICAL CORRELATES OF REGULATION

The vast majority of research on turn-taking and regulation has used either an experimental or a field-experimental paradigm in which conversations are conducted and the behaviors are coded for particular nonverbal behaviors such as silence, speech rate, vocal expressiveness, coordination of conversation, and so forth. Krueger (1986) took the observational study one step further with the use of LOGOPORT, discussed earlier in this chapter. His research suggested that turns occur in sequences over time and that vocal characteristics can help determine whatever lag time may exist in such sequences. For example, he reported that flirtation is characterized by highly synchronous behavior, so synchronous that neither participant actually holds the floor because both parties enact both dominant and submissive roles in the communication. When engaged in a quarrel, however, when neither party is dominant *or* submissive (or else one of them would have "won" the argument), the synchrony is lessened (Krueger 1986). LOGOPORT charts that are cued to the loudness of the interaction provide a convincing picture of the interactions. Interpretation of the charts is through the "hills" and "valleys" associated with measured loudness. In the case of flirtation, oscillation periods are short, indicating that the turns are progressing quite synchronously; a quarrel, however, yields longer oscillation periods, indicating that synchrony is less and that sequencing is rougher. Also, those hills and valleys converge in a flirtation segment but diverge in a quarrel segment.

Perhaps you are thinking, "So? Why should I care about this?" It is interesting to think of such scientific applications of technology to human communication. What social and behavioral scientists think we know about human nature can be confirmed by use of these technologies. We must always remember, however, that humans are not automatons, and they will not always "fit the mold" of what scientific research finds. Knowing the persons and the context is the best way to predict what their vocalic behaviors communicate about them, at least with any degree of accuracy.

SOCIOECONOMIC CLASS VARIABLES IN TURN-TAKING

It also appears that there may be a socioeconomic class difference in turn-taking behavior. Robbins, Devoe, and Wiener (1978) came to four conclusions regarding vocal behavior:

1. *Working-class speakers* emit unfilled pauses, upward inflection, and open inflection behaviors significantly more often and in significantly greater absolute numbers than do middle-class speakers.
2. *Middle-class speakers* emit filled pauses and downward inflection behaviors significantly more often and in significantly greater absolute numbers than do working-class speakers.
3. *Working-class speakers* emit a greater variety of regulators that can be considered ambiguous in significantly greater numbers and significantly more often than do middle-class speakers.
4. *Middle-class speakers* initiate continuation regulators significantly more often and in significantly greater numbers than do working-class speakers. (pp. 38–46)

Thus, the means of continuing or discontinuing conversations tend to vary according to socioeconomic class. It would be interesting to replicate this study in many different geographical regions from around the world to see if these findings would hold constant in other locations.

COMPUTER-MEDIATED COMMUNICATION AND TURN-TAKING

We would be remiss if we did not mention that in today's world, where just about everyone communicates via some form of technology, we sometimes are not attuned to the turn-taking aspects of *chat rooms* or chatting with someone over the Internet. For that reason, we have numerous "overlaps" of communication—be it questions or statements/comments—and this can affect the effectiveness of the process of communication taking place in that setting. We do the same thing vocally when we chat with someone face-to-face, but in chat rooms we can see this causing communication breakdown, misunderstandings, and sometimes ending of relationships (Jenks 2009). If you are an online "chatter," it would be to your advantage to pay attention to turn-taking cues discussed earlier, as the absence of visual and vocal nonverbal cues can cause communication breakdown, even on the simplest of topics.

RELATIONSHIP OF INTERACTANTS

Vocalics also function to establish certain relationships between people. These relationships may be on several levels, but those of most interest include vocal cues of *attraction, influence,* and *credibility,* and vocal cues of *emotion.* In this section, we briefly examine the impact of the voice on such relational topics. Specific cues produced by the voice become greater than their sum total. Hence, we may get multiple messages from one or two cues, messages that may complement or contradict each other. We turn first to messages that indicate the relationship one person may have with the other.

ATTRACTION, INFLUENCE, AND CREDIBILITY

As should be evident by now, vocal cues function not only to establish how one perceives the other, but also to establish whether one is trying to influence the other. Thus, relational vocal cues may provide indicators of social attractiveness, composure, extroversion, competence, benevolence, warmth, and influence (Hickson and Stacks 1991).

Vocal cues associated with perceptions of personality variables were discussed earlier. A review of this research from a relational perspective suggests that a slightly faster rate, more pitch change, and low loudness is associated with credible speakers, at least as concerns the perception of speaker competence and benevolence; pitch variation seems to be more important than loudness for benevolence. We perceive people to be socially attractive when our speech converges with that of the interactant, when there is slightly faster speech, and when there are shorter response latencies. Supportive conversations yield cues of expressiveness, with more interaction (fewer silences, latencies, and more coordinated or synchronous speech), more vocal warmth, interest, and pleasantness, and less anxiety (more vocal relaxation and attentiveness).

Research on communication apprehension, or reticence, suggests that the reticent speaker engages in more stressful vocal behavior. J. K. Burgoon, Pfau, Birk, and Manusov (1987), however, demonstrated that the speaker who avoids communication uses less vocal *potency* cues (loudness, tempo, intensity, and tempo).

Vocal cues have been shown to affect attempts to influence others. Research indicates that a faster rate of speech, more intonation, higher volume, and more fluent speech improves persuasiveness. This pattern is similar to what might also be labeled *pleasant* or *rewarding*. In 1980, J. A. Hall found that people complied with a request more often when the voice was pleasant (warm, friendly) than when it was neutral (stiffer, colder, more businesslike). In an extension of Hall's research, Buller and Burgoon (1986) added a neutral voice and also tested for receivers' sensitivity to nonverbal cues. Their results duplicated Hall's 1980 findings for the neutral and pleasant voices and found that hostile voices were perceived as non-intimate, tense, non-immediate, and dominant. When looking at good versus poor decoders, Buller and Burgoon found that:

> Poor decoders seem to discriminate the voices less on intimacy than good decoders and provide different arousal interpretations than good decoders to pleasant voices: the pleasant voices were seen as relatively tense by poor decoders and relatively relaxed by good decoders. . . . [Results indicated that] highly affiliative good decoders may employ positive, affiliative, composed, and sociable voices when attempting to gain compliance from them. . . . On the other hand, more socially anxious poor decoders may encode assertive, aloof, dynamic, and unsociable voices when attempting to gain compliance and prefer such voices when others attempt to gain compliance from them. (pp. 139–140)

Influence attempts, then, are at least in part a function of the relationship between the vocal cues and the decoding ability of the receiver.

EMOTION

Much of what we communicate is abstract, and this abstraction is further muddied when we attempt to label our inner feelings and, more particularly, others' feelings. Nonverbal communication is especially relevant when attempting to identify emotions and emotional states. The role of the voice in this process is significant, yet not as well researched as kinesics has been. What we know of the vocal relationships with emotion comes from research conducted by Scherer (1979). Scherer found that eight vocal characteristics were associated with how emotions were displayed through the voice:

1. *Amplitude variation*—*moderate* (pleasantness, activity, happiness) and *extreme* (fear).
2. *Pitch variation*—*moderate* (anger, boredom, disgust, fear), *extreme* (pleasantness, activity, happiness, surprise), *contour up* (potency, anger, fear, surprise), and *contour down* (pleasantness, boredom, sadness).
3. *Pitch level*—*high* (activity, potency, anger, fear, surprise) and *low* (pleasantness, boredom, sadness).
4. *Tempo*—*slow* (boredom, disgust, sadness) and *fast* (pleasantness, activity, potency, anger, fear, happiness, surprise).
5. *Duration*—*round* (potency, boredom, fear, disgust, sadness) and *sharp* (pleasantness, activity, happiness, surprise, sadness).
6. *Filtration*—*low* (sadness, pleasantness, boredom, happiness), *moderate* (pleasantness, boredom, happiness, potency, activity), and *extreme* (potency, activity, anger, disgust, fear, surprise).
7. *Tonality*—*atonal* (disgust), *tonal-minor* (disgust, anger), and *tonal-major* (pleasantness, happiness).
8. *Rhythm*—*not rhythmic* (boredom) and *rhythmic* (activity, fear, surprise).

More recent research has shown that as children age they are better able to recognize emotions (Rothman and Nowicki, 2004). Interestingly enough, Rothman and Nowicki not only conducted their own study to determine this, but they also looked back to 20 earlier studies to see if their results were similar to past studies, and they found a high degree of reliability and validity in their findings. It should be clear to you as college students that you have reached an age where you probably should be pretty good at determining the emotions that others are expressing through their vocalics.

We should take note at this time, however, that not everyone is adept at recognizing emotional messages through the use of voice. Wickline, Nowicki, Bollini, and Walker (2012) found that individuals who suffer from emotional illness, and schizophrenia in particular, are less able to identify emotions of others when talking with them. Perlov and Sawyer (2011) found similar results with children on the autism spectrum, although C. R. G. Jones et al. (2011) found that teenagers on the autism spectrum only had deficits on a few of the emotional recognitions, most notably on the emotion of surprise.

It is interesting when we look at vocal expressions of emotions as they are tied to facial expressions and body language. Hawk, Fischer, and Van Kleef (2012) determined that when it came to such primary emotions as anger, disgust, happiness, and sadness, vocal expressions and facial expressions are likely to be perceived as a matched set. Hawk et al. also discovered that when someone tried to mask his or her emotions in the facial areas, the recipients of the message were less likely to be able to decode the emotional message through the use of the voice. This should tell you that you really can fool people when trying to hide your emotions, but you need to make sure there is a match between your vocal expressions and your facial expressions.

As can be seen, vocal characteristics provide a lot of information relevant to emotional states, but note also that many of the emotional expressions overlap, making accurate judgments difficult with vocal cues alone. This even appears to happen interculturally, as Sauter, Eisner, Ekman, and Scott (2010) discovered, at least for the primary emotions (see also Wickline, Bailey, and Nowicki 2009). As always, the better you know the person with whom you are interacting and the better you know the context surrounding the interaction, the more accurate your judgments are likely to be.

SILENCE

Silence in interpersonal relationship contexts is an important factor. Damron and Morman (2011) report that in close interpersonal relationships, silence is important, but that men and women in same-sex friendships find it to be much more comfortable than people in opposite-sex relationships. Damron and Morman also discovered that silence in a relationship does predict how satisfied you will be with the relationship, how involved you are in the relationship, how committed you are to the relationship, and how close you are to the other person. In short, if you are comfortable just sitting in silence with someone, what we refer to as *comfortable silence*, it appears that your relationship is a positive one. Be sure not to think that silence does not communicate, however, because there are all kinds of messages that come from the use of silence, and especially in close relationships (see also Ephratt 2011; Acheson 2008).

BOX 9.8 OBSERVATIONAL STUDY

Test the hypothesis that we can actually communicate emotional meaning via the voice. Have your friends read a simple sentence and then ask them to express that sentence via Scherer's (1979) vocal characteristics. How good are they at conveying the emotional messages via the voice alone?

DISPLAY OF COGNITIVE INFORMATION

While the display of cognitive, or instructional, information is an important function of nonverbal communication in general, it is less important in vocalics than in some other areas, such as kinesics. It is important for us to remember, however, that often when we try to instruct someone else, we do use the voice to gain a person's attention and to emphasize a point. Sometimes, when we feel the other does not understand, we get louder, as if increasing our loudness will make us clearer.

The learning situation is the most common place where cognitive information is imparted to listeners via the use of vocalics. Research has shown that a *teacher's* vocalics will affect learning outcomes. Richmond and McCroskey (2000) report that a monotone voice is the most fatal vocalic flaw for teachers. They also report that a quicker pace (which doesn't allow for students' minds to wander as much), a variety in pitch, and fewer disfluencies are ideal for learning situations. Think about your own teachers for a moment; how many have problems with vocalics (monotone, nasality, too many disfluencies, or tempo problems)? Has that influenced your learning in any way?

DISPLAY OF AFFECTIVE INFORMATION

As has been indicated in other sections of this chapter, our vocal tone can tell others how we feel physically or psychologically—in essence, our emotional state. Certainly we can tell when someone we know is intoxicated, through vocal intonation, slurs, and the like. We can also usually tell when another is depressed, if we have a "normal" baseline from which to operate. Screams of anger, fear, joy, and surprise all differ from one another. Parents often know whether to go to an infant's room based on the kind of cry the baby is emitting. Accuracy in determining these judgments is dependent on how well you know the speaker and the context.

DECEPTION

We ask you to recall the discussion of deception in Chapter 9. In addition to the information provided earlier on deception, both vocalic and kinesic, there are other vocalic cues. Nonfluencies appear to be associated with spontaneous lying; however, the research is contradictory on the point. Most studies have found that pitch increased during deception; again, however, there is research that contradicts the point (see J. K. Burgoon, Buller, and Woodall 1996). While most research indicates that lying is "leaked" somewhere in nonverbal communication, the general conclusion is that one can tell much more about lying through the use of verbal communication, especially by asking specific questions. The more questions you ask, the more likely you are to *catch* the deception (or the deceiver). That, combined with observing nonverbal cues, is much more likely to be accurate than observing nonverbal behaviors on their own.

OTHER ENCODING AND DECODING ASPECTS OF VOCALICS

A. P. Smith (1991) studied the influence of noise on performing certain tasks and found that noise over 95 decibels was detrimental when the task lasts more than 30 minutes and when the situation is already stressful. Other researchers found that college students could detect children's emotions through vocalic cues only. In a study that supported what most of us know, C. R. Berger and diBattista (1993) found that when we provide another with directions, and the other indicates misunderstanding, we speak louder and slower to get them to understand. They also found that when we speak to someone whose first language is not ours, we tend to speak more loudly and slowly, too. Many people approach senior citizens in the same fashion, regardless of whether or not the person has a hearing loss. It is somewhat interesting in these cases that we use vocalics to re-code our communication rather than restructure our words. Other researchers have found that yawning appears to be voluntary; that is, participants did not yawn when they knew they were being observed, meaning they did not encode the message to yawn (Baenninger and Greco 1991). Clayman (1992) found that booing is a crowd response; each individual must decide whether to "go along with the crowd." He also found that booing is a much more delayed response than is applause; it takes people longer to encode their decision to "boo." Montpare, Steinberg, and Rosenberg (1992) found that there are vocalic differences in children when talking with their parents and their grandparents; the children encode the messages to these two sets of closely related interactants differently. Do you talk the same way, vocalically or verbally, with your grandparents as you do with your friends? Your answer to questions like this one will show you how you use your encoding abilities.

SUMMARY

Vocalics serve several functions. Of most importance are the regulation of interaction and the stereotypic expectations we have of other people based on their voices and vocal type. In many cases these expectations are either confirmed or disconfirmed. Thus, some of the more stereotypical judgments about sexual differences may not be true. Males may be the ones who talk the most, perhaps in compliance with a social norm that indicates they must be more assertive and dominant. In addition, the stereotypes we have of other groups (age, race, socioeconomic group, country of origin) may not be true either. Generalizing about any group (or class) of people is always dangerous, especially if you are seeking a high level of accuracy in your judgments.

This section has examined several diverse approaches to the study of vocalics. Trager's (1958) categorization system should provide us with a basic starting point, which today seems to have led to a more accurate voiceprint than earlier research found. At this time, however, identification (through electronic or interpersonal means) should still be approached with caution; we really are too good at masking our voices to concede complete effectiveness to such devices.

QUESTIONS FOR THOUGHT

1. Just how "normal" is normal speech?
2. How does a person consciously manipulate others through the use of his or her voice? How much weight can be placed on the voice as a manipulative tool as compared to other nonverbal subcodes?
3. How does the voice affect interpersonal relationships at different times in a relationship?
4. Why is vocalics sometimes referred to as "content free" speech? Is this an appropriate designation?
5. The research in vocalics appears to be "old"; that is, much of it was conducted between 1958 and the early 1990s. Why? What questions do you have that need to be addressed by contemporary nonverbal communication researchers? What changes in the study of nonverbal communication have created the move away from studying vocalics/paralanguage in as much depth as it once was?

FURTHER REFERENCES

Identification and Self-Presentation

DeGroot, T., and Gooty, J. (2009). Can nonverbal cues be used to make meaningful personality attributions in employment interviews? *Journal of Business and Psychology*, 24, 174–192.

Engstrom, E. (1994). Effects of nonfluencies on speaker's credibility in newscast settings. *Perceptual and Motor Skills*, 78, 739–743.

Haskard, K. B., DiMatteo, M. R., and Heritage, J. (2009). Affective and instrumental communication in primary care interactions: Predicting the satisfaction of nursing staff and patients. *Health Communication*, 24, 21–32.

Hughes, S., Farley, S., and Rhodes, B. (2010). Vocal and physiological changes in response to the physical attractiveness of conversational partners. *Journal of Nonverbal Behavior*, 34, 155–167.

Jaywant, A., and Pell, M. D. (2012). Categorical processing of negative emotions from speech prosody. *Speech Communication*, 54, 1–10.

Naidoo, S., and Pillay, G. (1990). Personal constructs of fluency: A study comparing stutters and nonstutters. *Psychological Reports*, 66, 375–378.

Puts, D. A., Apicella, C. L., and Cardenas, R. A. (2012). Masculine voices signal men's threat potential in forager and industrial societies. *Proceedings of the Royal Society B: Biological Sciences*, 279, 601–609.

Ray, G. B., Ray, E. B., and Zahn, C. J. (1991). Speech behavior and social evaluation: An examination of medical messages. *Communication Quarterly*, 39, 119–129.

Williams, F. (1970). The psychological correlates of speech characteristics: On sounding "disadvantaged." *Journal of Speech and Hearing Research*, 13, 472–788.

Yu, C. (2011). The display of frustration in arguments: A multimodal analysis. *Journal of Pragmatics*, 43, 2964–2981.

Controlling Interactions

Anderson, K., and Leaper, C. (1998). Meta-analyses of gender effects on conversational interruption: Who, what, when, where, why, and how. *Sex Roles*, 39 (3), 223–237.

Argyle, M., Lallijee, M., and Cook, M. (1968). The effects of visibility and introduction in a dyad. *Human Relations*, 21, 3–17.

Aries, E. (1987). Gender and communication. In P. Shaver and C. Hendrick (Eds.), *Sex and gender* (pp. 149–176). Newbury Park, CA: Sage.

Baird, J. E. (1976). Sex differences in group communication: A review of relevant research. *Quarterly Journal of Speech*, 62, 179–192.

Beck, A. T. (1988). *Love is never enough.* New York: Harper & Row.

Bernard, J. (1973). *The sex game: Communication between the sexes.* New York: Atheneum.

Clemmer, E. J., and Carrocci, N. M. (1984). Effects of experience on radio language performance. *Communication Monographs*, 51, 116–139.

Eakins, B. W., and Eakins, R. G. (1976). Verbal turn-taking and exchanges in faculty dialogue. In B. L. DuBois and I. Crouch (Eds.), *Papers in Southwest English: IV. Proceedings of the Conference on Sociology of the Languages of American Women* (pp. 53–62). San Antonio, TX: Trinity University Press.

Greene, J. O. (1984). Speech preparation processes and verbal fluency. *Human Communication Research*, 11, 61–84.

Henley, N., and Freeman, J. (1975). The sexual politics of interpersonal behavior. In J. Freeman (Ed.). *Women: A feminist perspective* (pp. 391–401). Palo Alto, CA: Mayfield Publishing.

Hickson, M. L., and Stacks, D. W. (1998). *Organizational communication in the personal context.* Needham Heights, MA: Allyn and Bacon.

Hodge, F. S., Maliski, S., Cadogan, M., Itty, T. L., and Cardoza, B. (2010). Learning how to ask: Reflections on engaging American Indian research participants. *American Indian Culture & Research*, 34, 77–90.

Jessen, S., and Kotz, S. A. (2011). The temporal dynamics of processing emotions from vocal, facial, and bodily expressions. *NeuroImage*, 58, 665–674.

Kalman, Y. M., and Rafaeli, S. (2011). Online pauses and silence: Chronemic expectancy violations in written computer-mediated communication. *Communication Research*, 38, 54–69.

Kennedy, C. W., and Camden, C. T. (1983). A new look at interruptions. *Western Journal of Speech Communication, 47,* 45–58.

Kramer, C. (1974). Women's speech: Separate but unequal. *Quarterly Journal of Speech, 60,* 14–24.

Kramer, C. (1978). Women's and men's ratings of their own and ideal speech. *Communication Quarterly, 26,* 2–11.

McComb, K. B., and Jablin, F. M. (1984). Verbal correlates of interviewer empathic listening and employment interview outcomes. *Communication Monographs, 51,* 353–371.

Mulac, A., Wiemann, J. M., Widenmann, S. J., and Gibson, T. W. (1988). Male/female language differences and effects in same-sex and mixed-sex dyads: The gender-linked language effect. *Communication Monographs, 55,* 315–335.

Strodtbeck, F., James, R., and Hawkins, C. (1973). Social status of jury deliberations. In R. A. Ofshe (Ed.), *Interpersonal behavior in small groups* (pp. 3–11). Englewood Cliffs, NJ: Prentice-Hall.

Tannen, D. (1990). *You just don't understand: Women and men in conversation.* New York: William Morrow and Company.

Thorne, B., and Henley, N. (Eds.). (1975). *Language and sex: Differences and dominance.* Rowley, MA: Newbury House.

Walker, G. (2012). Establishing Recipiency in Pre-Beginning Position in the Second Language Classroom. *Language & Speech, 55,* 141–163.

Walker, M. S. (1975). The sex of the speaker as a sociolinguistic variable. In B. Thorne and N. Henley (Eds.), *Language and sex: Difference and dominance* (pp. 76–83). Rowley, MA: Newbury House.

West, C., and Zimmerman, D. H. (1983). Small insults: A study of interruptions in cross-sex conversations between unacquainted persons. In B. Thorne, C. Kramarae, and N. Henley (Eds.), *Language, gender, and society* (pp. 103–117). Rowley, MA: Newbury.

Wood, J. T. (2007). *Gendered lives: Communication, gender and culture.* Belmont, CA: Wadsworth/Thompson Learning, Inc.

Zimmerman, D. W., and West, C. (1975). Sex roles: Interruptions and silences in conversation. In B. Thorne and N. Henley (Eds.), *Language and sex difference and domination* (pp. 105–129). Rowley, MA: Newbury House.

Deception

DePaulo, B. M., Stone, J. I., and Lassiter, G. D. (1985). Deceiving and detecting deceit. In B. R. Schlenker (Ed.), *The self and social life* (pp. 323–370). New York: McGraw-Hill.

Ekman, P., and Friesen, W. V. (1975). *Unmasking the face: A guide to recognizing emotion for facial cues.* Englewood Cliffs, NJ: Prentice-Hall.

Encoding and Decoding Aspects of Vocalics

Hortacsu, N., and Ekinci, B. (1992). Children's reliance on situational and vocal expressions of emotions: Consistent and conflicting cues. *Journal of Nonverbal Behavior, 16,* 231–245.

Relationship of Interactants

Duggan, A. P., Dailey, R. M., and Le Poire, B. A. (2008). Reinforcement and punishment of substance abuse during ongoing interactions: A conversational test of inconsistent nurturing as control theory. *Journal of Health Communication, 13,* 417–433.

Guerrero, L. K. (1994). "I'm so mad I could scream": The effects of anger expression on relational satisfaction and communication competence. *Southern Communication Journal, 59,* 125–138.

Jackob, N., Roessing, T., and Petersen, T. (2011). The effects of verbal and nonverbal elements in persuasive communication: Findings from two multi-method experiments. *The European Journal of Communication Research*, 36, 245–271.

Ray, G. B., and Floyd, K. (2006). Nonverbal expressions of liking and disliking in initial interaction: Encoding and decoding perspectives. *Southern Communication Journal*, 71, 45–65.

CHAPTER 10

THE COVERT SUBCODES: BIOFEEDBACK, OLFACTION, AND CHRONEMICS

KEY CONCEPTS

- Feedback Systems
- Gustatory
- Biofeedback
- Mood and Emotion
- Olfaction
- Olfactory Identification
- Olfactory Memory
- Chronemics
- Chronemic Structure
- Cultural Variation

OBJECTIVES

By the end of the chapter you should be able to:

- Explain how the covert subcodes operate.
- Distinguish between the biofeedback systems.
- Explain the olfactory process and how people identify with and remember smells.
- Discuss the impact of time as a communication medium.

This chapter attempts to expand your knowledge of nonverbal communication through the study of a subcode that is less apparent than kinesics and vocalics. Unlike proxemics, haptics, kinesics, and physical appearance, these subcodes cannot be seen. Unlike vocalics, these subcodes cannot be heard. Here we are talking about low-conscious perceptions, particularly the senses of taste, smell, and time, and especially the latter two.

FEEDBACK SYSTEMS

There are systems that operate at or just below consciousness and that are important to nonverbal functioning. These are the psychological and physical systems that operate to establish our daily rhythms, moods, and emotions.

GUSTATORY SYSTEMS

Gustatory tactile (oral taste) communication, we believe, is more a feedback system than it is an actual nonverbal subcode. We believe that gustatory systems operate more as an *information system* for humans than as a communication interaction system.

In a series of studies that examined the perceptual system's accuracy, Norman Lass and associates (Lass, Tekieli, and Eye 1971; Lass, Bell, Simcoe, McClung, and Park 1972) examined the feedback mechanisms that are associated with oral gustatory perception. According to this line of research, there are at least three monitoring systems that provide information: auditory feedback, tactile feedback, and kinesthetic feedback. Lass was more interested in the impact of oral *tactile* feedback, especially in light of visual versus tactile recognition of shapes. In a series of studies, when subjects were asked to identify objects by placing them in their mouths, Lass and his colleagues found that: (1) the tactile system is as accurate as, if not more accurate than, the visual system; (2) verbal feedback on shape did not affect performance on a test of oral form discrimination; (3) no specific learning appears to be operative (performance seems to be the same in the course of a number of trials); and (4) the location of the form in the mouth significantly affected performance. More recent research (Gotfredsen and Walls, 2007) reported that this concept of tactile perception of objects within the mouth is not very important to folks who study dentition and sound production. These findings suggest two conclusions: (1) human beings can receive messages from sources other than "normal" systems; (2) there are forms of communication, which may be unconscious, that affect our behavior and our assessment of things and that may influence our thoughts. Such forms may be examined as **biofeedback systems**. We mention this sort of off-beat study to have you realize that not all nonverbal communication research is "mainstream" communication research and that we can discover other communication theories if we "think outside the box."

BIOFEEDBACK SYSTEMS

Within the human being there are several types of biofeedback systems, each affecting the individual in a different way. In particular, the skin, the musculature, heart rate, blood pressure, and brain waves serve as potential biofeedback systems. We mention these because each operates most of the time at or below our consciousness. Of all major feedback systems, perhaps the *skin* is one of the most important. As Montagu (1971) noted, the skin is a tremendous communication receptor. It serves as more than a protection device; it also serves to communicate to the brain differences in the environment as well as the absence or presence of others. In an interesting recent study, Kim, Kim, Lee, Whang, and Cho (2011) developed and studied the use of an electronic computerized device that human beings can wear that allows the wearers to recognize their emotional states. Kim et al. believe that this might help people to better understand their biological responses to emotions, and thus be able to deal better with emotional reactions.

A second type of feedback is the *muscle system*. The muscle system, like the skin, serves an essential but not completely understood function. When we see someone we are attracted to, for instance, our muscle system changes, pulls or pushes, and alters our posture and even our pupils. Such changes are hardly noticed by the individual engaged in the communication, yet they are effective.

Heart rate and *blood pressure* are related biofeedback systems. These subtle changes also have a communicative function. In many instances, however, they are interpreted as stress or other negative behavioral indicators (see Floyd, Hesse, and Haynes, 2007). Such findings as the Sika deer studies and Calhoun's rat studies, discussed earlier in this volume, are indicative of biofeedback systems functioning abnormally. The same may be true of some of the studies of human crowding also examined earlier.

BOX 10.1   OBSERVATIONAL STUDY

How important is biofeedback? Try the following experiment with your friends. Take two coins or plastic playing pieces, clean them in boiling water, and then ask several friends to close their eyes and with one stimulus, place the object in their mouths. Ask each to describe the stimulus. Then ask each to feel with their fingers the same stimulus. How good were they at identifying through biofeedback (haptics/touch and taste) each stimulus? Was one form of biofeedback better than another?

Finally, there is the *olfactory system* and its influence on biofeedback systems. This area of study has been a part of nonverbal communication theory since the beginning of research into different factors of nonverbal communication (E. T. Hall 1966). There is evidence to indicate that pleasant odors produce a state of relaxation because "when we savor a pleasant fragrance, we take deeper and slower breaths, relaxing our respiratory pattern much as we do in meditation" (Weintraub 1986, 48–52, 114–116). Hence, olfaction—and perhaps olfactory memory—may be biofeedback systems that help control stress, hunger, and even pain. Research conducted at Duke University and Yale University in "aromatherapy" yielded promising outcomes for olfaction and biofeedback systems. You need not look very far to see the outcome of those studies; look at how popular the whole line of "aromatherapy" items has become. Indeed, they have even changed the concept they were researching into its own marketing term. From bath products to room fresheners to candles, aromatherapy came of age in the mid-1990s and thus far has remained a popular idea in our society. There has been some scientific evidence to prove that aromatherapy has at least some degree of effectiveness in calming and soothing troubled spirits, and creating smell memories (Kang-Ming and Chuh-Wei 2011; Fukumoto et al., 2008), but others dispute the degree of the effectiveness of scents in diminishing life's stress problems (Kiecolt-Glaser et al. 2008).

MOOD AND EMOTION

Feelings may be identified either as associated with a particular odor (e.g., fear, anger, disgust) or with a particular biofeedback device (including temporal rhythm). The mood state or emotive state we are in at any particular time may be influenced by the biofeedback we receive from ourselves and others (including our environment).

First to be examined is the biofeedback we receive that enables us to judge our own perceptions. In 1964, Stanley Schachter proposed a two-factor theory of emotion that takes into account the physiological reactions we have toward things and how we label those reactions. Schachter viewed emotion as a function of a state of physiological arousal and of an understanding of this state of arousal; that is, we physically respond and we comprehend the reason why we are responding. The cognition (comprehension), in a sense, exerts a steering function. Understanding, arising from the immediate situation, as interpreted by past experiences, provides the framework by which a person understands and labels his or her feelings. It is the cognition, or understanding, that determines how the person experiencing the physiological arousal labels it.

For an emotion to be correctly identified, both physiological arousal and past experience or other significant cues must be present. When one of these components is missing, the individual cannot identify the emotion.

Extending Schachter's argument one step further, one may surmise that the physiological arousal is in the form of some biofeedback system, one that is more perceptual than cognitive. A perceptual cue (temporal, olfactory, rhythm), then, could be responsible for the state of arousal. Cain's (1981) olfactory research looked at whether or not the odor given off by the individual aroused him or her to an emotional state. Wiener (1979) reported people being hypersensitive to others' emotive and mood states. Can we become more aware of our own internal states? Byers (1979) noted that we feel relaxed at the alpha brain wave state but when disturbed, that wave rhythm changes to a different cycle, possibly alerting us that *something* has changed. Clearly, physiological arousal in these cases can be measured by some form of response.

The argument here is that the feeling of mood or emotion is a two-part sequence. First, the individual reacts to some perceptual change, a change probably based either (1) on an unconscious cue received from outside our own biological systems or (2) on a form of synchronization between the self and others, meaning both individuals involved recognize the change. Second, based on this cue, the individual must then label the arousal. Such a biofeedback model of emotion would depend on a multi-channel form of communication. That is, we are constantly monitoring our system for change. This change may be perceptual, taking the form of unconscious events. Whatever we can attribute the change to in the near environment will produce a cognitive reaction to the event. If, for instance, we perceive the change as occurring olfactorily (such as anger), we may interpret our biofeedback as fear, and react appropriately, or we may mask that feeling (deceive the other person) and consciously react as though we are just fine. Can you think of a time when you did just that?

Part of the feedback system deals with the recognition of deception, which we discussed in depth in Chapter 9. Ekman (1981) evaluates this aspect of nonverbal behavior in two related situations: (1) when trying to withhold information, and (2) when trying to present false information in a credible fashion. These instances are labeled as "deceits." Sometimes an attempt at deceit is unsuccessful; a deceiver makes one of two basic mistakes. The first mistake is termed a "deception clue," an expression or gesture that indicates that a person is engaged in deception but does not reveal the content of the deception. The second mistake is termed "leakage" and occurs when a person accidentally reveals information he or she wished to conceal.

[handwritten: Smiles]

[handwritten margin notes: Felt = + emotion; 2/3 – 4 seconds]

An example of deception might be the smile. A smile is a simple expression requiring only one muscle movement. Ekman and Friesen (1982) contend that smiles can be the most misunderstood of all facial expressions. They not only conceal true feelings but can also convey false messages. Part of the interpretation of a smile—determining whether it is (1) *felt*, (2) *false*, or (3) *miserable*—is accomplished by the biofeedback and temporal aspects of the smile. Felt smiles are those used with a positive emotion, and they last from two-thirds of a second to 4 seconds. False smiles may be distinguished by the muscle used, laterality, location, and timing; they occur too early or too late, last too long, have short onset times, or they do not have a smooth offset. Miserable smiles do not mask emotion, as do the false smiles, but indicate accepted and contained misery. All three smiles are deliberate but are differentiated by both chronemic and biofeedback mechanisms.

Krumhuber, Manstead, and Kappas (2007), in a study trying to see how people are evaluated depending on onset, apex, and offset durations of smiles, defined these aspects of duration in this way: "Onset duration refers to the length of time from the start of the smile until its maximum intensity, apex duration to the length of time before this maximum smile starts to decrease, and offset duration to the length of time from the end of the apex until the smile disappears" (p. 40). In attempting this study, which was replicating some of their earlier studies, they discovered: "Smiles with longer onset and offset durations were judged as significantly more genuine than their shorter counterparts, whereas authenticity ratings decreased the longer the smile was held at the apex" (p. 40). As Krumhuber et al. also reported, "Stimulus persons displaying a smile with a long onset duration were rated as more attractive, more trustworthy, and less dominant than were persons showing a smile with a short onset duration. Furthermore, smiles with long onset durations were judged to be more flirtatious and more authentic" (p. 50). This is not only related to the issue of exhibiting moods, but also to chronemics, which we discuss later in this chapter.

[handwritten margin notes: Onset; offset; durations; apex]

When we look at this area of communication, there appears to be a general biological rhythm in all "interpersonal" communication. This rhythm, according to Byers (1979), consists of a ten-cycle-per-second synchrony between people engaged in nontask behavior. Any change in this cycle indicates a change in the relationship between the people. As the behavior moves in and out of synchrony—or phase relationships, as Byers called them—some perceptual feeling of the relationship is then observed by the people, codified (or organized in the brain), and reacted to. As Byers notes:

> Although one organism may not directly perceive his phase relationship to another, I believe that, in the case of humans, the phase relationship is systematically related to the biochemical (endocrinological) [to include olfactory] states, which are reflected in or perceived as feelings. It is particularly interesting to observe that the information carried by interpersonal rhythms does not move directionally from one person to another. This information cannot easily be conceptualized as "messages," since the information is always simultaneously shared and always about the state of the relationship. (p. 415)

Byers' perspective suggests an interpersonal synchrony that begins with self-rhythms meshing with another's self-rhythms. Once again, it is the dyadic effect (or the norm of reciprocity) discussed throughout this text; your "partner" is likely to adopt the time orientation that you adopt.

Emotion, mood, and deception, then, begin with the individual and move to encompass others. Once we begin an interaction, we perceive information from others and ourselves, based on perceptual systems, then act and react to it. We may be able to use such features as subconscious memory (e.g., olfactory) to provide a cue to the emotion; that is, we can self-cue as to the intended label for the arousal. If that self-cue is a particular odor in memory dealing with sex, the label might be identified as "love." If the cue were associated with being frightened or afraid, the label would then be "fear." Based on the perception, a mood state may be entered into, and possible interactions with others may be found to be either honest (mood shown) or deceptive (mood hidden).

BOX 10.2   OBSERVATIONAL STUDY

For the next week, keep track of your moods. Since chances are good that you are covering this chapter late in the semester, a time when many projects are probably due, you may have some stressful situations at this point in time. Surely there will be times when you are relaxed and in a positive mood, also. Try to keep track of how many times you show your "true emotions" through some nonverbal behaviors. Also try to keep track of how many times you mask your emotions by sending a nonverbal message contradictory to what you are really feeling. How good are you at expressing your true emotions? How good are you at masking them? Does this seem to be what you think of as the norm for our society?

OLFACTION

Leathers (1976) has suggested that "olfaction is truly the forgotten sense" (p. 155). Although we use our olfactory sense daily, we do not think about what we smell unless it is especially positive or negative. We associate certain odors with some visual aspect in the environment: a person, a place, a thing. Each has its own particular scent. In many ways, however, what we are smelling is a perceptual process, an action associated with the cognitive processes by which we label the odor (Cain 1981). Waskul and Vannini (2008) tell us that odors convey meaning, and because they do they become an important part of everyday life: "Odor is a subtle but significant component of the culturally normative and aesthetic rituals of expressive and impressive everyday life" (p. 68). Consider, for example, the odor of a field freshly fertilized with manure. What cognition comes to mind? Is it positive or negative? Before answering, consider a second example, the odor of a beach along the ocean or a lake just before sunset. What cognition comes to mind? Is it positive or negative? If the cognition is positive, then you probably designate such experiences with positive mental labels (perhaps you grew up on a farm or vacationed on a beach). Not only that, but the reaction to the smell will influence your behavior—as many advertisers have both found and demonstrated (Velasco-Sacristán and Fuertes-Olivera, 2006).

WHAT IS OLFACTION?

The olfactory process is a complex chemical exchange that has only recently begun to be understood. The role of odor or smell in human behavior, however, has been present for a long time. What we normally think of as olfaction, or the sense of smell, is different from the scientific notion of olfactory communication. The scientific view of olfactory communication is more concerned with how odor serves to communicate at a level just below the conscious; it concentrates more on how the particular chemical "signatures" we produce affect both our own behavior and that of others. We are also interested in this process, but we are more concerned with how scent influences us in our daily routines.

OLFACTORY PROCESSES

Olfaction is a process whereby we recognize certain scents around us. Those odors may come from the environment, from others around us, or from ourselves. We perceive the odor or scent through a pair of grooves high in our nasal passages. The cells there are closely linked to the lower, forward portion of the brain (the olfactory bulb), an area sensitive to odors that has a total surface smaller than the surface area of a dime. It consists, however, of about 600,000 specialized cells connected to the olfactory bulb. To be detected, an odor must first dissolve in the film or mucus of the olfactory bulb. Then, as it passes close to the sensory cells, it is captured and held just long enough to be analyzed by the brain.

It has been demonstrated, however, that odor remains in our memory much longer than things we see or hear. Engen (1980) theorized that the difference in terms of memory has been traced to survival as a species and to a linkage with the brain. He postulates that we possess an *odor memory* that lasts longer than other forms of memory (1) because of the nearness of sensory input to the brain area receptive to the information, (2) because a more direct, quicker, and less edited type of message comes from olfactory information, yielding (3) a memory that is stronger due to associations between the odor and the situation. The odor is received directly in the emotive centers of the brain; such associations of smell and emotion, then, follow naturally. As discussed later, advertisers take full advantage of this linkage. The survival value of such a message is something advertisers depend upon. Advertisers count on consumers remembering the odors and buying products based on the survival of those memories.

What research there is concerning subconscious exohormone effects indicates that males and females react differently to a sexual scent. Such research, however, is both mixed and contradictory. There are certain odors associated with menstrual cycles that differ in terms of both pleasantness and intensity as the cycle operates (Doty, Ford, Preti, and Huggins 1975). Further, analysis of vaginal secretions both before and after coitus produce different chemical analyses. Studies also infer that exposure to at least two exohormones (androstenol and copulins, both found in sexually excited women) affects how people perceive each other; this effect is more marked in females' perceptions of males than in males' perceptions of females. Another study (Cowley, Johnson, and Brooksbank 1977) concluded, possibly for the first time in a controlled experimental situation, that a complex human behavior was influenced by the odor of substances known to have sexual attractant properties in animals. In a more recent study, Havlicek et al. (2008) found that women were much more likely to rely on olfactory senses when choosing a mate; men are more likely to rely on the visual sense. Roberts et al. (2011) discovered that odors of other human beings do affect the perception of attractiveness of the other persons, and they also found that women and men look at this aspect of attractiveness differently.

In the early 1970s, researchers in both America and England found a social-grouping effect based in part on olfaction. This research reported that women who lived or worked together tended to synchronize their menstrual cycles (McClintock 1971). Such synchronization is limited to a very close circle of acquaintances and may be due to the smelling of exohormones and suppression of certain hormones, based on some not-too-well-understood processes. It is interesting to note, however, that "exposure to males" tends to counteract the synchronizing effect (see Wiener 1979). If the living situation includes a male, the synchronization is less likely to occur.

Aside from the sexual aspects of olfaction, there is also a social effect. There are some who suggest that emotions can be "smelled." That is, there are definite odors given off to communicate anger (Gottschalk 1969). Other emotions, such as fear and disgust, are also closely associated with differences in odor (de Groot, Smeets, Kaldewaij, Duijndam, and Semin 2012). Wiener (1979) theorizes that these odors of emotion may be associated with steroids. There is also evidence that psychotic behavior such as schizophrenia can be diagnosed through odor (Orlandi, Serra, and Sotgiu 1973). K. Smith and Sines (1960), for example, found that when the odor of sweat was compared, researchers could significantly differentiate schizophrenic from nonschizophrenic subjects. Wiener (1979) reports that some psychotic patients are also hypersensitive to others' emotional states, and the psychotic patient may become more sensitive to the chemical changes going through an individual as emotions change. This is a fascinating area of study for discussion, because most people are unaware that such factors can be determined by the olfactory sense.

OLFACTORY IDENTIFICATION

From what has been stated up to this point, it would appear that the only people who engage in olfaction are either sexually aroused or psychotic. This perception, of course, is not accurate. Each of us is influenced by the odors around us—more influenced than we might think, and we begin with those topics because they seem to be what has come to the forefront of our society's knowledge about scents. Besides the sexual attractant, there are hundreds of odors surrounding us at any given moment. How good we are at identifying them, however, may determine in part our inability to perceive them.

How good are we at identifying odors? According to some, we are "microsomatic," meaning we are poor sensors of smell. There is some evidence, however, that our sense of smell is much more developed than was thought earlier. This is especially true with an olfactory signature, which is your personalized scent that you carry with you. Research has demonstrated that parents can tell which children are their own on the basis of the child's own "smellprint" (R. Porter and Moore 1982). This same research confirmed earlier studies indicating that siblings could identify with high accuracy which shirts had been worn by their brothers or sisters. How many people can you identify by their olfactory signature? Does your significant other carry one that you recognize without having to see him or her? Your parents? Your roommate? The better we get to know someone, the better we know his or her olfactory signature.

According to research conducted by Cain (1981), the linkage between odor and label may be the significant feature of remembering and perceiving an odor. He infers that the cognitive process is inherently important in perceiving an odor. Cain further notes that "names define odors, locate them in relation to other odors, and even give them an internal 'address' for retrieval from memory storage" (p. 51). His research indicates that people, when presented with an odor, may fail to identify exactly what they smell but will decide upon some type of label (usually responding that the label is "on the tip of the tongue"). This label, right or wrong, is then associated with the odor at a later time. Whether or not the odor identified with a person is a good odor or a bad odor will likely influence others' evaluations of that person's social acceptability. Low (2006) found that people who equated foul odors with individuals judged those people to be socially and morally "defiled." Now that may seem a bit extreme to most of us, but think about it; how much do you like being around someone who does not smell very good? And how often have you "labeled" someone negatively because they smelled "foul" to you?

Interestingly, Cain has found that several features help increase our odor inventory. First, we must have an accurate label. The more accurate the label is, the better we can remember the odor; the more specific the label, the better we will remember it. Second, females are much better at identifying odors than are males, although with training males can approach the female's ability in odor identification. Finally, there are age differences; older people have more problems with odor identification than do younger people, perhaps because of decreased cognitive ability associated with age. There is some good news about this issue, though. Markovic et al. (2007) conducted a study that found that even if senior citizens have trouble with odor identification, pleasurable smells become more pleasurable as they age— something to look forward to in old age.

The importance of such a labeling process is not new. In the 1700s, Linnaeus suggested that odors could be best classified in a seven-fold category system:

1. Aromatic
2. Fragrant
3. Musky
4. Garlicky
5. Goaty
6. Repulsive
7. Nauseous

Use of such labels helps us both to remember and to identify the odor. Identification, then, provides significant cues to behavior, including survival behaviors, but some people now use these same findings to their advantage.

BOX 10.3 OBSERVATIONAL STUDY

How good are males and females at identifying odors? Are there certain odors that yield more agreement than others? For this study ask an equal number of male and female friends to close their eyes and smell a number of smells found in daily activities (coffee, chocolate, perfume, and so forth). Ask each to label the odor by the name and then to evaluate each on a seven-point scale ranging from unpleasant (1) to pleasant (7). What did you find? Do your results match those reported in the olfactory literature?

OLFACTORY INFLUENCE

As might be expected from the reported studies of the olfactory process, a certain amount of manipulation of others' behaviors is possible through smell. Olfaction can be used effectively to sell products, to make things more positive (or negative) than they are, and to help regulate other forms of communication.

(handwritten margin note: Smell influence in the economy)

Consider the following examples of olfactory manipulation. Car dealers find that by using a "new car" scent, they can sell used cars faster. A musty odor can be created to make objects smell "old" or antique. A bakery vents its ovens during morning rush hour, sending the smell of fresh doughnuts to people caught in traffic, and has youngsters selling doughnuts as people wait for the lights to change (Erb 1968). A cinnamon roll store leases space in a shopping mall near a major entrance/exit, hoping to attract customers on their way in and out of the mall.

These are but a few examples of how we are manipulated by smell. Consider, too, a study at Colgate University, which demonstrated the extent to which a person can be subconsciously influenced by odor (R. Winter 1976). Researchers used four batches of identical nylons (hose), scenting one with a floral fragrance (narcissus), one with a fruity fragrance, one with a sachet fragrance, and one with its own synthetic odor. Women shoppers were then observed touching and inspecting the stockings. When asked which of the four batches they would prefer, 50 percent of the women chose the floral-scented stockings as being "softer and more durable," 24 percent chose the fruity-scented stockings, and 18 percent chose the sacheted stockings. Only 8.5 percent of the shoppers chose the unscented pairs as being most desirable. Could Winter prove it was the scent that swayed their decision? Probably not, but the evidence is clear: People choose a scented product over an unscented product 91.5 percent of the time.

It is not only hosiery that is perfumed; even such items as paper, fabrics, underwear, socks, cosmetics, and prophylactics are deliberately given fragrances. In their initial stages, rugs are so strong smelling ("malodorous") that they would not sell unless they were *reodorized* (changed to smell different). Aromatic woods such as cedar, apple, sandalwood, and hickory sell for more than do stronger-smelling woods (pine, oak, birch); therefore, imitation aromatics are added to inferior-grade lumber to raise its price. Goldkuhl and Styvén (2007) conducted a study in European markets and discovered that the use of positive scents can improve competitive advantage with other retailers. It would be interesting to see a similar study to the one done on hosiery done on tissue—both facial and toilet—to see which sells better, the scented or the unscented. This could undoubtedly be used by retailers in every culture to improve sales.

Interestingly, in today's society, where there is advanced medical technology to determine what causes allergic reactions, many people have discovered that they are allergic to fragrances (especially perfumes). One of your authors once conducted a weekend-long workshop. Prior to arrival, an e-mail was sent to all participants as well as to the workshop leaders to let them know that there would be people attending the workshop who were allergic to all scents. They were all asked to refrain from using all scents, including deodorants. You can imagine that this was not an easy thing for people of American society to do. Due to so many people finding out that they are allergic to scented products, many products are now sold as "unscented" or "fragrance free." Chances are still good, however, that products with scents sell more than those without fragrances.

health impacts on body odor

How our bodies smell is most likely affected by our diet, medication, and health. People who eat red meat smell different from those who eat fish or vegetables. People who eat foods made with strong spices, especially garlic and curry, exude those smells through the pores of their skin. People on drugs such as penicillin have a distinctive odor. Many diseases can be diagnosed by the patient's smell alone (see, e.g., Manning 1994). Oral health problems are also closely associated with certain odors. Also, as R. Winter (1976) points out, the amount of body hair we have influences our odors; those with more body hair have a stronger smell than those with less hair since hair retains the odors more than skin does (a reason Asians, Caucasians, and those of African descent differ in their smells). Most college professors can give you examples of having discussions with students in early morning classes who have had more than their fair share of beer the night before. The smell of beer permeates their whole being, even though it may have been hours since they had any. The smell of curry stands out to Americans when they enter a place of business where the proprietors are from a culture that cooks with it (e.g., India or Pakistan) and where they have cooked food in that environment. Students in nonverbal classes often mention entering a place of business owned by those who cook with curry and being offended by the smell, since it is not a pleasurable smell to most Americans. Suffice it to say, odors are recognizable or distinguishable, and they do communicate things about people, environments, or objects.

PHOTO 10.1 Americans spend more money on fragrances than all other cultures in the world.

OLFACTORY MEMORY

Olfaction serves as a major influence on both our thinking and our behavior, but advertis-ers have also found that *olfactory memory* is a way to sell products. By means of such devices as "scratch and smell" advertisements and vivid emotional labels, advertisers can influence or awaken our olfactory memory, a form of remembrance that, as noted earlier, has the highest memory capacity of all five senses. Its sensation, according to Key (1976), is to awaken "vague and half-understood perceptions which are accompanied by very strong emotions" (p. 78). Ellen and Bone (1998), however, discovered that there is no empirical evidence that these "scratch and sniff" advertisements improve the attitude toward the brand or the product. How many times have you smelled something and suddenly you have a memory so strong you wonder where it came from? Was it something that reminded you of winter holidays? Thanksgiving? Halloween? Spring? Camping out by a campfire?

How lasting are these memories? Gilbert and Wysocki (1987) suggest that the memories associated with a smell tend to be recalled when the odor is perceived again, but these memories tend to fade with age. Morrin, Krishna, and Lwin (2011) found that this was only partially true, that even though some of it might be forgotten, the actual scent causes the individual to retrieve the memory. Willander and Larsson (2007) also discovered that this was not 100 percent true, that senior citizens were able to recall memories through the olfac-tory sense, but that the memories were more effective when the scents were coupled with the conceptual information to which they were connected. Willander and Larsson also discov-ered that the olfactory memories were more emotional than the verbal memories. Gilbert and Wysocki also reported that stronger odors produced more vivid memories. Women not only found all odors to be stronger than did men, except for the odor associated with flatu-lence, they reported more memories than did men. Both pleasant and unpleasant odors are more likely to produce memories than middle-ranged odors, and odors correctly identified are more likely to evoke a specific memory.

Malandro, Barker, and Barker (1989) note that a closely related aspect of olfactory memory is that of *smell adaptation*. Smell adaptation occurs when the odor you smell be-comes a part of your environment or general background. For instance, if you are wearing a perfume or cologne you like, you will notice that it tends to wear off as times goes on; it is adapted, and you feel a need to replenish. If, on the other hand, you are wearing something you do not like, its adaptation seems to take forever. An author of this text has his class wear a perfume or cologne they cannot stand for a class period. After about 20 minutes, the odor is so bad that doors and windows must be opened. On the next day, however, when the class members wear cologne they like, adaptation occurs.

Smell adaptation also occurs in environments. Have you ever walked into a room where it smells of something very strong (e.g., a gym, a restaurant, your kitchen when someone is cooking something you dislike)? After you have been there for a while (usually a short while, 5 to 10 minutes), you find that the smell seems to have disappeared. It has not; your olfactory senses have adapted to the smell. It often takes longer to adapt to odors you perceive to be negative than it does to ones you perceive positively.

One final aspect of olfactory memory needs to be addressed: *olfactory déjà vu*. When we have the feeling that we have experienced something before but have not in reality experienced it, we explain it away as *déjà vu*. In some ways this phenomenon may be related to the olfactory memory traces of people, places, and objects. Remember, the olfactory process is one that occurs very rapidly and one that may not have conscious labels attached to it. Remember also that odors can be identified by association; if the association is generalized enough, the odor will trigger a similar memory that may *not* match the new stimulus.

Consider, for example, an incident one of our colleagues tells us about. He was walking down the hall when he noticed a particular odor—a perfume—emanating from a female just ahead of him. He approached her, touched her, and mentioned her name. You can imagine his chagrin when she turned out to be someone else. Actually, the female was wearing the same perfume he associated with another person, and she was of the right size, build, and hair color he associated with that person. Has that ever happened to you?

Interpersonal versions of olfactory *déjà vu* like that described earlier may occur on a regular basis. Research supports this interpretation. D. C. Rubin, Groth, and Goldsmith (1984) examined the impact that olfactory cuing has on memory. They had undergraduate students describe the memory evoked by one of three cues: odors, photographs, or the names associated with 16 common objects. They were told to date the memory (when the focus of the memory occurred), rate its vividness and its pleasantness, and tell how many times they had thought of the memory before the experiment. The results indicated that odor cues evoked memories that were rarely evoked by photographs or words; that there were no distinct age differences in the memories; and that inaccessible memories can be evoked by the olfactory cue. They also suggested that odors might produce more pleasant memories than the other cues (Smets and Overbeeke 1989).

STUDENT VOICES

Briana: One of the strongest indicators of biofeedback influence, in my opinion, is the olfactory sense. For instance, whenever I smell bacon being cooked, I am immediately transported back to my childhood days spent at my grandparent's house in Indiana. My grandfather got up every morning at 5am and cooked bacon and eggs for himself, got the morning paper, and sat at the kitchen table and read while he ate. Writing about it now calms me and triggers a feeling of happiness and yearning for days gone by.

BOX 10.5 OBSERVATIONAL STUDY

For the next 24 hours, keep track of all the smells you notice (remember—we do not register all smells we encounter). Make a list of them and then indicate which olfactory processes are evoked for you by those scents—identification, influence, memory. Also, indicate if they are positive or negative responses.

TIME (CHRONEMICS)

Chronemics has to do with how we use and structure time. It is a significant area of nonverbal communication, because we generally perceive our actions and reactions as a time sequence. We talk about what we will do tomorrow, what we should have done yesterday, and how we have wasted time. Each of these statements reflects a general *Western* view of how time should be used, and how it is abused. This view sets forth expectations we use to identify others. All of us have heard of stereotypes of how different cultures use time, and the Latin culture is known to be a culture that uses time in a much less structured approach than mainstream American culture does (Klopf 2001). Consider how you view a Latin American through that person's use of time. Is this person as energetic as we are (assuming North American expectations)? Does this person value time as much as we do? How does this individual use time? If you decide that Latin Americans differ from us with respect to any of these criteria (or more), then you view their chronemic orientation as different. This is not necessarily a point of evaluation; it is simply a cultural difference. In the United States, we are very time-conscious; note how many clocks and watches you see in a day, or how many times you pull out your cellphone to see the time. Even our language choices often indicate time issues: "I'll be there in a minute"; "I don't have time for this"; "How long will it take?"

Time is generally perceived in three ways. First, we can examine time in an individual or psychological orientation. At this level, we are thinking about how we personally use and perceive time. We can also examine time on a more basic level, considering the biological "clocks" within us. This level also may differ from one individual to another. Finally, we can examine time on a cultural (and subcultural) level. It is at this level that we find major differences between people. Consider, for instance, E. T. Hall's (1959) description of Nigeria's Tiv and contrast it with your expectations:

> The Tiv equivalent of the week lasts five to seven days. It is not tied into periodic natural events, such as the phases of the moon. The day of the week is named after the things that are being sold in the nearest "market." If we had the equivalent, Monday would be "automobiles" in Washington, D.C., "furniture" in Baltimore, and "yard goods" in New York. Each of these might be followed by the days for appliances, liquor, and diamonds in the respective cities. This would mean that as you travel about, the day of the week would keep changing, depending upon where you were. (p. 27)

You may note that this type of division of time is not so different from what we Americans might have used a hundred years ago. Look at the *Farmer's Almanac* from that period, and you will find time divided by planting seasons in the several regions, a concept close to the Tiv's use of time.

THE STRUCTURE OF TIME

Many of us have asked the question, "What is time?" In answering this question, we provide others with a glimpse of how we view life itself, almost like answering the question of the glass that is filled to the halfway mark—is it half full or half empty? How we structure time offers us the same type of insight: Are our days numbered? Does time for the person ever end? Or does it, as one student suggested, continue on as long as the person is remembered? E. T. Hall (1984) suggests that it may better serve the student of time not to examine the specific "microstructure" of time but instead to examine the *kinds* of time we hold:

> As people do quite different things (write books, play, schedule activities, travel, get hungry, sleep, dream, meditate, and perform ceremonies), they unconsciously and sometimes consciously express and participate in different categories of time. (p. 13)

Hall further suggests that Western culture does not hold one specific view of time, which may differ from others, but that we Westerners perceive time as consisting of between six and eight *categories*. Further, these categories are functionally interrelated into four major time pairs in a *mandala* of time (a mandala is a classification device that shows a visual relationship between ideas or variables); it allows for multiple influences among the ideas or variables of time. The eight individual categories combine to create what Hall has labeled the ninth and ultimate category, *meta time*. Meta time refers to the study of time from philosophical to scientific orientations based on some theory of how time operates. Hall's theory of time is general and grounded in cultural derivations. He describes how the mandala characterizes time in both general and specific relationships between categories by noting:

> When one looks at the time mandala, several things become apparent. First, there are four pairs in which the categories appear to be functionally interrelated: (1) sacred and profane, (2) physical and metaphysical, (3) biological and personal, and (4) sync time and micro time. Second, the time positions on the opposite sides of the mandala also seem to bear a special relationship to each other. Sacred time and personal time are personal, and from what little is known of the metaphysical, it would seem that rhythm is shared with sync time in both. These common elements, such as rhythm, are links connecting the different kinds of time. Third, the two axes going from lower left to upper right and upper left to lower right set things apart in other ways: group, individual, cultural, and physical. Fourth, the left side is explicit and technical (low-context) while the right-hand side is situational (high-context). All of this suggests that there are clusters of ordered relationships between the different kinds of time. (p. 206)

To understand time, then, we must understand the different categories that function to make time "real."

HALL'S TIME CATEGORIES

Hall's (1984) eight time categories range from the "imaginary" to the "real." At one extreme, we find *sacred time*, or a time rooted in mythology; it is magical and helps to define consciousness by determining where we are in relation to something not of this world. Sacred time for hard-driving workers, for instance, may be found in the ability to lose themselves in

PHOTO 10.2 Americans are especially time-conscious , and today we find more people using cellphones as their "time pieces" than ever before.

Profane   numeric

their work, leaving the problems of relationships, family, and so forth, elsewhere. Closely related to this time is *profane time,* or a time that is deeply rooted in the explicit time system found in cultures. Profane time is formulated; it consists of centuries, decades, years, months, weeks, days, hours, and minutes. Tied closely to the sacred, profane time takes the magic and binds permanence to it—in Western culture; for instance, Christmas is celebrated on December 25, which may not be so in other cultures.

Micro time evolves from the sacred and the profane. Micro time is culture-specific and a product of the differences in how time units are perceived by the culture. Micro time includes informal time perspectives, such as the meanings we place on waiting, punctuality, and other uses of time. *Sync time* links the profane with the micro. According to Hall, sync time is a relatively new Western notion, yet one that has been around for centuries in other cultures. Sync time refers to the ability of people to move at various paces or beats. There are days, for instance, when we feel "out of sync" with others, when we operate on different time orientations. Sync time will differ both within a given culture and within a particular individual.

Because people differ in how they sync with each other and with themselves, Hall suggests that a *personal time* exists. Personal time is the experience of time by the individual. For the individual, time may fly or crawl. In dream analysis, a nightmare, for instance, may seem to last forever, yet it is typically over in less than a minute. Some students report that certain classes go "too fast," and others report that the exact same classes "drag." All are personal experiences of time within a given culture, closely linked perhaps to sync and profane time. *Metaphysical time* concerns the ability of the individual to escape from time and space—to go into a time warp for which contemporary science has no explanation. The concept of *déjà vu*, Hall suggests, is represented by this time category, as are the feelings associated with transcendental meditation. Metaphysical time is neither sacred nor profane; it is highly personal and mostly unexplainable, at least according to Western thought.

At the other end of this time continuum are physical and biological time. *Biological time* is cyclic, perhaps part of the sync between individual and environment. Biologically, we live a cycle; doomed from the beginning to die, we live through other time categories. Biological time—phasing expressed in terms of individual biological clocks—concerns the ability of individuals to recognize and alter behaviors they perform because of some cycle they are in. Hence, the biological interfaces with the social to produce a perception of time that differs from the more personal, psychological time orientations discussed earlier. Finally, there is *physical time*, which represents the scientific observation of time and its effect on life. From primitive cultures that determine time on the cycles of the sun or moon to the most advanced cultures, time represents a physical reality, something to be measured precisely and something that has a demonstrated impact.

What Hall has tried to communicate through his mandala is that time is not a simple continuum, as discussed previously. Instead, time is *nonlinear*; it does not follow a strictly logical path—hence the use of the mandala as his model. Attempting to follow Hall's eight categories, as his mandala presents them, is something neither he nor we could do *logically*. Instead, he suggests we look at the time categories in groupings.

Although most researchers prefer to examine time as a particular category or kind of time, the *meta time* perspective suggests that time categories function to establish usable groupings of categories. For example, at the cultural level, metaphysical, sacred, profane, and micro time function to define the particular culture's perception of time at a primary, or barely conscious, level. Time as a physical function is defined in terms of sync, personal, biological, and physical time categories, in which the emphasis is less on the sociological and more on the biological impact of time and time cycles. At the individual level, personal, sync, micro, and profane time become the focus of life. Here, we are more concerned with experiencing time and ourselves. Finally, at the group level, biological, physical, metaphysical, and sacred time interact to create a time perception suggesting permanence (physical and biological), which creates a subcultural life of its own.

The focus on meta time and its component categories suggests that all eight time categories interrelate to create our total perception of time. Theoretically, this phenomenon is both interesting and educational; it helps explain how cultures and individuals differ in their structure and use of time. It does not, however, tell much about the specifics of time. To establish a more formal structure of time, and to understand better how it communicates, we must turn to the work of Tom Bruneau.

BRUNEAU'S CHRONEMIC STRUCTURES

Just how is time structured? Bruneau's (1986, 2007) theorizing suggests that, much like kinesics and Birdwhistell's (1970) kinesic coding system, time can be studied as a *microstructure* that yields units from which time messages can be analyzed. Bruneau, opting for the term *chronemics* as the underlying construct of time, begins his analysis of time by noting that time is best equated with change and that change is a variation of *process* and *duration*. Further, chronemics is the study of the dynamic interrelationships of both process and duration explained in what follows. In attempting to structure chronemics, Bruneau operationalizes time at three levels: macrostructural, metastructural, and microstructural. The first two levels, much like Hall's mandala of time, establish the philosophical nature of time and make chronemics an area of study. At the microstructure level, however, the variables that create a notation system become operant.

Bruneau's philosophy of chronemic structure is found in the relationship between time as a process and time as duration. Philosophically, he differentiates between the events we process and how we perceive them (duration). In formulating this macrostructure of time, he suggests that cultures operate on a past–present–future trichotomy, but they differ in their perceptions of each leg of macrochronemics. The concepts may be easier to understand by examining the chronemic macrostructure from a *personal time perspective*—that is, how individuals relate process to duration. Bruneau (1986) argues that the interplay between personal time processes and durations alters how we perceive our world:

> We are basically and essentially temporal animals. Further, when we understand that our personal spatial realities expand and contract as our personal time varies through perceptions of the event and the event's duration], we can begin to see change and to dissolve temporal categories, as well as begin to think about the relativity of human experience. (p. 5)

What are the temporal categories that change? Bruneau suggests that time is inherently personal, that we view it as consisting of many things, most of which revolve around *becoming* and *being*. Becoming is related to the process of time, and being is related to the duration of the category of time that we become. Hence, he goes on to note, people view time as transitory and subjective and related to *now*. Where becoming and being are subjective, the now is measurable, it is the present moment. We may evaluate becoming and being as related to the now.

Those with a past orientation view change as a minimal element in their lives; they focus neither on potential change nor on the immediate impact of the now but on the stable and constant past. We often think of senior citizens as having this orientation, but there are plenty in the younger generation that are past-oriented. The future-oriented person views life in terms of novelty, seeking new perspectives on now and on old perceptions. Most college students are considered to be at least somewhat future-oriented, since being in college is meant to be preparation for the future. The present-oriented person focuses on the now, living without analysis of the event, living for the immediate duration of the event, rather than for the event as a process (with a past or future), and experiencing time in the now. Some say that people who do not plan for the future (i.e., not saving money, not establishing retirement contingencies, never staying in a job long enough to build any longevity) are considered to be present-oriented.

Note that this macrostructure, beginning with process and duration, eventually works itself down to the individual. At the metastructural level of chronemics, then, we deal not so much with society or culture but with what concerns the now. The now is tied to the individual who experiences through one of the three chronemic orientations—or through a combination of chronemic orientations—*time*. The metastructures of time, then, are found at the individual level and consist of issues that are centered on how the individual uses and values time. Chronemic metastructure becomes a biological–social relationship. How we view time may vary with changes in body rhythm and hormonal flux associated with our body clocks. These biological clocks then interrelate with social and psychological clocks—clocks that alter the biological rhythm we are born with and that create the unique orientation to time each of us has. Table 10.1 presents Bruneau's taxonomy of biological, social, and psychological clocks and their impact on our time-lives. The interaction of these clocks creates a *temporal environment*, yielding drives, cues, signals, estimates, beliefs, motives, judgments, and values from which we test "nowness." The impact of these temporal (time-oriented) codifications on behavior, as Bruneau (1986) notes, is such that they are unique to both individuals and groups, thus "When my time is not yours, or their time is not ours, dysrhythmia seems to occur" (p. 17).

The making of moments is what constitutes chronemic *microstructure*. A moment is the now; a moment contrasts with the future and the past, what will or did happen; they can be viewed as "nows," instances, or even points in time. Moments are potentially measurable and exist dynamically as units of the now. Bruneau suggests that we can define four levels of nowness. First is the *minimal unit*, the biological/physical/technical level of time. This level defines time as an objective, real concept that rarely changes and that exists at a level below consciousness. Minimal units include the speed of light, brain rhythms or waves, and perception. Minimal units have acquired labels such as *chrons, ergs,* and *oligons* and are measured in portions of seconds, or milliseconds, which exist at a level below consciousness.

When that minimal unit enters consciousness, it becomes a *standard interval unit*. The standard interval unit is found in the pacing, regularity, and synchronized use of multiple minimal units. It is the "formulation of nowness" in such a manner as to be objectively measured and studied. From the objective, time moves toward a subjective, personal level. Here time becomes a *variable unit*, a conceptual "thing" that extends into the past and future. At this level, we speak of the psychological impact of time. That is, at this level, the event may be initially labeled as a standard interval unit—objectively stating the event—and then psychologically adding duration as a measure of how the process/event is felt or perceived. In short, it adds the evaluative aspect to our communication by our use of time. Finally, Bruneau (1986) suggests that time is also something that transcends consciousness. At this *point-instant* level "flashes of awareness or insight (which appear to be acausal) arrive in consciousness as sudden awakenings, revelations, images, visions, and the like" (p. 23).

These four levels of time occur simultaneously. We are constantly guided by the physical into a perception of the present, which we may or may not use to enter the past or future. At times we are aware of sudden flashes of insight, intuition, or fear. These point-instances may be a function of one or all of the other chronemic levels. How to study such rhythms has been problematic. Bruneau suggests that a notation system similar to that developed by Birdwhistell for kinesics (discussed in Chapter 7) might be employed. At this time, Bruneau has identified four elements in his chronemic notation system: a *chron* (a now or moment at the level of primary momenting), which is similar to the kinesic kine; a *chroneme*

TABLE 10.1 CHRONEMIC TAXONOMY OF TEMPORAL VALUES

Level	Codification	Description
Biological	Temporal drive	Biorhythms; hormone periodicity; deals primarily with momenting in terms of stimulus detection
Physiological	Temporal cues	Sensing and recognition of temporal drives of self and others; involves the products of primary momenting
	Temporal signals	Sensing and recognition of duration from the perceptual moment; involves the recognition of nonverbal action
	Temporal estimates	The beginning of duration; a sense of time and timing, habit and tempo, pace and pacing
Physio-psychological	Temporal signals	The beginning of process; a sensing of succession, duration, change, permanence, and perspective (past, present, future); the beginning of symbolization and the I–Time interrelationship
Psychological	Temporal beliefs	The beginning of a process–duration relationship; of establishing assumptions about the role and value of time
	Temporal motives	Establishing intention–time relationship; establishment of influence on a conscious level of drives, cues, signals, etc.
Social	Temporal judgments	Creation and testing of temporal beliefs and motives as exercised by many individuals and groups
Cultural	Temporal values	Creation of a metaperspective on time as a commodity (interplay of process/event and duration) and its impact on behavior

Source: Bruneau, T. J. (1987). "The structure of chronemics," in *Current Trends in Nonverbal Communication*, ed. T. Bagley (Jonesboro, AR: Arkansas State University), pp. 95–120.

(chrons that occur regularly or habitually within the person, group, or culture), which is similar to the kinesic kineme; a *chronemorph* (the sequencing of chrons and/or chronemes into meaningful and symbolic patterns), which is similar to the kinesic kinemorph; and a *chrontax*, the utilization of chrons, chronemes, and chronemorphs in the conduct of individual and group communication behavior), which is similar to the kinesic kinemorphic class.

BOX 10.6 OBSERVATIONAL STUDY

Take a sheet of paper and lay out the time schedule you will follow for tomorrow from the time you wake up until you go to bed. How many of the things on your list are formal, meaning you can't change them (e.g., class, work, doctor's appointment)? How many are less formal? Count up how many activities you plan to do in a day. Does this surprise you? In what way? More than you thought? Less?

CULTURE AND TIME

Culture begins to educate each of us at an early age as to the value of and the means by which we distinguish time. Each culture has its own particular time norms, which are unconsciously followed until violated. When such violations occur, however, they are perceived as intentional messages associated with that particular culture. In this regard, each culture teaches its people what is appropriate or inappropriate with regard to time.

E. T. Hall (1976) has indicated that with respect to their use of time, cultures tend to fall into two general categories. The first is *monochronic*, which is defined as doing one thing at a time. Monochronic time is arbitrary, self-imposed, and learned. This is the way we Americans tend to operate. An arbitrary time device (clock, watch) controls us. We eat meals not when we are hungry but when the clock says it is time to eat. The second is polychronic, which is defined as doing many things at the same time. In polychronic cultures, several things may happen at once. Examples are found in Latin America and the Middle East, where emphasis is placed on interactions and people, rather than on an arbitrary time device. This orientation may also be seen in the Tiv example noted earlier.

INFORMAL TIME

E. T. Hall (1976) notes that each culture operates on three time systems, with each system operating simultaneously to create chronemic norms. Probably the most difficult to understand and adapt to is informal time. This concept of informal time is based on practice and takes on a more personalized or psychological orientation, depending on who we are dealing with. At least six factors influence our perception of informal time: duration, punctuality, urgency, activity, variety, and monochronic/polychronic orientation. Notice that each of these factors seems to be definable on the basis of a personal time orientation; that is, they tend to run as we "see" them. Notice also that these six factors lend themselves to stereotypical types of perceptions. (Refer back to your findings in Observational Study 10.6 as you read about these issues.)

Our North American culture (defined here as Canada and the United States) is readily definable in terms of how we perceive these six time factors. Consider, for instance, duration: How long does something last? In the North American culture, things last a short time, perhaps a vestige of our short history (compared to that of other, older cultures). Problems occur, even within the culture, in regard to such terms as *immediately, in a second* (as contrasted with *in a minute*), and *forever*. The importance of time has increased with the electronic age of television, radio, and cable. Speed and saving time are even more important in a digital age of personal computers. North Americans often become frustrated when events take "too long," such as a computer's taking 15 seconds to boot. As you can see, duration is subjective; your perception will affect it more than other factors.

Activity deals with what we perceive should be done in a given period. In North American culture, we perceive a great deal of activity as necessary, but not too much at any given time. We are more *monochronic*; we like to see things *varied* within a given period, not everything together at once. We create variety within a given period of time in a strange way in that we treat each activity as a separate entity. In this sense we are monochronic, but within that self-imposed period, we establish other monochronic periods that imply both activity and variety of content. Look at any summary of a daily TV schedule, and you will find examples of this. Other cultures, being more polychronic, do not place the same emphasis on activity and variety, which leads to a perspective of "things will get done when they get done"; North Americans view this perspective as lazy, nonambitious, and a waste of precious time. In some cultures, the polychronic norm may end with several people meeting to discuss business, whereas in our society, we would do so individually. The thought of meeting more than one person at a time upsets our monochronic norm.

An author of this text researched nonverbal communication in the Gulf War Crisis in the early 1990s and found that this issue of monochronic versus polychronic time was one to which the Americans had a difficult time adjusting. Since we are monochronic, when the Americans had a meeting arranged with the Saudis, they expected to be the only ones there for that purpose. The Saudi Arabians, who are polychronic, would just naturally schedule many things for the same time period, probably thinking to get the meetings done so they could move on to some other issues. You can imagine how the Americans reacted to such a situation, if not outwardly, at least among themselves. In the case of foreign affairs, especially in light of the area of the world in which our military actions have taken place in most recent years, it would seem like a good idea for Americans to be aware of cultural nonverbal differences such as this time usage example (as well as kinesics, physical appearance norms, touch, and space).

Probably the most important culturally defined informal time system is that of punctuality. In our culture, we expect people to be punctual. By this we mean that we expect people to arrive at the appointed time or just before then (five minutes); however, people tend to synchronize (or *sync*) differently. Hall has identified at least two major types of synchronizing that pertain to punctuality patterns; these types differ in their perceptions of where the time ends. For those of us who are *displaced*, who see a point in time as being the end, we operate as if a 4:45 meeting means just that: be there at 4:45 (actually, a couple of minutes early, just to be safe). For those of us who are more *diffused*, who see time as only an approximation, we would consider that same 4:45 meeting as an approximation and arrive around that time. For those who are displaced, there seems to be a need to be on time. For those who are diffused, the compulsion for punctuality is lessened. The diffused person, however, seems to operate more on a late basis than on an early basis. Some people, for instance, are always "*x* minutes" late, in fact, consistently late to such a degree that you can begin to depend on their "lateness." Do you know of someone who is always late, and so you tell them to meet you earlier than you really want to meet them just so they just might be there "on time"?

The issue of punctuality is not just about being concerned with being somewhere on time. In the workplace, it also deals with having your work in on time, and having others around you being punctual in the same way. Ballard and Seibold (2006) found in a study of the workplace that people "who perceive their task completion and activities as punctual are . . . more satisfied" (p. 329). As they stated further: "Organizational members who are able to successfully meet job demands are likely to be more satisfied . . ." (p. 333). Clearly, issues of punctuality affect us in many ways and in many contexts.

This issue of punctuality is one of the major chronemic communication issues for many Americans. We teach time usage to the young in our culture, and we continually learn more about it ourselves. We often discuss how being nonpunctual communicates something about the individual who is continually late, as well as about the person who is annoyed and irritated by nonpunctuality. Some of the messages we say are communicated by a habitual lack of punctuality include that you don't care about the person/event that was scheduled; that you are lazy, disorganized, careless, disrespectful, carefree, and so forth; that you think you are more important (since we allow people with a higher status more leeway when it comes to punctuality); and other such negative judgments (Emmert and Emmert 1984). In our culture it is unforgivable to be late for some meetings, such as employment interviews, meetings with a boss, professor, and so forth. Being late is expected in some other situations, such as parties. As you can imagine, the informal and formal nature of punctuality causes many people communication problems. Some who are late say, "Well, I have a reason," and even that does not completely "save" them. Many people believe that someone who is habitually nonpunctual, who always has a reason, is what is labeled as an *excuse giver*, which is something most people do not appreciate in a person. Professors who are hard on students who are habitually late to class sometimes get criticized. Students often think it is the professor's *quirk*, but informal research over the years has shown that the one thing that bothers students the most, as the most disruptive thing in a classroom, is when other students walk in after the class has begun. We suggest that you discover what a person's time orientation is when it comes to punctuality (including bosses, professors, group members for projects, friends, significant others, roommates, and so forth) so that you do not suffer the consequences of the message you send by your use (or misuse) of time, especially if the aftermath can be damaging to you personally or to your relationships.

One final issue of punctuality comes into being due to our society's reliance on technological communication that exists today. Since we are so dependent on things such as email, texting, *Twitter*, *Flickr*, etc. . . . , we expect instant answers when we send a message. If we do not receive that immediate answer, we judge the person we wish to hear from as nonpunctual. Larsen, Urry, and Axhausen (2008) believe that due to our dependence on such forms of communication, especially when we are trying to coordinate face-to-face meetings, our understanding of what is "timely" when it comes to asking for a meeting or calling a full-blown business meeting is skewed by the media we use. Bernstein (2010), in a *Wall Street Journal* article, finds that we use technology—especially calling on cell phones or texting messages—to circumvent social standards (or rules) for good manners when it comes to having set a meeting time with people. She believes that somehow we have allowed this to become the norm, and so that many of us think it is just fine if we are late if we have sent a message. One of your authors of this textbook had a student in the most recent semester that was late virtually every class meeting; when called out for it, his response was, "Well I sent you an email telling you I would be late."

STUDENT VOICES

Sean: In my opinion, punctuality displays an attitude. There are countless distractions and interruptions that can hinder anyone from staying on schedule, but it is truly a mindset of efficiency and maximization of time. I agree with professors' rules concerning late arrivals. I have a professor who instructs students to take a seat nearest the door so as to not disturb the current flow of communication taking place in the classroom. Also, this topic reminds me that I have a friend that still to this day, must be told that dinner plans will be an hour earlier than the actual reservation because she has been an running an hour behind since I have known her. Punctuality is not simply a time skill; it is a relationship quality and a demonstration of a personal character.

BOX 10.7 OBSERVATIONAL STUDY

Just how good are people at judging the correct time? In this study you are interested in formal time—that is, the time it is now. Go up to 10 strangers (five female, five male) who are not wearing watches. Ask each the time of the day and note what time they say it is and record their response and the correct time (obviously, they should not pull out their cell phones to look at the time—that defeats the purpose of the exercise). On average, how close were they? Did you find any differences between male and female "guesstimates"? If possible, conduct the study with people from different cultures and compare their results to those of students from the surrounding area.

Within each culture there are subcultures that view time a little differently. In the North American culture, for instance, a Southerner definitely views time differently than does a Northeasterner, who views time differently than a Californian does. These differences occur in all cultures and may be defined as time frames. Frames, as originally defined by Goffman (1974), are attitudes and perspectives for viewing performances. Within each culture there are subcultural "frames," or expectations based on appropriate time "performances." These time frames are unexpressed, or undefined, and are learned the hard way; we violate them in order to learn them, just as mentioned in the previous section on punctuality. In this sense, we encounter such time orientations as CPT ("Colored People's Time" from the vernacular of the day when it was labeled as such), or *street time* (Horton 1976); *haole time,* or *white person's time* ("haole" is a derogative Hawaiian term that referred to the early missionary's pallid complexion), is contrasted to Hawaiian time (J. K. Burgoon and Saine 1978). In each case, the subcultural time orientation (Hawaiian, CPT, and street time) refers to a more lax and unconscious perception of time. The haole time and white person's time refer to a more rigid time orientation.

Some of you may wonder about the existence of CPT, but it does still seem to exist, at least for some individuals. One of your authors, in the process of updating this edition of the textbook, asked racially mixed nonverbal communication classes (about 30 percent African American, the rest Caucasian) if there were any cultural differences, especially intercultural or subcultural ones, in the area of chronemics. A quick response from a number of the African American students in the class pointed out CPT and that in their experiences, for the most part, it still exists. Although once again, we caution you not to overgeneralize based on the findings of one study, and especially one as informal as this. The same author has a close African American friend who says this time concept is bogus, but then he was in the armed services for 25 years, not quite a culture that allows for such casual use of time. Again, as we have mentioned throughout this textbook, it is crucial to pay attention to the context and the actual individuals before you make any generalizations about any person or group of persons.

FORMAL TIME

Formal time refers to the way a culture views and teaches time as a conscious entity. It is this formality that creates the time system according to which we Americans operate: seconds, minutes, hours, days, weeks, months, years, decades, centuries. We attribute great importance to time systems in our culture, allocating salaries, wages, and time spent with someone on a continuum of positive to negative effect. Such a perspective concerning time is consciously taught to us as a function of five discrete time variables: order, cycle, value, duration, and tangibility. When we learn time, the first thing we learn is that time is *ordered*. That is, Monday comes after Sunday and before Tuesday. This time ordering indicates the beginning and the ending of a period (a week). We further order our time in terms of the number of days per week, weeks per month, months per year, years per century, and so on. Leap year, for example, is discomforting to many because they have an "extra day" with which they must deal.

A second feature of the formal time structure we learn is the *cycle*. We live in a cyclic society, one that expects things to occur in a particular order or cycle over a given number of units (days, weeks, months, years). We feel good when we can talk about something happening in a year or two, implying cycle, or when good or bad "seasons" occur (e.g., hurricane, monsoon, summer, winter, fall, spring). We view time as having a *duration*, temporal continuum, or depth. Our perception of depth, however, is not as long as that of some other cultures. For us, duration is short-lived, so much so that we want everything to go quickly. Finally, we view time as *tangible*. We spend time, we buy time (time-sharing, for instance), and we view how valuable we are based on our hourly pay. One of the first things people do when they obtain a job is figure out what they are worth per hour. This can be ego defeating for those on salary. By breaking down the hours people work (at home and office) in terms of the total weekly salary, they may find themselves actually working for less than the minimum wage.

Formal time, then, differs from informal time in that it is more conscious and is taught. Like informal time perception, formal time may differ in various situations, but this difference is more evident on the cultural level than on the subcultural level. We tend to stereotype people as being more different than they actually are, based on how they use formal time.

The last time system to discuss is technical time. Technical time is a precise way of measuring the relationship between a variable and time. We speak of ergs per square centimeter, of the atomic year (365 days, 5 hours, 48 minutes, and 45.51 seconds, give or take a millisecond), of $E = mc^2$ (where c equals time), and NASA time (or time used by the U.S. space program). Each of these times is precise and technical but not too useful in everyday communication. Listen to an engineer, physicist, or chemist, however, and you will hear him or her speak about different types of time. Hence, technical time becomes standard and useful.

In sum, cultural time orientations offer different frames from which to view time. We can begin with those taught and then see how informal orientations create differences. Conversely, we can begin with the informal and note the differences. We all need to remember that how we perceive time is based not only on cultural differences but also on subcultural differences.

BOX 10.8 OBSERVATIONAL STUDY

Take a magazine and survey the pictures in the ads or the stories. How many of the models are wearing watches (in ads other than watch company ads), and how many are not? How many environments have a clock on the wall? What message does their presence or absence send about the products or the stories?

SUMMARY

Perception is very important to nonverbal communication, and the areas of olfaction and chronemics are two such perceptual systems. A perceptual state exists when we are at least vaguely conscious that the information received exists. Biofeedback as a perceptual system may be used to explain emotion, mood state, and possibly deceptive communication.

Olfaction is an important nonverbal subcode. Not only are we subconsciously influenced by the odors around us, but we are much better at identifying odors than was previously thought. Olfaction serves several purposes. On one level, it deals with the basic survival needs: the scent of emotion and sexual attraction. On another level, it is associated with the labels we ascribe to the odors we perceive. Such perception can make us fair prey to those who would manipulate both our perceptions and our memory. Certain perfumes are associated with a strong and progressive young female; not too many traditional females would wear such a fragrance. Olfactory memory is used to sell us products that have some form of emotive connotation. Olfactory memory may, in this regard, act as a form of *déjà vu*; we sense that we have been there before, smell that we have been there before, and associate that perception with the present experience. In any event, our ability to manipulate and influence by means of smell has great potential, but this is an area that needs further research.

Time, or chronemics, is another perceptual area for the study of communication. We usually act and react to time as though we take it for granted, with little thought as to the messages we send and receive. On the cultural level, time sets forth expectations, and unfortunately time leads to stereotyped differences between and within cultures. How we use time and view time is important to the nonverbal messages we send.

QUESTIONS FOR THOUGHT

1. Just how important are the various biofeedback systems identified in this chapter to you on a daily basis? When do they rise above the unconscious? What effects do they have?
2. How do mood and emotion operate from a covert perspective? Which "traditional" nonverbal subcodes seem to be important? Why?
3. How important is olfaction in daily interpersonal encounters? Is it more than just a survival instinct, or does it actively play into our daily communication strategies?
4. Hall and Bruneau both look at time as a structured event. Which does a better job at presenting a *useful* perspective for daily communication?
5. Cultural variations in chronemic perception lie below conscious behavior—or do they? What impact does time have on subcultural interactions? On individual interactions?
6. When considering punctuality, what is your time orientation? Have you ever been upset, or have you ever upset someone else, because of a difference in your perceptions of punctuality? What was your reaction? The other person's?

FURTHER REFERENCES

Biofeedback

Byers, P. (1979). Biological rhythms as information channels in interpersonal communication behavior. In S. Weitz (Ed.), *Nonverbal communication: Readings with commentary* (2nd ed., pp. 398–418). New York: Oxford University Press.

Lane, L. L. (1971). Communicative behavior and biological rhythms. *Speech Teacher*, 20, 16–19.

McCutcheon, L. (1996). What's that smell? The claims of aromatherapy. *Skeptical Inquirer*, May/June, 1–4.

Parks, A. S., and Bruce, H. M. (1961). Olfactory stimuli in mammalian reproduction. *Science*, 134, 1049–1054.

Olfactory Issues

Aschenbrenner, K., Scholze, N., Joraschky, P., and Hummel, T. (2008). Gustatory and olfactory sensitivity in patients with anorexia and bulimia in the course of treatment. *Journal of Psychiatric Research*, 43, 129–137.

Bosmans, A. (2006). Scents and sensibility: When do (in)congruent ambient scents influence product evaluations? *Journal of Marketing*, 70, 32–43.

Croy, I., Negoias, S., Novakova, L., Landis, B. N., and Hummel, T. (2012). Learning about the functions of the olfactory system from people without a sense of smell. *PLoS ONE*, 7, 1–7.

Dominguez, P. R. (2011). The study of postnatal and later development of the taste and olfactory systems using the human brain mapping approach: An update. *Brain Research Bulletin*, 84, 118–124.

Durand, K., Baudon, G., Freydefont, L., and Schaal, B. (2008). Odorization of a novel object can influence infant's exploratory behavior in unexpected ways. *Infant Behavior & Development*, 31, 629–636.

Engen, T., and Lipsitt, L. P. (1963). Decrement and recovery of response to olfactory stimuli in the human neonate. *Journal of Comparative Physiological Psychology*, 56, 75–77.

Higuchi, T., Shoji, K., Taguchi, S., and Hatayama, T. (2005). Improvement of nonverbal behaviour in Japanese female perfume-wearers. *International Journal of Psychology*, 40, 90–99.

Holland, R. W., Hendriks, M., and Aarts, H. (2005). Smells like clean spirit. *Psychological Science*, 16, 689–693.

Honeyman, K. (2008). Catching the scent of a story: Why memories get so tied up with emotion. *Writer*, 121, 26–27.

Lipsitt, L. P., Engen, T., and Kaye, H. (1963). Development changes in the olfactory threshold of the neonate. *Child Development*, 34, 371–376.

Luka, T., Berner, E. S., and Kanakis, C. (1977). Diagnosis by smell? *Journal of Medical Education*, 52, 349–350.

Morrin, M., and Ratneshwar, S. (2003). Does it make sense to use scents to enhance brand memory? *Journal of Marketing Research*, 40, 10–25.

Riley, J. E. (1979). The olfactory factor in nonverbal communication. *Communication*, 8, 159–169.

Wen L., Moallem, I., Paller, K. A., and Gottfried, J. A. (2007). Subliminal smells can guide social preferences. *Psychological Science*, 18, 1044–1049.

Chronemics

Adam, B. (2006). Time. *Theory, Culture & Society*, 23, 119–126.

Ballard, D. I., and Seibold, D. R. (2004a). Communication-related organizational structures and work group temporal experiences: The effects of coordination method, technology type, and feedback cycle on members' construals and enactments of time. *Communication Monographs*, 71, 1–27.

Ballard, D. I., and Seibold, D. R. (2004b). Organizational members' communication and temporal experience. *Communication Research*, 31, 135–172.

Gudykunst, W. B. (1998). *Bridging differences: Effective intergroup communication.* Thousand Oaks, CA: Sage.

Rutkowski, A., Saunders, C., Vogel, D., and van Genuchten, M. (2007). "Is it already 4 a.m. in your time zone?" Focus immersion and temporal dissociation in virtual teams. *Small Group Research,* 38, 98–129.

Striano, T., Henning, A., and Stahl, D. (2006). Sensitivity to interpersonal timing at 3 and 6 months of age. *Interaction Studies,* 7, 251–271.

PART

2

APPLICATIONS

This part of the text brings closure to our study of nonverbal communication. To quickly review, we began our study of the nonverbal system by defining what we were studying, how it differs from the verbal system, how it functions with the verbal system, and finally what its subcodes are and how those subcodes function in communication. We are now ready to apply this knowledge in several contexts. At this stage in most textbooks, you would be on your own. We believe, however, that sufficient information is now available to indicate how the various subcodes operate in social situations, in the family, and on the job. At the outset, be aware that there is no way we could begin to cover all the application ramifications of what you have learned thus far. These three chapters are written to give you at least a partial view of how some of the subcodes can be studied in different contexts. It is our hope that you might become interested enough to pursue further research into the areas we cover here, as well as others.

We start with an examination of an area that has received some attention. Our discussion of how nonverbal communication is used in social situations begins by looking at the courtship and quasi-courtship behaviors in which we all engage (Chapter 11). It considers why we do so and things to look out for. We then move to power plays, or how we use nonverbal communication to increase our perceived power, status, credibility, and attraction. We also examine the process of identifying first impressions and how we manipulate them.

Next we move to the family and observe how we use nonverbal communication in day-to-day activities there (Chapter 12). We look specifically at the spatiotemporal subcodes, such as environment, time, and space; we also note how the physical appearance, zero-proxemic, vocalic, and kinesic areas impact home life. We look at the developmental aspects of nonverbal communication in childhood, in marriage, in adult life, and, finally, with the aged. The chapter examines the nonverbal processes by which we relate to people we care a great deal about, how that concern and that affection are communicated nonverbally, and their impact on the growth of a "nuclear" unit.

Chapter 13 examines nonverbal communication on the job. We are interested in how the environment, use and alteration of space, and the use of time interact to create impressions of how we work and who we are on the job. We consider the importance of building a non-verbal linkage through kinesics, physical appearance, and other nonverbal subcodes. Finally, we examine the process of getting a job—the nonverbal factors in the job interview—and how you can create an impression of power and credibility.

Chapter 14 sums up what we have been studying. It describes the problems associated with definition and functions. That chapter might be considered the "quick review" or "guide" chapter. It may be useful as a reference later in your academic or professional career.

By now you have the information needed to begin applying nonverbal communication. These final chapters expand upon the information found in Part I they provide applications of nonverbal communication in each subcode. They may change the impact of your own personal communication. Since they really are more contextual in nature, you will note fewer "Observational Studies" in this section. Perhaps some strategy or theory will emerge from this material that enables you to increase your awareness of how you are manipulated and, in turn, how to deal more effectively with your environment and those in it. At the very least, you now possess the necessary information to understand others' nonverbal commu-nication; based on this, you may be able to predict both intent and outcome.

CHAPTER 11

NONVERBAL COMMUNICATION IN SOCIAL SITUATIONS

KEY CONCEPTS

- Initial Interactions
- Intimate Behavior
- Male–Male Friendships
- Female–Female Friendships
- The "Matching Hypothesis"

OBJECTIVES

By the end of the chapter you should be able to:

- Describe the process by which people initiate interactions through subtle and not-so-subtle nonverbal behaviors.
- Explain how nonverbal communication is used to indicate a need for intimate behavior among people.
- Describe the 12 steps of courtship that lead to differing intimate behaviors.
- Explain how nonverbal subcodes operate in the establishment of intimacy.
- Describe and explain cross-sex friendships and how they turn into relationships.
- Explain the process through which cross-sex and same-sex relationships are formed and maintained through nonverbal cues.

The previous chapters provided us with the results and conclusions of historical and contemporary research on nonverbal communication, as obtained through laboratory investigations, survey questionnaires, field experiments, as well as observations by your authors over the years. In this chapter, we describe some of the nonverbal factors that operate in social situations (female–male; male–male; female–female).

The underlying assumption of this chapter is that social interactions are composed of the exchange of messages, or conversations. Ultimately, these conversations are combined into what we call a relationship. From a communication standpoint, then, a relationship is composed of a number of message exchanges between individuals. The focus of these messages certainly varies from person to person, from situation to situation, and from culture to culture. The types of nonverbal norms discussed in this chapter are especially pertinent to white, middle-class American society, since there is a paucity of research available about specific minority populations. The situations in this chapter are concerned primarily with non-job-related and non-family-related, heterosexual relationships, as well as general friendships, both cross-sex and same-sex. We also include discussion about less traditional relationships, such as committed couples living together and not married and homosexual couples living together as committed couples. The focus is liking, the primary ingredient in such relationships, as opposed to family and job relationships, both of which contain a number of complex power and status differentials. The family and job situations are covered in later chapters.

MEETING OTHERS

Let us look first at the old-fashioned "blind date" example. In this type of stranger-to-stranger interaction, both parties know the general type of situation in advance. For a number of reasons, the parties involved (we'll name them Kelly and Jaime) collect as much information as possible about one another before the face-to-face meeting, usually through an intermediary (Chris). One of the primary reasons for doing this is to increase the predictability about the other person. Chris knows both Kelly and Jaime and believes they would enjoy being with one another.

As a "matchmaker," Chris would probably use the *matching hypothesis* (Walster, Aronson, Abrahams, and Rohmann, 1966); that is, people tend to choose partners considered to be in the same category of physical attractiveness. Unfortunately, since *beauty is in the eye of the beholder,* Chris' perception is not the same as Kelly's or Jaime's. Thus, when Chris says, "Jaime has a nice personality," and "Everybody likes Jaime," the nonverbal message tells Kelly that Jaime probably is not very physically attractive. Kelly, like most people, is quite interested in physical attractiveness. As mentioned in Chapter 5, physical attractiveness is the single most important quality in initial romantic interest or dating interactions, and within cross-sex, heterosexual interactions, it is especially important for males.

STUDENT VOICES

Margaret: In my sorority, one of my sisters Cassie became recently engaged to her boyfriend of several years. They are perfect examples of the matching hypothesis. They are tall, blond, physically fit, and involved in Greek life. If anything, they seem to look more like brother and sister.

Assume for now that Kelly is male and Jaime is female, in order to apply some of the theories concerning heterosexism. While on the "blind date," Kelly is concerned primarily with physical appearance. His evaluation will be based on Jaime's bosom, general body shape, and eyes. Jaime's evaluation of Kelly will be based on overall physique, grooming and neatness, and eyes. Takeuchi (2006) tells us that "attitude similarity, and socioeconomic status are more likely to operate interactively once interactions between the seeker and the targets begin. Thus, the actual decision making . . . is based on the combination of various evaluative information about each target that the seeker possesses" (p. 43). *Although personality, intelligence, and socioeconomic status will have some effect on the probability of a second date, the single most important factor is likely to be physical appearance.*

A number of factors go into what the individual considers as physically attractive. For example, when people who are in love rate the physical attractiveness of others (third persons), they rate them as more attractive than do people who are not in love (Benassi 1985). Females are more in agreement about what constitutes physical attractiveness than are males (Donovan, Hill, and Jankowiak 1988). Rainville and Gallagher (1990) found that when a person is perceived as dominant, his or her physical attractiveness is greater, but less so for females than for males. In television commercials, baby-faced experts were considered less expert but more trustworthy than their mature-faced counterparts (Brownlow and Zebrowitz 1990). Thinner figures are associated with more positive characteristics (White, Brown, and Ginsburg 1999). While unattractive female faces were associated with higher homosexuality ratings, the same was not found to be true of males (Pratto and Bargh 1991). Clearly, the United States is a society that uses physical attractiveness as a measurement for sociability, regardless of sexual orientation.

As the night goes on, Kelly and Jaime begin to talk. At first this conversation may be awkward. The awkwardness of the conversation is noticeable to both parties because of certain verbal and nonverbal exchanges. Kelly and Jaime frequently switch topics; they ask seemingly meaningless questions; they repeat statements and questions. In terms of vocalics, there are many stutters and stammers, but of most importance, there are many meaningless pauses. Laughter is sometimes quelled because each is unfamiliar with the humor of the other. Neither wants to appear "too flighty." Even voice attractiveness of a potential mate can affect attractiveness judgments (S. Hughes, Pastizzo, and Gallup 2008).

GENERAL CHARACTERISTICS

The vocal cues just discussed are significant for another reason: Voice quality, assertiveness, response level, and intensity become meaningful aspects of physical attractiveness when two people interact in an intimate environment. Simply by being alone together in Kelly's or Jaime's car, the two find themselves in such an environment. If you had listened to Jaime and Kelly in their first phone conversation, you probably would have heard both of them lower their voices to sound more sexually attractive (S. Hughes, Farley, and Rhodes 2010).

Both Kelly and Jaime initially feel the need to increase the space between the two of them, to allow more freedom for each one. The initial interaction is *strained,* because neither knows what to expect from the other. In opposite-sex couples, Jaime is likely to defer to Kelly in making choices for the date since she probably has been socialized that it is "too forward" for her to make a decision about touching first or invading his personal space. Twenty years from now, this probably won't be the same scenario, but most of you in the college-age population are still being raised by parents who were taught that that was what was proper.

When Kelly and Jaime arrive at the basketball arena (the scene of their date), they find that some of the strain is gone and they are actually physically closer to one another. Like their home team, they are both somehow aware of "home territory."

PHOTO 11.1 People tend to choose partners in the same category of physical appearance. When this isn't the case, what do you think is the reason?

Kelly and Jaime are now seated together as close as they have ever been. The advantage of being in the arena is that there are thousands of distractions to keep each one from paying too much attention to the other. Each of them has friends at the game who come by to speak. Each of them introduces friends to the other. At this point, physical appearance enters the situation once again. Now Kelly is not only concerned about how Jaime looks to him, but he is also concerned about how Jaime looks *to his close friends*. Jaime has the same feelings about Kelly; Jaime wants her close friends to consider Kelly attractive, too.

Overall physical appearance is a factor, but what are the specific physical traits the two are seeking in one another? Essentially, each wants the other to "fit in" with his or her "crowd." Kelly would be quite disappointed if Jaime were excessively overweight. Perhaps Kelly would have decided to forgo the basketball game. Kelly may not have been pleased had Jaime been exceedingly underweight, appearing to have *anorexia nervosa*. Thus, Kelly prefers Jaime to be a medium-weight person. Jaime does not want Kelly to be overweight either, nor would Jaime like it if he were shorter than she.

Desired hair color is also an interesting attractiveness factor in cross-sex relationships. When Kelly first talked to Chris about Jaime, he also asked Chris about Jaime's hair color. As Malandro, Barker, and Barker (1989) have noted: "Blond hair has been the mark of both the princess and whore" (p. 61). Blonde women are known "to have more fun" and to be the ones "gentlemen prefer," and they are stereotyped as "dumb." The glut of *blonde jokes* over the last 25 years has done nothing to diminish this stereotype. Redheads are known for their tempestuousness and their tempers. Brunettes are probably found most often in American society. In a more recent study, Swami, Furnham, and Joshi (2008) discovered that women prefer darker colored hair (at least in the population in London that they studied). Sorokowski (2008) found that, at least in Poland, only the younger women with blonde hair were considered more attractive than brunettes. Kelly actually prefers brunettes himself, which is perhaps one reason why Chris selected Jaime. Though Kelly prefers brunettes, there is no evidence to show that males generally prefer females with any particular hair color. Kelly probably does not know whether Jaime dyes her hair, although more brunettes dye their hair blonde than vice versa. Jaime has a preference for a blonde male, but this is just Jaime's personal opinion. Likewise, there is no evidence to show that females prefer males with any particular hair color. Hair color is simply one more issue of personal preference when determining factors of attractiveness; there are no universal standards for what is more attractive, regardless of what advertising tries to tell us.

The conservative male also prefers hairstyles and lengths that are "typical" for the time. These variables may change from year to year, and they differ according to subculture. Kelly doesn't like very curly and long hair; he prefers long, straight hair. Conservative heterosexual females prefer short, clean-cut hairstyles on men. Jaime does not like long hair on men, nor does she like a "crew-cut." Just as Swami et al. (2008) discovered, there is no universal preferred hair length when trying to determine attractiveness.

Because Kelly perceives himself as conservative, he also prefers little makeup for his date (or at least he thinks he does). Although he likes a woman to wear some lipstick or lip gloss, he does not want makeup to be the first thing his male friends notice about Jaime. He wants Jaime to look "natural"; he really wants her to wear *appropriate* makeup to look natural rather than looking made-up or not wearing any makeup. Kelly is not alone in this opinion;

Huguet, Croizet, and Richetin (2004) reported that use of makeup on college-age women can even create a negative impression. Eye shadow was "out" for a number of years and has begun to make a comeback. Kelly is pretty sure, however, that he does not want it to be noticeable on Jaime. Mascara, as long as it isn't too thick, clumpy, or noticeable, is what Kelly thinks will give Jaime that "natural" look. Designer false eyelashes, and fingernails for that matter, would not have been a good choice for Jaime to apply prior to her date with Kelly.

In the college environment, Jaime has much more flexibility in clothing than she would have in other places. Designer clothes almost always appear appropriate. Traditional, but not "country," clothes are generally acceptable. Jaime should appear in attractive but not overly sexually appealing clothes. Kelly, as a male, has less to worry about than Jaime does. Kelly's clothes might also be designer brands, especially such brands as Aeropostale, *Abercrombie and Fitch, American Eagle*, and *Hollister* (at least at this writing), and the clothes should be the contemporary styles.

Realize that both are concerned about the appearance that each presents to the other's friends. As you may note, there are more stereotypes for women to live up to than there are for men, regardless of the person's sexual preferences. There are stronger stereotypes for female attractiveness, and society is more critical of women's physical appearance than it is of men's.

While Kelly and Jaime are still at the basketball game, the thoughts of intimacy or possible intimacy (fantasy) may run through their minds. The next section looks at what the research has to say about the issues of nonverbal intimacy, but first, there is a chance for you to practice what you have just learned.

BOX 11.1   OBSERVATIONAL STUDY

Choose a television program where you know one of the purposes is for the actors to "hook up" with another person and for the show to "play out" those relationships (e.g., *The Office, Two and a Half Men, Nip Tuck, Grey's Anatomy,* and the reruns of *Friends, Desperate Housewives,* and *Sex in the City*). Watch a relationship as it progresses during the show. What nonverbal communication behaviors show that it is more of an initial encounter than an established relationship, or vice versa? What do the characters do to send this message? Are there messages foreshadowing the end of the relationship? How can you tell (by their nonverbal behaviors, of course)?

INTIMATE BEHAVIOR

Desmond Morris (1971) delineated 12 steps in animal courtship that appear to apply generally to human beings. These steps vary from person to person, but they provide us a hypothetical sequence of events. Kelly and Jaime may not *physically* go through each step, but remember they are *fantasizing*. The first step is *eye-to-body*. Here the two parties examine the general physical appearance of the other. The second step is *eye-to-eye* (Laird and Lewis 1989), when the evaluation of the eye's attractiveness is made. Usually there is an initial gaze, looking away, and finally mutual gaze. A smile becomes important at this step, as Guéguen (2008a) reported. Women especially are judged to be more attractive and available for courtship if they smile at the potential mate. A gaze held and reciprocated for more than three

PHOTO 11.2 Which stage of Morris' stages of courtship behaviors do you notice here?

seconds usually indicates a desire to interact. At this stage, individuals attempt to gain information about character (especially trustworthiness). Staring is considered an act of aggression. As has been mentioned earlier, the third stage, *voice-to-voice*, is an important variable in determining physical attractiveness. As we mentioned at the outset, when the messages turn to conversations, a relationship can be developed.

The fourth stage is *hand-to-hand*. While hand holding may occur briefly early in the first interaction, this hand holding will be limited in time and restricted to semiprivate situations (such as in a movie theater or in an automobile while driving). *Arm-to-shoulder* is the fifth stage. This is the first stage toward intimacy. It can be used as an extension of the same method used with friends; however, it can be the first trunk-to-trunk interaction. *Arm-to-waist* is the next stage. This stage separates "friendly" arm-to-shoulder interaction from more intimate interaction. The hand is now closer to the genital region. The seventh stage is mouth-to-mouth. There is a likelihood that physiological arousal may first appear in this stage. "The female may experience genital secretions, and the male's penis may start to become erect" (Morris 1971, 77).

Tieffer (1979) has studied kissing behavior. She writes: "Nothing seems more natural than a kiss. Consider the French kiss, also known as the soul kiss, or tongue kiss (to the French, it was the Italian kiss, but only during the Renaissance). Western societies regard this passionate exploration of mouths and tongues as an instinctive way to express love and to arouse desire" (p. 28). According to Tieffer, the kiss may be used as (1) a sexual act, (2) a sign of friendship, (3) a gesture of respect, (4) a health threat, (5) a ceremonial celebration, or (6) a disgusting behavior. Regardless of the reason, the kiss is usually an intimate action.

Ford and Beach (1951) studied sexual customs in 190 tribal societies and found that only 21 mentioned kissing. Four of these kissed by sucking the lips and tongues of their partners. They also found that Lapps kissed the nose and the mouth at the same time. Even in the United States, Tieffer (1979) reports a study undertaken by Stein, which showed little kissing among call girls (prostitutes). In that study, the researcher was in the room, hidden from view, where she observed 64 call girls. In only 36 percent of these encounters did the partners engage in deep kissing. Thirteen percent of the encounters included sweet talk, seduction, adoration, and tongue kissing. In Japan, kissing is acceptable only between mother and child. For the Japanese, "Intercourse is 'natural'; a kiss, pornographic" (Tieffer 1979, 30). These findings show just a few of the ways cultures differ when it comes to the act of kissing. What others are you aware of?

In Western culture, there are also nonsexual uses of the kiss, including greetings and farewells, affection, religion, deference to higher authority, making the hurt go away, sealing a bargain, blessing sacred vestments, making up, and showing betrayal (known as the Judas kiss). The Hindus maintain four types of kissing that are not prevalent in Western society: tongue-sucking, tongue-tilting, tongue scraping, and lip biting.

In summing up the importance of the mouth in human interaction, Tieffer (1979) states:

> Deep kissing causes other physiological changes. The presence of a lover's tongue in one's mouth induces the secretion of saliva, which is under neural control (seventh and ninth cranial nerves) and thus appears in response to any stimulus in the mouth. Most societies find juicy kisses more desirable than dry ones, but they seek a balance. Excessively wet kisses are unpopular (as the Danes say, "He's nice to kiss—when one is thirsty."), but a dry, tight kiss is usually regarded as either immature or inhibited. (p. 23)

It is important to note that kissing is not a naturally sexually stimulating act. According to Tieffer, "sex researchers generally agree that the only way infants and young children can be sexually aroused is by direct stimulation of the genitals" (p. 35). The arousal from kissing is largely caused by the attachment of sexual symbols with the act itself. "The frequency and intensity of kissing [in the United States] varies according to gender, social class, sexual orientation, and the degree of emotional intimacy that the relationship calls for" (p. 36).

Kinsey and associates (reported in Tieffer 1979) found that 90 percent of the married women in the United States reported deep kissing during marital sex. Only 41 percent of men with an eighth-grade education, however, reported tongue kissing their wives, whereas 77 percent of college-educated males reported doing so. Tieffer also reported that Kinsey also found less tongue kissing among male than among female homosexuals. Since more than 20 years have passed since these studies were reported, it would be interesting to replicate some of their studies to see if and how these findings have changed.

Kissing, then, may or may not be sexually arousing. Kissing varies by culture, gender, social class, sexual orientation, and degree of intimacy. Even in sexual encounters, kissing may be absent as a stimulating factor. Nevertheless, since the kiss is an act of intimate spacing and touching, in our culture a degree of intimacy is almost always attached to a kiss.

Morris' eighth step is *hand-to-head.* As has been noted in the Jourard (1966) and Rosenfeld, Kartus, and Ray (1976) studies, the head is an intimate part of the body. In this stage, "Fingers stroke the face, neck, and hair. Hands clasp the nape and the side of the head" (Morris 1971, 77). The next three steps increase intimacy drastically. Step nine is *hand-to-body.* Step ten is *mouth-to-breast.* Step eleven is *hand-to-genitals.*

BOX 11.2 OBSERVATIONAL STUDY

On the same show you observed for Observational Study 11.1, how much kissing did you notice? How much of it was "deep kissing"? How much of it was "just a peck"?

What message did this send about the couples? Does that seem normal relative to what you know of kissing and the messages it sends in real-life relationships?

Whether the two parties engage in all of the preceding steps, the last step will be *genital-to-genital* or *mouth-to-genital*. Two irreversible acts can take place here. First, if the female is a virgin, the hymen is ruptured. Second, fertilization is often a possibility (see Hite 1976, 1981; Morris 1971, 78; J. H. Williams 1977, 219–233). Research also reports that the psychological effects of progressing to this step are monumental for those who make that decision. For women it is more likely to be a commitment decision (of mind and body); for men it is more of a cultural expectation, where men are expected to be more sexually active (Gaylin 1992; Wood 2007). This in no way means that some women do not engage in sexual intercourse out of pleasure and desire and that some men do not do so out of a sense of commitment; to say that would be an overgeneralization of the worst type.

There has been a significant trend when it comes to the issue of oral sex. The Diagram Group (1976, 1977) stated that more than 45 percent of the men reported receiving oral sex in heterosexual relations, but only about 16 percent of them reported giving oral sex. Objections to *mouth-to-genitals* encounters ranged from unnatural to sinful to unhygienic to unpleasant. The trend on this issue, however, has changed over the last 25 years since that research was reported. Reinholtz and Muehlenhand (1995), after studying a college population, reported that 79 percent of women and 82 percent of men had performed oral sex, and 81 percent of women and 89 percent of men had received it. Whether there was an increase in activity or an increase of willingness to disclose these activities would be an issue for further research and debate.

Let us point out one issue in light of the public admissions (albeit under duress) in the Clinton–Lewinsky affair. Some popular studies are reporting that more and more teenagers do *not* see oral sex as sexual intercourse. Stories on television magazine programs such as *Dateline NBC*, CBS's *60 Minutes*, and ABC's *20/20*, as well as regular fiction programs such as *ER* and newspapers and magazines such as *USA Today*, *TIME*, and *Newsweek* have all reported these findings frequently over the last 3 years. Reports of this type are not necessarily the most scientific, but they usually have at least some degree of credibility (see Appendix). Academic research has begun to publish more studies and scholarly research that further document these "pop research" results. For example, J. D. Brown and L'Engle (2009) found in a study of adolescents that being exposed to more sexually explicit media creates a belief that oral sex is acceptable. Bersamin, Walker, Fisher, and Grube (2006) discovered that adolescents tend to separate vaginal intercourse and oral sex into two different entities, and since most parents teach normative behaviors about vaginal sex but ignore oral sex, the adolescents do not look at oral sex to be the same as vaginal sex. Bersamin et al. (2008) found similar results when they replicated this study. Further scientific study would either confirm such findings of the aforementioned media sources as well as research studies, or give us reason to not accept them at face value.

We should point out that the first six steps of this process are considered *immediacy-type* behaviors; the last six are *intimacy-type* behaviors. We also point out that the steps are progressive, at least by most people's accounts. If you skip one step (or more), you are often considered to be "fast" or "loose" or "a player." (As an author of this text tells the class, you cannot get to step two of Morris' steps and jump to step eleven, at least in most cases.) Also, if you fail to respond to a step, you send the message either that you are "slow" or that you are not interested in more intimate relations with that person.

Since the first edition of this book, published 25 years ago, the degree to which sexual promiscuity has occurred has decreased tremendously. The always-present threat of venereal disease has had an upsurge. More significant, however, has been the media deluge of information about AIDS, a disease of startling proportions in which sexual histories are recorded in each sexual act. In addition, conservative organizations (religious and social movements in particular) have attempted to bring to the forefront of the public agenda the concept of total abstinence. Some groups support this idea on the basis of morality; others support it as prevention to AIDS, STDs (sexually transmitted diseases), and/or the psychological well-being of the younger generation. Certainly, sexual behaviors today are much more reserved than they were years ago.

ENVIRONMENT, PROXEMICS, CHRONEMICS

By now the basketball game has been completed. The next thought for Jaime is the uncertainty of where they are going next, how much intimacy Kelly will attempt, and when Kelly will take the next step. (We must remember that Kelly and Jaime are no longer strangers in the strictest sense; they have completed step three and may have completed Morris' step four if they held hands walking to the coliseum.) The environment in which the next interaction takes place will have a significant impact on the answers to the other questions.

Kelly decides to take Jaime to the local bar. Naturally, as Sommer (1969) has described them, bars are designed for drinking: "In the pub there is a general freedom from anxiety—any man with the money can be certain of a welcome" (p. 122). In the bar a person may have some privacy, but the general rule is to be open to interaction with others in the bar. The nature of the particular environment ranges from place to place, based upon legal restrictions and social customs. The duration of one's stay in a bar will depend upon lighting, noise level, others present, other stimuli, types of alcohol, and the amount of funds available.

College towns usually have bars that cater to various types of audiences. As Mehrabian (1976) notes: "At the high-load extreme, there should be a large dancing bar featuring 120-decibel hard rock, strobe lights, and a laughing, pushing, shouting, sweating mob" (p. 255). Remember, though, that was in 1976; is the bar scene still the same today, and if not, how does it differ? Going to a bar allows the two to eliminate some anxiety and inhibitions. If dancing is allowed, the amount of touching is increased. At this point, the two begin to know one another rather well. When Kelly takes Jaime home, she asks him to come in for one last drink. The nonverbal, interpersonal processes that occur after this are pretty much left up to the interactants, and we'll leave them to your imagination.

Keep in mind that the foregoing is one scenario only. The situation will depend on Kelly's and Jaime's personalities, intellects, communication tendencies, moral beliefs, even perhaps their religiosity (or lack thereof). The context will also affect this scenario, including anything from this being a first date—and a "blind date" at that,—the choice of the basketball game over a movie, whether or not Kelly and Jaime are "on the rebound," even the weather outside. If this were a homosexual couple, their interaction might also change somewhat. There are always many variables in relationship development, and we should never lose sight of that fact when we study the topic.

COMPUTER-MEDIATED RELATIONSHIP BUILDING

We would be remiss if we did not add to the mix that people today often meet and build romantic relationships online. If you notice the online dating websites, such as Match.com, E-Harmony.com, ChristianSingles.com, and Zoosk.com, among others, you'll find that online dating has become big business in our society. Some say since we have become so attuned to using the Internet for everything, why not use it for dating, while others say it makes it easier to make the not-so-physically attractive more attractive. Several studies have found that we are using the Internet to build relationships, and especially we use social networking sites like *Facebook* to create and build friendships. And regardless of what people tell you, we are influenced by the attractiveness of the photos that are posted on these websites. Wang, Moon, Kwon, Evans, and Stefanone (2010) discovered that both males and females are much more willing to develop friendships with individuals who post more physically attractive photos than those who post either unattractive photos or no photos at all (see also Wang, Moon, Kwon, Evans, and Stefanone 2009). In an interesting study of using computer-mediated communication (CMC) to develop friendships with others, Ramirez and Wang (2008) tell us that when you change the "modality" of building a relationship from online to face-to-face, you will more than likely find yourself in an expectancy violation situation. In other words, what you think you have been getting is not at all what you get when you meet with the person face-to-face.

Perhaps you are wondering if there any male and female differences in the use of CMC when it comes to building relationships. Ledbetter, Broeckelman-Post, and Krawsczyn (2011) discovered that cross-sex relationships interact less frequently in CMC than do same-sex friendships. Ledbetter et al. believed, however, that this may happen to protect the idea of a platonic relationship, and to do what they call "buffer intimacy" (p. 237). Recall that Ramirez and Wang (2008) found that the expectancy violations theory was likely to occur in CMC, and realize that relationships did not progress beyond the level of friendship created in the online medium. Van Cleemput (2012) found that we are likely to use CMC to develop friendships in more depth, and that we are likely to do this with our peers. Van Cleemput discovered that we are much more likely to use technologies to communicate with our peers/ friends—text messaging, social networking websites, etc. . . . —than ever before. Think of your own online friendships and how often you communicate in an online medium only. When you have met with the person face-to-face, were your nonverbal expectations violated? Was the person less attractive or more attractive due to his/her actual presence? Physically?

Perhaps kinesic mannerisms? Vocally? Surely you can see how much the prominence of CMC in our lives today can change our whole way of building and maintaining social relationships.

Another form of mediated communication is that of *texting* (also known as *SMS* in other cultures). M. A. Harrison and Gilmore (2012) discovered that we text a great deal in order to maintain our social relationships. As they say, "Because of our intrinsic need to affiliate, our society invents and employs increasingly convenient and rapid methods of staying in touch and sharing information" (p. 513). Because of this strong desire to stay connected, we see people texting at many times when perhaps it is not the most opportune time to text. This sends the nonverbal message of disinterest in the encounter you are in when this is done at a time when you are actually interacting with someone in a face-to-face setting. Has that ever happened to you? You are carrying on a conversation with a friend, who in the middle of a sentence whips out his or her cellphone and reads a text message and then replies to it. Have you ever thought about the message that comes from that? It often comes across as disinterest in what the other person involved is saying. You might be interested to know that Harrison and Gilmore also found that people text in "seemingly inopportune situations, such as while in the shower, while at work, during religious services, and while having sex" (p. 513). Furthermore, their study found that "most participants reported texting in situations that may be considered by some as social breaches, such as while on a date, while socializing in person with others, and to break up with and cheat on a romantic partner" (p. 513). Have you used text messaging for any social breaches of which you are aware? How do you react when someone crosses the line for your social rules with their texting habits?

BOX 11.3 OBSERVATIONAL STUDY

Go to whatever social media you use, and look through the contacts you have in that medium. Make a list of the people who violated your nonverbal expectations of how they would be in person, and list the ways in which their online persona is different from their "in person" persona. Was it their appearance? Their touch norms? Their voice? Etc. . . . Discuss what this means to you as far as your own online presence in your social networking Web presence.

CROSS-SEX FRIENDSHIPS

Male–female friendships almost always carry the undercurrent possibility of there being more to the relationship if the interactants are heterosexual. Particularly if the two individuals have known each other for an extended length of time, both will be aware of this undercurrent. Although the two may touch one another, and even kiss, they must be careful about the context, frequency, and nature of these tactile behaviors. Most people, however, report having few of these relationships because of the potential problems involved (Wood 2012). Booth and Hess (1974), for example, found in one study that only 35 percent of the men and 24 percent of women reported having cross-sex friendships. These low percentages are possibly due to the connotations of the cross-sex relationship. Today, in the 2000s, these may be changing behaviors. As American culture moves toward a more androgynous nature, more cross-sex friendships without romantic or sexual connotations are likely to develop. Henningsen, Kartch, Orr, and Brown (2009) discovered, however, that flirting is more likely to occur in cross-sex friendships, and that more often than the female, the male is the one likely to think the relationship just might have the opportunity of progressing to a more romantic one than just a platonic one. Have you ever seen this happen?

These statistics are not saying that cross-sex friendships do not exist; they certainly do. As L. West, Anderson, and Duck (1996) reported, many men and women do develop friendships with each other, and they find them very rewarding. Basow (1992) reported that one reason women like to develop friendships with men is that the relationships can be more fun and less emotionally involving than those they have with women. Men, according to Basow, say the opposite is true for them; with women, they are able to have a friendship where they can be more emotive and where the friend will be more emotionally supportive. Often an issue in these kinds of friendships is that one of the "friends" already has a romantic partner. S. Williams (2005) found that jealousy is almost always a part of the mix when one partner in a romantic relationship has a friendship with someone of the opposite sex. Guerrero and Chavez (2005) do say, however, that individuals maintain these cross-sex relationships differently depending on whether or not they see the friendship leading to a romantic relationship. Those who believe the friendship might (or could) progress to a romance, and who are interested in such a progression, spend more time trying to maintain more intimate communication than those who see the relationship as strictly platonic.

These cross-sex friendships, of course, will be influenced by the many gender communication differences as well as cultural communication differences discussed throughout this text. In a study targeting adolescents, both Caucasian and African American, Pagano and Hirsch (2007) found that black "adolescent boys and girls reported similar levels of self-disclosure in their romantic relationships as they did in their same-sex friendships" (p. 354). Caucasian adolescent girls, they found, report more self-disclosure in their friendships than in their romantic relationships. Hollenbaugh and Egbert (2009) found that men and women approach how they tell the other person they are romantically interested differently, mostly that there will be increases in self-disclosure when the person becomes interested in taking the relationship in a more romantic direction. Since men usually self-disclose less than women do in relationships, this might be something to watch for if you are trying to figure out if someone is thinking your cross-sex friendship should go in a new direction. Clearly, these findings show that this is an area wide open for further research; perhaps it is something you might like to pursue?

Finally, we would be remiss if we ignored a newer concept in today's society, what is known as *friends with benefits*. What this refers to is friendships that are labeled as platonic, but which clearly have sexual intimacy as part of the relationship (Morman and Green 2009). These seem to be occurring more in today's society than they have in the past, or perhaps people are admitting to them more today than they have in the past? Goodboy and Myers (2008) found that we will use different relationship maintenance behaviors in these types of friendships. Perhaps we will be less worried about our physical appearance, or less worried about violating nonverbal touch or spacing norms. If we are not so worried about where the friendship is going, do the nonverbal pressures lessen?

STUDENT VOICES

Raven: An example I have of when cross-sex relationships can go bad happened to two of my friends. We are all a part of the same social circle, and it was clear that the two were just friends, but there was some clear flirtation happening. The only problem was that the male in the relationship wasn't willing to take it past flirtation while the girl wanted more—a full-on relationship. The male also started to bring another girl around to parties and such which made the female upset. Unfortunately, they couldn't work through their issues and don't have the same relationship that they did before.

BOX 11.4   OBSERVATIONAL STUDY

Take the same set of magazine ads from Observational Study 11.3 and decide which ones appear to show a cross-sex friendship, not an intimate relationship. What nonverbal factors used by the advertisers send that message? What message is sent about the products by these nonverbal factors?

SAME-SEX RELATIONSHIPS

Usually the sex variable becomes less important in same-sex relationships, but the power variable increases in importance. The variable of power in relationships has been studied extensively by Haley (1963):

> If one took all the possible kinds of communicative behavior which two people might interchange, it could be roughly classified into behavior which defines a relationship as *symmetrical* and behavior which defines a relationship as complementary. A symmetrical relationship is one where two people exchange the same type of behavior. Each person will initiate action, criticize the other, offer advice, and so on. This type of relationship tends to be competitive; if one person mentions that he has succeeded in some endeavor, the other person points out that he has succeeded in some equally important endeavor. The people in such a relationship emphasize their symmetry with each other.
>
> A complementary relationship is one where the two people are exchanging different types of behaviors. One gives and the other receives, one teaches and the other learns. The two people exchange behavior that complements, or fits together. One is in a "superior" position and the other in a "secondary" in that one offers criticism and the other accepts it, one offers advice and the other follows it, and so on.
>
> This simple division of relationships into two types is useful for classifying different relationships or different sequences within a particular relationship. No two people will consistently have one of the types in all circumstances; usually there are areas of a relationship worked out as one type or another. Relationships shift in nature either rapidly, as when people take turns teaching each other, or more slowly over time. When a child grows up he progressively shifts from a complementary relationship with his parents toward more symmetry, as he becomes an adult. (p. 11)

Thus, we might say that some relationships are about "equal"—that is, no one person is always "in charge." Others carry status differences and are unequal. An equal relationship

PHOTO 11.3 Do you think that cross-sex friendships are more prevalent today than when Booth and Hess (1974) did their study?

may be defined as a "liking" relationship, and an unequal one may be considered a "power" relationship. Some of you will disagree with one of those models or the other, but you must realize that many people are comfortable with the one you disagree with. Just because you want a symmetrical relationship does not mean someone else is uncomfortable with a complementary one. Let us now investigate the nonverbal communication that accompanies male–male friendships and female–female friendships.

MALE–MALE NONVERBAL COMMUNICATION

The preoccupations that males share with one another appear to be sports (as participant, spectator, and Monday-morning quarterback), power (at work and at home), masculinity, and time (Wood 2007). The fourth preoccupation finds males in a chronemic dead-heat run with themselves and with society in general. In the United States, males find that there is a rush to do more than their contemporaries; they must be better and quicker than other males. The interactions that take place between males involve power plays at work, quasi-leisure at the basketball and racquetball courts, and externally induced leisure at bars. In all of these cases there is an underlying tension, as if there is more to do in life; thus the chronemic focus is on the future. Nonverbally, this also means that men will often show liking toward their male friends through restricted touch, for example in a sports situation, with affectionate punches and backslapping. This is especially true for heterosexuals.

Although the competition with time and other men is a significant factor in the life of American men, most also attempt various interpersonal, complementary relationships. Research has found that heterosexual men do communicate closeness and affection with their male friends; they just do it in a more covert fashion (Floyd 1997). For homosexual men, this seems to be less of an issue. Floyd and Morman (2000) also found that homophobia, and especially homophobia in heterosexual males, does affect the evaluation of expressions of affection in same-sex relationships, as did Derlega, Lewis, Harrison, Winstead, and Costanza (1989) a decade before them. Other studies report that men's friendships often have the men doing things for the people they care about and having a *give-and--take* approach to doing favors for and assisting others (Wood 2012). Be careful of stereotyping male relationships on the basis of what society says men are like; the stereotypes are often inaccurate.

MEETING THE SAME SEX

There are various contexts in which males meet one another: on the job, through mutual friends, or at recreation facilities. Unlike females, heterosexual males generally disregard physical appearance in establishing relationships with one another. Homosexual males seeking romantic partners, however, will pay as much attention to appearance as heterosexual men do when seeking female romantic partners. At the first meeting, there is a mutual attempt to determine the major interests of the other man. The conversation often leads to sports, when men define one another as baseball, football, or golf fans, for example. One primary separation is the sports fan versus the non–sports fan. Once such a separation is found, the likelihood of a long-term relationship is lessened. A second separation is between team sports and individual sports. Males are taught the concept of being a "team player" early in life, and they are expected to maintain an interest in the team phenomenon throughout life. Examples of non-team play may be "hogging" the ball when playing basketball, asking a best friend's significant other out on a date, and using "sneaky" means for beating out a competitor at work.

Males expect one another to be team players. They expect one another to accept differences (a fisherman versus a hunter versus a nonhunter) when working together on a common task. In addition, they expect one another to reward "good ol' boy" or "being one of the guys" behavior and penalize those who do not engage in it. Upon first meeting, if there is tacit agreement as to conversation topics, and if the other is perceived as a team player, the chances are good that the two will maintain at least a short-term relationship. Tiger (1974) suggested that the same-sex male relationship is likely to turn out better than a same-sex female relationship, although others would no doubt argue that point.

In a man's effort to be accepted into a group, it is necessary that he act as a team player, even at the cost of losing self-respect because of humiliation that may come as a result of harassment and discomfort. This procedure is seen in high school and fraternity initiation rites, as well as in the types of behavior needed to be promoted to colonel in the army or to full professor in academia. To be accepted, one must learn to work with men to the complete exclusion of women. Athletic teams and military units cannot allow the influence of females to destroy the team effort. The enforcement of legal statutes has changed the legality of these attitudes and behaviors, yet changing the mindset about this issue seems to be taking much longer. If you want to debate someone on a topic like this, be prepared for strong arguments about how women destroy the team spirit, or the *espirit de corps*, of the armed services. Legal or not, strong beliefs on this topic will not change easily.

The advantages of female "bonding" are found along the lines of spontaneity and confidences (Booth 1972). Male bonding is often based on machismo. According to this "real man" notion, males are viewed as independent, females as dependent. The independence carries with it a notion of control; therefore, for males, nonverbal communication is controlled. Emotions are generally covered up, whether the actual *felt* emotions are positive or negative.

Males must also be in control of their roles, for they do not generally look at one another as complete human beings but rather as complementary role players: a tennis partner, a co-worker, or a drinking buddy. We now investigate how some of these roles are demonstrated in nonverbal communication.

THE ENVIRONMENT

Many males prefer same-sex environments that exclude feminine content, at least for friendship situations: the bachelor apartment, the male bar, the poker game, a "pick-up game" of basketball at the gym, the tennis court, and often the office. The bachelor's apartment contains art objects but not of the same type as would be found in a woman's apartment. Flowery objects and flower-patterned coverings on furniture and drapes are usually omitted. Furniture fabrics are either solid or abstract, usually in earth tones. The music played on the stereo, while only males are present, is often of the hard-rock, soul, rap, or country variety. Generally, males do not prefer tender movies on television *in the presence of one another*. Instead, they usually opt for sports.

Bars with almost exclusively men present do not usually have flowers or candles on the tables. Tables do not usually have tablecloths. Beer is drunk from cans or bottles. Slot machines, pool tables, and game machines are likely to be present. In many ways, the dirtier the bar, the more *macho* it is. Interestingly, male *gay bars* take on much the same atmosphere of the male bars just described. Stereotyping gay bars to be effeminate would be a mistake.

Although this may be a little stereotypical, let us look at some other male gatherings. The poker game allows males to get down to their undershirts and smoke cigars. Here the place can be "messed up" as much as desired, without any female influence. Conversations may be continuous, but males do not feel the obligation to carry on a continuous conversation, as women do. Much of the conversation takes the form of sports talk, the poker game, kidding one another, racist and sexist jokes, and storytelling. At the tennis court, the game is all business. Multicolored tennis balls, outfits, or racquets are not acceptable. Even in these games, activity is important. According to Bell (1981), "A major value in the American masculine world is to do—to be active and get things done" (p. 79). This phenomenon does not seem to be changing.

The office is masculine, also. Technical (mechanical and electronic) "things" are present; feminine "things" are absent. Diplomas, trophies, awards, and abstract art are present. Wood and bronze occupy the office. Plastic and too many plants are absent. In many cases, however, pictures (of family or significant others) are present.

FRIENDLY INTERACTION

When male friends talk with one another, there is little touching after the initial greeting— the handshake (except for team sports, where they "pat" one another on the behind or back to signify, "Well done"). Today we also now have the much-used "man hug," where the two men begin the greeting with a handshake, bring the hand up to their chests, and reach around and pat the other on the upper back/shoulder. There is little eye contact. In terms of proxemics, males sit close enough to talk with one another, but no closer. In movie theaters, male friends often "skip" a seat between them if only two of them are there. At bars and in restaurants, they usually sit across from one another or sometimes at corners but not next to one another (if only two are present). Although some males have at least one good friend, they reveal little to one another except in times of crisis or after a number of alcoholic drinks. The following case serves as an example:

> I have three close friends I have known since we were boys and they live here in the city. There are some things I wouldn't tell them. For example, I wouldn't tell them much about my work because we have always been highly competitive. I certainly wouldn't tell them about my feelings of any uncertainties with life or various things I do. And I wouldn't talk about any problems I have with my wife or in fact anything about my marriage and sex life. But other than that I would tell them anything. [After a brief pause he laughed and said;] That doesn't leave a hell of a lot, does it? (Bell 1981, 79)

Bell also says that men will tend to have different friends for different areas of interest instead of doing everything with one person (see also Wood 2012). Although many males operate under a cloak of insecurity, this insecurity is rarely revealed to same-sex friends; however, many recent gender role changes as a by-product of feminism have allowed some freedom for the new male. He is allowed to be more emotive, to build closer relationships with male friends, and even to cry (but only if the stimulus is a critical one).

THE NEW MALE

H. Goldberg (1979, 35–38) described eight factors he felt were descriptive of the "old male." Goldberg defines the eight factors as self-destructive and feminine, as opposed to masculine,

PHOTO 11.4 What factors do you think play a role in male friends communicating their emotions nonverbally?

TABLE 11.1 GOLDBERG'S SELF-DESTRUCTIVE AND FEMININE BEHAVIORS

1. Emotional expression is feminine.
2. Giving in to pain is feminine.
3. Asking for help is feminine.
4. Paying too much attention to diet, especially when you're not sick, is feminine.
5. Alcohol abstinence is feminine.
6. Self-care is feminine.
7. Dependency is feminine.
8. Touching is feminine.

in nature (see Table 11.1). From this list, we see that factors 1 and 8 are particularly related to nonverbal communication. In the 1990s, the new male discovered that emotional expression is human, not feminine. This change in encoding behavior also gives the new male a greater sensitivity to the nonverbal communication of others. In addition, the new sensitivity allows the male to touch other males as well as females (Wood 2012). Like the European male, some American males have learned that hugging male relatives and friends is a positive action. Compare these findings with Goldberg's list in Table 11.1. How would you change Goldberg's list—or would you? If you think these characteristics are "spot on," then you indeed buy into the concept of the "old male." If you think they are passé and out of date, we could likely label you as the "new male."

Chronemics, however, remains the basic problem for the American male. Role-playing, or when men feel they must play the role of male that society has set, influences their behaviors. Both sexes go through a similar process of socialization and development, but men appear to feel a greater impact than women from aging, particularly in the middle years. McGill (1980) argues that, "mid-life crisis refers to a rapid and substantial change in personality and behavior during the age period forty to sixty" (p. 43). How many of you have noticed a nonverbal change in a male (perhaps your father or grandfather) who has reached middle age?

The mid-age crisis for a male may involve one or a combination of subcrises: (1) the goal gap, (2) vanity and virility, (3) the empty nest, (4) meeting mortality. The goal gap occurs when the individual finds that, in comparison with his peers, he is falling behind professionally. This "falling behind" is an example of the chronemic consciousness of the male. Some men accept their failure. Others go on to a new career and find new challenges; however, they often encounter failure in other areas of their lives. The wife of one man who started a new career in midlife said: "Art got what he wanted, and the kids and I lost what we wanted. We are separated now—legally, that is. The divorce will be final soon. We have been separated ever since he took the other job because he changed when he married the other job" (McGill 1980, 71). Other men have a crisis even when they have been successful in their work, sometimes because they begin to lack goals.

A second type of crisis in the middle-aged man is concerned with vanity and virility. Several physiological changes occur during this "male menopause" which is also known as "andropause." There is a slight change in gonadal functioning; there begins to be an inability to achieve erection or ejaculation. Other changes might also be occurring: "urinary irregularities;

fluid retention and resultant swelling, hot flashes; heart symptoms such as pseudo angina; peptic ulcers; itching; headaches; and dizziness. . . . [Changes most apparent to others include] liver spots, baldness, gradual weight gain, fatigue, insomnia, irritability, moodiness, and depression" (McGill 1980, 99). Males take drugs such as Viagra and Cialis to increase their sexual potency; indeed, a pharmaceutical industry related to "natural" and "herbal" treatments, from ginseng to gingko biloba, has sprung up to help men through their andropausal stage. One of your authors has observed numerous TV advertisements for an herbal product to increase male virility. The whole message of the ads, which cleverly use double entendre in every phrase of the commercials as well as numerous nonverbal phallic symbolic messages, is that a male is complete only if he is virile and is able to perform sexually. The women in the ads are only satisfied and happy when their men can perform sexually. It is no wonder men in this middle-aged group are obsessed with some of these issues, if the message the media send is one such as this example.

With these physiological changes, there are corresponding changes in behavior and personality. Males often turn to alcohol and other drugs. They may avoid sexual activity altogether, or they may seek new pleasures, often with a younger partner. As McGill (1980) relates, the daughter of one middle-aged man commented ". . . my father got old and he got horny. He began attacking every girl he got near—employees, patients, *my friends!* He cut Mom off physically and financially. He drove her to drink and worse. He's taken up with Marcia, who is my age, and their behavior together is disgusting. He's embarrassed and humiliated me and Mom just so he can stay young. This whole thing just makes me sick" (p. 96). To solve the problem of "looking young," men buy new clothes, jog, get hair transplants or use "HRT" (hair replacement therapy), dye their hair, buy sports cars, and so on, all behaviors that a few years ago would have been considered a woman's response, not a man's.

The third type of subcrisis is the empty nest. The father is concerned about his age because his last child has left home. The fourth subcrisis, mortality, is probably the core of all of the problems; who doesn't fear or even try to avoid their own mortality? Thus, both physical and psychological problems occur for many males in the middle years. Females go through a similar crisis during menopause (Money 1980). Female issues are addressed in the next section of this chapter.

BOX 11.5 OBSERVATIONAL STUDY

Call to mind a close male–male relationship you know of (if you are male, one of your own; if female, one that you think you know a lot about; if homosexual male, think about a friendship, not your romantic partner). What nonverbal communication have you seen between these men? Does that seem to fit what you have learned in this textbook is the norm for men? How? Or how not?

FEMALE–FEMALE NONVERBAL COMMUNICATION

Studies indicate that women are better encoders and decoders of nonverbal cues than are men (Richmond and McCroskey 2000; Wood 2012). Men, however, seem to be better at expressing positive emotion, whereas women are better at encoding negative emotions.

This statement may not pertain as much to encoding ability as it does to the perceptions of men and women. Because women typically smile more than men, negative emotions are detected more easily in women. On the other hand, smiles and positive expressions are less common in men; therefore, such positive expressions are more noticeable in men.

Women not only look at others more, but they also find conversation more difficult when they cannot see the person with whom they are conversing. Women, regardless of status, tend to use less personal space than men (the good old shrinkage behaviors we discussed in the chapters on kinesics). Moreover, both men and women approach women more closely. One study found that women dyads in waiting rooms sat closer than men pairs. Also, in crowded situations, women seem to become less irritated than men. F. N. Willis (1966), for instance, found that women stood closer to close friends than did males. These results seem to be the same in today's society.

Mehrabian's (1972) immediacy principle states that people are drawn to and touch those they like, withdrawing from and touching less those whom they dislike. In general, both women and men stand closer to people they like. Women, however, differ from men in that they use indirect body orientation with liked and disliked persons, using closer body orientation in neutral relationships. Body orientation also relates to status for both men and women. More direct body orientation is used with people of higher status.

FEMALE–FEMALE RELATIONSHIPS

Generalizations can be made about female–female relationships; however, these general statements seem to differ according to the intensity of the relationships. In other words, women behave differently with women who are considered mere acquaintances than with other women who are considered to be close friends. Moreover, women seem to make the distinction between friend and "close" friend more often than men do. These findings seem to be true for both heterosexual and homosexual women.

General research reports that women use conversation to build friendships with other women; they share more personal feelings, tell more details of their daily lives, and are more emotionally expressive and supportive than their male counterparts. In addition, they are not as comfortable with competition and the emotions of envy and jealousy. Women will selfdisclose more with their female friends, and they are less likely to limit those disclosures. Wood (2012) tells us that because women know each other's lives more intimately, women friends usually feel connected to each other even when separated.

In trying to distinguish among other nonverbal cues that women exhibit in same-sex relationships, consider a hypothetical situation. Cindy is an office clerk who has been employed by a company for several years. Lisa is a new employee of the company and is working in the same office as Cindy. Although their jobs are independent of each other, Cindy has more power in the relationship because she is more familiar with the procedures of the company and Lisa is just the "new kid on the block." Cindy and Lisa are acquaintances with the potential of becoming friends because of the amount of time that they must spend with each other at work. For a friendship to develop (beyond the level of acquaintance), however, Cindy's power within the relationship must be diminished. Reduction of power in a relationship, in turn, increases the level of liking.

Assuming that Cindy and Lisa are still at the acquaintance level, what are the general nonverbal norms that each one observes while playing the role of acquaintance? At this point, the perception of power in the relationship is very keen by both women; thus, Cindy's nonverbal cues tend to indicate her power. She may have more direct eye contact for longer durations with Lisa than Lisa has with her. Lisa, however, might maintain a greater distance when approaching Cindy. This may be Lisa's subconscious recognition of Cindy's power. Also, some vocalic cues might indicate more authority in Cindy's conversational voice and more friendliness (a subordinate role) in Lisa's.

At this point, although Cindy has the power in the relationship, there may be a third party whom both women would like to have as a friend. This creates an atmosphere of competition, especially if the third party is male and Cindy and Lisa are heterosexual. In this case, both Cindy and Lisa become sensitive to the nonverbal cues that each directs to the man. Each woman will monitor these cues, especially personal appearance, trying to evaluate herself as a competitor. Studies show that this situation will be the hardest part of the budding friendship, because women have a difficult time dealing with feelings of envy and competition, thinking it is wrong (Eichenbaum and Orbach 1987). If they survive the situation, the friendship can progress.

HOW FEMALE–FEMALE PAIRS REDUCE POWER AND INCREASE LIKING

One of the most common ways a woman removes a power barrier with another woman is to find a common enemy or antagonist. This enemy may be in the form of a person (perhaps a boss or a coworker), a situation (such as working conditions that neither Cindy nor Lisa likes), or a common goal. In the case of a common goal, the enemy the women have in common is what they perceive to be a barrier that may interfere with the accomplishment of the goal or project.

As Cindy and Lisa move from acquaintance to friendship, there is a consequent reduction in the amount of power that Cindy has in the relationship. In other words, as Cindy begins to consider Lisa a friend and not just a coworker, she must consequently relinquish some of the power she has over Lisa. This surrender of power is not usually a conscious act, but it is necessary. As these changes within the relationship take place, there are several nonverbal cues that may be noticed.

As the two women become friends, the nonverbal signals they exchange with each other become more equally balanced. As the relationship becomes friendlier and Cindy loses power, both women become more equal partners in the relationship. Because of this equality, Cindy's nonverbal cues are no longer indicative of power and, in turn, Lisa's are less indicative of subordination in the relationship. Some nonverbal power signs include initiating touch more, using more expansive gestures and postures, taking more liberties with the use of time and how the person dresses, having more expensive artifacts in the office environment (in this example), and even utilizing more space in the environment. Subordination cues would be the opposite, or at least the use of them to a lesser degree. Equity would mean that both women initiate these nonverbal behaviors equally. In addition, nonverbal immediacy will be important in this female–female friendship, more so than in a male–male relationship; it will be important to reducing power in the relationship (Santilli and Miller 2011). This change will increase the interpersonal interaction between Cindy and Lisa because, when a superior or a subordinate takes on the body language level of the other, the level of interpersonal communication increases.

FEMALE–FEMALE PAIRS LOSING FRIENDSHIP

Not only are there significant nonverbal cues indicative of people who are in the process of becoming friends, there are also a few cues that may indicate that the "closeness" in a relationship is being lost. This closeness is the immeasurable aspect of a relationship that distinguishes friends from acquaintances. Because we seldom choose to discuss changes in our relationships as they occur, most of these signals are nonverbal. These signals might include spending less time together, less eye contact, less touch, and things of that nature.

Often, women have very close relationships with other women. This is not to say that men are incapable or never experience this in same-sex relationships, but our society allows women to express emotion more openly than it allows men to express their feelings. Because women feel freer to express their emotions, they tend to do so more openly. This freedom of emotional expression causes the relationships of women to be more readily defined in emotional terms, rather than in terms of function or comradeship, as in male relationships.

The more open emotional aspect of female relationships is one factor that causes the nonverbal cues of women to differ from those of men in same-sex relationships. Because nonverbal signals are more indicative of emotion than of cognition, situations involving more emotional expression should draw different nonverbal responses than would those situations with less emotion.

BOX 11.6 OBSERVATIONAL STUDY

Call to mind a close female–female relationship you know of (if you are female, one of your own; if male, one that you think you know a lot about; if homosexual female, think about a friendship, not your romantic partner). What nonverbal communication have you seen between these women? Does that seem to fit what you have learned in this textbook is the norm for women? How? Or how not?

Friendships are important in everyone's lives. Ledbetter (2009) found that we are more likely to build friendships (of any type—cross-sex, same-sex) and work at maintaining them when we are raised in a family that is more oriented toward conversation. He also found that if you are raised in a more conversationally oriented family (meaning that conversation is an important part of familial life), you are more likely to work at maintaining friendships in face-to-face settings. These days, with the ever-present phenomenon of popular social networking websites (Facebook, MySpace, LinkedIn), we are seeing more and more people attempt relationship maintenance in online venues than we have seen in the past. This area of friendship and relational maintenance will surely be an area deserving of future research studies.

STUDENT VOICES

Olivia: My suitemate decided to set up her boyfriend's roommate with a mutual friend of ours on a double date. Though my suitemate thought they would make a good match, I did not have such high hopes as he did not seem like her type. I ended up being right as when they met for the first time, I could tell that he was more "into" her than she was to him. She smiled at him in a more polite way than an "I am attracted to you" way. After the initial introduction she told me that he was not her type at all and was way too short for her; he, on the other hand, had the perception they would make a good match. Their intimate behaviors were limited to the third stage of Morris' courtship behaviors, despite his best efforts. It was their lack of intimate behaviors that communicated to her date that there would not be a second.

SUMMARY

In social situations, nonverbal communication differs according to the gender and the relative power of the interactants. As has been noted, increasing power decreases liking, and vice versa. As we begin to enter into social relationships, certain nonverbal communication is expected. These expectations, however, differ according to both the sexual composition of the relationship and the outcome expected (simple friendship or an increasing bond toward intimacy) by one or both parties.

QUESTIONS FOR THOUGHT

1. In what way does nonverbal communication function in the initiation, establishment, and continuance of social interaction?
2. Based on Morris' (1971) stages of intimacy, how would you describe differing cultural mores toward not only the establishment of intimacy, but the way in which such stages are carried out (i.e., which are private, and why)?
3. Is the "new male" really new? Was Goldberg right to contrast "maleness" and "femaleness"? Based on your personal experiences with males, is the male of the new millennium any different than that of the latter half of the 1990s? How? What about earlier time periods, such as the 1960s, 1970s, 1980s, and the first half of the 1990s? How? If so, how have the changes happened?
4. Has the "bonding" between male–male and female–female interactions changed over the past 20 years? If so, how?
5. Based on the current research, how do nonverbal subcodes and the behaviors entered into via those subcodes facilitate the establishment of a social relationship? How do they facilitate the disintegration of that same social relationship?
6. Do you have any close friendships (not intimate or love relationships) with someone of the opposite sex? If yes, what difficulties of maintaining that relationship have you had? What have been the positive by-products? How have others reacted to your cross-sex relationship?

FURTHER REFERENCES

Meeting Others

Brown, S., Francis, P. L., and Lombardo, J. P. (1988). Sex role and opposite sex: Interpersonal attraction. *Perceptual and Motor Skills*, 58, 855–859.

Browning, J. R., Kessler, D., Hatfield, E., and Choo, P. (1999). Power, gender, and sexual behavior. *Journal of Sex Research*, 36, 342–347.

Dunkle, J. H., and Francis, P. L. (1990). The role of facial masculinity/femininity in the attribution of homosexuality. *Sex Roles*, 23, 157–158.

Furnham, A., and Radlye, S. (1989). Sex differences in perception of male and female body shapes. *Personality and Individual Differences*, 10, 633–642.

Guéguen, N. (2008). The effects of women's cosmetics on men's approach: An evaluation in a bar. *North American Journal of Psychology*, 10, 221–227.

Hill, R. A., Donovan, S., and Koyama, N. F. (2005). Female sexual advertisement reflects resource availability in twentieth-century UK society. *Human Nature*, 16, 266–277.

Koernig, S. K., and Page, A. L. (2002). What if your dentist looked like Tom Cruise? Applying the match-up hypothesis to a service encounter. *Psychology & Marketing*, 19, 91–110.

Nash, R., Fieldman, G., Hussey, T., Leveque, J., and Pineau, P. (2006). Cosmetics: They influence more than Caucasian female facial attractiveness. *Journal of Applied Social Psychology*, 36, 493–504.

Intimate Behavior

Grammer, K., Honda, M., Juette, A., and Schmitt, A. (1999). Fuzziness of nonverbal courtship communication unblurred by motion energy detection. *Journal of Personality & Social Psychology*, 77, 487–508.

Guéguen, N. (2010). The effect of a woman's incidental tactile contact on men's later behavior. *Social Behavior & Personality: An International Journal*, 38, 257–266.

Hettrich, E. L., and O'Leary, K. D. (2007). Females' reasons for their physical aggression in dating relationships. *Journal of Interpersonal Violence*, 22, 1131–1143.

Horn, J. C. (1986). Measuring man by the company he keeps. *Psychology Today*, 20, 12.

Jurich, A. P., and Polson, C. J. (1985). Nonverbal assessment of anxiety as a function of intimacy of sexual attitude questions. *Psychological Reports*, 57, 1247–1253.

Moore, M. M. (2002). Courtship communication and perception. *Perceptual & Motor Skills*, 94, 97–105.

Regan, P. C., Shen, W., De La Peña, E., and Gosset, E. (2007). "Fireworks exploded in my mouth": Affective responses before, during, and after the very first kiss. *International Journal of Sexual Health*, 19, 1–16.

St. Lawrence, J. S., Hansen, D. J., Cutts, T. F., Tisdelle, D. A., and Irish, J. D. (1985). Situational context: Effects of perceptions of assertive and unassertive behavior. *Behavior Therapy*, 16, 51–62.

Wagner, H. L., MacDonald, C. J., and Manstead, A. S. R. (1986). Communication of individual emotions by spontaneous facial expressions. *Journal of Personality and Social Psychology*, 50, 737–741.

Walsh, D. G., and Hewitt, J. (1985). Giving men the come-on: Effect of eye contact and smiling in a bar environment. *Perceptual and Motor Skills*, 61, 873–874.

Friendships—Cross-Sex and Same Sex

Bello, R. S., Brandau-Brown, F. E., Zhang, S., and Ragsdale, J. D. (2010). Verbal and nonverbal methods for expressing appreciation in friendships and romantic relationships: A cross-cultural comparison. *International Journal of Intercultural Relations*, 34, 294–302.

Bingham, S. (1996). Sexual harassment on the job, on the campus. In J. T. Wood (Ed.), *Gendered relationships: A reader* (pp. 233–252). Mountain View, CA: Mayfield.

Bourke, E. (2007, November). *Gendered perceptions of same-sex friendships.* Paper presented at the meeting of the National Communication Association, Chicago, IL

Comer, D., and Lindsey, A. (2007, November). *Cross-sex friendship challenges and maintenance strate-gies: Women's views of friendships with straight men vs. gay men.* Paper presented at the meeting of the National Communication Association, Chicago, IL

Emmers-Sommer, T. M. (1999). Negative relational events and event responses across relationship-type: Examining and comparing the impact of conflict strategy-use on intimacy in same-sex friendships, opposite-sex friendships and romantic relationships. *Communication Research Re-ports*, 16, 286–295.

Gomberg, E. S., and Franks, V. (1979). *Gender and disordered behavior: Sex differences in psychotherapy.* New York: Brunner/Mazel.

Guerrero, L. K., Eloy, S. V., and Wabnik, A. I. (1993). Linking maintenance strategies to relationship development and disengagement: A reconceptualization. *Journal of Social and Personal Relation-ships*, 10, 273–283.

Hite, S. (1976). *The Hite report: A nationwide study of female sexuality.* New York: Dell.

Hite, S. (1981). *The Hite report on male sexuality.* New York: Knopf.

Holmstrom, A. J. (2009). Sex and gender similarities and differences in communication values in same-sex and cross-sex friendships. *Communication Quarterly*, 57, 224–238.

Huneycutt, J. M. (1991). The role of nonverbal behaviors in modifying expectancies during initial encounters. *The Southern Communication Journal*, 56, 161–177.

Johnson, C. B., Stockdale, M. S., and Saal, F. E. (1991). Persistence of men's misperceptions of friendly cues across a variety of interpersonal encounters. *Psychology of Women Quarterly*, 15, 463–465.

Knight, K. (2009, November). *I'm just not that into him: A qualitative exploration of college students' friends with benefits relationships.* Paper presented at the meeting of the National Communication Association, Chicago, IL

Malachowski, C. C., and Dillow, M. R. (2011). An examination of relational uncertainty, romantic intent, and attraction on communicative and relational outcomes in cross-sex friendships. *Communication Research Reports*, 28, 356–368.

Morman, M. T., and Floyd, K. (1998). "I love you man": Overt expressions of affection in male–male interaction. *Sex Roles*, 38 (9/10), 871–882.

O'Meara, J. D. (1989). Cross-sex friendship: Four basic challenges of an ignored relationship. *Sex Roles*, 21, 525–543.

Phillips, G. M., and Wood, J. T. (1983). *Communication and human relationships: The study of interper-sonal communication.* New York: Macmillan.

Rubin, L. (1985). *Just friends: The role of friendships in our lives.* New York: Harper and Row.

Schachner, D., Shaver, P., and Mikulincer, M. (2005). Patterns of nonverbal behavior and sensivity in the context of attachment relationships. *Journal of Nonverbal Behavior*, 29, 141–169.

Sias, P. M., Smith, G., and Avdeyeva, T. (2003). Sex and sex-composition differences and similarities in peer workplace friendship development. *Communication Studies*, 54, 322–340.

Stacks, D. W., and Burgoon, J. K. (1981). The role of nonverbal behaviors as distracters in resistance to persuasion in interpersonal contexts. *Central States Speech Journal*, 32, 71–73.

Weger, H., Jr., and Emmett, M. C. (2009). Romantic intent, relationship uncertainty, and relationship maintenance in young adults' cross-sex friendships. *Journal of Social and Personal Relationships*, 26, 964–988.

Wright, P. H., and Scanlon, M. B. (1991). Gender role orientations and friendship: Some attenuation but gender differences still abound. *Sex Roles*, 24, 551–566.

Computer-mediated Communication in Relationship Building

Antheunis, M. L., Schouten, A., Valkenburg, P. M., and Peter, J. (2012). Interactive uncertainty reduction strategies and verbal affection in computer-mediated communication. *Communication Research*, 39, 757–780.

Ganster, T., Eimler, S. C., and Kramer, N. C. (2012). Same same but different? The differential influence of similies and emoticons on person perception. *CyberPsychology, Behavior and Social Networking*, 15, 226–230.

Kalman, Y. M., and Rafaeli, S. (2011). Online pauses and silence: Chronemic expectancy violations in written computer-mediated communication. *Communication Research*, 38, 54–69.

Parkinson, B. (2008). Emotions in direct and remote social interaction: Getting through the spaces between us. *Computers in Human Behavior*, 24, 1510–1529.

Riordan, M. A., and Kreuz, R. J. (2010). Cues in computer-mediated communication: A corpus analysis. *Computers in Human Behavior*, 6, 1806–1817.

Sheer, V. C. (2011). Teenagers' use of MSN features, discussion topics, and online friendship development: The impact of media richness and communication control. *Communication Quarterly*, 59, 82–103.

Vandergriff, I., and Fuchs, C. (2012). Humor support in synchronous computer-mediated classroom discussions. *Humor: International Journal of Humor Research*, 25, 437–458.

Walther, J. B. (2012). Interaction through technological lenses: Computer-mediated communication and language. *Journal of Language and Social Psychology*, 31, 397–414.

CHAPTER 12

NONVERBAL COMMUNICATION IN THE FAMILY

KEY CONCEPTS

- Nonverbal Communication in the Home
- Nonverbal Communication in the Family
- Nonverbal Communication in Marriage and Committed Relationships
- Nonverbal Communication with Children
- Nonverbal Communication with the Elderly

OBJECTIVES

By the end of the chapter you should be able to:

- Explain how nonverbal communication operates within the environment of the home and within the family.
- Describe how the various subcodes affect self-presentations both in the home and as a family.
- Describe how one's nonverbal communication changes as one's relationship with others moves from dating to marriage and committed relationships and to the creation of a family.
- Discuss the role nonverbal communication plays in helping to maintain a healthy marriage or committed relationship.
- Discuss how nonverbal communication functions in childhood.
- Explain nonverbal communication and its role in aging.

This chapter extends the study of nonverbal communication to the family. When we think of the family, we usually associate it with a continuing relationship between self and others, or "significant others," in terms of parent and peer or husband and wife. We use nonverbal communication in our family relationships in the home.

Much of our communication in the home is expressed nonverbally. As we become more intimate, more relaxed with one another in relational terms, we speak less, feel the need to speak less, and communicate more nonverbally; some refer to this as "comfortable silence."

The impact of nonverbal communication in the family can be found at a number of levels, fulfilling a number of functions. Many things change when two people move from the notion of the individual to that of the family. Many family conflicts are associated with nonverbal communication. In part, these conflicts occur because control in the family is different from control at work; the lines of authority are not as readily established at home. Additionally, families often identify and present themselves through their nonverbal communication.

Nonverbal communication associated with the home—where most family communication occurs—functions to establish a family self-presentation and the beginnings of relational development. We begin our study of the family here because most of us associate a home with a physical place, a sanctuary or refuge where we can hide from the world, an environment we sometimes use to express ourselves both publicly and privately. We do so, however, with the knowledge that little research has examined the impact of the home on communication per se. As we examine the home, keep in mind the identification and self-presentation functions associated with the nonverbal message.

THE HOME

The home may be more than a simple place of residence; the word may also have a psychological interpretation that affects communication. How many times have you heard someone say, "Would you act like that in your home?" even when that action takes place in your apartment, dormitory room, or a house you just bought? Home, then, means first of all some physical locale in which we place ourselves. It is environmental in that we express ourselves within it; it is spatial because we seek to use it as both territory and an extension of our personal space. We seem to think that time is different between home and other locations. Finally, we leave certain olfactory "signatures" in our homes. Our behaviors, especially those relating to touch, change greatly in the home and even more so in specific parts of the home.

SPATIOTEMPORAL DIMENSIONS

Within the home, we generally perceive the spatiotemporal factors first. Spatiotemporal factors are defined as nonverbal factors we perceive rather than factors we actually observe. The following section examines these spatiotemporal factors, or how the environment, space (territory and personal space), touch, and temporal and olfactory elements influence communication in the home.

ENVIRONMENTAL FACTORS

Anyone who has thought of buying a house knows that many considerations must be taken into account before selection. Consider, for instance, the appearance of the home; we usually live in a house that reflects our personality and satisfies our needs. There seems to be a relationship between the type of house we purchase and such factors as social status, degree of liberalism/conservatism, occupation, perceptions of self, and other variables. Our house becomes, to a degree, an extension of self.

One of the major decisions we make involves the physical layout of the rooms. Aside from cost and prestige (in terms of number of bedrooms and bathrooms), we want a layout that is pleasant and comfortable, as well as one that best reflects on us. Consider, for instance, a typical dormitory room. This may be square or slightly rectangular. It is usually "fixed" in that the objects are either too large to move or are bolted into position. Would you consider such a place as your home? Many students do for the greater part of a year. They act as owners (part-owners or co-owners in the case of sharing a room), and as such they have

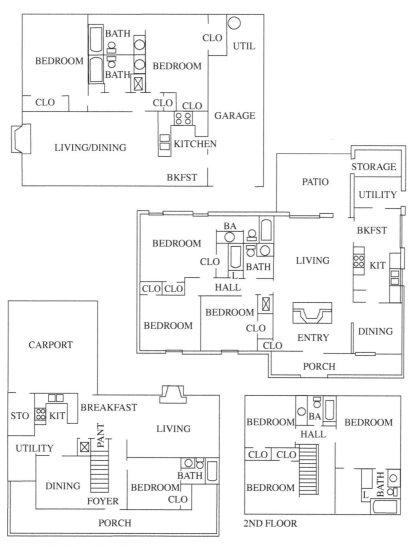

FIGURE 12.1   Which of these three housing plans best reflects your needs and desires?

many of the same needs and desires as others who live in apartments or homes. They place objects in and around the environment that reflect their own features or traits: their sex, things they like, and certain personality clues (e.g., posters, guitars, books) serve as self-presentational devices. In some instances, the student may even have "areas" of the room set off for study, sleep, relaxation, and social interaction.

This use of space is not much different from what goes on at home. What is the use of a living room, for instance, if there is also a den or family room in the house? Usually, we use the living room for more formal interactions and the den/family room for more relaxed activities. Some families even have a living room that is never used; it's just there "for show." How we use the space within the home reveals something about the owners. Some families spend a great amount of time in the kitchen. Most of us know people who always meet in the kitchen and talk (gossip) over a cup of coffee. We also know people who would never sit in the kitchen and talk, feeling that this location is improper and that the den is much better.

The environment, then, lets us know about the people living in the house. Whether it is *a home* may be better explained through the use of space: territorial demands and effects of personal spacing needs.

SPACE AND TERRITORY

An extension of the environmental factors in the home is the creation and use of space. How is the home used? As with the earlier treatment of space, this area is considered in terms of two subcomponents: territory and personal space.

According to Lyman and Scott's (1967) four types of territory, home territory is one of our most inviolate areas. J. E. Nash (1982) notes that defense of home territory extends from the physical home and its component parts to any territory the family defines as "the home." In a field study of family transformation of public territory (campsites) to home territory, Nash noted that a wide variety of territorial markers were used to establish home territory and that once these markers were established, typical home territory defenses occurred. This finding reinforces the impact of restricted access to home territory. Look at the prominence of the use of alarm systems to see just how much we want to defend our personal territory. When we are in our homes, we restrict access to specific others.

J. K. Burgoon (1983) formulated a theoretical overview of privacy. Although it does not deal directly with the home, the notion that we seek, need, or demand some form of privacy seems natural. We need privacy for a number of reasons, including a need to get away, to reduce stress in a relationship, to engage in behaviors that cannot be carried out in public (e.g., bathroom behaviors), and other reasons. In terms of the home, it seems that privacy is perceived in the following ranking: The most private are bathrooms, bedrooms, kitchens, dining rooms, and den/family rooms, and the least private are formal living rooms.

Other factors affecting how we perceive the home and various locations within it are defined by the uses we have for that space. For instance, from the historical studies on territory by Altman (Altman and Haythorn 1967; Altman, Nelson, and Lett 1972), we may find some significant parallels in the home. We usually use the bedroom as a place to cocoon, to withdraw from the pressures of day-to-day interactions. The bathroom, the most private, is treated very seriously. We do our most private things in the bathroom, but we also do other things when we treat it as a "reading room" or "library," as a place to address problems with children, and perhaps as somewhere to hide. Were you the type who used to go "hide" in the bathroom when there was a family chore—such as taking care of the dirty dishes—to be done?

Sometimes our personalities help establish territoriality in the home. Several examples include the office at home, the kitchen for the cook, and the workshop/garage for the handyperson. In addition, we sometimes have our own "places." These are perceived differently within the territory. As Roebuck and Hickson (1982) note about a stereotypical southern male, territoriality issues do exist:

> In the home the "man of the house" has his space reserved—like "Archie Bunker." Other space in the house is not reserved for anyone, except space for the redneck's few significant possessions (such as his truck, his tools, or his shotgun). Generally speaking, the woman in the house has no rights to social space and the children have few. (p. 117)

We do realize that the term *redneck* is pejorative, and we use it with great trepidation. The issue is that people do stereotype others from different geographical regions, and when Roebuck and Hickson wrote their book, the idea was to point out the phenomenon of how we stereotype and treat others based on their places of origin, in this case males from the southern region of the United States. This description, although aimed at a specific subculture of the greater public, could really be extended to many other people. For the most part, we establish a territory we deem "ours." Siblings, for instance, when possessing a room of their own, often lock their bedroom doors so that others cannot get in, especially ones with prying eyes. From this type of behavior—the notion of private property within the home—comes the feeling that a certain room is his or hers. What family has not had the argument with a teenage child about what is private in the home and how much privacy a child is allowed from his or her parents? Men and women view this concept differently, as we discussed earlier.

In addition, cultural backgrounds of families will affect privacy requirements and needs. Individuals from African American families will be different from Caucasian American individuals in their privacy needs and desires. People from Eastern cultures, such as Japan and China, who live differently than we do in the United States, will have different privacy needs. Many Japanese families all sleep together in the same room, which can also double as a living and eating area, so the privacy of going to their own rooms and closing the doors is virtually nonexistent.

An extension of the home is also perceived in how we use personal space. Most notably, we design our homes to create the best of all worlds. We establish enough space to "feel at home," yet we want our space close enough to feel like a family unit. Most dens or family rooms are laid out to accomplish two tasks: to view the television throughout the room and to make conversation convenient and easy. Most of the time, however, we only accomplish one or the other.

Probably the most important aspect of personal space, other than arrangement, is the perception of space we have—density. As noted earlier, density can cause interpersonal problems (McCain, Cox, and Paulus 1976). As space decreases within the home, members are forced to be with each other more. This may seem to be a positive feature, but as density increases, so also do family problems. The need to have some space, especially for males, who react more negatively to crowding, explains the need for privacy even within the home (J. L. Freedman 1971).

In sum, we plan our houses as comfortable yet personalized environments; within this environment we create special territories that may be set aside for the use of one or more family members. We then manipulate our contact by arranging the furniture in specific ways to increase or decrease distances for normal interactions.

BOX 12.1 OBSERVATIONAL STUDY

What does your "home" (dorm room, apartment, your parents' home) look like right now relative to these environmental factors we have discussed? What in that territory makes it yours? What messages are sent by your "home" territory (e.g., how have you decorated it, painted it, arranged it)?

TOUCH

We may expect touch norms to change in the home. Inside the home our touch behavior becomes more idiosyncratic as it relates to the level of intimacy within the family. In public there are the usual norms: touch is usually withheld unless a "proper" occasion allows for it. On the other hand, within the home, the frequency of touching increases. Not much research has really focused on this point; within the home, it would seem, touch is still a rather strong message.

Touch is used both to demonstrate intimacy and to serve as punishment. In this regard, the research demonstrating a context to touch (i.e., the location allows for touch or no touch) would seem to demonstrate that the home is one location where opposite-sex touch is allowed. The type of touch we might expect to observe would probably cover the entire range as noted by Nguyen, Heslin, and Nguyen (1975, 1976). Married couples, of course, should experience more intimate types of touch, such as the last five stages of courtship suggested by Morris (1971). The more private the room, the more arousing the touch; thus implying that a "love/intimacy" and "sexual arousal" type of touch change greatly even within the home, at least for most of the American public.

One area that the home and touch certainly affect is the degree of co-orientation found among family members. Co-orientation refers to the concept that members who live in that home have the same type of nonverbal orientation as the other members of that household; if one person is a "high toucher," then the rest of the household members are likely to be. This relationship, of course, is not true all the time, but there often is some degree of co-orientation in a home. In general, the more touch found in the home, the greater the liking and the less the stress. As demonstrated in research, people who are comfortable with each other engage in more other-oriented than self-oriented touch (Birchlier, Weiss, and Vincent 1975). The more touch one observes in a family, the better the relations between members. Further, within the home some of the more stringent norms for adult–adult and adult–child touch can be relaxed.

According to Prescott's (1975) findings on socialization, we should expect that as touch increases in the family, interpersonal relatedness should improve. Research, however, has not examined this question thoroughly, and perhaps this is an area that has grabbed your interest for researching on your own. Also, cultural differences will affect how much touch is normal in a family. For example, Asian cultures that touch even less than we do in the United States (since ours is considered a low-touch-oriented culture) would not communicate the same things reported here; they would not be likely to say that the use of touch communicates acceptance or a lessening of stress.

STUDENT VOICES

Colby: I experienced intimate touch over the Thanksgiving break with my family. My sister lives in Canada and my parents live nine hours from here, so needless to say we do not see each other very often. When we do get together it is a marathon of hugs and kisses, expression of our affection for each other, by way of touch.

TEMPORAL AND OLFACTORY ELEMENTS

Little is known about how time and olfaction are differentiated in the home, but each home seems to have an **olfactory signature** (R. Porter and Moore 1982). When we enter a home, we initially smell several things. Such smells tell us something about: (1) the ethnic background of the inhabitants, (2) the hygienic habits of the inhabitants, and (3) how long the inhabitants have lived there. Moreover, certain smells seem to linger: tobacco and animal odors; perfumes and other deodorizers; musty smells and other age indicators. Finally, there is a certain, perhaps unconscious, odor that we associate with *home*. Most of us have positive emotional attachments to such smells, which bring back memories of days gone by. When you walk into your home after having been away for a little while, do you take a deep breath and think, "Oh, yes. This is home"?

KINESIC FACTORS

Within the home, kinesic behaviors acquire different meanings. In public we typically mask our facial expressions and reduce the degree to which we emphasize other expressions. In the home, however, we engage in both facial and body displays that are more "open" yet idiosyncratic. First, considering the relative intimacy of the home, we may be more open with our gestures in conversation. Second, because we are more at ease in the home, our body posture is more relaxed, and our gestures become more expressive. Finally, we may create more emblems or emblematic illustrators in the home, using certain gestures with particular meanings.

Cultural backgrounds may well play a role in the actual eye behaviors of families. As we have discussed throughout, cultural backgrounds affect everything in the family, just as they do outside the family context. For example, Schofield, Parke, Castañeda, and Coltrane (2008) found some interesting results when looking at families of Mexican American (MA) and Euro-American (EA) descent. They discovered that MA families are less likely to engage in mutual gaze when conversing, but they discovered that EA children are much more likely to use gaze aversion than their MA counterparts. The difference in these eye contact patterns is that gaze aversion is usually considered a conscious and purposeful act, whereas not establishing mutual gaze is more of an unconscious or subconscious act of just not making eye contact with others. Schofield et al. surmised: "To the extent that gaze levels are a vehicle for expressing respect toward higher-status targets, these ethnic differences may be a result of the greater emphasis on signaling respect toward parents in MA than EA families" (p. 181). If we were to carry out studies about cultural differences in other cultures than the mainstream American culture, we would surely find many such differences. For that reason, we do not take a position that there are any "cut-and-dried rules" about how families communicate with their kinesics.

VOCALIC FACTORS

Closely associated with the kinesic behaviors are the vocalic cues found in the home. It seems that silence increases in the home. This may only be true for adults, however, because children view the home as the primary "work" and living place. As intimacy increases, the need for verbal communication appears to decrease. Long periods of silence are accepted and may become the norm.

STUDENT VOICES

Grady: You know, I never really thought about it, but vocalics really does play a role in my family. My father was born and raised in "The South" but has no noticeable accent to me. The interesting thing to me is that everyone who meets him says that they can tell he is a "good ole' boy" by his accent, the accent that I cannot hear. My best friend's mother has a thick Southern mountain accent that she hardly detects, yet all of our friends ask her to put her mother on speakerphone so they can hear her accent.

PHYSICAL APPEARANCE

The final subcode to be examined within the home is physical appearance. Within the home, physical appearance is often "let down." Behind the barriers of the home, we can relax the constant pressure to "look good." Unlike what we discussed in the previous chapter about reasons to look your best, we tend to place less emphasis on such normal activities as showering and shaving and we dress in a more relaxed manner in the home. In many ways, however, we change such behavior when we open the door. When the doorbell rings, we normally re-dress, smooth our clothing, and sometimes have the "most respectable" person answer the door. Within the home, we also place less stress on accessories.

REVIEW

Nonverbal communication in the home is a function of how we present ourselves to family members and to others. Because the home is considered a physical or territorial entity, it influences nonverbal communication. Indeed, the home may even establish "new" norms, such as silence and touch. But the home is more than just a physical entity; it also seems to engender the notion *of family*. We next examine the nonverbal aspect of the family in terms of control and relational development as well as the impact of nonverbal communication on children and the elderly.

BOX 12.2 OBSERVATIONAL STUDY

Take your own family situation and analyze it according to these five areas: touch, temporal and olfactory elements, kinesics, vocalics, and physical appearance. What issues about these nonverbal elements stand out to you? How many of your nonverbal behaviors are the same or similar to those of your parents and/or your siblings? Had you ever taken note of this before?

NONVERBAL COMMUNICATION IN THE MARRIAGE AND COMMITTED RELATIONSHIPS

Most people assume that a successful committed relationship, such as marriage or similar partnering, is one between two people of approximately equal attraction and of similar interests who are satisfied with each other's company. Within these relationships, and before the arrival of children, comes a time of adjustment. This adjustment deals partly with sharing an environment and partly with changing nonverbal behaviors.

Much of the research concerning nonverbal communication in committed relationships deals with marriages and comes from couples who are at a low ebb in their marriages. As Sillars (1984) noted, most of the previous marital research has been concerned with affective and dominance problems in the marriage. Koerner and Fitzpatrick (2002) tell us that one of the most important aspects of communication between spouses or partners is to be able to correctly decode the messages of the partner. Floyd and Riforgiate (2008) recently reported how important it is for spouses and committed partners to express affection toward each other. They especially point to the actual scientific confirmation of predicting lower stress levels experienced by couples who do express their affection toward each other. This bodes well for a quicker recovery from stress issues. This study opens up an area of study that combines both health issues as well as communication issues. Can you imagine a doctor prescribing a little dose of affection to "cure just what ails you"?

A natural progression of study would show similarities in other committed relationships, such as heterosexual and homosexual couples living together, or homosexual unions (some legal, some not, according to whatever state laws exist regarding this issue). Problems in marriages often end in a conflict *pattern* composed of verbal and nonverbal cues (Turner 1988). Although most research on marital communication has been on the verbal aspects of conflict, the nonverbal elements associated with conflict patterns are beginning to be recognized. As Turner notes, "conflicts are expressed in verbal *and* nonverbal behaviors [emphasis added]" (p. 3). The emphasis on conflict, however, tends to isolate some nonverbal behaviors from others and to ignore other behaviors that (a) may predate the distressed behavior and/or (b) may not recognize it. This section reviews the available research on marital satisfaction and conflict. We suggest that you also apply this information to other committed relationships you know of that do not meet the standard label of marriage, since many of the less traditional forms of committed relationships are similar in nature to what is considered the norm for marriages.

We have seen some research into other factors of committed relationships, including immediacy. Hinkle (1999) found that nonverbal immediacy between spouses plays a significant role in maintaining relational satisfaction. Hinkle's findings support earlier findings about successful relationships being dependent on "liking" and working at preserving the relationship (Canary, Stafford, Hause, and Wallace 1993). As Hinkle observes, the literature available has not yet "identified specific behaviors associated with liking" (p. 82). It is an area that deserves more scientific research. One interesting thought to hold on to is how much do media influence what our views of a home and family life are. Dickinson (2006) believes that movies especially depict specific norms for families, and this does influence how we think about what our lives should be like. As he reported, movies such as *Pleasantville, The Truman Show, American Beauty,* and *Far From Heaven* send us a specific message:

> The ethos of these films create spatialized imaginations in which safety, comfort, normalcy, are structured within the white heterosexist spaces of suburbia. More, however, the films point to the edges, the apparently unsayables, of contemporary life. Crossing over into this dangerous territory, these films seek to create the human subject in the suburb through the imagining of the sublimity (and thus the unsayability) of same-sex, cross-racial, cross-generational, and even cross-species (in *Edward Scissorhands)* sex. (p. 226)

ENVIRONMENTAL FACTORS

Some research extends the family to the social interactions in the community and infers a relationship between social and family relationships (see Proshansky, Ittelson, and Rivlin 1970). This analysis implies that family relations and social relations operate together; if the social aspect is altered, then the marital or committed relationship may change. For example, if one of the partners loses his or her job because of poor economic conditions, the family relationship is likely to go through some changes. The partner who loses the job may become depressed, which will affect communication. We saw a lot of this in the financial difficulties of the United States. from 2008 to the time of this writing.

A second feature of the environment deals with who creates the home. Which partner in the relationship is responsible for which room? The total decor? The exterior? These questions need to be answered. How many marriages and committed relationships, for instance, divide the environmental aspects and the placement of objects, according to one of the partners? As noted earlier, who "owns" which room? Informal analysis by students in classes we authors teach indicates that the female may have more of a voice than the male, but this arrangement is highly variable. In homosexual male committed relationships, it would be interesting to determine if one specific partner becomes responsible for what is commonly *assigned* to the female in heterosexual marriages and committed relationships. Conversely, it would be interesting to study which partner assumes the typically male environmental roles in lesbian committed relationships. In researching this updated edition, there were no such articles from scholarly journals found; perhaps that might be an area where you have some interest and you might be able to conduct some research into it.

SPACE

One of the best indicators of potential distress in a marriage or committed relationship is the increasing need for territory. Usually, satisfied committed couples spend much time in each other's company. However, as one female noted in a class analysis of her forthcoming divorce (the husband was still living in the home):

> My husband and I became informally separated but with his continuing to live in the house while we continued with our marital counseling. He lived in another part of the house, and our inter-personal contacts continued to decrease. . . . I beat a retreat to my bedroom, closing the door against the intrusion of the others. I began a lengthy siege there . . . emerging only when necessary.

During a positive committed relationship experience, we all expect that such behavior would not occur. However, there are times when we all need to get away from the presence of others, to "cocoon" for a while. Over time, we would also expect our personal space needs to change in our relationships. At the beginning of living together, personal space needs in the home are probably less than those at later stages. If the relationship continues and intensifies, the expected personal space would likely change from closer to farther and then back to closer as the years continued. As the transition from an extreme emotional bond to one of less intensity occurs, there may be a perceived need for more space (yet still less than that found in initial interaction and more than during courtship and "newlywed" stages). As the partners become comfortable with each other over time, the space need may decrease.

TOUCH

The amount of touch exhibited by both partners tends to be idiosyncratic, but as long as satisfaction with the relationship is high, the relative amount of touch, and the frequency of touch, should remain high. As dissatisfaction with the relationship increases, as it becomes distressed, touch between partners should decrease and self-touch increase (Birchlier, Weiss, and Vincent 1975). In most marriages, for example, touch decreases somewhat from the first years of marriage, but not as much as when dissatisfaction is present. Similar results would be natural for other committed relationships. Men and women in committed relationships experience touch differently. Hanzal, Segrin, and Dorros (2008) found that men had more positive reactions to intimate touch in marriage relationships than women did. They also found that in cases of non-intimate touch the responses between the two sexes were comparable.

In marriage and committed relationships, regardless of whether they are heterosexual or homosexual, touch seems to be the premier way the individuals indicate interest in sexual relations. We see many studies done on the heterosexual populations, and Beres, Herold, and Maitland (2004) conducted a study with a homosexual population (of both gay men and lesbians) and found that nonverbal behaviors are the most common way that partners indicate consent to have sexual relations with their partners. As discussed earlier in this textbook, Knöfler and Imhof (2007) reported that there are not too many differences in these areas concerning touch between heterosexuals and homosexuals. Whether this is a norm for committed relationships you know of will, as always, be influenced by the context as well as the participants.

KINESICS AND VOCALICS

Researchers have examined the impact of kinesics and vocalics on marital communication. In general, it has been found that (1) the nonverbal codes are better discriminators (indicators) of distress in a marriage than are the verbal messages we send, and that (2) when couples were asked to act happy, the nonverbal behaviors provided the only discriminating basis for distinguishing between distressed and nondistressed couples (Gottman 1980). These findings would no doubt carry over to other committed relationships.

A study by Gottman and Porterfield (1981) theorized that the ability to read the other's nonverbal cues may be related to the degree of satisfaction in the marriage. The results of this study indicate that when husbands receive their wives' cues, the relationship between marital satisfaction and nonverbal communication is positive. Comparing the ability to read the wives' nonverbal cues to strangers' ability to read them, Gottman and Porterfield found that satisfied husbands were better able to read their wives' nonverbal cues, whereas the husbands of dissatisfied wives were less able to read their wives' cues. Further research (Noller 1980) infers that marital adjustment and satisfaction are also influenced by the ability to send and receive ambiguous messages. Noller and Gallois (1986) examined the relationship between the type of message sent (positive, negative, neutral affect), the nonverbal cues used, and the degree of adjustment in the marriage. They found that wives were more accurate encoders and used more positive nonverbal behaviors (e.g., smiles) with positive messages. Husbands, however, tended to use *similar* nonverbal cues (eyebrow raises and flashes) for both positive *and* negative messages. When Noller and Gallois examined the degree of marital adjustment, no differences in nonverbal accuracy were found for wives, but highly adjusted husbands were more accurate when exposed to positive messages than to neutral or negative messages. Other research indicates that there is no general tendency for good nonverbal communicators to be married to good nonverbal communicators. Buck, Kenny, and Sabatelli (1986), for instance, analyzed 48 recently married couples; their research supports this contention and the contention that marital complaints were negatively associated with the wife's nonverbal sending ability. No relationship was found for the husband's ability to send nonverbal messages and the wife's complaints in the marriage. As critical thinkers, you probably can see how these findings would apply to committed relationships that are similar to marriages.

The type of nonverbal messages reported in these studies included both kinesic and vocalic messages. The nonverbal cues included messages transmitted by means of facial expression, vocal inflection and quality, body positions, and general movement cues. In most of these studies, the nonverbal channel conveyed the more accurate message. Swain, Stephenson, and Dewey (1982) examined the function of eye contact and the relational

PHOTO 12.1   People in close relationships tend to synchronize their nonverbal behaviors.

intimacy of couples, strangers, and friends in conversation. They found that married couples engaged in *less* eye contact than did strangers or friends, thus casting doubt on the belief that the intensity of a relationship is manifested by the amount of eye contact during conversation. One possible interpretation of this finding may be that eye contact diminishes after courtship as the partners become more comfortable with each other.

Within committed intimate relationships, we can also obtain an idea of the degree of satisfaction or adjustment by examining mirroring and synchrony behaviors. When two people are attracted to each other and are positively associating the other with self, we tend to find mirroring and synchrony behaviors. In many instances the partners do not even know they are mirroring the other's behaviors. Partners in committed relationships seem to synchronize their nonverbal behaviors, which helps increase the accuracy of the communication. It may also reinforce the other's behavior and lead to a greater prediction of what the intended message is. As distress increases in the relationship, we would expect that the degree of synchrony would decrease and the amount of mirroring would be reduced.

Finally, the paralanguage cue of silence is found in these relationships. In most instances the amount of silence between the two partners should indicate a degree of comfort in the relationship. Silence, however, can communicate just the opposite. The idea that "silence is golden" is only as true as the degree of satisfaction in the relationship. Much like the use of territory and increased personal space, we can hide behind our silences, using them as effective barriers against others. We would be remiss to neglect re-mentioning the "silent treatment" here. Have you seen this occur in your own family?

Carly: I am reminded when we discuss these factors of families of our annual summer vacation trips in the car. My sister and I, like most kids, would get bored, and then start picking at each other. Usually it was by just looking at the other one, which always brought on the famous complaint "Mom, she looked at me!" Of course, this always brought on a reprimand from our parents and a directive to "Behave!" Today I often think, did I ever really say "She looked at me" as an encroachment of my territory in the back seat? My sister and I are very close these days, and we often laugh at the ridiculousness of what we said in the back seat. I think I finally got the absurdity of it when I once caught my dad laughing after I said it.

CHRONEMICS

Some research indicates that the way we use time in the marriage may be related to marital satisfaction. M. L. Lewis (1983) examined the impact of how married couples used time (in this case how task-related [work] communication affected relations in the home) and found that as the amount of time spent in task-oriented communication increased, marital satisfaction decreased. This result suggests that bringing the office home, infringing on relational time with the partner, has a negative effect on relational satisfaction. Lewis' research included both the spouse who works keeping the home and the wife working outside of the home; hence, the impact of any differences due to the sex of the spouse working outside of the home should be negligible.

PHYSICAL APPEARANCE

The role of physical appearance and attractiveness has been examined in many interpersonal studies. As noted in Chapter 11, our physical appearance and attractiveness has an effect on whether or not we will interact with others. The relationship between physical appearance and marriage or committed relationships, however, has not been studied in any great detail. What we do know is generally divided into two viewpoints. One point of view maintains that attractiveness is more important during the dating stage; the other approach infers that dating is less of a commitment than marriage or deciding to live together as romantic partners, so that we might go out with someone less attractive during dating. Marriage, according to Murstein and Christy (1976), on the other hand, is of greater duration and importance and, hence, we would try to marry at or above our level of attractiveness.

Satisfaction in heterosexual committed relationships seems to be more influenced by whether the husband or male partner feels his wife or female partner is more attractive than he is. Nevertheless, as Pearson (1985) points out, physically attractive persons are not loved more by their partners, nor do they love their partners more than do unattractive persons. She further notes that the major factor in the relationship is found in the *differences* between attraction levels rather than overall attractiveness of one of the partners.

Amplifying the results of the attractiveness research, it appears that as the comfort level of the relationship progresses, there will be a different perception of what is "good" physical appearance. Here we can consider the type of clothing worn and the amount of time spent in preparing oneself for the other. At the initial interaction stage, it is extremely important for both partners to make themselves as attractive as possible. (This would include the olfactory component.) As time progresses, the amount of effort put into looking "good" may change. We may expect that the other person will be clean, but it is no longer expected that he or she will dress and put the same effort into dressing as he or she did earlier in the relationship. In heterosexual relationships, this would seem to hold truer for males than for females, perhaps because the stereotype for the attractive male is not as firm as that for the female.

For many women the home is the primary place of work. In traditional heterosexual marriages and committed relationships, males typically dress for their jobs, changing into something different once back at home. Females working in the home, on the other hand, may wear the same attire throughout the day. For females working outside the home, however, the same dress patterns as that of males usually apply.

BOX 12.3 OBSERVATIONAL STUDY

If you are married or living in a committed relationship, survey your own relationship for the role that nonverbal elements play. What messages do they send to you and your partner about your relationship? If you are not married or living in a committed relationship, choose a television program where a committed couple comprises the main characters. What nonverbal elements do you see portrayed in that relationship? What types of messages does the portrayal send you about marriage in general?

THE EXPANDING FAMILY—CHILDREN AND THE FAMILY RELATIONSHIP

The addition of a child to the home changes almost all nonverbal norms. Before the child, couples have a certain amount of privacy and perhaps an extra room, office, or sewing room; all this changes. Extra space is given to the child, even though many parents initially have the child sleep in the same room as they do. For a while, the child's room becomes the center of attention. Since many things must occur in the environment when a baby arrives, many marriage counselors counsel their clients to not add a baby to the mix the first year of marriage. Why? Because you must learn to live with one another in a new context, and to put a baby into that mix of nonverbal communication differences can lead to a great deal of turmoil in a young family.

In terms of space, privacy now becomes a secondary matter. Along with certain environmental sounds (noise, either external or internal), the general relationship between parents and home changes somewhat. As the child grows, parents probably find that they share everything with the child, including the bathroom. They also find that the child requires touch—reassurance—and sometimes the parents will need to touch each other simply for reassurance about dealing with the child. Perhaps the variable that changes the most is time: a child knows no time. Time becomes precious for the parent who works outside the home. At the same time, the child's caregiver begins to need some time to herself/himself because the child will monopolize that time if allowed to do so.

In some instances, special clothing may be worn, for protection. In addition, there will be a different odor around the house. Depending upon what type of diaper or baby products are used, the house will smell different. The brand of powder or diaper will have a distinctive smell, often like the one parents had as babies.

Interestingly, these changes occur rapidly and are apparently accepted rather quickly. Many new parents have trouble remembering what it was like without a child. Although such changes are not always positive and may lead to marital dissatisfaction, the changes are perceived to be in the child's best interest.

Some research has investigated the question of how the child–adult interaction affects the adult's own nonverbal cues. Bates (1976) found that children, through facial observation, positive expressions, negative expressions, and forward leans, are able to exert a subtle influence on adults. Bates found that when a child played a high-positive role, adults nonverbally reacted more positively to the child than when the child played a low-positive role. The adults also allowed the child's nonverbal cues to influence their written evaluations of intellectual and social abilities positively. Hence, we are more positive about children who indicate a more positive attitude toward us and react positively. Perhaps the idea that we train the child rather than the child training us should be reexamined. Indeed, Aronsson and Cekaite (2011) discovered that in families we do train each other to do what is acceptable nonverbally, and of course we try to discourage what is unacceptable nonverbal communication. Can you think of anything you were "trained" was something you were not allowed to do nonverbally? Perhaps roll your eyes at your mom? Perhaps touch your siblings in negative ways? Even down to dinner table conversations, we learn what works and what doesn't in our own families. When we go to someone else's home, we sometimes breach what the host family considers acceptable manners simply because we learn these behaviors in our own families (Brumark 2010).

Evidence indicates that the number of children in the family and the spacing of these births affect perceptions of marital satisfaction, as well as the parents' attitude toward the child and the care given. Mohan (1981), for instance, notes that although families with four or more children account for only about 20 percent of the U.S. population, they contribute about 40 percent of the cases of child abuse. Mohan implies that the number of children and their spacing are potential sources of stress. Parents who have a large number of children over a relatively short period of time are subject to more stress and may express more rejection and less protection toward their children, compared to parents who have fewer children over the same period of time.

Braithwaite, Baxter, and Harper (1998) add to the "mixture" the idea of "blended families" (families that come from divorced parents remarrying when both spouses have children by their previous spouses) and the communication problems that arise from combining the rituals of the two families. As Braithwaite and colleagues say, "Blended family members bring with them beliefs, norms, roles, and communication patterns developed in previous family structures" (p. 114). You can see how the nonverbal rituals of separate families can be a source of communication breakdown.

NONVERBAL COMMUNICATION IN CHILDREN

For the most part, the research on child nonverbal communication deals with developmental stages of emotional and social learning, when the interplay between family members begins to shape the child's outlook on life, his or her relational development, an understanding of social norms, and the encoding and decoding of affect.

INFANTS

The process of communication, of learning to communicate, begins at birth. Once a child is born, he or she begins to receive a number of stimuli from the environment: sounds, feeling of temperature, light, and touch, to name but a few. These are *stimuli* because the child probably has no way of analyzing such information as communicative, although it may be that some precommunicative function exists to account for rudimentary processing of such "communication" (see Stacks 1983a). What is known of infant nonverbal communication has come from research that examines how the infant relates to his or her parents, other infants, and strangers. In addition, there are the studies, mentioned earlier, by Langlois and colleagues (Langlois and Roggman 1990; Langlois, Ritter, Roggman, and Vaughn 1991) that discuss the infants' recognition of facial attractiveness. Beyond that, however, most people are at a loss to explain some of the nonverbal communication issues about infants since infants cannot explain them. In terms of the nature-versus-nurture debate discussed throughout this text, this development is the first place that debate has its application. If babies are not taught (nurtured) how to communicate something nonverbally, then is it just human nature that has them do the things they do? Some studies point to the fact that even blind babies smile when given positive stimuli; how do they learn to smile if they cannot see (Langlois et al. 1991)? The answers to those questions are what will fuel this nature-versus-nurture discussion for a long time to come.

The nonverbal code is the infant's major way of communicating. Infants do learn to use kinesic behaviors to communicate from their parents. Vallotton (2012), in a study of infants in economically deprived households, discovered that children of low-income families see and learn fewer bodily gestures. Vallotton believed that if these lower-income parents would learn to gesture more and use gestures as they raise their children, their children would become better communicators once they begin interacting with the world around them. Clearly, the infant communicates bodily and emotional needs through eye contact, touch, and smiling behavior. Because the infant has not yet progressed to the stage of verbal language, the immediate messages communicated are nonverbal in nature. At a later stage (between 2 and 6, for example, when the child is learning the language), the nonverbal code takes on a less important conscious role. As we shall see, however, the nonverbal code continues to provide information in several areas.

At birth, infants have some instinctive nonverbal communication potential. For example, some research indicates that an infant immediately after birth both recognizes and prefers human faces to abstraction (Franz 1961). After birth, facial display plays an important role in the child's adjusting to the parent. Kaye and Fogel (1980) studied the interaction of mother and infant over a 26-week period. They found that when a mother was "on"—engaged in smiling, exaggerated facial expressions, or bobbing her head—versus "off"—smaller facial expressions, less smiling—the infant's periods of attention changed. When the mother was "on," attention increased. This continued through the 26-week observation period; even though the total time spent gazing at the mother decreased with age, the time looking at the mother when she was "on" did not.

Kaye and Fogel also observed that when infants were 6 weeks old, the mother's facial greetings such as nodding and smiling were rarely effective in eliciting expressive greetings from the infant. However, without the greeting, the infant almost never generated any greeting behavior. By the time the study was completed, at age 26 weeks, the infant's spontaneous greetings had become as frequent as those elicited by the mother.

Research has shown that face-to-face gazing is one of the most crucial aspects of mother–infant interaction. Apart from its basic function as a setting for interaction, face-to-face interaction enables the infant to regulate the amount of social input at an age when other means are not available. Gazing at faces and particularly at the eyes has also been shown to correlate with the level of physiological arousal. One study, however, implies that, although eye contact is important, when it is extended beyond the period of normal development, it can slow the infant's social growth (J. Berger and Cunningham 1981).

Social perception is mirrored in the infant's facial expression. Brooks-Gunn and Lewis, for example (1981), showed pictures of parents and strangers (both male and female) to 72 infants ages 9 to 24 months and filmed the infants' facial expressions at 3- to 5-second intervals. Results indicated that infants smile more often and look longer at pictures of parents than at those of strangers. Older infants (18 to 24 months) were more likely to smile at familiar than at unfamiliar faces; younger infants were more likely to smile at strange women than at strange men; there appeared to be no difference in the response to either mother or father. This study infers that even at an early age—even prior to acquisition of verbal communication—infants can display likes and dislikes through nonverbal channels. Haviland (1977) found that, aside from mirroring expression, the type of emotion expressed by the infant (positive or negative) also influences how we perceive the infant. She found that infants who expressed "negative" emotions (distress, fear, wariness) were more likely to be judged "male," whereas infants who expressed "positive" emotions (laughing, smiling) were more likely to be judged "female." Mireault et al. (2012) also discovered that infants learn their humor and how to react to humor nonverbally through interactions with their parents.

Physical appearance, both in terms of attraction and clothing, serves an important developmental function in childhood. At least two studies reflect the impact of clothing on children. In one study, Weinberg and Weinberg (1980) were interested in how others perceived newborns dressed in either blue (masculine) or pink (feminine) gowns. As might be expected, infants dressed in blue were perceived as males and those in pink as females, regardless of the actual sex of the infant. A study of toddlers by Kaiser, Rudy, and Byfield (1985) reinforces the role of clothing on stereotypical judgments. They found that girls tend to associate dresses with traditionally feminine activities and pants with masculine activities, although they found no real association with the behaviors exhibited by the girls in actual play activities. Interestingly enough, this does seem to be a changing phenomenon as the authors were not able to find any more recent studies concerning this issue in contemporary communication scholarship. However, most of us still know of people who insist on buying pink gifts for little girl babies and blue ones for little boys.

In a study with potentially far-reaching ramifications, Berkowitz and Frodi (1979) found that physical attraction influenced the degree of punishment a child receives when making mistakes. Their findings indicate that unattractive children receive harsher punishments than do attractive children. This leads to a related question: Do abused or neglected children

PHOTO 12.2 (A) AND (B) Children learn to communicate nonverbally at an early age.

display different nonverbal behaviors than nonabused children? Abused and nonabused children do possess different nonverbal behaviors (Hecht et al. 1985). These researchers observed the kinesic, proxemic, and eye contact behaviors of children ages 1 to 3 and found that abused girls were more passive in their nonverbal cues than were abused boys, whereas with the "normal" children, girls were more nonverbally active than were the boys.

Other nonverbal subcodes of interest include proximity, haptics, and olfaction. Some research indicates (1) that infants 12 to 24 months seek more proximal interaction from their mothers than from strangers; (2) that older infants initiate more play with strangers than do younger infants and adopt closer distances; (3) that physical proximity and touch decreases between mother and infant as the infant grows older, and (4) that both visual and haptic frequency decrease with age (Bretherton, Stolberg, and Kreye 1981; Clarke-Steward and Hervey 1981). Finally, perhaps two of the most important initial nonverbal subcodes are touch and olfaction. Touch research indicates that mother–infant bonding is important and plays an important part in the socialization process, although just how important touch is to the process is questionable. Olfaction is one way the infant can identify with its parents. Olfactory memory may play a large part in the bonding between mother and child, although much more information is needed in this area.

Tronick (1989) has written about emotions in infants. He indicates that the affect of infants is influenced by the emotional experience of dealing with the mother and concludes that emotions motivate and organize an infant's behavior rather than disrupt it. Davidson and Fox (1989) elaborated on infant emotions as compared with hemisphere dominance. Using 35 ten-month-old female infants who were born to right-handed parents, they researched infants' emotions when the mother was in the room and when out of the room. They found that the brain's right hemispheric region was more active during negative experiences and the left more active during positive experiences. An infant who showed right-region activity during rest was likely to cry during periods of the mother's absence. Fernaid (1989) found that the mother's "melody" in her voice had a major impact on the behavior of an infant, and Legerstee (1987) found that infants do nonverbally respond more to humans than to dolls.

OLDER CHILDREN

Nonverbal communication in older children has been examined in much greater detail than that in infants. There is a large volume of research, however, seeming to indicate that a child has learned most of his or her nonverbal norms by about the age of 6 or 7 and that certain subcodes seem to change continually. Moreover, there are many theories and ways to analyze this learning. We take one perspective that postulates a developmental change in the way the child relates to self and others. That perspective has been most closely associated with George H. Mead, and it proposes a three-part developmental process: an imitation stage, a play stage, and a game stage (Hickson 1981).

Although Mead's three stages are more closely associated with socialization and verbal communication, the previous discussion of infant nonverbal communication suggests that the same developmental sequence can be found for socialization and nonverbal communication.

During the *imitation stage*, the child begins to expand his or her repertoire of nonverbal behaviors. Probably the most significant feature at this stage is the acquisition of emblems. It seems that the ability to encode and decode emblems increases with age, up to about age 5 (Kumin and Lazar 1974). The smile is acquired quite early, but the interpretation of that smile differs significantly by culture. Alexander and Babad (1981), for instance, compared children's smiles, their probability of smiling, and cultural norms as to how adults reacted to the smile. They found that American children with high probabilities of smiling were rated as more adjusted, more attractive, and more affiliative than those with low probabilities of smiling. They did not find a similar difference with an Israeli population. Hence, the imitation stage teaches the child not only what to do but also what expectations may be associated with the behavior. Additionally, Beek and Dubas (2008b) looked at children's and adolescents' (ages 9–15) perceptions of anger and joy in others faces, and found that the more anger they perceived there was, the more depressed they were likely to become in adolescence. Beck and Dubas (2008b) conjecture that this might be helpful in understanding how depression is manifested in adolescents, especially as it relates to individual and gender differences.

Since smiling is considered an immediacy behavior, this seems to be a good place to mention the S. A. Myers et al. (1999) findings that communication satisfaction in sibling relationships is related to "loving and liking" but that the "correlation was higher for liking" (p. 347). So the communication skills a child learns (in this case Myers et al. experimented with immediacy behaviors) may well influence how siblings interact as they grow up in the household.

There is also evidence to indicate that as early as age 2 the child begins to notice similarities in physical appearances (Golomb 1972). Knapp (1978), for instance, noted that most children before the age of 5 are able to note distinctions between proper and improper dress. Research on proxemics and touch also infers that during the imitation stage, communication behaviors are being learned. The research of Bretherton and others discussed earlier reported that children seek greater proxemic affiliation as age increases. Research also indicates that the norms associated with sex and distancing may begin as early as nursery-school age, with boys maintaining greater interaction distances than girls (Gifford and Price 1979). Finally, Brownlee and Bakeman (1981) reported that 2-year-olds used different kinds of touch/hitting patterns for different communication purposes. Interestingly, however, these patterns seem to disappear with age. It may be that after age 2 the child quickly learns the touch norms of his or her culture.

During the *play stage,* the child begins to learn which nonverbal behaviors are appropriate and which are inappropriate. Probably the most prominent subcodes at this stage are kinesics (emblems and facial expression), physical appearance, and vocalics. As early as age 6, children both know and understand what is physically attractive and unattractive (Cavior and Lombardi 1973). They seem to base such understanding on body type and stereotyped standards of attractiveness. Some children, for example, after being introduced to dolls such as Barbie and Ken, associate Barbie with sexiness and beauty. Note that both dolls are rather stereotypic of what the American culture associates with "good" body builds and attractiveness; she is "rail thin" and he is "buff."

In the area of kinesic behaviors, the child begins to understand what the particular emblems and facial expressions stand for (Dimitrovsky 1964). At this stage, the child begins to develop a repertoire of emotional messages. The child at the play stage begins to use the gestures and expressions for particular effect and within the understood meanings between children. About this same age, the child begins to understand the vocalizations associated with the same messages (Fenster and Goldstein 1971). Children are better able to read such emotions as disappointment at this stage, and Miller-Day and Lee (2001) discovered just that phenomenon. They did find an interesting result in their study of children and their parents; mothers are more likely to rely on nonverbal cues (as well as indirect messages) than fathers are when they wish to convey disappointment. Perhaps what this means is that

PHOTO 12.3   Which of Mead's three stages do you notice here?

children often learn their nonverbal decoding acuity from deciphering what their mothers are really saying beneath the indirect verbal messages and the nonverbal messages.

At the *game stage,* the well-understood norms are operating; it is at this stage that most of the nonverbal research cited earlier was conducted. Now children begin to actively manipulate their nonverbal communication to produce certain expected effects, and at this stage they move from being children to adults.

AFFECTIVE COMMUNICATION

There are two basic positions on the acquisition of emotion, although there are other theories as to how we acquire and interpret emotion. Many people agree with Charles Darwin, who believed that emotions are universal expressions that are inherited. Another perspective theorizes that we develop our emotions. This perspective, proposed by Wolff (1972), roughly parallels Mead's three stages of development. The stages overlap each other, as well as pass through periods of time where no new stages develop.

The first stage is labeled *instinctive.* This phase is found during the period immediately after birth up to about 6 months. During the instinctive phase, we find such behaviors as crying and smiling. At this stage there is no meaning directly associated with the behavior; the behavior is more instinctive and aimed more at survival and self-awareness than at communication. The second stage is called the *emotional phase.* It is during this phase (from the second week to about 2 years of age) that the child begins to associate his or her emotional repertoire with basic emotions. At this stage of development, for instance, we find the typical range of affection behaviors associated with infants. Early in this period, the child seems to behave at one or the other extreme of emotion. By the end of this stage, the child has developed, as Blurton-Jones (1972) demonstrated, more than a hundred emotional expressions. Floyd and Morr (2003) found that expressing affection in families was important for relational closeness as well as satisfaction, and that it was more likely to be expressed nonverbally between spouses than between siblings.

The third stage, the ***objective phase,*** is characterized by gestures and expressions that are related to thought. This stage begins around 6 years of age and indicates that the emotional message is now well integrated into the total communication repertoire of the child and can be used in day-to-day interactions.

A child can be very sensitive to the emotions and needs of others. In a study examining a child's ability to understand and label different kinds of emotions (happiness, sadness, anger, fear, disgust, and surprise), Cameras and Allison (1985) examined children from preschool to second-grade ages. They found that the child's accuracy in labeling increased with age but that the verbal label was recognized better than was the facial expression of emotion. They also found that some emotions were easier to recognize (i.e., happiness and sadness) than others (i.e., anger, fear, surprise), and that disgust was the most difficult emotion to identify. As noted earlier, however, children often mistake nonverbal communication or misinterpret it at other stages in their development. This may be due to the learning of their verbal language, a code that is quite complex and specific. Emphasis on this aspect of communication from age 2 to about 6 would obviously reduce their attention to the nonverbal messages they receive. They have already mastered the nonverbal, or so they might believe.

We would be remiss if we did not point out that the way a child is raised is not always what most of us would consider to be a positive situation. This can affect their ability to both encode and decode nonverbal messages. Bowen and Montepare (2007) truly believe that a child's ability to decode emotional nonverbal messages may have more to do with their upbringing than anything cultural or actual parenting styles. They believe that their research shows that "the association between experiences of maltreatment and family violence and children's decoding skills may be a function of the quality of family environment and expressiveness within the family, rather than parenting styles per se" (p. 185). What that means, in essence, is that children raised in a negative home environment will be less likely to understand nonverbal messages, and logically, that means they also will be more likely to violate the norms acceptable for emotional expression.

Sigelman and Adams (1990) used the naturalistic setting of parks to observe distance and touch behaviors between parents and their children. Consistent with other studies, they found that as the children got older, parents increased their distance and decreased the amount of touch. The presence of other children almost eliminated closeness between children and their parents. In a study of gender identity among children, Brody, Hay, and Vanderwater (1990) found that both boys and girls 6 to 12 years old were more hurt and disgusted by the opposite sex than by the same sex. Girls reported more fear than boys, and both sexes were more afraid of boys than girls.

B. Powell and Steelman (1990) studied the spacing of siblings as related to academic performance. They found that on standardized tests, having one brother had the same negative effect as having two sisters. Close spacing of siblings also had a detrimental effect. Density of family was more significant to children's scores on tests than was family income.

The amount of haptic behavior finds that parents gaze more than they touch, but infants touch more than they gaze (Peery and Roggman 1989); there are sex differences in decoding abilities of children (L. Beck and Feldman 1989). Children are reported to have more haptic behavior in a child-care setting than in a laboratory setting (A. Baxter and Walden 1989), and unpopular children tended to imitate negative responses of their peers (Nowicki and Oxenford 1988).

BOX 12.4 OBSERVATIONAL STUDY

Observe either a real-life situation or a television show for how infants and children are communicated with non-verbally. What nonverbal behaviors are used with either the children or the infants that are not ordinarily used with adults? What do these behaviors communicate to the child? What do they communicate to others observing them? If you watched a television program, what message did you receive about raising (or working with) children?

NONVERBAL COMMUNICATION WITH THE ELDERLY

An area that has acquired new importance is that of *gerontology*. The study of aging and the aged has become a popular concern as a result of the increasing age of the population. What we know about how the elderly communicate, both verbally and nonverbally, how-ever, is minimal, since it is only in the last 20 to 25 years that this group has become the target of research. Interestingly enough, in the rewrite of this new edition some 4 years after the last edition, the story is still the same. There are many articles about the physical and medical aspects of aging, but very few on how communication—and in particular nonverbal communication—is affected by the aging process. The one area that does seem to have gotten some attention in the last 4 years is the area of how dementia affects communication in families and with caregivers (Williams and Parker 2012; R. Wilson, Rochon, Mihailidis, and Leonarda, 2012). Completing this chapter with a survey of gerontological nonverbal communication seems fitting.

The elderly are an extension of the family, although not quite as integral in the United States as they were years ago. In the end, we all age, some graciously, some not so graciously. As we age, however, some of our nonverbal communication may change partly because of the restricted sensory input that may come with age: hearing loss, movement restrictions, and changes in our physical appearance. How we deal with each is something that will become more important in each of us as we age.

Some researchers believe that the differences in our communication in old age may stem from the problem of admitting to communication difficulties. With the onset of sensory problems and other communication difficulties, irritability, moodiness, and paranoia may appear. These changes may be due in part to a recognized dependency on others, and they may create a form of self-imposed isolation or at least the discovery that we are out of the information flow. Others believe that senior citizens can and do participate fully in a normal lifestyle, even if retired and no longer living the lifestyle they once did. For example, Seals, Clanton, Agarwal, Doswell, and Thomas (2008) recently studied how often elderly men and women have been learning to use the computer as a form of communication. The results show that more and more elderly people are learning this new technology. One of your authors' mother asked for a computer (her first) for her 85th birthday, so she could learn to do e-mail and search her genealogy. Also, we know of several folks over the age of 75 who have "Facebook" pages. So, the world does seem to be changing at least a little bit for senior citizens; if for no other reason, technology is allowing it to change.

What we know about the elderly and the process of aging is both limited and general. Perhaps the best way to study the elderly's use of nonverbal communication is to examine it, subcode by subcode. In so doing, we would describe what we know of this growing sub-population and, it is hoped, dispel some of the commonly held misperceptions.

ENVIRONMENT AND SPACE

The use of space by the elderly—the environment, territory, and personal space—has not been well researched. Most of the nonverbal research available is based on student populations or populations of middle-aged adults. What we know about spatial use may be best summarized in general terms. We know very little about environmental preferences. Sonnenfeld (1966) observed that young people prefer rugged, unfamiliar environments, and surroundings that they consider exotic.

This research does not infer that the elderly prefer an environment that is less exotic, less rugged, or more familiar. Due to economic restrictions, the elderly may not be able to seek different surroundings. Yet the move toward the Sun Belt by the elderly would seem to indicate that they, like their younger counterparts, seek different environments as they age. Lucas (2004) did a content analysis of retirement communities' promotional materials and discovered that most market to the idea of "successful aging" and the attributes of living in a community. Of course, part of the key is to have positive images—both in pictures and description—and to sell to the idea that these are functional, living human beings who are not headed toward the ends of their lives.

A perception held by many is that the type of environment influences how the elderly perceive themselves. There seems to be an understood, perhaps guilt-reasoned, perception that when we change an older person's environment drastically—taking the person out of his or her home—we induce a feeling of "institutionalism." According to J. F. Myers (1978), however, this perception may not be accurate. He studied both institutionalized and non-institutionalized elderly and found that (1) the institutionalized perceived themselves no differently, and (2) they were no more ill than were the noninstitutionalized. Although it may seem that when we institutionalize our elderly they appear to look worse, it may be that such a perception is based on our (a younger generation's) perception of what it would be like to be institutionalized.

Research is also scarce in the area of territory and personal space. What we know seems to indicate that the elderly are given more personal space and give each other more space than younger people. Such spatial norms are subject to the same intervening variables mentioned previously, except perhaps relationships between younger and older people. M. J. Smith, Reinheimer, and Gabbard-Alley (1988) demonstrated that the elderly, at least elderly females, do better on task performances with spatial intrusion or crowding than do younger females. They also found that the elderly exhibited more positive communication behaviors. Furthermore, as part of their study, they examined the problem of loneliness, inferring that part of the reason for increased loneliness might be the greater privacy af-forded to individuals in post-retirement periods. Although Smith and associates found that there were higher levels of loneliness among the elderly females they tested, the finding was influenced by educational differences, those with less education reporting more loneliness.

TOUCH

Very little is known about the effect of touch and the need for touch in the elderly. As early as 1978, Knapp noted:

> The use of touch to communicate emotional and relational messages to the elderly may be crucial—particularly as the reliance on verbal/cognitive messages wanes. Although we seem to give the aged in this country a greater "license" to touch others, it is not clear how much others touch them. No doubt the infirmities of age will require more touching, but it may make a big difference whether this increased touching is just "functional/professional" or expresses affectionate feelings. (pp. 245–246)

If we were to hypothesize a relationship between touch and the elderly, we would postulate that (1) there is probably less touch as people increase in age, regardless of sex; and that (2) even among family members, touch will probably decrease as the age difference in-creases. It is almost as if those in the younger generation are afraid they might "catch" the infirmities that growing old can bring, so they avoid touching elderly people. As one of your authors tells her class, "Lets all hope we do catch it!" If we don't, it means we die young. Older research indicates that the elderly may actually touch less and want to be touched less because of their sensitivity to touch (Axelrod and Cohen 1961). According to this body of thought, as we grow older, the number of touch "spots" we have decreases, and as the number of touch spots is reduced, our sensitivity to touch decreases. It may be that the elderly touch less and expect less touch as a result of reduced haptic sensitivity.

VOCALICS

The older voice sounds different from the younger voice; how that difference is produced may differ between older males and older females. According to research reported by Benjamin (1982), elderly males have greater hypovalving (allowing too much air to pass through the glottis) and less precise articulation than do elderly females. Other changes such as altera-tions in pitch level, speech rate, and vocal flexibility are not sex-related (McGlone and Hollien 1963). Furthermore, Addington (1968) implies that there are vocal quality differences between older and younger speakers. More recently, Hummert, Mazloff, and Henry (1999), although they had many counteracting influences, did find that women seniors are more likely to be evaluated negatively than older men are, and that the younger an elderly female sounds, the more likely she is to be evaluated positively. These evaluations were done by college-age students, which means, for the most part, individuals in your age bracket. It gives us a little insight into how our society values the elderly.

Although hearing is not actually a part of vocalics, at least directly, we believe this is a place we should point out one communication issue that seems to be a problem for the elderly. Younger people sometimes assume that a senior citizen has a hearing loss, so they often speak loudly to them. To add insult to injury, they often slow down their rate of speaking. If you do this, don't be surprised if you get a response such as, "Just because I am older doesn't mean I am deaf and dim-witted! And even if I was hard of hearing, my brain has not atrophied!" The 85-plus-year-old mother of one of your authors used to experience this quite frequently, especially by health care givers. Recall this the next time you talk with a senior citizen, and chances are good your communication will be much more effective.

PHYSICAL APPEARANCE

Our physical appearance changes as we age. Our skin becomes less elastic and dries out. Our hair grays or whitens, dries out, straightens, or falls out. Our bodies tend to soften, to lose their angular perspective. Other than our physical appearance, our clothing choices also seem to change. As a sociological function of age, we are usually forced to reduce the amount of money we spend on making ourselves attractive; we cannot pay as much for clothing, makeup, and accessories. It may be that young people are more fashion conscious, but given the changing median age in the United States today, more advertising money will probably be spent to appeal to the elderly in the future; hence, fashion may change in their direction. The concept of the "fixed income" might play a role in how fashionable an elderly person can be.

KINESICS

In the area of kinesics, we would expect that, given the usual frailties of age, the elderly will be less flexible, will be less expressive, and may differ in terms of posture. Although very little research has actually attempted to verify these expectations, common sense and day-to-day observations seem to indicate they are accurate. We may expect that dependence on kinesic expression will lessen as flexibility and visual acuity decrease. Once again, though, never assume that this is true, as most of us can probably name specific people who do not fit the stereotypical mold of being less agile, even if they are considered senior citizens.

CHRONEMICS AND OLFACTION

How the elderly perceive time has not really been examined in any great detail. Cottle (1976) suggests that time theories in our culture may make age something to deny, stressing instead a present or future time orientation. Cottle suggests that Americans view time as an hourglass, the two large portions being associated with the past and the future and the small middle part (where the sand passes) being the present. Thus, we associate time with the past and future, rather than with what occurs in the present. However, his research has concentrated only on younger people. This is one area that needs more research, especially in view of Americans' preoccupation with the present.

What we know about the elderly's olfactory communication is at best minimal. We have stated that the elderly, due to sensory restriction, may be less efficient in smell identification than younger people. It may be that they have more smell memories. The research, however, is at best contradictory. Although olfaction may be influenced by age, this really has not been

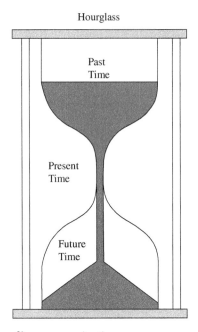

FIGURE 12.2 Cottle's perception of how we perceive time.
Source: Cottle, T. J. (1976). *Perceiving time: A psychological investigation with men and women.* New York: John Wiley and Sons.

proved one way or the other. Many people also mention how older people have more odors that are not pleasing to others. No research has shown this to be true, but look at advertising geared toward the senior population. We can find many products on the market that try to lessen or eliminate bad odors associated with aging.

BOX 12.5 OBSERVATIONAL STUDY

Observe advertising over the next week and see what products are targeted for the senior population. What types of products are marketed? How do the actors portray the seniors nonverbally? Are the actors really considered senior citizens? What messages do these ads send to you about the senior population?

REVIEW

Nonverbal communication is used at every stage of development, whether or not that development is associated with age or relationship. It is clear that we are continually learning and relearning what is normative for our nonverbal communication. We should also note that the influence of age on our nonverbal communication is a reciprocal process. As we influence the infant and child, so too is that same infant and child influencing us. The addition of a child can and does change both our lifestyles and our nonverbal expectations. What will happen when that child grows old and becomes a member of the elderly group is a subject that will be explored more as time goes on. At this stage, however, we know relatively little about this period.

SUMMARY

This chapter has examined how our nonverbal communication operates in a context that is very familiar: the family. We began with the home, indicating that it acts as a context for nonverbal communication. How nonverbal communication operates in marriage and formally committed relationships and how the addition of a child changes our expectations and the practices of nonverbal communication are also important to the concept of "family." In this section, we examined some of the developmental literature on the acquisition of nonverbal communication in infancy and childhood. The impact of extreme age on nonverbal communication is also an important aspect to consider when looking at this topic. In final review, however, it should be noted that we are really just beginning to understand how our nonverbal communication operates at both extremes: in the infant and in the elderly.

QUESTIONS FOR THOUGHT

1. What is the role of nonverbal communication in such private areas as the home? Does violating nonverbal norms in this environment yield stronger or harsher messages than outside the home?
2. If you were asked to identify the most powerful nonverbal subcode in the home, what would it be, and why do you believe it to be so powerful?
3. How do we use nonverbal messages at various stages in the marriage or committed relationship? Are such messages the same for nonmarried partners living in the same home as it is for married partners?
4. Nonverbal communication plays an important role in the development of children. Which subcodes do you think are the most important at what stages of a child's life? Why?
5. If you were to conduct a research project on the elderly's nonverbal communication, would you focus more on their use of nonverbal subcodes or the impact of nonverbal subcodes on their communication? Why?

FURTHER REFERENCES

The Home

Beier, E. G. (1974). Nonverbal communication: How we send emotional messages. *Psychology Today*, 8, 52–59.

Callister, M. A., and Robinson, T. (2010). Content analysis of physical affection within television families during the 2006–2007 season of U.S. children's programming. *Journal of Children and Media*, 4, 155–173.

D'Atri, D. A. (1975). Psychophysiological responses to crowding. *Environment and Behavior*, 7, 237–251.

Hunt, C., and Vaizey, J. (1966). Differential effects of group density on social behavior. *Nature*, 209, 1371–1372.

Mehrabian, A. (1970). Some determinants of affiliation and conformity. *Psychological Reports*, 27, 19–29.

Marriage and Committed Relationships

Beier, E. G. (1974). Nonverbal communication: How we send emotional messages. *Psychology Today*, 8, 52–59.

Cross, M., and Epting, F. (2005). Self-obliteration, self-definition, self-integration: Claiming a homosexual identity. *Journal of Constructivist*, 18, 53–63.

Children

Dailey, R. M. (2008). Assessing the contribution of nonverbal behaviors in displays of confirmation during parent–adolescent interactions: An actor–partner interdependence model. *Journal of Family Communication*, 8, 62–91.

Dion, K. K. (1972). Physical attractiveness and evaluations of children's transgressions. *Journal of Personality and Social Psychology*, 24, 207–213.

Dunsmore, J., Her, P., Halberstadt, A., and Perez-Rivera, M. (2009). Parents' beliefs about emotions and children's recognition of parents' emotions. *Journal of Nonverbal Behavior*, 33, 121–140.

Eibl-Eibesfeldt, I. (1970). Similarities and differences between cultures in expressive movement. In R. A. Hinde (Ed.), *Nonverbal communication* (pp. 297–314). Cambridge: Cambridge University Press.

Elfenbein, H. A. (2006). Learning in emotion judgments: Training and the cross-cultural understanding of facial expressions. *Journal of Nonverbal Behavior*, 30, 21–36.

Frisby, B. N., and Martin, M. M. (2010). Interpersonal motives and supportive communication. *Communication Research Reports*, 27, 320–329

Gerholm, T. (2011). Children's development of facework practices—An emotional endeavor. *Journal of Pragmatics*, 43, 3099–3110.

Langlois, J. H., and Roggman, L. A. (1990). Attractive faces are only average. *Psychological Science*, 1, 115–121.

Lau, J. Y. F., Burt, M., Leibenluft, E., Pine, D. S., Rijsdijk, F., Shiffrin, N., and Eley, T. C. (2009). Individual differences in children's facial expression recognition ability: The role of nature and nurture. *Developmental Neuropsychology*, 34, 37–51.

Mejía-Arauz, R., Rogoff, B., Dexter, A., and Najafi, B. (2007). Cultural variation in children's social organization. *Child Development*, 78, 1001–1014.

Michael, G., and Willis, F. N., Jr. (1968). The development of gestures as a function of social class, education, and sex. *Psychological Record*, 18, 515–519.

Miller, P. J., and Mangelsdorf, S. C. (2005). Developing selves are meaning-making selves: Recouping the social in self-development. *New Directions for Child and Adolescent Development*, 2005, 51–59.

Myers, S. A., and Bryant, L. E. (2008). The use of behavioral indicators of sibling commitment among emerging adults. *Journal of Family Communication*, 8, 101–125.

Myers, S. A., Byrnes, K. A., Frisby, B. N., and Mansson, D. H. (2011). Adult siblings' use of affectionate communication as a strategic and routine relational maintenance behavior. *Communication Research Reports*, 28, 151–158.

Shai, D., and Belsky, J. (2011). Parental embodied mentalizing: Let's be explicit about what we mean by implicit. *Child Development Perspectives*, 5, 187–188.

Tortora, S. (2010).Ways of seeing: An early childhood integrated therapeutic approach for parents and babies. *Clinical Social Work Journal*, 38, 37–50.

Visser, N., Alant, E., and Harty, M. (2008). Which graphic symbols do 4-year-old children choose to represent each of the four basic emotions? *Augmentative and Alternative Communication*, 24, 302–312.

Elderly

Fromm, D., and Holland, A. L. (1989). Functional communication in Alzheimer's disease. *Journal of Speech and Hearing Disorders*, 54, 535–540.

Mysak, E. D. (1959). Pitch and duration characteristics of older males. *Journal of Speech and Hearing Research*, 2, 46–54.

O'Hair, D., Allman, J., and Gibson, L. A. (1991). Nonverbal communication and aging. *The Southern Communication Journal*, 56 (2), 147–160.

Ryan, E. B., and Hummert, M. L. (1995) Communication predicaments of aging: Patronizing behavior toward older adults. *Journal of Language and Social Psychology*, 14, 144–166.

Schulman, M. D., and Mandel, E. (1988). Communication training of relatives and friends of institutionalized elderly persons. *The Gerontologist*, 28, 797–800.

CHAPTER 13

NONVERBAL COMMUNICATION AT WORK

KEY CONCEPTS

- Nonverbal Relational Messages on the Job
- Power
- Credibility
- Appraisal Interviews
- Nonverbal Communication in Business Situations
- Nonverbal Communication in the Classroom
- Nonverbal Communication in Court

OBJECTIVES

By the end of the chapter you should be able to:

- Explain how the various nonverbal subcodes influence decisions of power, credibility, liking, and leadership in the work environment.
- Discuss the relationship between nonverbal communication and success in the business world, in the classroom, and in the courts.

One of the major contexts in our communication is the occupation we choose to follow, and, as might be expected, nonverbal communication plays a major role in the success we enjoy at work. We now examine the nonverbal messages associated with the world of work. An occupation is the general area with which people choose to identify and from which they plan to make a living. Hence, occupations can be as general as education, business, and law, and as specific as cost accounting, elementary education, and contract law. Each occupation also comprises specific jobs, which might include positions as general manager, assembly-line worker, nightly news anchor, or third vice-president.

Although there are many occupations from which people may choose, we believe there are some general nonverbal messages associated with most occupations. For example, over time, researchers have shown in many studies that nonverbal immediacy is important to job satisfaction (Goodboy and McCroskey 2008; Teven 2007, 2010). We also know that certain jobs within occupations may differ in their nonverbal needs. We consider how people persuade others to think they are credible, how they create an appropriate communication environment for their duties, and how they build their nonverbal images.

You would think that because we spend so much time on the job, there would be volumes of research on the nonverbal aspects of work. This, unfortunately, is not true. Most of the books simply state the obvious. They list the subcodes the authors feel are appropriate and include a number of social science examples for illustration. There is also a paucity of specific research in what we know as organizational communication that deal with nonverbal communication issues. Books in the popular market tend to be more prescriptive and are often the result of the "it worked for me once, it'll work for you, too" type of reasoning (which we mention in the Appendix as a shortcoming of "pop books"). Let's see if we can't offer a little more perspective.

NONVERBAL RELATIONAL MESSAGES

The key to understanding nonverbal communication in any context is an awareness of how the various subcodes function to create messages consistent with their desired impact. The nonverbal communication found on the job is different from that found in social situations or in the family; it functions to establish an image or impression relative to someone else's in terms of control and power. (Recall that affinity was the main nonverbal function in social situations; accuracy and self-presentation were the major functions in the family.)

The relational impact of nonverbal messages is important on the job, especially a job that requires interaction with others, which most jobs do. Your image on the job may be directly affected by such factors as the size of your territory, the furnishings of your office, and your appearance, to name but a few nonverbal cues. Consider, for example, the impact of having to wait for someone else on your perceptions of his or her power, the impact of the layout of your work environment, and the impact of your first impressions of a new boss. Every perception will be heavily influenced by the nonverbal communication associated with each situation.

GENERAL NONVERBAL CONSIDERATIONS

This section identifies subcodes we feel are significant and examines them for their impact on the job. Most of the research has been conducted in environment and space, kinesics, and physical appearance. Additional material may be found in the spheres of chronemics, haptics, and vocalics, although little research has been reported in these areas. Perhaps the most important dimensions of nonverbal communication are found in the spatiotemporal, followed cosely by those we associate with the body.

SPATIOTEMPORAL DIMENSIONS

All jobs take place in space and time. The following section examines those spatiotemporal dimensions and their impact on how we relate to and behave on the job.

SPACE

The type of environment you work in does several things. First, the environment influences you. Two authors of this text, for example, were once asked by some friends in the real estate business to evaluate the physical layout of their office. The office was designed so that several agents could use the space at one time (see Figure 13.1). The supervisor could keep track of what was going on in the office through two large windows in his office, and next to the supervisor's office was a "conference" room for dosing deals (where the office soft-drink machine was located). The walls were white, and the office was carpeted. What was wrong? Two things: First, the supervisor's windows allowed no privacy for the agents; the agents felt they were continually under pressure as well as scrutiny. Second, there was no privacy for the agent working with a buyer in the business area, nor for the other agents in the office since all occupied the same space. As we know from earlier chapters, both of these issues are important to humans, and no less important in a work environment.

When you buy something as expensive as a house, there are certain private aspects of your life that must be made public: features such as salary, children (number and if you plan on having any), and other needs that are not meant for general or public knowledge.

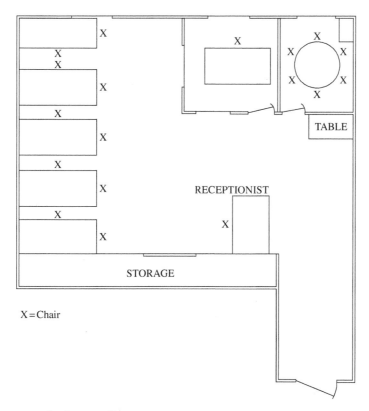

FIGURE 13.1 Layout of real estate office.

PHOTO 13.1 (A) AND (B). How work environments are structured can send a number of messages. What does this design convey to you about the person who works in this office space?

Having the soft-drink machine in the closing room was inappropriate; it was a distraction and invited interruptions by others. The recommendations we made were simple: (1) Have the windows in the supervisor's office curtained. (2) Place privacy walls between the desks. (3) Move the soft-drink machine.

This example may sound rather elementary, but if you visit most real estate offices, insurance offices, car dealers, or even banks, you will find similar situations. Taking into account the dimensions of environment, how would you rate the real estate office environment before the suggested changes? After?

A second aspect of the environment is where you are located. Korda (1975) contends that there are lines of power, and of prestige, based on where your office is located. The more windows and space you have, the greater your power and prestige (recall also the Bruneau studies discussed in Chapter 4). Sitton (1980) points out that some environments are designed to make the user feel powerless, and others are insensitive to the user's needs. Sitton targets the messages that schools provide to students and faculty—that they are untrustworthy and powerless. Not all environments, however, indicate insensitivity to the needs of others; modern environmental engineering has attempted to meet the needs of both employees and customers. Modern office buildings (such as the Chicago Willis Tower) have been designed with special consideration to such environmental features as quiet, comfort, and attractiveness. How we structure the environment can send various messages, many of which may yield less than satisfactory results.

Finally, we can examine the impact of color in the environment. Have you ever noticed that white is chosen for most businesses? Why? Two reasons might be offered. First, according to Biren (1956), white is associated with purity and perhaps honesty. Second, white is perceived to be environmentally cooler than other colors, and this can affect mental abilities. Hence, our work environments that are white may suggest an honest business and, at the same time, help control our tempers.

We should examine such environmental features as lighting, together with the general size and architectural design of the buildings in which we work. Research seems to indicate that lighting can increase productivity, but the lighting should be bright, not harsh. Lighting can also be used to reduce stress, as has been demonstrated by the simple addition of a fish tank in waiting rooms (Block 1975). Abdou (1997) found that lighting—both artificial and environmental—does affect productivity in the workplace as well as worker satisfaction.

Your own personal identity goes into the type of building in which you work—its size, design, and artifactual additions. From the type of building, we also learn how the company perceives itself. An author of your text knows of a company that was located in a suburban house. This company did a little over $6 million of business a year but had trouble convincing potential clients of its permanence and assets because it did not look like a prosperous business. When the company moved into an office complex, its problems were solved.

The same issues about developing "workspaces" may be true of the Willis Tower or other such buildings. In his memoirs, Speer (1970) noted that Adolf Hitler's perception of Berlin was a vision of such a grand style that the buildings would last for 1,000 years. In contrast, one of your authors has traveled to Auschwitz/Birkenau in Poland, and when Hitler designed those facilities (as well as similar other ones all over Europe), they were meant to last for 10 years only, at which time Hitler's "Final Solution" was to have been completed. This is yet another environmental issue that tells you about Hitler's view of how the world was supposed to look. Great buildings are large monuments to the people who build them, as are the lesser ones.

Finally, the environment you are in also provides information. Cooper (1979) describes some executives whose secretaries are in a separate building. The message of image is obvious: I'm extremely important—so important that I am located elsewhere. In a field study of factory workplaces, Peponis (1985) noted that many factories are designed to increase the distance between the powerful and the powerless. His research indicates that whereas management has offices away from the workplace, the foreman's office is on the shop floor.

Additionally, the managerial workplace is structured to allow for communication between and among the various managerial levels; the shop foreman's office, on the other hand, has no such connectivity.

TERRITORY

Not only does the location of the office give information about how the person is perceived—or wants to be perceived—but so does the arrangement of space and the treatment of space as territory. For instance, consider the door. Not an interesting object, but one that expresses something. What difference is there between an office with an open door and one with a closed door? What is the desire for privacy? Who is perceived as more important, the person with the open door or the one with the closed door? A closed door implies privacy. People who are more important are afforded more privacy.

If you are working in an environment where the person of higher status has many barriers you must pass through in order to gain access to him or her, it is incumbent upon you to realize who controls the barriers. In most work situations, this *gatekeeper* will be the office assistant, and some people have a negative attitude about dealing with clerical workers. Many secretaries will tell you about how some people's nonverbal treatment of them is very much a message of "I'm better than you," based simply on the issue of status in the organization. This attitude can be seen through many of the nonverbal subcodes discussed, but most often in invading the office assistant's territory (that, combined with condescending vocalics). Some people rifle through that person's desk as if it were their own, but if someone came into their office and did the same thing, the repercussions would be unspeakable. One rule of thumb to learn early in your career is how important clerical workers and any type of service assistants are to the organization; treat them with the respect due to any human being, especially one with more power than you. And, like it or not, your "boss' secretary" almost always wields more power than you, regardless of who has what "title." Usually they do have a whole lot more power than you do, especially if they control access to your superiors.

Traditionally, the chief executive has had a "dosed door," indicative of importance and privacy of conversation. Recently, however, an "open door" policy has evolved in business so that an executive might "meet" with the workers in a company cafeteria during lunch. The Chancellor (President) of one of your author's universities makes it a point to eat lunch in the student dining halls as often as possible to maintain contact with the students. All workers there feel they can talk with the "boss." The innovation of an "open door policy," however, has caused some unanticipated problems in that the chain of command has been broken, and officers in the middle range are "skipped" from decision making (Hickson, Stacks, and Padgett-Greely 1998).

A second feature of spatial use is the placement of objects in the office. The more permanent the object (as indicated by its value, its heaviness, and the space it takes up), the more prestige and/or power are indicated. Another feature is the size of the office; generally speaking, you can judge prestige and status by the amount of space provided for the person. An office may tell you something about that person's status in the organization (Is it shared? How much space? How many plants, decorations, diplomas, and so forth?)

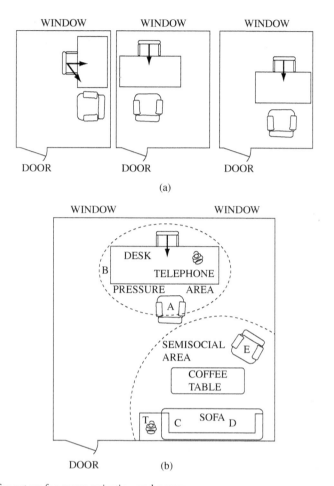

FIGURE 13.2 Office set up for communication and power.
Source: Michael Korda, *Power! How to Get It, How to Use It* (New York: Ballantine, 1975), 232–235. Reprinted with permission.

Figure 13.2 shows how Korda would establish power in two environments, one small and one large. If you look at these office spaces you will see a number of factors. The three offices labeled with (a) show how people create an environment that is either open or closed. The first office on the left is more open because the barrier of the desk is not set up as a "wall." The interactants are almost in a side-by-side setting, which has been deemed more intimate than a face-to-face one. The other two offices are set up with the barrier of the desk, although the office on the right causes fewer problems in communication since the door is not directly behind the seat where the one person is sitting. Office (b) is obviously the office of a person who has a higher status, due to the existence of a *pressure area* and a *social area*. If you are ever in offices of this type, and the business is conducted in the social areas, realize that the nonverbal message might be that the persons conducting the business do not take it as seriously as they would if it were conducted in the pressure areas. The other message,

PHOTO 13.2 Some offices are less organized than others. What do you think this communicates to others?

however, might be that the persons of higher status are trying to make the persons of lower status feel more comfortable and less intimidated.

One aspect of the office is the type of space it comes to represent. Because the office is a territory of sorts, it should fall into one of Lyman and Scott's (1967) four types of territory (**public**, **home**, **interactional**, or **body**). Unfortunately, however, the office tends to be viewed in more than one way. If the office is not shared with anyone else, then the territory should be considered *interactional*; that is, we expect others will enter, but they will have a reason, such as an office assistant. We tend to treat our offices as extensions of our homes; therefore, the office can become a *home territory*, assuming all the privacy and restrictions of the home.

When we enter an office, we tend to treat the other person's territory as if it were his or her home. Unless the person entering is of higher status or power, he or she is inclined to defer to the occupant of the office. Even if the door is open, we will probably stop, knock, or indicate our presence, and then enter. If the door is closed, we may even pass by. We value our offices and the privacy they afford; we do not expect others to enter without reason and permission.

BOX 13.1 OBSERVATIONAL STUDY

If you work in an environment, analyze your own; if you do not, analyze a past one (or one of your parents' work environments if you have not had a job). What factors

of the environment that we just discussed do you notice? What messages do these factors send to you? To other employees? To the public?

PERSONAL SPACE

Within the office territory, we have personal space and personal spacing expectations. Normally, on the basis of the arrangement of furniture, we know how we are to communicate. Figure 13.3 presents two offices, one arranged to restrict communication (a), and the other to encourage communication (b). The major difference is found in the blocking nature of

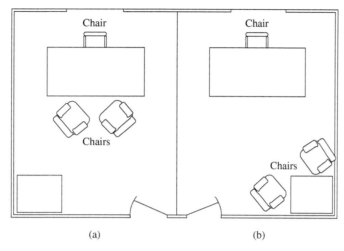

FIGURE 13.3 Two offices with different types of communication structures.

the desk. To reduce the distance between the occupant and the visitor, the occupant can move from behind the desk and sit with the visitor. Where we sit may indicate whether we are perceived as conversational and cooperative, or competitive and coactive (see Figure 13.4).

The *shape* of the table communicates impressions to others. A round table is equated with equality and unity; however, there is a particular *spot* from which power radiates in lessening degrees. The square table presents a problem because it sends messages of both equality and power. Because the sides are equally long, power struggles may ensue among equals; hence, unity is reduced. Finally, the rectangular table allows for power positions to

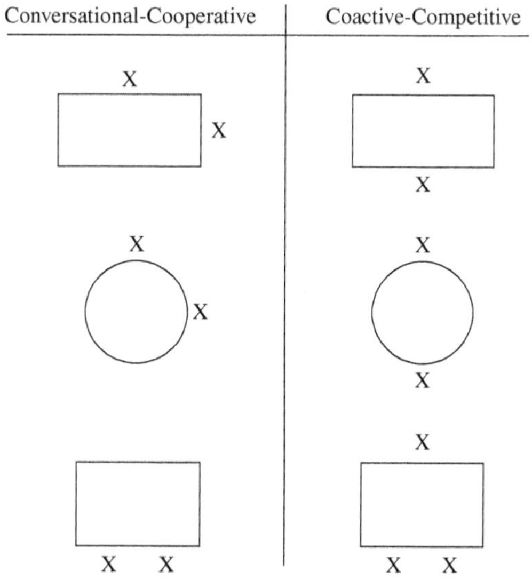

Conversational-Cooperative	Coactive-Competitive

FIGURE 13.4 Seating arrangements for cooperative and competitive interactions.

be identified (usually at the head—or short side—of the table), factions to be identified, and power struggles established (two equally powerful participants, one at each end of the table).

Seat placement may produce role differentiation. That is, your location at a particular table during a meeting or in a working group may help determine your role in the group. At least two studies suggest that such perceptions may be accurate, at least for those who either fail to contribute or wish to be perceived as noncontributing. In each study, the nonconforming member became isolated from the group (Riess and Rosenfeld 1980; Roger and Reid 1982).

In a larger space, the location of the seat taken during a training session may yield differing impressions (MacPherson 1984). For instance, sitting in the front of a group is associated with attention to what is being said, but it also indicates a dependence on the instructor. Sitting in the back of the group sends a message of independence and lack of concern. Sitting in the center of the group sends no particular message, although such a preference may indicate a need to avoid distraction.

In general, your choice of seating location within a space sends many messages. Some of these messages function to indicate power, unity, and interest. Some of the messages indicate independence, and others indicate subordination. Cooper (1979), for instance, suggests that to send an impression of power in group meetings, the person should avoid the table and locate himself or herself away from and above the rest. It may be that elevation is associated with perceptions of dominance and power in the meeting (B. Schwartz, Tesser, and Powell 1982). Recall, however, that this tip is not always fail-safe; it may cause undue stress (from being "on stage"), leading to poorer communication and the perception of less power.

A final factor that can be investigated but that has not received attention is the use of the automobile as an office. Each year there are hundreds of thousands of people who work out of their cars. What does the car tell us about them? Consider the following: Would you buy life insurance from someone who drove a large black automobile? Probably not, since it may appear "hearse-like," but you might if that same automobile were green or red. In a culture supposedly attached to automobiles, this use of territory, both as an office and as home territory, deserves more attention. Certainly, cellular telephones—especially *smart phones*—and increased wireless capabilities of computers have increased the use of automobiles as offices. With the advent—and prominence—of the use of 3G and 4G technology to access the Internet, we are likely to see the alteration of what is truly "office space" from here forward. Also, as the comfort level in cars has increased over the years (e.g., plush upholstery, seat design, accessories, more space), the car as an office and as a communicator is something to consider.

TIME

In the American culture we deem time to be important, especially on the job. We are paid for the time we spend working, sometimes even receiving bonuses for doing more work in a shorter period of time. In our culture, however, we use time in two ways on the job. First, we use time as an indicator of the prominence or prestige of the person we are dealing with. In this regard we either wait for people (the longer we wait, the more important they are) or keep people waiting for us. Second, the amount of time we spend with someone—customer or coworker—indicates how important he or she is to us.

We Americans also view time as a message that expresses something about the individual. L. Baxter and Ward (1975) interviewed secretaries about how they perceived people arriving early, late, and on time for an appointment. They found that people who arrived on time were perceived as being the most competent, composed, and sociable. The prompt person, however, was not rated as dynamic. The late arrivals were rated as more dynamic, but lower in competence, composure, and sociability. The early arriver was rated low to moderate in terms of these variables. In some cultures, however, these results would be quite different. We ask you to recall our earlier discussion on punctuality (Chapter 10) and the messages it sends.

Another time issue in the workplace is how much time you spend on the job. Some research has reported that to leave before your boss leaves sends the message that you are not dedicated to your employer; you are therefore judged to be less desirable for promotions. The other extreme that we have all heard about, however, is the person who spends too much time on the job, forsaking families, personal activities, health, and so on. This can be equally destructive to that employee, albeit in a different way.

TOUCH

Ordinarily, touch is not considered a nonverbal subcode operating on the job, but there are at least two important messages that touch communicates on the job. One is positive and expresses status and power relationships. The other deals more with sex differences and is probably perceived more negatively. In dealing with status and power, Henley (1977) has described how touch is perceived within superior–subordinate relationships. As you may observe, the superior initiates and controls touch more than the subordinate. Picture yourself with your "boss"; do you initiate touch with him or her? If the boss does a good job, do you walk up, put your hand on his or her shoulder and say, "Nice job!"? This scenario is more likely to occur with the boss touching the subordinate. Furthermore, as indicated in the research of J. D. Fisher, Rytting, and Heslin (1976), simple contact with another person may increase perceptions of credibility.

There are also negative perceptions based on touch. These are usually considered in the category of "sexual harassment," which is touch that differs from the "functional/professional" or "social-polite" touch we may expect on the job. As discussed in earlier chapters, men and women view touch differently from each other; personalities also affect attitudes toward touch (such as high- and low-touchers). Sometimes what one person thinks is social-polite touch (which is just barely acceptable in the workplace) may be perceived as friendship-warmth by another person, or perhaps even love-intimacy touch by a low- to non-toucher. You can imagine how these variables affect the workplace, and perhaps see how some sexual harassment accusations come about (McDonald, Backstrom, and Dear 2008).

Another negative perception found with touch is *self-touch*. Cooper (1979) points out that one of the basic indicators of stress in the business world is self-touch. Cooper writes that we indicate stress by "defensive beating" through such self-touch as rubbing the back of the neck, eyes, or forehead, and by pulling on our cheeks. As discussed earlier, adaptors (which include self-touch) are almost always seen as nervousness or boredom and are negatively perceived by others.

For the most part, we expect a handshake when we meet and when we leave someone, if the meeting pertains to the job. Although this may be an expectation, there are certain types of handshakes that are unexpected, as Nierenberg and Calero (1973) explain:

> Handshaking customs vary from country to country. The firmness of the typical male handshake in the United States probably originated in contests of strength. Many people consider themselves experts in analyzing character and attitude from a handshake, probably because perspiring palms usually indicate nervousness. The flaccid, or "dead fish," handshake is equally unpopular, although there may be mitigating circumstances. In the United States at least there is something vaguely un-American about a flaccid handshake. (p. 41)

A professional handshake has been considered so important in the workplace that many communication professors use specific activities to teach this skill (Hiemstra, 1999). Interestingly enough, however, the 2008 Presidential Campaign—and in particular Barack Obama's campaign—brought about a new norm of workplace hugging as a form of greeting. Whether or not this has become an acceptable form of greeting in all workplaces, though, remains to be seen.

In general, the environment conditions the type of touch, its location, and duration. Almost everyone has heard or read stories of bosses and secretaries touching each other. In reality, however, there seems to be a rather strict rule about touch in business. When it is possible that people are present, do not touch unless that touch is in the form of a ritualistic greeting. What types of touches go on behind the closed office door is unknown, but close your door while someone of the opposite sex is in the office with you, and others may perceive your touch behavior as less than "functional/professional." A good safety rule of thumb in this setting is to avoid touch in the workplace that is not functional-professional touch. One other tip is to observe the person whom you are wondering about with other individuals. If he or she touches you more than you think is acceptable and he or she is a high-toucher, that will become obvious to you by observing, and at least you have an explanation from which to proceed. If you seem to be singled out for touch by this person, and his or her norm is not to touch everyone the same way he or she is touching you, you have another decision to make. The first step, of course, is to resort to the verbal tactic, because regardless of what most of us think, people often cannot understand the nonverbal message we send, and often we are not accurate in our interpretations. Different people, and especially different genders, do not interpret (decode) nonverbal messages uniformly. The nonverbal message you are positive you are sending to that person may have been missed or, worse, misinterpreted.

BOX 13.2 OBSERVATIONAL STUDY

If you work in an environment, analyze your own; if you do not, analyze a past one (or one of your parents' work environments if you have not had a job). What factors of space that we just discussed do you notice? Time? Touch? What messages do these factors send to you? To other employees? To the public?

OVERT BODY DIMENSIONS

Much of what *you* communicate on the job is in the way your body communicates. This approach, commonly labeled "body language" in the popular literature, consists of the kinesic and vocal dimensions. Most of what we know about these expressions concerns the perceptions of credibility and status on the job. There are also attributions we make based on these dimensions that help interpret another person's awareness of you and the way that individual may react to you. Probably the most significant areas of the body are the face (the eyes and total facial expression) and gestures. The total body (posture, tenseness) apparently does not communicate as much as the other body parts. Finally, the voice is the object of perceived credibility and personality.

KINESIC BEHAVIORS

In most business situations, we seem to try to mask our faces. That is, people strive to maintain a noncommittal orientation or a positive emotional expression when dealing with others. This behavior seems to be reasonable. We want others to feel either that we like them or that we want to do business with them. We do not like to be placed in a situation where we are not entirely sure of how the other person perceives us (the "stone face"). Facial expression is perhaps one of the most important cues on the job. By your facial expression, others can ascertain how well or how poorly things are going.

We also try to deceive others. Significantly, research indicates that we may be better deceivers than we thought, although distortion of *factual* information seems an easier task than concealing or misrepresenting emotional information. On the job, then, there should be less emotional display because of expectations not to show emotions and because of the idea that it is more difficult to try to deceive someone with our facial expressions than to just be natural and show the factual information of what we are feeling and thinking.

Besides encoding and decoding emotional information, the face is important because of eye contact. Direct eye contact, for example, may be interpreted as a sign of credibility. What eye contact and gaze patterns can reveal to us about our relations with others includes the perception of status and power in the relationship. Perceptions of status and power are based on who is looked at more often, which is the higher status/power person, who looks with a steady, direct gaze (again, the higher status/power person), and who does not look at others (for some reason it is the higher status/power person who can avoid all eye contact and get away with it). This perception of power, however, is usually observed only when the power or status differential is known. The types of eye contact also affect perceptions of power and self -presentation. Recall from Chapter 8 that there are at least three types of eye contact: *mutual gaze, gaze omission*, and *gaze aversion* (R. G. Harper, Wiens, and Matarazzo 1978). Messages of equality are typically found in mutual gaze, or when two people are looking directly at one another (usually in the eyes). A one-sided look, or gaze omission, occurs when one person looks in the direction of the other's face while the other does not reciprocate the gaze; in this instance, the person gazing possesses more power or influence than the non-gazer. Finally, gaze aversion exists when one person intentionally avoids contact with the other. Gaze aversion is characterized by an impression of a lack of power and credibility (the perception may be that you are intentionally hiding something or being deceptive).

The smile is also a revealing feature of the face. Some research indicates that simply smiling helps in sales. Other research indicates that smiling people are perceived as being more intelligent than those who do not smile (Timmick 1982). The smile, however, is also associated with attempted emotional deception. Because in our culture the smile is perceived as a positive and reinforcing display, it should be a predominant facial feature; however, the face at rest (the face that people associate with you and your image on the job) does not ordinarily manifest a smile. Rather, the face at rest is more noncommittal. The smile, then, is one feature that we appear to manipulate but also tend to forget about. It is an indicator of positive affect/relations but is also one of deception.

In some professions it is very important to send the nonverbal message of being compassionate, an emotion that is often displayed through kinesics. K. I. Miller (2007) studied the importance of being able to show compassion, both verbally and nonverbally, and gives tips on how workers can appear more compassionate (when need be). Some of the nonverbal cues her subjects pointed out included more eye contact, appropriate touches, and nonverbal cues that indicate the other person is listening (backchanneling, postural leans toward the person being shown compassion, etc.).

GESTURES AND BODY MOVEMENT

How we elaborate our messages through body movement and gestures provides some information about our relation to others at work. Research indicates that mirroring the behaviors of others is a sign of conceding or according status or power to them. Further, the more relaxed the individual is in a situation, the more control this person perceives he or she has over the situation. This feeling usually comes from knowledge of where the individual is on the organizational ladder.

When it comes to gestures, we seem to interpret them in several ways. First, there are gestures that are positive and are attributed to confidence, competence, and sincerity. Such gestures as "steepling" and "readiness" are perceived as positive. The majority of the gestures described in the interpretations of popular literature, however, are negative. Nierenberg and Calero (1973) list more than 15 negative gestures observed in conversations, compared to only two or three positive gestures. Possibly the work context is such that we seldom furnish positive reinforcement. Competition for the other's job may be one reason. Another reason might be fear that giving positive reinforcement would be perceived as weakness in a world where the weak do not survive.

Facing behaviors are also indicative of who has power or status on the job. Obviously, we will defer to those in power; we normally do so by facing that person. This facing others Cooper (1979) calls the "choir effect," with the higher status/power person being faced by his or her "choir" of underlings. On the job, we normally face the person who has the expertise to do the job; facing behavior, then, may also indicate the attribution of credibility.

As mentioned earlier, adaptors are perceived negatively. These self-touching gestures are interpreted in one of three ways: as indicators of nervousness, indicators of boredom, or as quasi-courtship behaviors. These, obviously, are perceived negatively on the job; however, the use of illustrators is perceived positively. We expect those who are dynamic or in control to use slightly more animated gestures to accompany their verbal messages. Such gestures can also increase message acceptance.

An informative research project carried out by Remland (1984) indicates that people in either superior or subordinate positions are evaluated differently, depending upon the perceived status of their actions. Remland posited that a superior would be ranked as more *considerate* when displaying low-status rather than high-status nonverbal behaviors. He also posited that the superior would be rated as more considerate when the subordinate exhibited high-status rather than low-status behaviors. To conduct the research, Remland created the following videotapes of two men:

- *High-status superior:* Man was videotaped leaning back in his chair with hands clasped behind the neck; used an "invading" gesture (pointing at subordinate); did not establish eye contact.
- *High-status subordinate:* Man rested one arm on his desk and the other on the back of the chair; leaned back with ankle-on-knee leg cross; played with superior's pen at one point; did not look at superior while listening.
- *Low-status superior:* Leaned slightly in chair; rested both arms on the desk (close proximity to the desk); gazed at subordinate while subordinate spoke; looked away only occasionally while speaking; used a defensive gesture once while speaking (covering face with hands).
- *Low-status subordinate:* Leaned slightly forward in chair; faced superior directly; arms positioned on lap and feet on the floor; occasionally looked down while speaking; gazed at superior while superior spoke; nodded head approvingly while listening.

Remland found that people who viewed the videotaped interactions considered the low-status nonverbal communication of the superior as significantly more considerate than people who viewed the high-status nonverbal communication. He also found that the subordinate's nonverbal communication influenced the consideration rankings given to the superior. People who evaluated the superior when he was seen with the high-status subordinate judged him more considerate than did people who saw him interact with the low-status subordinate. Remland's findings suggest that status behaviors can also influence perceptions of leadership, but that the type of interaction displayed by the subordinate also influences perceptions of status and power. How do you see yourself in these settings? What would you do with your kinesics?

STUDENT VOICES

Tobi: I work with someone who has a distinct odor about him. By distinct I mean that he has awful body odor. I am aware that some people struggle with this issue, however it is very difficult to deal with. I don't know his personal story or if he has issues, but every time I walk past him I get the non-verbal that he doesn't take care of himself, and has little to no hygiene. In return, this makes me avoid close small talk because the smell is so bad.

VOCALICS

The degree to which our voice contributes to how we are perceived on the job is influenced by several factors. As noted in earlier chapters, the rate at which we speak influences perceptions of the speaker. In general, the good speaker uses a conversational, calm, slightly slower, slightly less tense, and lower voice than speakers not rated as positively. A speaker with such a voice, as pointed out by Pearce and Conklin (1971), is perceived as more trustworthy; is more favorably evaluated; is perceived as more attractive, as more educated, as possessing higher income, as possessing a better job; and is perceived as taller than a speaker using a dynamic voice. Use of a dynamic voice should be reserved for situations in which a perception of dynamism is needed.

Street and Brady (1982) determined that speech rate affected a listener's perceptions of competence and social attraction. The researchers found that listeners perceived a speaker to be more competent as the speaker's rate of speech increased—of course, within reason. They also found that listeners have a strong stereotype about the social attractiveness of speakers. Those who spoke with moderate and fast rates were perceived as being more socially attractive than speakers at the slowest rate.

Other than general style, voice quality, accent, and dialect seem to influence judgments about a speaker. The major accent and dialect accepted in this culture is the Great American or General American dialect. Those who speak "without an accent" (which is not really possible) may be perceived as more credible than those who speak with a New England or Southern accent and/or dialect. The issue discussed in Chapter 9 about grammatically incorrect dialectical issues certainly would be something to pay attention to in the workplace. Based on Addington's (1971) research, we note that certain voice types are perceived more negatively than others. Who, for example, wants to work with a person who has a nasal voice, with one who is whiny and argumentative, or with a breathy-voiced person on an assignment that requires bold and imaginative thought?

Finally, as a form of nonverbal communication, silence conveys messages of power and credibility. The more powerful and credible people can both initiate and break silences. Those less powerful or credible must endure the silence, which is often used as an indication of displeasure or punishment.

PHYSICAL APPEARANCE

At one time, this chapter might have begun with an examination of physical appearance. Today, however, there seem to be rather strong stereotypes of what is appropriate and inappropriate in terms of physical appearance on the job. (There are often even legal questions about what companies can and cannot stipulate for their employees' appearances.) Such prescriptions are probably truer for the white-collar than for the blue-collar worker, but even that seems to be changing quickly. What, or who, is responsible for this change? Most people would probably point to Molloy (1975, 1978, 1995, 1996) and his popular books on "dressing for success." Before examining Molloy's contribution to one's appearance on the job, we need to consider the general effect that our physical appearance has on the job.

BODY ASPECTS

We make major attributions based on a person's body size, height, and amount of hair. As mentioned previously, there are probably certain stereotypes that continue on the job. We expect that the taller person will be perceived as more credible and will have more power and status in the organization. As noted earlier, a person's physical height is highly correlated with his or her beginning wage. We may also assume that there is a relationship between status and height, that the greater the individual's status, the taller he or she is perceived to be.

A second physical feature is general somatotype, or body shape. Typically, people perceive endomorphic and ectomorphic body types more negatively than the mesomorphic (White, Brown, and Ginsburg 1999). Because the endomorph is usually perceived as being lazy and slow, you can imagine how that attribution is seen in the workplace. The ectomorph, on the other hand, is perceived as being high strung and tense, so the attribution there can be just as devastating in the workplace, albeit in a different way. Although the research on body type may be somewhat contrived, examination of popular trends gives evidence that our culture prefers its males and females to be more mesomorphic.

Some studies imply that physical attractiveness may be an asset for some and an encumbrance for others. Although we generally consider attractiveness an advantage, for people interested in managerial positions, physical attractiveness can be a liability. A study by Heilman and Saruwatari (1979), for instance, found that being attractive was an asset for males seeking a managerial position, but it was advantageous for females only if the position was nonmanagerial. Realize, however, that this was asserted more than 30 years ago. Whether this finding represents a general bias for males to be in managerial positions or is based on the stereotype that attractive women cannot succeed in managerial positions has yet to be ascertained. A clear sexual bias, however, exists at managerial levels. Wood (2012) says that this bias continues today in many forms, physical appearance being only one.

There appears to be a relationship between attractiveness and assertiveness, at least for females. Campbell, Kleim, and Olson (1986) examined the relationship between assertiveness and physical attractiveness. They found that more attractive females exhibited more assertive behavior than did less attractive females. They also found that attractive females reported a higher level of personal assertiveness (as ascertained by a self-expression measure) than did less attractive females. For males, however, there was no significant relationship between attractiveness and assertiveness. The reason is probably easy to see, but allow us to state the obvious here. This connection between attractiveness and assertion for females, and not for males, is no doubt based on self-esteem. More attractive women have been rewarded more than less attractive women, not only for their appearance, but, as we know, for just about everything they do (going to school, being in social settings, and so forth). Less attractive females have not been rewarded. If self-esteem is higher, the individual will naturally assert herself more than if it is lower. Since males are not judged as severely on the basis of their physical attractiveness, their assertiveness is likely to remain constant and is not as likely to be affected by the attractiveness variable.

Finally, the amount of hair you have may also affect how you are perceived. A general rule now is to moderate the amount of cranial hair; if facial hair is to be worn, limit it to a trimmed mustache. It would appear that the short-haired, well-kept individual is perceived as more masculine, mature, wise, and intelligent.

DRESS

What are the effects of dress on how a person is perceived? Although it may seem that this subject has received much research attention, this is not the case. Besides the work previously cited, little research has actually addressed the question of what clothing does for an individual. Much of what we now read and hear has come from Molloy's *Dress for Success* books (1975, 1978, 1995, 1996). These books have produced a stereotype saying that the well-dressed businessman or businesswoman looks a certain way. This stereotype seems to have become the norm and what we expect. More recently, a trend of independence in this area has emerged, with people rebelling against the idea that there is only one standard for dress in the workplace (C. L. Hughes, 2004). This trend, however, has not overcome the prevailing standard for dress. We continue to dress, for the most part, as is expected of us and not always as we want.

What do we know of how dress communicates on the job? Except for the use of a uniform, we know very little. As Bickman (1974a) found, uniforms convey special meanings. Although we do not, as a rule, expect to wear uniforms on the job (unless, of course, there is a uniform associated with the job), most jobs have *informal* uniform requirements. Such occupations as bank teller, stock-person, office assistant, and even teacher require some kind of informal uniform. We expect people in certain occupations to dress in certain ways; thus, we establish an expectation of a uniform as normative, allowing little deviance. With the uniform, we also find perceptions of similar attitudes and behaviors. Hence, the special garb, whether it is a police, fire, or business uniform, implies certain expected behavioral patterns. Cardon and Okoro (2009) discovered that most of us would like to work in a place that has a dress code, but that we would like for that dress code to be more casual than formal. Segrin (1993) analyzed 19 experiments on how clothing impacts perceptions of high and low status. One of Segrin's findings was that in most cases high-status dress elicits compliance more than does low-status dress. Most of us have certain ideas of how someone working for Microsoft dresses; in the same way we also have expectations about how other occupations and businesses expect their employees to observe certain dress, regardless of whether there is a dress code or not. Would you expect a person who waits on you at "Hooters" to be dressed in a business suit? What would you think if you saw that? Would you expect a CEO of a large company to be dressed in a "Hooters" uniform? What would you think if you saw that?

PHOTO 13.3 What impact does this person's clothing have on your perception of his credibility? Would its impact change if you saw a professor wearing this? Why or why not?

One study that examined the impact of clothing on perceptions of credibility was conducted by Bassett, Stanton-Spicer, and Whitehead (1979). Bassett and his colleagues asked their students to view photographs of two males and two females dressed in high- and low-status clothing. High-status dress for males consisted of a suit, dress shirt, tie, and dress shoes. High-status females wore a dress, heels, stockings, and jewelry. In the low-status conditions, male and female sources wore "blue-collar" dress: work jeans and shirts, tennis shoes or boots for males, and inexpensive skirts, blouses, shoes, and no stockings or jewelry for females. Students were then shown each dress condition, after which they rated each person on perceived source credibility. Their results indicated that males and females were perceived differently. Whereas high-status males were rated higher in terms of potency than were low-status males, females were not perceived differently. High-status females were rated as being more competent than low-status females, but for males there was no difference in the ratings of competence and status they received. Both males and females in the high-status conditions were perceived as being more competent than those in the low-status condition. And, finally, there was no difference between dress conditions in ratings for composure.

That these findings were and still seem to be valid in the working world was corroborated in part in a study carried out by Damhorst (1982). She had 64 employees of private businesses view four sketches of a male and a female interacting. In one sketch, both male and female were dressed in formal business attire, and in a second sketch the male and female were dressed less formally. Rather than the dress and suit and tie, as in the first sketch, the female wore pants and a simple knit or pullover top, and the male wore slacks and a knit pullover shirt. In the third and fourth sketches, the male and female wore dissimilar dress (in one the male was formal and the female informal, and vice versa in the other).

Damhorsf's results are significant in that men and women viewed the sketches differently. Although both sexes perceived the business suits worn in the sketches as highly informative about the level of managerial position, female respondents assumed that the man had a higher rank than the woman with whom he was interacting. The male respondents were more sensitive to the context of the situation, placing less importance on dress. Moreover, men in business suits interacting with casually dressed women were perceived to be more directive, rewarding, and punishing than when sketched with the formal female. The men who were dressed casually and interacting with formally dressed women were perceived as occupying nonmanagerial roles and as having ranks equivalent to or lower than those of the women.

In one final study to be described, Lawrence and Watson (1991) had a woman present a speech to ask people to contribute money for leukemia research. In one situation, she wore a nurse's uniform; in the other, a business suit. When she was dressed as a nurse, the pledges for donations were higher. The researchers found similar results for a woman dressed in a sheriff's uniform versus a business suit asking for support for a crime prevention program. Even the passage of time would likely not change those findings. Clearly, dress does seem to have an effect on people's credibility and ability to influence others.

All these studies imply that the type of clothing may have a significant effect on how others perceive your credibility and position, and thus, your effectiveness in persuading or influencing others (C. Hughes, 2004). Furthermore, the type of clothing you wear also tells others something about your communication style. Males in business attire are perceived as having a higher rank than females in business attire. It may be that the business "uniform" is perceived more strongly for males than for females. However, there appears to be a stereotypical "uniform" with which people identify in the "real" world.

How should you dress in the "real" world? If the position requires a uniform, then that uniform will be appropriate. If there is no uniform, then look around to see what others are wearing; you may find that an *informal* uniform policy exists. The relative success of books such as Molloy's indicates that there are uniform policies written nowhere that are known to none but understood by all. If all else fails, try something novel. Ask the people who seem to know and understand the unwritten code of exactly what is acceptable and what is not.

Finally, we consider accessories and artifacts. Molloy (1978) recommends that the artifacts and accessories we wear be kept to a minimum. Be smart, be fashion conscious, but do not become a display yourself. Other studies of artifacts include research that reports a difference in perceived credibility between smokers of cigars, pipes, and cigarettes. This study found that the nonsmoker was perceived as more credible than the smokers. This would certainly hold true in today's no-smoking, health-conscious society. Finally, eyeglasses also seem to say something about you. Molloy states that for a position in the business world, you should wear glasses that make you look authoritarian, traditional, and older. The styles of the day will affect this, but for the male, the glasses should be heavier; for the female, glasses on the job should be lighter and more feminine. It has been said that contacts should be worn for social occasions, although wearing contact lenses on the job provides more credibility because the disability of poor eyesight is less obvious.

STUDENT VOICES

Dana: Along with the long hair of the individual who was interviewing for the sale rep job, he had piercing in both ears and on his eyebrow. Piercings on a male are unprofessional and unattractive. Since the products sold by the company are targeted towards females, a male who is

clean cut, professionally dressed, and well spoken would be the most productive at this job, rather than a male with long hair and body piercings. I knew when I saw him walk into my mother's office, his outlook with this company did not look so positive.

BOX 13.4 OBSERVATIONAL STUDY

Observe a television program that depicts a workplace environment. How are the characters dressed in the

workplace? Do you see any status differentials? How are those differentials depicted through dress and artifacts? What message does this depiction send to the watcher?

IMPRESSION MANAGEMENT

One area that has produced considerable information in the last decade is called *impression management*. We all understand the need to make a good impression at certain times. Even children understand that to be able to ingratiate themselves to others is a way to be able get others to like them and do things for them (Watling and Banerjee, 2007). These children were not seen as self-promoters, which most would think would happen when they were ingratiating themselves, but were viewed more positively. Would this happen in the workplace? This is a good question, and one you probably could answer if you undertook it as a topic of research. The children did not see the ingratiation as being self-promotion, but when you see a fellow worker do that, how often do you label them a "brownnose"? Although many issues of impression management have been studied, most results reported in the literature of the field concern organizational settings, or the workplace. It is also important in interpersonal relationships, of course, but we look at it separately here so you might see how it is likely to be used in your future in organizational communication settings. It is our hope that you will recognize some nonverbal behaviors you might use to effectively manage the impressions you make once you begin your profession, and then as you maintain your career.

Impression management is defined as individuals making conscious efforts to control the impressions they make; we look at this as an aspect of controlling our nonverbal communication. When you wish to make a specific impression, you control such things as physical appearance, kinesics, face and eye behaviors, use of proxemics, and all of the nonverbal subcodes discussed in this textbook. Edinger and Patterson (1983) defined impression management as a person's "behavioral strategy to create some beneficial image" (p. 43). Leathers (1997), in his coverage of this topic, reports that various other scholars have discussed its importance in such professions as those in the courtroom (for lawyers, judges, and jurors), in medical fields, in classrooms, in job interviews, as well as in police interviews, in family settings, and, of course, in potential romantic situations. Patterson (1987) probably summed it up best when he reported that impression management was a function of self-presentation, and persons attempting to manage the impressions they make would be trying to exercise some control over the images others have of them.

You may be wondering how you might manage your impression to create the image of someone who can be perceived as a leader, or at least as someone who would like to be a leader. Peeters and Lievens (2006) discovered that it is not easy to actually control your nonverbal behaviors in a structured interview situation to improve the impression you make. They believe that this might be because we are less able to control our internal nonverbal reactions than we are to control our verbal reactions. One body of research in this area, however, shows how leaders and managers use impression management techniques to enhance their images. Palmer, Welker, Campbell, and Magner (2001) say that leaders and managers do this by presenting themselves as being more trustworthy, using attraction-seeking behaviors, attempting to ingratiate themselves to both their supervisors and their employees, supplication, and exemplifying positive behaviors, but also combining those positive qualities with intimidation. Although that last quality, intimidation, may seem negative at first reading, it becomes positive because it is perceived as a good manager being able to accomplish the assigned jobs and having "a 'thick skin' about failure" (p. 35). Harvey (2001) adds to this description by asserting that leaders, in their quest to manage the impressions they make, need to be charismatic in their self-presentation. As you know from earlier discussions, to lend a sense of charisma, you would choose nonverbal communication behaviors that augment your self-presentation. From the use of haptics and proxemics to physical appearance and kinesics to vocalics and face and eye behaviors, you have the capacity to create a positive impression or a negative one. Even chronemics and olfactics can play a crucial role in your impression management.

We will create a scenario, just to give you a clear idea of how people might use this material to create an image for their employers. Let's say you are a potential employee for a large corporation, and are in the interview process. When you go to the interview, you are careful about how you dress and how you smell, and you show up on time for the interview. You also pay attention to how you sit, how you gesture, how you make eye contact and use facial expressions, how you use touch when you shake hands with the interviewer, how much distance you keep between the interviewer and yourself, and the overall nonverbal impression you make. You have just concerned yourself with *image impression*. Let's say you get the job, and it is a job where you have the possibility of upward mobility within the company. You now concern yourself with making a nonverbal impression of being a person who is a leader, someone who is able to be in a position of management within the company. You concern yourself with the same nonverbal issues as you did for the interview: your appearance, your use of haptics, proxemics, face and eye behaviors, chronemics, kinesics, vocalics, and even olfactics. In short, you try to create the nonverbal impression that Palmer and colleagues say good managers make. True, the nonverbal impression has to be coupled with competencies in your position, but do not lose sight of the fact that your nonverbal impression is important.

STUDENT VOICES

Karyl: I was working at a summer camp over the summer, and the camp director was interviewing some folks for the position of office manager. Now mind you, it is a summer camp, BUT you still needed to take heed of things we have all been taught about concerning creating a positive impression. One young lady came to the interview wearing cut off shorts and a T-shirt where her stomach was showing. Then she proceeded to be over-relaxed in how she sat in the chair (I could see her from where I was working on my programming job). The topper was—she was chewing gum, and not the most polite way of chewing. Guess who did NOT get the job?.

REVIEW

The importance of nonverbal communication on the job can be demonstrated by our reactions and appearance. From the initial impression we have of the working environment to the type of accessories we wear, we are sending and receiving messages. Although there would seem to be many areas in which nonverbal research should be conducted, little has been done. What we know of nonverbal communication on the job seems to conform to stereotypic expectations. This is not surprising; we live in a world partially controlled by our nonverbal communication. Like Molloy's influence, once scholars begin to examine nonverbal communication and to report their findings, the findings take on a sort of permanence. This section should have provided you with some of the material needed to prepare for the needs of the job and, at the same time, provided you with enough information to make fairly accurate predictions about how you are expected to behave and how others want you to act on the job. Because most of us are periodically evaluated for job performance, we next discuss the performance appraisal interview.

BOX 13.5 OBSERVATIONAL STUDY

Consider a situation where you needed to manage your impression (either an organizational or interpersonal setting). What nonverbal subcodes did you manipulate? How? Why? Now consider a situation where you wish you had managed the impression you made, but you didn't. What would you have done differently? Why?

THE PERFORMANCE APPRAISAL INTERVIEW

In addition to the employment interview, most of us find that we are re-evaluated once or twice a year by our superiors. Such interviews are often referred to as **performance appraisal interviews**. In general, these are of two types or a combination of the two types: (1) a review for the purpose of determining salary increases and promotions and (2) a review for the benefit of the subordinate to determine what, if any, changes need to be made in our job performances. Stano (1992) has undertaken extensive research on these interviews, and he has found that in addition to the verbal and content aspects of such events, there are also nonverbal elements. Stano especially emphasizes the importance of the setting. According to him, it is best if such interviews are held in neutral places; this can help lessen any intimidation factors that might be created by the subordinate being evaluated in what is known as the "superior's home territory." Most of the effective nonverbal behaviors useful in the employment interview are also important for the performance appraisal interview. Galin and Benoliel (1990) indicate that dress is important for appraisal interviews, especially because how you dress affects your own behavior and level of confidence. Recall our earlier discussion on what is often an unwritten code of what is acceptable and unacceptable in the workplace, as well as how important it is to manage the impression you make. These factors will be especially important on any day you would need to meet with your superior, and especially when you will be evaluated.

NONVERBAL INTERACTION IN PARTICULAR PROFESSIONS

While nonverbal communication research in business is somewhat scant, there have been attempts to establish some guidelines in particular professions. These include the teacher in the classrooms, the attorney in court, and the businessperson in a leadership position.

THE TEACHER IN THE CLASSROOM

Most of us can name a really good teacher or a really bad one we have had in school or college. Unfortunately, we do not always know *why* we have singled one out as highly regarded or poorly regarded. Richmond and McCroskey (2000) have focused on the importance of *immediacy*, as have many recent nonverbal researchers. By using immediacy as the basic

PHOTO 13.4 Perceptions of a leader's credibility are strongly associated to kinesic and vocalic cues.

concept in effective teaching, Richmond and McCroskey have found that a teacher needs to be approachable, likable, and perceived as trustworthy. Frymier (1994) has indicated that immediacy in the classroom is determined by being, or appearing to be, "closer" to the students. In addition to distance, such factors as smiling, vocal expressiveness, moving around (and away from the lectern), eye contact, the use of humor, and talking with students before and after class all indicate a degree of openness not found in other factors. The dress of a teacher can gain one of two responses. A teacher who is dressed more formally will be perceived as organized, prepared, and knowledgeable; those dressed more casually will be seen as outgoing, fair, honest, receptive, and flexible. Richmond and McCroskey suggest that the teacher should dress more formally in the first days of class; as the term goes on, the teacher should dress more informally. However, we suggest that formality should be the "rule of the day," especially for new teachers. This advice is particularly pertinent for days when giving or returning tests and the last day of the course (Roach 1997). (And it may not be a bad idea for days when the students are evaluating the teacher.) In other words, when teachers wish to appear especially authoritative, they should dress formally—also these are clearly issues of impression management.

Pearson and West (1991) studied the asking of questions by students in the classroom; they found some gender differences. Male teachers received more questions than female teachers. When there was a male instructor, female students asked fewer questions than male students. Self-reported masculinity of the students (independence, assertiveness, and task-orientation) was associated with a greater likelihood of student question asking. These conclusions are supportive of Tannen's (1990) contention that males operate more overtly in public settings.

Some report that those who sit near the front of the class participate more and make better grades than other students. Mercincavage and Brooks (1990), however, found that such was not necessarily the case among business majors. They found that, among freshmen only, grades were better among those who sat in the front of the class. Among sophomores and juniors, it made no difference where they sat.

Regarding the chronemic element, Cinelli and Ziegler (1990) found some interesting results. Students with Type A personalities (a more tense and structured type) reported a higher incidence of hassles than Type B personalities (a more relaxed and fluid personality). There was no difference, however, between Types A and B regarding the intensity of hassles. Perhaps most interestingly, Type A's hassles involved having to wait, having concerns about physical appearance, and having a concern about meeting high standards. Type B subjects were more concerned about owing money and making decisions.

As can be seen in the list of sources for this section, there has been a great deal of nonverbal research in the last few years that has centered on nonverbal immediacy and the teacher. Most of these theorists believe that immediacy is the overriding factor in a teacher's overall effectiveness, although they find many nonverbal factors are not necessarily definitive determinants of immediacy for teachers. Immediacy can also be managed by controlling the behaviors you use to create an impression in this setting, whether you are a student or the instructor.

THE ATTORNEY IN COURT

There is an interesting difference drawn among laypersons and those in the legal profession regarding the use of nonverbal communication in courts of law. Huddleston and
Huddleston (1986), in a laboratory study, found that wearing a robe did have an impact on
what others thought of the judge's status, regardless of the sex of the judge. Most in the legal
profession, however, attach little credibility to the notion that nonverbal communication has
a significant impact on judgments in court. Recall, however, from our earlier discussion that
a great deal of the impression management research has been done in the courtroom setting.
Law schools devote some time—though little in comparison with other aspects of the law—
to studying nonverbal communication in the practice of law, inside or outside of the courtroom. Mauet (1988), in his text on courtroom behavior, writes:

> Prepare the witness for his courtroom appearance, explain that he should dress neatly and
> conservatively, with clothes appropriate to his background. Explain how the court is ar-
> ranged, where the judge, lawyers, court reporter, clerk, bailiff, and spectators sit, how the
> witnesses will enter and leave the courtroom, where and how he will take the oath, where he
> will sit while giving his testimony, and how he should act there. (p. 18)

Clearly, these are nonverbal communication issues, including issues of how the physical
environment affects the courtroom.

Mauet (1988) also mentions the "body language" method for selecting jurors, but the
explanation is less than a page long. The rationale behind those in the legal profession dis-
counting the importance of body language is that the record of the case is verbal—it is recorded via transcript, which later can be used as the basis for appeal. Those in the legal
profession believe that the verbal aspect of the communication process has the greatest
impact (Conley and O'Barr 1990). Perhaps, too, legal professionals feel that the law is a
cognitive, not an affective, process. Lay observers, such as those who view court television, as
well as regular viewers of *Law and Order*, and even the old stalwarts, *The Practice, Boston Legal,
Perry Mason, Matlock*, and *L. A. Law*, believe in the dynamism of the attorney, the sincerity in
the voice of the witness, and the arrogance portrayed in the guilty party.

In each case, observers believe that they can determine dynamism, sincerity, and arrogance through their interpretations of the nonverbal communication of others. Matlon's
(1988) text on communication and the legal process elaborates on nonverbal communication in interviews, negotiations, jury selection, opening statements, witness preparation, and
in closing arguments.

The study of nonverbal communication is important for attorneys during the jury selection process, since the jury ultimately decides the fate of the client. When potential jurors are asked questions, their eye contact with the attorneys, their positioning in their seats (erect or slouching), and the display of nervous habits help the attorney decide whether to "strike" (reject) a potential juror. Sannito (1983) has suggested that "wide-eyed" jurors are beneficial for plaintiff attorneys and for defendants in nonviolent criminal cases. Additionally, jurors physically leaning to the left or to the right may indicate which cliques may evolve if the pairs are chosen (Issacs 1987).

Wearing inappropriate clothing may elicit undesirable stereotyping. Accessories worn by jurors may help determine a final vote, especially as they indicate marital status, socioeconomic background, and religious affiliation. While many of these questions can be answered with a written form or through oral asking, the attorney who is quick in perceiving such items may be more successful, because the wearing of objects indicates a stronger commitment than simply completing a form (see Raiscott 1985).

Attorneys "prepare" their witnesses before trial, making certain that they do not appear "memorized" or "overrehearsed" (Varinsky 1992). Waltman (1984) has indicated that conservative dress should be worn in the courtroom by defendants and witnesses, and McElhaney (1987) has emphasized the importance of a clean and neat appearance. He does, however, recommend against overdressing a client. On the other side of the issue of dress, though, is that the client should not appear to be a prisoner (Fontaine and Kiger 1978). Eye behavior is crucial for all players in courts of law. Raiscott (1985) suggests that the first few minutes the person is seen are the most crucial. An accused criminal should be dressed in a manner that is inconsistent with the crime; in civil cases, the persons seeking damages need to look as if they need the damage settlement and that they deserve it. All courtroom appearances should be conservative in nature.

There is a joke told about the importance of eye behavior. The story is that a defense attorney in a murder case is giving a summation. In the attorney's talk to the jury, the final words are: "My client never committed murder. In fact, I think the victim may come through those doors in the back of this room at any time." All of the jurors looked at the doors. They came back with a verdict in minutes. "Guilty as charged," said the foreperson. As they were leaving the courtroom, the defense attorney said to the foreperson, "I don't understand. All of the jurors looked at the doors after I made my statement." "It's easy," responded the foreperson, "your client didn't."

BOX 13.7 OBSERVATIONAL STUDY

Observe a "lawyer show" on television (e.g., *Law and Order, Boston Legal, The Practice, L.A. Law, Perry Mason, Matlock*). Do the directors have the actors acting stereotypically as lawyers do? What nonverbal behaviors do they use that are indicative of lawyers? What messages are sent about lawyers by these nonverbal behaviors? Has the image of lawyers that directors portray in these programs changed over time?

THE HEALTH-CARE INDUSTRY

It should not come as a surprise to you that one area of the business world that has received more and more attention from the nonverbal communication field is that of health care workers. These include doctors, nurses, physicians' assistants, and support personnel, such as receptionists and "intake" personnel. The reason this has received so much attention in recent studies is probably that many academic programs now offer courses and majors in the area of Health Care Communication. Since most health care situations are nerve-wracking to begin with, add in the possibility of poor nonverbal communication on either the health care worker or the patient's part, and you have a recipe for disaster in an extremely important area of our society. Blanch-Hartigan (2011) found that it was important for health-care workers to try to recognize the emotions of the patients with which they worked. Albardiaz (2011) presented ideas to teach health care workers to utilize better nonverbal communication skills by paying attention to their body language (kinesics), their tone of voice, and the rate at which they speak. Chronemics would be an important aspect of health care workers, because all of us have been in a situation where we are rushed through, often so the doctor can fit more patients into an already busy schedule.

One area of the health care industry that has received a great deal of attention is the area of end-of-life care, especially hospice care, cancer treatment, and diseases of the aged, such as Alzheimers (see Kozlowska and Doboszynska 2012; and L. K. Sheldon et al. 2009). As you can imagine, people in dire health situations have many different aspects of their health care that need to be addressed. In addition, family members of individuals who are in crisis need to be approached in ways that convey the nonverbal message that they are worthy of care and treatment. Of course, as in all situations we have discussed throughout this book, health care workers must pay attention to contexts and to individuals' communication styles. Thinking they are giving compassionate touch to a person who has a low-touch persona would do nothing but add to the person's uneasiness with the situation. Paying attention to the patients' and family members' nonverbal communication will ensure that they can react "in kind"—the good old norm of reciprocity we have discussed throughout the material we present here.

THE BUSINESS PERSON IN A LEADERSHIP POSITION

This section examines nonverbal behaviors that affect perceptions of credibility and leadership. We believe that this discussion will provide you with the information needed (1) to promote an image associated with leadership and (2) to identify the nonverbal cues that are associated with leadership. How you use them, manipulate them, or simply defer to them may be important strategies in advancing your career.

Where you sit, how much eye contact you can control, and perhaps your physical size contribute to perceptions of leadership. These behaviors, with the exception of eye contact, may be less controllable in a group situation and, therefore, of less value to you than those that deal with your *presentational behaviors*. A number of researchers have stated that several nonverbal behaviors are important in establishing leadership. Mehrabian and Williams (1969) say that facial expression, gesturing, and head nodding are associated with influence.

Other researchers affirm that such behaviors are necessary for leadership, but they find that smiling is also an important feature for the leader. Smiles and gestures suggest that group members have conferred the approval necessary to emerge as a leader. In addition, a lack of positive nonverbal communication skills can be harmful to your credibility, especially as an emerging leader. Cole and McCroskey (2003), for example, discovered that if you show non-verbal signs of communication apprehension or verbal aggressiveness, then you are less likely to be considered a leader—or leadership material. These are all important issues to keep in mind as you go out into the working world.

Two studies that specifically examined the nonverbal behaviors under the control of the individual reported that gestures are probably most important in determining leadership emergence. O'Connor (1971) found that mouth movements (the amount of time a person moved his or her mouth), and arm and hand movement were significant predictors of lead-ership. Baird (1976) observed that as many as eight kinesic variables predicted leadership emergence, including gestures with arms and shoulders, head disagreement, eye contact, head agreement, gesticulation of hands and fingers, postural shifts, facial disagreement, and facial agreement. Streeck (2008) even supplies a list of possible types of gestures to use to depict what you are discussing, or at least ones discovered to be used in numerous situa-tions. When considered in the absence of other cues, each would be a significant predictor of leadership; however, when considered together, as would be the case in most interactions, only *arm and shoulder gesticulation* significantly differentiated the emerging leader from others. Obviously, other leadership qualities needed to be present as well, but this was one nonverbal kinesic behavior that did stand out in this study. People perceive someone who is fairly animated, who gestures with the arms and shoulders, as having leadership potential. Gesturing seems to be more important than control of eye contact, although this relation-ship has not been studied. Gestures may also be closely associated with a leader's credibility. Riggio and Friedman (1986) tell us that leaders exhibit relaxation kinesic behaviors. Kinesics do play an important role in creating an impression about communicators and their leader-ship abilities.

Leathers (1982) identified four factors that may affect a leader's credibility; all deal with either kinesic or vocal cues. Leathers postulated that eye behaviors, gestures, posture, and vocal qualities are useful in establishing a leader's credibility. There are, however, both posi-tive and negative behaviors associated with each set of cues. Many of these cues have been described previously, but their association with perceptions of credibility indicates that they should be reviewed here.

In terms of eye behavior, Leathers believed that we tend to form a strong cultural stereo-type specifying what is positive and negative in how we look at others. He stated that positive eye cues include sustaining and maintaining eye contact while talking and listening to others. Negative eye cues include looking down while responding, being "shifty-eyed," blinking excessively or fluttering the eyes, and avoiding eye contact or casting the eyes down and away from the person with whom you are speaking.

There are five positive types of gestures that enhance credibility perceptions. First, ges-tures should be used that add emphasis to the points you are making. Second, these gestures should be spontaneous, relaxed, and unrehearsed. Third, gestures should be used to signal that you wish to speak or that you want someone else to speak. Fourth, gestures with the hands and arms should be kept away from the body, thus increasing their persuasive impact. And fifth, gestures should indicate the feelings or emotion.

There are a number of negative gestures. These include defensive, nervous, and lack-of-confidence gestures such as tugging at clothing, lip licking, hand wringing, finger tapping, out of-context smiling and grimacing, and tentative gestures.

In terms of posture, Leathers suggested that credibility is enhanced when we spread our arms "expansively" in front of ourselves. Rapport will be established by leaning forward in response to a question, whereas responsiveness is indicated by frequent and forceful postural shifts while speaking. Negative postural indicators may include timid and constricted postures, body rigidity, crossed arms and legs, and bodily tension. Because posture and gesture are associated, it is not surprising that positive gestural and postural cues tend to reinforce each other.

Finally, there are a number of vocal cues that affect our perceptions of a person's credibility. Leathers stated that the vocal qualities assigned to credible individuals include conversational style; variation in pitch, rate, and volume (orchestration of the voice); and avoidance of a monotone delivery. Negative vocal qualities include nasalizing, flatness, and/or tenseness of the voice. Excessive rate (rapidity of speech) and frequent pauses may undermine perceptions of credibility, implying a lack of confidence and/or competence. Although not all nonfluencies are bad, too many *ahs*, the repetition of words, and stuttering have a negative impact on perceptions of credibility.

The credible leader, then, is one who communicates forcefully, in terms of both kinesic and vocalic cues. These cues can be used to increase your nonverbal repertoire of positive behaviors. They can also be used to discern possible flaws in others' credibility. You must remember, however, that some leaders, leaders by virtue of their position in the organization, do not worry about gesture, posture, or voice; they are credible simply because of their positions. Also realize that as you read over a list of positive factors for the perception of leadership qualities, many of those cues are what males are socialized to do; the negative cues show many things females are socialized to do. Lee (1999) discovered that there were gender differences in the exchanges that take place between leaders and members and that gender does make a difference in these exchanges. Logically, then, these are nonverbal cues you might have come by naturally by the nurturing process, or you may have been taught not to use them because they are behaviors your gender should not use. Recall the study by Palmer et al. (2001), mentioned earlier, that reported how important it was for people who wish to be in leadership or management roles to concern themselves with impression management. You might consider how you need to change your nonverbal messages to show your leadership abilities by manipulating the four factors Leathers says might do this (see also Leathers 1988).

A final note on this section involves the increased importance of *sexual harassment* cases in the workplace. Because the number of females in every type of workplace has increased in the past 30 years, more and more focus has been placed on male–female interactions there. Hickson, Grierson, and Linder (1991) have noted, however, that sexual harassment can also be a same-sex offense. In essence, most of us think of sexual harassment as a case (primarily) where a person in a superior position tries to use his or her influence over a subordinate employee for sexual favors (often called *quid pro quo*). Such cases do not necessarily involve having sex per se, but nonverbally they may involve inappropriate touch behavior, space usage, vocalizations, gazing, and the like. New employees, in particular, should be on guard for such violators of personal freedom. One area of nonverbal research does tell us that men and women interpret touch from the opposite sex differently, as we discussed in Chapter 3. In the past, men reported that they often saw female touch as flirting, or even as a sexual come-on (Henley 1977). With the changing norms of our society, and sexual harassment issues on the U.S. agenda for the workplace, the results of a similar study done today might yield different results.

The other aspect of sexual harassment that has become more recognizable is what the literature of the field calls *hostile environment*, or an environment that is uncomfortable for someone to work in because of his or her sex. Irizarry (2004) did an analysis of what causes women to feel more intimidated or, as she termed it, having their "face threatened" more in the workplace than men. She discovered that it was more likely to happen due to sex stereotyping, sex role constraints, and being treated differently. She also discovered that this is much more likely to happen to women who try to enter what has historically been known as a "man's profession." It is manifested in many ways, but one of the largest threats to face for women is a questioning of their professional knowledge and abilities. Although not many studies have been reported on this aspect of sexual harassment, it is safe to say that the majority of sexual harassment issues are of this nature. Hostile environments can be created by the same nonverbal cues we mentioned earlier in *quid pro quo* situations. The researchers have suggested that employees find out the employer's policy. If violations occur, they should be reported. If violations continue, victims should contact appropriate authorities.

BOX 13.8   OBSERVATIONAL STUDY

The next time you are a participant at a group meeting (as either a leader or a group member), observe the nonverbal differences that display power, status, and/or leadership that you notice between the leader and the group members. If the person is not your "boss," how do you respond to those nonverbal issues? If he or she is your boss, how do you respond?

SUMMARY

Nonverbal communication on the job is an important nonverbal area for study; it considers both physical and personal cues that a person can use in assessing power, status, credibility, leadership, and other variables. The appraisal interview is crucial, especially in terms of nonverbal behaviors that may have an impact on the chances of "surviving" in the workplace. It is important to learn the cues to exhibit in order to create a perception of credibility and, perhaps, of potential as an emergent leader. Finally, impression management seems to be an emerging field of study in the organizational communication field, and potential employees as well as employees and employers in all fields should pay attention to the nonverbal communication they use to create positive impressions. Because each job may be slightly different and may have different expectations, the suggestions made should be examined carefully and only within the specific work context you are considering. Like most of nonverbal communication, much of what we perceive may be idiosyncratic. There appears to be some rather strong stereotypes within the context of the job; such expectations and norms can be manipulated to your advantage. Knowledge of what is expected nonverbally and how these expectations are reinforced may provide the advantage needed for success on the job.

QUESTIONS FOR THOUGHT

1. How does nonverbal communication establish an individual's relationship with others at work? Are there certain nonverbal subcodes that are more important than others? At different points in the individual's career? If so, which?
2. How does a worker go about increasing her or his credibility and power on the job?
3. How would you conduct an appraisal interview now that you know the impact nonverbal messages have on the appraisal interview process? What nonverbal subcodes would you emphasize? Which would you de-emphasize? Why?
4. How would you create the nonverbal message of "I am a leader?" What changes would you have to make? What would you keep the same? Why?
5. How do nonverbal messages operate in professions other than business, education, and law? Are there any nonverbal subcodes important enough to be found across professions?

FURTHER REFERENCES

Relational Messages in the Workplace

Durr, M., and Harvey-Wingfield, A. M. (2011). Keep Your "N" in Check: African American Women and the Interactive Effects of Etiquette and Emotional Labor. *Critical Sociology, 37,* 557–571.
McCroskey, J. C., Richmond, V. P., Johnson, A. D., and Smith, H. T. (2004). Organizational orientations theory and measurement: Development of measures and preliminary investigations. *Communication Quarterly, 52,* 1–14.
Teven, J., McCroskey, J. C., and Richmond, V. P. (2006). Communication correlates of perceived Machiavellianism of supervisors: Communication orientations and outcomes. *Communication Quarterly, 54* (2), 127–142.
Wolf, K., Milburn, T., and Wilkins, R. (2008). Expressive practices: The local enactment of culture in the communication classroom. *Business Communication Quarterly, 71,* 171–183.

General Nonverbal Messages

Brief, A. P., and Weiss, H. M. (2002). Organizational behavior: Affect in the workplace. *Annual Review of Psychology, 53,* 279–307.
Kassing, J. W. (2008). Consider this: A comparison of factors contributing to employees' expressions of dissent. *Communication Quarterly, 56,* 342–355.

Impression Management

Johansson, C. (2007). Goffman's sociology: An inspiring resource for developing public relations theory. *Public Relations Review, 33* (3), 275–280.
Rozell, E. J., and Gundersen, D. E. (2003). The effects of leader impression management on group perceptions of cohesion, consensus, and communication. *Small Group Research, 34,* 197–222.

Performance Appraisal

Schraeder, M., Becton, J. B., and Portis, R. (2007). A critical examination of performance appraisals. *Journal for Quality and Participation*, 30, 20–25.

Teachers in the Classroom

Benzer, A. (2012). Teachers' opinions about the use of body language. *Education*, 132, 467–473.
Chory, R. M., and McCroskey, J. C. (1999). The relationship between teacher management communication style and affective learning. *Communication Quarterly*, 47, 1–11.
Hess, J. A., Smythe, M. J., and Communication 451. (2001). Is teacher immediacy actually related to student cognitive learning? *Communication Studies*, 52, 197–219.
Huhlaeva, O. V. (2012). Features of the interaction of teachers with students classes with mixed composition ethnocultural. *Psychological Science & Education*, 2, 71–75.
Mottet, T. P., and Beebe, S. A. (2002). Relationships between teacher nonverbal immediacy, student emotional response, and perceived student learning. *Communication Research Reports*, 19, 77–88.
Myers, S. A., Mottet, T. P., and Martin, M. M. (2000). The relationship between student communication motives and perceived instructor communicator style. *Communication Research Reports*, 17, 161–170.
Powell, L., Hamilton, T., Hickson, M., and Stuckey, J. (2001). The relationship of homophily to verbal and nonverbal immediacy in the classroom. *Communication Research Reports*, 18, 217–222.
Richmond, V. P., McCroskey, J. C., and Johnson, A. D. (2003). Development of the Nonverbal Immediacy Scale (NIS): Measures of self- and other-perceived nonverbal immediacy. *Communication Quarterly*, 51, 504–517.
Teven, J. J., and Gorham, J. (1998). A qualitative analysis of low-inference student perceptions of teacher caring and non-caring behaviors within the college classroom. *Communication Research Reports*, 15, 288–298.
Titsworth, B. S. (2001). Immediate and delayed effects of interest cues and engagement cues on students' affective learning. *Communication Studies*, 52, 169–179.

Attorneys

Smith, L. J., and Malandro, L. A. (1985). *Courtroom communication strategies*. New York: Kluwer.

Health Care Workers

Cutter, G. R. (2008). Effects of program exposure and engagement with tailored prevention communication on sun protection by young adolescents [Electronic version]. *Journal of Health Communication*, 13, 619–636.
Gorawara-Bhat, R., and Cook, M. A. (2011). Eye contact in patient-centered communication. *Patient Education and Counseling*, 82, 442–447.
Grossbach, I., Stranberg, S., and Chlan, L. (2011). Promoting effective communication for patients receiving mechanical ventilation. *Critical Care Nurse*, 31, 46–61.
Haskard, K. B., DiMatteo, M. R., and Heritage, J. (2009). Affective and instrumental communication in primary care interactions: Predicting the satisfaction of nursing staff and patients. *Health Communication*, 24, 21–32.
Jirwe, M., Gerrish, K., and Emami, A. (2010). Student nurses' experiences of communication in cross-cultural care encounters. *Scandinavian Journal of Caring Sciences*, 24, 436–444.

Stepanikova, I., Zhang, Q., Wieland, D., Eleazer, G., and Stewart, T. (2012). Non-verbal communication between primary care physicians and older patients: How does race matter? *Journal of General Internal Medicine, 27,* 576–581.

Business Person in Leadership

Halbe, D. (2012). "Who's there?": Differences in the features of telephone and face-to-face conferences. *Journal of Business Communication, 49,* 48–73.

Scarduzio, J. A., and Geist-Martin, P. (2008). Making sense of fractured identities: Male professors' narratives of sexual harassment. *Communication Monographs, 75,* 369–395.

CHAPTER 14

THE FUTURE OF NONVERBAL COMMUNICATION: A REVIEW

From its early beginnings almost 2,500 years ago as merely one of the five canons of rhetoric (pronuntiatio), the study of nonverbal communication has come a long way. Unquestionably, the theoretical views of Charles Darwin in the middle of the 19th century and the support of such theories through the recent work of Edward O. Wilson in sociobiology have supported the study of nonverbal communication. In addition to the adherence to nurture theory, new fields of study have developed—including anthropology, in which both biological and sociological data are included in the study of human beings—and have yielded additional knowledge about nonverbal communication. Since about 1960, the field we used to label as speech, but now call speech communication, communication, or communication studies, has transformed the study of nonverbal communication. The transformation has been from a field concerned only with the prescriptive *gesturing and vocal tone associated with public speaking to the understanding of varieties and eccentricities of nonverbal communication in all types of social situations.*

Nonverbal communication research has become more enlightening through photographs, films, and videotapes. Voiceprints and polygraphs have further enhanced the development of nonverbal communication research. The scientific method of the social scientist has improved with the use of computers for statistics, the addition of new statistical methods (which have in some instances made researchers revise their earlier findings), and the evolution from simplistic data gathering to more sophisticated techniques. Research methods of the qualitative researchers have also changed with the times, resulting in more reliability and validity from the studies that are conducted.

The application of nonverbal communication research has seen a major resurgence. Industry uses information on chronemics, physical appearance, impression management, environment, and territory in making decisions that affect many. Clothing and impression management studies have also changed the business field. Although the research thus far has presented a prescriptive approach, it is likely that future studies will add even more. Proxemic and haptic studies are used as a basis for determining sexual harassment charges as well as other aspects in the legal field. The overall study of facial expression, dress, and gestures is useful to lawyers and students of law in selecting jurors who are likely to see one particular side of the case or the other. The study of gestures in everyday life is

PHOTO 14.1 Those who understand nonverbal messages will have an advantage over those who have not learned to identify what these behaviors communicate.

useful in studying dramatic order to imitate the gestures of people in real-life situations as well as the various dialects used in daily speech. Film directors study nonverbal communication to make their actors appear more real. Students pursuing advertising find the study of all nonverbal subcodes important to how successful advertisements actually are. Advertisers who know the messages that specific nonverbal characteristics and behaviors send will have an advantage over those who have not studied these phenomena and how they communicate. Those of you going into the field of advertising should use this knowledge to your advantage, from the development of your resumes, to your job interviews, to the actual positions you hold.

Thus, the study of nonverbal communication has changed significantly over the years regarding the theoretical bases of study, the methods used for study, and the applications of research it has produced. Now, from all we have studied, what do we know about nonverbal communication? What do we need to know? Where will nonverbal communication research be in 2020, 2030?

WHAT WE KNOW ABOUT NONVERBAL COMMUNICATION

At the beginning of this book we examined what we believe to be the major considerations for the study of nonverbal communication. We noted that nonverbal communication, although recognized as important, has not really received the attention that has been directed to verbal communication. It was pointed out that there is a number of diverse opinions as to what constitutes nonverbal communication, and no particular approach is actually more correct than any other. We stated that nonverbal communication operates or functions with the verbal message intentionally or unintentionally, to reinforce, contradict, complement, accentuate, regulate, or replace the verbal message. In this connection, we indicated that approximately two-thirds of our total communication is nonverbal in nature. We then examined how nonverbal research is undertaken, and we described several ways to conduct research.

In Part I, we examined eight major subcodes, each consisting of one or more "minor" subcodes. Our focus has been on establishing how nonverbal communication functions to provide the communicators with information regarding identification, control of the interaction, relational information, cognitive processing, affective processing, and deception. *areas of study* A summary of this discussion is found in Table 14.1.

We began with a study of touch, where we pointed out that one of the most powerful communication tools we have is touch, but touch is also one of the tools we use least. We also examined the impact of violating proxemic and haptic norms and expectations, stating that people may be influenced and may influence others by means of the systematic creation and violation of spatial/touch norms. We also discussed some contemporary issues of the usage of touch, including its use in persuasive situations and sexual harassment cases. Next we looked at the space in which we communicate, indicating that the environment and the territory in which we communicate may be considered our first lines of communication. We then examined the environment to determine its effect on communication, noting that any environment has both perceptual and situational features. How our environment is structured also indicates something about its creator and about how others are expected to act and communicate in that setting.

TABLE 14.1   NONVERBAL FUNCTIONS BY SUBCODE

Function	Space	Gestures	Physical Appearance	Vocalics	Covert
Identification	Intimate fragrance	Personal hug	Face	Voice	Natural walk
Control of interaction	Moving away	Raising hand	Puzzling expression	Raising pitch at the end of a question	Looking at one's watch to indicate "hurry"
Relationship of interactants	Intimate	Hand holding	Wedding band	Whispering	Passing time slowly
Display of cognitive information	Placing markers in seats	Placing finger & thumb to indicate "okay"	Fraternity pin	Speaking slowly as in giving directions	Sweaty palms when anxious
Display of affective information	Sitting adjacent in seats at a restaurant	Hugging	Facial expression of emotion: happiness, sadness, fear, anger, etc.	Whispering	Fidgeting
Deception	Socially appropriate hug	Hand-to-face (excessive)	Looking away at inappropriate times	Stuttering unusually; stammers; stops	Talking too fast

PHOTO 14.2 Most people gesture while talking.

The territories we establish were then examined. Based on this discussion, we inferred that territory consists of areas of space that are marked and possess boundaries, and that certain communications are appropriate based on the access others have to that territory.

Personal space, we noted, has no markers and is flexible. Our personal space is treated like a zone around us—larger in some areas and smaller in others. A number of features influence how much personal space we expect from others; these include age, sex, race, intimacy, and formality of interaction. The ultimate violation of personal space is touch, or zero-proxemics.

Next we examined how the body and its coverings communicate. Physical appearance was defined as body shape, clothing, cosmetics, and accessories. We indicated that because of its power, physical appearance plays a major factor in how people perceive us. The effect of the perception is attributable to the fairly strong stereotypes we associate with body shape, hair, skin color and texture, and the clothing people wear. We noted that one's appearance is a major factor in the development of self-image. Finally, we stated that (1) by means of our appearance, we can influence others, and in turn we can be influenced by them, and that (2) we are placed in certain social categories on the basis of our "uniforms."

A major nonverbal area that deals with communication is the body. In examining the kinesic subcode, we looked at several approaches to the study of bodily motion, discussing specific areas of the body and including gesture and facial expression. We then examined the impact of the voice on communication and stereotyping, observing what the voice communicates (e.g., in terms of accent, intonation), what perceptions we have of people based on their vocalizations, and what potential there is for identification through the voice.

We rounded out our study of the various subcodes by describing those based on some type of perceptual "set." These subcodes include the chronemic and olfactory modes of communication associated with internal states. Chronemics, our perception of time, was classified in terms of the impact of time that we acquire through (1) culture, (2) subculture, and (3) our psychological orientations toward time. We then considered how smell affects communication, noting that people differ in their ability to smell, that smell communicates a variety of meanings, and that it is used as a manipulative tool.

Part II applied what we had covered in the preceding chapters. In this part we correlated the study of nonverbal communication in three critical contexts: the social situation (initial interaction), the family (both physical and psychological aspects) and home situation, and the job situation. It was pointed out that nonverbal communication plays a large role in our initial interactions with others, including courtship and courtship readiness cues. We then examined how the concepts of the physical and the psychological "home" influence our nonverbal communication. In this connection we described how people use nonverbal communication from birth through old age. Finally, we examined nonverbal communication on the job, describing how you can demonstrate leadership and credibility and create either a more successful or a less-than-satisfactory work life for yourself simply by your use of nonverbal communication.

WHERE IS THE STUDY OF NONVERBAL COMMUNICATION GOING?

In the area of theory, Ekman and his colleagues continue to seek support for their nature theory of nonverbal communication. Such research is certainly beneficial in establishing cultural similarities. Recent work on human genes will probably bring up additional support for the nature theory. At the same time, nurture theorists have been assisting us in establishing micro-units of nonverbal behavior, which may (or may not) vary from culture to culture. The functionalists are much more concerned with how nonverbal communication is used than they are with where similarities and differences developed.

Regarding method, technology has been a major factor in the resurgence of nonverbal communication research and study. Film and broadcasting have brought about significant changes, as has the field of advertising. Significantly, the relationships between the way communication is processed, both verbally and nonverbally, and the resultant behaviors may provide insight not only into the *how* of communication but also into the *why*. The study of nonverbal internal states may yield answers as basic as the systems under study.

The area of application is expanding significantly. In the job field, for example, applications are being used in various professions to make services more efficient and productive, especially in interpersonal encounters with other human beings. As mentioned, transportation companies are looking at chronemics, businesses are looking at environmental engineering, and service companies are looking at making the individual worker more sensitive to nonverbal cues in general and to specific cues in particular (e.g., sales, leadership). The medical and health care professions are looking at proxemics and haptics, and more recently at the territory in which they serve their patients. Graphic arts areas have used impression management findings to further their profession in new and different ways. The field of psychology is becoming more concerned with kinesic behavior and the way in which nonverbal cues are processed by clients. In mass communication professions, especially media—advertising, broadcasting, and public relations—the knowledge and application of nonverbal communication theories will be invaluable.

There is still more to know. Specifically, we believe that the following represent just some significant questions still unanswered:

1. How does the internal state compare to external behavior during deception?
2. Can changing one's external behavior change one's internal state?
3. Is nonverbal communication as important to the transmitter (via internal states) as it is to the receiver (as perceived through external behavior)?
4. Are general solutions to problems of depression, anxiety, conflict, and deception available through the enhanced study of nonverbal communication?
5. How can we better teach individuals to improve their nonverbal communication for an improved lifestyle? For better situations in their families? On the job? In their intimate relationships?
6. What impact does nonverbal communication have on our lives as we progress from birth to death?
7. How have technological changes, especially in areas of media (film, broadcasting, advertising, and the Internet), changed our understanding of nonverbal messages, especially in light of the belief by some theorists that media play a large role in socializing people?
8. How have social media changed our nonverbal communication with others? Are we more open than we have been? Are we more deceptive than we are in face-to-face settings?
9. If we agree that media socialize us, what can media do to teach us new roles and rules? Have they accepted that responsibility?
10. Has nonverbal genderization of children changed since the initial research on gender differences was done? Were you raised as a stereotypical child of your sex, or were you raised more androgynously?
11. What areas (subcodes) of nonverbal communication interest you enough to try some research studies of your own? What types of things would you like to find the answers to by use of research studies?
12. With our world becoming such a global village, how important will cultural differences in nonverbal communication become to you as you progress through life?
13. Will the changes the country saw in the presidential elections of 2008 and 2012 (both the primaries and the actual election) bring any changes in how we view minorities nonverbally (including women)?

These are relatively abstract questions that barely scratch the surface, but ultimately the study of small, seemingly insignificant variables may help us understand the larger, more significant questions about who we are and about how we can assist others in understanding who we are.

GENERAL REVIEW

To conclude this study of nonverbal communication, we present 18 general statements summarizing the present content and scope of the subject. This list provides a convenient reference and review:

1. Nonverbal communication is "more" important than verbal communication in face-to-face situations.
2. Nonverbal communication can be approached in a variety of ways, each offering a slightly different interpretation of the behavior(s) observed.
3. Nonverbal communication, unlike verbal communication, may only need to be *perceived* as intentional to be considered communication.
4. Verbal and nonverbal communication may differ according to which brain hemisphere is dominant, or which side of the brain receives and interprets the communication.
5. Kinesics, proxemics, haptics, vocalics, chronemics, olfaction, and physical appearance interact with verbal communication to transmit a message.
6. Positive messages are commonly associated with forward leans, increased eye contact, relaxed posture, increased touching, and decreased distance; negative messages are transmitted by means of the opposite cues.
7. Nonverbal communication varies with microcultures, subcultures, cultures, personality, age, sex, and race.
8. Females are more sensitive to nonverbal cues—except for deception—and transmit more accurate nonverbal messages to others.
9. When contradictory messages are sent through verbal and nonverbal channels, most adults consider the nonverbal message to be more accurate; most children consider the verbal message to be more accurate.
10. Social situations provide a setting for determining the quality of relationships through nonverbal cues.
11. Nonverbal cues provide families with a means for achieving better understanding between their members.
12. Nonverbal communication is used differently and is perceived differently at various stages of a relationship.
13. We use nonverbal communication differently at various stages in our lives.
14. In job situations, we should be very careful about nonverbal cues, for they demonstrate power, credibility, assertiveness, and awareness of others.
15. Although we usually assume that nonverbal cues are sincere and spontaneous, they are often manipulated with some particular outcome in mind.
16. We should always remember what we call the *Accuracy Rule*: The better you know the person and context (when perceiving someone's nonverbal message), the more accurate your perception will be.
17. We should always remember the dyadic effect (or norm of reciprocity): What I do to you nonverbally, I should expect you to do in return.
18. We are really just beginning to become aware of our nonverbal potential.

We hope that by now you are a better nonverbal communicator. You should be able to understand your nonverbal communication better and should also be more qualified to interpret the research being reported. We hope that the research reported has given you a better understanding of the field, of what you see and do nonverbally. Perhaps you now have some reasons and understanding behind what you have always perceived as nonverbal quandaries. You may have picked up some tips to use for your own nonverbal communication, but we caution you again about instructing others on how they should communicate nonverbally. We also caution you one final time about your accuracy in interpreting others' nonverbal communication; remember that your accuracy will depend on how well you know the person(s) and the context. It is our hope that we have opened your minds to what sorts of things you might be interested in discovering about nonverbal communication. This book should serve both as a good reference guide in specific contexts and later situations and as a starting point for a lifelong study of communication, whether the emphasis is on verbal *or* nonverbal communication.

METHODS OF NONVERBAL COMMUNICATION RESEARCH

OBJECTIVES OF THE APPENDIX

After studying the Appendix you should be able to:

- Explain the process of research in nonverbal communication.
- Conduct a literature review and establish a theoretical perspective.
- Explain what constitutes "data."
- Explain the relative advantages and disadvantages of different data collection techniques.
- Explain how data are analyzed and applied to nonverbal research.
- Discuss the limitations of nonverbal communication research, including idiosyncratic findings and the impact of context on research.

You are sitting in a public speaking class, and your professor is discussing audience analysis. The professor says, "People who are able to 'tap into the audience demographics' are much more successful when giving a persuasive speech." How many times have you sat in a class all semester and thought to yourself, "Where do they come up with all these theories we read about in our textbooks and that the professors tell us about?" They are found through research studies, and we believe it important that students gain a basic understanding of how nonverbal communication research is conducted. This knowledge should (1) help you to better understand the limitations of the research reported in this and other books, (2) help make you more critical of what you read, and perhaps (3) enable you to conduct nonverbal communication research projects on your own. In Chapter 1 you probably got at least some knowledge of nonverbal communication in general, and also of how nonverbal communication functions to influence your communication in a variety of contexts. The remaining chapters of this book then enumerate many theories of how nonverbal communication functions in our society. This Appendix examines how nonverbal communication research is undertaken and reported, and it will, we hope, clarify the often-misunderstood components of research—hopefully before you begin to read the results of others' research included in this text. If you are reading this material after covering the chapters in the text, we hope you will reflect on the studies you have read about and come to an understanding about how the studies were conducted and reported, and theories drawn from those studies.

We are trying to simplify a very complex topic in a brief section; we do not aim to make researchers out of all of you. We do hope you will have at least an understanding of the basics of how research is conducted and how results are reported, especially in your textbooks (including this one). In many of your classes you will be expected to complete practical projects; indeed, your professor in this course might require that of you. It is important for you to know something about the good and bad ways you can accomplish research. It is also important that you know some of the pitfalls that you might encounter when you conduct your own research. Our vision in covering this is that you might also become interested enough to pursue this topic in a research methods course, and for that reason we try to have you put yourself into the role of the researcher.

NONVERBAL RESEARCH

We believe that nonverbal communication research involves at least six steps: (1) reviewing the pertinent literature, (2) establishing a theoretical perspective, (3) finding a methodology, (4) collecting "data," (5) analyzing that data, and (6) applying the findings to *real-world* situations. Most research in nonverbal communication includes the methods of laboratory experiment, survey, field experiment, and/or field study. The first step is the literature review, and it seeks to combine and consolidate the many areas of study by compiling the available materials that have been published on given topics. We begin by analyzing how such a review is undertaken, with the understanding that all research really begins with a thorough review of the literature.

REVIEW OF THE LITERATURE

Like research of any type, nonverbal communication research requires that researchers first look at what has previously been investigated in the topic. Although many consider the literature review a method that looks at the history of what has been done, it is quite precise and may even lead to formal predictions of what the outcome of the research will be; these predictions are known as hypotheses. According to Stacks and Hocking (1999), the literature review, as a component method of critical investigation, serves several functions. These functions include the collection and verification (confirmation, corroboration) of primary sources (or original research) and secondary sources (or reports of other research) of information, as well as interpreting that information and making conclusions based on it. Review of the relevant literature often brings together existing knowledge and assigns data into categories. These are categories that are theoretically interesting and that will provide you with the background for asking questions or developing hypotheses to be tested.

The general procedure you will need to use in the review of literature is to examine journal articles, books, and published papers to determine what research has been undertaken. Stacks and Hickson (1974) have provided a systematic way to undertake a library search, which has been modified slightly to account for today's electronic library (see Figure A.1).

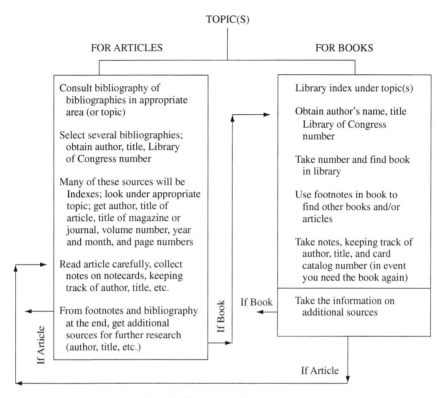

FIGURE A.1   A programmed approach to the literature review.
Source: D. W. Stacks & M. L. Hickson, III. "Research: A programmed approach." *Florida Speech Communication Journal,* 2 (1974), 22.

In addition, indices devoted to communication research have been compiled (e.g., *CommSearch* 1999), as have specialized annotated bibliographies of specific content areas that have been researched (e.g., Stacks, 1985).

The review of literature should be as exhaustive as possible. You should try to obtain all relevant material during this phase of your research, looking for data and studies that support your position as well as material that nullifies or invalidates your hypothesis, which is the outcome you project will happen in the study. The best procedure is the oldest: Prepare note cards on each article or section of a book. You may also cross-index each area of study, such as proxemics, personal space, and violations (see Figure A.2). A list of journals that often publish articles on nonverbal communication is found in Table A.1.

Sources other than academic journals also contribute to your understanding of the literature; however, you must be careful about drawing inferences from sources that have not gone through a peer-review process (required of academic journals before they can be published). John L. Gray's (1992) *Men Are from Mars, Women Are from Venus* is an excellent example to turn to when discussing this issue of peer review. Although many people in the United States, and people around the world, took Gray's work to be a definitive guidebook on male–female communication differences, most scholars of communication viewed this

Willis, F. N., & Rawdon, V.A. (1994). Gender and national differences in attitudes toward same-gender touch. Perceptual and Motor Skills. 78,1027–1034.

SUMMARY: Willis and Rawdon tested the hypotheses that (1) women would be more positive about same-gender touch than men; (2) participants from the Far East would be more negative about same-gender touch; and (3) since Chilean and Spanish persons share the category, "Hispanic," and have a common language, their attitudes about same-gender touch would be similar. Participants were volunteer undergraduates from one university in each of four countries: Spain, Chile, Malaysia, and the United states. All respondents completed the Same-Sex Touch Scale,which had been translated into the languages of the participants. Women had higher scores than men, overall and for each country. However, only the U.S. sample was statistically significant (p < .01). Malaysian students scored lower, indicating a less positive position about same-gender touch. Spanish and American students scored higher than Chilean students. American females scored higher than any other group, followed by Spanish women. Malaysian males had the lowest scores, followed by Chilean males.

METHODOLOGY: Survey Questionnaire
SUB-CODE: Haptics
KEY Words: Gender, same-gender, touch

FIGURE A.2   Example of notecard for literature review.

work guardedly. Why? It did not follow scholarly requirements for good research; many of the conjectures made in this book came from Gray's personal observance of people over the years, not from conducting scientific research. There was a lack of controlled studies. Also—and this is one of the major issues for social scientists—it was not "peer reviewed." Fellow psychologists were not consulted about whether the work was acceptable for publication, nor were communication scholars who specialize in conducting scientific research in the gender differences of communication practices consulted. This lack of peer review does not mean the work has no merit. It simply means that it does not meet the requirements of good academic research, which all scholars hope to produce.

Many other popular authors have published books about nonverbal communication issues, such as dressing professionally, being persuasive, giving good presentations, and even gender communication issues (Molloy 1975, 1978, 1995, 1996; Tannen 1983, 1990). Does this mean that these works are worthless? By no means; it means they are simply not considered scientific research. Interestingly, most of these "pop authors" have also published works that are considered scholarly research (Tannen 1990). When the author of a popular book also has scholarly works published on the subject, the academic community considers the popular literature as more credible than when it is written by someone who has not published scholarly works.

BOX A.1   OBSERVATIONAL STUDY

Find an article in a scholarly journal on some issue of nonverbal communication. This can usually be done through your library (either their online resources or in bound archives of past journals), through your professors, or perhaps even in a department library. Realize that some of the nonverbal communication studies can be found in journals other than those in the field of communication (try psychology, sociology, and anthropology indexes at the very least). Try to discern the following from the article you read: (1) What did the researcher(s) set out to discover? (2) How did they go about it? (3) What did they discover, and what does it mean for nonverbal communication theories? and (4) What do you think about these findings?

TABLE A.1 · PERTINENT JOURNALS WITH ARTICLES ON NONVERBAL COMMUNICATION

Acta Psychologica	Central States Communication Journal
American Anthropologist	Communication Education
American Journal of Psychiatry	Communication Monographs
American Journal of Psychoanalysis	Communication Quarterly
American Journal of Psychology	Communication Research
American Journal of Sociology	Communication Research Reports
American Psychologist	Communication Studies
American Sociological Review	Communication Theory
Archives of General Psychiatry	Developmental Psychology
Behavior Therapy	Discourse Processes
Behavioral Science	Ergonomics
British Journal of Psychiatry	Ethology and Sociobiology
British Journal of Social and Clinical Psychology	Human Communication Research
	Human Ethology
Child Development	Human Factors
Current Anthropology	International Journal of Social Psychiatry
Journal of Abnormal Psychology	Nature
Journal of the American Institute of Planners	Perceptual and Motor Skills
	Psychological Bulletin
Journal of Applied Communication Research	Psychological Reports
	Psychological Review
Journal of Clinical Psychology	Psychology
Journal of Communication	Psychology Today
Journal of Communication Therapy	Psychological Record
Journal of Consulting and Clinical Psychology	Psychonomic Science
	Psychotherapy
Journal of Counseling Psychology	Science
Journal of Cross-Cultural Psychology	Scientific American
Journal of Experimental Psychology	Semiotica
Journal of Nonverbal Behavior	Sex Roles
Journal of Personality	Signs
Journal of Personality and Social Psychology	Southern Communication Journal
	Western Journal of Communication
Journal of Social Psychology	World Communication
Language and Speech	

PHOTO A.1   Studies conducted by researchers are often found in periodicals such as these.

As students in the 21st century, you have a number of options available to you in order to complete your review of literature. One excellent resource will be your library's database. Many scholarly journals, as well as other types of scholarly articles, are available online, and access to them is usually via a database search engine. For example, one author of this text, in the process of updating this edition, read some statistics that seemed incorrect, or at the very least outdated. A database search engine turned up a few scholarly journal articles as well as newspaper and newsmagazine articles that gave newer, updated statistics. You should become familiar with your library's capabilities for accessing online resources, not just the regular search engines you use when surfing the Internet, which are considerably different. Realize, too, that many websites are not considered credible resources when it comes to doing scientific, scholarly research, a point many college professors spend a considerable amount of time trying to impress upon their students. Many college professors limit the number of websites you may use as primary sources because people can put anything they want on a website. There is no guarantee of peer review; there are no restrictions or standards an author must follow when "posting" to a website. Remember, though, that an online source (such as a published journal article that is found online) is not the same as a website source; it is an electronic version of a published product.

As a good researcher, conducting your review of literature will include consulting many different types of works, being sure that the bulk of your literature has merit as peer-reviewed scholarship. When all the sources have been consulted, you should consider your theoretical perspective.

THEORETICAL PERSPECTIVE

Normally, we would begin a literature review already having a theoretical perspective. When studying nonverbal communication, you will theorize that certain relationships exist between the variables that interest you. In some cases, you may not have developed a theoretical perspective. In others, your position or outlook may be changing. In the course of time, most perspectives tend to change as researchers and disciplines mature.

Nonverbal research today is very different from what it was in the 1970s and 1980s, when its study seemed to have peaked. Less nonverbal communication research is published today than during those two decades, and a survey of the most recent *CommSearch* (1999) revealed some interesting statistics. The earliest reported article under the index heading of "Nonverbal Communication" was published in 1938, but between that date and the 1960s, only three such articles were published. In the 1960s, there was a total of 16 articles; in the 1970s, 99 articles; in the 1980s, 75 articles; and in the 1990s, 71 articles (the index includes articles published through 1997). This means that out of a total of 264 articles in professional communication journals over those seven decades, almost 72 percent of them were published prior to 1990; 66 percent were published in the 1970s and 1980s. In addition, what was published in the 1990s seems to be of a different nature. The early studies, especially in the 1970s, seemed to be more subcode oriented, looking at specific subcodes of nonverbal communication and how they affect different situations, types of people, contexts, and the like. The studies of the 1990s seem to be more contextually bound, looking at issues of multiculturalism, use of nonverbal immediacy characteristics (immediacy is defined in a few words as the appearance of being approachable), deception detection, gender differences, and gay and lesbian issues in nonverbal communication, to name just a few. Because the later studies (of the 1990s) are more contextually oriented than subcode oriented, we often cite the earlier research (of the 1970s and 1980s) when we wish to show you the original theories that were found to be the effects when specific subcodes were studied, and we add newer research when it has been conducted.

For the new researcher, there are several available sources in which to search for theoretical views. Among these are books by Stacks, Hill, and Hickson (1991); Infante, Rancer, and Womack (2003); and Littlejohn (2007). Stacks, Hill, and Hickson and Littlejohn, in particular, note two approaches to the study of nonverbal communication: the structural and the functional approaches. In the structural approach, each variable is singled out and looked at separately. The functional approach, often called an external variable or gestalt approach, looks at how selected nonverbal variables (subcodes) function together in the totality of a given situation. This distinction is especially important when one considers the perspectives of Birdwhistell and Hall (structuralists) versus Ekman and Friesen (functionalists). In addition, J. K. Burgoon and Saine (1978) present an excellent overview of many perspectives on the study of nonverbal communication. If you become interested in conducting your own research, we suggest examining these sources to advance your position on processing differences, the origin of nonverbal communication, intentionality, and so forth.

Your theoretical perspective, then, provides guidance for interpreting the literature. This perspective influences how you put forward and test research questions or hypotheses. Another issue about the perspective chosen by a researcher would be to consider your discipline; a psychologist would take a different theoretical view than would a sociologist, or an anthropologist, or a communication scholar. Understanding the theoretical background of a researcher also may help you interpret a study's results; then, if these findings differ from yours, the difference in backgrounds may provide a reason for such differences.

METHODOLOGY

Once the research literature has been reviewed and a theoretical approach formed, it is essential to consider what methodologies might be used. To do this, you must first state the research question, or hypothesis, which states what you hope to discover by your research. After this has been done, you consider the methodology. Usually, the training you have had will likely influence the methods you select in your research. As students, you often will choose methodologies similar to your professors' choices, usually for a safety net; if you need assistance, you can seek it from someone who knows what you are doing.

Pearce, Cronen, and Harris (1982) have outlined seven methodological approaches to social science research. They note that several questions must be asked about the method you use. These questions can be grouped into two major areas: (1) What counts as "data," and (2) How do "data" count? (Data are what we observe and use for analysis, or they are collections of facts from which conclusions may be drawn.) How you answer these two questions determines what method you follow. For example, when you consider what counts as data, you specify which units of analysis you will use, what type of observational unit you will approve, and what kind of data you will accept. You also decide whether the data serves to support your hypothesis.

When we study space usage (proxemics), for instance, where the unit of analysis—what counts as data—is typically *discrete* (separate or distinct), we might break continuous spatial use into four subareas: public space, social space, personal space, and intimate space. For intimate space, we will assign the *interval* of 0 to 18 inches. The personal space interval will be 18 to 48 inches (4 feet), and so on until all four subareas are assigned a specific space zone according to the actual space kept between the people being observed for the study. These space zones are known as *proxemes* (because proxemics is the scientific study of the use of space; it derives from the concept of proximity), and these intervals and how they are

PHOTO A.2   Computers have accelerated the process of researching and analyzing data.

manipulated and used in this study will become the data that we "count." We should point out that we did not determine the intervals ourselves; those measurements came from prior research into space usage (E. T. Hall 1968). It is common practice, when deciding on what data to count, to draw on earlier studies that are considered credible. These materials need to come from scientific studies that have been peer-reviewed before publication. You would discover these types of things when you set out to read the literature to create your Literature Review. In our example, the data we count will come from a questionnaire that we ask the participants in the completed study, and then we will make decisions about how those data counted.

As you can see, you should always consider which approach is going to be used before attempting data collection. The approach you use defines the unit of data and how it is perceived. It also indicates how you should analyze the data and interpret your findings within the general theoretical framework you have adopted.

DATA COLLECTION

Generally speaking, the data for study in nonverbal communication come in four forms: (1) information from laboratory investigations, (2) information from surveys, (3) information from field experiments, or (4) information from field studies. The first three methods of data collection generate *quantitative* data (data that focus on isolating, counting, and analyzing units of phenomena); the fourth generates *qualitative* data. Qualitative data are observed by the researcher or participants in the study and are then evaluated by the knowledgeable scholar, who explores and describes the qualities and then draws conclusions based on what has been studied and observed. You should realize that most quantitative studies include aspects of a qualitative nature, and many qualitative studies use some statistical analyses to clarify qualitative points being made. All four methods are important and contribute to the body of knowledge concerning nonverbal communication; each has advantages and disadvantages. Finally, each has researchers who advocate one approach over the other, just as you will. Table A.2 illustrates the levels of research.

What really makes each approach different, however, is the amount of *control* you have over the variables under study. Generally, control is most evident in the laboratory experiment and is reduced as you approach the field study. Whereas the laboratory experiment isolates the particular variables under study from others, thus deriving as "pure" a finding as possible, the field study places few or no constraints on the variables. Participants being studied simply operate as they do normally in social interactions. One major problem with laboratory research is that it is rarely possible to generalize results from the laboratory to the general population because the effects of other variables are artificially controlled in the lab setting. Similarly, the field study encounters difficulties when you try to specify causes and effects because in the end, as educated as you might be, your findings are ultimately based on the conjectures you make. You can see why peer review is crucial: Peer review allows for confirmation of the researchers' conjectures and research findings. Each form of data collection, however, contributes to our knowledge of nonverbal communication (this textbook, for example, cites research from a variety of the four types of data collection).

TABLE A.2   LEVELS OF RESEARCH

	Person	Nature	Method
More "objective"	1st	Act	Act
		Recording VTR Audio recording Paper recording Participant-observation • as participant • as participant-observer • as observer-participant • as observer	
2nd	Synthesis	Self-report (and interpretation by subjects)	
3rd		Historical report and interpretation—from primary source	Historical report and interpretation—from secondary source • Self-report • Historical report • Interpretation • Self-report with stimulus (lab) • Historical report with stimulus
More "subjective"	Omniscient narrator	Fiction	Contrived

Source: M. Hickson, III, J. B. Roebuck, and K. S. Murty, "Creative Triangulation: Toward a Methodology for Studying Social Types," in *Studies in Symbolic Interaction*, ed. N. K. Denzin (Greenwhich, CT: JAI Press, 1990) 114.

LABORATORY EXPERIMENTS

A portion of the research reported in this book comes from studies conducted in the laboratory. In the laboratory experiment, you attempt to control all the variables in a situation with the exception of those being tested. Even those being tested, however, are controlled in that they are carefully manipulated and limited, and their effects are then noted. The typical laboratory experiment begins with some research questions or hypotheses in mind, which are derived from a review of the literature in a particular area of interest. You then state specific questions or hypotheses concerning the relationship(s) between the variables under study. In the space study example mentioned earlier, for example, the research questions might ask about relationships, "Does personal spacing influence persuasion?" Hypotheses predict relationships. The hypothesis might be "Extreme personal space violations reduce the persuasiveness of 'space invaders' who are low in charisma." In other words, persuaders who are interpersonally unattractive will be less successful at persuasion if they violate the space norms of the persons they are trying to persuade. (Because of scientific publication constraints, most language in research is more complex than everyday common language usage.) You then create procedures to maximize any potential sources of information. At the same time, you try to reduce other sources of information that might "contaminate" the manipulations of these space variables. The idea is to keep the manipulations and findings as "pure" as possible.

In the laboratory experiment, there are two types of variables. First, there is the **independent variable**. This is the variable that you can control or manipulate. In the space usage example, such manipulations may include dress of *confederates* (those individuals helping you to conduct your experiment), distance kept, time spent in close proximity, or all three. Second, there is the **dependent variable**, a factor with which you judge the effects of the independent variable(s) when you compare your findings. Dependent variables may include source credibility, attitude change, attraction, decision to purchase, and so forth. You usually test the independent variables to determine how they produce different results among the dependent variables, either in isolation or in combination.

When the procedures and variables have been identified, you initiate the study. To carry out a research project you need **participants**, people who have been chosen, either randomly or for a particular reason, to participate in the research. Participants are normally assigned to a **condition**, a particular group that receives one or more "treatment" manipulation(s). Usually, participants are *randomly* assigned to a condition, which reduces the probability of error due to the participant's past or knowledge and enables you to exercise some form of control over the results. Once participants have been manipulated, they are then exposed to the dependent measures, which become data to be analyzed. If the dependent measure tested how participants "reacted" to the manipulation (say a smile compared to a frown), and the reactions were filmed, then the reactions could be coded by assistants and become *data.*

Let us look at an example of how these variables work in a study, using the same example of space usage and how it affects persuasion. Realize that you will need to have done your review of literature and to have determined your research questions and hypotheses prior to initiating the study. Once done, you begin the actual study. You might manipulate the attire worn to attempt to persuade, the distance the persuaders put between the persuadees and themselves, and how long the persuaders stand at a given difference from the persuadees. Those would be the independent variables because you manipulate them to conduct your study. The dependent variable you might determine to be the subjects' decisions to purchase products. You manipulate the independent variable to change the distances you use between different participants (persuadees in this example), and you compare the effectiveness of the confederates (persuaders in this example) at different distances.

A scientific example of the laboratory experiment can be seen in a study conducted by Hickson, Powell, Hill, Holt, and Flick (1970). The study randomly assigned college students to one of four groups: three treatment groups or a control group. One group viewed 16 slides of a man smoking a pipe. Another, the **control group**, viewed 16 slides of the same man in the same poses, except he was not smoking. Two other groups viewed a set of slides of the same man, in the same poses, smoking either a cigarette or a cigar. After viewing the slides, each group completed forms on the man's attractiveness, credibility (believability), and perceived similarity with the participant. The independent variable was seeing the man either smoking one of the three types of artifacts (pipe, cigarette, or cigar) or not smoking.

PHOTO A.3   Smoking affects people's perceptions of the smoker.

The answers to the questionnaire comprised the dependent variables. One major criticism of this study is that participants were not asked whether they smoked; hence, some loss of control might be expected (especially for the perceived similarity variable).

Realizing this possible loss of control, researchers replicated this study later (Amsbary, Vogel, Hickson, Wittig, and Oakes 1994). A **replication** is a second study that duplicates the first, except that it may use different participants and take place at a different time, and it may consider variables that should have been considered in the previous study. Replicating a study can either strengthen the original findings or disconfirm the findings, or add to the findings. In this case, Armsbary and colleagues included information about whether the participants smoked or not. They found that being a smoker made no difference in the findings. They also found that smokers were perceived to be lower in credibility and interpersonal attractiveness than in the earlier study, which was not surprising in light of the antismoking campaigns that became prevalent in the 1980s and 1990s. In addition, they found that the pipe smokers' credibility had significantly diminished over the 15-year period. It would be an interesting study to replicate once again post-2000, since the tenor of society about smoking has become even more negative after the millennium.

SURVEYS

A second way to gather data is to administer surveys to randomly selected people. A survey is one way to collect data in the field while still exercising some control over the research. Typically, surveys are carefully devised questionnaires that ask specific questions. The questions should be *pre-tested* so that results are not biased. Moreover, there are specific and rigorous ways of ensuring that people selected to be surveyed come from the general population under study. The people selected compose the study's **sample**. There are two different types of surveys—one that uses random selection of participants and the other that employs what is called a "convenience sample." An example of a representative convenience sample study is one done on body image that was reported in *Psychology Today* (Berscheid, Walster, and Bohrnstedt 1973). This study consisted of questionnaires cut out of the magazine and mailed back to the editors. Because only readers of the magazine completed the survey, the sample was biased in favor of college-educated, middle-class participants—the typical reader of *Psychology Today*. Some surveys found in research journals employ a random sample, which allows comparisons to the larger population under study. It is hard to generalize findings to the larger population if the study's sample is biased, such as in the body image survey.

Surveys enable researchers to obtain as much data as possible while still exercising some control. You maintain control through the selection of the sample and the careful development of the questionnaire used to gather the data. A second form of surveying is the face-to-face interview. Much of what is reported on job interviews is obtained through such dialogues. This type of data may differ from that obtained from the laboratory experiment. Often you must analyze the results of the interview by using a content analysis system. Such systems may include how respondents reacted to open-ended questions (questions asked for a general response), in contrast to how they reacted to closed-ended questions (ones that restrict the answers by giving the respondents several responses to choose from).

The survey is often the most economical and feasible way of collecting data. Consider, for example, a study that seeks to find out whether college students perceive a professor's manner of dress differently from noncollege persons. To conduct this study by means of a laboratory experiment would be both time-consuming and almost impractical. You could induce some students to participate, but finding nonstudents would be a real problem. A survey questionnaire, with pictures of professors in various types of dress, might work very well. You would randomly select the college sample and the noncollege sample, transmit the questionnaires to your respondents by mail or the Internet, and then compare the results. The use of Internet surveying has become so prevalent in today's society that it has become the tool that many, many researchers use when running research studies. You still exercise a degree of control by randomly selecting your sample (being careful to include all possible respondents), and you also maintain control by formulating your questionnaire and pre-testing it to avoid biased responses.

FIELD EXPERIMENTS

The field experiment attempts to combine the advantages of the two procedures previously discussed. First, it tries to control the variables under study as much as possible by manipulating degrees or levels of the variable under study. Second, the field experiment allows other variables that would normally be controlled in the laboratory to influence results. The major advantage of the field experiment, however, is that it allows the study to be carried out in a "natural" setting.

Research conducted by J. K. Burgoon and Aho (1982) on how dress affects a salesperson's perception of a shopper is a good example of the field experiment in nonverbal communication. In this case, the researchers had confederates (students engaged in the research project) dress either "up" (defined as well-dressed) or "down" (defined as sloppy, unkempt). The students then observed salespeople in different shops at a mall and their reactions to the confederates as the "customers." Similar studies include those conducted by Bickman (1974b), in which he examined how dress influenced the response to requests for a dime to be returned from a telephone booth, or the one by Stillman and Hensley (1980), where a waitress' wearing of a flower in her hair influenced tipping behaviors of restaurant customers.

Cant (2009) found, when replicating other studies, that clients of dieticians do look at the dress as well as body shape and size when being counseled by dieticians. The independent variables were clearly manipulated in these field studies. Some would say that the dependent variables are less controllable and therefore you are less likely to find the results as reliable as you would with a laboratory experiment (meaning that the same results would not occur consistently each time you manipulated the variables).

The field experiment can exercise some degree of control for randomization of participants. Although most field experiments do not control for participants, claiming that the value of the data collected in a natural setting offsets any loss of scientific rigor for experiments, you still can manipulate some type of control. Suppose you were interested in how different types of handshakes influence perceptions of another person's credibility. Your independent variable in this case is the handshake, *operationalized* (explained in terms of what the handshake is to be like in the experiment) as strong (a "bone crusher"), moderate/ firm ("normal"), and weak ("wet fish"). In addition, based on your review of the literature, you found that the "normal" handshake in this culture consisted of one-and-a-half pumps of the hand with a moderate/ firm grip. If you are concerned that the sex of the initiator of the handshake may make a difference (and sex often *does* make a difference), you would decide to ensure that you have both a male and a female confederate (the subject who shakes the participants' hands) that are equally attractive. You would also need to pre-test for attractiveness (as in an experiment) to ensure that the results you attribute to the attractiveness factor were valid.

After training each confederate to "squeeze" equally in each of the three conditions, you then go out and randomly select your participants. You can have another confederate approach randomly selected people at randomly selected times and places (on campus, for example) and ask that they "participate in an interview." The interview begins with a handshake and some questions on some topic. After the interview is over, a third confederate asks that the interviewee complete some data on the interviewer (e.g., credibility, attraction, persuasiveness).

The data are then coded and entered into a computer program, and statistical tests are conducted to see which handshake produced which perceptions of the dependent variables. If some experimental research exists on this same topic, you could then compare your results to those conducted in the lab to determine whether the participants reacted in the same way to the same (or similar) variables under different conditions. In some field study research, the results conform to laboratory findings; in many, however, they do not.

FIELD STUDIES

Whereas the field experiment is controlled for the most part, except for the actual sampling of participants, field studies have little control except for the objectivity of the researcher (Diesing 1971; Rossiter 1977). In the field study, the researcher enters a natural setting in an attempt to answer general research questions. Hickson (1977), for example, studied the nonverbal and verbal communication of people on a commuter bus in Washington, D.C. His participants were people who regularly rode the bus. In this type of study, he could examine what he labeled "typical" and "atypical" situations as they occurred naturally.

Should Hickson decide to study this today, although his base of knowledge exists from the original study, he would need to control for new factors, such as the prominence of the use of mass transit in the D.C. area, the more prevalent use of the Metro system 25 years later, and the more accessible ways of reaching downtown Washington, D.C., via modes other than the personal car. New factors would mean new research questions and hypotheses, although the base of the field study would remain the same.

One problem with the field study is that you are both the participant and the observer (hence the method is known as participant-observation). You must find a way to *unobtrusively* record the variables of interest while still acting as a participant in the interaction. Hickson solved this problem on the bus by pretending to read a book while he recorded subjects' behaviors. A second problem facing you in this type of research, however, is the subjective nature of the data. You cannot control, as you might have in the handshake field experiment, the handshake. Instead, you would have to observe the handshake as it was done, guess the force applied, and try to count the number of "pumps." The situation is similar to A. Mazur's (1977) study of cultural differences in personal spacing norms on public benches. The study was biased because benches in different locations were of different sizes: Was the space between subjects on a bench a cultural artifact, or did it reflect the bench size? Mazur could have created a field experiment by inserting benches of the same size into the various locations, thereby increasing the study's reliability. However, the results would not have occurred naturally, which was the goal of his research.

Although there are several disadvantages to the field study, the major advantage is that you obtain truly natural results. The primary disadvantage, other than questionable objectivity of the researcher and loss of control over participant selection, is the fact that the field study usually will take much longer to conduct than other methods. Over time, many things can happen that might influence how participants behave. The field study, however, has produced some significant findings for most nonverbal subcodes.

BOX A.2 OBSERVATIONAL STUDY

Conduct a study that at least partially replicates A. Mazur's (1977) study (the one done on park benches), but choose a location you are familiar with—perhaps on your own campus, the local town, the local mall, etc. . . . Begin by reading how Mazur conducted his study; this will mean finding his article (it is available through EBSCO). Lay out the observational procedures you plan to follow, and then begin to observe. What problems did you find replicating his study? Do you think you found similar results to what he found? If so, what does this say about the findings? Does it strengthen them? If so, how so? Or have the years made a difference in spacing patterns? How so?

Source: Mazur, A. (1977). Interpersonal spacing on public benches in "contact" vs. "noncontact" cultures. *Journal of Social Psychology,* 101, 53–58.)

DATA ANALYSIS AND APPLICATION

After the data have been collected, you must analyze what you observed or collected. At this stage, you will make some kind of interpretation based on the analytical method appropriate for your theoretical position and type of data collected. Most nonverbal communication researchers use some type of inferential or descriptive statistics (based on mean or average response per condition or percent of participants responding to a question). In the case of qualitative data, nonverbal researchers examine the data accumulated in their "coding systems" and make some type of inference based on what is found. In most cases, the reporting will be based on the probability that only 5 percent of the results, or less, are the result of chance. This means that the outcome is the result of how the independent variable was manipulated 95 out of 100 times. If all this seems complex to you, realize that a course in research methods and statistics is really necessary to fully understand this process of analyzing data. If you have a basic idea of what to look at when analyzing data, you probably have enough knowledge to understand the results you will be reading in this textbook.

Once the data have been analyzed, you must demonstrate their usefulness. This analysis is usually found in the discussion section of a report. Here you summarize what you set out to find, what was actually found, and what impact this might have on any number of things. The application section should point out: (1) where the study broke new ground and how it can be used in dealing with other communication phenomena, (2) what limitations there are on the findings, and (3) suggestions for future studies. Keep in mind that sometimes the limitations on the research reveal more about the study and its impact than do the discussion or the literature review.

LIMITATIONS OF NONVERBAL COMMUNICATION RESEARCH

We need to pause for a minute to caution you about a phenomenon we have observed when students are about to finish their nonverbal communication courses. At this stage (although it may happen earlier), other people become interested in what you have been studying during the term, and they ask you to do "analyses." At this point your knowledge is like a loaded gun in the hands of a novice shooter; it can go off in any direction and possibly injure those around you.

At the end of this course, you will be acquainted with the basic concepts from which to study and analyze nonverbal communication. Like most people who possess only the fundamentals, you might apply what you have learned where it is not applicable. When someone approaches you and asks, "What does doing this mean?" you are at a disadvantage if you try to reply. You must rely on data, and you must know how the participant has reacted in the past before you make judgments; this is referred to as "baseline" data. Because you are not in control of the situation and have not carefully conditioned or controlled the other person, the reactions may be *idiosyncratic*; that is, your results might be from an unusual case. We point you back to the cardinal rule of interpreting nonverbal behaviors: *the better you know the person and the context, the more accurate your interpretations will be.*

At one time, a colleague was called on the office intercom to ask what was going on in the parking lot below his window. The caller noted that a male and female (ages uncertain) were kissing each other. "What nonverbal message was this?" he was asked. The only response possible was, "I guess that they like each other." Although other responses could have been given, lack of knowledge about a number of factors prevented this. You must be careful, especially if you say that something may be occurring because you once read a study about it. Some people, such as psychiatrists and psychologists as well as certain police personnel, can and do "read" other people's nonverbal communication with *some* degree of accuracy. These individuals, however, have been trained over a period of years to make this type of analysis, and they do it on a regular basis, some of them every hour of their working day. You will not have the experience after taking one semester-long course in nonverbal communication to give definitive statements about what a specific nonverbal behavior communicates.

Your initial knowledge of what constitutes nonverbal communication and how it is used should provide you with the information needed to better understand the communication of others. In many cases you will conclude that people use nonverbal communication as a manipulative tool; by knowing how this is done, you will be better prepared to counter such influence. By now you have probably created your own manipulative nonverbal strategies and tested a few of them. As you will discover in the chapters on application of nonverbal communication, we use our nonverbal communication in a number of contexts, and the context may change the expected nonverbal message. The rule of thumb to always keep in mind, as mentioned earlier, is that the accuracy of the conclusions you make becomes crucial. Your conclusions will be based on how well you know the persons, how many times you have encountered them (so that you know that these nonverbal behaviors are either normal or out of the ordinary), and how well you know the nonverbal communication theories you learn about in this course. A second rule would be to always consider the context or situation of the communication taking place. We call these *rules of thumb,* and we refer to them numerous times throughout this textbook.

AN EXAMPLE OF CONTEXT

The context is not only important in everyday use of nonverbal information, but it is also important in nonverbal communication research. These studies in nonverbal communication that yield the most useful results are those that have been conducted at different times, under different conditions, using different methods, incorporating the most recent reviews of literature, and undertaken by a number of different researchers in differing locations. This is what Denzin (1989) refers to as "**triangulation**," where research not only builds off other research (replication), but also provides a different "angle" for interpreting results.

A good example of such triangulation is a series of studies beginning in the late 1960s with Jourard's (1966) study of touch and human body parts. Jourard surveyed students by having them fill out a questionnaire that showed 24 human body areas. The students were asked whether they had seen touch by any of four other persons, or whether they had been touched by any of four other persons (mother, father, same-sex friend, opposite-sex friend) on each of the 24 body areas. In general, the results indicated that females allowed greater access to their bodies than did males; opposite-sex friends and mothers were found to do the most touching, whereas fathers usually touched no more than hands.

In 1976, 10 years later, Rosenfeld, Kartus, and Ray replicated Jourard's study, using only 14 basic body areas (but including the front and back areas for a total of 28 body areas). Rosenfeld et al. found that over the 10-year period, there had been some dramatic shifts in body access. For instance, they found females were less accessible in the neck area but had increased accessibility from the chest to knees. Thus, the results of Rosenfeld et al. and Jourard's works illustrate that sex and relationship are important variables in understanding the norms of touch, which change over time.

Basing their study on a review of the literature, S. E. Jones and Yarbrough replicated these studies in 1985. In addition, they asked their participants to write down information about actual touches. Their data were gathered over 18 months. The participants (five distinct groups) kept track of who initiated the touch, who the other person was, where the physical location of the touch was, the time of day, what was said, whether the touch was accepted or rejected, the type of touch, who else was present, the relationship with the other person, and whether the touch took place while sitting or standing.

More than 1,500 touches were recorded in the 18-month period. Using this combination of field study and survey methods, much information was collected. Jones and Yarbrough found that most touches were *cross-sex*. They also found that both males and females initiated touch but that females initiated touch more often. And, as might be expected, they found a wider range of touch meanings and ambiguity than was suggested in the previous research. Finally, they found that context, meaning the situation, was a critical factor in touching behavior. In the case of touch studies such as this one, this would mean touch was more prevalent in social settings than in business settings, in giving advice rather than getting advice, when receiving worry messages, at funerals, and so on (Richmond, McCroskey, and Hickson, 2011).

Thus, when a particular nonverbal cue is analyzed many times, we accumulate more significant data. As you go through this text, or if you are reading this section after you have read the textbook, you should take special care to note whether a study has been replicated, when it was conducted, how many researchers were involved, the academic discipline of the researchers, who the participants were, and so forth. Allow us to emphasize that in your use of the results found in this or any communication text, be extremely cautious. *Do not overgeneralize your discoveries.*

You should remember that verbal and nonverbal communication function together to create a "total" message and that the nonverbal communication theory information you possess is only basic, entry-level information. If you find this subject exciting and wish to learn more, enroll in other courses on interpersonal communication, nonverbal communication, communication theory, and research methods. We have made nonverbal communication a lifelong study. It is not a study that is isolated from our verbal messages, because of the ways verbal and nonverbal communication function together. We hope that you, too, will find the study of nonverbal communication both productive and something you want to continue.

BOX A.3 OBSERVATIONAL STUDY

Have touching norms changed since they were reported by Jones and Yarbrough in 1985? Create your own observational study of touch and see if they have. When analyzing your data, watch for several limiting conditions—whose format for collection, for example, did you follow? Did you change how the observations were recorded? If so, how? What conclusions can you draw from your results?

SUMMARY

Nonverbal communication can be an exciting topic, as you can see by the many ways available to study it. In particular, the ways that research studies are carried out present some fascinating ideas for extending your knowledge about nonverbal communication. We recommend a six-step process for the study of nonverbal communication: (1) review the literature, (2) develop a theoretical perspective, (3) develop a methodology, (4) collect the data, (5) analyze the data, and (6) apply the findings. We also suggest one or more of four general methods for research: (1) laboratory experiments, (2) surveys, (3) field experiments, and (4) field studies. Although this chapter constitutes just a glimpse at a very complex topic—research methods—we hope you have gleaned enough basic information to understand the research reported here. When studying a topic as important to the field of communication as nonverbal communication, you should analyze how the studies cited were conducted.

QUESTIONS FOR THOUGHT

1. How important is method to the study of nonverbal communication?
2. Context often plays an important role in nonverbal communication research. In what ways do you think context may have influenced previous research on communication in general?
3. In what ways has context affected your own communication encounters? Have you encountered people who do not concern themselves with understanding the context of a given communication encounter?
4. What method of nonverbal communication research is best suited to *your* needs? Your interests? Why?
5. In your chosen career, how will nonverbal communication research be used? Looking ahead to other specific courses in your major, how do you think what you have learned about nonverbal communication research will add to your knowledge of that specific course area?
6. If someone asked you to discuss the limitations placed on nonverbal communication research (or any type of social science research), what would you say?
7. If you were to conduct a nonverbal communication research project on a specific subcode—for example, proxemics or touch—how do you think you would design it? What research method would you use? What variables would you manipulate?

FURTHER REFERENCES

Indexes Available

Frye, J. K. (1980). *FIND: Frye's index to nonverbal data.* Duluth: University of Minnesota Press.

Hore, T., and Paget, N. S. (1975). *Nonverbal behaviour: A select annotated bibliography.* Hawthorn, Victoria, Australia: Australian Council for Educational Research.

Matlon, R. J. (1988). *Communication in the legal process.* New York: Holt, Rinehart, and Winston. Ebsco Host: Academic Search Premier.

Theoretical Perspectives

Burgoon, J. K., Buller, D. B., and Woodall, G. W. (1989). *Nonverbal communication: The unspoken dialogue.* New York: Harper and Row.

Approaches to Research

Babbie, E. R. (2000). *Survey research methods* (9th ed.). Belmont, CA: Wadsworth.

Budd, R. W., Thorp, R. K., and Donohew, L. (1967). *Content analysis of communications.* New York: Macmillan.

Burgoon, J. K., Stacks, D. W., and Burch, S. A. (1982). The role of interpersonal rewards and violations of distancing expectations in achieving influence. *Communication,* 11, 114–128.

Denzin, N. K., and Lincoln, Y. S. (1994). Introduction: Entering the field of qualitative research. In N. K. Denzin and Y. S. Lincoln (Eds.), *Handbook of qualitative research* (pp. 1–17). Thousand Oaks, CA: Sage.

Floyd, K., and Morman, M. T. (1998). The measurement of affective communication. *Communication Quarterly,* 46, 144–162.

Hickson, M. L., and Stacks, D. W. (1998). *Organizational communication in the personal context.* Needham Heights, MA: Allyn and Bacon.

Stacks, D. W., and Burgoon, J. K. (1981). The role of nonverbal behaviors as distracters in resistance to persuasion in interpersonal contexts. *Central States Speech Journal,* 32, 71–73.

Stacks, D. W., and Hocking, J. E. (1999). *Communication research* (2nd ed.). New York: Longman.

Limitations of Nonverbal Research

DiMatteo, M. R. (1977, May). *Nonverbal skill and the physician–patient relationship.* Paper presented at the meeting of the American Psychological Association, Toronto, Canada.

Edgar, T., and Samter, W. (1983, April). *Feminist therapy and nonverbal behavior.* Paper presented at the meeting of the Eastern Communication Association, Ocean City, MD.

Gergerian, E. (1979, May). *Facial expression in mania and schizophrenia.* Paper presented at the meeting of the Eastern Communication Association, Philadelphia, PA.

Leather, D. G. (1982a, November). *An examination of police interviewers' beliefs about the utility and nature of nonverbal indicators of deception.* Paper presented at the meeting of the Speech Communication Association, Louisville, KY.

Leathers, D. G. (1982b). *The role of nonverbal factors in shaping perceptions of leadership.* Seminar presentation, University of Southern Mississippi, Hattiesburg, MS.

GLOSSARY

Terms that have specific theorists linked with them are indicated in parentheses after the definition.

ACCENT How the words sound as they are pronounced by individuals.

ADAPTORS Gestures learned early in life that relate to the touching of the body or objects; often seen as nervous movements (Ruesch and Kees).

AFFECT BLENDS Nonverbal expressions of two or more emotions at the same time; in essence, blending of these emotions.

AFFECT DISPLAYS Nonverbal displays of emotions you are experiencing.

ALLOKINE Smallest unit in the structure-centered approach to kinesics; cultural variation of a kine (Birdwhistell).

ANALOGICAL Continuous, infinite, and natural representations of what people observe.

ANDROGYNOUS Having both feminine and masculine characteristics; being neither distinguishably masculine nor feminine, as in dress, appearance, or nonverbal behaviors.

APPEALS TO INVITATION Gestures inviting others to engage in quasi-courtship behaviors (Schlefen).

APPROACH The way a person sees that which is around him or her.

AROUSAL–NONAROUSAL Responsiveness. High levels of emotional and/or physical responses, both internally and externally; shows when we are interested in something or someone, or when we dislike something or someone.

ARTICULATION Clearness and control of the voice in oral communication.

BACKCHANNELING Kinesic behaviors used to make the speaker feel he or she is being listened to, to confirm interest in the speaker, or to suppress the taking of a turn; may include head nods, "mm-hmm," eye contact.

BEHAVIORAL CONSTRAINT Occurs when your freedom of movement is reduced; when you cannot spread out.

BIOFEEDBACK SYSTEM Perceptual state consisting of feedback from brain waves, the skin, muscles, heart rate, and blood pressure.

BODY ALTERATIONS Changes involving hairstyle, skin changes, and additions, that are less drastic than plastic surgery but more involved than a change of clothing.

BODY BUFFER ZONE Implies a definite psychological need for personal space; the need for personal territory.

BODY ORIENTATION   The extent to which your shoulders, trunk, and legs are turned toward, rather than away from, the person with whom you are communicating.

BODY TERRITORY   The space immediately surrounding us, marked by the skin and clothing (Lyman and Scott). Continuous, infinite, and natural units of information.

CHANNEL   *See* subcode.

CHRONEMICS   The study of how we use and structure time.

COCOON   To withdraw from the pressures of day-to-day interactions; to isolate oneself.

COCOONING   A withdrawing into oneself; creating a personal territorial behavior.

COLLECTIVISTIC   A culture that sees group membership as most important; the group takes priority over the individual.

COMMUNICATION   An interactive process whereby people seek to induce change through the sending and receiving of messages by means of a commonly understood code system.

COMMUNICATION APPREHENSION   Fear of communicating with others, creating an unwillingness to communicate; can be in face-to-face settings or public venues.

COMPLEMENTATION FUNCTION   The concept that your nonverbal behaviors/messages complement—or add to—the verbal message you send.

COMPUTER-MEDIATED COMMUNICATION (CMC)   Communication that takes place through the use of mediated venues—computers, cellphones, SKYPE, etc.

CONDITION   A grouping of participants in a research study, providing for a particular manipulation based on an independent variable.

CONFEDERATES   People who assist in the conducting of a research project.

CONJUGATE LATERAL EYE MOVEMENTS (CLEMS)   What are known as lateral shifts of the eyes to either the right or left; thought to indicate which side of the brain is dominant for the function of communication that is taking place.

CONTEXT   The background against which communication occurs; the situation in which it occurs.

CONTINUITY DISTINCTION   Assumes that verbal interactions have a distinct start and finish; that they are discontinuous. Nonverbal interactions do not have a distinct start and finish; they are continuous.

CONTROL GROUP   The group in an experiment where no variables have been manipulated to see their effects on the experimental outcome.

CONTROL OF INTERACTION   Influenced by one's nonverbal behaviors; a person can nonverbally initiate an interaction more easily and maintain control of the conversation by various nonverbal subcodes; initially influenced by physical appearance.

CONVERSATION PRESERVE   Involves who can summon others into offices or areas to talk and when we can be summoned to talk; one of Goffman's territories of the self.

COURTSHIP READINESS   Physiological changes in people as they prepare to engage in quasi-courtship behavior (Schlefen).

COVERINGS   Clothing; *see also* body alterations.

CREDIBILITY   The appearance of being believable, trustable.

CROWDING   When you perceive that there are restrictions on your use of space due to the presence of too many other people (or objects); an issue of perception.

DATA (IN RESEARCH)   What we observe and use for analysis; or collections of facts from which conclusions may be drawn.

DECODING   Interpreting of messages received in order to send effective feedback.

DEFERENCE   Deferring to others, usually out of status differentials or respect, in terms of conversations and other communication interactions.

DELIVERY   One of the five important components of effective public presentation; usually refers to physical and vocal delivery of messages.

DENSITY The number of people in a given territory or space.

DEPENDENT VARIABLES The variables with which you judge the effects of the independent variable(s) when you compare your findings.

DERIVATION SYSTEM Morris' approach to kinesics that says we derive our kinesic behaviors in a number of ways: inborn, discovered, absorbed, trained, etc.

DIALECT The use of unique words or phrases common to a specific group; may also include grammatical issues.

DISPLAY OF COGNITIVE AND AFFECTIVE INFORMATION Nonverbal behaviors that indicate specific pieces of information or emotions.

DOMINANCE–SUBMISSIVENESS Status or power difference. People stand with a more direct body orientation and rigid posture when talking with a higher-status person.

DURATION How long a sound is made in oral communication (paralanguage); informal time dimension relating to how long something lasts (chronemics).

DYNAMIC ENVIRONMENTS Space that changes as people change.

ECTOMORPHIC A body type typified as tall, frail, and thin.

ELOCUTIONARY MOVEMENT Early school of communication education that focused on the proper use of voice and gesture.

EMBLEMS Gestures with direct verbal translations (Ekman and Friesen).

ENCODING Putting together the message in your own brain so that you can send it to the person(s) with whom you communicate.

ENDOMORPHIC A body type typified as soft, plump, short, and round.

EXPECTATIONS VIOLATION THEORY When someone violates your expectations of their nonverbal behaviors, you will respond in either a positive or negative way, depending on if it is a positive violation or a negative one.

FEMININE CULTURES People in highly feminine cultures value quality of life and nurturance; they value fluid sex roles, service, and interdependence.

FILTER Something that influences our perceptions and interpretations; could be the function or purpose of the communication, process structure, age, culture and race, status, or sex and gender.

FIXED-FEATURE ENVIRONMENTS An environment with a particular architectural arrangement based on specific cultural configurations.

FUNCTIONAL APPROACH TO RESEARCH Looks at how selected nonverbal variables (subcodes) function together in the totality of a given situation; often called an external variable or gestalt approach.

FUNCTIONAL APPROACH TO NONVERBAL COMMUNICATION Focuses on the types and functions of nonverbal communication.

GAME STAGE A developmental stage at which a child has well-understood nonverbal norms operating (Mead in da Silva 2011).

GAZE AVERSION When one person intentionally avoids eye contact with the other.

GAZE OMISSION A one-sided look; the person who does not make the eye contact does not realize he/she is not reciprocating gaze from someone else.

GENDER The psychological determination of individuals; masculine, feminine, or androgynous.

HAPTICS The study of touch and touching; also known as *zero-proxemics*.

HEMISPHERIC STYLE The way each of the brain's hemispheres processes communication; commonly thought of as left-brain/right-brain issues.

HIGH-CONTEXT COMMUNICATION Information is either in the physical context or internalized in the coded, explicit, transmitted part of a message.

HIGH POWER DISTANCE Cultures that believe individuals with more power should be in control and that their nonverbal communication behaviors will reflect this.

HOME A physical place, a barrier behind which we can hide from the world, and an environment we sometimes use to express ourselves both publicly and privately; a place of residence.

HOME TERRITORY The physical territory to which an individual lays claim, marked by legal and physical barriers (Lyman and Scott).

HOMOPHILY Similarity; people are likely to be drawn more to people who are nonverbally similar to themselves.

INDIVIDUALISTIC A culture where individuals' goals take precedence over the group's goals; people are expected to look after self and immediate family only; the "I" identity takes precedence over the "we" identity (Gudykunst).

IDENTIFICATION The most important function of physical appearance; self-presentation helps to create an individual's identity *(see* self-presentation).

ILLUSTRATORS Gestures that support what is being said orally: cannot stand alone and must accompany or follow the oral message (Ekman and Friesen).

IMITATION STAGE A development stage at which a child begins to expand his or her repertoire of nonverbal behaviors (Mead).

IMMEDIACY Appearance of being likeable, open, and friendly, likened to "approachability"; an extremely important idea to consider when looking at what factors of nonverbal communication make us more immediate or less immediate.

IMPRESSION MANAGEMENT Individuals making conscious efforts to control the impressions they make; another aspect of controlling our nonverbal communication.

INDEPENDENT VARIABLES The variables that you can control or manipulate when conducting a research study.

INDIVIDUALISTIC CULTURES Cultures where individuals' goals take precedence over the group's goals; more likely to promote self-realization, see each person as having a unique set of talents and potential.

INFORMATION PRESERVE Territories that contain facts about the self we wish to control; one of Goffman's territories of the self.

INTENSITY One of three variables important in evaluating the touch we receive from another; the amount of emotional arousal determines the intensity.

INTENTIONALITY A nonverbal behavior done on purpose; as it relates to nonverbal communication it is an act an individual deems appropriate or inappropriate given the environment and the act itself; purposeful communication by use of nonverbal behaviors.

INTERACTIONAL TERRITORY An area, mobile or fixed, that is restricted in terms of accessibility by someone (Lyman and Scott).

INTERPERSONAL COMMUNICATION Communication between at least two individuals, usually up to five to seven individuals.

INTIMATE SPACE A distance zone measuring from touching to about 18 inches between interactants (E. T. Hall).

INTRAPERSONAL COMMUNICATION Internal communication within a communicator's own mind.

KINEME A combination of kines in the structure-centered approach to kinesics that creates the first meaningful level of analysis (Birdwhistell).

KINEMORPHEMES Sequential movements in the structure-centered approach to kinesics, consisting of kineme combinations (Birdwhistell).

KINES Combinations of allokines in the structure-centered approach to kinesics, still below meaningful analysis (Birdwhistell).

KINESICS The study of body movement and facial expression.

LANGUAGE The use by human beings of words, placed together in organized combinations and patterns, in order to express and communicate thoughts and feelings.

LEFT HEMISPHERE The side of the brain responsible for most people's verbal communication; specialized in an abstract, logical, and analytical way; best used for the analysis of language. Also known as the side of the brain that most often processes the cognitive information you receive.

LINGUISTIC DISTINCTION Relies on language as opposed to nonverbal communication.

LINGUISTIC ANALOGY OF KINESICS The categories of kinesics—allokines, kines, kinemes, and kinomorphemes—function similarly to language, from allophones to full sentences.

LOCATION One of three variables important in evaluating the touch we receive from another; locations on body where we are touched.

LOUDNESS Intensity of the voice.

LOW-CONTEXT COMMUNICATION When the mass of the information is vested in the explicit code; more detailed and explicit verbal language is used.

LOW POWER DISTANCE Cultures that believe people should be treated as equals even if there is a status difference between them, such as the American culture.

MARASMUS Translated from the Greek; means "wasting away"; believed to be a by-product of not receiving touch.

MARKERS Signs that denote ownership of a territory.

MASCULINE CULTURES In cultures that are considered masculine, gender roles are clearly distinct; men are supposed to be assertive, tough, and focused on material success.

MESOMORPHIC A body type typified as properly proportioned, athletic, trim, muscular, and average in height.

METAMESSAGE A message about how to communicate in a given context or environment.

MONOCHRONIC Doing one thing at a time, not everything together at once.

MUTUAL GAZE Interactants making direct eye contact with each other.

NATURE APPROACH TO NONVERBAL The nonverbal behaviors we use are innate; they are a product of heredity.

NONVERBAL COMMUNICATION A process of creating meaning in the minds of receivers, whether intentionally or unintentionally, by use of actions other than, or in combination with, words or language; includes norms and expectations, usually imposed by society, for the expression of experiences, feelings, and attitudes.

NONVERBAL INTERACTIONS Communication through the use of nonverbal messages.

NORM OF RECIPROCITY Expectation that those with whom we communicate will respond in a manner similar to our original communication; also known as the *dyadic effect*.

NORMATIVE EXPECTATIONS Expectations of behavior that, over a period of time, become the norms that govern our behavioral and communication patterns.

NURTURE APPROACH TO NONVERBAL The nonverbal behaviors we use are learned or cultivated over time by our interactions in society.

OFFENSIVE DISPLAYS Can be accomplished by the posture an individual assumes, the stance one takes, or the gestures one uses; used to accomplish dominance or to keep someone from invading our territory or personal space.

OLFACTICS The study of how we use and perceive odors; olfaction.

OLFACTORY SIGNATURE A "smell print" or identification based on some odor that classifies people, places, or things.

OPERATIONALIZED Factors are explained in terms of how they are to be used in an experiment.

OVERLAPS Negative interruptions in a conversation, or overlapping someone else's speech by over-running their verbal message with your own.

PARAKINESIC PHENOMENA Those physiological features that influence kinesic expression (intensity, duration, and range of expression) (Birdwhistell).

PARALANGUAGE Aspects of the voice and other sounds made by an individual that have communicative value; vocalics.

PARAVOCAL BEHAVIORS Content-free speech, which are the sounds that accompany speech; create paralanguage/vocalics.

PARTICIPANTS People who have been chosen, either randomly or for a particular reason, to participate in research.

PAUSE Silence within a turn or between turns.

PERCEPTIONS The way we look at things through sensation, recognition of the sensation, and interpretation; our own view of things.

PERFORMANCE APPRAISAL INTERVIEWS The evaluation by a superior at an individual's place of employment to determine salary increase or promotion; a review for the subordinate to determine a change in job performance.

PERSONAL SPACE (1) An invisible space immediately surrounding the person, a body buffer zone, micro-space; (2) a distance zone measuring from 18 inches to about 4 feet between interactants (E. T. Hall); (3) Goffman's equivalent of *body territory*; includes touch, one of the territories of the self.

PHYSICAL APPEARANCE The impression people have of others based on the body, personal aesthetics, clothing, body adaptors, and additions.

PITCH Range of voice during conversation.

PLAY STAGE A developmental stage during which a child begins to learn which nonverbal behaviors are appropriate and which are inappropriate (Mead).

PLEASURE–DISPLEASURE Liking–disliking; relaxation is low when talking to a disliked person showing displeasure, moderate to relaxed when talking with a friend.

POLYCHRONIC Doing many things at the same time; several things may happen at once.

POSITIONAL CUES Kinesic cues that exclude some persons from an interaction while including another person in quasi-courtship behavior (Schlefen).

POSSESSION TERRITORY Objects that we view as our own; one of Goffman's territories of the self.

POWER DISTANCE A variable that affects the use of nonverbal communication in situations involving interactions between people of different statuses; the degree to which we are comfortable with someone showing nonverbal power or control.

PREENING BEHAVIOR Preparation for quasi-courtship, including adjustments of clothing and primping (Schlefen).

PRONUNCIATION Clearness and control of sound; the rhythm and rate of speech.

PROXEMES Units of space within each distance "zone" we have; generally classified as "inner" or "outer" zones.

PROXEMICS The interrelated observations and theories of our use of space as a specialized elaboration of culture; usually divided into territory and personal space.

PUBLIC Of, concerning, or affecting the community or the people. One of Lyman and Scott's four types of territory.

PUBLIC SPACE A distance of 10 feet or more between people (E. T. Hall).

PUBLIC TERRITORY An area people may enter freely; an area open to people with a legitimate use for that space (Lyman and Scott).

QUALITY A speaker's timber, tonality, and production of air flow through the glottis.

QUALITATIVE RESEARCH Focuses on observed phenomena which are then evaluated by a knowledgeable scholar, who explores and describes the qualities and then draws conclusions based on what has been studied and observed.

QUANTITATIVE RESEARCH Focuses on isolating, counting, and analyzing units of phenomena; takes a statistical approach to analyzing the phenomena.

QUASI-COURTSHIP BEHAVIOR Schlefen's model of kinesic behavior, according to which both sexes note and display a sexual interest in one another.

RECEIVER The person who receives a message sent to them by a speaker (or sender).

REGULARITY The rate at which we speak, which includes stress within the speech.

REGULATORS Gestures that indicate when to talk or when to allow others to talk; signal a desire to enter, exit, or maintain the floor in a conversation (Ekman and Friesen).

RELATIONSHIP OF INTERACTANTS A connection, association, or involvement between people when dealing with one another.

REPLICATION A second (third, fourth, etc.) study duplicating the first, but may use different participants, different times, and may consider variables not considered; done to confirm or disconfirm what was discovered in the original study.

RIGHT HEMISPHERE Side of the brain specialized for the spatiotemporal, gestalt, emotive forms of communication for which nonverbal communication is best suited; often called the side of the brain that processes more of the affective (or emotional) information as well as more of the creative information received.

SAMPLE People selected to participate in research from among the population under study.

SECONDARY SPACE Space that you deem important but that you could live without; space not crucial to your emotional or physical environment.

SELF-PRESENTATION The way you nonverbally present yourself, including all subcodes of nonverbal communication.

SEMIFIXED ENVIRONMENT Space in which people can increase or decrease their interactions with others and provide some control over others.

SEQUENCING Structuring of an interaction in a "my turn, your turn" format.

SEX Biological determination of individuals; male or female.

SHEATH The territory of the skin and its coverings (clothing); one of Goffman's territories of the self.

SIGN The natural representation of an event or act.

SILENCE The lack of sound; does not mean a lack of communication.

SIMILARITY HYPOTHESIS We tend to like those who do not distort our own view of ourselves (self-image) or those who do not depreciate our own level of attractiveness.

SITUATION As perceived by the sender or receiver, it is the part of nonverbal communication that includes context, environment, and the time of the interaction.

SMELL ADAPTATION Occurs when the odor you smell becomes a part of your environment or general background; olfactory senses adapt to the smells in an environment.

SOCIAL COGNITION When a communicator weighs the social consequences of a nonverbal act; also includes issues such as decision making, the perceptions of others, and the attribution of characteristics to a specific nonverbal behavior.

SOCIAL SPACE A distance zone measuring from 4 feet to 10 feet between interactants (E. T. Hall).

SPEAKER The sender of a message to be processed by a receiver.

STALL A well-bounded space used by one person at a time; one of Goffman's territories of the self.

STIGMA The possession of an attribute that makes one different from others in the category of people available, and of a less desirable kind.

STIMULI OVERLOAD Occurs when there are just too many things (noises, sights, sounds, people talking) going on and you feel bombarded by their presence, creating unease in that setting.

STRUCTURAL APPROACH TO RESEARCH Each variable is singled out and looked at separately.

SUBCODE A specific category or type of nonverbal communication; also known as a channel.

SUPER TERRITORY The desire by humans to attempt to maintain more territory than is actually needed for them to survive.

SURVEILLANCE Occurs when one perceives that he or she is being watched or observed by strangers, which can cause a crowded feeling.

SYMBOL Something that represents an abstraction; a symbol takes the place of the referent.

TACTICS The study of touch and touching in reference to tactile behaviors.

TEMPORAL COMMUNICATION How the use of time communicates messages; chronemics.

TENURE Another way to maintain your territory; concerns the length of time you have held your space.

TERRITORIALITY Laying claim to an area and defending it against members of the same species.

TERRITORIES OF THE SELF Goffman's eight territories that humans possess: personal space, stall territory, use space, the turn, the sheath, possession territory, information preserve, and conversation preserve.

TRIANGULATION Research builds off other research (replication); also provides a different "angle" for interpreting results.

TURN (1) Goffman's temporal element in space that relates to space and time, a territory of the self; (2) the time you speak or have the "floor" in a conversation.

TURN CUES Nonverbal cues used to maintain a turn, signal the listener that it is their turn to talk, or to signal a desire to take a turn.

UNCERTAINTY AVOIDANCE Cultural concept that deals with how comfortable we are with being uncertain about how communication progresses in our society; people high in uncertainty avoidance establish nonverbal communication rules so as to be clear about how to communicate with them; people low in uncertainty avoidance are more relaxed in terms of what is acceptable and what is not when communicating.

UNINTENTIONALITY People are often unaware that their nonverbal behaviors are sending nonverbal messages; communicating a message through nonverbal behaviors not done on purpose.

USE SPACE Space claimed by people within their line of vision, or as instrumental in performing a function; one of Goffman's territories of the self.

VOCAL CHARACTERIZERS Vocalization as nonverbal sounds, such as laughing, crying, whimpering, and so forth.

VOCAL SEGREGATES Nonwords that are used to fill pauses, or words and phrases used as meaningless fillers.

VOCALICS The study of the communicative value of the voice and other sounds made by an individual; paralanguage.

VOCALIZATIONS Specific features of the voice that characterize the voice at specific points in time.

VOICEPRINT An analysis based on the uniqueness of the voice; an individual's voice is unique, much like a fingerprint; it is possible to identify people on the basis of certain vocal qualities.

VOICE QUALIFIERS All factors that affect sound production, such as loudness, pitch height, and duration.

VOICE QUALITIES Modifications of the voice: includes pitch range, vocal lip control, glottis control, pitch control, articulation control, tempo control, resonance, rhythm control.

VOICE SET Prelinguistic area of vocalics, establishes a context from which the voice is to be evaluated; provides the background against which we hear the voice. Includes an identification aspect; people will recognize others by their voice set.

VOICE TYPES Certain voice qualities that stereotype people one way or another.

ZERO PROXEMICS Touching; no space between the involved individuals.

REFERENCES

Abel, E. L., and Kruger, M. L. (2011). Facial resemblances between heterosexual, gay, and lesbian couples [Electronic version]. *Psychological Reports*, 3, 688–692.

Abele, A. (1986). Functions of gaze in social interaction: Communicating and monitoring. *Journal of Nonverbal Behavior*, 10, 3–101.

Abdou, O. A. (1997). Effects of luminous environment on worker productivity in building spaces [Electronic version]. *Journal of Architectural Engineering*, 3, 124–132.

Acheson, K. (2008). Silence as gesture: Rethinking the nature of communicative silences [Electronic version]. *Communication Theory*, 18, 535–555.

Adam, B. (2006). Time [Electronic version]. *Theory, Culture & Society*, 23, 119–126.

Adamczyk, A. (2010). Forum for the ugly people—Study of an imagined community [Electronic version]. *Sociological Review*, 58, 97–113.

Adamo, G. E. (2011). Nigerian dress as a symbolic language [Electronic version]. *Semiotica*, 184, 1–9.

Adams, G. R., and Crossman, S. M. (1978). *Physical attractiveness: A cultural imperative*. Roselyn Heights, NY: Libra.

Adams, R. S., and Biddle, B. (1970). *Realities of teaching: Explorations with video tape*. New York: Holt, Rinehart, & Winston.

Addington, D. W. (1968). The relationship of selected vocal characteristics to personality perception. *Speech Monographs*, 35, 492–503.

Addington, D. W. (1971). The effect of vocal variations on ratings of source credibility. *Speech Monographs*, 38, 242–247.

Addison, W. E. (1989). Beardedness as a factor in perceived masculinity. *Perceptual and Motor Skills*, 68, 921–922.

Adler, R. B., and Proctor, R. F., II. (2010). *Looking out, looking in.* (13th ed.). Belmont, CA: Wadsworth/ Cengage Learning, Inc.

Adler, R., and Towne, N. (1975). *Looking out/looking in*. San Francisco: Rinehart Press.

Agnosto, D. E., Paone, K. L., and Ipock, G. S. (2007). The female-friendly public library: Gender differences in adolescents' uses and perceptions of U.S. public libraries [Electronic version]. *Library Trends*, 56, 387–401.

Aguilar, A. (2007, November). *Tattoos as worldviews: A journey into tattoo communications using standpoint theory* [Electronic version]. Paper presented at the National Communication Association, Chicago, IL.

Ahmed, S. M. S. (1979). Invasion of personal space: A study of departure times as affected by sex of the intruder, sex of the subject, and saliency condition. *Perceptual and Motor Skills*, 49, 85–86.

Aiello, J. R., and Aiello, T. C. (1974). The development of personal space: Proxemic behavior of children 6 through 16. *Human Ecology*, 2, 177–189.

Aiken, L. R. (1963). The relationship of dress to selected measures of personality in undergraduate women. *Journal of Social Psychology*, 59, 119–128.

Akert, R. M., and Panter, A. T. (1988). Extraversion and the ability to decode nonverbal communication. *Personality and Individual Differences*, 9, 965–972.

Albardiaz, R. (2011). Teaching non-verbal communication skills [Electronic version]. *Education for Primary Care*, 22, 423–424.

Albert, S., and Dabbs, J. M. (1970). Physical distance and persuasion. *Journal of Personality and Social Psychology*, 15, 265–270.

Alexander, I. E., and Babad, E. Y. (1981). Returning the smile of a stranger: Within-culture and cross-culture comparisons of Israeli and American children. *Genetic Psychological Monographs*, 103, 31–77.

Aliakbari, M., Faraji, E., and Pourshakibaee, P. (2011). Investigation of the proxemic behavior of Iranian professors and university students: Effects of gender and status [Electronic version]. *Journal of Pragmatics*, 43, 1392–1402.

Alibeik, H., Angaji, S. A., Pouriamanesh, S., and Movallali, G. (2011). The correlation between left-sidedness and intelligence as an advantage for persistence of left-handed frequency in human evolutionary pathway [Electronic version]. *Australian Journal of Basic & Applied Sciences*, 5, 1517–1524.

Allgeir, A. R., and Byrne, D. (1973). Attraction toward the opposite sex as a determinant of physical proximity. *Journal of Social Psychology*, 90, 213–219.

Altman, I. (1973). An ecological approach to the functioning of social groups. In J. G. Rasmussen (Ed.), *Individual and group behavior in isolation and confinement* (pp. 241–269). Chicago: Aldine Press.

Altman, I. (1975). *The environment and social behavior: Privacy, personal space, territoriality, and crowding.* Monterey, CA: Brooks/Cole.

Altman, I., and Haythorn, W. W. (1967). The ecology of isolated groups. *Behavioral Science*, 12, 169–182.

Altman, I., Nelson, R. A., and Lett, E. E. (1972). The ecology of home environments. *Man-Made Systems*, 2, 189–191.

Altman, I., Taylor, D. A., and Wheeler, L. (1971). Ecological aspects of group behavior in isolation. *Journal of Applied Social Psychology*, 1, 76–100.

Ambler, B. (1977). Information reduction, internal transformation, and task difficulty. *Bulletin of Psychonomic Science*, 10, 43–46.

Amsbary, J. H., Vogel, R., Hickson, M., III, Wittig, J., and Oakes, B. (1994). Smoking artifacts as indicators of homophily, attraction, and credibility: A replication. *Communication Research Reports*, 11, 161–167.

Anastasi, A. (1958). *Differential psychology.* New York: Macmillan.

Andersen, J. F., Andersen, P. A., and Lustig, M. W. (1987). Opposite-sex touch avoidance: A national replication and extension. *Journal of Nonverbal Behavior*, 11, 89–109.

Andersen, P. A. (1999). *Nonverbal communication: Forms and functions.* Mountain View, CA: Mayfield Publishing Company.

Andersen, P. A., Andersen, J. F., and Mayton, S. M. (1985). The development of nonverbal communication in the classroom: Teachers' perceptions of students in grades K–12. *Western Journal of Speech Communication*, 49, 188–203.

Andersen, P. A., Garrison, J. D., and Andersen, J. F. (1979). Implications of a neurological approach for the study of nonverbal communication. *Human Communication Research*, 16, 74–89.

Andersen, P. A., and Leibowitz, K. (1978). The development and nature of the construct touch avoidance. *Environmental Psychology and Nonverbal Behavior*, 3, 89–106.

Andersen, P. A., and Sull, K. K. (1985). Out of touch, out of reach: Tactile predispositions as predictors of interpersonal distance. *Western Journal of Speech Communication*, 49, 57–72.

Anderson, K., and Leaper, C. (1998). Meta-analyses of gender effects on conversational interruption: Who, what, when, where, why, and how. *Sex Roles*, 39 (3), 223–237.

Antheunis, M. L., Schouten, A., Valkenburg, P. M., and Peter, J. (2012). Interactive uncertainty reduction strategies and verbal affection in computer-mediated communication. *Communication Research*, 39, 757–780.

Antonijevic, S. (2008). From text to gesture: A microethnographic analysis of nonverbal communication in the Second Life virtual environment. *Information, Communication & Society*, 11, 221–238.

Archer, D., Kimes, D. D., and Barrios, M. (1976). Face-ism. *Psychology Today*, 20, 65–66.

Archer, J., Hay, D. C., and Young, A. W. (1992). Face processing in psychiatric conditions. *British Journal of Clinical Psychology*, 31, 45–61.

Ardrey, R. (1966). *The territorial imperative: A personal inquiry into the animal origins of property and nations*. New York: Dell.

Arendsen, J. (2008). Garrick Mallery (1891): Greeting by gesture [Electronic version]. *Gesture*, 8, 386–390.

Argyle, M. (1975). *Bodily communication*. New York: International Universities Press.

Argyle, M., and Cook, M. (1976). *Gaze and mutual gaze*. Cambridge: Cambridge University Press.

Argyle, M., and Dean, J. (1965). Eye contact, distance, and affiliation. *Sociometry*, 28, 289–304.

Argyle, M., Lallijee, M., and Cook, M. (1968). The effects of visibility and introduction in a dyad. *Human Relations*, 21, 3–17.

Argyle, M., and Williams, M. (1976). Observer or observee? A reversible perspective in person perception. *Sociometry*, 39, 170–173.

Aries, E. (1987). Gender and communication. In P. Shaver and C. Hendrick (Eds.), *Sex and gender* (pp. 149–176). Newbury Park, CA: Sage.

Arik, E. (2012). Space, time, and iconicity in Turkish sign language (TID) [Electronic version]. *TRAMES: A Journal of the Humanities & Social Sciences*, 16, 345–358.

Arnold, L. B., and Doran, E. (2007). Stop before you hurt the kids: Communicating self-control and self-negation in femininity, mothering, and eating disorders [Electronic version]. *Women's Studies in Communication*, 30, 310–339.

Aronsson, K., and Cekaite, A. (2011). Activity contracts and directives in everyday family politics [Electronic version]. *Discourse & Society*, 22, 137–154.

Arroyo, A., and Harwood, J. (2012). Exploring the causes and consequences of engaging in fat talk. *Journal of Applied Communication Research*, 40, 167–187.

Aschenbrenner, K., Scholze, N., Joraschky, P., and Hummel, T. (2008). Gustatory and olfactory sensitivity in patients with anorexia and bulimia in the course of treatment [Electronic version]. *Journal of Psychiatric Research*, 43, 129–137.

Ashikali, E., and Dittmar, H. (2012). The effect of priming materialism on women's responses to thin-ideal media [Electronic version]. *British Journal of Social Psychology*, 4, 514–533.

Astrom, J., Thorell, L. H., and D'Elia, G. (1992). Psychotherapists' attitudes towards and observations of nonverbal communication in a greeting situation: II. Relationships to background variables. *Psychological Reports*, 70, 183–194.

Atkinson, M. (2004). Tattooing and civilizing processes: Body modification as self-control [Electronic version]. *Canadian Review of Sociology & Anthropology*, 41, 125–146.

Aucoin, J. W., and Lane P. L. (2004). Space invasion [Electronic version]. *Nursing*, 34, 32.

Austad, C., Bugglin, C., Burns, C. L., Farina, A., and Fisher, E. H. (1985). Physical attractiveness in the readjustment of discharged psychiatric patients. *Journal of Abnormal Psychology*, 95, 139–143.

Austin, G. (1966). Chironomia or a treatise on rhetorical delivery. In M. M. Robb and L. Thonssen (Eds.), *Bibliography in speech education* (pp. 583–598). Carbondale: Southern Illinois University Press.

Avery, A. Pallister, C., Allan, J., Stubbs, J., and Lavin, J. (2012). An initial evaluation of a family-based approach to weight management in adolescents attending a community weight management group [Electronic version]. *Journal of Human Nutrition and Dietetics*, 25, 469–476.

Aviezer, H., Trope, Y., and Todorov, A. (2012). Body cues, not facial expressions, discriminate between intense positive and negative emotions [Electronic version]. *Science*, 338, 1225–1229.

Axelrod, S., and Cohen, L. D. (1961). Senescence and embedded-figure performance in vision and touch. *Perceptual and Psychophysiology*, 12, 283–288.

Axtell, R. E. (1991). *Gestures: The do's and taboos of body language around the world*. New York: John Wiley & Sons.

Axtell, R. E., and Fornwald, M. (1997). *Gestures: The do's and taboos of body language around the world*. New York: John Wiley & Sons, Inc.

Aylor, B., and Dainton, M. (2001). Antecedents in romantic jealousy experience, expression, and goals. *Western Journal of Communication*, 65, 370–391.

Ayres, J., Hopf, T., Brown, K., and Suek, J. M. (1993). The impact of communication apprehension, gender, and time on turn-taking behavior in initial interactions. *Southern Communication Journal*, 59, 142–150.

Babbie, E. R. (2000). *Survey research methods* (9th ed.). Belmont, CA: Wadsworth.

Back, M. D., Schmukle, S. C., and Egloff, B. (2010). Why are narcissists so charming at first sight? Decoding the narcissism-popularity link at zero acquaintance [Electronic version]. *Journal of Personality & Social Psychology*, 98, 132–145.

Baenninger, R., and Greco, M. (1991). Some antecedents and consequences of yawning. *Psychological Record*, 41, 453–460.

Bagdasarov, Z., Banerjee, S., Greene, K., and Campo, M. (2007, May). *Indoor tanning and problem behavior theory: Systems of influence* [Electronic version]. Paper presented at the meeting of the International Communication Association, San Francisco, CA.

Bagley, C. (1989). Urban crowding and the murder rate in Bombay, India. *Perceptual and Motor Skills*, 69, 1241–1242.

Bailey, P. E., and Henry, J. D. (2009). Subconscious facial expression mimicry is preserved in older adulthood [Electronic version]. *Psychology and Aging*, 24, 995–1000.

Bailey, R. C., and Schreiber, T. S. (1981). Congruency of physical attractiveness perception and liking. *Journal of Social Psychology*, 115, 285–286.

Baird, J. E. (1976). Sex differences in group communication: A review of relevant research. *Quarterly Journal of Speech*, 62, 179–192.

Baker, A. H., and Ledner, A. I. (2004). Body asymmetry affects conjugate lateral eye movement [Electronic version]. *Journal of General Psychology*, 131, 36–51.

Balcetis, E., Cole, S., Chelberg, M. B., and Alicke, M. (2013). Searching out the ideal: Awareness of ideal body standards predicts lower global self-esteem in women [Electronic version]. *Self and Identity*, 12, 99–113.

Baldaro, B., Rossi, N., Caterina, R., Codispoti, M., Balsamo, A., and Trombini, G. (2003). Deficit in the discrimination of nonverbal emotions in children with obesity and their mothers [Electronic version]. *International Journal of Obesity and Related Metabolic Disorders*, 27, 191–195.

Ballard, D. I., and Seibold, D. R. (2004). Communication-related organizational structures and work group temporal experiences: The effects of coordination method, technology type, and feedback cycle on members' construals and enactments of time. *Communication Monographs*, 71, 1–27.

Ballard, D. I., and Seibold, D. R. (2006). The experience of time at work: Relationship to communication load, job satisfaction, and interdepartmental communication. *Communication Studies*, 57, 317–340.

Ballenson, J., and Yee, N. (2007). Virtual interpersonal and digital chameleons [Electronic version]. *Journal of Nonverbal Behavior*, 31, 225–242.

Banton, M. (2012). The colour line and the colour scale in the twentieth century [Electronic version]. *Ethnic & Racial Studies*, 35, 1109-1131.

Banziger, G., and Simmons, R. (1984). Emotion, attractiveness, and interpersonal space. *Journal of Social Psychology*, 124, 255–256.

Barker, R. G. (1942). The social interrelatedness of strangers and acquaintances. *Sociometry*, 5, 176–179.

Barrios, B. A., Corbitt, L. C., Estes, J. P., and Topping, J. S. (1976). Effect of a social stigma on interpersonal distance. *Psychological Record*, 26, 343–348.

Bar-Tal, D., and Saxe, L. (1976). Physical attractiveness and its relationships to sex-role stereotyping. *Sex Roles*, 2, 123–133.

Bartz, A. (2011). Plugging in. *Psychology Today*, 44, 18.

Basow, S. A. (1992). *Gender: Stereotypes and roles* (3rd ed.). Pacific Grove, CA: Brooks/Cole.

Bass, J. K., and Lambert, S. F. (2004). Urban adolescents' perceptions of their neighborhoods: An examination of spatial dependence [Electronic version]. *Journal of Community Psychology*, 32, 277–293.

Bassett, R. E., Stanton-Spicer, A. Q., and Whitehead, J. L. (1979). Effects of attire and judgments of credibility. *Central States Speech Journal*, 30, 282–285.

Bates, J. E. (1976). Effects of children's nonverbal behavior upon adults. *Child Development*, 47, 1079–1088.

Bauchner, J. E., Kaplan, E. A., and Miller, G. R. (1980). Detecting deception: The relationship of available information to judgmental accuracy in initial encounters. *Human Communication Research*, 6, 253–264.

Bauer, E. A. (1973). Personal space: A study of blacks and whites. *Sociometry*, 36, 402–408.

Bauman, K. (2008, November). *Tattoo stories: Bodies revealing life in India* [Electronic version]. Paper presented at the National Communication Association, San Diego, CA.

Baxter, A., and Walden, T. A. (1989). The effect of context and age on social referencing. *Child Development*, 60, 1511–1518.

Baxter, L. C. (1970). Interpersonal spacing in natural settings. *Sociometry*, 33, 444–456.

Baxter, L., and Ward, J. (1975). Newsline. *Psychology Today*, 8, 28.

Beattie, K. (1975). *Eyeglasses as nonverbal credibility indicators*. Unpublished manuscript, Mississippi State University.

Beatty, J. (1977). Activation and attention in the human brain. In M. C. Wittrock (Ed.), *The human brain* (pp. 63–85). Englewood Cliffs, NJ: Prentice-Hall.

Becher, D., Sommer, R., Bee, J., and Osley, B. (1973). College classroom ecology. *Sociometry*, 36, 514–525.

Beck, A. T. (1988). *Love is never enough*. New York: Harper & Row.

Beck, L., and Feldman, R. S. (1989). Enhancing children's decoding of facial expression. *Journal of Nonverbal Behavior*, 13, 269–277.

Beckman, S. J. (1975, August). *Sex differences in nonverbal behavior*. Paper presented at the meeting of the American Psychological Association, Chicago.

Beebe, S. A. (1974). Eye contact: A nonverbal determinant of speaker credibility. *Speech Teacher*, 23, 21–25.

Beek, Y., and Dubas, J. (2008a). Age and gender differences in decoding basic and non-basic facial expressions in late childhood and early adolescence [Electronic version]. *Journal of Nonverbal Behavior*, 32, 37–52.

Beek, Y., and Dubas, J. (2008b). Decoding basic and non-basic facial expressions and depressive symptoms in late childhood and adolescence [Electronic version]. *Journal of Nonverbal Behavior*, 32, 53–64.

Begley, S. (1997). Gray matters. *Newsweek*, March 27, 48–54.

Beier, E. G. (1974). Nonverbal communication: How we send emotional messages. *Psychology Today*, 8, 52–59.

Belk, R. W. (1988). My possessions, myself. *Psychology Today*, 22, 51–52.

Bell, R. R. (1981). *Worlds of friendship*. Beverly Hills, CA: Sage.

Bello, R. S., Brandau-Brown, F. E., Zhang, S., and Ragsdale, J. D. (2010). Verbal and nonverbal methods for expressing appreciation in friendships and romantic relationships: A cross-cultural comparison [Electronic version]. *International Journal of Intercultural Relations*, 34, 294–302.

Benassi, M. A. (1985). Effects of romantic love on perceptions of stranger's physical attractiveness. *Psychological Reports*, 56, 355–358.

Benjamin, B. J. (1982, April). *Sex differences in the older voice*. Paper presented at the meeting of the Southern Speech Communication Association, Hot Springs, AR.

Bennett, A. (1981). Interruption and the interpretation of conversation. *Discourse Processes*, 4, 171–188.

Benzer, A. (2012). Teachers' opinions about the use of body language [Electronic version]. *Education*, 132, 467–473.

Berenbaum, H., and Rotter, A. (1992). The relationship between spontaneous facial expressions of emotion and voluntary control of facial muscles. *Journal of Nonverbal Behavior*, 16, 179–190.

Beres, M. A., Herold, E., and Maitland, S. B. (2004). Sexual consent behaviors in same-sex relationships [Electronic version]. *Archives of Sexual Behavior*, 33, 475–486.

Berger, C. R., and Calabrese, J. J. (1975). Some explorations in initial interactions and beyond: Toward a developmental theory of interpersonal communication. *Human Communication Research*, 1, 99–112.

Berger, C. R., and diBattista, P. (1993). Communication failure and plan adaptation: If at first you don't succeed, say it louder and say it slower. *Communication Monographs*, 60, 220–237.

Berger, J., and Cunningham, C. C. (1981). The development of eye contact between mothers and normal versus Down's syndrome infants. *Developmental Psychology*, 17, 678–689.

Berkowitz, L., and Frodi, A. (1979). Reactions to a child's mistakes as affected by his/her looks and speech. *Social Psychology Quarterly*, 42, 420–425.

Bernard, J. (1973). *The sex game: Communication between the sexes*. New York: Atheneum.

Bernstein, E. (2007). Laser tattoo removal [Electronic version]. *Seminars in Plastic Surgery*, 21, 175–192.

Bernstein, E. (2010). Sick of this text: "Sorry I'm late." [Electronic version]. *Wall Street Journal*, 81, D1–D2.

Berry, D. S. (1990). Vocal attractiveness and babyishness: Effects on stranger, self, and friend. *Journal of Nonverbal Behavior*, 14, 141–153.

Berry, D. S. (1992). Vocal types and stereotypes: Joint effects of vocal attractiveness and vocal maturity on person perception. *Journal of Nonverbal Behavior*, 16, 41–54.

Berry, D. S., and McArthur, L. Z. (1986). Perceiving character in faces: The impact of age-related craniofacial changes on social perception. *Psychological Bulletin*, 100, 3–18.

Berry, D. S., Hansen, J., Landry-Pester, J., and Meier, J. (1994). Vocal determinants of first impressions of young children. *Journal of Nonverbal Behavior*, 18, 187–197.

Bersamin, M. M., Todd, M., Fisher, D. A., Hill, D. L., Grube, J. W., and Walker, S. (2008). Parenting practices and adolescent sexual behavior: A longitudinal study [Electronic version]. *Journal of Marriage and Family*, 70, 97–112.

Bersamin, M. M., Walker, S., Fisher, D. A., and Grube, J. W. (2006). Correlates of oral sex and vaginal intercourse in early and middle adolescence [Electronic version]. *Journal of Research on Adolescence*, 16, 59–68.

Berscheid, E., and Walster, E. H. (1969). *Interpersonal attraction*. Reading, MA: Addison-Wesley.

Berscheid, E., Walster, E., and Bohrnstedt, G. (1973). Body image. *Psychology Today*, 7, 119–131.

Bhattacharya, B. B., and Mandal, M. K. (1985). Recognition of facial affect in depression. *Perceptual and Motor Skills*, 61, 13–14.

Biaggio, M. (1989). Sex differences in behavioral reactions to provocation of anger. *Psychological Reports*, 64, 23–26.

Bickman, L. (1974a). Social roles and uniforms: Clothes make the person. *Psychology Today*, 7, 48–51.

Bickman, L. (1974b). Clothes make the person. *Psychology Today*, 8, 49–51.

Biernat, M. (1993). Gender and height: Developmental patterns in knowledge and the use of an accurate stereotype. *Sex Roles*, 29, 691–713.

Bilton, N. (2011). A new purpose for wristwatches [Electronic version]. *New York Times*, February 21, 4.

Bingham, S. (1996). Sexual harassment on the job, on the campus. In J. T. Wood (Ed.), *Gendered relationships: A reader* (pp. 233–252). Mountain View, CA: Mayfield.

Birchlier, G., Weiss, R., and Vincent, J. (1975). Multi-method analysis of social reinforcement exchange between maritally distressed and nondistressed spouse and stranger dyads. *Journal of Personality and Social Psychology*, 31, 349–360.

Birdwhistell, R. L. (1960). Kinesics and communication. In E. Carpenter and M. McLuhan (Eds.), *Explorations in communication: An anthology* (pp. 54–64). Boston: Beacon Press.

Birdwhistell, R. L. (1967). Some body motion elements accompanying spoken American English. In L. Thayer (Ed.), *Communication: Concepts and perspectives* (pp. 53–76). Washington, DC: Spartan.

Birdwhistell, R. L. (1970). *Kinesics and context: Essays on body motion communication.* Philadelphia: University of Pennsylvania Press.

Birdwhistell, R. L. (1974). The language of the body: The natural environment of words. In A. Silverstein (Ed.), *Human communication: Theoretical explorations* (pp. 203–220). New York: John Wiley & Sons.

Birdwhistell, R. L. (1983). Masculinity and femininity as display. In A. M. Katz and V. T. Katz (Eds.), *Foundations of nonverbal communication: Readings, exercises, and commentary* (pp. 81–86). Carbondale: Southern Illinois University Press.

Biren, F. (1956). *Selling color to people.* Secaucus, NJ: Lyle Stuart, University Books.

Bissell, K., and Hays, H. (2010). Exploring the influence of mediated beauty: Examining individual and social factors in white and black adolescent girls' appearance evaluations [Electronic version]. *Howard Journal of Communications, 21,* 385–411.

Bissell, K. L., and Zhou, P. (2004). Must-see TV or ESPN: Entertainment and sports media exposure and body-image distortion in college women [Electronic version]. *Journal of Communication, 54,* 5–21.

Blake, J., and Dolgoy, S. J. (1993). Gestural development and its relation to cognition during the transition to language. *Journal of Nonverbal Behavior, 17,* 87–102.

Blanch-Hartigan, D. (2011). Measuring providers' verbal and nonverbal emotion recognition ability: Reliability and validity of the Patient Emotion Cue Test (PECT) [Electronic version]. *Patient Education and Counseling, 82,* 370–376.

Bloch, P. H., and Richins, M. L. (1993). Attractiveness, adornments, and exchange. *Psychology and Marketing, 6,* 467–470.

Block, C. (1975). Design to dispel fear of oral surgery. *Dental Surgery: The Journal of Dental Practice, 4,* 85–89.

Blurton-Jones, N. G. (1972). Non-verbal communication in children. In R. A. Hines (Ed.), *Non-verbal communication* (pp. 271–295). Cambridge: Cambridge University Press.

Bockler, A., Knoblich, G., and Sebanz, N. (2011). Observing shared attention modulates gaze following [Electronic version]. *Cognition, 120,* 292–298.

Bodary, D. L., and Miller, L. D. (2000). Neurobiological substrates of communicator style. *Communication Education, 49,* 82–89.

Boden, S. (2006). Dedicated followers of fashion? The influence of popular culture on children's social identities [Electronic version]. *Media, Culture & Society, 28,* 289–298.

Bodie, G. D., and Villaume, W. D. (2008). Men and women holding hands revisited: Effects of mutual engagement and hand dominance on attributions of cross-sex handholding. *Communication Research Reports, 25,* 243–254.

Bodin-Danielsson, C., and Bodin, L. (2008). Office type in relation to mental health, well-being, and job satisfaction among employees [Electronic version]. *Environment and Behavior, 40,* 636–668.

Bohn, E., and Stutman, R. (1983). Sex role differences in the relational control dimension of dyadic interaction. *Women's Studies in Communication, 6,* 96–104.

Bond, C. F., Jr., Omar, A., Pitre, U., Lashley, B. R., Skaggs, L. M., and Kirk, C. T. (1992). Fishy-looking liars: Deception judgment from expectancy violation. *Journal of Personality and Social Psychology, 63,* 969–997.

Bond, C. F., Omar, A., Mahmoud, A., and Bonser, R. N. (1990). Lie detection across cultures. *Journal of Nonverbal Behavior, 14,* 189–203.

Bond, M. H., and Shiraishi, D. (1974). The effect of body lean and status of an interviewer on non-verbal behavior of Japanese interviewers. *International Journal of Psychology, 9,* 117–128.

Bonta, J. (1986). Prison crowding: Searching for the functional approach. *American Psychologist*, 41, 99–101.

Booth, A. (1972). Sex and social participation. *American Sociological Review*, 37, 186–187.

Booth, A., and Edwards, J. N. (1976). Crowding and family relations. *American Sociological Review*, 41, 308–321.

Booth, A., and Hess, E. (1974). Cross-sex friendship. *Journal of Marriage and Family*, 44, 38–147.

Booth-Butterfield, M., and Booth-Butterfield, S. (1994). The affective orientation to communication: Conceptual and empirical distinctions. *Communication Quarterly*, 42, 331–344.

Booth-Butterfield, M., and Jordan, F. (1989). Communication adaptation among racially homogeneous and heterogeneous groups. *Southern Communication Journal*, 54, 253–272.

Bosmajian, H. A. (1971). *The rhetoric of nonverbal communication: Readings.* Glenview, IL: Scott, Foresman and Co.

Bosmans, A. (2006). Scents and sensibility: When do (in)congruent ambient scents influence product evaluations? [Electronic version]. *Journal of Marketing*, 70, 32–43.

Boucher, J. D., and Ekman, P. (1975). Facial areas and emotional information. *Journal of Communication*, 25, 21–29.

Bourke, E. (2007, November). *Gendered perceptions of same-sex friendships* [Electronic version]. Paper presented at the National Communication Association, Chicago, IL.

Bowen, E. E., and Montepare, J. (2007). Nonverbal behavior in a global context dialogue questions and responses [Electronic version]. *Journal of Nonverbal Behavior*, 31, 185–187.

Bowers, D., Bauer, R. M., and Heilman, K. M. (1993). The nonverbal affect lexicon: Theoretical perspectives from neuropsychological studies of affects perception. *Neuropsychology*, 7, 433–444.

Bowlby, J. (1961). *Maternal care and mental health.* Geneva: World Health Organization.

Bradley, P. H. (1980). Sex, competence, and opinion deviation: An expectation status approach. *Communication Monographs*, 47, 101–110.

Braithwaite, D. O., Baxter, L. A., and Harper, A. M. (1998). The role of rituals in the management of the dialectical tension of "old" and "new" in blended families. *Communication Studies*, 49, 102–120.

Breed, G., and Porter, M. (1972). Eye contact, attitudes, and attitude change among males. *Journal of Genetic Psychology*, 120–122, 211–217.

Brennan-Parks, K., Goddard, M., Wilson, A. E., and Kinnear, L. (1991). Sex differences in smiling as measured in a picture taking task. *Sex Roles*, 24, 375–382.

Brenner, J. B., and Cunningham, J. G. (1992). Gender differences in eating attitudes, body concept, and self-esteem among models. *Sex Roles*, 27, 413.

Bretherton, I., Stolberg, U., and Kreye, M. (1981). Engaging strangers in proximal interaction: Infants' social development. *Developmental Psychology*, 17, 746–755.

Brief, A. P., and Weiss, H. M. (2002). Organizational behavior: Affect in the workplace [Electronic version]. *Annual Review of Psychology*, 53, 279–307.

Broadstock, M. (1992). Effects of suntan on judgments of healthiness and attractiveness by adolescents. *Journal of Applied Social Psychology*, 22, 151–171.

Brody, L. R., Hay, D. H., and Vanderwater, E. (1990). Gender, gender role identity, and children's reported feelings toward the same and opposite sex. *Sex Roles*, 23, 363–387.

Brooks-Gunn, J., and Lewis, M. (1981). Infant social perception: Responses to pictures of parents and strangers. *Developmental Psychology*, 17, 647–649.

Brown, I., and Thompson, J. (2007). Primary care nurses' attitudes, beliefs, and own body size in relation to obesity management [Electronic version]. *Journal of Advanced Nursing*, 60, 535–543.

Brown, J. D., and L'Engle, K. L. (2009). X-rated: Sexual attitudes and behaviors associated with U.S. early adolescents' exposure to sexually explicit media. *Communication Research*, 36, 129–151.

Brown, S., Francis, P. L., and Lombardo, J. P. (1988). Sex role and opposite sex: Interpersonal attraction. *Perceptual and Motor Skills*, 58, 855–859.

Brownell, K. D. (1991). Dieting and the search for the perfect body: Where physiology and culture collide. *Behavior Therapy*, 22, 1–12.

Browning, J. R., Kessler, D., Hatfield, E., and Choo, P. (1999). Power, gender, and sexual behavior. *Journal of Sex Research*, 36,342–347.

Brownlee, J. R., and Bakeman, R. (1981). Hitting in the toddler—peer interaction. *Child Development*, 52, 1076–1079.

Brownlow, S. (1992). Seeing is believing: Facial appearance, credibility, and attitude change. *Journal of Nonverbal Behavior*, 6, 101–115.

Brownlow, S., and Zebrowitz, L. A. (1990). Facial appearance, gender, and credibility in television commercials. *Journal of Nonverbal Behavior*, 14, 51–60.

Brumark, A. (2010). Behaviour regulation at the family dinner table: The use of and response to direct and indirect behavior regulation in ten Swedish families [Electronic version]. *Journal of Child Language*, 37, 1065–1088.

Bruneau, T. J. (1973). Communicative silences: Forms and functions. *Journal of Communication*, 23, 17–46.

Bruneau, T. J. (1986, April). *The structure of chronemics*. Paper presented at the Conference on Current Trends in Nonverbal Communication: A Multidisciplinary Approach, Jonesboro, Arkansas.

Bruneau, T. J. (2007). Time, change, and sociocultural communication: A chronemic perspective [Electronic version]. *Sign Systems Studies*, 35, 89–117.

Buck, R. (1982). Spontaneous and symbolic nonverbal behavior and the ontogeny of communication. In R. S. Feldman (Ed.), *Development of nonverbal behavior in children* (pp. 29–62). New York: Springer-Verlag.

Buck, R. (1984). *The communication of emotion*. New York: Guilford Press.

Buck, R., Kenny, D. A., and Sabatelli, R. (1986). A social relations analysis of nonverbal communication accuracy in married couples. *Journal of Personality*, 3, 513–527.

Buck, R., Miller, R. E., and Caul, W. F. (1974). Sex, personality and psychological variables in the communication of affect via facial expression. *Journal of Personality and Social Psychology*, 30, 587–596.

Bull, P., and Connelly, E. (1985). Body movement and emphasis in speech. *Journal of Nonverbal Behavior*, 9, 169–187.

Buller, D. B. (1988). Communication apprehension and reaction to proxemic violations. *Journal of Nonverbal Behavior*, 11, 13–25.

Buller, D. B., and Aune, R. K. (1987). Nonverbal cues to deception among intimates, friends, and strangers. *Journal of Nonverbal Behavior*, 11, 269–289.

Buller, D. B., and Aune, R. K. (1992). The effects of speech rate similarity on compliance: Application of communication accommodation theory. *Western Journal of Communication*, 56, 37–53.

Buller, D. B., and Burgoon, J. K. (1986). The effects of vocalics and nonverbal sensitivity on compliance: A replication of extension. *Human Communication Research*, 13, 126–144.

Buller, D. B., Comstock, J., Aune, R. K., and Strzyzewski, K. D. (1989). The effect of probing on deceivers and truthtellers. *Journal of Nonverbal Behavior*, 13, 155–170.

Burgoon, J. K. (1978). Further explication and an initial test of the theory of violations of personal space expectations. *Human Communication Research*, 4, 129–142.

Burgoon, J. K. (1982). Privacy and communication. In M. Burgoon (Ed.), *Communication yearbook 6* (pp. 206–249). Beverly Hills, CA: Sage.

Burgoon, J. K. (1983). Nonverbal violations of expectations. In J. M. Weimann and R. P. Harrison (Eds.), *Nonverbal interaction* (pp. 77–111). Beverly Hills, CA: Sage Publications.

Burgoon, J. K. (1991). Relational message interpretations of touch, conversational distance, and posture. *Journal of Nonverbal Behavior*, 15, 233–259.

Burgoon, J. K., and Aho, L. (1982). Three field experiments on the effects of violations of conversational distance. *Communication Monographs*, 49, 70–88.

Burgoon, J. K., and Buller, D. B. (1994). Interpersonal deception III: Effects of deceit on perceived communication and nonverbal behavior dynamics. *Journal of Nonverbal Behavior*, 18, 155–184.

Burgoon, J. K., Buller, D. B., and Woodall, G. W. (1989). *Nonverbal communication: The unspoken dialogue.* New York: Harper and Row.

Burgoon, J. K., Buller, D. B., and Woodall, G. W. (1996). *Nonverbal communication: The unspoken dialogue.* (2nd ed.). New York: McGraw-Hill.

Burgoon, J. K., Coker, D. A., and Coker, R. A. (1986). Communicative effects of gaze behavior: A test of two contrasting explanations. *Human Communication Research*, 12, 495–524.

Burgoon, J. K., Guerrero, L. K., and Floyd, K. (2010). *Nonverbal Communication.* Boston: Pearson

Burgoon, J. K., and Hale, J. L. (1988). Nonverbal expectancy violations: Model elaboration and application to immediacy behaviors. *Communication Monographs*, 55, 58–79.

Burgoon, J. K., and Jones, S. B. (1976). Toward a theory of personal space expectations and their violations. *Human Communication Research*, 2, 131–146.

Burgoon, J. K., Manusov, V., Mineo, P., and Hale, J. L. (1985). Effects of gaze on hiring, credibility, attraction, and relational message interpretation. *Journal of Nonverbal Behavior*, 9, 133–146.

Burgoon, J. K., and Newton, D. A. (1991). Applying a social meaning model to relational message interpretations of conversational involvement: Comparing observer and participant perspectives. *Southern Communication Journal*, 56, 96–113.

Burgoon, J. K., Pfau, M., Birk, T., and Manusov, V. (1987). Nonverbal communication and perceptions associated with reticence: Replications and classroom implications. *Communication Education*, 36, 117–130.

Burgoon, J. K., and Saine, T. J. (1978). *The unspoken dialogue: An introduction to nonverbal communication.* Boston: Houghton Mifflin.

Burgoon, J. K., Stacks, D. W., and Burch, S. A. (1982). The role of interpersonal rewards and violations of distancing expectations in achieving influence. *Communication*, 11, 114–128.

Burgoon, J. K., Stacks, D. W., and Woodall, W. G. (1977, December). *Personal space expectations and reward as predictors of recall, credibility, and attraction.* Paper presented at the meeting of the Speech Communication Association, Washington, DC.

Burgoon, J. K., Stacks, D. W., and Woodall, W. G. (1979). Personal space expectations and reward as predictors of recall, credibility, and attraction. *Western Journal of Communication*, 43, 153–167.

Burgoon, J. K., and Walther, J. B. (1990). Nonverbal expectancies and the evaluative consequences of violations. *Human Communication Research*, 17, 232–265.

Burgoon, J. K., Walther, J. B., and Baesler, E. J. (1992). Interpretations, evaluations, and consequences of interpersonal touch. *Human Communication Research*, 19, 237–263.

Burton, A. M., and Bruce, V. (1992). I recognize your face but I can't remember your name: A simple explanation. *British Journal of Psychology*, 83, 45–60.

Buss, D. M (2001). Cognitive biases and emotional wisdom in the evolution of conflict between the sexes [Electronic version]. *Current Directions in Psychological Science*, 10, 219–223.

Byers, P. (1979). Biological rhythms as information channels in interpersonal communication behavior. In S. Weitz (Ed.), *Nonverbal communication: Readings with commentary* (2nd ed., pp. 398–418). New York: Oxford University Press.

Cain, W. S. (1981). Educating your nose. *Psychology Today*, 15, 48–56.

Calhoun, J. B. (1950). The study of wild animals under controlled conditions. *Annals of the New York Academy of Sciences*, 51, 113–122.

Calhoun, J. B. (1962). Population density and social pathology. *Scientific American*, 206, 130–146.

Callen, V., and Gallios, C. (1986). Decoding emotional messages: Influences of ethnicity, sex, message type, and channel. *Journal of Personality and Social Psychology*, 51, 755–762.

Callister, M. A., and Robinson, T. (2010). Content analysis of physical affection within television families during the 2006–2007 season of U.S. children's programming [Electronic version]. *Journal of Children and Media*, 4, 155–173.

Cameras, L., and Allison, K. (1985). Children's understanding of emotional facial expressions and verbal labels. *Journal of Nonverbal Behavior*, 9, 84–93.

Campbell, K. E., Kleim, D. M., and Olson, K. (1986). Gender, physical attractiveness, and assertiveness. *Journal of Social Psychology*, 125, 297–698.

Canary, D. J., Stafford, L., Hause, K. S., and Wallace, L. A. (1993). An inductive analysis of relational maintenance strategies: Comparisons among lovers, relative, friends, and others. *Communication Research Reports*, 10, 5–14.

Cann, A. (1991). Stereotypes about physical and social characteristics based on social and professional competence information. *Journal of Social Psychology*, 313, 225–231.

Cant, R. P. (2009). Communication competence within dietetics: dietitians' and clients' views about the unspoken dialogue - the impact of personal presentation. *Journal of Human Nutrition & Dietetics*, 22, 504–510.

Cardon, P. W., and Okoro, E. A. (2009). Professional characteristics communicated by formal versus casual workplace attire [Electronic version]. *Business Communication Quarterly*, 72, 355–360.

Carmen, R. A., Guitar, A. E., and Dillon, H. M. (2012). Ultimate answers to proximate questions: The evolutionary motivations behind tattoos and body piercings in popular culture [Electronic version]. *Review of General Psychology*, 16, 134–143.

Carre, J. M., McCormick, C. M., and Mondloch, C. J. (2009). Facial structure is a reliable cue of aggressive behavior [Electronic version]. *Psychological Science*, 20, 1194–1198.

Casasanto, D. (2011). Different bodies, different minds: The body specificity of language and thought [Electronic version]. *Current Directions in Psychological Science*, 20, 378–383.

Casasanto, D., and Jasmin, K. (2010). Good and bad in the hands of politicians: Spontaneous gestures during positive and negative speech [Electronic version]. *PLoS ONE*, 5, 1–5.

Cash, T. F. (1987). The psychology of cosmetics: A review of the scientific literature. *Social and Behavioral Science Documents*, 17, 1–62.

Cash, T. F., and Green, G. K. (1986). Body weight and body image among college women: Perception, cognition, and affect. *Journal of Personality Assessment*, 50, 290–300.

Cash, T. F., Noles, S. W., and Winstead, B. A. (1985). Body image, physical attractiveness, and depression. *Journal of Consulting and Clinical Psychology*, 53, 88–94.

Cash, T. F., Winstead, B. A., and Janda, L. H. (1986). The great American shape-up. *Psychology Today*, 20, 30–77.

Caso, L., Maricchiolo, F., Bonaiuto, M., Vrij, A., and Mann, S. (2006). The impact of deception and suspicion on different hand movements [Electronic version]. *Journal of Nonverbal Behavior*, 30, 1–19.

Castelli, L., Carraro, L., Pavan, G., Murelli, E., and Carraro, A. (2012). The power of the unsaid: The influence of nonverbal cues on implicit attitudes [Electronic version].*Journal of Applied Social Psychology*, 42, 1376–1393.

Castle, D. J., Honigman, R. J., and Phillips, K. A. (2002). Does cosmetic surgery improve psychosocial wellbeing? *The Medical Journal of Australia*, 176 (8), 601–604.

Cavior, N., and Lombardi, D. A. (1973). Developmental aspects of judgments of physical attractiveness in children. *Developmental Psychology*, 8, 67–71.

Cayanus, J. L., Martin, M. M., and Weber, K. D. (2005). The relationships between driver anger and aggressive communication traits. *Communication Research Reports*, 22, 189–197.

CBS News (2013). 10 most popular plastic surgery procedures. Retrieved from http://www.cbsnews.com/2300-204_162-10007103.html

Chambers, C., and Sparks, J. (2009, November). *Judging a book by its cover: The influence of personality presentation on perceptions of physical attractiveness and memory* [Electronic version]. Paper presented at the National Communication Association, Chicago, IL.

Cheng, S. C. (2003, May). *My body is the book: An ethnographic study of the tattooing practice among U. S. youth [Electronic version]*. Paper presented at the meeting of the International Communication Association, San Diego, CA.

Childress, H. (2004). Teenagers, territory and the appropriation of space [Electronic version]. *Childhood*, 11, 195–205.

Cho, S. (2007). TV news coverage of plastic surgery 1972–2004. *Journalism and Mass Communication Quarterly*, 84, 75–89.

Chock, T. (2007, November). *Is it all in the looks? Approval of cosmetic surgery, gender role stereotypes, and the effects of graphic surgical depictions* [Electronic version]. Paper presented at the meeting of the National Communication Association, Chicago, IL.

Chory, R. M., and McCroskey, J. C. (1999). The relationship between teacher management communication style and affective learning. *Communication Quarterly*, 47, 1–11.

Christian, J. J. (1963). The pathology of overpopulation. *Military Medicine*, 128, 571–603.

Christian, J. J., and Davis, D. E. (1964). Social and endocrine factors are integrated in the regulation of growth of mammalian population. *Science*, 146, 1550–1560.

Christian, J. J., Flyger, V., and Davis, D. E. (1961a). Phenomena associated with population density. *Proceedings of the National Academy of Science*, 47, 428–449.

Christian, J. J., Flyger, V., and Davis, D. E. (1961b). Factors in mass mortality of a herd of Sika deer (Cervus nippon). *Chesapeake Science*, 47, 79–95.

Chung, V. Q., Gordon, J. S., Veledar, E., and Chen, S. C. (2010). Hot or not: Evaluating the effect of artificial tanning on the public's perception of attractiveness[Electronic version]. *Dermatologic Surgery.* 36, 1651-1655.

Church, R. B., Garber, P., and Rogalski, K. (2007). The role of gesture in memory and social communication [Electronic version]. *Gesture*, 7, 137–158.

Cinelli, L. A., and Ziegler, D. J. (1990). Cognitive appraisal of daily hassles in college students showing Type A and Type B behavior patterns. *Psychological Reports*, 67, 83–88.

Clarke-Stewart, A., and Hervey, C. (1981). Longitudinal relations in repeated observations of mother—child interaction from 1–2 1/2 years. *Developmental Psychology*, 17, 127–145.

Clay, V. S. (1966). *The effect of culture on tactile communication.* Unpublished dissertation, Columbia University, New York.

Clayman, S. (1992). Booing: The anatomy of a disaffiliative response. *American Sociological Review*, 28, 110–129.

Clemmer, E. J., and Carrocci, N. M. (1984). Effects of experience on radio language performance. *Communication Monographs*, 51, 116–139.

Clifford, M. M., and Walster, E. H. (1973). The effect of physical attractiveness in teacher expectation. *Sociological Education*, 46, 248–258.

Cline, R. J. (1986). The effects of biological sex and psychological gender on reported and behavioral intimacy and control of self-disclosure. *Communication Quarterly*, 34, 41–54.

Cline, R. J., and Musolf, K. E. (1985). Disclosure of social exchange: Anticipated length of relationships, sex roles, and disclosure intimacy. *Western Journal of Speech Communication*, 49, 43–56.

Clynes, M. (1988). Human emotion communication by touch: A modified replication of an experiment. *Perceptual and Motor Skills*, 66, 419–424.

Cohen, A. A. (1977). The communicative functions of hand gestures. *Journal of Communication*, 27, 54–63.

Coker, D. A., and Burgoon, J. K. (1987). The nature of conversational involvement and nonverbal encoding patterns. *Human Communication Research*, 14, 463–494.

Cole, J. G., and McCroskey, J. C. (2003). The association of perceived communication apprehension, shyness, and verbal aggression with perceptions of source credibility and affect in organizational and interpersonal contexts. *Communication Quarterly*, 51, 101–110.

Comer, D., and Lindsey, A. (2007, November). *Cross-sex friendship challenges and maintenance strategies: Women's views of friendships with straight men vs. gay men* [Electronic version]. Paper presented at the National Communication Association, Chicago, IL.

CommSearch (3rd ed.). (1999). Annandale, VA: National Communication Association.

Conigliaro, L., Cullerton, S., Flynn, K., and Rueder, S. (1989). Stigmatizing artifacts and their effect on personal space. *Psychological Reports*, 65, 897–898.

Conley, J. M., and O'Barr, W. M. (1990). *Rules versus relationships: The ethnography of legal discourse.* Chicago: University of Chicago Press.

Conners, J. (2007, November). *Ethics in plastic surgery TV portrayals: Cautions and warnings, or only the "Wow"?* [Electronic version]. Paper presented at the meeting of the National Communication Association, Chicago, IL.

Cook, M. (1970). Experiments in orientation and proxemics. *Human Relations*, 23, 71–76.

Cooper, K. (1979). *Nonverbal communication for business success.* New York: AMACOMM.

Corbett, E. P. J. (1971). *Classical rhetoric for the modern student* (2nd ed.). New York: Oxford University Press.

Cornell, E., and McManus, I. C. (1992). Differential survey response rates in right- and left-handers. *British Journal of Psychology*, 83, 39–43.

Cortes, J. B., and Gatti, F. M. (1965). Physique and self-description of temperament. *Journal of Consulting Psychology*, 29, 434.

Costa, M. (2012). Territorial behavior in public settings [Electronic version]. *Environment and Behavior*, 44, 713–721.

Cottle, T. J. (1976). *Perceiving time: A psychological investigation with men and women.* New York: John Wiley and Sons.

Courtwright, J., Millar, F., and Rogers-Millar, L. E. (1979). Domineeringness and dominance: Replication and expansion. *Communication Monographs*, 46, 179–192.

Cowley, J. J., Johnson, A. L., and Brooksbank, B. (1977). The effects of two odorous compounds on performance in an assessment-of-people test. *Psychoneuroendocrinology*, 2, 159–172.

Craig, A. B., Martz, D. M., and Bazzini, D. G. (2007). Peer pressure to "fat talk": Does audience type influence how women portray their body image [Electronic version]. *Eating Behaviors*, 8, 244–250.

Crandall, C. S. (1991). Do heavy-weight students have more difficulty paying for college? *Personality and Social Psychology Bulletin*, 17, 606–611.

Crandall, C. S. (1995). Do parents discriminate against their heavyweight daughters? *Personality and Social Psychology Bulletin*, 21, 724–735.

Cross, M., and Epting, F. (2005). Self-obliteration, self-definition, self-integration: Claiming a homosexual identity [Electronic version]. *Journal of Constructivist*, 18, 53–63.

Croy, I., Negoias, S., Novakova, L., Landis, B. N., and Hummel, T. (2012). Learning about the functions of the olfactory system from people without a sense of smell [Electronic version]. *PLoS ONE*, 7, 1–7.

Culturegram: China (People's Republic). (1981a). *Culturegram.* Provo, UT: Brigham Young University Press.

Culturegram: Italy. (1981b). *Culturegram.* Provo, UT: Brigham Young University Press.

Culturegram: The Commonwealth of Puerto Rico. (1981c). *Culturegram.* Provo, UT: Brigham Young University Press.

Culturegram: Western Canada and Ontario. (1981d). *Culturegram.* Provo, UT: Brigham Young University Press.

Culturegram: Kingdom of Saudi Arabia. (1982). *Culturegram.* Provo, UT: Brigham Young University Press.

Cunningham, M. R. (1986). Measuring the physical in physical attractiveness: Quasi-experiments on the sociobiology of female facial beauty. *Journal of Personality and Social Psychology*, 50, 925–935.

Cutter, G. R. (2008). Effects of program exposure and engagement with tailored prevention communication on sun protection by young adolescents [Electronic version]. *Journal of Health Communication*, 13, 619–636.

Dabbs, J. M., Jr., and Stokes, N. A., III. (1975). Beauty is power: The use of space on the sidewalk. *Sociometry*, 38, 551–557.

Dailey, R. M. (2008). Assessing the contribution of nonverbal behaviors in displays of confirmation during parent—adolescent interactions: An actor—partner interdependence model [Electronic version]. *Journal of Family Communication*, 8, 62–91.

Damhorst, M. L. (1982, November). *Influences of context upon the use of nonverbal symbols.* Paper presented at the meeting of the Speech Communication Association, Louisville, KY.

Damron, J. C. H., and Morman, M. T. (2011). Attitudes toward interpersonal silence within dyadic relationships. *Human Communication*, 14, 183–203.

Daniels, M. C., and Adair, L. S. (2005). Breast-feeding influences cognitive development in Filipino children [Electronic version]. *Journal of Nutrition*, 135, 2589–2595.

Darwin, C. (1998). *The expression of the emotions in man and animals.* (Definitive ed.). New York: Oxford University Press. (Original work published 1871.)

D'Atri, D. A. (1975). Psychophysiological responses to crowding. *Environment and Behavior*, 7, 237–251.

Dauterive, R., and Ragsdale, J. D. (1986). Relationship between age, sex, and hesitation phenomena in young children. *Southern Speech Communication Journal*, 52, 22–34.

Davidson, R. J., and Fox, N. A. (1989). Frontal brain asymmetry predicts infants' responses to maternal separation. *Journal of Abnormal Psychology*, 20, 127–131.

Davies, J., Zhu, H., and Brantley, B. (2007). Sex appeals that appeal: Negative sexual self-schema as a moderator of the priming effects of sexual ads on accessibility [Electronic version]. *Journal of Current Issues and Research in Advertising*, 29, 79–89.

Davis, C., and Cowles, M. (1991). Body image and exercise: A study of relationships and comparisons between physically active men and women. *Sex Roles*, 25, 33–44.

Davis, K. (1995). *Reshaping the female body: The dilemma of cosmetic surgery.* New York: Routledge Press.

Dean, L. M., LaRocco, J. M., and Willis, F. N. (1976). Invasion of personal space as a function of age, sex, and race. *Psychological Reports*, 58, 959–964.

Deaux, K. (1976). *The behavior of men and women.* Monterey, CA: Brooks/Cole Publishing Co.

Debevac, K., Madden, T. J., and Kernan, J. B. (1986). Physical attractiveness, message evaluation, compliance: A structural examination. *Psychological Reports*, 58, 503–508.

DeBono, K. G., and Harnish, R. J. (1988). Source expertise, source attractiveness, and the processing of persuasive information: A functional approach. *Journal of Personality and Social Psychology*, 55, 541–550.

Deffenbacher, J. L., Oetting, E. R., and Lynch, R. S. (1994). Development of a driving anger scale. *Psychological Reports*, 74, 83–91.

DeGroot, T., and Gooty, J. (2009). Can nonverbal cues be used to make meaningful personality attributions in employment interviews? [Electronic version] *Journal of Business and Psychology*, 24, 174–192.

de Groot, J. H. B., Smeets, M. A. M., Kaldewaij, A., Duijndam, M. J. A., and Semin, G. R. (2012). Chemosignals communicate human emotions [Electronic version]. *Psychological Science*, 23, 1417–1424.

Denzin, N. K. (1989). *The research act: A theoretical introduction to sociological methods* (3rd ed.). Englewood Cliffs, NJ: Prentice–Hall.

Denzin, N. K., and Lincoln, Y. S. (1994). Introduction: Entering the field of qualitative research. In N. K. Denzin and Y. S. Lincoln (Eds.), *Handbook of qualitative research* (pp. 1–17). Thousand Oaks, CA: Sage.

DePaulo, B. M. (1992). Nonverbal behavior and self-presentation. *Psychological Bulletin*, 111, 203–243.

DePaulo, B. M., Stone, J. I., and Lassiter, G. D. (1985). Deceiving and detecting deceit. In B. R. Schlenker (Ed.), *The self and social life* (pp. 323–370). New York: McGraw-Hill.

DePaulo, B. M., Zuckerman, M., and Rosenthal, R. (1980). Detecting deception: Modality effects. In L. Wheeler (Ed.), *Review of personality and social psychology* (Vol. 1, pp. 129–131). Beverly Hills, CA: Sage Publications.

Derlega, V. J., Lewis, R. J., Harrison, S., Winstead, B. A., and Costanza, R. (1989). Gender differences in the initiation and attribution of tactile intimacy. *Journal of Nonverbal Behavior*, 13, 83–96.

Despert, J. L. (1941). Emotional aspects of speech and language development. *International Journal of Psychiatry and Neurology*, 105, 193–222.

deTurck, M. A., and Miller, G. R. (1985). Deception and arousal: Isolating the behavioral correlates of deception. *Human Communication Research*, 12, 181–201.

deTurck, M. A., Bodhorn, J. J., and Texter, A. (1990). The effects of training social perceivers to detect deception from behavioral cues. *Communication Quarterly*, 38, 189–199.

Diagram Group. (1976). *Man's body: An owner's manual*. New York: Bantam.

Diagram Group. (1977). *Woman's body: An owner's manual*. New York: Bantam.

Dicker, R. L., and Syracuse, V. R. (1976). *Consultation with a plastic surgeon*. Chicago: Nelson-Hall.

Dickinson, G. (2006). The Pleasantville effect: Nostalgia and the visual framing of (white) suburbia. *Western Journal of Communication*, 70, 212–233.

Diesing, P. (1971). *Patterns of discovery in the social sciences*. Chicago: Aldine.

Dietz, S. R., and Byrnes, L. E. (1981). Attribution of responsibility for sexual assault: The influence of observer empathy and defendant occupation and attractiveness. *Journal of Psychology*, 108, 17–30.

Dimitrovsky, L. (1964). The ability to identify the emotional meaning of vocal expression at successive age levels. In J. R. Davitz (Ed.), *The communication of emotional meaning* (pp. 69–86). New York: McGraw-Hill.

Dinardo, L., and Rainey, D. (1991). The effects of illumination level and exposure time on facial recognition. *Psychological Record*, 41, 329–334.

Dindia, K. (1986). Antecedents and consequences of awkward silence: A replication using revised lag sequential analysis. *Human Communication Research*, 13, 108–125.

Dindia, K. (1987). The effects of sex of subject and sex of partner on interruptions. *Human Communication Research*, 13, 345–371.

Dion, E., Berschied, E., and Walster, E. (1972). What is beautiful is good. *Journal of Personality and Social Psychology*, 24 (2), 285–290.

Dion, K. K. (1972). Physical attractiveness and evaluations of children's transgressions. *Journal of Personality and Social Psychology*, 24, 207–213.

Dion, K. K., and Berscheid, E. (1972). Physical attractiveness and evaluation of children's transgressions. *Journal of Personality and Social Psychology*, 30, 207–213.

Dittman, A. T. (1971). Review of kinesics and context by R. L. Birdwhistell. *Psychiatry*, 34, 334–342.

Dittman, A. T. (1972). *Interpersonal messages of emotion*. New York: Springer.

Dixon, H. G., Hill, D. J., Karoly, D. J., Jolley, D. J., and Aden, S. M. (2007). Solar UV forecasts: A randomized trial assessing their impact on adults' sun-protection behavior [Electronic version]. *Health Education and Behavior*, 34, 486–502.

Dixon, J. A., and Foster, D. H. (1998). Gender, social context, and backchannel responses [Electronic version]. *Journal of Social Psychology*, 138, 134–136.

Dixson, B. J., and Vasey, P. L. (2012). Beards augment perceptions of men's age, social status, and aggressiveness, but not attractiveness [Electronic version]. *Behavioral Ecology*, 23, 481–490.

Doering, N., and Poeschl, S. (2007, May). *Nonverbal cues in mobile phone text messages: The effects of chronemics and proxemics* [Electronic version]. Paper presented at the meeting of the International Communication Association, San Francisco, CA.

Dolin, D. J., and Booth-Butterfield, M. (1993). Reach out and touch someone: Analysis of nonverbal comforting responses. *Communication Quarterly*, 41, 383–393.

Dolinski, D. (2010). Touch, compliance, and homophobia [Electronic version]. *Journal of Nonverbal Behavior*, 34, 179–182.

Dolphin, C. Z. (1988). Beyond Hall: Variables in the use of personal space in intercultural transactions. *Howard Journal of Communications*, 1, 23–38.

Dominguez, P. R. (2011). The study of postnatal and later development of the taste and olfactory systems using the human brain mapping approach: An update [Electronic version]. *Brain Research Bulletin*, 84, 118–124.

Doniger, W. (2000). The mythology of the face-lift. *Social Research*, 67, 99–125.

Donovan, J., Hill, E., and Jankowiak, W. R. (1988). Gender, sexual orientation, and truth of consensus in studies in physical attractiveness. *Journal of Sex Research*, 26, 264–271.

Dosey, M., and Meisels, M. (1969). Personal space and self-protection. *Journal of Personality and Social Psychology*, 11, 93–97.

Doss, K., and Ebesu-Hubbard, A. S. (2009). The communicative value of tattoos: The role of public self-consciousness on tattoo visibility. *Communication Research Reports*, 26, 62–74.

Doty, R. L., Ford, M., Preti, G., and Huggins, G. R. (1975). Changes in the intensity and pleasantness of human vagina odors during the menstrual cycle. *Science*, 190, 1316–1318.

DuBrin, A. J. (1991). Sex and gender differences in tactics of influence. *Psychological Reports*, 68, 635–645.

Duggan, A. P., Dailey, R. M., and Le Poire, B. A. (2008). Reinforcement and punishment of substance abuse during ongoing interactions: A conversational test of inconsistent nurturing as control theory [Electronic version]. *Journal of Health Communication*, 13, 417–433.

Dunbar, N. E., and Burgoon, J. K. (2005). Perceptions of power and interactional dominance in interpersonal relationships [Electronic version]. *Journal of Social and Personal Relationships*, 22, 207–233.

Duncan, S. (1972). Some signals and rules for turn taking in conversations. *Journal of Personality and Social Psychology*, 23, 283–292.

Duncan, S. (1975). Interaction units during speaking turns in face-to-face conversations. In A. Kendon, R. Harns, and M. Key (Eds.), *Organization of behavior in face-to-face interaction* (pp. 199–212). The Hague: Mouton.

Duncan, S. (1983). Speaking turns: Studies of structure and individual differences. In J. M. Wiemann and R. P. Harrison (Eds.), *Nonverbal interaction* (pp. 149–178). Beverly Hills, CA: Sage Publications.

Dunkle, J. H., and Francis, P. L. (1990). The role of facial masculinity/femininity in the attribution of homosexuality. *Sex Roles*, 23, 157–158.

Dunsmore, J., Her, P., Halberstadt, A., and Perez-Rivera, M. (2009). Parents' beliefs about emotions and children's recognition of parents' emotions [Electronic version]. *Journal of Nonverbal Behavior*, 33, 121–140.

Durand, K., Baudon, G., Freydefont, L., and Schaal, B. (2008). Odorization of a novel object can influence infant's exploratory behavior in unexpected ways [Electronic version]. *Infant Behavior and Development*, 31, 629–636.

Durr, M., and Harvey-Wingfield, A. M. (2011). Keep Your 'N' in Check: African American Women and the Interactive Effects of Etiquette and Emotional Labor [Electronic version]. *Critical Sociology*, 37, 557–571.

Eakins, B. W., and Eakins, R. G. (1976). Verbal turn-taking and exchanges in faculty dialogue. In B. L. DuBois and I. Crouch (Eds.), *Papers in Southwest English: IV. Proceedings of the Conference on Sociology of the Languages of American Women* (pp. 53–62). San Antonio: Trinity University Press.

Eakins, B. W., and Eakins, R. G. (1978). *Sex differences in human communication*. Boston: Houghton Mifflin.

Eason, K. A., and Hodges, N. (2011). Reading contemporary female body modification as a site of Cixous' L'ectriture Feminine [Electronic version]. *The Journal of Dress, Body and Culture*, 15, 323–343.

Eaves, M., and Leathers, D. G. (1991). Context as communication: McDonald's versus Burger King. *Journal of Applied Communication Research*, 19, 263–289.

Ebesu-Hubbard, A., Sur, J., Saito, N., Hanna, A., Nishigaya, K., Nakamura, L., and Doi, R. (2009, November). *Men's facial hair as a mate signal: An evolutionary perspective* [Electronic version]. Paper presented at the National Communication Association, Chicago, IL.

Edgerton, M. T., Jacobson, W. E., and Meyer, E. (1960). Surgical-psychiatric study of transsexual patients seeking plastic (cosmetic) surgery: Ninety-eight consecutive patients with minimal deformity. *British Journal of Plastic Surgery*, 13, 144.

Edgerton, M. T., and Knorr, N. J. (1971). Motivational patterns of patients seeking cosmetic (esthetic) surgery. *Plastic and Reconstructive Surgery*, 48, 553–554.

Edinger, J. A., and Patterson, M. L. (1983). Nonverbal involvement and social control. *Psychological Bulletin* 93, 30–56.

Edney, J. J. (1974). Human territoriality. *Psychological Bulletin*, 81, 959–975.

Edney, J. J. (1976). Human territories. *Environment and Behavior*, 8, 31–47.

Edney, J. J., and Jordan-Edney, N. L. (1974). Territorial spacing on a beach. *Sociometry*, 37, 92–104.

Edwards, D. J. A. (1972). Approaching the unfamiliar: A study of human interaction distances. *Journal of Behavioral Science*, 1, 249–250.

Edwards, J. N., and Booth, A. (1977). Crowding and human sexual behavior. *Social Forces*, 55, 791–808.

Egan, K., Harcourt, D. and Rumsey, N. (2011). A qualitative study of the experience of people who identify themselves as having adjusted positively to a visible difference [Electronic version]. *Journal of Health Psychology*, 16, 739–749.

Egolf, D. B., and Corder, L. E. (1991). Height differences of low and high job status, female and male corporate employees. *Sex Roles*, 24, 365–373.

Eibl-Eibesfeldt, I. (1970). Similarities and differences between cultures in expressive movement. In R. A. Hinde (Ed.), *Nonverbal communication* (pp. 297–314). Cambridge: Cambridge University Press.

Eichenbaum, L., and Orbach, S. (1987). *Between women: Love, envy, and competition in women's friendships.* New York: Viking.

Eiland, R., and Richardson, D. (1976). The influence of race, sex, and age on judgments of emotion portrayed in photographs. *Communication Monographs*, 43, 167–175.

Ekman, P. (1965). Communication through nonverbal behavior: A source of information about an interpersonal relationship. In S. S. Tompkins and C. E. Izard (Eds.), *Affect, cognition, and personality* (pp. 390–442). New York: Springer.

Ekman, P. (1976). Movements and precise meanings. *Journal of Communication*, 26, 14–26.

Ekman, P. (1981). Mistakes while deceiving. *Annals of the New York Academy of Sciences*, 364, 269–278.

Ekman, P. (1982). Facial expression and nerve name surgery. In M. D. Graham and W. F. House (Eds.), *Disorders of the facial nerve* (pp. 363–368). New York: Raven Press.

Ekman, P. (1985). *Telling lies: Clues to deceit in the marketplace, politics, and marriage.* New York: Norton.

Ekman, P. (1989). Would a child lie? *Psychology Today*, 23, 62–65.

Ekman, P. (1993). Facial expression and emotion. *American Psychologist*, 48, 384–392.

Ekman, P. (1994). Strong evidence for universals in facial expressions: A reply to Russell's mistaken critique. *Psychological Bulletin*, 115, 268–287.

Ekman, P., and Friesen, W. V. (1968). Nonverbal behavior in psychotherapy research. *Research in Psychotherapy*, 3, 179-216.

Ekman, P., and Friesen, W. V. (1969). The repertoire of nonverbal behavior: Categories, origins, usage and codings. *Semiotica*, 1, 49–98.

Ekman, P., and Friesen, W. V. (1975). *Unmasking the face: A guide to recognizing emotion for facial cues.* Englewood Cliffs, NJ: Prentice-Hall.

Ekman, P., and Friesen, W. V. (1982). Felt, false, and miserable smiles. *Journal of Nonverbal Behavior*, 6, 238–252.

Ekman, P., and Friesen, W. V. (1985). Is the startle reaction an emotion? *Journal of Personality and Social Psychology*, 49, 1416–1426.

Ekman, P., and Friesen, W. V. (1986). A new pan-cultural facial expression of emotion. *Motivation and Emotion*, 10, 159–168.

Ekman, P., Friesen, W. V., and Tompkins, S. S. (1971). Facial affect scoring technique: A first validity study. *Semiotica*, 3, 37–58.

Ekman, P., O'Sullivan, M., Friesen, W. V., and Scherer, K. R. (1991). Face, voice, and body in detecting deceit. *Journal of Nonverbal Behavior*, 15, 125–135.

Elfenbein, H. A. (2006). Learning in emotion judgments: Training and the cross-cultural understanding of facial expressions [Electronic version]. *Journal of Nonverbal Behavior*, 30, 21–36.

Elfenbein, H. A., and Eisenkraft, N. (2010). The relationship between displaying and perceiving nonverbal cues of affect: A meta-analysis to solve an old mystery [Electronic version]. *Journal of personality and Social Psychology*, 98, 301–318.

Ellen, P. S., and Bone, P. F. (1998). Does it matter if it smells? Olfactory stimuli as advertising executional cues [Electronic version]. *Journal of Advertising*, 27, 29–39.

Elliott, R., and Elliott, C. (2005). Idealized image of the male body in advertising: A reader-response exploration [Electronic version]. *Journal of Marketing Communications*, 11, 3–19.

Ellis, R. (2009). Understanding interpersonal relationships in the Chinese context [Electronic version]. *Journal of Intercultural Communication*, 20, 3.

Ellsworth, P. C., and Carlsmith, J. M. (1968). Effect of eye contact and verbal content on affective response to a dyadic interaction. *Journal of Personality and Social Psychology*, 10, 15–24.

Ellsworth, P. C., and Ludwig, L. M. (1972). Visual behavior in social interaction. *Journal of Communication*, 22, 375–403.

Elman, D. (1977). Physical characteristics and the perception of masculine traits. *Journal of Social Psychology*, 103, 157–158.

Emmers-Sommer, T. M. (1999). Negative relational events and event responses across relationship-type: Examining and comparing the impact of conflict strategy-use on intimacy in same-sex friendships, opposite-sex friendships and romantic relationships. *Communication Research Reports*, 16, 286–295.

Emmert, P., and Emmert, V. J. L. (1984). *Interpersonal communication* (3rd ed.). Dubuque, IA: Wm. C. Brown.

Engelbretsen, D., and Fullmer, D. (1970). Cross-cultural differences in territoriality: Interaction distance of native Japanese, Hawaii Japanese, and American caucasians. *Journal of Cross-Cultural Psychology*, 1, 261–269.

Engelin-Maddox, R., Salk, R. H., and Miller, S. A. (2012). Assessing women's negative commentary on their own bodies: A psychometric investigation of the negative body talk scale. *Psychology of Women Quarterly*, 36, 162–178.

Engen, T. (1980). Why the aroma lingers. *Psychology Today*, 14, 13.

Engen, T., and Lipsitt, L. P. (1963). Decrement and recovery of response to olfactory stimuli in the human neonate. *Journal of Comparative Physiological Psychology*, 56, 75–77.

Engstrom, E. (1994). Effects of nonfluencies on speaker's credibility in newscast settings. *Perceptual and Motor Skills*, 78, 739–743.

Ephratt, M. (2011) Linguistic, paralinguistic and extralinguistic speech and silence [Electronic version]. *Journal of Pragmatics*, 43, 2286–2307.

Erb, R. C. (1968). *The common scents of smell: How the nose knows and what it all shows!* Cleveland: World.

Erbe, B. M. (1975). Race and socioeconomic segregation. *American Sociological Review*, 40, 801–812.

Erceau, D., and Guéguen, N. (2007). Tactile contact and the evaluation of the toucher [Electronic version]. *Journal of Social Psychology*, 147, 441–444.

Ericksen, S. J. (2012). To cut or not to cut: Cosmetic surgery usage and women's age-related experiences [Electronic version]. *International Journal of Aging and Human Development*, 74, 1–24.

Erickson, W., and Billick, S. (2012). Psychiatric issues in cosmetic plastic surgery [Electronic version]. *Psychiatric Quarterly*, 83, 343–352.

Esposito, E. (1979). Sex differences in children's conversations. *Language and Speech*, 22, 213–220.

Ewing, L., Rhodes, G., and Pellicano, E. (2010). Have you got the look? Gaze direction affects judgments of facial attractiveness [Electronic version]. *Visual Cognition*, 18, 321–330.

Exline, R. (1963). Exploration in the process of person perception: Visual interaction in relation to competition, sex, and the need for affiliation. *Journal of Personality*, 31, 1–20.

Fabricant, S. M., and Gould, S. J. (1993). Women's makeup careers: An interpretive study of color cosmetic use and "face value." *Psychology and Marketing*, 10, 531–548.

Falk, J. (1980). The conversational duet. *Proceedings of the sixth annual meeting of the Berkeley Linguistics Society*, 6, 507–514.

Farris, C., Treat, T. A., Viken, R. J., and McFall, R. M. (2008). Perceptual mechanisms that characterize gender differences in decoding women's sexual intent [Electronic version]. *Psychological Science*, 19, 348–354.

Fast, J. (1970). *Body language*. New York: M. Evans.

Fay, M., and Price, C. (1994). Female body-shape in print advertisements and the increase in anorexia nervosa [Electronic version]. *European Journal of Marketing*, 28, 5–18.

Feeley, T. H., and Young, M. J. (1998). Humans as lie detectors: Some more thoughts. *Communication Quarterly*, 46, 109–126.

Feiman, S., and Gill, G. W. (1978). Sex differences on physical attractiveness preferences. *Journal of Social Psychology*, 105, 43–52.

Feingold, A. (1992). Good-looking people are not what we think. *Psychological Bulletin*, 111, 304–341.

Felipe, N., and Sommer, R. (1966). Invasions of personal space. *Social Problems*, 14, 206–214.

Felson, R. (1981). Physical attractiveness and perceptions of deviance. *Journal of Social Psychology*, 114, 85–90.

Fenske, M. (2007). Movement and resistance: (Tattooed) bodies and performance [Electronic version]. *Communication and Critical/Cultural Studies*, 4, 51–73.

Fenster, A., and Goldstein, A. M. (1971). The emotional world of children "vis-à-vis" the emotional world of adults: An examination of vocal communication. *Journal of Communication*, 21, 353–362.

Fernaid, A. (1989). Intonation and communicative intent in mother's speech to infants: Is the melody the message? *Child Development*, 6, 1497–1510.

Fernandez-Dols, J., Wallbott, H., and Sanchez, F. (1991). Emotion category accessibility and the decoding of emotion from facial expression and context. *Journal of Nonverbal Behavior*, 15, 107–123.

Finkelstein, J. C., and Walker, L. A. (1976). Evaluation apprehension as a mediator of responses to pupil-size cues. *Personality and Social Psychology Bulletin*, 2, 474–477.

Finn, A. N., and Schrodt, P. (2012). Students' perceived understanding mediates the effects of teacher clarity and nonverbal immediacy on learner empowerment. *Communication Education*, 61, 111–130.

Firmin, M. W., Tse, L. M., Foster, J., and Angelini, T. (2008). Christian student perceptions of body tattoos: A qualitative analysis [Electronic version]. *Journal of Psychology and Christianity*, 27, 195–204.

Fisher, J. D., and Byrne, D. (1975). Too close for comfort: Sex differences in response to invasions of personal space. *Journal of Personality and Social Psychology*, 32, 15–21.

Fisher, J. D., Rytting, M., and Heslin, R. (1976). Hands touching hands: Affective and evaluative effects of an interpersonal touch. *Sociometry*, 39, 416–421.

Fisher, K. D. (2009). Placing social interaction: An integrative approach to analyzing past built environments [Electronic version]. *Journal of Anthropological Archaeology*, 28, 439–457.

Fisher, R. (1967). Social schema of normal and disturbed school children. *Journal of Educational Psychology*, 58, 88–92.

Fisher, S., and Cleveland, S. (1968). *Body image and personality*. New York: Dover.

Fitzpatrick, L. (2009). Are hugs the new handshakes? [Electronic version]. *Time*, 173, 91.

Floyd, K. (1997). Communicating affection in dyadic relationships: An assessment of behavior and expectancies. *Communication Quarterly*, 45, 68–80.

Floyd, K. (2000a). Attributions for nonverbal expressions of liking and disliking: The extended self-serving bias. *Western Journal of Communication*, 64, 385–404.

Floyd, K. (2000b). Affectionate same-sex touch: The influence of homophobia in observers' perceptions. *Journal of Social Psychology*, 140, 774–788.

Floyd, K., Hesse, C., and Haynes, M. T. (2007). Human affection exchange: XV. Metabolic and cardiovascular correlates of trait expressed affection. *Communication Quarterly*, 55, 79–94.

Floyd, K., and Morman, M. T. (1998). The measurement of affective communication. *Communication Quarterly*, 46, 144–162.

Floyd, K., and Morman, M. T. (2000). Reacting to the verbal expression of affection in same-sex interaction. *Southern Communication Journal*, 65, 287–299.

Floyd, K., and Morr, M. C. (2003). Human affection exchange: VII. Affectionate communication in the sibling/spouse/sibling-in-law triad. *Communication Quarterly*, 51, 247–261.

Floyd, K., and Riforgiate, S. (2008). Affectionate communication received from spouses predicts stress hormone levels in healthy adults. *Communication Monographs*, 75, 351–368.

Flugel, J. C. (1950). *The psychology of clothes*. London: Hogarth Press.

Fogot, B. I. (1991). Attractiveness in young children: Sex-differentiated reactions of adults. *Sex Roles*, 25, 269–284.

Folwell, A. L. (2000). A comparison of professors' and students' perceptions of nonverbal immediacy behaviors. *Journal of the Northwest Communication Association*, 29, 41–58.

Fong, L. (2007). Playing keepaway [Electronic version].*Psychology Today*, 40, 15.

Fontaine, G., and Kiger, K. (1978). The effects of defendant dress and supervision of judgments of simulated jurors: An exploratory study. *Law and Human Behavior* 2, 63.

Ford, C., and Beach, F. (1951). *Patterns of sexual behavior*. New York: Harper and Row.

Forgas, J. P., and East, R. (2008). How real is that smile? Mood effects on accepting or rejecting the veracity of emotional facial expressions [Electronic version]. *Journal of Nonverbal Behavior*, 32, 157–170.

Forrester, L., Crumbley, J., Powell, L., Hill, S. R., Jr., and Hickson, M. L., III. (1981). *The effects of hair color on homophily, attraction, and credibility*. Unpublished manuscript, Mississippi State University.

Forston, R. F., and Larson, C. U. (1968). The dynamics of space: An experimental study in proxemic behavior among Latin Americans. *Journal of Communication*, 18, 109–116.

Fortenberry, J. H., Maclean, J., Morris, P., and O'Connell, M. (1978). Mode of dress as a perceptual cue to deference. *Journal of Social Psychology*, 104, 139–140.

Fowles, J. (1974). Why we wear clothes. *ETC: A Review of General Semantics*, 21, 343.

Frank, L. K. (1957). Tactile communication. *Genetic Psychology Monographs*, 56, 209–255.

Franklin, T. W., Franklin, C. A., and Pratt, T. C. (2006). Examining the empirical relationship between prison crowding and inmate misconduct: A meta-analysis of conflicting research results [Electronic version]. *Journal of Criminal Justice*, 34, 401–412.

Franz, R. L. (1961). The origin of form perception. *Scientific American*, 204, 66.

Freed, H. (1973). Nudity and nakedness. *Sexual Behavior*, 3, 3–5.

Freedman, D. G. (1969). The survival value of the beard. *Psychology Today*, 3, 36–39.

Freedman, J. L. (1971). The crowd: Maybe not so maddening after all. *Psychology Today*, 4, 58–61, 86.

Freeman, D. N., Roach, D., and Gladney, K. (1980, April). *The nonverbal persuasive influence of the supermarket in food purchasing behavior*. Paper presented at the meeting of the Southern Speech Communication Association, Birmingham, AL.

Fried, M. K., and DeFazio, V. J. (1974). Territory and boundary conflicts in the subway. *Psychiatry*, 34, 47–58.

Friedman, H. S., and Riggio, R. E. (1981). Effect of individual differences in nonverbal expressiveness and transmission of emotion. *Journal of Nonverbal Behavior*, 6, 96–104.

Friedman, H. S., Riggio, R. E., and Casella, D. F. (1988). Nonverbal skill, personal charisma, and initial attraction. *Personality and Social Psychology Bulletin*, 14, 203–211.

Friedman, S., and Mehrabian, A. (1986). Analysis of fidgeting and associated individual differences. *Journal of Personality*, 84, 406–429.

Frieze, I. H., and Ramsey, S. J. (1976). Nonverbal maintenance of traditional sex roles. *Journal of Social Issues*, 32, 133–141.

Frisby, B. N., and Martin, M. M. (2010). Interpersonal motives and supportive communication. *Communication Research Reports*, 27, 320–329.

Frith, K., Shaw, P., and Cheng, H. (2005). The construction of beauty: A cross-cultural analysis of women's magazine advertising [Electronic version]. *Journal of Communication*, 55, 56–70.

Fromm, D., and Holland, A. L. (1989). Functional communication in Alzheimer's Disease. *Journal of Speech and Hearing Disorders*, 54, 535–540.

Frymier, A. (1993). The impact of teacher immediacy on students' motivation: Is it the same for all students? *Communication Quarterly*, 41, 454–464.

Frymier, A. (1994). A model of immediacy in the classroom. *Communication Quarterly*, 42, 133–144.

Fukumoto, S., Morishita, A., Furutachi, K., Terashima, T., Terashima, T., and Yokogoshi, H. (2008). Effect of flavour components in lemon essential oil on physical or psychological stress [Electronic version]. *Stress and Health: Journal of the International Society for the Investigation of Stress*, 24, 3–12.

Furnham, A., and Dias, M. (1998). The role of body weight, waist-to-hip ratio, and breast size in judgements of female attractiveness. *Sex Roles*, 39, 311–327.

Furnham, A., and Radlye, S. (1989). Sex differences in perception of male and female body shapes. *Personality and Individual Differences*, 10, 633–642.

Futch, A., and Edwards, R. (1999). The effects of sense of humor, defensiveness, and gender on the interpretation of ambiguous messages. *Communication Quarterly*, 47, 80–97.

Galin, A., and Benoliel, B. (1990). Does the way you dress affect your performance? *Personnel*, 67, 49–52.

Ganster, T., Eimler, S. C., and Kramer, N. C. (2012). Same same but different!? The differential influence of similies and emoticons on person perception [Electronic version]. *CyberPsychology, Behavior & Social Networking*, 15, 226–230.

Gapinski, K. D., Brownell, K. D., and LaFrance, M. (2003). Objectification and "fat talk": Effects on emotion, motivation, and cognitive performance [Electronic version]. *Sex Roles*, 48, 377–388.

Gardin, H., Kaplan, K. J., Firestone, I. J., and Cowen, G. A. (1973). Proxemic effects of cooperation, attitude, and approach-avoidance in a Prisoner's Dilemma game. *Journal of Personality and Social Psychology*, 27, 13–18.

Garrido, L., Eisner, F., McGettigan, C., Stewart, L., Sauter, D., Hanley, J. R., Schweinberger, S. R., Warren, J. D., and Duchaine, B. (2009). Developmental phonagnosia: A selective deficit of vocal identity recognition [Electronic version]. *Neuropsychologia*, 47, 123–131.

Gaylin, W. (1992). *The male ego.* New York: Viking/Penguin.

Gendrin, D. M., and Rucker, M. L. (2007). Student motive for communicating and instructor immediacy: A matched-race institutional comparison [Electronic version]. *Atlantic Journal of Communication*, 15, 41–60.

Gerholm, T. (2011). Children's development of facework practices—An emotional endeavor [Electronic version]. *Journal of Pragmatics*, 43, 3099–3110.

Gettleman, T. E., and Thompson, J. K. (1993). Actual differences and stereotypical perceptions in body image and eating disturbance: A comparison of male and female heterosexual samples. *Sex Roles*, 29, 545–562.

Gifford, P., and Price, J. (1979). Personal space in nursery school children. *Canadian Journal of Behavioral Science*, 11, 318–326.

Gilbert, A. V., and Wysocki, C. J. (1987). The smell survey: Its results. *National Geographic*, 172, 514–525.

Giles, H. (1970). Communication effectiveness as a function of accented speech. *Speech Monographs*, 40, 330–331.

Giles, H., Scholes, J., and Young, L. (1983). Stereotypes of male and female speech: A British study. *Central States Speech Journal*, 34, 255–256.

Gillath, O., McCall, C., Shaver, P. R., and Blascovich, J. (2008). What can virtual reality teach us about prosocial tendencies in real and virtual environments? [Electronic version]. *Media Psychology*, 11, 259–282.

Gilman, S. L. (1998). *Creating beauty to cure the soul: Race and psychology in the shaping of aesthetic surgery.* Durham, NC: Duke University Press.

Gilman, S. L. (1999). *Making the body beautiful: A cultural history of aesthetic surgery.* Princeton, NJ: Princeton University Press.

Gittelson, N. (1975). What your clothes say about you. *McCalls*, 102, 23.

Gleeson, M., and Higgins, A. (2009). Touch in mental health nursing: An exploratory study of nurses' views and perceptions [Electronic version]. *Journal of Psychiatric and Mental Health Nursing*, 16, 382–389.

Goffman, E. (1963). *Stigma: Notes on the management of spoiled identity*. Englewood Cliffs, NJ: Prentice Hall.

Goffman, E. (1971). *Relations in public: Microstudies of the public order*. New York: Harper Colophon Books.

Goffman, E. (1974). *Frame analysis*. New York: Harper and Row.

Goffman, E. (1976). Gender advertisements. *Studies in the Anthropology of Visual Communication*, 3, 64–154.

Gold, S. (2010). Voice biometrics: Real-world issues and solutions [Electronic version]. *Biometric Technology Today*, 2010, 6–7.

Goldberg, H. (1979). *The new male: From self-destruction to self-care*. New York: Signet.

Goldberg, S., and Rosenthal, R. (1986). Self-touching behavior in the job interview: Antecedents and consequences. *Journal of Nonverbal Behavior*, 10, 65–80.

Goldin-Meadow, S. (2005). The two faces of gesture: Language and thought [Electronic version]. *Gesture*, 5, 241–257.

Goldkuhl, L., and Styvén, M. (2007). Sensing the scent of service success [Electronic version]. *European Journal of Marketing*, 41, 1297–1305.

Goldman, M., Kiyohara, O., and Pfanners, D. A. (1985). Interpersonal touch, social labeling, and the foot-in-the-door effect. *Journal of Social Psychology*, 125, 143–147.

Golomb, C. (1972). Evolution of the human figure in a three-dimensional medium. *Developmental Psychology*, 6, 385–391.

Gomberg, E. S., and Franks, V. (1979). *Gender and disordered behavior: Sex differences in psychotherapy*. New York: Brunner/Mazel.

Goodboy, A. K., and McCroskey, J. C. (2008). Toward a theoretical model of the role of organizational orientations and Machiavellianism on nonverbal immediacy behavior and job satisfaction. *Human Communication*, 11, 293–307.

Goodboy, A. K., and Myers, S. A. (2008). Relational maintenance behaviors of friends with benefits: Investigating equity and relational characteristics. *Human Communication*, 11, 71–85.

Goodman, J. R. (2005). Mapping the sea of eating disorders: A structural equation model of how peers, family, and media influence body image and eating disorders [Electronic version]. *Visual Communication Quarterly*, 12, 194–213.

Gorawara-Bhat, R., and Cook, M. A. (2011). Eye contact in patient-centered communication [Electronic version]. *Patient Education and Counseling*, 82, 442–447.

Gorawara-Bhat, R., Cook, M. A., and Sachs, G. A. (2007). Nonverbal communication in doctor—elderly patient transactions (NDEPT): Development of a tool [Electronic version]. *Patient Education and Counseling*, 66, 223–234.

Gotfredsen, K. L., and Walls, A. W. G. (2007). What dentition assures oral function? [Electronic version]. *Clinical Oral Implants Research*, 18, 34–45.

Gottman, J. M. (1980). Consistency of nonverbal affect and affect reciprocity in marital interaction. *Journal of Consulting and Clinical Psychology*, 48, 711–717.

Gottman, J. M., and Porterfield, A. (1981). Communicative competence in the nonverbal behavior of married couples. *Journal of Marriage and the Family*, 43, 454–464.

Gottschalk, L. A. (1969). Phasic circulating biochemical reflections of transient mental content. In A. J. Mandril and M. P. Mandeli (Eds.), *Psychochemical research in man: Method, strategy, and theory* (pp. 357–378). New York: Academic Press.

Graham, G. H., Unruh, J., and Jennings, P. (1991). The impact of nonverbal communication in organizations: A survey of perceptions. *Journal of Business Communication*, 28, 45–62.

Grammer, K., Honda, M., Juette, A., and Schmitt, A. (1999). Fuzziness of nonverbal courtship communication unblurred by motion energy detection [Electronic version]. *Journal of Personality & Social Psychology*, 77, 487–508.

Gray, J. (1992). *Men are from Mars, women are from Venus: A practical guide for improving communication and getting what you want in your relationships.* New York: HarperCollins.

Graziano, W. G., Jensen-Campbell, L. A., Shebilske, L. J., and Lundgren, S. R. (1993). Social influence, sex differences, and judgments of beauty: Putting the interpersonal back in interpersonal attraction. *Journal of Personality and Social Psychology,* 65, 522–531.

Greene, J. O. (1984). Speech preparation processes and verbal fluency. *Human Communication Research,* 11, 61–84.

Greene, J. O., and Frandsen, K. (1979). Need fulfillment and consistency theory: Relationships between self-esteem and eye contact. *Western Journal of Speech Communication,* 43, 123–133.

Greene, J. O., O'Hair, H. D., Cody, M. J., and Yen, C. (1985). Planning and control of behavior during deception. *Human Communication Research,* 11, 335–364.

Gregersen, T., Olivares-Cuhat, G., and Storm, J. (2009). An examination of L1 and L2 gesture use: What role does proficiency play? [Electronic version]. *Modern Language Journal,* 93, 195–208.

Gregory S. W., Jr., and Webster, S. (1996). A nonverbal signal in voices of interview partners effectively predicts communication accommodation and social status perceptions [Electronic version]. *Journal of Personality & Social Psychology,* 70, 1231–1240.

Griffit, W. (1970). Environment effects of interpersonal affective behavior: Ambient effective temperature and attraction. *Journal of Personality and Social Psychology,* 15, 240–244.

Grossbach, I., Stranberg, S., and Chlan, L. (2011). Promoting effective communication for patients receiving mechanical ventilation [Electronic version]. *Critical Care Nurse,* 31, 46–61.

Grugg, H. J., Sellers, M. I., and Waligroski, K. (1993). Factors related to depression and eating disorders: Self-esteem, body image, and attractiveness. *Psychological Reports,* 72, 1003–1010.

Guarino, M., Fridrich, P., and Sitton, S. (1994). Male and female conformity in eating behavior. *Psychological Reports,* 75, 603–609.

Gudykunst, W. B. (1998). *Bridging differences: Effective intergroup communication.* Thousand Oaks, CA: Sage.

Guéguen, N. (2008a). The effect of a woman's smile on men's courtship behavior [Electronic version]. *Social Behavior and Personality: An International Journal,* 36, 1233–1236.

Guéguen, N. (2008b). The effects of women's cosmetics on men's approach: An evaluation in a bar [Electronic version]. *North American Journal of Psychology,* 10, 221–227.

Guéguen, N. (2008). The effect of a woman's smile on men's courtship behavior [Electronic version]. *Social Behavior and Personality,* 36, 1233–1236.

Guéguen, N. (2010). The effect of a woman's incidental tactile contact on men's later behavior [Electronic version]. *Social Behavior and Personality: An International Journal,* 38, 257–266.

Guéguen, N. (2012a). Tattoos, piercings, and sexual activity [Electronic version].*Social Behavior and Personality,* 40, 1543–1547.

Guéguen, N. (2012b). Gait and menstrual cycle: Ovulating women use sexier gaits and walk slowly ahead of men [Electronic version]. *Gait & Posture,* 35, 621–624.

Guéguen, N., and Jacob, C. (2002). Direct look versus evasive glance and compliance with a request [Electronic version]. *Journal of Social Psychology,* 142, 393–396.

Guerrero, L. K. (1994). "I'm so mad I could scream": The effects of anger expression on relational satisfaction and communication competence. *Southern Communication Journal,* 59, 125–138.

Guerrero, L. K., and Andersen, P. A. (1991). Nonverbal involvement across interactions with same-sex friends, opposite-sex friends, and romantic partners: Consistency or change? *Journal of Social and Personal Relationships,* 8, 147–165.

Guerrero, L. K., and Andersen, P. A. (1994). Patterns of matching and initiation: Touch behavior and touch avoidance across romantic relationship settings. *Journal of Nonverbal Behavior,* 18, 137–153.

Guerrero, L. K., and Chavez, A. M. (2005). Relational maintenance in cross-sex friendships characterized by different types of romantic intent: An exploratory study. *Western Journal of Communication,* 69, 339–358.

Guerrero, L. K., Eloy, S. V., and Wabnik, A. I. (1993). Linking maintenance strategies to relationship development and disengagement: A reconceptualization. *Journal of Social and Personal Relationships*, 10, 273–283.

Guido, G., Peluso, A. M., and Moffa, V. (2011). Beardedness in advertising: Effects on endorsers credibility and purchase intention [Electronic version]. *Journal of Marketing Communications*, 17, 37–49.

Gullberg, M., and Kita, S. (2009). Attention to speech-accompanying gestures: Eye movements and information uptake [Electronic version]. *Journal of Nonverbal Behavior*, 33, 251–277.

Gunson, N., Marshall, D., McInnes, F., and Jack, M. (2011). Usability evaluation of voiceprint authentication in automated telephone banking: Sentences versus digits [Electronic version]. *Interacting with Computers*, 23, 57–69.

Gur, R., and Gur, R. (1975). Defense mechanisms, psychosomatic symptomatology and conjugate lateral eye movements. *Journal of Consulting and Clinical Psychology*, 43, 416–420.

Guy, R. F., Rankin, B. A., and Norvell, M. J. (1980). The relation of sex role stereotyping to body image. *Journal of Psychology*, 105, 167–174.

Hadar, V., Steiner, F., and Rose, F. C. (1985). Head movements during listening turns in conversation. *Journal of Nonverbal Behavior*, 9, 214–221.

Halbe, D. (2012). "Who's there?": Differences in the features of telephone and face-to-face conferences [Electronic version]. *Journal of Business Communication*, 49, 48–73.

Halberstadt, A. (1986). Family socialization of emotional expression and nonverbal communication styles and skills. *Journal of Personality and Social Psychology*, 51, 827–836.

Halberstadt, A. G., Hayes, C. W., and Pike, K. M. (1988). Gender and gender role differences in smiling and commitment consistency. *Sex Roles*, 19, 589–604.

Haley, J. (1963). *Strategies of psychotherapy*. New York: Grune and Stratton.

Hall, E. T. (1959). *The silent language*. Garden City, NY: Doubleday.

Hall, E. T. (1966). *The hidden dimension*. Garden City, NY: Anchor Books.

Hall, E. T. (1968). Proxemics. *Current Anthropology*, 9, 33–95, 106–108.

Hall, E. T. (1972). Proxemics: The study of man's spatial relations. In L. A. Samovar and R. E. Porter (Eds.), *Intercultural communication: A reader* (pp. 205–220). Belmont, CA: Wadsworth.

Hall, E. T. (1976). *Beyond culture*. Garden City, NY: Anchor.

Hall, E. T. (1984). *The dance of life: The other dimension of time*. New York: Anchor.

Hall, E. T., and Hall, E. (1976). How cultures collide. *Psychology Today*, 10, 66–74, 97.

Hall, J. A. (1980). Voice and tone persuasion. *Journal of Personality and Social Psychology*, 36, 924–934.

Hall, J. A. (1984). *Nonverbal sex differences: Communication accuracy and expressive style*. Baltimore, MD: Johns Hopkins University Press.

Hall, J. A. (1996). Touch, status, and gender at professional meetings. *Journal of Nonverbal Behavior*, 20, 23–44.

Hall, J. A., and Veccia, E. M. (1990). More "touching" observations: New insights on men, women, and interpersonal touch. *Journal of Personality and Social Psychology*, 59, 1155–1162.

Hall, N., Millings, A., and Boucas, S. (2012). Adult attachment orientation and implicit behavioral mimicry [Electronic version]. *Journal of Nonverbal Behavior*, 36, 235–247.

Hamburger, A. C. (1988). Beauty quest. *Psychology Today*, 22, 29–32.

Hamid, P. N. (1968). Style of dress as a perceptual cue in impression formation. *Perceptual and Motor Skills*, 26, 904–906.

Hamid, P. N. (1972). Some effects of dress cues on observational accuracy: A perceptual estimate, and impression formation. *Journal of Social Psychology*, 86, 279–289.

Hanzal, A., Segrin, C., and Dorros, S. (2008). The role of marital status and age on men's and women's reactions to touch from a relational partner [Electronic version]. *Journal of Nonverbal Behavior*, 32, 21–35.

Hare, A. P., and Bales, R. F. (1963). Seating position and small group interaction. *Sociometry*, 26, 480–486.

Harlow, H. F., and Zimmerman, R. R. (1958). The development of affectional responses in infant monkeys. *Proceedings, American Philosophical Society*, 102, 501–509.

Harlow, M. (2008, November). *UnConventional beauty: Bodies that speak*. [Electronic version]. Paper presented at the National Communication Association, San Diego, CA.

Harper, L. V., and Sanders, K. M. (1975). Preschool children's use of space: Sex differences in outdoor play. *Developmental Psychology*, 11, 119.

Harper, R. G., Wiens, A. N., and Matarazzo, J. D. (1978). *Nonverbal communication: The state of the art*. New York: Wiley.

Harris, M. B., Waschull, S., and Walters, L. (1990). Feeling fat: Motivations, knowledge, and attitudes of overweight women and men. *Psychological Reports*, 67, 1191–1202.

Harrison, A. A., Hwalek, M., Raney, D. F., and Fritz, J. G. (1978). Cues to deception in the interview situation. *Social Psychology*, 41, 156–161.

Harrison, C. (2008). Real men do wear mascara: Advertising discourse and masculine identity [Electronic version]. *Critical Discourse Studies*, 5, 55–74.

Harrison, K., Taylor, L. D., and Marske, A. L. (2006). Women's and men's eating behavior following exposure to ideal-body images and text. *Communication Research*, 33, 507–529.

Harrison, M. A., and Gilmore, A. L. (2012). U txt WHEN? College students' social contexts of text messaging. *Social Science Journal*, 49, 513–518.

Harvey, A. (2001). A dramaturgical analysis of charismatic leader discourse. *Journal of Organizational Change Management*, 14, 253–265.

Harvey, J. (2007). Showing and hiding: Equivocation in the relations of body and dress [Electronic version]. *The Journal of Dress, Body and Culture*, 11, 65–94.

Haskard, K. B., DiMatteo, M. R., and Heritage, J. (2009). Affective and instrumental communication in primary care interactions: Predicting the satisfaction of nursing staff and patients [Electronic version]. *Health Communication*, 24, 21–32.

Haviland, J. M. (1977). Sex-related pragmatics in infants' nonverbal communication. *Journal of Communication*, 27, 80–84.

Havlicek, J., Saxton, T. K., Roberts, S. C., Jozifkova, E., Lhota, S., Valentova, J., and Flegr, J. (2008). He sees, she smells? Male and female reports of sensory reliance in mate choice and non-mate choice contexts [Electronic version]. *Personality and Individual Differences*, 45, 565–570.

Hawhee, D. (2006). Language as sensuous action: Sir Richard Paget, Kenneth Burke, and gesture-speech theory. *Quarterly Journal of Speech*, 92, 331–354.

Hawk, S. T., Fischer, A. H., and Van Kleef, G. A. (2012). Face the noise: Embodied responses to nonverbal vocalizations of discrete emotions [Electronic version]. *Journal of Personality and Social Psychology*, 102, 796–814.

Hayduk, L. A. (1978). Personal space: An evaluative and orienting overview. *Psychological Bulletin*, 85, 117–134.

Hayduk, L. A. (1983). Personal space: Where we stand now. *Psychological Bulletin*, 94, 293–335.

Hearn, G. (1957). Leadership and the spatial factor in small groups. *Journal of Abnormal and Social Psychology*, 54, 269–272.

Hecht, M., Foster, S. H., Dunn, D. J., Williams, J. K., Anderson, D. R., and Pulbratek, D. (1985). Nonverbal behavior of young abused and neglected children. *Communication Education*, 35, 134–142.

Heilburn, A. B., and Witt, N. (1990). Distorted body image as a risk factor in anorexia nervosa: Replication and clarification. *Psychology Reports*, 66, 407–416.

Heilman, M. E., and Saruwatari, L. R. (1979). When beauty is beastly: The effects of appearance and sex on evaluations of job applicants for managerial and non-managerial jobs. *Organizational Behavior and Human Performance*, 23, 360–372.

Heilman, M. E., and Stopeck, M. H. (1985). Being attractive, advantage or disadvantage? Performance-based evaluations and recommended personnel actions as a function of appearance, sex, and job type. *Organizational Behavior and Human Decision Processes, 35*, 202–215.

Heilville, I. (1976). Deception and pupil size. *Journal of Clinical Psychology, 32*, 675–676.

Heinberg, P. (1964). *Voice training for speaking and reading aloud.* New York: Ronald Press.

Heisel, M. J., and Mongrain, M. (2004). Facial expressions and ambivalence: Looking for conflict in all the right faces [Electronic version]. *Journal of Nonverbal Behavior, 28*, 35–52.

Hendricks, M., and Bootzin, R. (1976). Race and sex as stimuli for negative affect and physical avoidance. *Journal of Social Psychology, 98*, 111–120.

Henley, N. M. (1977). *Body politics: Power, sex, and nonverbal communication.* Englewood Cliffs, NJ: Prentice-Hall.

Henley, N., and Freeman, J. (1975). The sexual politics of interpersonal behavior. In J. Freeman (Ed.), *Women: A feminist perspective.* Palo Alto, CA: Mayfield Publishing.

Henningsen, D. D., Kartch, F., Orr, N., and Brown, A. (2009). The perceptions of verbal and nonverbal flirting cues in cross-sex interactions. *Human Communication, 12*, 371–381.

Hensley, W. E. (1981). The effect of attire, location, and sex on aiding behavior: A similarity explanation. *Journal of Nonverbal Behavior, 6*, 3–11.

Hertenstein, M., and Keltner, D. (2011). Gender and the communication of emotion via touch [Electronic version]. *Sex Roles, 64*, 70–80.

Heslin, R. (1974, April). *Steps toward a taxonomy of touching.* Paper presented at the meeting of the Western Psychological Association, Chicago, IL.

Hess, E. H. (1965). Attitude and pupil size. *Scientific American, 212*, 46–54.

Hess, E. H. (1975). The role of pupil size in communication. *Scientific American, 222*, 110–119.

Hess, E. H. (1985). Telephone conversation with authors and as published in *Experimetelle unt Angewandte Psychologie, 26* (February 13, 1979), 436–447.

Hess, E. H., and Polt, J. M. (1960). Pupil size as related to interest value of visual stimuli. *Science, 132*, 349–350.

Hess, E. H., Seltzer, A. L., and Schlien, J. M. (1965). Pupil responses of hetero- and homo-sexual males to pictures of men and women: A pilot study. *Journal of Abnormal Psychology, 70*, 165–168.

Hess, J. A., Smythe, M. J., and Communication 451. (2001). Is teacher immediacy actually related to student cognitive learning? *Communication Studies, 52*, 197–219.

Heston, J. K., and Garner, P. (1972). A study of personal space and desk arrangement in a learning environment. Paper presented at the International Communication Association convention, Atlanta, GA.

Hettrich, E. L., and O'Leary, K. D. (2007). Females' reasons for their physical aggression in dating relationships [Electronic version]. *Journal of Interpersonal Violence, 22*, 1131–1143.

Hewig, J., Trippe, R. H., Hecht, H., Straube, T., and Miltner, W. H. R. (2008). Gender differences for specific body regions when looking at men and women [Electronic version]. *Journal of Nonverbal Behavior, 32*, 67–78.

Hewitt, J., and German, K. (1987). Attire and attractiveness. *Perceptual and Motor Skills, 64*, 558.

Hickson, M. L., III. (1977). Communication in natural settings: Research tool for undergraduates. *Communication Quarterly, 25*, 23–28.

Hickson, M. L., III. (1981). *Toward a biosocial theory of human communication.* Unpublished master's thesis, Mississippi State University.

Hickson, M. L., III, Grierson, R. D., and Linder, B. C. (1991). A communication perspective on sexual harassment: Affiliative nonverbal behaviors in asynchronous relationships. *Communication Quarterly, 39*, 111–118.

Hickson, M. L., III, Powell, L., and Sandoz, M. L. (1987). The effects of eye color on credibility, attraction, and homophily. *Communication Research Reports, 4*, 20–23.

Hickson, M. L., III, Powell, S., Hill, S. R., Jr., Holt, G. B., and Flick, H. (1970). Smoking artifacts as indicators of homophily, attraction, and credibility. *Southern Speech Communication Journal, 44*, 191–200.

Hickson, M. L., III, and Self, W. (2003). Biological foundations of territoriality: Nonverbal communication, language, and the law. *Journal of Intercultural Communication Research*, 32, 265–283.

Hickson, M. L., III, and Stacks, D. W. (1991). *Nonverbal communication: Studies and applications* (3rd ed.). Dubuque, IA: Brown and Benchmark.

Hickson, M. L., III, Stacks, D. W., and Padgett-Greely, M. (1998). *Organizational communication in the personal context: From interview to retirement.* Needham Heights, MA: Allyn and Bacon.

Hiemstra, K. M. (1999). Shake my hand: Making the right first impression in business with nonverbal communications [Electronic version]. *Business Communication Quarterly*, 62, 71–74.

Higdon, J. F. (1982). Roles of power, sex and inadequate attractiveness in paranoid women. *Psychological Reports*, 50, 399–402.

High, T., and Sundstrom, E. (1977). Room flexibility and space use in a dormitory. *Environment and Behavior*, 9, 81–90.

Higuchi, T., Shoji, K., Taguchi, S., and Hatayama, T. (2005). Improvement of nonverbal behaviour in Japanese female perfume-wearers [Electronic version]. *International Journal of Psychology*, 40, 90–99.

Hildreth, A. M., Derogatis, L. R., and McClusker, K. (1971). Body buffer zone and violence: A reassessment and confirmation. *American Journal of Psychology*, 127, 77–81.

Hill, A. J., Oliver, S., and Rogers, P. J. (1992). Eating in the adult world: The rise of dieting in childhood and adolescence. *British Journal of Clinical Psychology*, 31, 95–105.

Hill, R. A., Donovan, S., and Koyama, N. F. (2005). Female sexual advertisement reflects resource availability in twentieth-century UK society [Electronic version]. *Human Nature*, 16, 266–277.

Hill, T., Lewicki, M., Czyzewska, M, and Schuller, G. (1990). The role of learned intentional encoding rules in the perception of faces: Effects of nonconscious self-perception of a bias. *Journal of Experimental Social Psychology*, 26, 350–371.

Hillman, J., Vrij, A., and Mann, S. (2012). Um … they were wearing … : The effect of deception on specific hand gestures [Electronic version]. *Legal and Criminological Psychology*, 17, 336–345.

Hilton, S., Hunt, K., Emslie, C., Salinas, M., and Ziebland, S. (2008). Have men been overlooked? A comparison of young men and women's experiences of chemotherapy-induced alopecia [Electronic version]. *Psycho-Oncology*, 17, 577–583.

Hinkle, L. L. (1999). Nonverbal immediacy communication behaviors and liking in marital relationships. *Communication Research Reports*, 16, 81–90.

Hinkle, L. L. (2001). Perceptions of supervisor nonverbal immediacy: Vocalics and subordinate liking [Electronic version]. *Communication Research Reports*, 18, 128–136.

Hinsz, V. B., and Tomhave, J. A. (1991). Smile and (half) the world smiles with you, frown and you frown alone. *Personality and Social Psychology*, 17, 586–592.

Hirst, E., and Cooper, M. (2008). Keeping them in line: Choreographing classroom spaces [Electronic version]. *Teachers and Teaching: Theory and Practice*, 14, 431–445.

Hite, S. (1976). *The Hite report: A nationwide study of female sexuality.* New York: Dell.

Hite, S. (1981). *The Hite report on male sexuality.* New York: Knopf.

Ho, R., and Mitchell, S. (1982). Students' nonverbal reactions to tutors' warm/cold nonverbal behavior. *Journal of Social Psychology*, 114, 121–130.

Hocking, J. E. (1976). *Detecting deceptive communication from verbal, visual, and paralinguistic cues: An exploratory experiment.* Unpublished doctoral dissertation, Michigan State University, East Lansing, MI.

Hocking, J. E., Bauchner, J. E., Miller, G. R., and Kaminski, E. P. (1979). Detecting deceptive communication from verbal, visual, and paralinguistic cues. *Human Communication Research*, 6, 33–46.

Hocking, J. E., Walker, B. A., and Fink, E. L. (1982). Physical attractiveness and judgments of morality following an "immoral act." *Psychological Reports*, 48, 111–116.

Hodge, F. S., Maliski, S., Cadogan, M., Itty, T. L., and Cardoza, B. (2010). Learning how to ask: Reflections on engaging American Indian research participants [Electronic version]. *American Indian Culture and Research*, 34, 77–90.

Hoek, J., and Gendall, P. (2006). Advertising and obesity: A behavioral perspective [Electronic version]. *Journal of Health Communication*, 11, 409–423.

Holland, R. W., Hendriks, M., and Aarts, H. (2005). Smells like clean spirit [Electronic version]. *Psychological Science*, 16, 689–693.

Hollenbaugh, E. E., and Egbert, N. (2009). A test of communication privacy management theory in cross-sex friendships [Electronic version]. *Ohio Communication Journal*, 47, 113–136.

Hollender, M. H. (1961). Prostitution, the body, and human relatedness. *International Journal of Psychoanalysis*, 42, 403–413.

Hollender, M. H. (1970). The need or wish to be held. *Archives of General Psychiatry*, 22, 445–453.

Holler, J., and Wilkin, K. (2011). Co-speech gesture mimicry in the process of collaborative referring during face-to-face dialogue [Electronic version]. *Journal of Nonverbal Behavior*, 35, 133–153.

Holmstrom, A. J. (2009). Sex and gender similarities and differences in communication values in same-sex and cross-sex friendships. *Communication Quarterly*, 57, 224–238.

Honeyman, K. (2008). Catching the scent of a story: Why memories get so tied up with emotion [Electronic version]. *Writer*, 121, 26–27.

Hopson, M. C., and Orbe, M. P. (2007). Playing the game: Recalling dialectical tensions for black men in oppressive organizational structures [Electronic version]. *Howard Journal of Communications*, 18, 69–86.

Horn, J. C. (1986). Measuring man by the company he keeps. *Psychology Today*, 20, 12.

Horne, J., Knox, D., Zusman, J., and Zusman, M. (2007). Tattoos and piercings: Attitudes, behaviors, and interpretations of college students [Electronic version]. *College Student Journal*, 41, 1011–1020.

Horowitz, M. J., Duff, D. F., and Stratton, L. O. (1964). Body buffer zones. *Archives of General Psychiatry*, 11, 651–656.

Hortacsu, N., and Ekinci, B. (1992). Children's reliance on situational and vocal expressions of emotions: Consistent and conflicting cues. *Journal of Nonverbal Behavior*, 16, 231–245.

Horton, J. (1976). Time and cool people. In L. A. Samovar and R. E. Porter (Eds.), *Intercultural communication: A reader* (pp. 84–94). Belmont, CA: Wadsworth Publishing.

Hosman, L. A., and Wright, J. W., II (1987). The effects of hedges and hesitations on impression formation in a simulated courtroom context. *Western Journal of Speech Communication*, 51, 173–188.

Hoult, T. F. (1954). Experimental measurement of clothing as a factor in some social ratings of selected American men. *American Sociological Review*, 19, 326–327.

Houston, G. S. (2006). Ally McBeal as allegory: Setting the eating-disordered subject in opposition to feminism. *Communication and Critical/Cultural Studies*, 3, 288–306.

Howells, L. T., and Becker, S. W. (1962). Seating arrangement and leadership emergence. *Journal of Abnormal and Social Psychology*, 64, 148–150.

Hu, F., and Wang, M. (2009, November). *Beauty and fashion magazines and college-age women's appearance-related concerns* [Electronic version]. Paper presented at the National Communication Association, Chicago, IL.

Huang, A. J. (2001). Rethinking the approach to beauty in medicine. *Journal of the American Medical Association*, 286 (17), 2158.

Huang, L. T., Phares, R., and Hollender, M. H. (1976). The wish to be held: A transcultural study. *Archives of General Psychiatry*, 33, 41-43.

Huddleston, B. M., and Huddleston, J. H. (1986). An experimental test of perceptions regarding credibility of judicial decisions: The cult of the robe. In *Proceedings: Current trends in nonverbal communication: A multidisciplinary approach* (pp. 72–87). Jonesboro: Arkansas State University Press.

Hugenberg, K., and Sczesny, S. (2006). On wonderful women and seeing smiles: Social categorization moderates the happy face response latency advantage [Electronic version]. *Social Cognition*, 5, 516–539.

Hughes, C. L. (2004). Class and other identifications in managerial careers: The case of the lemon dress [Electronic version]. *Gender, Work & Organization*, 11, 526–543.

Hughes, J., and Goldman, M. (1978). Eye contact, facial expression, sex, and the violation of personal space. *Perceptual and Motor Skills*, 46, 579–584.

Hughes, S., Farley, S., and Rhodes, B. (2010). Vocal and physiological changes in response to the physical attractiveness of conversational partners [Electronic version]. *Journal of Nonverbal Behavior*, 34, 155–167.

Hughes, S., Pastizzo, M., and Gallup, G. (2008). The sound of symmetry revisited: Subjective and objective analyses of voice [Electronic version]. *Journal of Nonverbal Behavior*, 32, 93–108.

Huguet, P., Croizet, J., and Richetin, J. (2004). Is "What has been cared for" necessarily good? Further evidence for the negative impact of cosmetics use on impression formation [Electronic version]. *Journal of Applied Social Psychology*, 34, 1752–1771.

Huhlaeva, O. V. (2012). Features of the interaction of teachers with students classes with mixed composition ethnocultural [Electronic version]. *Psychological Science and Education*, 2, 71–75.

Hummert, M. L., Mazloff, D., and Henry, C. (1999). Vocal characteristics of older adults and stereotyping [Electronic version]. *Journal of Nonverbal Behavior*, 23, 111–132.

Huneycutt, J. M. (1991). The role of nonverbal behaviors in modifying expectancies during initial encounters. *The Southern Communication Journal*, 56, 161–177.

Hunt, C., and Vaizey, J. (1966). Differential effects of group density on social behavior. *Nature*, 209, 1371–1372.

Hurd, K., and Noller, P. (1988). Decoding deception: A look at the process. *Journal of Nonverbal Behavior*, 12, 217–232.

Hurley, C. M., and Frank, M. G. (2011). Executing facial control during deception situations [Electronic version]. *Journal of Nonverbal Behavior*, 35, 119–131.

Huston, T. L. (Ed.). (1974). *Foundations of interpersonal attraction*. New York: Academic Press.

Iizuka, Y. (1993). Regulators in Japanese conversation. *Psychological Bulletin*, 72, 203–209.

Iizuka, Y. (1994). Gaze during speaking as related to shyness. *Perceptual and Motor Skills*, 78, 1259–1264.

Illife, A. H. (1960). A study of preference in feminine beauty. *British Journal of Psychology*, 61, 267–273.

Infante, D. A., Rancer, A. S., Pierce, L. L., and Osborne, W. J. (1980). Effects of physical attractiveness and likeableness of first name on impressions formed of journalists. *Journal of Applied Communications Research*, 8, 1–9.

Infante, D., Rancer, A. S., and Womack, D. F. (2003). *Building communication theory* (4th ed.). Prospect Heights, IL: Waveland.

Innala, S. M., and Ernulf, K. E. (1994). When gay is pretty: Physical attractiveness and low homophobia. *Psychological Reports*, 74, 827–831.

Irizarry, C. A. (2004). Face and the female professional: A thematic analysis of face-threatening communication in the workplace [Electronic version]. *Qualitative Research Reports in Communication*, 5, 15–21.

Issacs, S. G. (1987). Evaluating the panel: Understanding implied and nonverbal communication. *Trial*, 23, 21–25.

Izard, C. E. (1994). Innate and universal facial expressions: Evidence from developmental and cross-cultural research. *Psychological Bulletin*, 115, 288–299.

Jackob, N., Roessing, T., and Petersen, T. (2011). The effects of verbal and nonverbal elements in persuasive communication: Findings from two multi-method experiments [Electronic version]. *The European Journal of Communication Research*, 36, 245–271.

Jackson, D., and Engstrom, E. (2004, May). *Effects of sex and proxemics on perceptions of leadership* [Electronic version]. Paper presented at the meeting of the International Communication Association, New Orleans.

Jaffe, S., and Feldstein, S. (1970). *Rhythms of dialogue*. New York: Academic Press.

James, D., and Drakich, J. (1993). Understanding gender differences in amount of talk. In D. Tannen (Ed.), *Gender and conversational interaction* (pp. 281–312). New York: Oxford University Press.

Janisse, M. P., and Peavler, W. S. (1974). Pupillary research today: Emotion in the eye. *Psychology Today*, 7, 60–73.

Jason, L. A., and Jung, R. (1984). Stimulus control techniques applied to handicapped-designated parking spaces. *Environment and Behavior*, 16, 675–686.

Jaywant, A., and Pell, M. D. (2012). Categorical processing of negative emotions from speech prosody. *Speech Communication*, 54, 1–10.

Jenks, C. J. (2009). When is it appropriate to talk? Managing overlapping talk in multi-participant voice-based chat rooms. *Computer Assisted Language Learning*, 22, 19-30.

Jensen, M., and Rosenfeld, L. B. (1974). Influence of mode of presentation, ethnicity, and on teachers' evaluations of students. *Journal of Educational Psychology*, 66, 540–547.

Jerslev, A. (2006). The mediated body [Electronic version]. *NORDICOM Review*, 2, 133–151.

Jessen, S., and Kotz, S. A. (2011). The temporal dynamics of processing emotions from vocal, facial, and bodily expressions [Electronic version]. *NeuroImage*, 58, 665–674.

Jirwe, M., Gerrish, K., and Emami, A. (2010). Student nurses' experiences of communication in cross-cultural care encounters [Electronic version]. *Scandinavian Journal of Caring Sciences*, 24, 436–444.

Johansson, C. (2007). Goffman's sociology: An inspiring resource for developing public relations theory [Electronic version]. *Public Relations Review*, 33 (3), 275–280.

Johnson, C. B. (1994). Gender, legitimate authority, and leader-subordinate conversations. *American Sociological Review*, 59, 122–135.

Johnson, C. B., Stockdale, M. S., and Saal, F. E. (1991). Persistence of men's misperceptions of friendly cues across a variety of interpersonal encounters. *Psychology of Women Quarterly*, 15, 463–465.

Johnson, K. R. (1972). Black kinesics: Some nonverbal communication patterns in the black culture. In L. A. Samovar and R. E. Porter (Eds.), *Intercultural communication: A reader* (pp. 181–189). Belmont, CA: Wadsworth.

Johnson, K. R. (2004). Black kinesics: Some non-verbal communication patterns in the black culture [Electronic version]. In R. L. Jackson (Ed.), *African American communication and identities: Essential readings* (pp. 39–46). Thousand Oaks, CA: Sage.

Jones, C. R. G., Pickles, A., Falcaro, M., Marsden, A. J. S., Happe, F., Scott, S. K., Sauter, D., Tregay, J., Phillips, R. J., Baird, G., Simonoff, E., and Charman, T. (2011). A multimodal approach to emotion recognition ability in autism spectrum disorders [Electronic version]. *Journal of Child Psychology & Psychiatry*, 52, 275–285.

Jones, R. M., and Adams, G. R. (1982). Assessing the importance of physical attractiveness across the life-span. *Journal of Social Psychology*, 118, 131–132.

Jones, S. E. (1986). Sex differences in tactile communication. *Western Journal of Speech Communication*, 50, 227–241.

Jones, S. E., and Aiello, J. R. (1972). *The acquisition of proxemic norms of behavior: A study of the lower-class black and middle-class white children at three grade levels.* Unpublished manuscript.

Jones, S. E., and Aiello, J. R. (1973). Proxemic behavior of black and white first-, third-, and fifth-grade children. *Journal of Personality and Social Psychology*, 25, 21–27.

Jones, S. E., and Brown, B. C. (1996). Touch attitudes and touch behaviors: Recollections of early childhood touch and social self-confidence. *Communication Monographs*, 52, 19–56.

Jones, S. E., and Yarbrough, A. E. (1985). A naturalistic study of the meanings of touch. *Communication Monographs*, 52, 19–56.

Jones, S. M., and Wirtz, J. G. (2007). "Sad monkey see, monkey do:" Nonverbal matching in emotional support encounters. *Communication Studies*, 58, 71–86.

Jordan, J. W. (2004). The rhetorical limits of the "plastic body." *Quarterly Journal of Speech*, 90, 327–358.

Jourard, S. M. (1966). An exploratory study of body-accessibility. *British Journal of Social and Clinical Psychology*, 5, 221–231.

Jourard, S. M. (1968). *Disclosing man to himself.* Princeton, NJ: Van Nostrand.

Jurich, A. P., and Polson, C. J. (1985). Nonverbal assessment of anxiety as a function of intimacy of sexual attitude questions. *Psychological Reports*, 57, 1247–1253.

Kaiser, S. (1990). *The social psychology of clothing: Symbolic appearances in context* (2nd ed.). New York: Macmillan.

Kaiser, S., Rudy, M., and Byfield, P. (1985). The role of clothing in sex role socialization: Person perceptions versus overt behavior. *Child Study Journal*, 15, 83–98.

Kalick, S. M. (1988). Physical attractiveness as a status cue. *Journal of Experimental Social Psychology*, 24, 469–489.

Kalman, Y. M., and Rafaeli, S. (2011). Online pauses and silence: Chronemic expectancy violations in written computer-mediated communication. *Communication Research*, 38, 54–69.

Kana, R. K., and Travers, B. G. (2012). Neural substrates of interpreting actions and emotions from body postures. *Social Cognitive and Affective Neuroscience*, 7, 446–456.

Kanekar, S., and Kisawalla, M. B. (1980). Responsibility of a rape victim in relation to her respectability, attractiveness, and provocativeness. *Journal of Social Psychology*, 112, 153–154.

Kanekar, S., Mayundar, D., and Kolsawalla, M. B. (1981). Perception of an aggressor and his victim as a function of physical attractiveness and retaliation. *Journal of Social Psychology*, 113, 289–290.

Kang, Y., and Hamilton, M. (2003, May). *The effect of sex appeal on believability, attitude toward the advertisement and brand, and purchase intention* [Electronic version]. Paper presented at the meeting of the International Communication Association, San Diego, CA.

Kang-Ming, C., and Chuh-Wei, S. (2011). Aromatherapy benefits autonomic nervous system regulation for elementary school faculty in Taiwan [Electronic version]. *Evidence-Based Complementary and Alternative Medicine*, 8, 1–7.

Karris, J. (1977). Prejudice against obese renters. *Journal of Social Psychology*, 101, 159–160.

Kassing, J. W. (2008). Consider this: A comparison of factors contributing to employees' expressions of dissent. *Communication Quarterly*, 56, 342–355.

Kaye, K., and Fogel, A. (1980). The temporal structure of face-to-face communication between mothers and infants. *Developmental Psychology*, 16, 454–464.

Kearney, P., Plax, T. G., Smith, V. R., and Sorensen, G. (1988). Effects of teacher immediacy and strategy on college student resistance to on-task demands. *Communication Education*, 37, 54–67.

Keating, C. F. (1985). Gender and the physiognomy of dominance and attractiveness. *Social Psychology Quarterly*, 48, 61–70.

Keisanen, T., and Rauniomaa, M. (2012). The organization of participation and contingency in prebeginnings of request sequences [Electronic version]. *Research on Language and Social Interaction*, 45, 323–351.

Keith, V., and Herring, C. (1991). Skin tone and stratification in the black community. *American Journal of Sociology*, 97, 760–771.

Kelly, J. (1969, May). *Dress as non-verbal communication*. Paper presented at the meeting of the American Association for Public Opinion Research Lake George, NY.

Kelly, S. D., and Lee, A. L. (2012). When actions speak too much louder than words: Hand gestures disrupt word learning when phonetic demands are high [Electronic version]. *Language and Cognitive Processes*, 27, 793–807.

Kendon, A. (1976). Some functions of gaze direction in social interaction. *Acta Psychologica*, 26, 22–63.

Kendon, A., and Ferber, A. (1973). A description of some human greetings. In R. P. Michael and J. H. Crook (Eds.), *Comparative ecology and behavior of primates* (pp. 591–668). London: Academic Press.

Kendrick, D. T., and MacFarlane, S. W. (1986). Ambient temperature and horn honking. *Environment and Behavior*, 18, 179–191.

Kenealy, P., Frude, N., and Shaw, W. (1988). Influence of children's physical attractiveness on teacher expectations. *Journal of Social Psychology*, 128, 373–383.

Kennedy, C. W., and Camden, C. T. (1983). A new look at interruptions. *Western Journal of Speech Communication*, 47, 45–58.

Kerr, N. L., Raymond, H. C. B., MacCoun, R. J., and Rathborn, J. (1985). Effects of victim attractiveness, care, and disfigurement on the judgments of American and British mock jurors. *British Journal of Social Psychology*, 24, 54–58.

Kerssen-Griep, J., and Witt, P. L. (2012). Instructional feedback II: How do instructor immediacy cues and facework tactics interact to predict student motivation and fairness perceptions? *Communication Studies*, 63, 498–517.

Key, W. B. (1976). *Media sexploitation*. Englewood Cliffs, NJ: Prentice-Hall.

Kiecolt-Glaser, J. K., Graham, J. E., Malarkey, W. B., Porter, K., Lemeshow, S., and Glaser, R. (2008). Olfactory influences on mood and autonomic, endocrine, and immune function [Electronic version]. *Psychoneuroendocrinology*, 33, 328–339.

Kim, D., Kim, J., Lee, E., Whang, M., and Cho, Y. (2011). Interactive emotional content communications system using portable wireless biofeedback device [Electronic version]. *IEEE Transactions on Consumer Electronics*, 57, 1929–1936.

Kimbara, I. (2008). Gesture form convergence in joint description [Electronic version]. *Journal of Nonverbal Behavior*, 32, 123–131.

Kimble, C. E., and Seidel, S. D. (1991). Vocal signs of confidence. *Journal of Nonverbal Behavior*, 15, 99–105.

King, A. S. (1973). The eye in advertising. *Journal of Applied Communications Research*, 1, 1–12.

Kirouac, G., and Dore, F. Y. (1985). Accuracy of the judgment of facial expression of emotions as a function of sex and level of education. *Journal of Nonverbal Behavior*, 9, 3–7.

Kitchens, J. T., Herron, T. P., Behnke, R. R., and Beatty, M. J. (1977). Environmental esthetics and interpersonal attraction. *Western Journal of Speech Communication*, 41, 126–130.

Kleck, R., Buck, P. L., Goller, R. S., London, J. R., Pfieffer, J. R., and Vukcevic, D. P. (1968). Effect of stigmatization conditions on the use of personal space. *Psychological Reports*, 23, 111–118.

Kleinke, C. (1980). Interaction between gaze and legitimacy of request on compliance in a field setting. *Journal of Nonverbal Behavior*, 5, 3–12.

Kleinke, C. L. (1986). Gaze and eye contact: A research review. *Psychological Review*, 100, 78–100.

Kleinke, C., and Staneski, R. (1980). First impressions of female bust size. *Journal of Social Psychology*, 110, 123–134.

Klopf, D. W. (2001). *Intercultural encounters: The fundamentals of intercultural communication* (5th ed.). Denver: Morton Publishing Company.

Knapp, M. L. (1978). *Nonverbal communication in human interaction* (2nd ed.). New York: Holt, Rinehart, and Winston.

Knapp, M. L. (1980). *Essentials of nonverbal communication*. New York: Random House.

Knapp, M. L., and Comandena, M. E. (1979). Telling it like it isn't: A review of theory and research on deceptive communications. *Human Communication Research*, 5, 270–285.

Knapp, M. L., and Hall, J. A. (1992). *Nonverbal communication in human interaction* (3rd ed.). New York: Holt, Rinehart and Winston.

Knapp, M. L., Hart, R., and Dennis, H. (1974). An exploration of deception as a communication construct. *Human Communication Research*, 1, 15–29.

Knight, K. (2009, November). *I'm just not that into him: A qualitative exploration of college students' friends with benefits relationships* [Electronic version]. Paper presented at the annual convention of the National Communication Association, Chicago, IL.

Knöfler, T., and Imhof, M. (2007) Does sexual orientation have an impact on nonverbal behavior in interpersonal communication? [Electronic version] *Journal of Nonverbal Behavior*, 31, 189–204.

Knorr, N. J., Edgerton, M. T., and Hooper, J. E. (1967). The "insatiable" cosmetic surgery patient. *Plastic and Reconstructive Surgery*, 40, 285–289.

Knowles, E. S. (1972). Boundaries around social space: Dyadic responses to an invasion. *Environment and Behavior*, 4, 437–445.

Knuf, J. (1992). Spit first and then say what you want! Concerning the use of language and ancillary codes in ritualized communication. *Quarterly Journal of Speech*, 78, 466–482.

Koch, J. R., Roberts, A. E., Armstrong, M. L., and Owen, D. C. (2007). Frequencies and relations of body piercing and sexual experience in college students [Electronic version]. *Psychological Reports*, 101, 159–162.

Koch, S. C. (2005). Evaluative affect display toward male and female leaders of task-oriented groups [Electronic version]. *Small Group Research*, 36, 678–703.

Koerner, A. F., and Fitzpatrick, M. A. (2002). Nonverbal communication and marital adjustment and satisfaction: The role of decoding relationship relevant and relationship irrelevant affect. *Communication Monographs*, 69, 33–51.

Koernig, S. K., and Page, A. L. (2002). What if your dentist looked like Tom Cruise? Applying the match-up hypothesis to a service encounter [Electronic version]. *Psychology & Marketing*, 19, 91–110.

Kolber, R. H., and Albanese, P. J. (1996). Man to man: A content analysis of sole-male images in male-audience magazines [Electronic version]. *Journal of Advertising*, 4, 1–20.

Koljonen, V., and Kluger, N. (2012). Specifically requesting surgical tattoo removal: Are deep personal motivations involved? [Electronic version]. *Journal of the European Academy of Dermatology & Venereology*, 26, 685–689.

Koppensteiner, M., and Grammer, K. (2011). Body movements of male and female speakers and their influence on perceptions of personality [Electronic version]. *Personality and Individual Differences*, 51, 743–747.

Korda, M. (1975). *Power! How to get it, how to use it*. New York: Ballantine Books.

Korn, J. (1971). *The studio*. New York: Time-Life Books.

Kozlowska, L., and Doboszynska, A. (2012). Nurses' nonverbal methods of communicating with patients in the terminal phase [Electronic version]. *International Journal of Palliative Nursing*, 18, 40–46.

Krail, K. A., and Leventhal, G. 1976. The sex variable in the invasion of personal space. *Sociometry*, 39, 170–173.

Kramer, C. (1974). Women's speech: Separate but unequal. *Quarterly Journal of Speech*, 60, 14–24.

Kramer, C. (1977). Perceptions of female and male speech. *Language and Speech*, 20, 151–161.

Kramer, C. (1978). Women's and men's ratings of their own and ideal speech. *Communication Quarterly*, 26, 2–11.

Krcmar, M., Giles, S., and Helme, D. (2008). Understanding the process: How mediated and peer norms affect young women's body esteem. *Communication Quarterly*, 56, 111–130.

Krueger, H.-P. (1986). Nonverbal characteristics of verbal behavior: A biological approach to personality and syntality. In *Proceedings, Conference of Current Trends in Nonverbal Communication: A Multidisciplinary Approach* (pp. 121–168). Jonesboro: Arkansas State University Press.

Krumhuber, E., Manstead, A., and Kappas, A. (2007). Temporal aspects of facial displays in person and expression perception: The effects of smile dynamics, head-tilt, and gender [Electronic version]. *Journal of Nonverbal Behavior*, 31, 39–56.

Kumin, L., and Lazar, M. (1974). Gestural communication in preschool children. *Perceptual and Motor Skills*, 38, 708–710.

LaCrosse, M. B. (1975). Nonverbal behavior and perceived counselor attractiveness and persuasiveness. *Journal of Counseling Psychology*, 22, 563–566.

LaFrance, M., and Carmen, B. (1980). The nonverbal display of psychological androgyny. *Journal of Personality and Social Psychology*, 38, 36–49.

LaFrance, M., and Mayo, C. (1979). A review of nonverbal behaviors of women and men. *Western Journal of Speech Communication*, 43, 96–107.

Laird, J., and Lewis, J. (1989). Looking and loving: The effects of mutual gaze on feelings of romantic love. *Journal of Research in Personality*, 23, 145–161.

Lamb, C. S., Jackson, L. A., Cassiday, P. B., and Priest, D. J. (1993). Body figure preferences of men and women: A comparison of two generations. *Sex Roles*, 28, 345–358.

Lamb, M. E. (1982a). Paternal influences on early socio-emotional development. *Journal of Child Psychology*, 23, 185–190.

Lamb, M. E. (1982b). The bonding phenomenon: Misinterpretations and their implications. *Journal of Pediatrics*, 101, 555–557.

Lamb, M. E. (1982c). Early contact and maternal-infant bonding: One decade later. *Pediatrics*, 70, 763–768.

Lambrey, S., Voisin, C., Roucault, R., Canet, P., Rauturau, G., Jouvent, R., and Pelissolo, A. (2011). How do patients with social phobia manage interpersonal distance during social interactions? [Electronic version] *European Psychiatry*, 26, 162.

Lane, L. L. (1971). Communicative behavior and biological rhythms. *Speech Teacher*, 20, 16–19.

Lang, G. T., Calhoun, L. G., and Selby, J. W. (1977). Personality characteristics related to cross-situational consistency of interpersonal distance. *Journal of Personality Assessment*, 41, 274–278.

Lang, P. J., Bradley, M. M., and Cuthbert, B. N. (1990). Emotion, attention, and the startle reflex. *Psychology Review*, 97, 377–395.

Langlois, J. H., Ritter, J. M., Roggman, L. A., and Vaughn, L. S. (1991). Facial diversity and infant preferences for attractive faces. *Developmental Psychology*, 27, 79–84.

Langlois, J. H., and Roggman, L. A. (1990). Attractive faces are only average. *Psychological Science*, 1, 115–121.

Langman, L. (2008). Punk, porn and resistance: Carnivalization and the body in popular culture [Electronic version]. *Current Sociology*, 56, 657–677.

Lapinski, M. K. (2006). Starvingforperfect.com: A theoretically based content analysis of pro-eating disorder web sites [Electronic version]. *Health Communication*, 20, 243–253.

Larsen, J., Urry, J., and Axhausen, K. (2008). Coordinating face-to-face meetings in mobile network societies [Electronic version]. *Information, Communication & Society*, 11, 640–658.

Lasikiewicz, N., Hendrickx, H., Talbot, D., and Dye, L. (2013). Exploring stress-induced cognitive impairment in middle aged centrally obese adults [Electronic version]. *Stress: The International Journal of the Biology of Stress*, 16, 44–53.

Lass, N. J., and Harvey, L. A. (1976). An investigation of speaker photograph identification. *Journal of the Acoustical Society of America*, 59, 1232–1236.

Lass, N. J., Bell, R. R., Simcoe, J. C., McClung, N. J., and Park, W. E. (1972). Assessment of oral tactile perception: Some methodological considerations. *Central State Speech Journal*, 23, 165–173.

Lass, N. J., Tekieli, M. E., and Eye, M. P. (1971). A comparative study of two procedures for assessment of oral tactile perception. *Central States Speech Journal*, 22, 21–26.

Lau, J. Y. F., Burt, M., Leibenluft, E., Pine, D. S., Rijsdijk, F., Shiffrin, N., and Eley, T. C. (2009). Individual differences in children's facial expression recognition ability: The role of nature and nurture. *Developmental Neuropsychology*, 34, 37–51.

Lawrence, S. G., and Watson, M. (1991). Getting others to help: The effectiveness of professional uniforms in charitable fundraising. *Journal of Applied Communication Research*, 19, 170–185.

Leal, S., and Vrij, A. (2010). The occurrence of eye blinks during a guilty knowledge test [Electronic version]. *Psychology, Crime & Law*, 16, 349–357.

Leathers, D. G. (1976). *Nonverbal communication systems*. Boston: Allyn and Bacon.

Leathers, D. G. (1982). *The role of nonverbal factors in shaping perceptions of leadership*. Seminar presentation, University of Southern Mississippi, Hattiesburg, MS.

Leathers, D. G. (1988). Impression management training: Conceptualization and application to personal selling. *Journal of Applied Communication Research*, 16 (2), 126–145.

Leathers, D. G. (1997). *Nonverbal communication systems: Principles and applications* (3rd ed.). Boston: Allyn and Bacon.

Leathers, D. G., and Eaves, M. H. (2008). *Successful nonverbal communication: Principles and application*. Englewood Cliffs, NJ: Prentice-Hall

Leathers, D. G., and Emigh, T. H. (1980). Decoding facial expressions: A new test with decoding norms. *The Quarterly Journal of Speech*, 66, 418–435.

Leathers, D. G., and Hocking, J. E. (1982, November). *An examination of police interviewers' beliefs about the utility and nature of nonverbal indicators of deception.* Paper presented at the meeting of the Speech Communication Association, Louisville, KY.

Lechelt, E. (1975). Occupational affiliation and ratings of physical height and personal esteem. *Psychological Reports, 36,* 943–946.

Ledbetter, A. M. (2009). Family communication patterns and relational maintenance behavior: Direct and mediated associations with friendship closeness. *Human Communication Research, 35,* 130–147.

Ledbetter, A. M., Broeckelman-Post, M. A., and Krawsczyn, A. M. (2011). Modeling everyday talk: Differences across communication media and sex composition of friendship dyads [Electronic version]. *Journal of Social and Personal Relationships, 28,* 223–241.

Lee, J. (1999). Leader—member exchange, gender, and members' communication expectations with leaders. *Communication Quarterly, 47,* 413–429.

Lefkowitz, M., Blake, R. R., and Mouton, J. S. (1955). Status of actors in pedestrian violation of traffic signals. *Journal of Abnormal and Social Psychology, 51,* 704–706.

Legerstee, M. (1987). The development of infants' responses to people and a doll: Implications for research in communication. *Infant Behavior and Development, 10,* 81–95.

Leipold, W. (1963). *Psychological distance in dyadic interviews.* Unpublished dissertation, University of North Dakota, Grand Forks.

LePoire, B. A. (1991). Orientation and defensive reactions as alternatives to arousal in theories of nonverbal reactions to changes in immediacy. *Southern Communication Journal, 56,* 138–146.

Lerner, R. M. (1973). The development of personal space schemata toward body build. *Journal of Psychology, 84,* 229–235.

Lerner, R., and Brackney, B. (1976). The importance of inner and outer body parts on attitudes in the self concept of late adolescence. *Sex Roles, 2,* 225–238.

Lester, D. (1981). Ectomorphy and suicide. *Journal of Social Psychology, 113,* 135–136.

Levine, T. R., Asada, K. J. K., and Park, H. S. (2006). The lying chicken and the gaze avoidant egg: Eye contact, deception, and causal order. *Southern Communication Journal, 71,* 401–411.

Levine, T. R., McCornack, S. A., and Avery, P. B. (1992). Sex differences in emotional reactions to discovered deception. *Communication Quarterly, 40,* 289–296.

Levy, R., and Poll, A. P. (1976). Through a glass, darkly. *Dun's Review, 107* (2), 77–78.

Lewis, C. (2002). Botox cosmetic: A look at looking good. FDA *Consumer, 36* (4), 11–14.

Lewis, M. L. (1983, April). *Communication rules and work motivation patterns as predictors of marital satisfaction.* Paper presented at the meeting of the Southern Speech Communication Association, Orlando, FL.

Li, H. Z. (2006). Backchannel responses as misleading feedback in intercultural discourse [Electronic version]. *Journal of Intercultural Communication Research, 35,* 99–116.

Lipsitt, L. P., Engen, T., and Kaye, H. (1963). Development changes in the olfactory threshold of the neonate. *Child Development, 34,* 371–376.

Little, K. B. (1965). Personal space. *Journal of Experimental Social Psychology, 1,* 237–247.

Littlejohn, S. W. (2007). *Theories of human communication* (9th ed.). Belmont, CA: Wadsworth.

LoBue, V. and Larson, C. L. (2010). What makes and angry face look so … angry? Examining visual attention to the shape of threat in children and adults [Electronic version]. *Visual Cognition, 18,* 1165–1178.

Locher, P., Unger, R., Sociedade, P., and Wahl, J. (1993). At first glance: Accessibility of the physical attractiveness stereotype. *Sex Roles, 28,* 729–743.

Lomranz, J., Shapira, A., Choresa, N, and Gilat, Y. (1975). Children's personal space as a function of age and sex. *Developmental Psychology, 11,* 541–545.

Lorenz, J. (1976). Cultural variations in personal space. *Journal of Social Psychology, 99,* 21–27.

Lott, D. F., and Sommer, R. (1967). Seating arrangement and status. *Journal of Personality and Social Psychology, 7,* 90–94.

Low, K. E. (2006). Presenting the self, the social body, and the olfactory: Managing smells in everyday life experiences [Electronic version]. *Sociological Perspectives*, 49, 607–631.

Lozano, S. C., and Tversky, B. (2006). Communicative gestures facilitate problem solving for both communicators and recipients [Electronic version]. *Journal of Memory and Language*, 55, 47–63.

Lu, L., Kao, S., Chang, T., and Lee, Y. (2009). Individual differences in coping with criticism of one's physical appearance among Taiwanese students [Electronic version]. *International Journal of Psychology*, 44, 274–281.

Lucas, S. (2004). The images used to "sell" and represent retirement communities [Electronic version]. *Professional Geographer*, 56, 449–459.

Lucker, W., Beane, W., and Helmreich, R. L. (1981). The strength of the halo effect in physical attractiveness research. *Journal of Psychology*, 197, 69–76.

Luka, T., Berner, E. S., and Kanakis, C. (1977). Diagnosis by smell? *Journal of Medical Education*, 52, 349–350.

Luscher, M. (1971). *The Luscher color test* (I. Scott, Ed. and Trans.). New York: Pocket Books.

Luther, C. A. (2009). Importance placed on physical attractiveness and advertisement-inspired social comparison behavior among Japanese female and male teenagers [Electronic version]. *Journal of Communication*, 59, 279–295.

Lyman, S. M., and Scott, M. B. (1967). Territoriality: A neglected sociological dimension. *Social Problems*, 15, 236–249.

Machado-Casas, M. (2012). Pedagogies of the chameleon: Identity and strategies of survival for transnational indigenous Lation immigrants in the U.S. south [Electronic version]. *Urban Review*, 44, 534–550.

MacPherson, J. C. (1984). Environments and interaction in row and column classrooms. *Environment and Behavior*, 16, 481–502.

Madden, S. J. (1999). Proxemics and gender: Where's the spatial gap? [Electronic version] *North Dakota Journal of Speech and Theatre*, 12, 41–46.

Mahl, G. F. (1956). Disturbances and silences in patients' speech in psychology. *Journal of Abnormal Social Psychology*, 53, 1–15.

Maines, D. R. (1977). Tactile relationships in the subway affected by racial, sexual, and crowded situations. *Environmental Psychology and Nonverbal Behavior*, 2, 100–107.

Major, B. (1981). Gender patterns in touching behavior. In C. Mayo and N. M. Henley (Eds.), *Gender and nonverbal behavior* (pp. 15–37). New York, Springer-Verlag.

Mak, A. K. Y. (2007). Advertising whiteness: An assessment of skin color preferences among urban Chinese [Electronic version]. *Visual Communication Quarterly*, 14, 144–157.

Makaremi, A. (1990). Anger reactions of Iranian adolescents. *Psychological Reports*, 67, 259–262.

Malachowski, C. C., and Dillow, M. R. (2011). An examination of relational uncertainty, romantic intent, and attraction on communicative and relational outcomes in cross-sex friendships. *Communication Research Reports*, 28, 356–368.

Malandro, L. A., Barker, L. L., and Barker, D. (1989). *Nonverbal communication* (2nd ed.). Reading, MA: Addison-Wesley.

Mallenby, T. W. (1974). Personal space—Direct measurement techniques with hard of hearing students. *Environment and Behavior*, 6, 117–121.

Manning, A. (1994, February 22). Doctors do tests to solve body fumes mystery. *USA Today*, pp. D-1, D-2.

Manusov, V. (1991). Perceiving nonverbal messages: Effects of immediacy and encoded intent on receiver judgments. *Western Journal of Speech Communication*, 55, 235–253.

Manusov, V. (1992). Mimicry or synchrony: The effects of intentionality attributions for nonverbal mirroring behavior. *Communication Quarterly*, 40, 69–83.

Margalit, M. (1977, February). *Ethnic differences in expressions of shame feelings by mothers of severely handicapped children*. Paper presented at the congress of the Israel Psychology Association, Jerusalem.

Markham-Shaw, C., and Edwards, R. (1997). Self concepts and self presentations of males and females: Similarities and differences. *Communication Reports*, 10, 55–62.

Markley-Rountree, M., and Davis, L. (2011). A dimensional qualitative research approach to understanding medically unnecessary aesthetic surgery [Electronic version]. *Psychology & Marketing*, 28, 1027–1043.

Markovic, K., Reulbach, U., Vassiliadu, A., Lunkenheimer, J., Lunkenheimer, B., Spannenberger, R., and Thuerauf, N. (2007). Good news for elderly persons: Olfactory pleasure increases at later stages of the life span [Electronic version]. *Journals of Gerontology Series A: Biological Sciences & Medical Sciences*, 62A, 1287–1293.

Martin, J. G. (1964). Racial ethnocentrism and judgment of beauty. *Journal of Social Psychology*, 63, 59–63.

Martin, M. M., and Anderson, C. M. (1993). Psychological and biological differences in touch avoidance. *Communication Research Reports*, 10, 141–147.

Martino, S. (2008). Perceptions of a photograph of a woman with visible piercings [Electronic version]. *Psychological Reports*, 103, 134–138.

Martz, D. M., Petroff, A. B., Curtin, L., and Bazzini, D. G. (2009). Gender differences in fat talk among American adults: Results from the psychology of size survey [Electronic version]. *Sex Roles*, 61, 34–41.

Marwit, S. J. (1982). Students' race, physical attractiveness, and teachers' judgments of transgressions: Follow-up and clarification. *Psychological Reports*, 50, 242.

Maslow, A. H., and Mintz, N. L. (1956). Effects of esthetic surroundings: I. Initial effects of three esthetic conditions upon perceiving "energy" and "well-being" in faces. *Journal of Psychology*, 41, 247–254.

Matarasso, A., and Hutchinson, O. H.-Z. (2001). Liposuction. *Journal of the American Medical Association*, 265 (3), 266–268.

Mathes, E., and Kempher, S. B. (1976). Clothing as a nonverbal communicator of sexual attitudes and behavior. *Perceptual and Motor Skills*, 43, 495–498.

Matlon, R. J. (1988). *Communication in the legal process*. New York: Holt, Rinehart, and Winston.

Matsumoto, D. (1980). Face, culture and judgments of anger and fear: Do the eyes have it? *Journal of Nonverbal Behavior*, 13, 171–188.

Matsumoto, D. (1991). Cultural influences on facial expressions of emotion. *Southern Communication Journal*, 56, 128–137.

Matsumoto, D., and Assar, M. (1992). The effects of language on judgments of universal facial expressions of emotion. *Journal of Nonverbal Behavior*, 16, 85–99.

Mauet, T. A. (1988). *Fundamentals of trial techniques* (2nd ed.). Boston: Little, Brown.

May, J. (1980). What tips tippers to tip. *Psychology Today*, 14, 98–99.

Mazur, A. (1977). Interpersonal spacing on public benches in "contact" vs. "noncontact" cultures. *Journal of Social Psychology*, 101, 53–58.

Mazur, E., and Richards, L. (2011). Adolescents' and emerging adults' social networking online: Homophily or diversity? [Electronic version] *Journal of Applied Developmental Psychology*, 32, 180–188.

McCain, G., Cox, V. C., and Paulus, P. B. (1976). The relationship between illness complaints and the degree of crowding in a prison environment. *Environment and Behavior*, 8, 283–289.

McCauley, M. M., Mintz, L., and Glenn, A. A. (1988). Body image, self esteem, and depression-proneness: Closing the gender gap. *Sex Roles*, 18, 381–391.

McClave, E., Kim, H., Tamer, R., and Mileff, M. (2007). Head movements in the context of speech in Arabic, Bulgarian, Korean, and African-American vernacular English [Electronic version]. *Gesture*, 7, 343–390.

McClelland, D. (1961). *The achieving society*. New York: Van Nostrand Reinhold.

McClintock, M. K. (1971). Menstrual synchrony and suppression. *Nature*, 229, 244–245.

McClure, E. B. (2000). A meta-analytic review of sex differences in facial expression processing and their development in infants, children, and adolescents [Electronic version]. *Psychological Bulletin*, 126, 424–453.

McComb, K. B., and Jablin, F. M. (1984). Verbal correlates of interviewer empathic listening and employment interview outcomes. *Communication Monographs*, 51, 353–371.

McCroskey, J. C., Richmond, V. P., Johnson, A. D., and Smith, H. T. (2004). Organizational orientations theory and measurement: Development of measures and preliminary investigations. *Communication Quarterly*, 52, 1–14.

McCutcheon, L. (1996). What's that I smell? The claims of aromatherapy. *Skeptical Inquirer*, May/June, 1–4.

McDaniel, E., and Andersen, P. A. (1998). International patterns of interpersonal tactile communication: A field study [Electronic version]. *Journal of Nonverbal Behavior*, 22, 59–75.

McDonald, P., Backstrom, S., and Dear, K. (2008). Reporting sexual harassment: Claims and remedies [Electronic version]. *Asia Pacific Journal of Human Resources*, 46, 173–195.

McElhaney, J. W. (1987). Horse-shedding the witness: Techniques for witness preparation. *Trial*, 23, 80–84.

McGehee, F. (1937). The reliability of the identification of the human voice. *Journal of General Psychology*, 17, 249–271.

McGill, M. E. (1980). *The 40- to 60-year-old male*. New York: Simon and Schuster.

McGinley, R., LeFevre, R., and McGinley, P. (1975). The influence of a communicator's body position on opinion change in others. *Journal of Personality and Social Psychology*, 31, 686–690.

McGlone, R. E., and Hollien, H. (1963). Vocal pitch characteristics of aged women. *Journal of Speech and Hearing Research*, 6, 164–170.

McKeachie, W. (1952). Lipstick as a determiner of first impressions on personality: An experiment for the general psychology course. *Journal of Social Psychology*, 36, 241–244.

McLaughlin, M. L. (1984). *Conversation: How talk is organized*. Beverly Hills, CA: Sage.

McLaughlin, M. L., and Cody, M. J. (1982). Awkward silences: Behavioral antecedents and consequences of the conversational lapse. *Human Communication Research*, 8, 299–316.

McNaughton, M. J. (2007). Hard cases: Prison tattooing as visual argument [Electronic version]. *Argumentation and Advocacy*, 43, 133–143.

Meehan, T. (1999). *Suit yourself: A practical guide to men's attire*. Birmingham, AL: Meehan.

Mehrabian, A. (1968). Relationship of attitude to seated posture, orientation, and distance. *Journal of Personality and Social Psychology*, 10, 26–30.

Mehrabian, A. (1970). Some determinants of affiliation and conformity. *Psychological Reports*, 27, 19–29.

Mehrabian, A. (1971a). Nonverbal betrayal of feeling. *Journal of Experimental Research in Personality*, 5, 64–73.

Mehrabian, A. (1971b). Verbal and nonverbal interaction of strangers in a waiting situation. *Journal of Experimental Research in Psychology*, 5, 127–138.

Mehrabian, A. (1972). *Nonverbal communication*. Chicago: Aldine-Atherton.

Mehrabian, A. (1976). *Public places and private spaces: The psychology of work, play, and living environments*. New York: Basic Books.

Mehrabian, A. (1981). *Silent messages: Implicit communication of emotions and attitudes* (2nd ed.). Belmont, CA: Wadsworth.

Mehrabian, A., and Diamond, S. (1971). Effects of furniture arrangement, props, and personality on interaction. *Journal of Personality and Social Psychology*, 20, 18–30.

Mehrabian, A., and Williams, M. (1969). Nonverbal concomitants of perceived and intended persuasiveness. *Journal of Personality and Social Psychology*, 13, 87–58.

Mejía-Arauz, R., Rogoff, B., Dexter, A., and Najafi, B. (2007). Cultural variation in children's social organization [Electronic version]. *Child Development*, 78, 1001–1014.

Melinger, A., and Levelt, W. J. (2004). Gesture and the communicative intention of the speaker [Electronic version]. *Gesture*, 4, 119–141.

Menz, F., and Al-Roubaie, A. (2008). Interruptions, status and gender in medical interviews: The harder you brake, the longer it takes. *Discourse & Society*, 19, 645–666.

Mercincavage, J. E., and Brooks, C. I. (1990). Differences in achievement motivation of college business majors as a function of year in college and classroom seating position. *Psychological Reports*, 66, 632–634.

Merrill, E., and Grassley, J. (2008). Women's stories of their experiences as overweight patients [Electronic version]. *Journal of Advanced Nursing*, 64, 139–146.

Mesquita, B., and Frijda, N. H. (1992). Cultural variations in emotions: A review. *Psychological Bulletin*, 112, 179–204.

Metalis, S. A., and Hess, E. H. (1982). Pupillometric analysis of two theories of obesity. *Perceptual and Motor Skills*, 55, 87–92.

Meunier, H., Vauclair, J., and Fagard, J. (2012). Human infants and baboons show the same pattern of handedness for a communicative gesture [Electronic version]. *PLoS ONE*, 7, 1–3.

Michael, G., and Willis, F. N., Jr. (1968). The development of gestures as a function of social class, education, and sex. *Psychological Record*, 18, 515–519.

Milgram, S., Liberty, H. J., Toledo, R., and Wackenhut, J. (1986). Response to intrusion into waiting lines. *Journal of Personality and Social Psychology*, 61, 683–689.

Millar, D. P., and Millar, F. E. (1976). *Messages and myths*. New York: Alfred Publishing.

Miller, K. I. (2007). Compassionate communication in the workplace: Exploring processes of noticing, connecting, and responding. *Journal of Applied Communication Research*, 35 (3), 223–245.

Miller, P. J., and Mangelsdorf, S. C. (2005). Developing selves are meaning-making selves: Recouping the social in self-development [Electronic version]. *New Directions for Child and Adolescent Development*, 2005, 51–59.

Miller-Day, M., and Lee, J. W. (2001). Communicating disappointment: The viewpoint of sons and daughters [Electronic version]. *Journal of Family Communication*, 1, 111–131.

Miller-Day, M., and Marks, J. D. (2006). Perceptions of parental communication orientation, perfectionism, and disordered eating behaviors of sons and daughters [Electronic version]. *Health Communication*, 19, 153–163.

Mills, J., and Aronson, E. (1965). Opinion change as a function of the communicator's attractiveness and desire to influence. *Journal of Personality and Social Psychology*, 1, 73–77.

Mintz, N. L. (1956). Effects of esthetic surrounds: II. Prolonged and repeated experience in a "beautiful" and "ugly" room. *Journal of Psychology*, 41, 459–466.

Mireault, G., Poutre, M., Sargent-Hier, M., Dias, C., Perdue, B., and Myrick, A. (2012). Humour perception and creation between parents and 3- to 6-month-old infants [Electronic version]. *Infant and Child Development*, 21, 338–347.

Mirivel, J. C. (2008). The physical examination in cosmetic surgery: Communication strategies to promote the desirability of surgery [Electronic version]. *Health Communication*, 23, 153–170.

Miura, M. (1991). Relationship between nonverbal decoding ability and cognitive mode. *Psychological Reports*, 68, 803–806.

Modesti, S. (2008). Home sweet home: Tattoo parlors as postmodern spaces of agency. *Western Journal of Communication*, 72, 197–212.

Mohan, P. J. (1981). Child raising attitudes, family size, and the value of children. *Journal of Psychology*, 107, 97–104.

Molloy, J. T. (1975). *Dress for success*. New York: Warner.

Molloy, J. T. (1978). *The woman's dress for success book*. New York: Warner Books.

Molloy, J. T. (1995). *The new dress for success book*. New York: Warner Books.

Molloy, J. T. (1996). *New women's dress for success book*. New York: Warner Books.

Money, J. (1980). *Love and love sickness: The science of sex, gender difference, and pair bonding*. Baltimore: Johns Hopkins University Press.

Montagu, A. (1971). *Touching: The human significance of the skin*. New York: Perennial Library.

Montepare, J. M., and Zebrowitz, L. A. (1993). A cross-cultural comparison of impressions created by age-related variations in gait. *Journal of Nonverbal Behavior*, 17, 55–68.

Montpare, J. M., Steinberg, J., and Rosenberg, B. (1992). Characteristics of vocal communication between young adults and their parents and grandparents. *Communication Research*, 19, 479–492.

Moore, M. M. (1985). Nonverbal courtship behaviors in women: Context and consequences. *Ethology and Sociobiology*, 6, 237–247.

Moore, M. M. (1995). Courtship signaling and adolescents: "Girls just wanna have fun?" *The Journal of Sex Research*, 32, 319–328.

Moore, M. M. (2002). Courtship communication and perception [Electronic version]. *Perceptual & Motor Skills*, 94 97–105.

Moore, M. M., and Butler, D. L. (1989). Predictive aspects of nonverbal courtship behavior in women. *Semiotica*, 3, 205–215.

Morgan, G. (1997). *Images of organization* (2nd ed.). Thousand Oaks, CA: Sage Publications.

Moriarty, C. M., and Harrison, K. (2008). Television exposure and disordered eating among children: A longitudinal panel study [Electronic version]. *Journal of Communication*, 51, 361–381.

Morimoto, H. M., Hirose, S., Chikazoe, J., Jimura, K., Asari, T., Yamashita, K., Miyashita, Y., and Konishi, S. (2008). On verbal/nonverbal modality dependence of left and right inferior prefrontal activation during performance of flanker interference task [Electronic version]. *Journal of Cognitive Neuroscience*, 20, 2006–2014.

Morman, M. T., and Floyd, K. (1998). "I love you man": Overt expressions of affection in male—male interaction. *Sex Roles*, 38 (9/10), 871–882.

Morman, M. T., and Floyd, K. (1999). Affectionate communication between fathers and young adult sons: Individual and relational-level correlates. *Communication Studies*, 50, 294–309.

Morman, M., and Green, K. (2009, November). *Perceived benefits of the friends with benefits relationship* [Electronic version]. Paper presented at the National Communication Association, Chicago, IL.

Morrin, M., Krishna, A., and Lwin, M. O. (2011). Is scent-enhanced memory immune to retroactive interference? [Electronic version] *Journal of Consumer Psychology*, 21, 354–361.

Morrin, M., and Ratneshwar, S. (2003). Does it make sense to use scents to enhance brand memory? [Electronic version] *Journal of Marketing Research*, 40, 10–25.

Morris, D. (1971). *Intimate behavior*. New York: Random House.

Morris, D. (1976). "Please touch" is message of Morris. In L. B. Rosenfeld and J. M. Civikly, *With words unspoken: The nonverbal experience* (pp. 129–132). New York: Holt, Rinehart and Winston.

Morris, D. (1977). *Manwatching: A field guide to human behavior*. New York: Henry N. Abrams.

Morris, D. (1985). *Bodywatching*. New York: Crown.

Morris, D., Collett, P., Marsh, P., and O'Shaughnessy, M. (1979). *Gestures: Their origins and distribution*. New York: Stein and Day.

Mortensen, K. (2009). Establishing recipiency in pre-beginning position in the second language classroom [Electronic version]. *Discourse Processes, 46*, 491–515.

Moszkowski, R. J., Stack, D. M., and Chiarella, S. S. (2009). Infant touch with gaze and affective behaviors during mother-infant still-face interactions [Electronic version]. *Infant Behavior and Development*, 32, 392–403.

Motley, M. T. (1993). Facial affect and verbal context in conversation. *Human Communication Research*, 20, 3–40.

Mottet, T. P., and Beebe, S. A. (2002). Relationships between teacher nonverbal immediacy, student emotional response, and perceived student learning. *Communication Research Reports*, 19, 77–88.

Mucherah, W. and Frazier, A. D. (2013). How deep is skin-deep? The relationship between skin color satisfaction, estimation of body image, and self-esteem among women of African descent. *Journal of Applied Social Psychology*, 43, 1177–1184.

Mufson, L., and Nowicki, S., Jr. (1991). Factors affecting the accuracy of facial affect recognition. *Journal of Social Psychology*, 131, 815–822.

Mulac, A. (1976). Assessment and application of the revised speech dialect attitudinal scale. *Communication Monographs*, 43, 238–245.

Mulac, A., Studley, L. B., Wiemann, J. M., and Bradac, J. J. (1987). Male/female gaze in same-sex and mixed-sex dyads. *Human Communication Research*, 13, 323–343.

Mulac, A., Wiemann, J. M., Widenmann, S. J., and Gibson, T. W. (1988). Male/female language differences and effects in same-sex and mixed-sex dyads: The gender-linked language effect. *Communication Monographs*, 55, 315–335.

Murray, D. C., and Deabler, H. L. (1957). Colors and mood-tones. *Journal of Applied Psychology*, 41, 279–283.

Murstein, B., and Christy, P. (1976). Physical attractiveness and marriage adjustment in middle-aged couples. *Journal of Personality and Social Psychology*, 34, 537–542.

Myers, J. F. (1978). Institutionalization and sick role identification among the elderly. *American Sociological Review*, 43, 508–521.

Myers, S. A., and Bryant, L. E. (2008). The use of behavioral indicators of sibling commitment among emerging adults [Electronic version]. *Journal of Family Communication*, 8, 101–125.

Myers, S. A., Byrnes, K. A., Frisby, B. N., and Mansson, D. H. (2011). Adult siblings' use of affectionate communication as a strategic and routine relational maintenance behavior. *Communication Research Reports*, 28, 151–158.

Myers, S. A., Cavanaugh, E. K., Dohem, L. M., Freeh, J. L., Huang, V. W., Kapler, M. R., Leonatti, A., Malicay, M. M., Schweig, V., Sorensen, H. J., Vang, M. M., and Wise, D. C. (1999). Perceived sibling use of relational communication message and sibling satisfaction, liking, and loving. *Communication Research Reports*, 16, 339–352.

Myers, S. A., Mottet, T. P., and Martin, M. M. (2000). The relationship between student communication motives and perceived instructor communicator style. *Communication Research Reports*, 17, 161–170.

Mysak, E. D. (1959). Pitch and duration characteristics of older males. *Journal of Speech and Hearing Research*, 2, 46–54.

Nabi, R. L. (2009). Cosmetic surgery makeover programs and intentions to undergo cosmetic enhancements: A consideration of three models of media effects. *Human Communication Research*, 35, 1–27.

Naidoo, S., and Pillay, G. (1990). Personal constructs of fluency: A study comparing stutterers and nonstutterers. *Psychological Reports*, 66, 375–378.

Nash, J. E. (1982). The family camps out: A study in nonverbal communication. *Semiotica*, 39, 331–334.

Nash, R., Fieldman, G., Hussey, T., Leveque, J., and Pineau, P. (2006). Cosmetics: They influence more than Caucasian female facial attractiveness [Electronic version]. *Journal of Applied Social Psychology*, 36, 493–504.

Nathan, J. (1986). *Uniforms and nonuniforms: Communication through clothing*. New York: Greenwood Press.

Nechamkin, Y., Salganik, I., Modai, I., and Ponizovsky, A. M. (2003). Interpersonal distance in schizophrenic patients: Relationship to negative syndrome. *International Journal of Social Psychiatry*, 49, 165–173.

Neff, J. (2004). Marketers betting on big-hair bounce [Electronic version]. *Advertising Age*, 75, 3–53.

Neijer, M. D. (1991). The attribution of aggression and grief to body movements: The effect of sex-stereotypes. *European Journal of Social Psychology*, 21, 249–259.*New York Times* (2008, Oct. 6). The measure of a President. Retrieved from http://www.nytimes.com/interactive/2008/10/06/opinion/06opchart.html?_r=0

Nguyen, M. L., Heslin, R., and Nguyen, T. (1974, April). *The meaning of four modes of touch as a function of sex and body area*. Paper presented at the Central States Speech Association convention, Chicago, IL. [Electronic version]

Nguyen, M. L., Heslin, R., and Nguyen, T. (1975). The meaning of touch: Sex differences. *Journal of Communication*, 25, 93–103.

Nguyen, M. L., Heslin, R., and Nguyen, T. (1976). The meaning of touch: Sex and marital status differences. *Representative Research in Social Psychology*, 7, 13–18.

Nierenberg, G. I., and Calero, H. H. (1973). *How to read a person like a book*. New York: Pocket Books.

Nitz, M., Reichert, T., Aune, A. S., and Velde, A. V. (2007). All the news that's fit to see? The sexualization of television news journalists as a promotional strategy [Electronic version]. *Journal of Promotion Management*, 13, 13–33.

Noller, P. (1980). Misunderstandings in marital communication: A study of couples' nonverbal communication. *Journal of Personality and Social Psychology*, 39, 1135–1148.

Noller, P., and Gallois, C. (1986). Sending emotional messages in marriage: Non-verbal behavior, sex, and communication clarity. *British Journal of Social Psychology*, 25, 287–297.

Norum, G. A., Gergen, J. K., Peele, S., and van Ryneveld, J. (1977). Reactions to receiving expected and unexpected help from a person who violates or does not violate a norm. *Journal of Experimental Psychology*, 13, 397–402.

Norum, G. A., Russo, N. J., and Sommer, R. (1967). Seating patterns and group task. *Psychology in the Schools*, 4, 240.

Novelli, D., Drury, J., and Reicher, S. (2010). Come together: Two studies concerning the impact of group relations on "personal space" [Electronic version]. *British Journal of Social Psychology*, 49, 223–236.

Nowicki, S., and Oxenford, C. (1988). The relationship of hostile communication styles to popularity in preadolescent children. *Journal of Genetic Psychology*, 150, 39–44.

O'Brien, F. (1990). A crowding index for finite populations. *Perceptual and Motor Skills*, 70, 3–11.

O'Connor, J. (1971). *The relationship of kinesic and verbal communication to leadership perception in small group discussions.* Unpublished doctoral dissertation, Indiana University.

Ogden, J., and Clementi, C. (2010). The experience of being obese and the many consequences of stigma [Electronic version]. *Journal of Obesity*, 2010, 1–9.

O'Grady, K. E. (1989). Physical attractiveness, need for approval, social self-esteem, and maladjustment. *Journal of Social and Clinical Psychology*, 8, 62–69.

O'Hair, D., Allman, J., and Gibson, L. A. (1991). Nonverbal communication and aging. *The Southern Communication Journal*, 56 (2), 147–160.

O'Hair, D., Cody, M. J., and Behnke, R. R. (1985). Communication apprehension and vocal stress as indices of deception. *Western Journal of Speech Communication*, 49, 286–300.

O'Hair, D., Cody, M. J., Wang, X.-T., and Chao, E. Y. (1990). Vocal stress and deception detection among Chinese. *Communication Quarterly*, 38, 158–169.

Ohira, H., and Kurona, K. (1993). Facial feedback effects on impression formation. *Perceptual and Motor Skills*, 77, 1251–1258.

O'Meara, J. D. (1989). Cross-sex friendship: Four basic challenges of an ignored relationship. *Sex Roles*, 21, 525–543.

O'Neil, E. C., Schultz, J., and Christensen, T. E. (1987). The menstrual cycle and personal space. *Journal of Nonverbal Behavior*, 11, 26–32.

Orbe, M. P. (1995). African American communication research: Toward a deeper understanding of inter-ethnic communication. *Western Journal of Communication*, 59, 61–79.

Orbe, M. P. (1996). Laying the foundation for co-cultural communication theory: An inductive approach to studying non-dominant communication strategies and the factors that influence them. *Communication Studies*, 47, 157–177.

Orbe, M. P. (1998). An outsider within perspective to organizational communication: Explicating the communicative practices of co-cultural group members [Electronic version]. *Management Communication Quarterly*, 12, 230–280.

Orbe, M. P. (2008). Representations of race in reality TV: Watch and discuss. *Critical Studies in Media Communication*, 25, 345–352.

Orbe, M. P., and Warren, K. T. (2000). Different standpoints, different realities: Race, gender, and perceptions of intercultural conflict [Electronic version]. *Qualitative Research Reports in Communication*, 1, 51–57.

Orlandi, F., Serra, D., and Sotgiu, G. (1973). Electric stimulation of olfactory mucosa: A new test for the study of hypothalamic functionality. *Hormone Research*, 4, 141–152.

Orlando Sentinel (997, July 31). Baywatch' beauty secrets uncovered: Not everything is what it seems with those gorgeous people running along the beach. Retrieved from http://articles.orlandosentinel.com/1997-07-31/lifestyle/9707300562_1_baywatch-connell-sunless-tanning-lotion

Orton, J. (2006). Responses to Chinese speakers of English [Electronic version]. *International Review of Applied Linguistics in Language Teaching*, 44, 287–309.

O'Sullivan, M., Ekman, P., and Friesen, W. V. (1988). The effect of comparisons on detecting deception. *Journal of Nonverbal Behavior*, 12, 203–213.

Othony, A., and Turner, T. J. (1990). What's basic about basic emotions? *Psychological Review*, 97, 315–331.

Otte, M. (2007). The mourning after: Languages of loss and grief in post-Katrina New Orleans [Electronic version]. *Journal of American History*, 94, 828–836.

Owen, L. (2012). Living fat in a thin-centric world: Effects of spatial discrimination on fat bodies and selves [Electronic version]. *Feminism & Psychology*, 22, 290–306.

Ozdemir, A. (2008). Shopping malls: Measuring interpersonal distance under changing conditions and across cultures [Electronic version]. *Field Methods*, 20, 226–248.

Pagano, M., and Hirsch, B. (2007). Friendships and romantic relationships of black and white adolescents [Electronic version]. *Journal of Child & Family Studies*, 16, 347–357.

Palanica, A., and Itier, R. (2012). Attention capture by direct gaze is robust to context and task demands [Electronic version]. *Journal of Nonverbal Behavior*, 36, 123–134.

Palchoudhury, S., and Mandal, M. K. (1985). Perceptual skills in decoding facial affect. *Perceptual and Motor Skills*, 60, 96–98.

Palmer, R. J., Welker, R. B., Campbell, T. L., and Magner, N. R. (2001). Examining the impression management orientation of managers. *Journal of Managerial Psychology*, 16 (1), 35–49.

Parameswaran, R. (2009, May). *E-raceing color: Gender and transnational visual economies of beauty in India* [Electronic version]. Paper presented at the International Communication Association, Chicago, IL.

Parameswaran, R., and Cardoza, K. (2007, May). *Fairness/lightness/whiteness in advertising: The mobility of beauty in globalizing India* [Electronic version]. Paper presented at the meeting of the International Communication Association, San Francisco, CA.

Park, E. S., Levine, T. R., Harms, C. M., and Ferrara, M. H. (2002). Group and individual accuracy in deception and detection. *Communication Research Reports*, 19, 99–106.

Park, S., Ku, J., Kim, J., Jang, H. J., Kim, S. Y., Kim, S. H., Kim, C., Lee, H., Kim, I. Y., and Kim, S. I. (2009). Increased personal space of patients with schizophrenia in a virtual social environment [Electronic version]. *Psychiatry Research*, 3, 197–202.

Park, S. Y. (2005). The influence of presumed media influence on women's desire to be thin. *Communication Research*, 32, 594–614.

Parkinson, B. (2008). Emotions in direct and social interaction: Getting through the spaces between us [Electronic version]. *Computers in Human Behavior*, 24, 1510–1529.

Parks, A. S., and Bruce, H. M. (1961). Olfactory stimuli in mammalian reproduction. *Science*, 134, 1049–1054.

Parsons, T. J., Manor, O., and Power, C. (2008). Television viewing and obesity: A prospective study in the 1958 British birth cohort [Electronic version]. *European Journal of Clinical Nutrition*, 62, 1355–1363.

Patterson, M., Iizuka, Y., Tubbs, M., Ansel, J., Tsutsumi, M., and Anson, J. (2007). Passing encounters East and West: Comparing Japanese and American pedestrian interactions [Electronic version]. *Journal of Nonverbal Behavior*, 31, 155–166.

Patterson, M. L. (1987). Presentational and affect-management functions of nonverbal involvement. *Journal of Nonverbal Behavior*, 11 (2), 110–122.

Patterson, M. L., and Holmes, D. S. (1966). Social interaction correlates of the MPI Extroversion-Introversion Scale. *American Psychologist*, 21, 724–745.

Patterson, M. L., Powell, J. L., and Lenihan, M. G. (1986). Touch, compliance and interpersonal effect. *Journal of Nonverbal Behavior*, 10, 41–50.

Patterson, M. L., and Tubbs, M. E. (2005). Through a glass darkly: Effects of smiling and visibility on recognition and avoidance in passing encounters. *Western Journal of Communication*, 69, 219–231.

Patton, T. O. (2006). Hey girl, am I more than my hair? African American women and their struggles with beauty, body image, and hair [Electronic version]. *NWSA Journal*, 18, 24–51.

Patzer, G. L. (1985). *The physical attractiveness phenomena*. New York: Plenum.

Payne, L., Martz, D., Tompkins, K., Petroff, A., and Farrow, C. (2011). Gender comparisons of fat talk in the United Kingdom and the United States [Electronic version]. *Sex Roles*, 65, 557–565.

Pearce, W. B., and Conklin, F. (1971). Nonverbal vocalic communication and perception of speaker. *Speech Monographs*, 38, 235–241.

Pearce, W. B., Cronen, V. E., and Harris, L. M. (1982). Methodological considerations in building human communication theory. In F. E. X. Dance (Ed.), *Human communication theory: Comparative essay* (pp. 212–218). New York: Harper and Row.

Pearson, J. C. (1985). *Gender and communication*. Dubuque, IA: William C. Brown.

Pearson, J. C., and West, R. (1991). An initial investigation of the effects of gender on student questions in the classroom: Developing a descriptive base. *Communication Education*, 40, 22–32.

Pedersen, D. M. (1973). Developmental trends in personal space. *Journal of Psychology*, 83, 3–9.

Pedersen, D. M., and Heaston, A. B. (1972). The effects of sex of subject, sex of approaching person, and angle of approach on personal space. *Journal of Psychology*, 82, 277–286.

Peery, C. J., and Roggman, L. A. (1989). Parent—infant social play in brief encounters: Early gender differences. *Child Study Journal*, 19, 65–79.

Peeters, H., and Lievens, F. (2006). Verbal and nonverbal impression management tactics in behavior description and situational interviews [Electronic version]. *International Journal of Selection and Assessment*, 14, 206–222.

Peixoto, L. M. (2002). The Brazilian wax: New hairlessness norm for women? [Electronic version]. *Journal of Communication Inquiry*, 26, 113–133.

Pell, M. D. (2005a). Nonverbal emotion priming: Evidence from the "Facial Affect Decision Task" [Electronic version]. *Journal of Nonverbal Behavior*, 29, 45–73.

Pell, M. D. (2005b). Prosody—face interactions in emotional processing as revealed by the facial affect decision task [Electronic version]. *Journal of Nonverbal Behavior*, 29, 193–215.

Pelligrini, R. J. (1973). Impressions of a male personality as a function of beardedness. *Psychology Today*, 10, 29–33.

Peponis, J. (1985). The spatial culture of factories. *Human Relations*, 38, 357–390.

Perlov, J., and Sawyer, A. (2011). Almost autism [Electronic version]. *European Psychiatry*, 26, 344.

Pertschuk, M. J., Sarwer, D. B., Wadden, T. A., and Whitaker, L. A. (1998). Body image dissatisfaction in male cosmetic surgery patients. *Aesthetic Plastic Surgery*, 22 (1), 20–24.

Peterson, J. L., and Miller, C. (1980). Physical attractiveness and marriage adjustment in older American couples. *Journal of Psychology*, 105, 247–252.

Peterson, K., and Curran, J. C. (1976). Trait attribution as a function of hair length and correlates of subject preference for hair style. *Journal of Psychology*, 93, 331–339.

Phillips, G. M., and Wood, J. T. (1983). *Communication and human relationships: The study of interpersonal communication*. New York: Macmillan.

Philpott, J. S. (1983). *The relative contribution to meaning of verbal and nonverbal channels of communication*. Unpublished master's thesis, University of Nebraska, Lincoln.

Piercy, M. (1973). Small changes. New York: Doubleday.

Ping, Y. (2011). Nonverbal aspects of turn taking in Mandarin Chinese interaction [Electronic version]. *Chinese Language & Discourse*, 2, 99–130.

Pisano, M., Wall, S. M., and Foster, A. (1986). Perceptions of nonreciprocal touch in romantic relationships. *Journal of Nonverbal Behavior*, 10, 29–40.

Plant, E. A., Kling, K. C. and Smith, G. L. (2004). The Influence of Gender and Social Role on the Interpretation of Facial Expressions. *Sex Roles*, 51, 187–196.

Placement Manual. (1976). (Fall). Gainesville: University of Florida.

Plax, T. G., Kearney, P., McCroskey, J. C, and Richmond, V. P. (1986). Power in the classroom VI: Verbal control strategies, nonverbal immediacy, and affective learning. *Communication Education*, 35, 43–55.

Pliner, P., and Chaiken, S. (1990). Eating, social motives, and self-presentation in women and men. *Journal of Experimental Social Psychology*, 26, 240–254.

Pompper, D., Soto, J., and Piel, L. (2007). Male body image and magazine standards: Considering dimensions of age and ethnicity. *Journalism and Mass Communication Quarterly*, 84, 525–545.

Pool, R. (1991). Can lefties be right? *Nature*, 350, 545.

Poole, G. D., and Craig, K. D. (1992). Judgments of genuine, suppressed, and faked facial expressions of pain. *Journal of Personality and Social Psychology*, 63, 797–805.

Porter, H. H. (2012). Tattooist v. tattoo: Separating the service from the constitutionally protected message [Electronic version]. *Brigham Young University Law Review*, 2012, 1071–1107.

Porter, R., and Moore, J. (1982). Newsline. *Psychology Today*, 16, 19.

Porter, S., ten Brinke, L., and Wallace, B. (2012). Secrets and lies: Involuntary leakage in deceptive facial expressions as a function of emotional intensity [Electronic version]. *Journal of Nonverbal Behavior*, 36, 23–37.

Portnoy, E. J. (1993). The impact of body type on perceptions of attractiveness by older individuals. *Communication Reports*, 6, 101–108.

Powell, B., and Steelman, L. C. (1990). Beyond sibship size: Sibling density, sex composition, and educational outcomes. *Social Forces*, 69, 181–206.

Powell, L., Hamilton, T., Hickson, M., and Stuckey, J. (2001). The relationship of homophily to verbal and nonverbal immediacy in the classroom. *Communication Research Reports*, 18, 217–222.

Powell, L., Hill, S. R., Jr., and Hickson, M., III (1980). Path analysis of attitudinal, dispositional, and situational predictions in impression formation. *Psychological Reports*, 47, 327–333.

Powell, R. G., and Harville, B. (1990). The effects of teacher immediacy and clarity on instructional outcomes: An intercultural assessment. *Communication Education*, 39, 369–379.

Powers, W. G. (1993). The effects of gender and consequence upon perceptions of deceivers. *Communication Quarterly*, 41, 328–337.

Prabu, D., Liu, K., and Cortese, J. (2003, May). *Effect of thin vs. plus-size models: A comparison of body image ideals by gender* [Electronic version]. Paper presented at the meeting of the International Communication Association, San Diego, CA.

Pratto, F., and Bargh, J. A. (1991). Stereotyping based on apparently individuating information: Trait and global components of sex stereotypes under attention overload. *Journal of Experimental Social Psychology*, 27, 26–47.

Prescott, J. L. (1975). Body pleasure and the origins of violence. *The Futurist*, 9, 64–74.

Pressner, B. E. (1978). *The therapeutic implications of touch during articulation therapy*. Unpublished master's thesis, University of Florida, Gainesville.

Prochnow, D., Hoing, B., Kleiser, R., Lindenberg, R., Wittsack, H. J., Schafer, R., Franz, M., and Seitz, R. J. (2013). The neural correlates of affect reading: An fMRI study on faces and gestures [Electronic version]. *Behavioural Brain Research*, 237, 270–277.

Proshansky, H. M., Ittelson, W. H., and Rivlin, L. G. (1970). *Environmental psychology: Man and his physical setting*. New York: Holt, Rinehart, and Winston.

Pujols, Y., Meston, C. M., and Seal, B. N. (2010). The association between sexual satisfaction and body image in women [Electronic version]. *Journal of Sexual Medicine*, 7, 905–916.

Punyanunt-Carter, N. M., and Wrench, J. S. (2009). Development and validity testing of a measure of touch deprivation. *Human Communication*, 12, 67–76.

Puts, D. A., Apicella, C. L., and Cardenas, R. A. (2012). Masculine voices signal men's threat potential in forager and industrial societies [Electronic version]. *Proceedings of the Royal Society B: Biological Sciences*, 279, 601–609.

Rainville, R. E., and Gallagher, S. G. (1990). Vulnerability and heterosexual attraction. *Sex Roles*, 23, 25–31.

Raiscott, J. (1985). *Jury selection, body language and the visual trial*. Minneapolis, MN: AB Publications.

Raiscott, J. (1986). *Silent sales*. Minneapolis, MN: AB Publications.

Ramirez, A., and Wang, Z. (2008). When online meets offline: An expectancy violations theory perspective on modality switching [Electronic version]. *Journal of Communication*, 58, 20–39.

Rasnake, L. K., Laube, E., Lewis, M., and Linscheid, T. R. (2005). Children's nutritional judgments: Relation to eating attitudes and body image [Electronic version]. *Health Communication*, 18, 275–289.

Ray, G. (1986). Vocally cued personality prototypes: An implicit personality theory approach. *Communication Monographs*, 53, 266–276.

Ray, G. B., and Floyd, K. (2006). Nonverbal expressions of liking and disliking in initial interaction: Encoding and decoding perspectives. *Southern Communication Journal*, 71, 45–65.

Ray, G. B., Ray, E. B., and Zahn, C. J. (1991). Speech behavior and social evaluation: An examination of medical messages. *Communication Quarterly*, 39, 119–129.

Ray, M. L., and Webb, E. J. (1966). Speech duration effects in the Kennedy news conference. *Science*, 153, 899–901.

Read, D., and Craik, F. I. M. (1995). Earwitness identification: Some influences on voice recognition. *Journal of Experimental Psychology: Applied*, 1, 6–18.

Reeder, H. M. (1996). A critical look at gender difference in communication research. *Communication Studies*, 47, 318–331.

Regan, P. C., Shen, W., De La Peña, E., and Gosset, E. (2007). "Fireworks exploded in my mouth": Affective responses before, during, and after the very first kiss [Electronic version]. *International Journal of Sexual Health*, 19, 1–16.

Reich, A. R., Moll, K. L., and Curtis, J. F. (1976). Effects of selected vocal disguises upon spectrographic speaker identification. *Journal of the Acoustical Society of America*, 60, 919–925.

Reiman, T. (2008). First impressions really matter. *Communication World*, 25, 28–31.

Reinhold, B. (1999). *Toxic work: How to overcome stress, overload and burnout and revitalize your career*. New York: Dutton.

Reinholtz, R. K., and Muehlenhand, C. L. (1995). Genital perceptions and sexual activity in a college population. *Journal of Sex Research*, 32, 155–167.

Remland, M. S. (1984). Leadership impressions and nonverbal communication in a superior-subordinate interaction. *Communication Quarterly*, 32, 41–48.

Remland, M. S. (2000). *Nonverbal communication in everyday life*. Boston: Houghton Mifflin Co.

Remland, M. S., Jones, T. S., and Brinkman, H. (1991). Proxemic and haptic behavior in three European countries. *Journal of Nonverbal Behavior*, 15, 215–232.

Remland, M. S., Jones, T. S., and Brinkman, H. (1995). Interpersonal distance, body orientation, and touch: Effects of culture, gender, and age. *Journal of Social Psychology*, 135, 281–298.

Resenhoeft, A., Villa, J., and Wiseman, D. (2008). Tattoos can harm perceptions: A study and suggestions [Electronic version]. *Journal of American College Health*, 56, 593–596.

Reynolds, K. D., Buller, D. B., Yaroch, A. L., Maloy, J., Geno, C. R., and Cutter, G. R. (2008). Effects of program exposure and engagement with tailored prevention communication on sun protection by young adolescents [Electronic version]. *Journal of Health Communication*, 13, 619–636.

Riby, D. M., Doherty-Sneddon, G., and Whittle, L. (2012). Face-to-face interference in typical and atypical development [Electronic version]. *Developmental Science*, 15, 281–291.

Rich, M. K., and Cash, T. F. (1993). The American image of beauty: Media representatives of hair color for four decades. *Sex Roles*, 29, 113–124.

Richardson, L. W. (1981). *The dynamics of sex and gender*. Boston: Houghton Mifflin.

Richmond, V. P., and Gorham, J. S. (1998). *Communication, learning, and affect in instruction*. Acton, MA: Tapestry Press.

Richmond, V. P., Gorham, J. S., and McCroskey, J. C. (1987). The relationship between selected immediacy behaviors and cognitive learning. In M. McLaughlin (Ed.), *Communication yearbook* 10 (pp. 574–590). Beverly Hills, CA: Sage.

Richmond, V. P. and McCroskey, J. C. (2000). *Nonverbal behavior in interpersonal relations (4th ed.)*. Boston: Allyn and Bacon.

Richmond, V. P., McCroskey, J. C., and and Hickson, M. L (2007). *Nonverbal behavior in interpersonal relations* (6th ed.). Boston: Allyn and Bacon.

Richmond, V. P., McCroskey, J. C., and and Hickson, M. L (2011). *Nonverbal behavior in interpersonal relations* (7th ed.). Boston: Allyn and Bacon.

Richmond, V. P., McCroskey, J. C., and Johnson, A. D. (2003). Development of the Nonverbal Immediacy Scale (NIS): Measures of self- and other-perceived nonverbal immediacy. *Communication Quarterly*, 51, 504–517.

Ridgeway, C. L., Berger, J., and Smith, L. (1985). Nonverbal cues and status: An expectation states approach. *American Journal of Sociology*, 90, 995–978.

Ries, H. T., Nezlek, J., and Wheeler, L. (1980). Physical attractiveness in social interaction. *Journal of Personality and Social Psychology*, 38, 604–617.

Riess, M., and Rosenfeld, P. (1980). Seating preferences as nonverbal communication: A self-presentational analysis. *Journal of Applied Communications Research*, 8, 22–28.

Riggio, R. E., and Friedman, H. S. (1986). Impression formation: The role of expressive behavior. *Journal of Personality and Social Psychology*, 30 (4), 421–427.

Riley, J. E. (1979). The olfactory factor in nonverbal communication. *Communication*, 8,159–169.

Rinck, C. M., Willis, F. N., and Dean, L. M. (1980). Interpersonal touch among residents of homes for the elderly. *Journal of Communication*, 30, 44–47.

Rintamaki, L. S., Scott, A. M., Kosenko, K. A., and Jensen, R. E. (2007). Male patient perceptions of HIV stigma in health care contexts [Electronic version]. *AIDS Patient Care & STDs*, 21, 956–969.

Riordan, M. A., and Kreuz, R. J. (2010). Cues in computer-mediated communication: A corpus analysis [Electronic version]. *Computers in Human Behavior*, 6, 1806–1817.

Rivardo., M. G. and Keelan, C. M. (2010). Body modifications, sexual activity, and religious practices [Electronic version]. *Psychological Reports*, 106, 467–474.

Roach, K. D. (1997). Effects of graduate teaching assistants' nonverbal communication, attire, dress, student learning, student misbehaviors, students' ratings of instruction. *Communication Quarterly*, 45, 125–141.

Robbins, O., Devoe, S., and Wiener, M. (1978). Social patterns of turn-taking: Nonverbal regulators. *Journal of Communication*, 28, 38–46.

Roberts, S., Kralevich, A., Ferdenzi, C., Saxton, T., Jones, B., DeBruine, L., Little, A., and Havlicekk, J. (2011). Body odor quality predicts behavioral attractiveness in humans [Electronic version]. *Archives of Sexual Behavior*, 40, 1111–1117.

Roebuck, J. B., and Hickson, M., III. (1982). *The Southern redneck: A phenomenological case study*. New York: Praeger.

Roese, N. J., and Olson, J. M. (1992). Same-sex touching behavior: The moderating role of homophobic attitudes. *Journal of Nonverbal Behavior*, 16, 249–260.

Rogels, P. L. J., Roelen, E., and VanMeel, J. M. (1990). The function of self-touchings, posture shifts, and motor discharges in children from 3 to 6 years of age. *Perceptual and Motor Skills*, 70, 1169–1178.

Roger, D. B., and Reid, R. L. (1982). Role differentiation and seating arrangements: A further study. *British Journal of Social Psychology*, 21, 23–29.

Roger, D. B., and Schalekamp, E. E. (1976). Body-buffer zone and violence: A cross-cultural study. *Journal of Social Psychology*, 98, 153–158.

Romano, S. T., and Bordieri, J. E. (1989). Physical attractiveness stereotypes and students' perceptions of college professors. *Psychological Reports*, 64, 1099–1102.

Rosegrant, T. J., and McCroskey, J. C. (1975). The effects of race and sex on proxemic behavior in an interview setting. *Southern Speech Communication Journal*, 40, 408–240.

Rosencrantz, M. L. (1962). Clothing symbolism. *Journal of Home Economics*, 54, 18–22.

Rosenfeld, L. B., and Civikly, J. M. (1976). *With words unspoken: The nonverbal experience.* New York: Holt, Rinehart, and Winston.

Rosenfeld, L. B., Kartus, S., and Ray, C. (1976). Body accessibility revisited. *Journal of Communication, 26,* 27–30.

Rosenfeld, L. B., and Plax, T. G. (1977). Clothing as communication. *Journal of Communication, 27,* 24–31.

Rosenthal, R., Hall, J. A., Di Matteo, M. R., Rogers, P. L., and Archer, D. (1979). *Sensitivity to nonverbal communication: The PONS test.* Baltimore, MD: Johns Hopkins University Press.

Ross, E. D., Reddy, A. L., Nair, A., Mikawa, K., and Prodan, C. I. (2007). Facial expressions are more easily produced on the upper-lower compared to the right-left hemiface [Electronic version]. *Perceptual & Motor Skills, 104,* 155–165.

Rossiter, C. M. (1977, December). *Qualitative methodology in communication theory development.* Paper presented at the meeting of the Speech Communication Association, Washington, DC.

Rothman, A. D., and Nowicki, S., Jr. (2004). A measure of the ability to identify emotion in children's tone of voice [Electronic version]. *Journal of Nonverbal Behavior, 28,* 67–92.

Rotter, N. G., and Rotter, G. S. (1988). Sex differences in encoding and decoding of negative facial emotions. *Journal of Nonverbal Behavior, 12,* 139–148.

Rozell, E. J., and Gundersen, D. E. (2003). The effects of leader impression management on group perceptions of cohesion, consensus, and communication [Electronic version]. *Small Group Research, 34,* 197–222.

Rozin, P., and Fallon, A. (1988). Body image, attitudes toward weight, and misperceptions of figure preferences of the opposite sex: A comparison of men and women in two generations. *Journal of Abnormal Psychology, 97,* 342–345.

Rozin, P., Lowery, L., and Ebert, R. (1994). Varieties of disgust faces and the structure of disgust. *Journal of Personality and Social Psychology, 66,* 870–881.

Rubin, D. C., Groth, E. G., and Goldsmith, D. J. (1984). Olfactory cuing and autobiographical memory. *American Journal of Psychology, 97,* 493–505.

Rubin, L. (1985). *Just friends: The role of friendships in our lives.* New York: Harper and Row.

Rubin, M., and Sabatelli, R. (1986). Nonverbal expressiveness and physical attractiveness as mediators of interpersonal perceptions. *Journal of Nonverbal Behavior, 10,* 120–133.

Ruesch, J., and Kees, W. (1956). *Nonverbal communication: Notes on the visual perception of human relations.* Berkeley, CA: University of California Press.

Russell, J. A. (1994). Is there universal recognition of emotion from facial expression? A review of the cross-cultural studies. *Psychological Bulletin, 115,* 102–141.

Russo, N. (1967). Connotation of seating arrangements. *Cornell Journal of Social Relations, 2,* 37–44.

Rustemili, A. (1988). The effects of personal space invasion on impressions and decisions. *Journal of Psychology, 122,* 113–118.

Rutkowski, A., Saunders, C., Vogel, D., and van Genuchten, M. (2007). "Is it already 4 a.m. in your time zone?" Focus immersion and temporal dissociation in virtual teams [Electronic version]. *Small Group Research, 38,* 98–129.

Ruys, K. I., and Stapel, D. A. (2008). Emotion elicitor or emotion messenger? Subliminal priming reveals two faces of facial expressions [Electronic version]. *Psychological Science, 19,* 593–600.

Ryan, E. B., and Hummert, M. L. (1995) Communication predicaments of aging: Patronizing behavior toward older adults. *Journal of Language and Social Psychology, 14,* 144–166.

Saarni, C. (1988). Children's understanding of the interpersonal consequences of dissemblance of nonverbal emotional-expressive behavior. *Journal of Nonverbal Behavior, 12,* 275–293.

Sabatilli, R. M., and Rubin, M. (1986). Nonverbal expressiveness as mediators of interpersonal perceptions. *Journal of Nonverbal Behavior, 10,* 120–133.

Saine, T. J. (1976, March). *Synchronous and concatenous behavior: Two models of rule-violation in conversational interaction.* Paper presented at the meeting of the Southeastern Psychological Association, New Orleans.

St. Lawrence, J. S., Hansen, D. J., Cutts, T. F., Tisdelle, D. A., and Irish, J. D. (1985). Situational context: Effects of perceptions of assertive and unassertive behavior. *Behavior Therapy*, 16, 51–62.

Salk, R. H., and Engelin-Maddox, R. (2012). Fat talk among college women is both contagious and harmful. *Sex Roles*, 66, 636–645.

Salk, R. H., and Engelin-Maddox, R. (2011). "If you're fat, then I'm humongous!": Frequency, content and impact of fat talk among college women. *Psychology of Women Quarterly*, 35, 18–28.

Salt, R. E. (1991). Affectionate touch between fathers and preadolescent sons. *Journal of Marriage and the Family*, 53, 545–554.

Samar, R. G., and Alibakhshi, G. (2007). The gender linked differences in the use of linguistic strategies in face-to-face communication. *Linguistics Journal*, 2, 59–71.

Samovar, L. A., Porter, R. E., McDaniel, E. R., and Roy, C. S. (2013). *Communication between cultures* (8th ed.). Boston: Wadsworth.

Sanders, J. A., and Wiseman, R. L. (1990). The effects of verbal and nonverbal teacher immediacy on perceived cognitive, affective, and behavioral learning in the multicultural classroom. *Communication Education*, 39, 341–353.

Sandoval, V. A., and Adams, S. H. (2001). Subtle skills for building rapport [Electronic version]. *FBI Law Enforcement Bulletin*, 70, 1–5.

Sanfilipo, M. P. (1993). Depression, gender, gender role traits and the wish to be held. *Sex Roles*, 28, 583–605.

Sanfilipo, M., and Stein, N. (1985). Depression and the wish to be held. *Journal of Abnormal Psychology*, 41, 3–9.

Sannito, T. (1983). Nonverbal communication in the courtroom. *Trial Diplomacy Journal*, 6, 22–28.

Santilli, V., and Miller, A. N. (2011). The effects of gender and power distance on nonverbal immediacy in symmetrical and asymmetrical power conditions: A cross-cultural study of classrooms and friendships [Electronic version]. *Journal of International and Intercultural Communication*, 4, 3–22.

Sapir, E. (1949). The unconscious patterning of behavior in society. In E. Mandelbaum (Ed.), *Selected writings of Edward Sapir in language, culture, and personality*. Berkeley, CA: University of California Press.

Sarwer, D. B., Bartlett, S. P., Bucky, L. P., La Rossa, D., Low, D. W., Pertschuk, M. J., Wadden, T. A., and Whitaker, L. A. (1998). Bigger is not always better: Body image dissatisfaction in breast reduction and breast augmentation patients. *Plastic & Reconstructive Surgery*, 101 (7), 1956–1961.

Sarwer, D. B., Pertschuk, M. J. Wadden, T. A., and Whitaker L. A. (1998a). Body image and body dysmorphic disorder in 100 cosmetic surgery patients. *Plastic & Reconstructive Surgery*, 101 (4), 1644–1649.

Sarwer, D. B., Pertschuk, M. J., Wadden, T. A., and Whitaker L. A. (1998b). Psychological investigations in cosmetic surgery: A look back and a look ahead. *Plastic & Reconstructive Surgery*, 101 (4), 1136–1142.

Sarwer, D. B., Pertschuk, M. J., Wadden, T. A., and Whitaker L. A. (1998c). The psychology of cosmetic surgery: A review and reconceptualization. *Clinical Psychology Review*, 1, 1–22.

Sattel, J. W. (1983). Men, inexpressiveness, and power. In B. Thorne, C. Kramarae, and N. Henley (Eds.), *Language, gender, and society* (pp. 119–124). Rowley, MA: Newbury House.

Sauter, D. (2010). More than happy: The need for disentangling positive emotions [Electronic version]. *Current Directions in Psychological Science*, 19, 36–40.

Sauter, D. A., Eisner, F., Ekman, P., and Scott, S. K. (2010). Cross-cultural recognition of basic emotions through nonverbal vocalizations [Electronic version]. *Proceedings of the National Academy of Sciences of the United States of America*, 107, 2408–2412.

Scarduzio, J. A., and Geist-Martin, P. (2008). Making sense of fractured identities: Male professors' narratives of sexual harassment. *Communication Monographs*, 75, 369–395.

Schachner, D., Shaver, P., Mikulincer, M. (2005). Patterns of nonverbal behavior and sensivity in the context of attachment relationships [Electronic version]. *Journal of Nonverbal Behavior*, 29, 141–169.

Schachter, S. (1964). The interaction of cognitive and physiological determinants of emotional states. In L. Berkowitz (Ed.), *Advances in experimental social psychology* (pp. 49–80). New York: Academic Press.

Scheflen, A. E. (1964). The significance of posture in communication systems. *Psychiatry*, 28, 316–331.

Scheflen, A. E. (1965). Quasi-courtship behavior in psychotherapy. *Psychiatry*, 28, 245–257.

Scherer, K. R. (1979). Acoustic concomitants of emotional dimensions: Judging affect from synthesized tone sequences. In S. Weitz (Ed.), *Nonverbal communication: Readings with commentary* (2nd ed., pp. 249–253). New York: Oxford University Press.

Schiller, D. (2008). China in the United States [Electronic version]. *Communication & Critical/Cultural Studies*, 5, 411–415.

Schmid, P., Schmid-Mast, M., Bombari, D., and Mast, F. (2011). Gender effects in information processing on a nonverbal coding task [Electronic version]. *Sex Roles*, 65, 102–107.

Schmidt, K., Ambadar, Z., Cohn, J., and Reed, L. (2006). Movement differences between deliberate and spontaneous facial expressions: Zygomaticus major action in smiling [Electronic version]. *Journal of Nonverbal Behavior*, 30, 37–52.

Schmidt-Fajlik, R. (2007). Introducing nonverbal communication to Japanese university students: Determining content [Electronic version]. *Journal of Intercultural Communication*, 15, 2.

Schneider, K., and Josephs, I. (1991). The expressive and communicative functions of preschool children's smiles in an achievement situation. *Journal of Nonverbal Behavior*, 15, 185–198.

Schofield, T. J., Parke, R. D., Castañeda, E. K., and Coltrane, S. (2008). Patterns of gaze between parents and children in European American and Mexican American families [Electronic version]. *Journal of Nonverbal Behavior*, 32, 171–186.

Schonfield, J., Taylor, R. W., Boutin, S., Humphries, M. M., and Andrew, G. (2012). Territorial defence behavior in red squirrels is influenced by local density [Electronic version]. *Behaviour*, 149, 369–390.

Schraeder, M., Becton, J. B., and Portis, R. (2007). A critical examination of performance appraisals [Electronic version]. *Journal for Quality and Participation*, 30, 20–25.

Schramme, T. (2008). Should we prevent non-therapeutic mutilation and extreme body modification? [Electronic version] *Bioethics*, 22, 8–15.

Schulman, M. D., and Mandel, E. (1988). Communication training of relatives and friends of institutionalized elderly persons. *The Gerontologist*, 28, 797–800.

Schulz, J., Karshin, C., and Woodiel, D. K. (2006). Body art: The decision making process among college students [Electronic version]. *American Journal of Health Studies*, 21, 123–127.

Schwartz, B. (1975). *Queuing and waiting: Studies in the social organization of access and delay.* Chicago: University of Chicago Press.

Schwartz, B., Tesser, A., and Powell, E. (1982). Dominance cues in nonverbal behavior. *Social Psychology Quarterly*, 45, 114–120.

Seals, C. D., Clanton, K., Agarwal, R., Doswell, F., and Thomas, C. M. (2008). Lifelong learning: Becoming computer savvy at a later age [Electronic version]. *Educational Gerontology*, 34, 1055–1069.

Segrin, C. (1993). The effects of nonverbal behavior on outcomes of compliance gaining attempts. *Communication Studies*, 44, 169–187.

Seiter, J. S., and Dunn, D. (2000). Beauty and believability in sexual harassment cases: Does physical attractiveness affect perceptions of veracity and the likelihood of being harassed? *Communication Research Reports*, 17, 203–209.

Seiter, J. S., and Sandry, A. (2003). Pierced for success? The effects of ear and nose piercing on perceptions of job candidates' credibility, attractiveness, and hirability. *Communication Research Reports*, 20, 287–298.

Semnani-Azad, Z. and Adair, W. L. (2011). The display of "dominant" nonverbal cues in negotiation: The role of culture and gender [Electronic version]. *International Negotiation*, 3, 451–479.

Sengupta, S. (2000). In the eyes of the beholder: The relevance of skin tone and facial features of African American female models to advertising effectiveness. *Communication Research Reports*, 17, 210–220.

Shai, D., and Belsky, J. (2011). Parental embodied mentalizing: Let's be explicit about what we mean by implicit [Electronic version]. *Child Development Perspectives*, 5, 187–188.

Sharifabad, M. R. and Vali, S. (2011). A comparative study of native and non-native body language: The case of Americans' kinesics vs. Persian English speakers [Electronic version]. *Journal of Intercultural Communication*, 26, 6.

Shariff, A. F., and Tracy, J. L. (2009). Knowing who's boss: Implicit perceptions of status from the nonverbal expression of pride [Electronic version]. *Emotion*, 9, 631–639.

Sharkey, W. F., and Stafford, L. (1990). Responses to embarrassment. *Human Communication Research*, 17, 315–342.

Sheer, V. C. (2011). Teenagers use of MSN features, discussion topics, and online friendship development: The impact of media richness and communication control. *Communication Quarterly*, 59, 82–103.

Sheldon, L. K., Ellington, L., Barrett, R., Dudley, W. N., Clayton, M. F., and Rinaldi, K. (2009). Nurse responsiveness to cancer patient expressions of emotion [Electronic version]. *Patient Education & Counseling*, 76, 63–70.

Sheldon, W. H. (1942a). *The varieties of human physique*. New York: Harper and Row.

Sheldon, W. H. (1942b). *The varieties of temperament*. New York: Harper and Row.

Sherertz E. F., and Hess S. P. (1993). Stated age. *New England Journal of Medicine*, 329, 281–282.

Shields, S. A., Mallory, M. E., and Simon, A. (1990). The experience and symptoms of blushing. *Journal of Nonverbal Behavior*, 14, 171–186.

Shuter, R. (1976). Proxemics and tactility in Latin America. *Journal of Communication*, 26, 46–76.

Shuter, R. (1977). A field study of nonverbal communication in Germany, Italy, and the United States. *Communication Monographs*, 44, 298–305.

Sias, P.M., Smith, G., and Avdeyeva, T. (2003). Sex and sex-composition differences and similarities in peer workplace friendship development. *Communication Studies*, 54, 322–340.

Sigelman, C. K., and Adams, R. M. (1990). Family interactions in public: Parent-child distancing and touching. *Journal of Nonverbal Behavior*, 14, 63–75.

Sillars, A. L. (1984, July). *The semantics of family relationships*. Paper presented at the Lambert Family Communication Conference, Northwestern University, Chicago, IL.

Silverstone, P. H. (1990). Low self-esteem in eating disordered patients in the absence of depression. *Psychological Reports*, 67, 276–278.

Sime, D. (2006). What do learners make of teachers' gestures in the language classroom? [Electronic version]. *International Review of Applied Linguistics in Language Teaching*, 44, 211–230.

Siminoff, L. A., Traino, H. M., and Gordon, N. H. (2011). An exploratory study of relational, persuasive, and nonverbal communication in requests for tissue donation [Electronic version]. *Journal of Health Communication*, 16, 955–975.

Sims, C. (2008, November). *Living (body) art: Framing the art and losing the body* [Electronic version]. Paper presented at the National Communication Association, San Diego, CA.

Singer, J. E. A. (1964). The use of manipulative strategies: Machiavellianism and attractiveness. *Sociometry*, 27, 128–151.

Singer, J. E., and Lamb, P. F. (1966). Social concern, body size, and birth order. *Journal of Social Psychology*, 68, 143–151.

Singer, M., Radinsky, J., and Goldman, S. R. (2008). The role of gesture in meaning construction [Electronic version]. *Discourse Processes*, 45, 365–386.

Singh, D. (1993). Adaptive significance of female physical attractiveness: Role of waist-to-hip ratio. *Journal of Personality and Social Psychology*, 65, 293–308.

Sinha, S. P., and Mukherjee, N. (1996). The effect of perceived cooperation on personal space require-ments [Electronic version]. *Journal of Social Psychology*, 136, 655–657.

Sitton, T. (1980). Inside school spaces: Rethinking the hidden dimensions. *Urban Environment*, 15, 62–82.

Skegg, K., Nada-Raja, S., Paul, C., and Skegg, D. (2007). Body piercing, personality, and sexual behavior [Electronic version]. *Archives of Sexual Behavior*, 36, 47–54.

Slavutzkaya, A., Gerasimenko, N., and Mikhailova, E. (2012). Recognition of spatially transformed objects in men and women: Analysis of behavior and evoked potentials [Electronic version]. *Human Physiol-ogy*, 38, 238–248.

Slevec, J., and Tiggemann, M. (2011). Media exposure, body dissatisfaction, and disordered eating in middle-aged women: A test of the sociocultural model of disordered eating [Electronic version]. *Psychology of Women Quarterly*, 35, 617–627.

Smets, G. J. F., and Overbeeke, C. J. (1989). Scent and sound of vision: Expressing scent or sound as visual forms. *Perceptual and Motor Skills*, 69, 227–333.

Smith, A. P. (1991). Noise and aspects of attention. *British Journal of Psychology*, 82, 313–324.

Smith, K., and Sines, J. O. (1960). Demonstration of specific odor in the sweat of schizophrenic patients. *Archives of General Psychiatry*, 2, 184–188.

Smith, L. J., and Malandro, L. A. (1985). *Courtroom communication strategies*. New York: Kluwer.

Smith, M. J., Reinheimer, R. E., and Gabbard-Alley, A. (1988). Crowding, task performance, and commu-nicative interaction in old age. *Human Communication Research*, 7, 259–272.

Smith, S. M., and Shaffer, D. R. (1991). Celerity and cajolery: Rapid speech may promote or inhibit persua-sion through its impact on message elaboration. *Personality and Social Psychology Bulletin*, 17, 663–669.

Sobel, R. S., and Liffith, N. (1974). Determinants of nonstationary personal space invasion. *Journal of Social Psychology*, 97, 39–45.

Sogon, S., and Masutani, M. (1989). Identification of emotion from body movements: A cross-cultural study of Americans and Japanese. *Psychological Reports*, 65, 35–46.

Solomon, M. R. (1986). Dress for effect. *Psychology Today*, 19, 20–22, 26–28.

Solomon, N. P., Helou, L. B., Dietrich-Burns, K., and Stojadinovic, A. (2011). Do obesity and weight loss affect vocal function? [Electronic version]. *Seminars in Speech and Language*, 32, 31–42.

Sommer, R. (1969). *Personal space: The behavioral basis of design*. Englewood Cliffs, NJ: Prentice-Hall.

Sonnenfeld, J. (1966). Variable values in space and landscape: An inquiry into the nature of environmen-tal necessity. *Journal of Social Issues*, 22, 71–82.

Sorokowski, P. (2008). Attractiveness of blonde women in evolutionary perspective: Studies with two Polish samples [Electronic version]. *Perceptual & Motor Skills*, 106, 737–744.

Speer, A. (1970). *Inside the Third Reich* (R. Winston and C. Winston, Trans.). New York: Macmillan.

Spence, P., Westerman, D., Skalski, P., Seeger, M., Ulmer, R., Venette, S., and Sellnow, T. (2005). Proxemic effects on information seeking after the September 11 attacks. *Communication Research Reports*, 22, 39–46.

Stacks, D. W. (1982 April). *Hemispheric and evolutionary use: A re-examination of verbal and nonverbal com-munication and the brain*. Paper presented at the meeting of the Eastern Communication Association, Hartford, CT.

Stacks, D. W. (1983a). Toward a preverbal stage of communication. *Journal of Communication Therapy*, 2, 39–60.

Stacks, D. W. (1983b). *When reward fails: An examination of high reward and the violations of distancing expec-tations model*. Unpublished manuscript, University of South Alabama, Mobile.

Stacks, D. W. (1985). *Nonverbal communication: Theory assessment and instruction: A selected annotated bibli-ography*. Washington, DC: ERIC Clearinghouse on Reading and Communication Skills.

Stacks, D. W., and Andersen, P. A. (1989). The modular mind: Implications for interpersonal communication. *Southern Communication Journal*, 54, 273–293.

Stacks, D. W., Browning, C., Browning, S., Busby, L., Carrol, A., Devery, M., Flowers, D., Graham, K., Henderson, P., Kendrick, K., Kozoroski, K., Leverett, D., Milne, J., Turnipseed, M., Walker, M. K., Walters, L., Weaver, K., and Wiedeimer, L. (1980). *Hands touching hands: An examination of the ritualistic handshake on attitude and credibility*. Unpublished paper, University of South Alabama, Mobile.

Stacks, D. W., and Burgoon, J. K. (1979, April). *The effects of violating spatial distance expectations in small groups*. Paper presented at the meeting of the Southern Speech Communication Association, Biloxi, MS.

Stacks, D. W., and Burgoon, J. K. (1981). The role of nonverbal behaviors as distracters in resistance to persuasion in interpersonal contexts. *Central States Speech Journal*, 32, 71–73.

Stacks, D. W., and Hickson, M., III. (1974). Research: A programmed approach. *Florida Speech Communication Journal*, 2, 21–25.

Stacks, D. W., Hill, S. R., Jr., and Hickson, M. (1991). An *introduction to communication theory*. Dallas: Holt, Rinehart and Winston.

Stacks, D. W., and Hocking, J. E. (1999). *Communication research* (2nd ed.). New York: Longman.

Stacks, D. W., and Sellers, D. E. (1989). Understanding intrapersonal communication: Neurological processing implications. In C. Roberts and K. Watson (Eds.), *Intrapersonal communication processes: Original essays* (pp. 243–267). Auburn, AL: Spectra Publishers.

Stacks, D. W., and Stacks, F. W. (1982). Getting on board for the CME. *Tri-Lakes Division News U.S.C.G. Auxiliary*, 3, 5–7.

Stanners, R. F., Byrd, D. M., and Gabriel, R. (1985). The time it takes to identify facial expressions: Effects of age, gender of subject, sex of sender, and type of expression. *Journal of Nonverbal Behavior*, 9, 201–211.

Stano, M. (1992). The performance appraisal interview: Guidelines for academic department chairs. In M. Hickson, III, and D. W. Stacks (Eds.), *Effective communication for academic chairs* (pp. 107–220). Albany: State University of New York Press.

Steele, J. (1968). Prosodia rationalis. London. As reprinted in M. M. Robb, *Oral interpretation literature in American colleges and universities*. New York: H. W. Wilson Company. (Original work published 1779.)

Stepanikova, I., Zhang, Q., Wieland, D., Eleazer, G., and Stewart, T. (2012). Nonverbal communication between primary care physicians and older patients: How does race matter? [Electronic version]. *Journal of General Internal Medicine*, 27, 576–581.

Stewart, C. J., and Cash, W. B. (2003). *Interviewing principles and practices*. Boston, MA: McGraw-Hill.

Stewart, L. P., Stewart, A. D., Friedley, S. A., and Cooper, P. J. (1990). *Communication between the sexes: Sex differences, and sex role stereotypes* (2nd ed.). Scottsdale, AZ: Gorsuch Sacrisbrick.

Stiff, J. B., Hale, J. L., Garlick, R., and Rogan, R. G. (1990). Effect of cue congruence and social normative influences on individual judgments of honesty and deceit. *Southern Communication Journal*, 55, 206–229.

Stiff, J. B., and Miller, G. R. (1986). "Come to think of it …": Interrogative probes, deceptive communication and deception detection. *Human Communication Research*, 12, 339–357.

Stiff, J. B., Miller, G. R., Sleight, C., Mongeau, P., Garlick, R., and Rogan, R. (1989). Explanations for visual cue primacy in judgments of honesty. *Journal of Personality and Social Psychology*, 56, 555–564.

Stillman, J., and Hensley, W. E. (1980). She wore a flower in her hair: The effect of ornamentation on nonverbal communication. *Journal of Applied Communications Research*, 8, 31–39.

Stirn, A., and Hinz, A. (2008). Tattoos, body piercings, and self-injury: Is there a connection? Investigations on a core group of participants practicing body modification [Electronic version]. *Psychotherapy Research*, 18, 326–333.

Stodtbeck, F. L., and Hook, L. H. (1961). The social dimensions of a twelve man jury table. *Sociometry*, 24, 397–415.

Stolte, K. M., and Friedman, P. G. (1980). Patients' perceptions of touch during labor. *Journal of Applied Communication Research*, 8, 10–21.

Storrs, D., and Kleinke, C. L. (1990). Evaluation of high and equal status male and female touchers. *Journal of Nonverbal Behavior*, 14, 87–95.

Stoykov, L. (2007). Language of corporate dress in cross-cultural business communication [Electronic version]. *Language in India*, 7, 1–8.

Streeck, J. (2008). Depicting by gesture [Electronic version]. *Gesture*, 8, 285–301.

Street, R. L., Jr. (1984). Speech convergence and speech evaluation in fact-finding interviews. *Human Communication Research*, 11, 139–169.

Street, R. L., Jr., and Brady, R. M. (1982). Speech rate acceptance ranges as a function of evaluative domain, listener speech rate, and communication context. *Communication Monographs*, 49, 290–308.

Street, R. L., Brady, R. M., and Lee, R. (1984). Evaluative responses to communicators: The effects of speech rate, sex, and interaction content. *Western Journal of Speech Communication*, 48, 14–27.

Street, R. L., and Murphy, T. L. (1987). Interpersonal orientation and speech behavior. *Communication Monographs*, 54, 42–62.

Streeter, L. A., Krauss, R. M., Geller, V., Olsen, C., and Apple, W. (1977). Pitch changes during attempted deception. *Journal of Personality and Social Psychology*, 35, 345–350.

Stretch, R. H., and Figby, C. R. (1980). Beauty and the beast: Predictors of interpersonal attraction in a dating experiment. *Psychology*, 17, 35–44.

Striano, T., Henning, A., and Stahl, D. (2006). Sensitivity to interpersonal timing at 3 and 6 months of age [Electronic version]. *Interaction Studies*, 7, 251–271.

Strodtbeck, F., James, R., and Hawkins, C. (1973). Social status of jury deliberations. In R. A. Ofshe (Ed.), *Interpersonal behavior in small groups* (pp. 3–11). Englewood Cliffs, NJ: Prentice-Hall.

Stromwall, L. A. and Willen, R. M. (2011). Inside criminal minds: Offenders' strategies when lying [Electronic version]. *Journal of Investigative Psychology and Offender Profiling*, 8, 271–281.

Struckman-Johnson, C., and Johnson, D. (1993). College men's and women's reactions to hypothetical sexual touch varied by initiator gender and coercion level. *Sex Roles*, 29, 371–385.

Stulp, G., Buunk, A. P., Verhulst, S., and Pollet, T. V. (2012). Tall claims? Sense and nonsense about the importance of height of US Presidents [Electronic version]. *The Leadership Quarterly*, 23, 729–739.

Subramani, R. (2010). Insight through body language and non-verbal communication references in Tirukkural [Electronic version]. *Language in India*, 10, 261–271.

Sullivan, D. A. (2001). *Cosmetic surgery: The cutting edge of commercial medicine in America*. New Brunswick, NJ: Rutgers University Press.

Swain, J., Stephenson, G. M., and Dewey, M. E. (1982). Seeing a stranger: Does eye-contact reflect intimacy? *Semiotica*, 42, 2–4, 107–108.

Swami, V., Furnham, A., and Joshi, K. (2008). The influence of skin tone, hair length, and hair colour on ratings of women's physical attractiveness, health and fertility [Electronic version]. *Scandinavian Journal of Psychology*, 49, 429–437.

Swann, W. B., Jr., Stein-Seroussi, A., and McNulty, S. E. (1992). Outcasts in a white-lie society: The enigmatic worlds of people with negative self-conceptions. *Journal of Personality and Social Psychology*, 62, 618–624.

Tait, S. (2007). Television and the domestication of cosmetic surgery [Electronic version]. *Feminist Media Studies*, 7, 119–135.

Takeuchi, S. A. (2006). On the matching phenomenon in courtship: A probability matching theory of mate selection [Electronic version]. *Marriage & Family Review*, 40, 25–51.

Taniguchi, E., and Lee, H. E. (2012). Cross-cultural differences between Japanese and American female college students in the effects of witnessing fat talk on facebook. *Journal of Intercultural Communication Research*, 41, 260–278.

Tanke, E. D. (1982). Dimensions of the physical attractiveness stereotype: A factor/analytic study. *Journal of Psychology*, 110, 63–74.

Tannen, D. (1983). *Lilika Nakos*. Boston: G. K. Hall.

Tannen, D. (1990). *You just don't understand: Women and men in conversation.* New York: William Morrow and Company.

Tarrant, D. (1999, October 10). Tears at work reduce stress … and credibility. *The Miami Herald*, p. 1F.

Tassinary, L. G., and Hansen, K. A. (1998). A critical test of the waist-to-hip-ratio hypothesis of female physical attractiveness. *Psychological Science*, 9, 150–156.

Tate, J. C., and Shelton, B. L. (2008). Personality correlates of tattooing and body piercing in a college sample: The kids are alright [Electronic version]. *Personality and Individual Differences*, 45, 281–285.

Taylor, L. D. (2008). Cads, dads, and magazines: Women's sexual preferences and articles about sex and relationships. *Communication Monographs*, 75, 270–289.

Tennis, G. H., and Dabbs, J. M., Jr. (1975). Sex, setting and personal space: First grade through college. *Sociometry*, 38, 385–394.

Teven, J. J. (2007). Effects of supervisor social influence, nonverbal immediacy, and biological sex on subordinates' perceptions of job satisfaction, liking, and supervisor credibility. *Communication Quarterly*, 55, 155–177.

Teven, J. J. (2010). The effects of supervisor nonverbal immediacy and power use on employees' ratings of credibility and affect for the supervisor. *Human Communication*, 13, 69–85.

Teven, J. J., and Gorham, J. (1998). A qualitative analysis of low-inference student perceptions of teacher caring and non-caring behaviors within the college classroom. *Communication Research Reports*, 15, 288–298.

Teven, J., McCroskey, J. C., and Richmond, V. P. (2006). Communication correlates of perceived Machiavellianism of supervisors: Communication orientations and outcomes. *Communication Quarterly*, 54, 127–142.

Thayer, S. (1988). Touch encounters. *Psychology Today*, 22, 31–36.

Thomas-Maddox, C. (2003). Creating Perceptions of Closeness in the Classroom: Exploring the Concept of Nonverbal Immediacy [Electronic version]. *Communication Teacher*, 17, 3–15.

Thomas, C. D. (1991). Stable vs. unstable weight history, body image, and weight concerns in women of average body weight. *Psychological Reports*, 68, 491–498.

Thomas, C. E., Richmond, V. P., and McCroskey, J. C. (1994). The association between immediacy and socio-communicative style. *Communication Research Reports*, 11, 107–115.

Thomas, C. K. (1958). An *introduction to phonetics of American English.* New York: Ronald.

Thomas, D. R. (1976). Interaction distances in same-sex and mixed-sex groups. *Perceptual and Motor Skills*, 36, 15–18.

Thomas, K., Hevey, D., Pertl, M., Ni Chuinneagáin, S., Craig, A., and Maher, L. (2011). Appearance matters: The frame and focus of health messages influences beliefs about skin cancer [Electronic version]. *British Journal of Health Psychology*, 16, 418–429.

Thompson, E. H., and Hampton, J. A. (2011). The effect of relationship status on communicating emotions through touch [Electronic version]. *Cognition & Emotion*, 25, 295–306.

Thompson, J. K. (1986). Larger than life. *Psychology Today*, 20, 39–44.

Thorne, B., and Henley, N. (Eds.). (1975). *Language and sex: Differences and dominance.* Rowley, MA: Newbury House.

Thorpe, W. H. (1972). The lower vertebrates and the invertebrates. In R. A. Hinde (Ed.), *Nonverbal communication* (pp. 297–314). Cambridge: Cambridge University Press.

Thourlby, W. (1980). *You are what you wear.* New York: New American Library.

Tieffer, L. (1979). The kiss. *Human Nature*, 1, 20–38.

Tiger, L. (1974). Sex-specific friendship. In E. Leyton (Ed.), *The compact.* St. John's, Newfoundland, Canada: University of Newfoundland Press.

Timmick, J. (1982). How you can learn to be likeable, confident, socially successful for only the cost of your present education. *Psychology Today*, 16, 42–49.

Tipton, R. M., Bailey, K. G., and Obenchain, J. P. (1975). Invasion of male's personal space by feminists and nonfeminists. *Psychological Reports*, 37, 99–102.

Titsworth, B. S. (2001). Immediate and delayed effects of interest cues and engagement cues on students' affective learning. *Communication Studies*, 52, 169–179.

Toma, C. L., and Hancock, J. T. (2010). Looks and lies: The role of physical attractiveness in online dating and self-presentation and deception. *Communication Research*, 37, 335–351.

Tompkins, C. J., and Perkinson, M. A. (2006). Are we really teaching our students an aging perspective when we use the term intergenerational? Are we encouraging the stigmas associated with aging if we use a "backdoor approach" in recruiting students to become interested in working with older adults? [Electronic version]. *Journal of Intergenerational Relationships*, 4, 109–112.

Tortora, S. (2010).Ways of seeing: An early childhood integrated therapeutic approach for parents and babies. *Clinical Social Work Journal*, 38, 37–50.

Tracy, J. L., and Robins, R. W. (2008). The nonverbal expression of pride: Evidence for cross-cultural recognition [Electronic version]. *Journal of Personality & Social Psychology*, 94, 516–530.

Trad, L., Baker, N., Blackman, H., Glynn, K, Wright, A., and Miller, A. N. (2012). Student incivility and instructor communication in the college classroom [Electronic version]. *Florida Communication Journal*, 40, 47–53.

Trager. G. L. (1958). Paralanguage: A first approximation. *Studies in Linguistics*, 2, 1–12.

Tronick, E. Z. (1989). Emotions and emotional communication in infants. *American Psychologist*, 44, 112–119.

Trussoni, S. J., O'Malley, A., and Barton, A. (1988). Human emotion communication by touch: A modified replication of an experiment by Manfred Clynes. *Perceptual and Motor Skills*, 66, 419–424.

Tsai, W., Huang, T., and Yu, H. (2012). Investigating the unique predictability and boundary conditions of applicant physical attractiveness and nonverbal behaviours on interviewer evaluations in job interviews [Electronic version]. *Journal of Occupational and Organizational Psychology*, 85, 60–79.

Tucker, I. (2010). Mental health service user territories: Enacting "safe spaces" in the community [Electronic version]. *An Interdisciplinary Journal for the Study of Health, Illness, and Medicine*, 14, 434–448.

Tucker, K. L., Martz, D. M., Curtin, L. A., and Bazzini, D. G. (2007). Examining "fat talk" experimentally in a female dyad: How are women influenced by another woman's body presentation style? *Body Image: An International Journal of Research*, 4, 157–164.

Tucker, J. S., and Riggio, R. E. (1988). The role of social skills in encoding posed and spontaneous facial expressions. *Journal of Nonverbal Behavior*, 12, 87–97.

Tuminello, E. R. and Davidson, D. (2011). What the face and body reveal: In-group emotion effects and stereotyping of emotion in African American and European American children [Electronic version]. *Journal of Experimental Child Psychology*, 110, 258–274.

Turner, L. H. (1988, May). *Communication patterns in marital conflict: An examination of conceptual models.* Paper presented at the meeting of the International Communication Association, New Orleans, LA.

Vallotton, C. D. (2012). Infant signs as intervention? Promoting symbolic gestures for preverbal children in low-income families supports responsive parent—child relationships [Electronic version]. *Early Childhood Research Quarterly*, 27, 401–415.

Van Cleemput, K. (2012). Friendship type, clique formation and the everyday use of communication technologies in a peer group [Electronic version]. *Information, Communication and Society*, 15, 1258–1277.

Vandergriff, I., and Fuchs, C. (2012). Humor support in synchronous computer-mediated classroom discussions [Electronic version]. *Humor: International Journal of Humor Research*, 25, 437–458.

Van der Meer, G. T., Schultz, W., and Nijman, J. M. (2008). Intimate body piercings in women [Electronic version]. *Journal of Psychosomatic Obstetrics & Gynaecology*, 29, 235–239.

Varinsky, H. (1992). Non-verbal communication enhances witness credibility. *For the Defense*, 34, 28–31.

Velasco-Sacristán, M., and Fuertes-Olivera, P. A. (2006). Olfactory and olfactory-mixed metaphors in print ads of perfume [Electronic version]. *Annual Review of Cognitive Linguistics*, 4, 217–252.

Vergados, D. (2010). Service personalization for assistive living in mobile ambient healthcare-networked environment [Electronic version]. *Personal and Ubiquitous Computing*, 14, 575–590.

Vevea, N. (2008, November). *Body art: Performing identity through tattoos and piercing* [Electronic version]. Paper presented at the annual convention of the National Communication Association, San Diego, CA.

Vingerhoets, J. J. M., and Breed, W. P. M. (2009). Scalp cooling to prevent chemotherapy-induced hair loss: Practical and clinical considerations [Electronic version]. *Supportive Care in Cancer*, 17, 181–189.

Visser, N., Alant, E., and Harty, M. (2008). Which graphic symbols do 4-year-old children choose to represent each of the four basic emotions? [Electronicversion] *Augmentative and Alternative Communication*, 24, 302–312.

Von Neuforn, D. S. (2007). Gender gap in the perception of communication in virtual learning environments [Electronic version]. *Interactive Learning Environments*, 15, 209–215.

Vrig, A. (1994). The impact of information and setting on detection of deception by detectives. *Journal of Nonverbal Behavior*, 18, 117–136.

Vrij, A. Mann, S., Leal, S., and Fisher R. (2010). "Look into my eyes": Can an instruction to maintain eye contact facilitate lie detection? [Electronic version] *Psychology, Crime & Law*, 16, 327–348.

Wagner, H. L., MacDonald, C. J., and Manstead, A. S. R. (1986). Communication of individual emotions by spontaneous facial expressions. *Journal of Personality and Social Psychology*, 50, 737–741.

Walker, G. (2012). Establishing recipiency in pre-beginning position in the second language classroom [Electronic version]. *Language and Speech*, 55, 141–163.

Walker, M. S. (1975). The sex of the speaker as a sociolinguistic variable. In B. Thorne and N. Henley (Eds.), *Language and sex: Difference and dominance* (pp. 76–83). Rowley, MA: Newbury House.

Walker, M., Harriman, S., and Costello, S. (1980). The influence of appearance on compliance with a request. *Journal of Social Psychology*, 112, 159–160.

Walkosz, W., Buller, D., Andersen, P., Scott, M., Dignan, M., Cutter, G., and Maloy, J. (2007, May). Increasing sun protection in outdoor recreation: A theory-based health communication program [Electronic version]. Paper presented at the meeting of the International Communication Association, San Francisco, CA.

Walsh, D. G., and Hewitt, J. (1985). Giving men the come-on: Effect of eye contact and smiling in a bar environment. *Perceptual and Motor Skills*, 61, 873–874.

Walster, E., Aronson, V., Abrahams, D., and Rohmann, L. (1966). Importance of physical attractiveness in dating behavior. *Journal of Personality and Social Psychology*, 4, 508–516.

Walther, J. B. (2012). Interaction through technological lenses: Computer-mediated communication and language [Electronic version]. *Journal of Language and Social Psychology*, 31, 397–414.

Walther, J. B., Loh, T., and Granka, L. (2005). Let me count the ways: The interchange of verbal and nonverbal cues in computer-mediated and face-to-face affinity [Electronic version]. *Journal of Language and Social Psychology*, 24, 36–65.

Waltman, J. (1984). Nonverbal elements in courtroom demeanor. *F.B.I. Law Enforcement Bulletin*, 53, 21–23.

Wang, D., and Li, H. (2007). Nonverbal language in cross-cultural communication [Electronic version]. *US-China Foreign Language*, 5, 66–70.

Wang, S. S., Moon, S., Kwon, K. H., Evans, C. A., and Stefanone, M. A. (2009, May). *Better Without Face? Gender Difference in Visual Cue Use When Initiating Friendship on Facebook.* [Electronic version] Paper presented at the meeting of the International Communication Association, Chicago, IL.

Wang, S. S., Moon, S., Kwon, K. H., Evans, C. A., and Stefanone, M. A. (2010). Face off: Implications of visual cues on initiating friendship on Facebook [Electronic version]. *Computers in Human Behavior*, 26, 226–234.

Waskul, D. D., and Vannini, P. (2008). Smell, odor, and somatic work: Sense-making and sensory management [Electronic version]. *Social Psychology Quarterly*, 71, 53–71.

Watling, D., and Banerjee, R. (2007). Children's differentiation between ingratiation and self-promotion [Electronic version]. *Social Development*, 16, 758–776.

Watson, K. W., and Smeltzer, L. R. (1982). Perceptions of nonverbal communication during the selection interview. *ABCA Bulletin*, 30–34.

Watts, E. K., and Orbe, M. P. (2002). The spectacular consumption of "true" African American culture: "Whassup" with the Budweiser guys? *Critical Studies in Media Communication*, 19, 1–20.

Watzlawick, P., Beavin, J., and Jackson, D. (1967). *Pragmatics of human communication: A study of interpersonal patterns, pathologies, and paradoxes*. New York: Norton.

Weger, Jr., H., and Emmett, M. C. (2009). Romantic intent, relationship uncertainty, and relationship maintenance in young adults' cross-sex friendships [Electronic version]. *Journal of Social and Personal Relationships*, 26, 964–988.

Wein, B. (2002). The changing face of cosmetic surgery. *Biography*, 6, 7, 62–66.

Weinberg, S., and Weinberg, J. (1980). The influence of clothing on perceptions of infant sex roles. *Journal of Applied Communications Research*, 8, 111–119.

Weintraub, P. (1986). Scentimental journeys. *Omni*, 8, 48–52, 114–116.

Weisel, A. (1985). Deafness and perception of nonverbal expression of emotion. *Perceptual and Motor Skills*, 61, 515–523.

Weiss, P. (2013). Do you have an "annoying girl voice"? [Electronic version]. *Shine from Yahoo*. Retrieved from http://shine.yahoo.com/healthy-living/8220-annoying-8221-girl-voice-164900387.html.

Weiten, W., and Etaugh, C. (1974). Lateral movement as a function of cognitive mode, question sequence, and sex of subject. *Perceptual and Motor Skills*, 38, 439–444.

Weitz, S. (Ed.). (1974). *Nonverbal communication: Readings with commentary*. New York: Oxford University Press.

Weitz, S. (1979). *Nonverbal communication: Readings with commentary* (2nd ed.). New York: Oxford University Press.

Wen L., Moallem, I., Paller, K. A., and Gottfried, J. A. (2007). Subliminal smells can guide social preferences [Electronic version]. *Psychological Science*, 18, 1044–1049.

Wenz, F. V. (1984). Household crowding, loneliness, and suicide ideation. *Psychology: A Quarterly Journal of Human Behavior*, 21, 25–28.

West, C. (1979). Against our wills: Male interruptions of females in cross-sex conversations. *Annals of the New York Academy of Science*, 327, 81–97.

West, C., and Zimmerman, D. H. (1983). Small insults: A study of interruptions in cross-sex conversations between unacquainted persons. In B. Thorne, C. Kramarae, and N. Henley (Eds.), *Language, gender, and society* (pp. 103–117). Rowley, MA: Newbury.

West, L., Anderson, J., and Duck, S. (1996). Crossing the barriers to friendship between women and men. In J. T. Wood, *Gendered relationships: A reader* (pp. 111–127). Mountain View, CA: Mayfield.

Wexner, L. B. (1954). The degree to which colors (hues) are associated with mood-tones. *Journal of Applied Psychology*, 38, 432–435.

White, S. E., Brown, N. J., and Ginsburg, S. L. (1999). Diversity of body types in network television programming: A content analysis. *Communication Research Reports*, 16, 386–392.

Wickline, V. B., Bailey, W., and Nowicki, S. (2009). Cultural in-group advantage: Emotion recognition in African American and European American Faces and voices [Electronic version]. *Journal of Genetic Psychology*, 170, 5–30.

Wickline, V. B., Nowicki, S., Bollini, A. M., and Walker, E. F. (2012) Vocal and facial emotion decoding difficulties relating to social and thought problems: Highlighting schizotypal personality disorder [Electronic version]. *Journal of Nonverbal Behavior*, 36, 59–77.

Widgery, R. N., and Webster, B. (1969). The effects of physical attractiveness upon perceived initial credibility. *Michigan Speech Journal*, 4, 9–15.

Wiemann, J. M., and Knapp, M. L. (1975). Turn-taking in conversations. *Journal of Communication*, 25, 75–92.

Wiener, H. (1979). Human exocrinology: The olfactory component of nonverbal communication. In S. Weitz (Ed.), *Nonverbal communication: Studies with commentary* (pp. 338–345). New York: Oxford University Press.

Wilbur, M. P., and Roberts-Wilbur, J. (1985). Lateral eye-movement responses to visual stimuli. *Perceptual and Motor Skills, 61,* 167–177.

Willander, J., and Larsson, M. (2007). Olfaction and emotion: The case of autobiographical memory [Electronic version]. *Memory and Cognition, 35,* 1659–1663.

Willems, E. P., and Campbell, D. E. (1976). One path through the cafeteria. *Environment and Behavior, 8,* 125–140.

Williams, C. L., and Parker, C. (2012). Development of an observer rating scale for caregiver communication in persons with Alzheimer's disease [Electronic version]. *Issues in Mental Health Nursing, 33,* 244–250.

Williams, D. E., and Hughes, P. C. (2005). Nonverbal communication in Italy: An analysis of interpersonal touch, body position, eye contact, and seating behaviors [Electronic version]. *North Dakota Journal of Speech and Theatre, 18,* 17–24.

Williams, F. (1970). The psychological correlates of speech characteristics: On sounding "disadvantaged." *Journal of Speech and Hearing Research, 13,* 472–488.

Williams, H. J., Wagner, H. L., and Calam, R. M. (1992). Eating attitudes in survivors of unwanted sexual experiences. *British Journal of Clinical Psychology, 31,* 203–206.

Williams, J. H. (1977). *Psychology of women: Behavior in a biosocial context.* New York: W. W. Norton.

Williams, J. L. (1963). *Personal space and its relation to extroversion—introversion.* Unpublished master's thesis, University of Alberta.

Williams, S. A. (2005). Jealousy in the cross-sex friendship [Electronic version]. *Journal of Loss and Trauma, 10,* 471–485.

Willis, F. N. (1966). Initial speaking distances as a function of the speaker's relationship. *Psychonomic Science, 5,* 221–222.

Willis, F. N., and Briggs, L. F. (1992). Relationship and touch in public settings. *Journal of Nonverbal Behavior, 16,* 55–63.

Willis, F. N., and Hoffman, G. E. (1975). Development of tactile patterns in relation to age, sex, and race. *Developmental Psychology, 11,* 866.

Willis, F. N., and Rawdon, V. A. (1994). Gender and national differences in attitudes toward same-gender touch. *Perceptual and Motor Skills, 78,* 1027–1034.

Willis, J. (1994). *Beautiful again: Restoring your image and enhancing body changes.* Santa Fe, NM: Health Press.

Wilson, G., and Nias, D. (1976). Beauty can't be beat. *Psychology Today, 10* (4), 96–98, 103.

Wilson, R. (2010). Being hot leaves some professors cold [Electronic version]. *Chronicle of Higher Education, 56,* A1–A10.

Wilson, R., Rochon, E., Mihailidis, A., and Leonarda, C. (2012). Examining success of communication strategies used by formal caregivers assisting individuals with Alzheimer's disease during an activity of daily living [Electronic version]. *Journal of Speech, Language and Hearing Research, 55,* 328–341.

Wing, C. S. (2010). Cross-cultural transfer in gesture frequency in Chinese-English bilinguals [Electronic version]. *Language and Cognitive Processes, 25,* 1335–1353.

Winge, T. M. (2008). "Green is the new black": Celebrity chic and the "green" commodity fetish [Electronic version]. *The Journal of Dress, Body, and Culture, 12,* 511–523.

Winograd, E., Kerr, N. H., and Spence, M. J. (1984). Voice recognition: Effects of orienting task and the blind versus sighted listeners. *American Journal of Psychology, 97,* 57–69.

Winter, D. D., Widell, C., Truitt, G., and George-Falvy, J. (1989). Empirical studies of posture-gesture mergers. *Journal of Nonverbal Behavior, 13,* 207–223.

Winter, R. (1976). *The smell book: Scents, sex, and society.* New York: J. P. Lippincott.

Wispe, L., and Kiecolt, J. (1980). Victim attractiveness and nonhelping. *Journal of Social Psychology*, 112, 67–74.

Wohlrab, S., Fink, B., Kappeler, P. M., and Brewer, G. (2009). Perception of human body modification [Electronic version]. *Personality and Individual Differences*, 46, 202–206.

Wohlrab, S., Stahl, J., Rammsayer, T., and Kappeler, P. M. (2007). Differences in personality characteristics between body-modified and non-modified individuals: Associations with individual personality traits and their possible evolutionary implications [Electronic version]. *European Journal of Personality*, 21, 931–951.

Wolf, K., Milburn, T., and Wilkins, R. (2008). Expressive practices: The local enactment of culture in the communication classroom [Electronic version]. *Business Communication Quarterly*, 71, 171–183.

Wolfe, J. (2005). Gesture and collaborative planning: A case study of a student writing group [Electronic version]. *Written Communication*, 22, 298–332.

Wolff, C. (1972). *A psychology of gesture*. New York: Arno.

Woliver, L. R. (1990). Feminism at the grass roots: The recall of Judge Archie Simonson [Electronic version]. *Frontiers*, 11, 111-119.

Wood, J. T. (1998). *But I thought you meant …: Misunderstandings in human communication*. Mountain View, CA: Mayfield.

Wood, J. T. (2007). *Gendered lives: Communication, gender and culture* (7th ed.) Belmont, CA: Wadsworth/ Thompson Learning, Inc.

Wood, J. T. (2012). *Gendered lives: Communication, gender and culture* (10th ed.) Belmont, CA: Wadsworth/ Cengage Learning, Inc.

Woodstock, L. (2008, May). *Tattoo therapy: Gender and healing on reality TV* [Electronic version]. Paper presented at the meeting of the International Communication Association, Montreal, Canada.

Woodzicka, J. (2008). Sex differences in self-awareness of smiling during a mock job interview [Electronic version]. *Journal of Nonverbal Behavior*, 32, 109–121.

Worthington, M. E. (1974). Personal space as a function of the stigma effect. *Environment and Behavior*, 6, 289–294.

Wrench, J. S., and Knapp, J. L. (2008). The effects of body image perceptions and sociocommunicative orientations on self-esteem, depression, and identification and involvement in the gay community [Electronic version]. *Journal of Homosexuality*, 55, 471–503.

Wright, P. H., and Scanlon, M. B. (1991). Gender role orientations and friendship: Some attenuation but gender differences still abound. *Sex Roles*, 24, 551–566.

Wright, S. (2012). Grow a 'tache, save a life [Electronic version]. *Nursing Standard*, 27, 24.

Yang, P. (2011). Nonverbal aspects of turn taking in **Mandarin** Chinese interaction [Electronic version]. *Chinese Language & Discourse*, 2, 99-130,

Yang, P. (2007). Nonverbal Affiliative Phenomena in **Mandarin** Chinese Conversation [Electronic version]. *Journal of Intercultural Communication*, 15, 7.

Ye, Y., and Zhou, S. (2006, June). *Is it the content or the person? Examining sexual content in promotional announcements and sexual self schema* [Electronic version]. Paper presented at the meeting of the International Communication Association, Dresden, Germany.

Yeomans, T. (2009, November). *Communicating initial interest and attraction: Quasi-courtship versus courtship behaviors* [Electronic version]. Paper presented at the National Communication Association, Chicago, IL.

Young, M., Henderson, M. M., and Marx, D. (1990). Attitudes of nursing students toward patients with AIDS. *Psychological Reports*, 67, 491–497.

Youngquist, J. (2009). The effect of interruptions and dyad gender combination on perceptions of interpersonal dominance. *Communication Studies*, 60, 147–163.

Yu, C. (2011). The display of frustration in arguments: A multimodal analysis [Electronic version]. *Journal of Pragmatics*, 43, 2964–2981.

Yun, Y., Xiaoyi, H., and Jie, Z. (2007). A research on sexual difference in the resident space [Electronic version]. *Canadian Social Science*, 3, 92–100.

Zahavi, A., and Zahavi, A. (1997). *The handicap principle: A missing piece of Darwin's puzzle*. New York: Oxford University Press.

Zakahi, W. R., and Duran, R. L. (1988). Physical attractiveness as a contributing factor to loneliness: An exploratory study. *Psychology Reports*, 63, 747–751.

Zebrowitz, L. A., and Rhodes, G. (2004). Sensitivity to "bad genes" and the anomalous face overgeneralization effect: Cue validity, cue utilization, and accuracy in judging intelligence and health [Electronic version]. *Journal of Nonverbal Behavior*, 28, 167–185.

Zick, A., Granieri, M., and Makoul, G. (2007) First-year medical students' assessment of their own communication skills: A video-based, open-ended approach [Electronic version]. *Patient Education and Counseling*, 68, 161–166.

Zimmerman, D. W., and West, C. (1975). Sex roles: Interruptions and silences in conversation. In B. Thorne and N. Henley (Eds.), *Language and sex difference and domination*. (pp. 105–129). Rowling, MA: Newbury House.

Zucker, N., Moskovich, A., Bulik, C. M., Merwin, R., Gaddis, K., Losh, M., Piven, J., Wagner, H. R., and Labar, K. S. (2013). Perception of affect in biological motion cues in anorexia nervosa [Electronic version]. *International Journal of Eating Disorders*, 46, 12–22.

Zuckerman, M., De Paulo, B. M., and Rosenthal, R. (1981). Verbal and nonverbal communication of deception. In L. Berkowitz (Ed.), *Advances in experimental social psychology* (Vol. 14, pp. 1–60). New York: Academic Press.

Zuckerman, M., Driver, R., and Guadango, N. S. (1985). Effects of segmentation patterns on the perception of deception. *Journal of Nonverbal Behavior*, 9, 160–168.

Zuckerman, M., Hodgins, H., and Miyake, K. (1990). The vocal attractiveness stereotype: Replication and elaboration. *Journal of Nonverbal Behavior*, 14, 97–112.

Zuckerman, M., and Miyake, K. (1993). The attractive voice: What makes it so? *Journal of Nonverbal Behavior*, 17, 119–135.

AUTHOR INDEX

SUBJECT INDEX

Page numbers followed by *t* or *f* indicate a table or figure respectively. Italicized page numbers indicate a photograph